The

SELF~SUFFICIENT LIFE
AND HOW TO LIVE IT
THE COMPLETE BACK-TO-BASICS GUIDE

The

SELF-SUFFICIENT LIFE
AND HOW TO LIVE IT

THE COMPLETE BACK-TO-BASICS GUIDE

JOHN SEYMOUR

WITH WILL SUTHERLAND

Contents

London • New York • Munich • Melbourne • Delhi

For this edition
Editor Andrew Roff
Designer William Hicks
Managing Editor Dawn Henderson
Managing Art Editor Christine Keilty
Production Editor Ben Marcus
Production Controller Wendy Penn
For original edition, *see page 408*

Illustrators
David Ashby, David Bryant, Peter Bull Associates,
Sally Launder, Kathleen McDougall,
Robert Micklewright, Peter Morter, Jim Robins,
Simon Roulstone, Jeremy Sancha, Eric Thomas,
John Woodcock

This edition first published in 2009
in the United States by DK Publishing, Inc.
375 Hudson Street, New York, New York 10014

09 10 11 12 13 10 9 8 7 6 5 4 3 2 1

175232—October 2009

All material in this book is taken from *The Self-Sufficient
Life and How to Live It,* first published in 1976, and the
additional material in Food From The Garden is taken from
The New Self-Sufficient Gardener, first published in 1978.

Copyright © 1976, 1978, 1996, 2003, 2008, 2009
Dorling Kindersley Ltd.
Text copyright © 1976, 1978, 1996, 2003, 2008, 2009
John Seymour, Anne Sears, Will Sutherland

Published in Great Britain by Dorling Kindersley Limited.
A catalog record for this book is available from
the Library of Congress.

ISBN 978-0-7566-5450-4

DK books are available at special discounts when purchased
in bulk for sales promotions, premiums, fund-raising,
or educational use. For details, contact: DK Publishing
Special Markets, 375 Hudson Street, New York, New York
10014 or SpecialSales@dk.com.

Color reproduction by Colourscan, Singapore
Printed and bound in China by Toppan

Discover more at
www.dk.com

WARNING
The text in this book was first written in the 1970s by
John Seymour. Dorling Kindersley has republished these
classic texts with only minimal changes. However, some
of the pesticides recommended in the Food From The
Garden section of the book are either no longer readily
available or no longer recommended; the publisher has
made every effort to identify these by inserting asterisks
throughout the text in this section. If you are in any
doubt about these or any of the other recommendations
given in this book, in the light of today's changing
world, please seek current advice. The publisher does not
accept any liability for any damage or injuries resulting
from the use of any pesticides or from following any of
the advice in this book.

Preface

FOR THIS EDITION, **Will Sutherland**

I first met John Seymour in 1991. I had just resigned from my job in the City of London as a Senior Management Consultant and was organizing a conference on alternative political ideas where John was one of the main speakers. I had previously discovered John's writings and was immediately attracted to his common sense, wisdom, and wide knowledge of the world. John's message was direct and simple—people (like you and me) can change the world by changing what they do in their own lives. We don't need to wait for governments or giant corporations to tell us how. The only problem is that most of the skills and knowledge we need to do this have been lost in the consumer frenzy that has dominated the last 50 years. *The Complete Book of Self-Sufficiency*, published by Dorling Kindersley in 1976, was, and remains, John's answer to the problem.

After I had attended the first UN Earth Summit in Rio I decided it was time for me to explore the book's philosophy for myself. I will never forget that first trip to visit John and his companion Angela. The blackest of winter nights swallowed up my old BMW motorcycle as it lurched onward unsteadily through a remote Irish farmyard knee-deep in cow slurry. With all the studied objectivity of my old days as a government civil servant, I weighed up the prospect of ending my first trip to Ireland lost in bottomless manure! But the fates were kind, the slurry released me, and a kind Irish family redirected me to the smallholding here at Killowen. Supper was delicious, the stove was warm, and I found myself part of a totally different approach to life and living. We had eaten home-reared beef, drunk home-brewed beer, and supped extraordinarily delicious homemade ice cream. Over a whisky after supper John took out his accordion and Angela sang songs.

Now, so many years later, John has sadly passed away—in 2004 at the ripe old age of 90. We buried him on his old farm in Wales and erected a memorial headstone in his favorite spot overlooking the Atlantic in the graveyard of the Star of the Sea church at Duncannon. Fortunately, with help from Dorling Kindersley, we were able to improve and expand *The Complete Book of Self-Sufficiency* with *The Self-Sufficient Life and How to Live It* in 2003. So John's work lives on and, indeed, has probably never been more important. His ideas may have seemed marginal or even outlandish when they first appeared in print but they are now rapidly entering the mainstream.

Of course, my own journey did not end at Killowen. I realize now that this was only the beginning of a new and better way of life. I moved to Ireland and later fell in love with Angela, who is now my wife. There was much to learn and there is much still to learn. Together with our two children, Roisin and Liam, we continue to run the smallholding, which John and Angela started so long ago. This is now our home and our business as we try through our courses and writing to show others a different approach to life.

Most of those who come on our courses are already highly successful people in conventional terms. They are at the top of their game in all sorts of professional jobs and they come from all over the world. The one thing they have in common is a feeling that their lives are lacking some key ingredient that money cannot buy. They want to take back control of their own lives, they want healthier food, and a less stressful lifestyle. They have a belief, a dream, if you like, that they can achieve this by moving out of the mainstream, moving closer to nature, and getting out of the office and into the air. Dreams can, of course, quite easily become nightmares, as many a popular sitcom has shown! It is the purpose of this book to ensure that your dream does not become a nightmare. We will give you the knowledge and, I hope, the inspiration to turn at least some of your dream into reality. But don't be hasty and don't be surprised if your desire for change takes you in unexpected directions—it is the unexpected, after all, that gives life its sparkle. So pick up your spade and live!

FOREWORD TO THE FIRST EDITION (1976), **Dr E. E. Schumacher, CBE**

We can do things for ourselves or we can pay others to do them for us. These are the two "systems" that support us; we might call them the "self-reliance system" and the "organization system." The former tends to breed self-reliant men and women; the latter tends to produce organization men and women. All existing societies support themselves by a mixture of the two systems; but the proportions vary.

In the modern world, during the last hundred or so years, there has been an enormous and historically unique shift: away from self-reliance and toward organization. As a result, people are becoming less self-reliant and more dependent than has ever been seen in history. They may claim to be more highly educated than any generation before them; but the fact remains that they cannot really do anything for themselves. They depend utterly on vastly complex organizations, on fantastic machinery, on larger money incomes. What if there is a hold-up, a breakdown, a strike, or unemployment? Does the state provide all that is needed? In some cases, yes; in other cases, no. Many people fall through the meshes of the safety net; and what then? They suffer; they become dispirited, even despondent. Why can't they help themselves? Generally, the answer is only too obvious: they would not know how to; they have never done it before and would not even know where to begin.

John Seymour can tell us how to help ourselves, and in this book he does tell us. He is one of the great pioneers of self-sufficiency. Pioneers are not for imitation but for learning from. Should we all do what John Seymour has done? Of course not. Total self-sufficiency is as unbalanced and ultimately stultifying as total organization. The pioneers show us what *can* be done, and it is for every one of us to decide what *should* be done, that is to say, what we should do to restore some kind of balance to our existence.

Should I try to grow *all* the food my family and I require? If I tried to do so, I probably could do little else. And what about all the other things we need? Should I try to become a jack-of-all-trades? At most of these trades I would be pretty useless and horribly inefficient. But to grow or make some things by myself; for myself: what fun, what exhilaration, what liberation from any feelings of utter dependence on organizations! What is perhaps even more: what an education of the real person! To be in touch with the *actual processes of creation*. The inborn creativity of people is no mean or accidental thing; neglect or disregard it, and it becomes an inner source of poison. It can destroy you and all your human relationships; on a mass scale, it can—nay, it inevitably will—destroy society.

Contrariwise, nothing can stop the flowering of a society that manages to give free rein to the creativity of its people—*all* its people. This cannot be ordered and organized from the top. We cannot look to government, but only to ourselves, to bring about such a state of affairs. Nor should anyone of us go on "waiting for Godot," because Godot never comes. It is interesting to think of all the "Godots" modern humanity is waiting for: this or that fantastic technical breakthrough or automation so that nobody, or hardly anybody, will have to lift a finger anymore; government policies to solve all problems once and for all: multinational companies to make massive investments in the latest and best technologies; or simply "the next upturn in the economy."

John Seymour has never been found "waiting for Godot." It is the essence of self-reliance that you start now and don't wait for something to turn up; and though the technology behind John Seymour's self-sufficiency is still quite rudimentary, it can, of course, be improved. The greater the number of self-supporters, the faster will be the rate of improvement, that creation of technologies designed to lead people to self-reliance, work-enjoyment, creativity, and therefore *the good life*. This book is a major step along that road, and I wholeheartedly commend it to you.

Forewords

THE FIRST EDITION (UK)
The cover of the first British edition, published in 1976.

FOR THIS BOOK, **Anne Sears (John Seymour's daughter)**
As far back as I can remember there was always a feeling of abundance and worthwhile activity on our farm. Activities that have happened on small farms for centuries with no thought to them. In our case, it was a life consciously chosen by John and Sally with a will to learn old methods as well as integrating new ideas and technologies into the smallholder's life. It was an informed decision to live a moderate, worthy existence in a world of increasing extravagance and waste.

With the help of his books, especially *The Self-Sufficient Life and How to Live It*, *The Self-Sufficient Gardener*, and *The Fat of the Land*, he has managed to reach many thousands of people, encouraging them to believe that they can make positive changes themselves. He made them realize that if they could take responsibility and be more self-reliant they would find that there is fun and fulfillment in this lifestyle.

For most of his life, John worked tirelessly, trying to increase awareness of the damage that we are inflicting on our planet. He tried to show that there was a much simpler, more satisfying way of living, to be in harmony with nature, not against her. John's writing has always been light-hearted and accessible, but the underlying message is urgently serious, to be ignored at our peril.

FOR *THE SELF-SUFFICIENT LIFE AND HOW TO LIVE IT* (2003), **John Seymour**
This book first came out over 25 years ago, created by Dorling Kindersley, with a little help from me, but published by Faber and Faber. It is now being delivered into the new millennium kicking and screaming! Since I first wrote it the book has certainly gotten around. I have traveled in at least dozens of countries since I wrote it (to say nothing of four continents) and in every one of them people have come up to me with their copy for me to sign. I have been delighted to find wine stains on the wine-making pages, and good honest dirt on the gardening pages. I have indeed updated it for the new millennium, but have not sacrificed any of the techniques and tips that have stood me well all that time and continue to do so.

Since I first wrote the first version of this book back in 1975, I now think there is a far more urgent reason for it. Very few people today can fail to see that the present course that man- and woman-kind is embarked upon is unsustainable. We are changing our atmosphere with frightening rapidity—we are altering the world's climate—we are burning up the Earth's enormous stores of carbon as quickly as possible. We are utterly dependent on cheap fossil fuels, so any interruption in supply would bring disaster. Imagine trying to feed and service our huge cities if the fuel ran out! It is now urgently necessary to dismantle the whole fabric of world trade and replace it with a far less fuel-hungry, less polluting, less dangerous arrangement.

Most people know all this, but they are afraid that their quality of life will decline if we change course. Well, the purpose of this book is to show that this is not the case. We could live without pillaging our planet—and live very well indeed! We have allowed ourselves to get where we are because of the "blind workings of the market." But we are not blind, so we must now start using our good sense to "break this sorry scheme of things and then remold it to our hearts' desire," as old Omar Khayam said it.

To allow ourselves to be dependent on some vast "Thing created by the Merchants of Greed" is madness. It is time to cut out what we do not need so we can live more simply and happily. Good food, comfortable clothes, serviceable housing, and true culture—those are the things that matter. The only way this can happen is by ordinary people, us, boycotting the huge multinational corporations that are destroying our Earth—and creating a new Age—an Age of Healing in place of the current Age of Plunder.

I would like to acknowledge my fellow self-supporters, Will Sutherland and Angela Ashe, for their unfailing help over the last three decades. They have shared the trials and labors as well as the joys of this way of life, and have come into partnership with me to start a school of self-sufficiency in Ireland, to which all honest men, women, and children are welcome, provided they can find the fees!

Of course, I have learned a lot since I wrote it (when you cease learning things they take you away in a box), and I continue to live a pretty self-sufficient life. There are very few processes described in this book that I have not performed myself—albeit, perhaps, some of them ineptly. I have embarked on many an enterprise without the faintest idea of how to do it—but I have always ended up with the thing done and with a great deal more knowledge than I had when I started.

Would I advise other people to follow this lifestyle? I wouldn't advise anybody to do anything. The purpose of this book is not to shape other people's lives but simply to help people to do things if they decide to. This way of life suits me—it has kept me fighting fit and at least partly sane into my 88th year, and it has prevented me from doing too much harm to our poor planet.

I would offer this advice: do not try to do everything at once. This is an organic way of life and organic processes tend to be slow and steady. I would also like to offer this motto: "I am only one. I can only do what one can do. But what one can do, I will do!" Happy grub-grubbing! (Better than money-grubbing any day!)

Introduction

In the lives we lead today, we take much for granted, and few of us remember why so many "advanced" civilizations of the past simply disappeared. When I left college, I went to Africa and roamed for six years. I rode the veld in the Karroo, in South Africa, looking after sheep; I managed a sheep farm in Namibia on the verge of the Namib Desert; I hunted buck and shot lions. I spent a year deep-sea fishing and six months working in a copper mine in what is now Zambia. And then I traveled all over central Africa for two years, inoculating native cattle.

One of the best friends I made during my time in Africa was a man of the Old Stone Age. White people, unable to get their tongues around his real name, which was a conglomeration of clicks, called him Joseph. He was a Bushman of the Namib desert, but he had been caught by a white farmer and made to work, so he knew Afrikaans. I knew some of this language and so could communicate with him.

I used to go hunting with Joseph. First he would hand over the flock of sheep to his wife, and then we would walk out into the bush in search of gemsbok or oryx. Joseph had what seemed to be an amazing knack for knowing where they were. When he knew me better he asked me to leave my rifle behind, and he used to put his arm into a thorn bush and pull out the head of a spear. It was quite illegal for a "native" to own a spear. He would cut a shaft from a bush and fit the spearhead, and, using three dogs, we would bring a buck to bay and Joseph would kill it with the spear. Later, Joseph took me on an expedition to meet his people. They lived in the most desolate and inhospitable part of Africa, but they still lived well. They hunted food by lying in wait near waterholes and shooting game with small poisoned arrows. They found water by cutting open the stomach of the gemsbok and drinking the contents—as I learned to do myself. Or they would find an insignificant-looking creeper, dig down under it, and bring up a soggy mass of vegetation as big as a football. They sucked the liquid from this, and very nasty it tasted, too, but very welcome when it could keep you alive.

These people did not "work." They could walk 40 miles in a night and had endless patience while waiting for game. Life was hard in this fierce climate, but they spent most nights dancing and singing and telling stories in the light of their fires. They were completely at home in the natural world and they knew every living being in it. They never felt that they were in any way special or apart from the rest of nature.

I tell all this because I want to point out the enormous change in lifestyle that took place when humans began to practice agriculture. Suddenly, only 10,000–12,000 years ago, people discovered they could plant crops and, just as important, domesticate animals. But there were only a few places (mostly fertile river valleys) where natural conditions made this possible year after year and thus allowed the development of cities. As history shows, very few civilizations developed cultures sufficiently wise and robust to last for more than a thousand years: they simply exhausted their soils or were conquered by more aggressive neighbors.

Now we have had the Industrial, the Technological, and are in the midst of the Information Revolution, which again is bringing about great changes. It is bringing great material prosperity to the few who have their hands on or adjacent to the levers of power. Elsewhere, most of humankind lives in appalling conditions, forced to work in slum cities for starvation wages and sing to the tunes of the big multinationals. Farmers and farmworkers are either starving or being forced to adopt methods that they know are damaging the land. All over the earth the soil is going, eroded by tractor cultivation and slowly poisoned by chemicals from agribusinesses. And so we have created lifestyles that are simply not sustainable or pleasant. But there are many simple changes that individuals can make to their lifestyles that could change all this. And, if we are wise, we will not wait for the apocalypse before making some adjustments. I do not ask you to follow my suggestions blindly, but merely to consider them as you think about the future.

ENERGY

One day I was invited to attend a public symposium on energy, and a public relations officer for the nuclear power industry was there. He showed us all a frightening graph showing the world's energy consumption from 1800 to the present day. The graph started at virtually zero and went up at ever-increasing speed until it was almost vertical. What he had not noticed was that the line pointed straight at the "EXIT" sign above!

Now, surely a moment's reflection is enough to tell us that everyone in the world simply cannot live at the energy levels favored by the 21st-century Western ideal. Of course, for thousands of years, muscle energy and the heat from fires was all that humans had to depend on. When I was born in 1914, things began to change radically with the discovery of how to exploit oil, and today we have released so much carbon back into the atmosphere that no one can predict the consequences. But what difference will it make (you may ask) if I walk up the stairs instead of using the elevator, or turn down the heat a couple of degrees, or use my bike instead of the car? I get no substantial cash benefits because no one can really pay me for benefiting the "commons." This is called the tragedy of the commons—no one pays us to keep the oceans or the air clean.

But if it is true that the only person over whom I have control of actions is myself, then it does matter what I do. It may not matter a jot to the world at large, but it matters to me. And there is, by good fortune, one important factor that can help us make progress in saving energy. For not only does using our muscles help the planet, but it also keeps us fit and healthy.

Of course, there are many other sources of benign energy, and we discuss these later in this book. Solar energy, wind energy, and water power are three obvious alternatives that are increasingly easy to harness with modern technology. I count planned tree planting and coppicing as one of the best solar energy collecting devices. And let us never forget that energy saved is as good as energy bought. It is often much cheaper to buy energy-saving equipment than to pay for the energy used by less effective arrangements.

TRANSPORTATION

Unless we come from a race of traveling people, we are all pretty much "locals." We live somewhere, and what goes on in the locality of where we live is much more important than what goes on in Paris, London, or Washington, D.C. If we could once again run our world on a local scale, with decisions made on a local basis, then many of our problems would be stopped in their tracks. Let me explain "local" by comparing two villages: these are in Crete, but they could be anywhere. One village is high up in the mountains, just to the south of the cave where the god Zeus was born, according to Greek myth. It can only be reached by an unpaved road full of potholes and quite unsuitable for buses. The only contact with the outside world that I could see was that a man with a very tough truck would brave the potholes once each week and bring a load of fish from the small fishing port down on the coast. Sheep were exported from the village to bring in the cash for this transaction.

Apart from this exchange, the community on this mountain was self-supporting. There were enough tiny terraced fields to grow wheat, wine, and olives. There was an oil mill for pressing the olives. There were plenty of nut trees as well as lemon groves, fig trees, and many other kinds of fruits. There were beehives, and the sheep provided meat in abundance. The mountain village houses were beautiful, simple, and comfortable in that climate. Clothes were made by the women. There was a loom-maker in a neighboring village, a boot-maker in another, and a knife-maker in yet another. Was there culture? Well, there was singing and dancing and music aplenty. There were few books, but if the villagers had wanted them, they could have been made available. The villagers paid no taxes and had just one policeman. They knew their own laws and kept to them.

Now, the other Cretan village I wish to describe was lower down the mountain and had a "good" road. This gave access to the city, but also gave the city access to the country. City money came in and bought much of the land, uprooting the old trees and vineyards and planting quick-growing olive trees, so providing an olive crop for cash sale. Now the villagers had to pay for their olive oil and were dragged quickly into the money economy. All sorts of traders had access to the village, and a small supermarket opened. Suddenly, the villagers found they "needed" all sorts of things they had never needed before. Television arrived and brought with it aspirational visions. Young people in the village no longer sang or danced; they wanted Western pop music and Coca-Cola. Even though their fine road looked like a road to freedom, it was actually a road to sadness, wage slavery, and discontent, from which the youngsters could not return.

WORK

I once knew an old lady who lived by herself in the Golfen Valley of England. She was one of the happiest people I have met. She described to me all the work she and her mother used to do when she was a child: washing on Monday, butter-making on Tuesday, market on Wednesday, and so on. "It all sounds like a lot of hard work," I said to her. "Yes, but nobody ever told us then," she said. "Told you what?" "Told us there was anything wrong with work!" Today, "work" has become a dirty word, and most people would do anything to get out of it. To say that an invention is labor-saving is the highest praise, but it never seems to occur to anyone that the work might have been enjoyable. I have plowed all day behind a good set of horses and been sad when the day came to an end!

This book is about changing the way we live, and I am aware that the subject is fraught with difficulties. The young couple who have mortgaged themselves to buy a house, or are struggling with personal loans and credit card debts, are in no position to be very choosy about what work they do.

But why get into such a situation? Why labor to enrich the banks (for that is what we are doing)? There is not necessarily anything wrong with doing things that are profitable. It is when "profit" becomes the dominant motive that the cycle of disaster begins.

In my work with self-sufficiency I have met hundreds of people in many countries and four continents who have withdrawn themselves from conventional work in big cities and moved out to the country. Almost all of them have found good, honest, and useful ways of making a living. Some are fairly well off with regard to money; others are poor in that regard, but they are all rich in the things that really matter. They are the people of the future. If they are not in debt, they are happy men and women.

HOME

A true home should be the container for reviving real hospitality, true culture and conviviality, real fun, solid comfort, and above all, real civilization. And the most creative thing that anybody can do in this world is to make a real home. Indeed, the homemaker is as important as the house, and being a "housewife" is the most creative, most important job on Earth.

One of the essential characteristics of a good home is "craftsmanship." It seems to me that all human artifacts give off a sort of cultural radiation, depending on how much love and art has gone into their production. A mass-produced article of furniture comes from a high-speed, high-tech factory, using plastics and often working with wood that has been destroyed by chipping and gluing. The noise and smell of these places is quite terrifying. And this factory-made rubbish, although it may look fine for a few years, is fit only for the landfill site (burning it would release dioxins). Furniture made by a craftsman, on the other hand, is made with sympathy for the wood. It will last for generations and be a constant beacon of beauty in the home. Of course, I am not suggesting that everyone should build their own home or furniture. After all, if houses were well built and the population were stable, everyone would inherit a good house. But if you can build your own furniture, or indeed house, either with your own hands or with the help of a contractor, it is a marvelous thing to do.

FOOD

Supermarkets have made many "advances" in pre-prepared meals. But the sad fact is that our food now travels thousands of miles before it reaches our mouths. Most people never taste real, locally grown food—they do not know what they are missing. This book is about quality of life, and I submit that if there is no quality in the food we eat, then we must just hope to get through life as quickly as possible. Because the sources of our food are getting farther away, and the food goes through more and more industrial processing, the only quality now deemed important is shelf life. Such food is dead food: all the life has been taken out of it. The best food of all comes from our own land. Next best is food from a local farm or farmer's market, and then food from a local store. If we make the effort to seek out real, "flavor-full" food, we benefit ourselves and, just as important, support those who produce such food. The flavors of homemade cheese or home-reared meat are in a different league from those of processed food. There is a much a self-supporter can do either to encourage local stores to find better food. Better still, get together with others to source food from local farmers (if you cannot produce it yourselves, of course!).

"We had never had any real conscious drive to self-sufficiency. We had thought, like a lot of other people, that it would be nice to grow our own vegetables. But living here has altered our sense of values. We find that we no longer place the same importance on artifacts and gadgets as other people do. Also, every time we buy some factory-made article, we wonder what sort of people made it—if they enjoyed making it or if it was just a bore—what sort of life the maker, or makers, lead. I wonder where all this activity is leading. Is it really leading to a better or richer or simpler life for people? Or not? I wonder about the nature of progress. One can progress in so many different directions. Up a gum-tree, for example. I know that the modern factory worker is supposed to lead an 'easier' life than, say, the peasant. But I wonder if this supposition is correct. And I wonder if, whether 'easier' or not, it is a better life? Simpler? Healthier? More spiritually satisfying? Or not? So far as we can, we import our needs from small and honest craftsmen and tradesmen. We subscribe as little as we can to the tycoons, and the ad men, and the boys with their expense accounts. If we could subscribe to nothing at all, we would be the better pleased."

JOHN SEYMOUR FAT OF THE LAND 1976

CHAPTER ONE

THE MEANING OF SELF-SUFFICIENCY

The Way to Self-Sufficiency

The first questions we must answer are: What is this book about? What is self-sufficiency, and why do it? Now self-sufficiency is not "going back" to some idealized past in which people grubbed for their food with primitive implements and burned each other for witchcraft. It is going forward to a new and better kind of life; a life that is more fun than the overspecialized round of office or factory life; a life that brings challenge and the use of daily initiative back to work, and variety, and occasional great success and occasional abysmal failure. It means the acceptance of complete responsibility for what you do or what you don't do, and one of its greatest rewards is the joy that comes from seeing each job through—from sowing your own wheat to eating your own bread, from planting a field of pig food to slicing a side of bacon.

Self-sufficiency does not mean "going back" to the acceptance of a lower standard of living. On the contrary, it is the striving for a higher standard of living; for food that is fresh and organically grown and good; for the good life in pleasant surroundings; for the health of body and peace of mind that come with hard, varied work in the open air; and for the satisfaction that comes from doing difficult and intricate jobs well and successfully.

A further preoccupation of the self-sufficient person should be the correct attitude to the land. If it ever comes to pass that we have used up all, or most of, the oil on this planet, we will have to reconsider our attitude to our only real and abiding asset—the land itself. We will one day have to derive our sustenance from what the land, unaided by oil-derived chemicals, can produce. We may not wish in the future to maintain a standard of living that depends entirely on elaborate and expensive equipment and machinery, but we will always want to maintain a high standard of living in the things that really matter—good food, clothing, shelter, health, happiness, and fun with other people. The land can support us, and it can do it without huge applications of artificial chemicals and fertilizers or use of expensive machinery.

But everyone who owns a piece of land should husband that land as wisely, knowledgeably, and intensively as possible. The so-called "self-supporter" sitting among a riot of docks and thistles talking philosophy ought to go back to town. He is not doing any good at all, and is occupying land that should be occupied by somebody who can really use it.

Other forms of life, too, besides our own, should merit our consideration. Humans should be a husbandmen, not exploiters. This planet is not exclusively for our own use. To destroy every form of life except such forms as are obviously directly of use to us is immoral, and ultimately, quite possibly, will contribute to our own destruction. The kind of varied, carefully thought-out husbandry of the self-supporting farm fosters a great variety of life forms, and every self-supporter will wish to leave some areas of true wilderness on his farm, where wild forms of life can continue to flourish undisturbed and in peace.

And then there is the question of our relations with other people. Many people move from the cities back to the land precisely because they find city life, surrounded by people, too lonely. A self-supporter, living alone and surrounded by giant commercial farms, may be lonely, too; but if there are other self-supporters nearby, he or she will be forced into cooperation with them and become, very quickly, part of a living and warm community. There will be shared work in the fields, there will be relief milking and animal feeding duties when other people go on vacation, there will be sharing of babysitting duties, there will be barn-raisings and corn-shuckings and celebrations of all kinds. This kind of social life already happens in those parts of Europe and North America where self-supporting individuals, or communities, are becoming common.

Good relations with the indigenous population of the country are important, too. In my area, the old country people are very sympathetic to the new "drop-ins." They rejoice to see us reviving and preserving the old skills they practiced in their youth, and they take pleasure in imparting them to us. They wax eloquent when they see the hams and flitches of bacon hung up in my chimney. "That's real bacon," they say, "better than the stuff we get at the store." "My mother used to make that when I was a boy; we grew all our own food then," they might add. "Why don't you grow it now?" I ask. "Ah! times have changed." Well, they are changing again.

Self-sufficiency on a small scale

Self-sufficiency is not only for those who have five acres of their own country. A city-dweller who learns how to mend her own shoes becomes, to some extent, self-sufficient. She saves money and increases her own satisfaction and self-respect, too. We were not meant to be a one-job animal. We do not thrive as parts of a machine. We are intended by nature to be diverse, to do diverse things, to have many skills. The city person who buys a sack of wheat from a farmer on a country visit and grinds his own flour to make his own bread cuts out the middlemen and furthermore gets better bread. He gets good exercise turning the handle of the grinding machine, too. And any suburban gardener can dig up some of that useless lawn, put some of those dreary hardy perennials on the compost pile, and grow some cabbages. An urban garden or a community garden can provide a sound base for a would-be self-supporter (*see pp.26–29*), and a good-sized suburban garden can practically keep a family. I knew a woman who grew the finest outdoor tomatoes I ever saw in a window box 12 stories up in a high-rise. They were too high up to get the blight.

So good luck and long life to all self-supporters! And if every reader of this book learns something useful that he or she did not know before, and could not very easily find out, then I, and the dedicated people who have done the very arduous and difficult work of putting it together, will be happy and feel it has not been in vain.

THE FIRST PRINCIPLES OF SELF-SUFFICIENCY

The only way that the homesteader can farm his piece of land as well and intensively as possible is to institute some variant of what was called "High Farming" in Europe in the 19th century. This was a carefully worked out balance between animals and plants, so that each fed the other: the plants feeding the animals directly, the animals feeding the soil with their manure, and the land feeding the plants. A variety of both animals and plants were rotated around the same land so that each species took what it needed out and put what it had to contribute back, and the needs of the soil were kept uppermost always in the husbandman's mind. Each animal and crop was considered for what beneficial effect it might have on the soil.

If the same crop is grown on a piece of land year after year, the disease organisms that attack that crop will build up in the area until they become uncontrollable. Nature abhors monoculture: any cursory inspection of a natural plant and animal environment will reveal a great variety of species. If one species becomes too predominant, some pest or disease is sure to develop to strike it down. Man has managed to defy this law, to date, by the application of stronger and stronger chemical controls, but the pests (particularly the fast-evolving viruses) adapt very quickly to withstand each new chemical and so far the chemist has managed to keep only a short jump ahead of the disease.

The new homesteader will wish to husband his land in accordance with the principles of High Farming. He will have to substitute the labor of his hands for imported chemicals and sophisticated machinery. He will have to use his brain and his cunning to save the work of his hands. For instance, if he can get his animals to go out into his fields and consume their share of his crops there, then he will save himself the work of harvesting the crops for them and carrying them in. In other words, take the animals to the crops, not the crops to the animals. So, also, if he can get the animals to deposit their dung on his land, then this will save him the labor of carrying the dung out himself. Thus the keeping of animals on limited free range will appeal to him: sheep can be "folded" on arable land (folding means penning animals on a small area of some fodder crop and moving the pen from time to time), chickens can he housed in coops that can be moved over the land so as to distribute the hens' manure while allowing the hens to graze fresh grass, and pigs can be kept behind electric fences that can also be easily moved. Thus the pigs harvest their food for themselves and also distribute their own manure. (To say nothing of the fact that pigs are the finest free cultivators that were ever invented! They will clear your land, and plow it, and dung it, and harrow it, and leave it nearly ready for you to put your seed in, with no more labor to you than the occasional shifting of an electric fence.)

In planning the layout of the small farm, the homesteader will take careful account of natural shelter, considering especially the effects of the prevailing wind. Trees will be planted to create a barrier on the north and east (in the northern hemisphere) and permanent thorn hedges established to divide the holding into sensible stockproof fields. Existing water and streams will be carefully assessed for possible use in irrigation, water power, or suitable ponds for duck and geese. Care will be taken to make good advantage of all natural features of the site. Walls will be constructed to create a south-facing shelter suitable for excellent fruit trees. The buildings will be sited where they are most convenient both to each other and to the productive areas of the smallholding.

Now the true husbandman will not keep the same species of animal on a piece of land too long, just as he will not grow the same crop year after year in the same place. He will follow his young calves with his older cattle, his cattle with sheep, his sheep with horses, while geese and other poultry either run free or are progressively moved over his grassland and arable land (land that gets plowed and planted with crops as opposed to land that is grass all the time).

All animals suffer from parasites, and if you keep one species on one piece of land for too long, there will be a buildup of parasites and disease organisms. As a rule, the parasites of one animal do not affect another and therefore following one species with another over the land will eliminate parasites.

Also, the true husbandman will find that every enterprise on his holding, if it is correctly planned, will interact beneficially with every other. If he keeps cows their dung will manure the land, which will provide food not only for the cows but for the humans and pigs also. The by-products of the milk of the cows (skim milk from butter-making and whey from cheese-making) are a marvelous whole food for pigs and poultry. The dung from the pigs and poultry helps grow the food for the cows. Chickens will scratch around in the dung of other animals and salvage any undigested grain.

All crop residues help to feed the appropriate animals and such residues as not even the pigs can eat, they will tread into the ground, and activate with their manure, and turn into the finest in-situ compost without the husbandman lifting a spade. All residues from slaughtered birds or animals go either to feed the pigs or the sheepdogs, or to activate the compost pile. Nothing is wasted. Nothing is an expensive embarrassment to be taken away to pollute the environment. There should be no need for a garbage man on the self-sufficient farm. Even old newspapers can make litter for pigs, or be composted. Anything that has to be burned makes good potash for the land. Nothing is wasted—there is no "garbage."

However, before the potential self-supporter or homesteader decides to embark on the pursuit of "true husbandry," he should acquaint himself with some of the basic laws of nature, so that he can better understand why certain things will happen on his holding and why other things will not.

Humans & the Environment

True homesteaders will seek to husband their land, not exploit it.

They will wish to improve and maintain the "heart" of this land: its fertility.

They will learn by observing nature that growing one crop only, or keeping one species of animal only, on the same piece of land is not in the natural order of things.

They will therefore wish to nurture the animals and plants on their land to ensure the survival of the widest possible variety of natural forms.

They will understand and encourage the interactions between living things.

They will even leave some areas of wilderness on their land, where wild forms of life can flourish.

Where they cultivate, they will always keep in mind the needs of the soil, considering each animal and each plant for what beneficial effect it might have on the land.

Above all, they will realize that if they interfere with the chain of life (of which they are a part) they do so at their peril, for they cannot avoid disturbing the natural balance.

THE FOOD CHAIN

Life on this planet has been likened to a pyramid: a pyramid with an unbelievably wide base and a small apex.

All life needs nitrogen, for it is one of the most essential constituents of living matter, but most creatures cannot use the free, uncombined nitrogen that makes up a great part of our atmosphere. The base of our biotic pyramid, therefore, is made up of the bacteria that live in the soil, sometimes in symbiosis with higher plants, and have the power of fixing nitrogen from the air. The number of these organisms in the soil is unimaginably great: suffice it to say that there are millions of them in a speck of soil only as big as a pinhead.

On these, the basic and most essential of all forms of life, lives a vast host of microscopic animals. As we work up the pyramid, or the food chain, whichever way we like to consider it, we find that each superimposed layer is far less in number than the layer it preys upon.

On the higher plants graze the herbivores. Every antelope, for example, must have millions of grass plants to support it. On the herbivores "graze" the carnivores. And every lion must have hundreds of antelopes to support it. The true carnivores are right at the apex of the biotic pyramid. Humans are somewhere near the top, but not at the top, because we are omnivores. We are one of those lucky animals that can subsist on a wide range of food: vegetable and animal.

INTERRELATIONSHIPS

Up and down the chain, or up and down between the layers of the pyramid, there is a vast complexity of inter-relationships. There are, for example, purely carnivorous microorganisms. There are all kinds of parasitic and saprophitic organisms: the former live on their hosts and sap their strength; the latter live in symbiosis, or in friendly cooperation, with other organisms, animal or vegetable. We have said that the carnivores are at the apex of the food chain. Where in it stands a flea on a lion's back? Or a parasite in a lion's gut?

And what about the bacterium that is specialized (and you can bet there is one) to live inside the body of the lion flea? A system of such gargantuan complexity can best, perhaps, be understood by the utter simplification of the famous verse:

Little bugs have lesser bugs upon their backs to bite 'em,
And lesser bugs have lesser bugs and so ad infinitum!

This refers to parasitism alone, of course, but it is noteworthy that all up and down the pyramid, everything is consumed, eventually, by something else. And that includes us, unless we break the chain of life by the purely destructive process of cremation.

Now humans, the thinking monkeys, are wont to interfere with this system (of which we should never forget that we are a part), but we do so at our peril.

If we eliminate many carnivores among the larger mammals, the herbivores on which these carnivores preyed become overcrowded, overgraze, and create deserts. If, on the other hand, we eliminate too many herbivores, the herbage grows rank and out of control, and good pasture goes back to scrub and cannot, unless it is cleared, support many herbivores. If we eliminate every species of herbivore except one, the grazing is less efficiently grazed.

Sheep graze very close to the ground, biting the grass off with their front teeth. Cows, on the other hand, rip the grass up by wrapping their tongues around it, and they prefer long grass. So the hills produce more and better sheep if cattle graze on them, too. It is up to us as husbandmen and women to consider very carefully, and act very wisely, before we use our powers to interfere with the rest of the biotic pyramid.

Plants, too, exist in great variety in natural environments and for very good reasons. Different plants take different things out of the soil, and put different things back. Members of the pea, bean, and clover family, for example, have nitrogen-fixing bacteria in nodules on their roots. Thus they can fix their own nitrogen. But you can wipe the clovers out of a pasture by applying artificial nitrogen. It is not that the clovers do not like the artificial nitrogen, but that you remove the "unfair advantage" that they had over the grasses (which are not nitrogen-fixing) by supplying the latter with plenty of free nitrogen, and, being naturally more vigorous than the clovers, the grasses smother them out.

It is obvious from observing nature that monoculture is not in the natural order of things. We can only sustain a one-crop-only system by adding the elements that the crop needs from the fertilizer bag and destroying all the crop's rivals and enemies with chemicals. If we wish to farm more in accordance with the laws and customs of nature, we must diversify as much as we can, both with plants and animals.

Ultimately, it all comes back to the first rule in becoming self-sufficient: that is, to understand the "Natural Cycle": namely, the soil feeds the plants, the plants feed the animals, the animals manure the land, the manure feeds the soil, the soil feeds the plants (*see pp.22–23*). True "husbanding" homesteaders will wish to maintain this natural cycle, but they have to become part of the cycle themselves; as plant-eaters and carnivores they are liable to break the chain unless they observe at all times the "Law of Return." The Law of Return means that all residues (animal, vegetable, and human) should be returned to the soil, either by way of the compost heap, or the guts of an animal, or the plow, or by being trodden into the ground by livestock. Whatever cannot be usefully returned to the soil, or usefully used in some other way, should be burned; this will make potash for the land. Nothing should be wasted on the self-sufficient farm and I believe this applies as much to a modest community garden as it does to a farm of several acres.

THE SOIL

Because soil derives from many kinds of rock, there are many varieties of soil. Since we cannot always get exactly the kind of soil that we require, self-supporters must learn to make the best of the soil that they have. Depending on the size of their particles, soils are classified as light or heavy, with an infinite range of gradations in between. Light means composed of large particles. Heavy means composed of small particles. Gravel can hardly be called soil, but sand can, and pure sand is the lightest soil you can get. The kind of clay that is made of the very smallest particles is the heaviest. The terms "light" and "heavy" in this context have nothing to do with weight but with the ease of working of the soil. You can dig sand, or otherwise work with it, no matter how wet it is, and do it no harm. Heavy clay is very hard to dig or plow, gets very "puddingy" and sticky, and is easily damaged by working it when it is wet.

What we call soil generally has a thickness to be measured in inches rather than feet. It merges below with the subsoil, which is generally pretty humus-free but may be rich in mineral foods needed by plants. Deep-rooting plants such as some trees, alfalfa, comfrey, and many herbs, send their roots right down into the subsoil, and extract these nutriments from it.

The nature of the subsoil is very important because of its influence on drainage. If it is heavy clay, for example, then the drainage will be bad and the field will be wet. If it is sand, gravel, decayed chalk, or limestone, then the field will probably be dry. Below the subsoil lies rock, and rock goes on down to the center of the Earth. The rock, too, can affect drainage: limestone, sandstone, chalk, and other pervious rocks make for good drainage: clay (geologists consider this a rock, too), slate, mudstone, some shales, granite, and other igneous rocks generally make for poor drainage. Badly drained soils can always be drained—provided enough expenditure of labor and capital is put into doing it.

Types of soil

Let us now consider various types of soil:

Heavy clay This, if it can be drained and worked with great care and knowledge, can be very fertile soil, at least for many crops. Wheat, oak trees, field beans, potatoes, and other crops do superbly on well-farmed clay. Farmers often refer to it as strong land. But great experience is needed to farm it effectively. This is because of the propensity of clay to "flocculate"—that is, the microscopic particles that make up clay gather together in larger particles. When this happens, the clay is more easily worked, drains better, allows air to get down into it, and allows the roots of plants to penetrate it more easily. In other words it becomes good soil. When it does the opposite of flocculate it "puddles": it forms a sticky mass, such as the potter uses to make his pots, becomes almost impossible to cultivate, and gets as hard as brick when it dries out. The land forms big cracks and is useless.

Factors that cause clay to flocculate are alkalinity rather than acidity, exposure to air and frost, incorporation of humus, and good drainage. Acidity causes it to puddle; so does working it while wet. Heavy machines tend to puddle it. Clay must be plowed or dug when in exactly the right condition of humidity, and left strictly alone when wet.

Clay can always be improved by the addition of humus (compost, "muck" or farmyard manure, leaf mold, green manuring: any vegetable or animal residue), by drainage, by plowing it up at the right time and letting the air and frost get to it (frost separates the particles by forcing them apart), by liming if acid, even, in extreme cases, by incorporating sand with the clay. Clay soil is "late" soil, which means it will not produce crops early in the year. It is difficult soil. It is not "hungry" soil—that is, if you put humus in it, the humus will last a long time. It tends to be rich in potash and is often naturally alkaline, in which case it does not need liming.

Loam This is intermediate between clay and sand, and has many gradations of heaviness or lightness. A medium loam is perhaps the perfect soil for most kinds of farming. Most loam is a mixture of clay and sand, although some loams probably have particles all of the same size. If loam (or any other soil) lies on a limestone or chalk rock, it will probably be alkaline and will not need liming, although this is not always the case: there are limestone soils that, surprisingly, do need liming. Loam, like every other kind of soil, will always benefit from humus addition.

Sand Sandy soil, or the lighter end of the spectrum of heavy light soils, is generally well-drained, often acid (in which case it will need liming), and often deficient in potash and phosphates. It is "early" soil; that is, it warms up very quickly after the winter and produces crops early in the year. It is also "hungry" soil; when you put humus into it, the humus does not last long. In fact, to make sandy soil productive you must put large quantities of organic manure into it, and inorganic manure gets quickly washed away from it. Sandy soils are favored for market gardening, being early and easy to work and very responsive to heavy dressings of manure. They are good soils for such techniques as folding sheep or pigs on the land. They are good for wintering cattle on because they do not "poach" (turn into a quagmire when trodden) like heavy soils do. They recover quickly from treading when under grass. But they won't grow as heavy crops of grass or other crops as heavier land. They dry out very quickly and suffer from drought more than clay soils do.

Peat Peat soils are in a class of their own, but unfortunately are fairly rare. Peat is formed of vegetable matter that has been compressed in anaerobic conditions (underwater) and has not rotted away. Sour wet peatland is not much good for farming, although such soil, if drained, will grow potatoes, oats, celery, and certain other crops. But naturally drained peatlands are, quite simply, the best soils in the world. They will grow anything, and grow it better than any other soil. They don't need manure, they are manure!

The Natural Cycle

One of the most important maxims you may remember from your high school science classes is that matter can be neither created nor destroyed. Nowhere is the principle more critical than in understanding the process by which the fertility of the land can be increased. The major life processes on earth require large quantities of certain basic elements: carbon, oxygen, and nitrogen in particular. And the energy that makes all this life shake, rattle, and roll is provided by sugars that are essentially made by photosynthesis, driven by the sun. While carbon and oxygen are both common and reactive, nitrogen is not quite so easy for our life processes to manage. Even though there is a huge quantity of nitrogen gas in our atmosphere, plants cannot absorb nitrogen directly. Apart from a small amount of nitrogen that is made water-soluble by the action of thunderstorms, we depend upon bacteria to fix nitrogen and change it into forms that can be used by plants. The animals that run around have to get their nitrogen second-hand, courtesy of the plant kingdom. The bacteria we need are present by the million in healthy soil.

MUCH-NEEDED NITROGEN
Huge quantities of usable nitrogen are present in human, animal, and plant wastes. It is much easier for the soil to recycle these than for soil bacteria to "fix" nitrogen from scratch. This is why all effective husbandry places such emphasis on the importance of composting and healthy soil. It is easy to understand the cycle from this simple diagram.

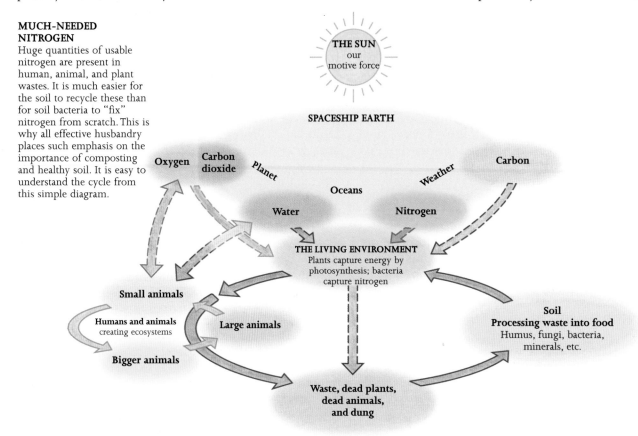

THE ECOLOGICALLY SOUND HOLDING
One of the chief features of 18th-century English farming was the famous "Norfolk four-course rotation." This was an ecologically sound system of husbandry—a model for the productive growing of a variety of crops in both large- and small-scale farming. It worked like this:

1 One-year Ley A ley was grass and clover sown for a temporary period. The grass and clover were grazed off by stock. The ley's purpose was to increase the fertility of the land with the nitrogen fixed in the root nodules of the clover, with the dung of the grazing animals, and ultimately with the mass of vegetation plowed into the land when the ley was plowed up.

2 Root break The crops in the root break might have been turnips or rutabagas to be fed to cattle, sheep, or pigs, potatoes to be fed mostly to humans, mangels for cattle, and various kinds of kale—the latter not actually "roots," of course, but taking the same place in the root break. The effect of the root break was to increase the fertility of the soil, because nearly all the farmyard manure produced on the farm was used to nourish the root crop and to "clean" (remove weeds from) the land. Root crops are "cleaning crops" because, being planted in rows, they have to be hoed several times. The third effect of the root break was to produce crops that stored the summer's growth for winter feeding.

3 Winter cereal break This was wheat, beans, barley, oats, or rye sown in the fall. It drew out the fertility put into the land by the ley and the roots, benefited from the cleanliness of the land after the roots, and was the farmer's chief cash crop—the crop from which he made his money. The beans, however, were for feeding to livestock.

4 Spring cereal break This was possibly spring-sown wheat, but it was more likely to be barley. After the barley had been drilled, grass and clover seed was undersown—that is, broadcast on the ground along with the cereal seed. As the barley grew, the grass and clover grew, and when the barley was harvested, a good growth of grass and clover was left to be grazed off the next spring and summer, or to be cut for hay and grazed the following winter, too. The barley went principally to feed stock, but the best of it went to be malted for beer. The oats and barley straw were fed to the cattle; the wheat straw went under their feet to provide all that vast tonnage of farmyard manure (the best compost ever invented); rye straw was used for thatching; the roots were mostly fed to the cattle or to the sheep; and wheat, malting barley, beef, and wool went off to be sold to city folk.

Historically, land properly managed in this way often grew two tons of wheat to the acre, and this was with no input of oil-derived chemicals whatsoever, because there weren't any back then. Now we can emulate this ecologically sound system, changing it to suit our different needs. We may not wish to live primarily on the bread, beef, and beer of the 18th-century Englishman. We may need more dairy products—butter, cheese, and milk—more vegetables, a greater variety of food altogether. Also, we are blessed with new crops and modern equipment: Jerusalem artichokes, fodder radish, fodder beet, corn in northern climates, and devices such as the electric fence, which widen our possible courses of action.

So, whether our would-be self-supporter has nothing more than a backyard garden, or perhaps a community garden plot, or whether he or she has, say, a hundred-acre farm, or whether we are part of a community that owns a thousand acres, the principles we should follow are the same. We should try to work with Nature, not against it, and we should, as far as we can while still serving our own ends, emulate Nature in our methods.

EIGHT POINTERS TO A HEALTHY PLOT

If you want to improve and maintain the heart of your land, you should remember these eight pointers:

1 Monoculture, or the growing of the same crop on land year after year, should be avoided. Disease organisms that attack any particular crop always build up in land on which that crop is grown year after year. Also, each crop has different requirements from the soil, and its residues return different materials to the soil.

2 The keeping of only one species of animal on the soil should also be avoided. The old farmers in England used to say: "A full bullock yard makes a full stack yard." In other words, the manure from the animals is good for the soil. Mixed stocking is always better than mono-stocking, and best of all is rotational grazing: the penning or folding of a species of animal over varying sections of the land, so that the animals leave their droppings (and inevitable parasite eggs) behind and so break the parasites' life cycle.

Following one species with another in such a rotation should be practiced wherever possible.

3 Grow leys, graze them, and ultimately plow them in.

4 Practice "green manuring." That is, if you don't want to grow a crop for grazing or producing animal feed, grow the crop anyway and then plow it in, or, better still, work it in with discs or other instruments.

5 Avoid plowing too much or too deep. To bury the topsoil and bring the subsoil to the surface is not good. On the other hand, chisel plowing (the cutting of furrows in the soil by dragging knives through it) does not invert the soil, helps drainage, breaks "pans" (hard layers under the surface), and can only do good.

6 Don't let land remain bare and exposed to the weather and elements any more than is absolutely necessary. When it is covered with vegetation, even with weeds, the soil will not erode or deteriorate. If left bare, it will. A growing crop will take up and store the nitrogen and other elements of the soil and release them when it rots down. In bare soil, many soluble plant foods are leached out (washed away).

7 Attend to drainage. Waterlogged soil is no-good soil and will deteriorate unless, of course, you are growing rice or keeping water buffalo.

8 Observe, at all times, the Law of Return. All crop and animal residues should be returned to the soil. If you sell anything off the holding, then you should import something of equal manurial value back onto it. (The Law of Return should apply to human excrement, too.) Now if the Law of Return is properly observed, it is theoretically possible to maintain, if not increase, the fertility of a piece of land without animals at all. Careful composting of vegetable residue is necessary, but it is noteworthy that on holdings where no animals are kept, but a high standard of fertility is maintained, vegetable matter is almost always brought in from outside the holding, and very often other high-energy substances, such as compost activator, are also imported. Seaweed, leaf mold from the woods, dead leaves from city street-cleaning services, waste vegetables from grocery stores, straw or spoiled hay, nettles or bracken mown on public land or waste ground or neighbors' land: all such inputs of vegetable residues are possible, and will keep up the fertility of land that has no animals.

It is difficult to see why putting vegetable matter into animals and then returning it to the land as manure should be better than putting it directly on to the land, but it is demonstrably so. There is no doubt about it: as any farmer with any experience knows, there is some potent magic that transmutes vegetable residues into manure of extraordinary value by putting it through the guts of an animal. But when it is realized that animals and plants have evolved together on this planet, perhaps this is not surprising. Nature does not seem to show any examples of an animal-free vegetable environment. Even the gases inhaled and exhaled by these two different orders of life seem to be complementary: plants breathe in carbon dioxide and breathe out oxygen, animals do the opposite.

The Seasons

EARLY SPRING

Plow and rototill your land when the winter frosts have broken up the soil. Rototill beds several times in dry weather at two-week intervals to knock out the weeds. Harrow fields for sowing with discs or spikes. Spread compost or well-rotted animal manure on the land before cultivation. Start ordering or buying the seeds you will need when the weather warms up. Plant up your onion sets.

LATE SPRING

Sow seeds when the ground is warm and mark rows carefully for future hoeing. Sow batches every two weeks and make sure you take every chance to hoe and give the weeds a beating when the weather is dry. Put in your early potatoes and use cloches to protect melons and other squashes from late frosts. Harvest your delicious sprouting broccoli. Turn out animals onto grass. Make sure you have plenty of home brew in the making to prepare you for the thirsty work of shearing and hay-making later on. Buy in young piglets for fattening over the summer. Expect to start milking again as soon as your cow has calved.

EARLY SUMMER

Shear your sheep and look forward to the fact that wool from five of them will clothe a large family. With the summer flush of grass, your cow(s) will pour out milk and you should make butter nearly every day. Make a good cheese each week for storing for the winter. In midsummer comes the backbreaking but satisfying job of hay-making. Make sure your equipment is in good shape and line up friends to give you a hand. Check again that you have ample supplies of home brew. Prune plum trees now while there is still vigorous growth. Keep weeding the vegetable beds. Plant out tender plants such as tomatoes and corn.

LATE SUMMER

Harvest your wheat and barley when it is good and ripe. The harvest is the crown of the year, and you will need help from friends. Tree fruit from the orchard will start being ready to pick; soft fruits must be picked and processed. The early potatoes will be lifted: lovely fresh ones for lunch each day. Wild berries can be gathered for jams and canning. Wine-making continues throughout the late summer period. Many parts of the garden will now need harvesting daily: peas and beans to be processed for the freezer, lettuce and tomatoes to be eaten fresh. By now you will have beaten the weeds and your plants are pretty well strong enough to stand up for themselves.

FALL

This is the time to harvest root crops and get them into winter storage. Now you will be in full production of hard cider, both from your own apples and from those you pick up from friends. Mushrooms of all shapes and sizes will be a tasty addition to your rations, and if there are any extra, they will go into the freezer. Take some time now to prepare your firewood for the winter. Bring wood in to cut and split before it gets too wet. Begin spinning of flax and wool in preparation for winter weaving. Pickle the remainder of your beets and dry out and string up your onions. Rototill and tidy up all parts of the garden that have been harvested.

WINTER

This is the time to rebuild hedges and plant new ones. Now you must dig in and press on with repair work on gates and fences. Tools and implements must be sharpened and repaired. Bring in grazing animals if the weather turns nasty. When the weather is cold, plan to slaughter livestock and butcher meat in a fly-free environment. Kill pigs and make ham and bacon. Prepare areas for your winter tree planting program. Consider racking off your demijohns of summer wine. Above all, take time out to enjoy the fruits of your labors with new friends and old.

The Urban Garden

It is amazing what can be packed into an urban garden. Even the smallest space can be made productive, and what could be more appealing than the sight of well-tended fruit and vegetables right outside your back door? If you have enough space, think about a small greenhouse to extend your growing season and let you grow more exotic produce. And don't forget that a beehive will send your little foragers out to gather nectar from all the flowers in your neighborhood and make pounds of lovely honey.

I remember meeting a fascinating man when I was in California who made his living creating "easy-run" urban vegetable gardens for the elderly and disabled. These were all based on raised beds made of either brick or treated wood. The beds raised the soil level to a comfortable height for weeding and picking, at the same time, giving the plants more light and providing the garden with a pleasing 3-dimensional effect. This kind of garden layout is expensive, but when land is scarce in a city, it provides maximum planting areas.

The raised gardens I saw in California were of the "deep bed" type. They were raised containers constructed by using old railroad ties, bricks, or blocks, and then filled up with extremely good-quality topsoil to a depth of at least 18 in (45 cm). This depth of soil allows for very dense planting, high output, and vigorous, drought-resistant rooting. The smaller your plot, the more intensively you will be able to cultivate.

Planning your urban garden

It's a lovely occupation and a great luxury to sit in your armchair dreaming about your future garden in the depths of winter, but finally crunch time comes: what exactly are you going to put where?

The first essential is to think about the orientation of the site: where is the sun and where is the shade? You will not want to have tall plants on the south side of your garden; equally, you will want to use any south-facing fence or wall for sun-loving plants—for example, espaliered fruit trees. Ideally, you will want to break up the cultivated area into smaller blocks by using perennials, such as the soft fruit bushes or artichokes.

Next, you have to decide what kind of crops you want to grow. In part, this is a matter of personal preference, but also it is a question of what the site will support. Some plants—for example, squash or blackberries—tend to be very large and aggressive. These "plants with attitude" will not make comfortable plantings for your small urban garden. Equally, potatoes take up a great deal of space for very little real gain; you can easily obtain first-rate potatoes from other sources. As a compromise, you might want to plant just a few earlies. The green salad crops are wonderful to grow because they taste so much better pulled up fresh from the garden. Snow peas or sugar-snap peas are also especially delicious when fresh. Runner beans are very exciting to grow. They are a real 3-D plant that produces a mass of food from a very small space. A few soft fruit bushes and raspberries will pay their way well in terms of labor and space, as will espaliered fruit trees. You might also consider rhubarb, which is a nice early fruit crop, but asparagus would be a real space guzzler, as would corn.

Carrots are an ideal vegetable to grow, too, and they taste absolutely delicious when pulled fresh from the soil. Tomatoes can also be a brilliantly productive plant in a tight space. Strawberries grow well in specially designed pots, but make sure the pot you buy is frost-proof, because many cheaper ones are not and will crack, causing you to lose your lovely crop. As well as growing strawberries in pots, you can also grow them in little crevices made in stone walls. In the urban garden, I think this is the best place for them. The best piece of advice I can give you when planning your urban garden is to remember that the more use you can make of all three dimensions, the better your garden—and produce—will be.

And finally… it is a notable feature of the natural world that pests such as aphids or rabbits breed extremely fast. Once they get going, their numbers soon go exponential and your vegetable plot is rapidly consumed. So there is vital value in having predators ready and waiting right at the start of the breeding season so no bubbles of aphid population get out of control. One or two bushy perennials—such as currant bushes or raspberry canes—will provide shelter for these predators over the winter. You might even consider making a hedge out of them to create a border and discourage cats and dogs from wandering into your plantings.

There are many suitable perennials that you can use to break up your cultivated areas of cultivation. The soft fruits, especially currants, work well for this purpose. Alternatively, you can use the vigorous globe artichoke or something like asparagus or even strawberries

Central deep bed
This is the workhorse of your garden. Keep fertility and soil condition high with regular applications of rotted manure and compost. Make sure you vary the choice of crop each year to avoid disease.

AN URBAN MICRO-GARDEN
Make use of all your urban garden space by using all three dimensions. Paving and bricks cut out mud and eliminate weeds.

Wire supports
Use rot-proof timbers and galvanized wire for supports. Even better, find stainless steel wire, which is less abrasive on bark.

Fruit espalier hedges
Apples and plums can be trained to make attractive and productive "hedges." These should face south or west.

Productive climbers
Raspberries and runner beans provide a 6-foot "wall" of productivity.

Larger plants
Use tomatoes, artichokes, rhubarb, or even zucchini as a lower layer of robust productivity.

Beehive
Keep a clear space around your hive to allow the bees access.

Composting
An enclosed bin keeps out rats and flies. A perforated metal sheet underneath will let in worms but keep out rats and mice.

Paving slabs
Cover access areas and walkways with paving slabs, block paving or concrete. Put plastic membrane underneath to make sure the weeds do not come through.

Raised bed
Make this from bricks, stone, or treated wood. Make sure drainage is good.

Raised planting
Tasty salad crops are ideal for the raised bed. Grow seedlings here for transplanting to the central deep bed.

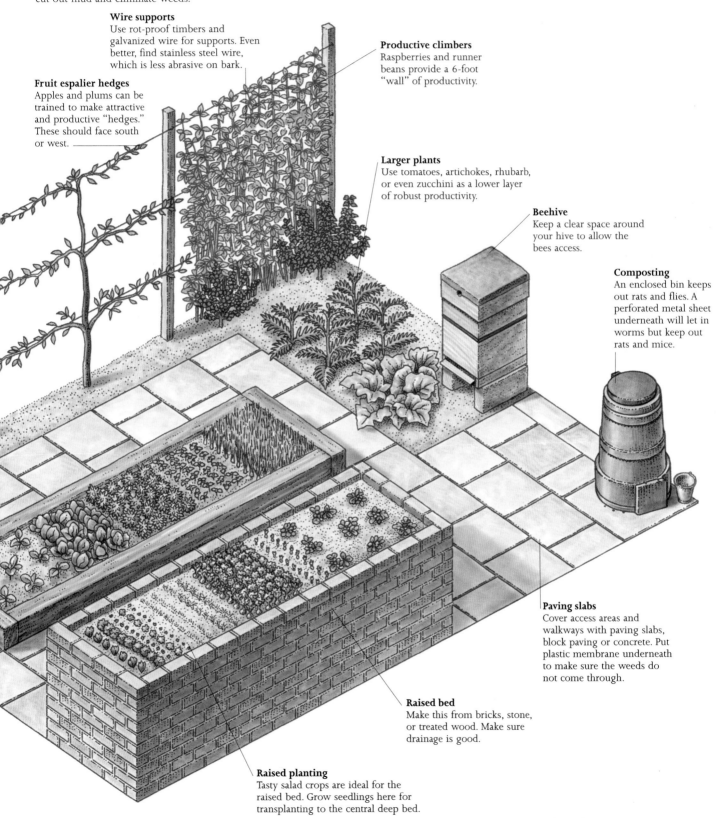

The Community Garden

If you have no land of your own, find out whether your city or town has a community garden where you can rent a plot. This will not only give you a chance to get your hands dirty and grow your own good, fresh produce, but will also allow you to meet like-minded neighbors and take an active role in developing your community.

Think about how your plot will develop over a number of years. Plants like soft fruit bushes and fruit trees will grow more than you imagine, or at least that has been my experience—I always seem to end up having to thin out my currant and gooseberry bushes after five or six years.

The layout of paths, hedges, and perennial plantings needs to be thought about carefully. Once hedges and trees have grown, it is very difficult to move them! I always tell people to leave enough space to take a small tractor into the center of the plot, in case they decide to bring in building materials or farmyard manure.

COMMUNITY SPIRIT
A community garden can become part of a long-term relationship between your neighborhood and the natural world. Even "bad" areas often improve when a disused urban lot or street corner is cleared of junk and transformed into an attractive green space that gives residents a sense of achievement and pride.

Training espaliers
Be brutal when training espaliers; pinch out shoots, and prune off unwanted branches.

Row crops
Grow row crops like lettuce, onions, and peas in six-year rotation.

Espaliered fruit trees
Buy new trees and train them to make a productive hedge, preferably facing south or west. This is an attractive and space-efficient way to grow tree fruit.

Central bed
Grow beets for a heavy yield. They also make a great winter salad substitute when pickled.

Cultivated beds
Make these long but not too wide so you can use a rototiller to make life easy. 5 feet (1.5 m) is maximum for a deep bed garden; use 6–12 feet (1.8–3.5 m) for conventional row planting.

Permanent posts
Use either rot-resistant wood or concrete posts for your fencing.

Brassicas
Well-spaced mature brassicas are a great crop for winter greens.

Raspberry supports
Always use rot-proof wooden posts to make secure supports that can be reused year after year.

Beech hedges
These are an ideal way to shelter your garden from blustery winds. They are easily controlled, good-looking, and very durable. Keep height down to about 4 feet (1.2 m) to prevent shade.

Seedbeds
Plant brassicas and salad crops in seedbeds for transplanting later in the year, when there is more room in the garden.

Runner beans
These are a brilliantly productive "aerial" crop. Slugs love the young shoots, and don't forget they grow at least 8 feet (2.5 m) tall, casting lots of shade.

Compost bins
Use a two-bin compost system, layering the material in square stacks, not loose heaps. Add farmyard manure if you can get it.

Paving
Well-laid paving helps restrain weeds and generally makes working the garden easier.

Soft fruits
Use soft fruits and other large perennials to break up the garden and provide shelter.

Avoid the temptation to get everything done overnight, and you will happily make haste in clearing a weedy plot! If you leave any perennial deep-rooted weeds (nettles, thistles, and docks, for example) lurking in your soil, it will be impossible to keep them at bay later.

To start clearing a plot, first remove all the surface vegetation and set up a composting area. You will probably need a space about 5 feet square (2.5 sq m) for this. A scythe is the perfect tool for cutting the weeds as close

to the earth as your skill allows (*see pp.378–379*). Rake off the cut vegetation with a garden fork. Press the fork down firmly as you pull it toward you to get the surface weeds pulled out. When the surface clearing is complete, get to work with your fork again. By using a fork, you will avoid cutting up the deep roots of perennial weeds such as docks or the dreaded quack grass. You will not be able to dig if it is too wet, and you will not be able to dig if it is too dry. A nice, cool, breezy day in winter is best of all—especially if the sun is shining to keep your spirits high. Fork the land over in large lumps, pulling out deep roots and quack grass by hand. Don't worry too much about surface-rooting annual weeds, since you are going to give them a hard time anyway in the weeks to come. Just turn over the biggest square sods that you can with the green side down.

When you are digging, it is essential to pace yourself and develop a sort of meditational rhythm. Let your mind wander as your body steadily does the work. It may take several hours or even days to dig the plot, but that's fine. We cannot hurry nature, and your next meal will taste much better after a good session. When the job is finished, you will have a brown and lumpy plot spread out in front of you. Now you must leave things as they are for at least three or four weeks. This will allow the weather, the wind, and the sun to work on your soil.

The ideal next step is to find yourself a good rototiller. This should not go down too deep—9 inches (23 cm) is about right. Try to choose a bright, sunny morning, as warm and windy as possible. Before you start to rototill, take a quick walk over the plot and pull out any remaining deep-rooted perennials. Now you can start your rototiller and make at least two passes over the plot. On the last pass, try not to leave any footprints. You want the soil to be left as fluffed up as possible so that weed roots will dry out and die. You are now going to leave your plot again for a couple of weeks, although at this stage you may want to put in some of the larger plantings—for example, rhubarb, soft fruits, artichokes, and fruit trees.

As you work, keep your wheelbarrow nearby and throw in any leftover weeds and roots. Later, take them to your compost pile and spread them in layers to make a stack.

Caring for compost
Choose a shady place for your composting piles—preferably with a bit of shelter from the prevailing wind, so that they do not get too soaked with rain. And always remember that the compost pile is the foundation of a successful garden. Nowadays you will find many foolish folks who will readily part with their animal manure—whether local horse owners or local farmers. Their loss is your gain, since well-rotted farm manure is going to make your garden the best on the block. Manure added to the compost pile also greatly assists in turning weeds and garden waste into good humus for your soil.

The One-Acre Farm

Everyone will have an entirely different approach to husbanding his or her land, and it is unlikely that any two self-supporters with one acre each will adopt the same plan or methods. Some people like cows; other people are afraid of them. Some people like goats; other people cannot keep them out of the garden. (I never could, and I don't know many people who can.) Some people will not kill animals and have to sell their surplus stock off to people who will kill them; others will not sell surplus stock off at all because they know that the animals will be killed. Some people are happy to keep more stock than their land can support and to buy in fodder from outside, while other people regard this as contrary to the principles of self-sufficiency.

For myself, if I had an acre of good, well-drained land, I think I would keep a cow and a goat, a few pigs, and maybe a dozen hens. The goat would provide me with milk when the cow was dry. I might keep two or more goats, in fact. I would have the cow (a Jersey) to provide me and the pigs with milk, but more importantly I would keep her to provide me with heaps and heaps of lovely manure. For if I was to derive any sort of living from that one acre, without the application of a lot of artificial fertilizer, it would have to be heavily manured.

Now the acre would only just support the cow and do nothing else, so I would, quite shamelessly, buy in most of my food for the cow from outside. I would buy all my hay, plenty of straw (unless I could cut bracken on a nearby field), all my barley meal and some wheat meal, and maybe some concentrated protein in the form of bean meal or fish meal (although I would aim to grow beans).

It will be argued that it is ridiculous to say you are self-supporting when you have to buy in all this food. True, you would grow much of the food for cows, pigs, and poultry: fodder beet, mangels, kale, "chat" (small potatoes), comfrey, alfalfa, and all garden produce not actually eaten by people. But you would still have to buy, say, a ton or a ton and a half of hay a year, a ton a year of grain of different sorts, including your own bread wheat, and a ton or two of straw. I would not envisage growing wheat or barley on such a small area as an acre; instead, I would choose to concentrate on more expensive things than cereals, and things that it was more important to harvest and eat fresh. Also, the growing of cereals on very small acreages is often impossible because of excessive bird damage, although I have managed to grow wheat successfully on a garden scale.

A cow or not a cow?

The big question here is: cow or no cow? The pros and cons are many and various. In favor of having a cow is the fact that nothing keeps the health of a family, and a farm, at a high level better than a cow. If you and your children have ample good, fresh, unpasteurized, unadulterated milk, butter, buttermilk, soft cheese, hard cheese, yogurt, sour milk, and whey, you will simply be a healthy family,

and that is the end of it. A cow will give you the complete basis of good health. If your pigs and poultry get their share of the milk by-products, they also will be healthy and will thrive. If your garden gets plenty of cow manure, that too will be healthy and thrive. This cow will be the wellspring of all your health and well-being.

On the other hand, the food that you buy in for this cow will cost you hundreds of dollars each year. Against this you can set whatever money you would pay for dairy products in that year for yourself and your family (and if you work that out, you will find it to be quite substantial), plus the increased value of the eggs, poultry meat, and pig meat that you will get (you can probably say that, in value, a quarter of your pig meat will be creditable to the cow), plus the ever-growing fertility of your land. But a serious counter-consideration is that you will have to take on the responsibility of milking the cow. Twice a day for at least 10 months of the year, rain or shine, you will have to milk the cow. It doesn't take very long to milk a cow (perhaps eight minutes), and it is very pleasant if you know how to do it and if she is a quiet nice cow, but you will have to do it. So the buying of a cow is a very important step, and you shouldn't do it unless you do not intend to go away very much, or you can make arrangements for somebody else to relieve you with milking. (Of course, even if you only have a hamster, somebody has to feed it.)

So let us plan our one-acre farm on the assumption that we are going to keep a cow.

ONE-ACRE FARM WITH A COW

Half the land will be put down to grass, leaving half an acre arable. (I am not allowing for the land on which the house and other buildings stand.) Now the grass half could remain permanent pasture and never be plowed up at all, or it could be rotated by plowing it up, say, every four years. If the latter is done, it is better done in strips of a quarter of the half-acre each, so each year you grass down an eighth of an acre of your land. Thus, there is some freshly sown pasture every year, some two-year-old ley, some three-year-old ley, and some four-year-old ley. The holding will be more productive if you rotate your pasture this way every four years.

The holding may break naturally in half: for example, an easily worked half-acre of garden, and a half-acre of roughish pasture. You will begin then by plowing up or pigging (allowing pigs to root it up, confined by an electric fence) or rototilling half of your land. This land you will put down to a grass, clover, and herb mixture.

If you sow the seed in the fall, you can then winter your cow indoors, feeding her on bought hay, and hope for sufficient grazing next spring. If your timetable favors your sowing in the spring, and if you live in a moist enough climate to do so, then you will be able to do a little light grazing that summer. It is better not to cut hay the first summer after spring-sowing of grass, so just graze it lightly with your little cow.

Grazing

At the first sign of poaching (destruction of grass by treading), take the cow away. Better still, tether her, or strip-graze behind an electric fence. Just allow the cow to have, say, a sixth of the grass at one time, leave her on that for perhaps a week, then move her to the next strip. The length of time she stays on one strip must be left to your common sense (which you must develop if you are to become a self-supporter).

The point about strip-grazing is that grass grows better and produces more if it is allowed to grow for as long as possible before being grazed or cut, then grazed or cut right down, then rested again. If it is grazed down all the time, it never really has a chance to develop its root system. In such intensive husbandry as we are envisaging now, it is essential to graze as carefully as possible.

Tether-grazing on such a small area might well be better than electric fencing. A little Jersey quickly gets used to being tethered and this was, indeed, the system that they were developed for on the island of Jersey, where they were first bred. I so unequivocally recommend a Jersey to the one-acre man, incidentally, because I am convinced that for this sort of purpose, she is without any peer. I have tried Dexters, with complete lack of success, but if you really know of a Dexter that gives anything like a decent amount of milk (my two gave less than a goat) and is quiet and amenable, then go ahead and get a Dexter and good luck to you. But remember, a well-bred Jersey gives plenty of milk (quite simply the richest in butterfat of any milk in the world) and is small, healthy, very hardy, moderate in her eating demands, and so lovable and docile that you will be tempted to take her into the house with you.

Now your half-acre of grass, once established, should provide your cow with nearly all the food she needs for the summer months. You are unlikely to get any hay off it as well, but if the grass grows faster than the cow can eat it, then you could cut some of it for hay.

A highly intensive garden

The remaining half of your farm—the arable half—will then be farmed as a highly intensive garden. It will be divided, ideally, into four plots, around which all the annual crops that you want to grow will follow each other in strict rotation. (I discuss this rotation in more detail on p.40.) The only difference that you will have to make in this rotation is that every year you will have to grass a quarter down, and every year plow a quarter of your grassland up. I suggest that your potatoes come after the newly plowed phase.

An ideal rotation might go something like this:

—Grass (for four years)
—Potatoes
—Legumes (pea and bean family)
—Brassicas (cabbage family)
—Root vegetables (carrots, beets, parsnips, and so on)
—Grass again (for four years)

To sow fall-sown grass after your roots, you will have to lift them early. In a mild climate, it would be quite practicable to do this; however, in regions with more severe winters, it might be necessary to wait until the following spring. In areas with dry summers, unless you have irrigation, it would probably be better to sow in the fall. In some climates (dry summers and cold winters) it might be best to sow your grass in the late summer after the pea and bean break instead of after the root break, for the peas and beans are off the ground earlier than the roots. It might then pay you to follow the grass with potatoes, and your succession could be like this:

—Grass (for four years)
—Potatoes
—Brassicas (cabbage family)
—Root vegetables (carrots, beets, parsnips, and so on))
—Legumes (pea and bean family)
—Grass again (for four years)

A disadvantage of this might be that the brassicas, following main-crop potatoes, might have to wait until the summer following the fall in which the potatoes were lifted before they could be planted. When brassicas are planted after the pea and bean family, they can go in immediately, because the brassica plants have been reared in a nursery bed and it is not too late in the summer to transplant them after the peas and beans have been cleared. But potatoes cannot be lifted (main crop can't, anyway) until fall, when it is too late to plant brassicas. Actually, with this regimen, you will be able to plant some of your brassicas that first summer, after early potatoes. Or if you grow only earlies, you may get it all in.

One possibility would be to follow the potatoes immediately with brassicas (thus saving a year) by lifting some earlies very early and planting immediately with the earliest brassicas, then following each lifting of potatoes with more brassicas, ending with spring cabbages after the main crop has come out. This would only be possible in fairly mild climates, though.

All this sounds complicated, but it is much easier to understand when you do it than when you talk about it. And consider the advantages of this kind of rotation. It means that a quarter of your arable land is newly plowed-up, four-year-ley every year: intensely fertile because of the stored-up fertility of all the grass, clover, and herbs that have just been plowed in to rot, plus the dung of your cow for four summers. It means that because your cow is in-wintered, on bought-in hay, and treading and dunging on bought-in straw, you will have an enormous quantity of marvelous muck to put on your arable land. It means that all the crop residues that you cannot consume go to help feed the cow, or the pigs or poultry, and I would be very surprised if, after following this regimen for a few years, you did not find that your acre of land increased enormously in fertility, and that it was producing more food for humans than many a 10-acre farm run on ordinary commercial lines.

DIVIDING UP YOUR ONE ACRE

If you had one acre of good, well-drained land, you might choose to use all of it to grow fruit and vegetables. Myself, I would divide it in half and put half an acre down to grass, on which I would graze a cow, and perhaps a goat to give milk during the short periods when the cow would be dry, a sow for breeding, and a dozen chickens. I would admittedly have to buy in food from outside to feed these animals through the winter, but this is preferable to buying in dairy products and meat, which would be the alternative.

My remaining half-acre I would divide into four plots for intensive vegetable production, devoting a plot each to potatoes, legumes (peas and beans), brassicas (cabbage family), and roots. I would divide the grass half-acre into four plots as well, and rotate the whole holding every year. This means I would be planting a grass plot every year and it would stay grass until I plowed it up four years later. I would not have enough grass to keep the cow outdoors all year. I would have a greenhouse for tomatoes and hives for bees, and I would plant a vegetable patch with extra household vegetables, herbs, and soft fruit.

Peas and beans

Grow at least three kinds of beans— say, French, runner (pole), and broad, and plenty of peas. Plan to put brassicas on this plot next year.

Brassicas

On your brassica plot, grow a variety of cabbages, cauliflower, broccoli, and Brussels sprouts for yourself. Grow kale, turnips, and rutabagas, which are roots but also brassicas, to feed to your animals. Next year this plot should be planted with roots.

A HALF-ACRE OF GRASS

Your half-acre of grass will feed your cow all through the summer. Let your hens run on it and give them a movable chicken coop. When you want to plow up your annual eighth of an acre, put the pigs on it and let them do the work for you.

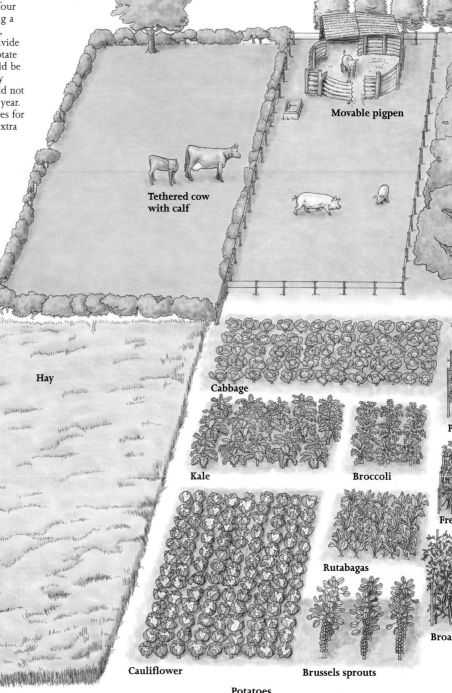

Movable pigpen

Tethered cow with calf

Hay

Cabbage

Kale

Broccoli

Peas

French be

Rutabagas

French be

Brussels sprouts

Broad bean

Cauliflower

Potatoes

Each year plant your potatoes in the plot that has just been plowed up from grass.

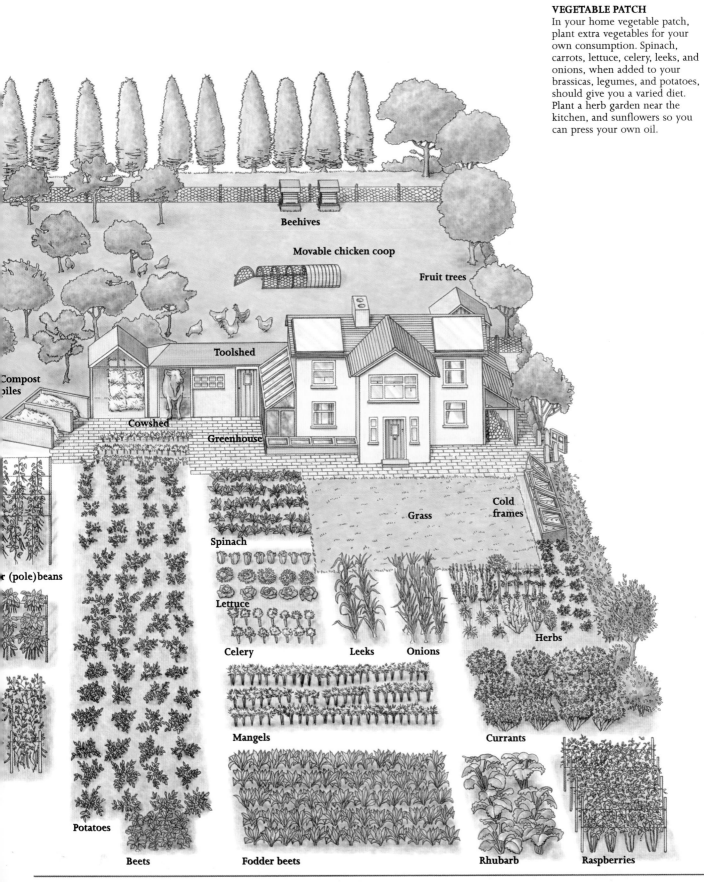

Beehives

Movable chicken coop

Fruit trees

Toolshed

Compost piles

Cowshed

Greenhouse

(pole) beans

Spinach

Grass

Cold frames

Lettuce

Celery

Leeks

Onions

Herbs

Mangels

Currants

Potatoes

Beets

Fodder beets

Rhubarb

Raspberries

Half-acre rotation

You may complain that by having half your acre down to grass, you confine your gardening activities to a mere half-acre. But actually, half an acre is quite a lot, and if you garden it really well, it will grow more food for you than if you "scratch" over a whole acre. And the effect of being under grass, and grazed and dunged, for half its life will enormously increase the fertility of it. I believe you will grow more actual vegetables than you would on the whole acre if you had no cow or grass break.

Small-acreage tips

Here are a few pointers to bear in mind:

Cows First, the cow will not be able to stay outdoors all year. On such a small acreage, she would poach it horribly. She should spend most of the winter indoors, only being turned out during the daytime in dry weather to get a little exercise and fresh air. Cows do not really benefit from being out in any weather in the wintertime, although they put up with it. Your cow is, for the most part, better kept in, where she makes lovely manure for you, and she will have plenty of greenstuffs and roots that you will grow for her in the garden. In the summer you will let her out, night and day, for as long as you find the pasture stands up to it. You could keep the cow on deep litter: that is, she would dung on a layer of straw and turn it into good manure, and you would add more clean straw every day. I have milked a cow for years like this, and the milk was perfect, made good butter and cheese, and kept well.

Or you could keep the cow on a concrete floor (insulated if possible), giving her a good bed of straw every day and removing the soiled straw, and putting it carefully on the muck-heap—that fount of fertility for everything on your acre—every day. You would probably find that your cow did not need hay at all during the summer, but she would be entirely dependent on it throughout the winter, and you could plan on having to buy her at least a ton. If you wished to rear her yearly calf until he reached some value, you would need perhaps a further half-ton of hay.

Pigs You would have to be prepared to confine pigs in a house for at least part of the year (and provide straw for them). This is because on a one-acre farm, you are unlikely to have enough fresh land to keep them healthy. The best thing would be a movable house with a strong movable fence outside it, or you could have a permanent pigpen as well. But the pigs would have a lot of outdoor work to do: they would spend part of their time plowing up your eighth of an acre of grassland; they could run over your potato land after you had lifted the crop; they could clear up after you had lifted your roots, or after you had lifted any crop. But they could only do this if you had time to let them do it. Sometimes you would be in too much of a hurry to get the next crop in. As for food, you would have to buy in some wheat, barley, or corn. This, supplemented with the skim milk and whey you would have from your cow, plus a share of the garden produce and such specially grown fodder crops as you could spare the land for, would keep them excellently.

If you could find a neighbor who would let you use his boar, I would recommend that you kept a sow and bred from her. She might well give you 20 piglets a year. Two or three of these you would keep to fatten for your bacon and ham supply. The rest you would sell as "weaners" (piglets 8–12 weeks old, depending on the requirements of your particular market), and they would probably bring in enough money to pay for every scrap of food you had to buy for them, the poultry, and the cow, too. If you could not get the service of a boar, you would probably buy weaners yourself—just enough for your own use—and fatten them.

Poultry Poultry could be kept on the Balfour method (*described on p.220*), in which case they would stay for years in the same corner of your garden. Or, better in my opinion, they could be kept in movable coops on the land. They could then be moved over the grassland, where their scratching and dunging would do it good. I would not recommend keeping very many birds. A dozen hens should give you enough eggs for a small family, with a few occasionally to sell or give away in the summertime. You would have to buy a little grain for them, and in the winter some protein supplement, unless you could grow enough beans. You might try growing sunflowers, buckwheat, or other food especially for them. You might consider confining them in a small permanent house, with two outdoor runs as in the Balfour system, during the worst months of the winter, with electric lights on in the evenings to fool them into thinking it was the time of the year to lay, and thus get enough winter eggs.

Goats If you decided to keep goats instead of a cow (and who am I to say this would not be a sensible decision?), you could manage things in much the same way. You would only get a small fraction of the manure from goats, but on the other hand you would not have to buy anything like as much hay and straw—indeed, perhaps not any. You would have nothing like as much whey and skim milk to rear pigs and poultry on, and you would not build up the fertility of your land as quickly as you would with a cow.

Crops Crops would be all the ordinary garden crops, plus as much land as you could spare for fodder crops for the animals. But bear in mind that practically any garden crop that you grew for yourself would be good for the animals too, so everything surplus to your requirements would go to them. You would not have a compost pile: your animals would be your compost pile.

Half an acre If you kept no animals at all, or maybe only some poultry, you might well try farming half an acre as garden and growing wheat in the other half-acre. You would then rotate your land as described above, but substituting wheat for the grass and clover ley. If you were a vegetarian, this might be quite a good solution. But you could not hope to increase the fertility, and therefore the productiveness, of your land as much as with animals.

The Five-Acre Farm

The basic principles I have described for running a one-acre farm will also broadly apply to larger acreages. The main difference would be that if you had, say, five acres of medium to good land in a temperate climate, and the necessary knowledge, you could grow all the food needed for a large family, except such things as tea and coffee, which can only be grown in the tropics. And you could, of course, do without such things. You could grow wheat for bread, barley for beer, every kind of vegetable, every kind of meat, eggs, and honey.

Just as every person in the world is different, so is every five-acre plot, but here is a possible pattern. Assuming one acre was set aside for house and buildings, orchard, and kitchen garden, the remainder could be divided up into eight half-acre plots. It would be necessary to fence them permanently: electric fencing would do. Or, if you are a tetherer, you might tether your cows, and your pigs, and your goats if you have any, and not have any fencing at all. I tried tethering a sheep once, but the poor thing died of a broken heart, so l wouldn't recommend it.

The rotation could be something like this:

—*Grass (for three years)*
—*Wheat*
—*Root vegetables (carrots, beets, parsnips, and so on)*
—*Potatoes*
—*Legumes (pea and bean family)*
—*Barley, undersown with grass and clover (for three years)*

This would, of course, only leave you one and a half acres of grassland, but it would be very productive grassland, and in a good year it could be supplemented with something like: a ton of wheat; 20 tons of roots; four tons of potatoes; half a ton of peas or beans; three-quarters of a ton of barley. You might well manage to get two tons of hay off your grassland, and then have enough "aftermath" (grass that grows after you have cut the hay) to give grazing to your cows until well into the fall.

Flexibility: the essence of good husbandry

There are a thousand possible variations of this plan, of course. Flexibility is the essence of good husbandry. You could, for example, plant potatoes after your plowed-up grassland, and follow that with wheat. You could grow oats as well as barley, or oats as well as wheat. You could grow some rye: very useful if you have dry, light land, or want good thatching straw, or like rye bread. You could grow fewer legumes. You could try to grow all your arable crops in four half-acre plots instead of five, and thus leave two acres for grassland instead of one and a half. You might find you had some grassland to spare in your "home acre"—in your orchard, for example, if your trees were standards and therefore too high to be damaged by the stock. Of course if you were in corn-growing country, you would grow corn, certainly instead of barley, maybe instead of roots or potatoes. A good tip is to seek out farming neighbors and ask them which crops grow best in your area.

Stock As for stock, you might well consider keeping a horse to help you do all that cultivating, or you might have a small garden tractor instead. Your plowing could be done with pigs. With five acres you might consider keeping enough sows to justify a boar. Four is probably the minimum; we kept six sows and a boar for many years, and they were astonishingly profitable. Indeed, in good years and bad, they paid all our bills for us: the Irish call the pig "the gentleman who pays the rent," and it's easy to see why. But pigs won't pay you very well unless you can grow a great deal of their food for them. You could look upon your pig herd, whether large or small, as your pioneers: they would plow up your half-acre of grass every year for you, plow your stubbles after grain, clean up your potato and root land after harvest, and generally act as rooters-up and scavengers.

Poultry Poultry, too, would be rotated around the holding as much as possible. Put on wheat or barley stubble, they will feed themselves for some time on spilled grain, besides doing great good scrapping out leatherjackets and wireworm. Following the pigs, after the latter have rooted up a piece of land, they will also do good by eating pests and will do themselves good, too. Ducks, geese, turkeys, tame rabbits, pigeons: your five acres will provide enough food and space for them all, and they will vary your diet.

Cows I would recommend keeping two cows, so you would have ample milk year-round. You would have enough milk to make decent hard cheese during the summer to last you through the winter, and enough whey and skim milk to supplement pig and poultry feed. If you reared one calf a year, and kept him 18 months or two years, and then slaughtered him, you would have enough beef for family use. That is, if you had a chest freezer. If you did not, then you could sell your bullock and use that money for buying beef from the butcher, or, much better, you could make an arrangement with self-supporting neighbors in which you each took turns slaughtering a beast, then divided the meat up among you so it could all be eaten before it went bad. In a cold winter, you can keep beef at least a month without a freezer.

Sheep On such a small acreage, sheep are a more doubtful proposition because they need very good fencing, and also because it is uneconomic to keep a ram for less than, say, six sheep. But you could keep some pet ewes, get them mated with a neighboring ram, rear the lambs, and keep yourself in mutton and wool.

The above is only an introductory outline of how a prospective self-supporter might organize a five-acre holding. Each person will wish to adapt according to his or her circumstances, the size of his or her family or community, and the nature of the land. But the main body of this book is aimed at providing you with as much practical help as possible in selecting and managing your acreage, your crops, and your livestock, and in making them the productive agents in your search for self-sufficiency and the good life.

DIVIDING YOUR FIVE ACRES

If you had five acres of good well-drained land, you could support a family of, say, six people and have occasional surpluses to sell. Of course, no two five-acre plots are ever the same, but in an ideal situation, I would set aside one of my acres for the house, farm buildings, kitchen garden, and orchard, and the other four acres I would divide into eight half-acre plots. Three of them I would put down to grass every year, and there I would run two cows for dairy produce; four sows, a boar, some sheep and some geese for meat; and some chickens for eggs. I would keep ducks, rabbits, pigeons, and bees wherever I could fit them in.

Now, in the five remaining plots, I would sow wheat, roots, Jerusalem artichokes or potatoes, peas and beans, oats, and barley undersown with grass and clover. I would rotate all eight plots every year so no plot ever grew the same crop two years running, unless it was grass. A grass plot would stay grass for three years before being plowed.

Pasture

Your pasture can cover one and a half acres. Here you can graze cows, sheep, geese, and chickens; and when you want to plow up some of your grassland, you can bring pigs back from the woods and fold them on small areas at a time. The top end of the field has not yet been cut for hay.

Hay

Grazing pasture

Spare paddock

Paddock

Grass

Peas

Barley

Runner (pole) beans

French beans

Broad beans

Oats

Spring crops

In the spring, sow a plot with peas and beans, and another with barley and oats for a late harvest. Undersow your barley with grass and clover that can be grazed after the harvest.

Root break
Divide your half-acre for roots into several small plots and grow a selection of roots for feeding to your animals in winter. When you have dug your roots and stored them in a clamp or root cellar, put your pigs on the land.

Woodland
If you have some woodland, farm it for timber and firewood just as you would farm the rest of your farm. Each year, fell the old, mature trees and clear the undergrowth with your pigs. Plant new trees like ash, larch, oak, and spruce.

The home acre
This is the hub of your farm. Around the farmyard are your house, barn, cowsheds, and dairy. Keep a horse in the paddock, ducks in the pond, and bees in the orchard, but be sure to allow plenty of space for the vital business of growing vegetables and soft fruit.

ots   Fodder beets   Kale   Potatoes   Mangels   Beets

Young spruce plantation

Farm buildings

Soft fruit

Orchard

Timber

Beehives

Duck houses

Pigs

Wheat

Winter crops
Sow wheat and potatoes, or Jerusalem artichokes, as winter crops or an early harvest. Harvest your crop, then fold pigs on that plot and let them dig out the remnants of the roots, dung the land, and plow it ready for next year's pea and bean break.

"We don't bother to do a lot of things in our garden. We let things take their chance, and every year some crops are good and others are bad; but at least there is always enough to eat and we always get a taste of everything. If we did all the spraying and sprinkling and dusting and fumigating that one is told to do in books, we would spend a fortune on chemicals and have no time left over for anything else. In fact, growing a big variety of crops and never the same crop two years on the same ground, and heavily manuring with the dung of a variety of animals, seems to give our crops the strength to resist most pests and diseases. Only sometimes do we come a cropper...

The failure to use artificials is not crankiness. It is simply this: our aim is to grow our food for nothing. If we spend money on buying artificial manures, we are not doing this. Also, we realize now that food tastes a lot nicer if it has been grown with natural and not artificial manures."

JOHN SEYMOUR FAT OF THE LAND 1976

CHAPTER TWO

FOOD
FROM THE
GARDEN

The Food-Producing Garden

The country garden of my childhood was a mixture of vegetables, flowers, soft fruit, tree fruit (oh, those greengages!), and very often tame rabbits, almost certainly a hen run, often pigeons, and often ferrets. It was a very beautiful place indeed. Now, unfortunately, the whole things has disappeared under a useless velvety lawn and a lot of silly bedding plants and hardy perennials—because, of course, the current owner feels compelled to keep up with the people next door.

However limited the space available, you only need the determination to abandon your space-wasting lawn and flowerbeds in exchange for a program of planned crop rotation for every inch of your garden to become a highly productive unit. You will save money, your end products will be fresh and delicioius, and your garden will be a fine example of a dying breed: the cottage garden of yesteryear. But how can we best reproduce the old cottage garden, which was one of the most productive places on earth? Well, start by dividing the garden area into six parts—or seven if you want a small lawn-and-flower area for the sublime fragrance of flowers.

The clever thing to do is to use perennial food plants as hedges to divide up the garden into plots. Perennials are plants that go on from year to year, thus providing valuable overwintering homes for beneficial insects, as well as shelter from the wind and weather. Plants for this purpose include asparagus, globe artichoke, horseradish, rhubarb, and many of the soft fruits, including raspberries. Avoid large, open areas that encourage the spread of disease. At the same time, you do not want a garden so claustrophobic that you cannot maneuver the rototiller effectively for spring cultivation. Larger trees, like the fruit trees, are best kept separate in the orchard, since they really do shade and sterilize a large area of soil. Of course, neat espaliered fruit trees can and do make excellent and very productive hedges for dividing up beds.

Our six parts can then be used in a six-part rotation (*see also* p.190), which will keep potatoes and brassicas from being grown too frequently in the same position. The six yearly crops I use are:

—Potatoes
—Legumes (*pea and bean family*)
—Brassicas (*cabbages, broccoli, turnips, etc.*)
—Greedy plants like corn, pumpkins, and cucumbers
—Salad and catch crops, onions, shallots
—Root vegetables (*carrots, beets, parsnips, celery, and so on*)

Liming

If the soil on your land is acid, it will need lime. You can test for acidity with a simple device that you can buy from any garden center—or just ask your neighbor. You should lime before the pea and bean crop. Peas and beans like the lime, and the cabbage tribe that follows them likes what is left of it. Lime has more time to combat the dreaded clubroot disease, which is carried by brassicas, if it is in the soil for a few months before the brassicas are planted.

Mucking and mulching

If you have muck (farmyard manure)—and I hope you have—or if you have compost, concentrate this on your potato plot. The potatoes benefit enormously from it. In fact, you won't grow very many without it. It is better not to put it on the root plot because some root vegetables, carrots and turnips in particular, tend to "fork" if they have too much fresh muck. It is better not to put muck on the pea and bean plot, because you lime that, and lime and muck don't go together very well in the same year.

It is advantageous to put a mulch, a covering of some dead greenstuff, on the surface of the soil between the cabbage-family plants, but only after you have hoed them two or three times to suppress the weeds. If you mulch on top of weeds, the weeds will simply grow through the mulch and the mulch will then impede the hoe.

Organic gardening

The goal of the organic gardener should be to get as much humus into the land as possible. Muck, compost, seaweed, leaf mold, spoiled hay, nettles, roadside cuttings, or nearly anything of vegetable or animal origin can be composted (*see* p.334) and put on the land, or just put on the land directly. If you dig it in well, you dig it in. If you just leave it on top, the worms will dig it in for you.

PERCENTAGE VALUES OF ORGANIC FERTILIZERS

	Nitrogen	Phosphorus	Potash	Calcium
Average farmyard manure	0.64	0.23	0.32	–
Pure pig manure	0.48	0.58	0.36	–
Pure cow manure	0.44	0.12	0.04	–
Compost	0.50	0.27	0.81	–Δ
Deep litter on peat*	4.40	1.90	1.90	2.20
Deep litter on straw	0.80	0.55	0.48	–
Fresh poultry manure	1.66	0.91	0.48	–
Pigeon manure	5.84	2.10	1.77	–

ΔUnless lime has been added

Unless you keep animals on your garden, you will have to bring organic matter, or inorganic matter if you are not "organically minded," in from outside if you want a really productive garden. I subsidize my garden with manure made by animals that eat grass, hay, and crops grown on the rest of the farm. There is much wild talk by would-be organic gardeners who think a garden will produce enough compost material to provide for itself. Well, let them try it. Let them take a plot of land, grow the bulkiest compost-making crop they can, compost it, and then see how far the resulting material goes. It will not go very far.

True, deep-rooting plants, such as comfrey and alfalfa, can do great work in bringing up minerals, and phosphates and potash as well, from the subsoil to add to your soil. Trees do an even better job. But the land that is devoted to growing the comfrey or the trees is out of use for growing food crops.

Of course, if your own sewage went back into the soil of your garden, one big leakage of plant nutriments would be stemmed. The old cottage gardens of the past had all their sewage returned, because the sewage system was a bucket and the contents of that were buried in the garden. Provided the sewage was buried and left undisturbed for a time, any pathogens would die a natural death. These country gardens owed their phenomenal fertility to the fact that the inhabitants were importing food from outside all the time, as well as eating their garden's own produce, and matter from both sources ended up in the soil. But if you annually extract large amounts of produce from a piece of soil, and either export it or eat it and export the resulting waste via a modern sewage system, and don't import any manure or fertilizer, the laws of nature are such that you will ultimately exhaust the soil.

It is vital that your garden be well drained, and it is an advantage if the land beneath it is not too heavy.

GARDEN TOOLS

1 Dutch hoe, for pushing; good for using backward, leaving the ground free of footprints. **2** Draw hoe, for pulling; much faster, goes deeper, and tackles tougher weeds. **3** Mattock, excellent for cutting through tree roots. **4** Spade, essential for inverting soil and digging in manure; keep clean. **5** Fork, for loosening up soil quickly without inverting it, or incorporating compost or manure in first few inches and forking out roots of creeping weeds; a must for digging up potatoes. **6** Backpack (pressure) sprayer, essential for large areas. **7** Pruning shears, quicker and kinder for pruning than a knife; also for severing chickens' neckbones when gutting them. **8** Trowel, for setting out plants. **9** Pruning knife. **10** Dibber, for setting out seedlings; make one by cutting down a broken spade or fork handle. **11** Garden reel, wooden or iron, for winding up line. **12** Garden line; use light cord that does not get tangled up like string. **13** Watering can, preferably big and galvanized. **14** Rake; use a large steel one for fine seed beds and covering seed. **15** Precision drills, which pick seeds up one at a time and drop them at exactly the right intervals, save seed and save work later by reducing the need for thinning.

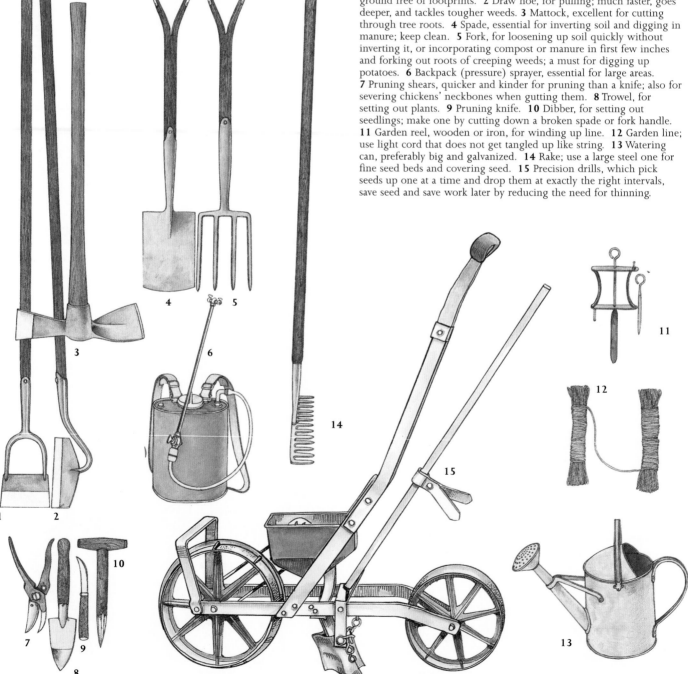

A well-drained medium loam is most desirable, but sandy soil, provided you muck it well, is very good, too. Heavy clay is difficult to manage, but will grow good brassica crops. Whatever your soil is, you can scarcely give it too much muck, or other humus or humus-forming material.

Green manuring

Green manuring is the process of growing a crop and then digging or plowing it into the soil, or else just cutting or pulling the crop and throwing it down on top of the soil. This latter form of green manuring is called "mulching." Ultimately, the green matter will rot and the earthworms will drag it down into the soil in their indefatigable manner. If you dig in green manure crops, you should do it at least three weeks before you sow the next crop on top of them. The only way around this is to add plenty of available nitrogen to help the green manure rot down without robbing the soil.

Green manuring improves the quality of the soil because the vegetable matter rots down into humus. The amount of humus added by an apparently heavy crop of green manure is smaller than you might think, but the great value of such crops is that they take up the free nitrogen in the soil. Bare soil would lose this nitrogen to the air, but the green crop retains nitrogen and only releases it when it has rotted, by which time the subsequent crop should be ready to use it.

It should be the aim of the organic gardener to keep as much of his land as possible covered with plants. Bare soil should be anathema, unless for a very good reason it has to be bare temporarily. The old gardener's idea of "turning up land rough in the fall to let the frosts get in it in the winter" should not stop us from encouraging a green covering of vegetation after harvesting—a green covering that can be readily scythed off for the compost pile before it seeds and before the soil is broken up. The key here is to leave large lumps, 12 inches (30 cm) square, that will weather well without leading to erosion. Soil dug over like this in January will be perfectly ready to rototill down into a seedbed in late March. If you can manage two or three passes in dry weather with at least a week between each, you will ensure that your seedbed is quite free of weeds.

Using weeds

Even weeds can be a green manure crop. Many annual weeds will pop out of nowhere after your crops have been harvested. Tolerate these with good heart, for they make an excellent addition to the compost pile when scythed off to the ground before they seed. Their roots will also help bind the ground against winter rains. But whatever you do, don't let them seed. For one thing, "one year's seeding is seven years' weeding," and for another, all green manure crops should be cut or pulled at the flowering stage, or earlier, when their growth is young, succulent, and high in protein. They then have enough nitrogen in them to provide for their own rotting down.

So look upon annual weeds as friends, provided you can keep them under control. Perennial weeds (weeds that go on from year to year) should not be tolerated at any cost. They will do you nothing but harm, except perhaps nettles and bracken. If you grow these two crops on unused land, you can cut them and add them to the compost pile. They will do great good—they are both deep-rooting and thus full of nutrients they bring up from below.

Planting green manure

Green manure crops can be divided into winter and summer crops, and legumes and non-legumes. People with small gardens will find winter crops more useful than summer ones, for the simple reason that they will need every inch of space in summer for growing food crops. Legumes make better green manure than non-legumes, because they have bacteria at their roots that take nitrogen from the air, and this is added to the soil when they rot.

Grazing rye

Of winter green manure crops, grazing rye is probably the best. It can be broadcast at a rate of 2 ounces of seed per square yard (70 g/sq m) after early potatoes have been lifted. Rake the seed in, leave it to grow all winter, and dig it in during spring. You can plant grazing rye as late as October, although you won't get such a heavy crop.

Comfrey

Comfrey is a perennial to grow for either magnificent green manure or good compost. Plant root cuttings from existing plants 2 feet (60 cm) apart in really weed-clear land in spring and just let it grow. The roots will go down into the soil as far as there is soil for them to penetrate, and they will live for a decade, giving heavy yields of highly nitrogenous material, rich in potash, phosphate, and other minerals, too.

Other green manure and compost crops

Vetches are both legumes and winter crops, and so are doubly valuable. They can be sown from August to October, and dug in the next spring. As a summer crop, they can be sown any time in spring and dug in when in flower. Sow the much-used mustard after early potatoes are lifted. Give the dug-over ground a good raking, broadcast the seed tightly, and rake it in. Dig the crop into the ground as soon as the first flowers appear. Red clover seed is expensive, but it is a fine, bulky, nitrogen-rich legume to sow after early potatoes and dig in in the fall. Lupins are a large legume. Put the seeds in at 6-inch (15-cm) intervals both ways, in the spring or early summer. *Tagetes minuta* is a kind of giant marigold, and it is an interesting crop to plant for compost material. It grows 10 feet (3 m) high and has two marvelous effects: it kills nematodes and it wipes out thistles and bindweed. Sunflowers make bulky compost material. Plant the seeds half an inch (1 cm) deep and 12 in (30 cm) apart both ways in the spring, and cut when it is in flower.

The Deep Bed

When we face a semicircle of eager students raring to get their teeth into something tough and physical, our favorite question is, "How would you like to dig a deep bed?" General puzzlement all around is the usual response, followed by, "What is a deep bed?"

A deep bed is a highly intensive and effective method of producing vegetables in a small space—especially if you are looking for drought resistance and vigorous growth. The idea seems to have originated in California—at least that is where I first saw it. The technique is ideal for those with limited space.

The first essential is obviously to understand how to create the bed. Then we have to learn to get the best out of it. The principles of the deep bed system follow these three simple steps:

1 Create a highly fertile, deep, and well-drained block of topsoil, working in plenty of good compost so it will give you vigorous root growth as well as drought resistance.

2 Work your plot from the edges, without walking on it. A deep bed should not be any more than 5 feet (1.5 m) wide—and it might need to be narrower for those who have short arms! This way, you can do your planting and weeding from the sides.

3 Plant your vegetables in a close pattern that will reduce the need for weeding (much of which you will have to do by hand).

Marking out

Begin by marking out the area you have chosen for your bed. This may well be in established grassland turf—or it may be an area of already cultivated soil convenient for the purpose (perhaps a specifically created area within an urban garden).

The area may be 5 feet (1.5 m) wide by 20 feet (6 m) long. Note that the deep bed is an excellent way to bring old grassland into vegetable production; the turf is turned over well below two "spits" of earth—a "spit" is the country term for the depth of one good spadeful of earth, that is, about 9 inches (22 cm).

If your bed is 5 feet (1.5 m) wide, you begin by marking off six widths using a line or batten to guide you. Before you start, it is useful to find a large piece of old plastic or even some old pieces of plywood. This will provide a convenient place to dump the diggings from the first row. After cutting the turf, dig out the first row.

Next, you are going to go back to where you started and dig out the next spit of soil. Do not worry if the second spit of soil contains some subsoil. By bringing some subsoil to the top, you make it available to mix with compost. And as your deep bed matures over the years, you will be regularly turning over the top 18 inches (45 cm) or so of soil, creating a massively expanded layer of topsoil for your plants.

After finishing your first trench you can fork in a 2–3-inch (5–8-cm) layer of good manure into the bottom before turning over the next sod.

If you don't have manure, don't worry; your bed will work well anyway—but manure does form a superb reservoir of moisture for plants during a dry period. Give the turves a few chops with your spade if they are too lumpy and uneven to fit in the trench.

Continue the process until you have dug the final trench. At this point you take in the turf and then the soil from the very first trench (from your plastic of plywood sheet). Presto! Your deep bed is dug.

The process can be tough work, especially if you are working with land that has not been cultivated before. In our Irish garden, we have many huge stones—well hidden underground, for the most part. You will need to be prepared for this kind of thing. Have your wheelbarrow ready, a pickaxe, and a good, strong iron bar.

Be prepared, too, to find tree roots many yards away from large trees. When dealing with roots or a stone, always hold the spade with both hands grasping the shaft. This way you can use the momentum of the spade's own weight to cut roots or loosen stones without hurting your hands. It is a useful tip, believe me.

Don't be surprised when you find that your deep bed is now raised 9 inches (22 cm) above the surrounding garden. This is quite normal; indeed, the "heaped" effect is beneficial for the use of the bed. But, of course, this is what happens to all soil when it is disturbed, and there will be considerable subsidence with weather and rain.

Making the edges

One feature that makes a deep bed more effective is to add substantial edging of some kind once the bed has been created. I like to use large paving slabs, but you can use old railroad ties or rot-resistant wood or anything similar. Put the slabs onto sheets of building plastic (you can buy these at the home improvement store) to stop weeds from growing through the cracks. Not only does the solid edging allow you to cultivate and harvest the bed more comfortably, but it also lets you rest heavy equipment on it without disturbing the bed. There are several other beneficial effects:

1 Rainfall from both sides of the deep bed is gathered from the edges, almost doubling the effective summer rainfall into the cultivated area.

2 Edging prevents the constant spread of creeping weeds, and warm concrete acts as a major deterrent for the slugs (especially if you sprinkle on a little salt or ash from time to time), which are always wandering around in the garden looking for their next meal.

3 Surprisingly, the sheer capacity of slabs to soak up heat during the day helps to keep off frost and maintain a better temperature through the short days of winter. I have used this feature very effectively to keep frost away from tender young trees like walnuts—you can use a couple of 9-inch (22-cm) concrete blocks on either side of each young tree. And it keeps children and beasts from accidentally damaging the trees, too!

DIGGING A DEEP BED

1 First, mark the boundaries of your bed. Using all your weight on a sharp spade, cut the turf in two parallel lines all the way down the first row of the plot before you start to dig.

2 The cut lines should be about 12 inches (30 cm) apart, allowing you now to dig out square lumps of turf 6 inches (15 cm) thick. Pull out deep-rooted weeds, such as thistles.

3 Put the turves (the first "spit") in a row on a board or a sheet of plastic that you have placed close to the edge of the plot. Put the row at the far side of the board so there is enough space for the soil that comes out next.

4 When you have taken out the whole top layer of turf (the top "spit"), continue to dig the trench by taking out the next "spit" of soil. Put this onto the board next to the turf.

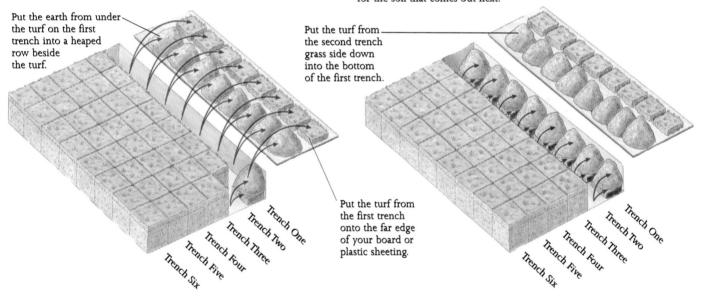

Put the earth from under the turf on the first trench into a heaped row beside the turf.

Put the turf from the second trench grass side down into the bottom of the first trench.

Put the turf from the first trench onto the far edge of your board or plastic sheeting.

Trench One
Trench Two
Trench Three
Trench Four
Trench Five
Trench Six

Trench One
Trench Two
Trench Three
Trench Four
Trench Five
Trench Six

5 When you have dug out all the soil from the first row, you begin the second trench by cutting squares of turf as for the first row, but these go grass side down into the trench you have already dug.

6 The second trench is now completed by digging out. the next "spit" of soil and turning it on top of the upturned turf in the first row. Put any large stones into the wheelbarrow.

7 Continue the sequence with each row going upside down into the trench. Add rotted manure under each turf for the ideal result.

8 Finally, take the turf from your first trench and put it face down into the last trench. When you cover this with the soil from the first trench, your bed is complete.

Using the deep bed

Let your new bed settle for at least a week before you get it ready for seeding (depending, of course, on the time of year). Fork over the top layer, and then smooth it out with your fork or a sturdy rake. Ideally, you will want to work some good compost into the top layer if it contains a high proportion of subsoil. If you don't do this, your germination may be poor. You can avoid this risk if you transplant seedlings from elsewhere, and this, in my view, is the best approach. If you do this, you will find that crops such as onions, lettuce, sweet corn, cucumbers, squash, and strawberries simply race away, as will the brassicas. However, plants like carrots and beets must obviously start from seed.

Sowing & Planting

Some people are said to have a "green thumb," meaning that when they plant a seed or a tree, it grows. I suspect that this mysterious power is merely common sense and sympathy—sympathy for the new life that you are helping to nurture. After all, what does a seed want? Moisture, warmth, and soil friable enough for its shoots to grow upward and its roots downward. This soil should be in close contact with the seed, and there shouldn't be too much soil between the seed and the light, because the plant's growth depends on the energy collected from the sun by photosynthesis in its green leaves. This energy takes over from the energy stored in the seed when that is exhausted, and helps to protect the plant from its enemies.

Plants vary in their requirements, of course, but broadly speaking, there are two ways to establish vegetables. One is by sowing the seed directly into the ground where it will grow. The other is by sowing it somewhere else, and then transplanting it in due course. And there are even occasions when we transplant the plants from where we sowed the seed into another bed, leave them there to grow for a while, and then transplant them again into their final bed.

There are two quite sensible reasons for this seemingly laborious and time-consuming procedure. First, by crowding the seed in a seed bed, we can release the land that the plants will ultimately take up and use it for another, earlier crop. So nearly all our brassicas (cabbage tribe), leeks, and those other plants that will grow through the fall and possibly part of the winter occupy very little ground for the first half of the summer. Then we put them in ground vacated by earlier crops, such as early potatoes or peas, and so we get two crops off the land in one year. The second reason for transplanting is to give seeds a good start.

This is done by sowing seeds in a seed bed, but under glass, plastic, or some other covering. This way, those of us who live in temperate climates can start them earlier and give them an initial boost, so that they will come to harvest during our short summer. After all, many of our vegetable crops evolved in warmer climes than the ones we grow them in.

Peat* pots

There are certain crops that respond far better to being grown in peat* pots before they are transplanted, rather than in flats or seed boxes. These are crops that don't like having their roots interfered with. When you plant the peat* pot directly in the ground, the roots will simply drive their way through the wet peat* and the plant won't suffer. Corn, melons, squash, and many other semihardy plants benefit from this treatment.

Soil for seed boxes

The kind of soil you put in your flats, or seed boxes, or pots, or whatever, is very important. If you just put in ordinary topsoil, it will tend to crack and dry out, and it will have insects and disease organisms in it that may flourish in the hot air of the greenhouse. This won't give you very good results.

If you can get, and afford, prepared potting composts, then use them. The expense is justified by results. These composts are carefully blended and well sterilized. If you can't or don't want to buy them, then you will have to manufacture potting composts of your own from various components. The fundamental ingredients of prepared composts are loam, peat*, and sand.

SOWING

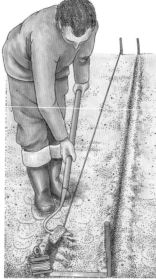

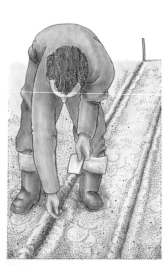

1 Fork over the ground. Mark out the rows, and stretch a garden line along each one. Drive a drill with a draw hoe at a suitable depth.

2 Sprinkle tiny seeds thinly. Large seeds like peas and beans should be planted at regular intervals, as recommended by the supplier. Water them gently.

3 When sowing is finished, rake the bed all over, so the entire surface becomes a fine tilth. This top layer of crumbly soil is the most important feature.

4 After you have raked the soil, tamp it down firmly with your feet or the head of the rake. This ensures that the seeds are in close contact with the earth.

You can make the loam by digging top-quality meadow turves and stacking them, grass side down, with a sprinkling of good compost or farmyard manure in between each layer of turves. Stack them in 6-foot (1.8-m) layers, and leave them for six months to a year. The loam should be sterilized. This is best done by passing steam through it: put the loam in any container with holes in the bottom and place it over a vessel of boiling water.

Peat* can be bought in bales, but make sure you buy environmentally friendly peat* from sustainable bogs.

Seed compost, for putting in flats or seed boxes, is, by volume: 2 parts sterilized loam; 1 part sterilized peat*; 1 part coarse sand. To each bushel (25.5 kg) of the above add 1½ ounces (40 g) superphosphate of lime and ¾ ounce (20 g) of ground chalk or ground limestone.

Potting compost is, by volume: 7 parts sterilized loam; 3 parts sterilized peat*; 2 parts coarse sand. To each bushel (25.5 kg) add ¼ pound (115 g) of base fertilizer and ¾ ounce (20 g) ground chalk or limestone.

Base fertilizer is by weight: 2 parts hoof and horn meal; 2 parts superphosphate of lime; 1 part sulfate of potash.

Transplanting

The same qualities are needed for transplanting a growing plant successfully as are needed for sowing seed: sympathy and common sense. Think for a moment what a trauma transplantation must be for a plant, which is a life form evolved for growing all its life in one place. It is wrenched out of the ground, and most of the friendly earth is shaken from its tender roots, which themselves are probably severely damaged. Then it is shoved roughly into some alien soil, possibly with much of its root system not in contact with the soil at all and the rest jammed together into a matted ball. It is quite amazing that transplanted seedlings ever survive, let alone grow into mature plants.

So dig plants out gently and be sure that as much soil adheres to their roots as possible. Transplant them gently into friable soil with their roots spread naturally, as they were before. Make sure the soil is well firmed, but not so roughly trampled as to break off tender roots. Then water them well. Puddling transplants, which means completely saturating them, is nearly always a good idea. It is drying out that kills most transplants. Of course, if we have hundreds of brassicas to plant, we can't be too particular— we just have to get them all in as well possible in a reasonable amount of time. But even then, it is surprising how some people will have 100% success with their plantings, while others have many failures.

Putting the plant in

Plant when it is raining, or when rain is forecast. Put large plants in with a trowel and smaller ones with a dibber (a pointed stick). Farm laborers transplanting thousands of brassicas go along at a slow walking pace, jabbing the dibber in beside the plant and moving the dibber over toward it to jam the earth tight around its roots. If a moderate tug on the plant doesn't pull it out, it will be all right.

With larger or more delicate plants, such as tomatoes or corn, keep a ball of soil on the roots and very carefully place them in a hole dug with a trowel. Then firm the soil around them. If you have grown them in pots, carry them in the pots to their planting station. Water them well, then take them gently out of the pots immediately before you place them in the ground.

PLANTING

1 Crowd the seeds into a seed box, so that the land where they will eventually grow will be free to bear another early crop in the meantime.

2 Or you can plant your seeds in pots. As the seedlings grow, thin them out to allow the strongest seedlings more room for their roots to develop.

3 When the seedlings of your first seed box look over-crowded, prick them out. This means thinning and moving to a box or bed to give more room.

4 Give your seeds a good start by putting them in pots or seed boxes under glass. They will grow and thrive earlier than they would if left in the open air.

Growing under Cover

You can get a greenhouse that has an interior like a space module about to make a landing on the Moon, with thermostats, propagators, electric fumigators, and all sorts of gadgets. But if you buy this kind of equipment, you are spending the money that would buy you out-of-season vegetables at the nearest supermarket for many decades. Is it really worth going to great trouble and expense in order to have some vegetable or fruit ready two weeks earlier than you would otherwise? If you are growing produce for sale, the answer is yes.

Greenhouse production or intensive cloche production for sale is a very sensible and valid way of making the small amount of money that every self-supporter must have to conduct their limited trade with the rest of the world. I write books, one of my neighbors gives piano lessons, and another makes wooden articles. If anyone wants to make under-glass cultivation their money-making enterprise, then they must get some good specialized books on the subject, which is a very complex one and requires a great deal of knowledge to make the difference between success and complete, expensive failure.

But unless the self-supporter intends to make greenhouse production a main source of income for mortgages, bills, health insurance, and so on, only the simplest of greenhouses is justified, with maybe some cold frames, hot frames, or a variety of cloches. You can buy your greenhouse ready-made or build it yourself. Buying the frames with glass in them is often the best thing, since you can then build your own lean-to greenhouse (*see pp.190–191 for more details*).

Cold frames

If you make four low walls and put a pane of glass on them, sloping to face the sun, you have a frame. The walls can be made of wood, bricks, concrete blocks, rammed earth, or whatever you have. The glass must be set in wooden frames so that it can be raised or lowered. Frames are fine for forcing on early lettuces and cabbages, for growing cucumbers later in the summer, or for melons and other things. Most are too low for tomatoes.

Hot frames

These are much used by experienced truck gardeners, and are a fine and economical way to force on early plants, but they do need skill. Step one is to make a hotbed: this is a pile of partly rotted farmyard manure or compost.

The best is stable manure: horse dung mixed with straw, mixed with an equal part of leaves or other composting material so it won't be too hot. Turn this a couple of times, until the first intense heat of fermenting has faded along with the strong smell of ammonia, and then lay it down in your frame with a shallower layer of earth on top.

You should manure 2½ feet (75 cm) deep with a foot (30 cm) of soil over it. The seed should be put in when the temperature falls to about 80°F (27°C). You can transplant plants into the bed. You would need to do this

in the late winter or early spring, so that as the hotbed cools, the spring advances, and the heat of the sun replaces the heat of the manure, which will be gone by the time you no longer need it. You will then have lovely, well-rotted horse manure.

Growing in a hot frame is not as easy as it sounds, but if you get it right, it is highly effective. It is sad that it is not used more often. Maybe as heating greenhouses with gas or electricity becomes more expensive, it will be. Of course, it helps to have a horse. A well-made compost heap with some activator will work, too.

Cloches

The first cloches were bell-shaped glass bowls, and they were much used in France. They were simply inverted over the plants to be forced. These were replaced by continuous cloches, which are tent- or barn-shaped glass sheds placed end to end to form long tunnels. These are much cheaper,

HOT FRAME
Enough heat to last from late winter all the way through spring comes from a thick layer of decomposing manure or compost. Cover with a layer of soil.

CARDBOARD BOX
A cardboard box painted black absorbs the sun's heat and aids germination.

PLASTIC SHEETING
A transparent plastic sheet will help germination and force on early vegetables.

which is a good thing, because if you are half as clumsy as I am, your cloche-managing career will be incessantly punctuated by the merry tinkling sound of breaking glass. If I just look at a glass cloche, it falls to pieces, so when you reflect that you have to hoe around crops, hand-weed, water (very necessary for crops under cloches, since they do not get the rain), thin, inspect and harvest, and that the cloches have to keep coming off and going back on every time you do one of these operations, you will realize that cloche mortality can be very high.

Polyethelene tunnels supported by inverted U-shaped wires were the next development. They don't shatter, but can very easily be blown away or flattened by high winds. However, they do work, and many people use them now; many truck gardeners have them on a large scale. Getting them on and off enormously increases the labor involved in growing a crop, but harvesting two weeks early may well make the difference between profit and loss. PVC, by the way, retains the heat more efficiently than polyethelene, but it is more expensive. And don't neglect the humble jelly jar. One of these inverted over an early-sown seed or plant of some tender species will protect it as well as any cloche. A sheet of any transparent plastic spread on the ground and weighted down on the edges with earth is fine for forcing on early potatoes and so on. When you do this sort of thing, you must be careful to harden off the plants sensibly and gradually.

Propagators

To get very early seeds going, you can use a propagator. This is an enclosed glass box containing soil and an under-soil electric heater. It produces the condition known as "warm feet but cold head," which many plants like. Tomato seeds can be germinated in one of these in January in a temperate climate, but as well as the soil being warm, the temperature of the air above it must be kept at 45°F (7°C) at least. A propagator is probably a worthwhile investment if you have the time and skill to grow your own tomato plants from seed.

CLOCHES AND A COLD FRAME
A cold frame is four walls with glass across them (*far right, top*). Cloches are portable, and there are many types: (*left to right*) hard plastic cloche; glass barn cloche; soft plastic tunnel cloche; simple corrugated plastic cloche; glass tent cloche. A weighted-down plastic "fleece" (*top center*) will also do.

Protection from Pests

The weeds that grow so merrily in our gardens, in defiance of all our efforts to wipe them out, are tough organisms, and well-adapted to protect themselves from most enemies and diseases. They wouldn't be there otherwise. But our crops have evolved gradually through artificial selection so as to be succulent, good to eat, and productive of high yields. As a result, their natural toughness and immunity against pests and diseases have often been sacrificed for other qualities. We must therefore protect them instead; but avoiding attacks by pests and diseases is not so easy. You will always get them, but they should not reach serious proportions. An organic farmer I know who farms a thousand acres with never an ounce of chemicals, and whose yields for every crop he grows are well above the national average, says that in his wheat he can show you examples of every wheat disease there is, but never enough of any one for it to make the slightest difference to his yield.

If you observe the principles of good husbandry, by putting plenty of animal manure or compost on the land, and by keeping to strict crop rotations (never grow the same annual crop on a piece of land two years running, and always leave the longest possible gap between two crops of the same plant), you will avoid many troubles.

It's also important to encourage a highly diversified floral and faunal environment for balance between species: plenty of predators of various kinds kill the pests before they get out of hand. Destroy all forms of life with poisonous chemicals and you destroy all the predators, too.

WORK WITH NATURE, NOT AGAINST IT

Nasturtiums repel cucumber beetle and Mexican bean beetle.

Toads will eat nasties such as slugs, aphids, and mosquitoes.

Thrushes eat snails that would otherwise damage your plants.

Hedgehogs (Europe) and moles (North America) eat millipedes.

Mint with its smell keeps white fly off beans.

Lacewings and their larvae destroy aphids.

Centipedes eat slug eggs and are the gardener's friend.

Ladybugs aren't just pretty. They consume aphids by the thousand.

So when you do get a plague of some pest, there will be no natural control, and you will be forced to use chemicals again. Still, no matter how organically you farm, there are times when some pest or disease gets the upper hand and something must be done if you are not to lose the crop.

Chemical pest control

Orthodox gardeners will use poison. You can indeed use some poison, and maybe sometimes you will have to; but surely it is far better and more skillful gardening practice to save your crops without using poison. Any fool can keep disease at bay simply by dousing his crop with chemicals, but what of the effect on other, benign, forms of life? If a chemical is poisonous to one thing, you can be certain it will be poisonous to other forms of life, too—including human life—and will do damage even if it doesn't kill.

The only chemicals I use are Bordeaux mixture* (*see* p.164) against blight in potatoes, various poisoned baits against slugs, and rotenone or pyrethrum, or a mixture of both, against caterpillars and aphids. Rotenone and pyrethrum are both derived from plants and are nonpersistent in the environment. They can be toxic to fish and some mammals, though, so use them with caution.

Biological pest control

Comparatively little research has been done into natural, or biological, means of defense, simply because there is no money to be made out of doing such research. No big company will look into ways of controlling pests and diseases that aren't going to make it any profit (and that will even operate against the profits it already makes from selling poisonous chemicals).

Here are some tips recommended from research into natural controls conducted by Lawrence D. Hills of the Henry Doubleday Association in England. Many of the findings are merely confirmations of tried and true methods that have been used for centuries. The Association also sells a little book called *Organic Pest and Disease Management*, which is very useful.

- Tie sacking strips or corrugated cardboard around fruit trees in late summer, then take it off and burn it, complete with weevils, codling moth grubs, and other nasties.
- Put a good old-fashioned grease-band around tree boles to catch nasties crawling up the trunks. Most predators fly.
- Cut off all dead wood from stone fruit trees in early summer and burn it as a guard against dieback.
- Spray dormant oil on fruit trees in winter only if needed, since it kills useful predators as well as nasties.
- Use plenty of potash to prevent chocolate-spot in beans.
- Grow winter-sown broad beans instead of spring-sown to avoid aphids. Pick out (and cook and eat!) the tips of broad bean plants at the first sign of aphid attack.
- Avoid carrot fly by interplanting with onions. The smell of the one is said to "jam" the smell of the other; thus you avoid both carrot and onion fly. Covering carrot plants with spun-bonded fabrics (floating row covers) is even more effective.
- Rigorously get rid of every brassica weed (wild mustard and shepherd's purse) so as not to harbor clubroot.
- Drop bits of rhubarb down each hole before you plant out brassica seedlings, or better still, water seed beds and seedlings with rhubarb-water. Rhubarb is said to contain substances that deter clubroot. This is an old remedy.
- Sink saucers full of beer into the ground to trap slugs. Or save the beer and use milk and water instead.

My own experience is that, except for potato blight, if you don't spray occasional plagues of caterpillars on brassicas, and occasional aphid attacks, there is no need to worry as long as you work with nature, not against it. A few pests on healthy crops do very little harm—certainly not enough to worry about.

SIMPLE METHODS OF PROTECTION

Young plants and bushes need protection from birds. Four sticks and some soft netting can cage in a growing bush. Cover seedlings with wire netting stretched across hoops, or with a mesh of string wound on wooden pegs.

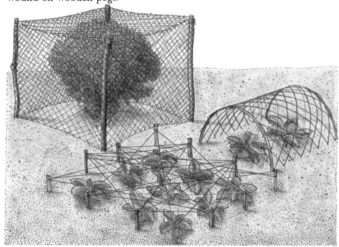

Intercropping works wonders. Carrots and onions, for example, repel each other's enemies.

Strips of sand or diatomaceous earth can keep slugs away from tender seedlings.

A piece of rhubarb under a brassica seedling is said to deter clubroot.

Slugs like beer. Trap them by sinking a saucerful in the ground.

Pests, Fungus, & Diseases

The mere mention of pests, fungi, and diseases can seem like a startling exposure to topics best left out of the upbeat miasma of many expositions on organic gardening. Most members of the human race are fixed on the idea that there should be "magic bullets" to cure all ills. You will indeed find many promises of such in most garden centers. In fact, many of their brightly-colored, heavily promoted, and very nasty products are simply offshoots from chemical warfare. Most selective weedkillers, defoliants, insecticides, and fungicides are deadly poison. And it is no accident that statistics show that the use of garden chemicals is closely correlated with increases in rates of serious cancers—especially for children who play so often in and around our gardens. Suffice it to say we do not want to pollute our own small havens of the natural world with by-products of chemical warfare or, at the very least, chemicals whose effects we know very little about. So what is our answer?

First, it must be clear that in the natural world there is an enormous and very beautiful variety of healthy plants with all their attendant bugs and fungi. Nature itself does have a multitude of checks and balances that militate against epidemics and vegetative wipeouts. We can try to mirror some of these strategies in our planting and management.

We want variety. We want to avoid large areas of single-species planting. We want to mix perennials with annuals. We want areas of wilderness close by. We want birds and insects in profusion. We want invertebrates, dragonflies, frogs, and toads. We want a vibrant and healthy soil. We want to avoid planting the same plant in the same place year after year. We want to dispose of garden waste and keep our boxes and tools clean. We want to limit damage from domestic animals and children. We want to keep out the nuisance birds and animals that are encouraged by human activities, such as pigeons, deer, and rabbits.

By incorporating all these features into the design and management of our land, we can give ourselves a head start on maintaining a natural balance. And where there is a natural balance, there are no epidemics, just minor damage. Good soil, wise garden layout, effective garden hygiene, and sensible precautions against ineffective composting—these are the number-one priority. Burning garden waste (if local regulations allow) is the number-two priority, and having sheds and buildings with easily cleaned concrete floors is number three. Be ruthless about tearing up and composting or burning diseased material, always use good seed, and never try to store anything other than top-quality produce.

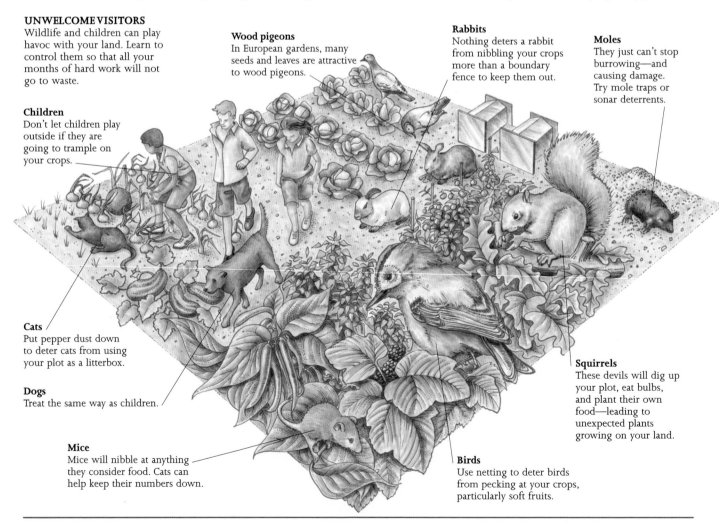

UNWELCOME VISITORS
Wildlife and children can play havoc with your land. Learn to control them so that all your months of hard work will not go to waste.

Children
Don't let children play outside if they are going to trample on your crops.

Cats
Put pepper dust down to deter cats from using your plot as a litterbox.

Dogs
Treat the same way as children.

Mice
Mice will nibble at anything they consider food. Cats can help keep their numbers down.

Wood pigeons
In European gardens, many seeds and leaves are attractive to wood pigeons.

Rabbits
Nothing deters a rabbit from nibbling your crops more than a boundary fence to keep them out.

Moles
They just can't stop burrowing—and causing damage. Try mole traps or sonar deterrents.

Squirrels
These devils will dig up your plot, eat bulbs, and plant their own food—leading to unexpected plants growing on your land.

Birds
Use netting to deter birds from pecking at your crops, particularly soft fruits.

PLANNING FOR PREVENTION

A well-managed garden with a vibrant soil and varied planting will have few problems from fungus, pests, and diseases. Slugs, birds, and four-legged pests are likely to be the main threat—mostly taken care of by good protection and being "slug wise." There are a few essential principles to bear in mind.

Variety—We know it is the spice of life! Mix your plantings, have no large pots of a single vegetable, and ensure you have plenty of perennials scattered about the garden to give winter shelter to helpful bugs.

Build up your soil Your annual applications of compost are key here. Make it, spread it, and your plants will enjoy it.

Fencing, walls, and netting You cannot beat sheer physical protection—the stronger you can make it the happier you and your plants will be.

Encourage helpful beasts—Frogs and toads are your allies and a well-behaved dog can help keep off those annoying cats. Falcons and hawks are the ultimate bird deterrent, although they may not be in everyone's bag of tricks.

Companion planting—Use the smells and chemicals produced by one plant to mask those given off by others—onions with carrots, for example, or arugula with lettuce.

Sacrificial cropping—Just plant a few extra plants on the outside of your rows then you won't mind if the slugs take their share since your main crop should escape unscathed.

Good garden hygiene—Keep down rough grass and weeds, don't leave rotting vegetation on your beds, keep your tools clean, and make sure you rotate your crops rigorously.

FRIENDS IN THE GARDEN
Bees
Not only do bees supply us with copious quantities of honey, but they also provide a vital service in pollinating our garden crops. Make sure you have a healthy bee population in and around your garden.

Birds
Although some birds cause us trouble by stealing our fruit and nibbling our vegetables, there are many that eat insects, and you would be wise to encourage these. Blackbirds, robins, starlings, and thrushes constantly search out insects, caterpillars, and slugs.

Centipedes
These are fast-moving little hunters that eat mites, bugs, and slugs. (Do not confuse centipedes with millipedes, which are slower and have more legs.)

Frogs and toads
These require water for breeding and are extremely sensitive to poisons. Both eat insects in large quantities. They will travel all over your garden, provided you have areas of long grass or shade for them to lurk in.

Ground beetles
There is a large family of beetles, mostly large black ones, that live on the ground and eat other insect pests, including the root fly larvae. These beetles need cover to survive the winter—hence the importance of perennial crops and hedges.

Hedgehogs
This little fellow is the great consumer of slugs in British backyards. Gardeners like to encourage them by leaving out bowls of pet food or bread and milk. They need rough hedges and plenty of leaves to build winter nests for hibernating in.

Hoverfly
Looking like small wasps, these pretty insects have larvae with a voracious appetite for aphids. The larvae are nasty-looking little creatures with a pair of nippers to hold their aphid prey. Encourage hoverflies by growing flowers in your vegetable garden—they seem to be particularly fond of yellow flowers.

Lacewings
These delicate insects so beloved by trout are encouraged by water. Their larvae, which are flattish with a brown body, have a great appetite for aphids.

Ladybugs
The ladybug is the best-known predator for aphids. The adult and larvae both eat aphids. The larvae are gray colored and are very active killers.

Worms
Earthworms and manure worms are the two species of worm that we most want to see in our gardens. Earthworms are the master soil builders, constantly aerating the soil and bringing new soil to the surface as worm castes and dragging organic material down. If you have ever wondered why ancient ruins are so often buried under several feet of earth, you only need to watch what happens on your lawn. Worms are constantly bringing up new soil in their castes. Tests have shown that on healthy soil this little miracle creates about 2 inches (5 cm) of new topsoil every 20 years.

Manure worms, on the other hand, are thinner and redder than earthworms. They rapidly turn organic material into compost and are the essential basis of worm composting.

ANIMAL PESTS
Birds
Many birds will dig up seeds, pull out onion sets, eat emerging leaves of peas and brassicas, and steal your soft fruits. A cat or two may well help keep damage down, but the cat itself will do damage of its own kind. A tethered hawk or falcon is much more effective—but, realistically, physical protection is an effective remedy against bird damage.

Nets will protect your fruit and your plants but they can be hard work, easily torn, and tangled. The best solution is to invest time in making wire mesh frames using roofing battens and wire or fine netting. Choose a size that suits your cropping—I have both large and small. Something perhaps 10 feet (3 m) long and 4 feet square (0.5 sq m) at the ends would do the job. This will even keep the white butterflies off it if the mesh is small enough. And the frames are an excellent place to dry onions, potatoes, and carrots before storage.

Cats and Dogs
Our lovely household pets can easily become monsters in the vegetable garden. You can train dogs to KEEP OUT and if you are wise you will make this a strict rule, but cats will always please themselves. I have found a good water pistol (an old dishwashing-liquid bottle will do!) makes an admirable training device. Temporary use of wire rabbit fencing may help and even a sprinkling of red pepper can work wonders if all else fails.

Cattle and Deer
You are looking at mega-damage here so if you think you may suffer it is time to start building strong walls and fences. It was not for nothing that the traditional vegetable garden had a 10 feet (3 m) high boundary wall.

Children
Kids love the garden but their attention span is short and those that come from towns may go a bit crazy in your fine open space. This is definitely a case where ignorance is very definitely not bliss: education and information is the best way to avoid damage. If you can find simple jobs for them to do you will find they soak up knowledge very quickly. They love harvesting and animals but don't forget to warn them if you have aggressive rooster or geese.

Mice
Not only do mice destroy stored food, they also steal pea and bean seeds very effectively. Keep your mouse popullation down with cats, or alternatively, use mousetraps. Soaking the seeds in kerosene* or pregerminating them before planting will also help.

Moles
If you get moles in your garden, then set traps immediately. Setting a mole trap is a strange black art. The trap must be left outside in the soil for at least a month before you use it. Some experts say you should rub the traps with the skin of another mole you have caught. But the vital thing is that the trap should not be touched by human hands or contaminated by oil or grease. The mole lives through his nose and will immediately be wary of a strange smell. Dig the trap into his run and hope you catch him.

Rabbits and hares
Keep rabbits and hares out of your garden by making sure you have a good boundary fence.

Squirrels
These agile pests can do a great deal of damage. Netting is the only cure.

INSECT PESTS
Ants
Unless you are unlucky or there is a very hot summer, ant infestations are unlikely to cause you much trouble.

Ants can be killed with boiling water or, if necessary, with a solution of equal parts of borax and powdered sugar.

Aphids

Believe it or not, healthy plants will almost instantly create their own chemical defenses to limit attacks by aphids.

If your plants are weak and your garden has few natural aphid predators, then you will have to resort to other control methods. Soft soap* mixed with warm water and then sprayed on will reduce small infestations.

Beetles

There are a range of beetles that are harmful to the garden—mostly through the appetites of their larvae. The most common are the chafer beetle and the flea beetle. Chafer beetles feed mainly on the leaves, flowers, and fruits of plants, while the grub destroys the roots, making the leaves wilt and the plant die. Continuous cultivation and good weed control are the main preventive measures.

Flea beetles eat small, round holes in the leaves of plants, while their grubs tunnel into stems and eat roots. Control the beetle by making sure the soil is kept clear of debris in the winter to deprive them of wintering quarters. Keep seedlings growing fast in dry weather by watering.

Big bud mite

This small mite attacks currants in Europe and New Zealand. As the name implies, it creates "big buds" in early spring—these contain the mites and can be broken off and burned.

Capsid bugs

Similar to aphids but smaller and more virulent, capsid bugs cause small brown patches to appear on leaves, making them distorted and causing them to fall off. Keep the bottoms of your fruit trees well cleaned out during winter and replace mulches to prevent overwintering. Dormant oil sprays are helpful, but the only effective summer control is spraying with nicotine*.

Caterpillars

The white butterfly is the great creator of caterpillars—and is a pretty unwelcome guest in our summer gardens. The main control is to net seedlings with lightweight wire frames. Then, when plants are too large for the frames, remove the caterpillars by hand each day and destroy them. If plants are really badly affected, they are better destroyed than simply abandoned.

Gooseberry sawfly

Their larvae may strip your bushes bare but usually after fruiting. Keep bases well weeded and you will still get a good crop of gooseberries next year.

Pea moth

The larvae tunnel into the peas in their pods. Early or late varieties of pea are less affected. Once an attack has started, there is no cure. The best control is good cultivation after the peas have been lifted.

Cutworms

Cutworms are the caterpillars of any of several night-flying moths, which attack the stems of seedlings at ground level. Keep weeds down to discourage them.

Rootfly

Cabbage and carrots have their own particular kind of rootfly. Affected plants will discolour and wilt before they die. Cure is by prevention. Attack to cabbages is likely after seedlings have been transplanted. Make sure these are well-watered and earthed up.

Attack to carrots is encouraged by damage to plants when thinning or weeding. Always remove thinnings immediately—thin when the ground is damp and ensure the remaining plants are well covered with soil at ground level.

Red spider mites

These little mites suck sap from leaves, which get yellow spots and then turn brown.

Keep greenhouse plants cool and moist to avoid attack by spraying them with water twice a day. There are biological controls available that are used to treat red spider mites in greenhouses. With fruit trees, control is more difficult—remove and burn affected leaves.

Slugs

Slugs are an ever present hazard for the gardener but for all their cunning they have one great weakness—they cannot run fast. Picking off slugs with a torch after midnight is easy and effective if you put out tempting bait to attract them—like a bowl of milk or even dried dog food! Keep weeds and grass controlled to minimize their habitat. Put down a large plank of wood at least 1½ inches (4 cm) thick beside your favorite vegetable and then lift it during the day and destroy the slugs that will be hiding there.

Dressing your soil with diatomaceous earth or fresh wood ash will also limit attacks, since slugs dislike traveling over sharp, dry material.

Wasps

These are another of the gardener's love–hate insects. In early summer, wasps hunt a large range of insects, and their larvae consume thousands of aphids, so helping the gardener. But, as the summer wears on, the wasps develop a longing for sweet food as they begin to transform into queens for their winter hibernation. The only effective control is to find and destroy nests.

Weevils

The larvae of weevil beetles attack a wide range of plants—particularly apple blossom, peas and beans, and turnips. In the orchard, this pest can be controlled by catching the pupating larvae in bands of sacking around the tree trunks in June, then burning the sacking. Keeping the soil clean, free from debris, and full of fertility will also reduce damage, as will good crop rotation.

Wireworms

These worms inhabit grassland and can be very destructive when it is first cultivated. They are the larvae of the click beetle and live as brown, wiry worms, about 1 inch (2.5 cm) long, for 4 or 5 years before pupating. They are particularly harmful to potatoes in late summer. Newly cultivated grassland may be affected for up to 3 years, so you can plant resistant crops such as peas and beans. Catch wireworms and destroy them by punching holes in a tin can, filling it with potato peelings, and burying in the ground.

DISEASES

Blight

This is the most serious fungal disease of potatoes (and tomatoes). Once affected, there is no cure. Blight needs warm humid weather with little wind in order to develop. Dark patches develop on top of leaves and a white mold develops underneath. Prevent by spraying with Bordeaux mixture* (see p.264). Spray both sides of leaves every two weeks, starting in late June.

Canker

The bark on pear and apple trees may shrink and crack, and a deep, swollen wound develops. In the winter, small red growths cover the affected area. In the worst cases, whole trees may be destroyed. The fungus attacks trees where drainage is poor. All affected branches must be cut off and burned. Make sure that cuts are clean, with no damage to surrounding bark that could lead to reinfection.

Clubroot

This is the most serious of the diseases affecting brassicas. Roots become swollen (and smell foul), and the plants wilt. The disease organisms lie in the soil—sometimes for more than 20 years. There is no cure, so good crop rotation is a must. All affected plants must be burned, not composted.

Damping off

This fungus affects young seedlings; stems turn black and rot. Overwatering and overcrowding, combined with a lack of ventilation, can cause this problem. Also, be careful not to touch stems or roots as you transplant small seedlings—hold them by the seed leaves only.

Fire blight

This is a deadly disease of pears and sometimes apple trees. Affected leaves turn dark brown but do not drop off; whole branches may be affected. In some countries, you must notify government authorities if this disease is contracted and control must be carried out under their supervision. Severely affected trees must be uprooted and burned.

Mildew

There are many fungal mildews. Some, such as downy mildew, occur in damp, overcrowded conditions; others, like powdery mildew, grow in hot, dry, overcrowded conditions on light soils. Bordeaux mixture* will offer some protection, but avoiding poor conditions is the priority. Seriously affected plants should be burned.

Rusts

There is a huge variety of fungal rusts affecting plants. In most cases, strong plants will be no more than discolored with brown or yellow rusty spots. Bordeaux mixture* will control but not cure. Badly affected plants should be burned.

Scab

Common scab affects potatoes, beets, radishes, and rutabagas. It is not a very serious disease, simply causing ugly "scabs" on the surface of these vegetables. There are some potato varieties that are resistant to scab. More important, you can reduce the alkalinity of the soil (you can buy a simple test kit for testing your soil pH values).

The Illustrated Index of Vegetables, Herbs, & Fruits

Containing the edible roots, stems, leaves, flowers, seeds,
pods, and fruits that constitute the produce
of the kitchen garden.

The Edible Parts of Plants

I was once extremely hungry in a jungle and almost overwhelmed by plant life. However, I could not find a single edible plant. I was made to realize that for human beings, few of the thousands of plants that grow on this planet are edible. Most of them are far too tough. Humans cannot digest cellulose, which is the basis of much plant tissue.

Of the comparatively few plants that humans can eat, most are only edible in part. The larger and more complex edible plants have, just like animals, evolved separate and specialized organs that are quite different from each other and serve quite different purposes. We, and other herbivorous and omnivorous animals, eat different parts of different plants, on the basis of what tastes best and does us the most good.

For the purposes of the gardener, the main parts of plants can be classified as: roots, stems, leaves, flowers, fruits, and seed. Most plants have all of these parts. There are some oddities that don't, like cacti, which don't have leaves—their stems serve instead. The tissues of which the various organs are composed are different in kind, and the botanist can tell, quite easily, whether an organ is, for example, a stem or a root. The non-botanist is in for a few surprises. This is because some plants have developed some of their organs for very particular purposes—storing nourishment through the winter, for example—and the resulting organ is often a unique and strange-seeming example of its type.

Many of the plants we eat, particularly root and stem vegetables, are naturally biennial. The plant uses a swollen root or stem to store in its first year of growth much of the energy that it will use in its second year to produce flowers and seeds. Gardeners harvest these biennial plants after their first year of growth, so as to get the full benefit of this stored-up nourishment before it is dissipated. This is why lettuces should not be allowed to "bolt," and why many vegetables should not be permitted to go to seed. If you leave a beet or carrot, for example, in the ground for more than a year, the edible roots will become tough and shrink as the energy stored in them is used to make the plants flower.

Roots

When analyzing plants, it seems sensible to start at the bottom, with roots. Most roots have the specialized function of absorbing from the soil the nonorganic nutrients that plants need to grow and survive. These include: water, in which all the other nutrients have to be dissolved; nitrogen; potash; phosphates; and all the many trace elements that are essential to plants. Roots force themselves far down into the soil in their search for water and nutrients. Fortunately for humans, some plants also use their roots for storing food as well as gathering it. Gardeners are able to harvest this stored food to keep themselves going in the lean times of winter or drought.

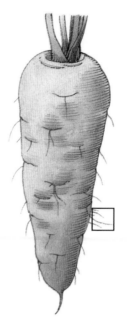

Swollen taproot

ROOTS
Most edible roots are swollen taproots. Laterals, or side roots, grow from the tap root, and toward the ends of these are the microscopic root hairs that feed the plant by absorbing moisture and nutrients from the soil.

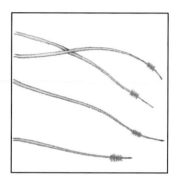

Edible roots are nearly all taproots. A taproot is the main support root of the plant, out of which grow the searching side roots and their absorbent root hairs. A number of common vegetables are swollen taproots. These include carrots, parsnips, radishes, rutabagas, turnips, and beets. Red beet is the beet that is eaten; sugar beet stores the plant's energy in the form of sugar and is grown commercially for that very reason.

Most plant energy is stored in the form of starch, but energy can only be transported around a plant in the form of sugar. This is because starch is not soluble. This fact is important to the gardener. If you want the sweetness of certain vegetables—new potatoes and sweet corn are cases in point—you must harvest the crop when the energy is still in the form of sugar and not wait until the plants grow older and the sugar has been stored away as starch. If you make wine, you will find that you need certain enzymes to turn the starch into sugar, for only sugar, and not starch, can be turned into alcohol by yeast.

Stems

There are some very unusual stems. Potatoes, for example, although they grow underground and are swollen to store food, are not roots but stems.

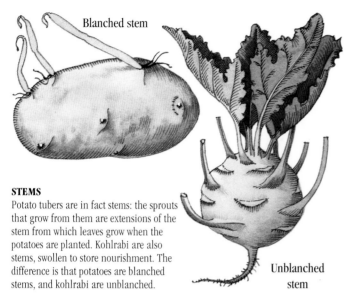

Blanched stem

Unblanched stem

STEMS
Potato tubers are in fact stems: the sprouts that grow from them are extensions of the stem from which leaves grow when the potatoes are planted. Kohlrabi are also stems, swollen to store nourishment. The difference is that potatoes are blanched stems, and kohlrabi are unblanched.

Potatoes have all the morphological characteristics of stems. They don't put off lateral roots, and the "eyes" in them are in fact growth buds from which normal stems and leaves develop when the potatoes are planted below ground. Exposed to the light, potatoes immediately develop chlorophyll—turn green—as most stems do, so that they can engage in photosynthesis.

Photosynthesis is not only the very basis and mainspring of the gardener's art, but it is the one process that keeps every single living being, animal or vegetable, alive on this planet. It is the miraculous process—no scientist has ever been able to duplicate it—that uses the energy of the Sun to make carbohydrate or starch, which is the basis of all plant and animal energy.

Photosynthesis is carried out by molecules of chlorophyll—the green pigment of plants—and in the total absence of light, no green plant can live. Non-green plants (for example, Indian pipe) live, like fungi, as parasites or saprophytes on the living or dead tissue of other organisms. They lack chlorophyll and cannot derive energy from the Sun.

Many stems are very tough—consider the stem of an oak tree—because they have to support the upper parts of the plant in the air. Some stems are only pleasant for us to eat if they are blanched—that is, kept from the light so they do not develop chlorophyll and stay white instead of turning green. Potatoes are like this, and so are celery stems, sea kale, and chards, which are the stems of cardoons. The stem is the edible part of a rhubarb plant: the leaves are actually poisonous. Kohlrabi and celeriac are both stems, swollen so that they can store food. Notice the leaf buds and the scars left by leaves on the stems of kohlrabi.

Leaves

Leaves are often edible, and some of them have evolved to become storehouses of energy, just like the specialized roots and stems. For example, onions, leeks, garlic, and shallots are really layered clusters of leaf bases adapted to store food throughout the winter. The leaves of hearted cabbages behave in much the same way, and other plants, like lettuces, are halfway along this line of evolution toward tight clumps of leaves that store energy through the winter, so that, if you allow it to, the plant gets away the second year to produce a flowering head and early seed.

All plants are either monocotyledons (monocots) or dicotyledons (dicots). The difference lies in the seed, the leaves, and the mode of growth. The seed of a dicot—a bean, for example—is made up of two halves. You can see this for yourself: a fava bean will readily split in two if you just press into it with your fingernail. A monocot seed, on the other hand, is self-contained and cannot be split.

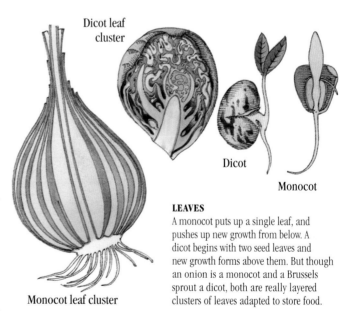

Dicot leaf cluster

Dicot

Monocot

Monocot leaf cluster

LEAVES
A monocot puts up a single leaf, and pushes up new growth from below. A dicot begins with two seed leaves and new growth forms above them. But though an onion is a monocot and a Brussels sprout a dicot, both are really layered clusters of leaves adapted to store food.

Dicots produce two seed leaves. Thereafter the stem grows upward and new leaves issue from a growing point at its tip, or from growing points at the tips of branches. Monocots grow in a completely different way. They begin by pushing up a single leaf—a blade of grass or an onion is a good example. Thereafter they continue to grow by pushing from the seed upward. The first leaf is pushed up and to one side and new ones push their way up beside it. Dicots add new growth above existing growth, while monocots push existing growth upward, adding new growth beneath it. Most vegetables are dicots, but some, notably onions, leeks, asparagus, and sweet corn, are monocots. An easy way to distinguish between a monocot and a dicot is to look at their leaves. If they have almost parallel veins, the chances are they are monocots, but if the veins of the leaves splay out away from each other, they are almost certainly dicots.

Flowers

Flowers are the next step upward in a plant, and they are not as a rule an important food for humans. But they are important to the plant, of course, for they ensure its posterity.

Sex reared its beautiful head in a new and elaborate form millions of years ago in the Jurassic Period, when insects and plants developed their amazing symbiosis. The plants provide nectar and other delights to attract the insects, and the insects unwittingly cross-fertilize the plants by going from one to the other, carrying pollen from the male organs of one flower to the female organs of another. The extraordinary elaboration of devices to attract the right insects, and ensure that they collect pollen on their bodies, and do not self-fertilize the flower they are visiting, but instead fertilize the next flower, has been the life study of many botanists, including, notably, Charles Darwin. It is a very good thing to keep bees, particularly if you have fruit trees, for not only do you get honey from them but they pollinate your trees and flowering plants.

Some flowers are pollinated by the wind. Corn is one of them, and because of this, you should plant your sweet corn in a wide block and not in one long row. You must try to make sure that when the wind blows from any direction, it blows pollen from one plant to another.

FLOWERS
Flowers are essential to the reproduction of plants. Their nectar **1** attracts insects that pick up pollen from the male part **2** of one plant and carry it to the female part **3** of the next. The ovary **4** of a flower after it has been fertilized is the fruit.

There are not many flowers that are edible. The main ones are cauliflower and broccoli, which are immature flowers. If you leave these to continue growing instead of eating them, they will produce inedible mature flowers, just as an abandoned cabbage will. Globe artichokes are flowers, although

only a small part is actually edible. Nasturtium seeds make good substitutes for capers, and some herb flowers are good for flavoring and coloring. But, if you had to live exclusively on flowers, you would get very thin indeed. Seed and fruit, which come from the reproductive part of flowers, are more important to the self-sufficient gardener.

When the female element of a flower has been pollinated, the flower forms a fruit. The fruit grows and produces seed within it. The seed is spread far and wide by a number of amazingly ingenious methods that plants have evolved so as to propagate their species. A gardener who wishes to enjoy his craft will study all these things, for a knowledge of them will increase enormously the pleasure he gets from his labors. The more you learn about plants, the more you will wonder at the extraordinary cunning and elaboration that selection has evolved for their survival and perpetuation.

Fruits

To a botanist, fruit is the ovary of a flower after it has been fertilized. Fertilization causes the ovules, which are inside the ovary, to turn into seeds and the ovary itself to turn into a fruit. Some fruits don't bear much resemblance to what most people would call fruit. A whiff of dandelion fluff is a fruit, and so are all nuts. Tomatoes, eggplants, peppers, beans, and pods full of peas are all fruits; an individual pea, and a bean threshed from its pod for drying, are both seeds.

To a cook and a gastronome, and to most people, in fact, fruit means the sort of sweet succulent fruit that is eaten as a dessert. I have used this common classification in ordering this chapter. The only exception I have made is rhubarb, which though eaten as a dessert is not naturally sweet and is grown like a vegetable, which in fact it is.

Botanically, a blackberry or raspberry is not one fruit but a cluster of fruits. Each tiny globe that goes to make up such a "berry" is a complete fruit. The word "berry" means something different to a botanist. A tomato is a true berry, because its seeds are embedded in soft pulp. Grapes, gooseberries, and oranges are also berries. The fruits that contain single pits or stones—plums, cherries, and peaches—are called drupes. Fruits like apples and pears are called pomes. Only the core of a pome is a cluster of true fruits; the edible part surrounding the core is just a layer of stored food. Each tiny seed in a strawberry is a single fruit. They are all held together by a succulent mass. If you take the trouble to cut open pomes, berries, and drupes at various stages of their growth, you will see how all of this works.

Every part of the fruit is in embryo in the flower, and you can follow the development of each part of the flower as it becomes a fruit.

Generally speaking, fruits contain little nourishment, and most of the little they have is in the form of sugar. All the stored energy of the plant is going to go into the seed, not the fruit. If you tried to live on fruits alone, you would soon become seriously undernourished. Fruits tend to be rich in certain vitamins, however, particularly vitamin C, and this makes them valuable to humans. Many years ago a learned doctor said: "Apples have no nutritive value whatever and it does not matter whether you eat them or not." He was completely mistaken, but then he did not know about vitamins. Cobbett made the same mistake when advising his cottagers not to grow fruit trees. He thought they were good for nothing but giving children bellyaches.

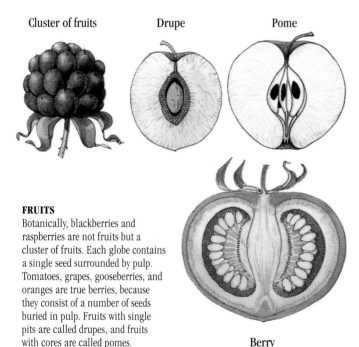

Cluster of fruits   Drupe   Pome

FRUITS
Botanically, blackberries and raspberries are not fruits but a cluster of fruits. Each globe contains a single seed surrounded by pulp. Tomatoes, grapes, gooseberries, and oranges are true berries, because they consist of a number of seeds buried in pulp. Fruits with single pits are called drupes, and fruits with cores are called pomes.

Berry

All the members of the squash tribe are fruits. Some, like melons, seem to have developed their large, water-filled fruit so that they can store water. They come from parts of the world with short rainy seasons. The stored water gives the seeds a head start—one good watering—to enable them to stay alive until the next rain. Other fruits have undoubtedly developed to attract animals. Apples, plums, peaches, and cherries have all evolved in this way. Man has taken many of these slightly succulent and somewhat sour wild fruits and, by artificial selection, evolved improved varieties, containing a lot of sugar, extra flavor, plenty of succulent flesh, and not too much

acid. If you compare the wild crabapple with a Cox's Orange Pippin apple, you will understand what has happened. Most cultivated fruits have been improved beyond recognition from their wild form.

Seeds
If it were not for edible seeds, humans could scarcely survive. Some seeds have to pass through the guts of an animal in order to germinate. So it is important for plants that their fruit should be eaten. Many seeds are not strictly edible; humans eat them but they pass through them intact without doing them any good. It is the fruit that they benefit from.

Other seeds, especially the cereals, such as wheat, rice, and corn, are eaten for direct nutrition, and it is these seeds that keep humanity alive in many parts of the globe. Before an annual plant dies, it puts all the nourishment it has into its seeds, which are to carry its life on into future generations. Thus seeds are generally far more nutritious than any other parts of plants and, if you grind them or cook them and make them palatable, they will give you the energy to keep alive. Without seeds, a vegetarian would live on a very sparse diet indeed: it would be scarcely adequate to sustain life.

Seeds of certain plants, notably leguminous ones, are quite rich in protein. Pea and bean seeds of all kinds are very important. A vegan can enjoy a near-perfect diet by eating plenty of soybeans, some other vegetables, and a little comfrey, which is almost the only edible plant that contains vitamin B12. The great thing about seeds is that they are easy to dry and store.

Herbs
Many herb seeds are used to flavor food, for the essential oils and other virtues of herbs are often concentrated in their seeds. Many of the more aromatic herbs come from dry, warm regions. Their aromatic oils have evolved largely to protect them from dessication in dry, hot weather. The small leaves of many of them—often mere needles— are that size and shape to prevent moisture from being transpired by the plant too fast.

Some of the delicious flavors and aromas of culinary herbs are there for reasons that are not yet fully understood: attracting and repelling various insects may well be one of them. But plants are endlessly fascinating and mysterious, and happily, it is improbable that we will ever know all there is to know about them. It should be enough for us that thyme and rosemary smell and taste as they do, without worrying why.

Roots

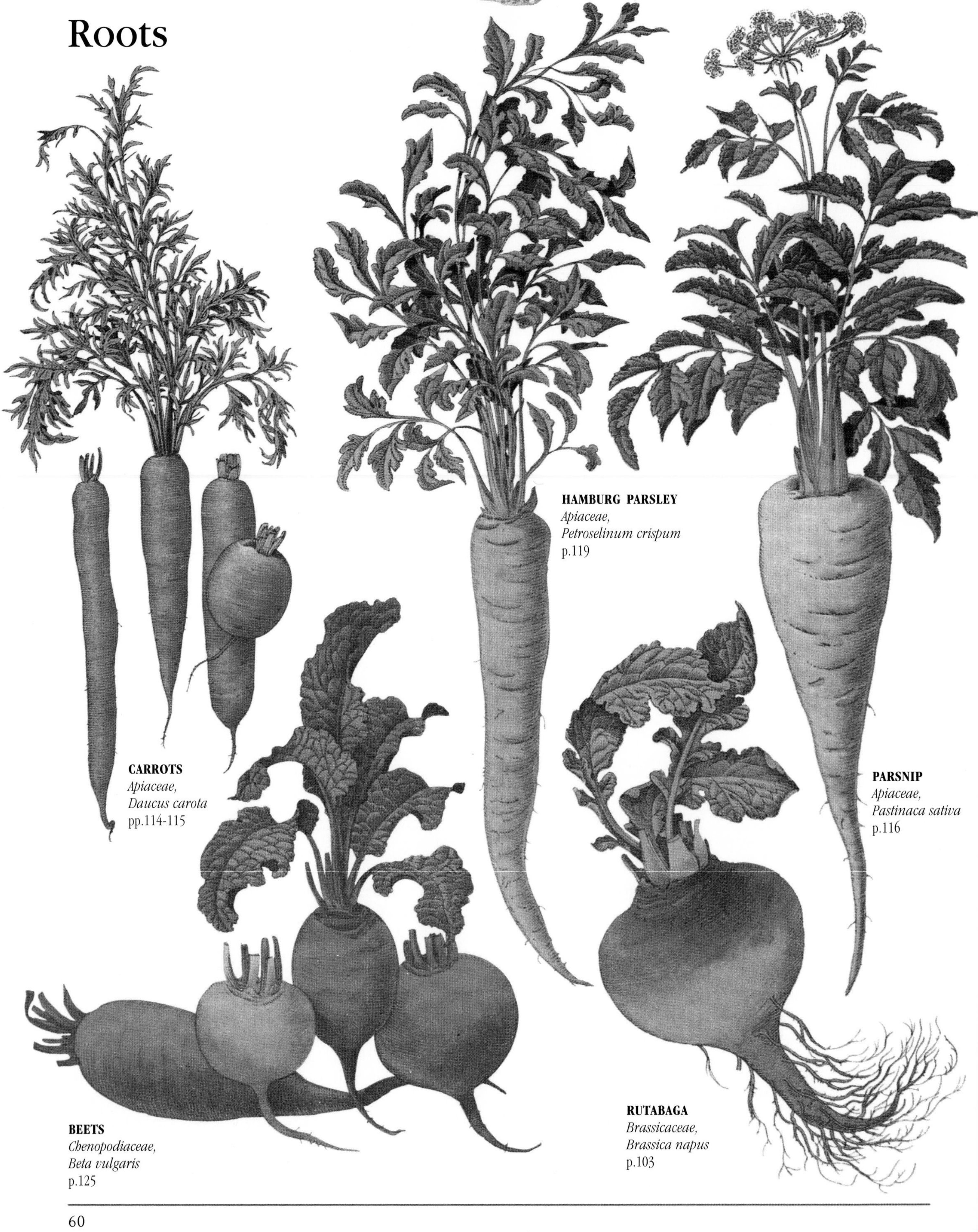

HAMBURG PARSLEY
Apiaceae,
Petroselinum crispum
p.119

CARROTS
Apiaceae,
Daucus carota
pp.114-115

PARSNIP
Apiaceae,
Pastinaca sativa
p.116

BEETS
Chenopodiaceae,
Beta vulgaris
p.125

RUTABAGA
Brassicaceae,
Brassica napus
p.103

TURNIPS
Brassicaceae,
Brassica rapa
p.103

RADISHES
Brassicaceae,
Raphanus sativus
p.104

HORSERADISH
Brassicaceae,
Armoracia rusticana
p.147

SCORZONERA
(**BLACK SALSIFY**)
Asteraceae,
Scorzonera hispanica
p.134

SALSIFY
Asteraceae,
Tragopogon
porrifolius
p.134

Stems

CELTUCE
p.133

CELERIAC
Apiaceae,
Apium graveolens
var. rapaceum
p.118

CARDOON
Asteraceae,
Cynara cardunculus
p.136

JERUSALEM
ARTICHOKE
Asteraceae,
Helianthus
tuberosus
p.137

CHINESE
ARTICHOKE
Asteraceae,
Stachys affinis
p.137

ANGELICA
Asteraceae,
Angelica archangelica
p.142

SELF-BLANCHING
CELERY

CELERY
Apiaceae,
Apium graveolens
var. dulce
p.117

CHINESE CABBAGE
Brassicaceae, Brassica rapa
p.99

POTATOES
Solanaceae,
Solanum tuberosum, p.106

SEAKALE
Brassicaceae,
Crambe
maritima
p.105

KOHLRABI
Brassicaceae,
Brassica oleracea
p.104

RUBY CHARD

RHUBARB
Polygonaceae,
Rheum
rhabarbarum
p.139

ASPARAGUS
Liliaceae,
Asparagus officinalis
p.123

SWISS CHARD
(SEAKALE BEET)
Chenopodiaceae,
Beta vulgaris
p.127

Leaves

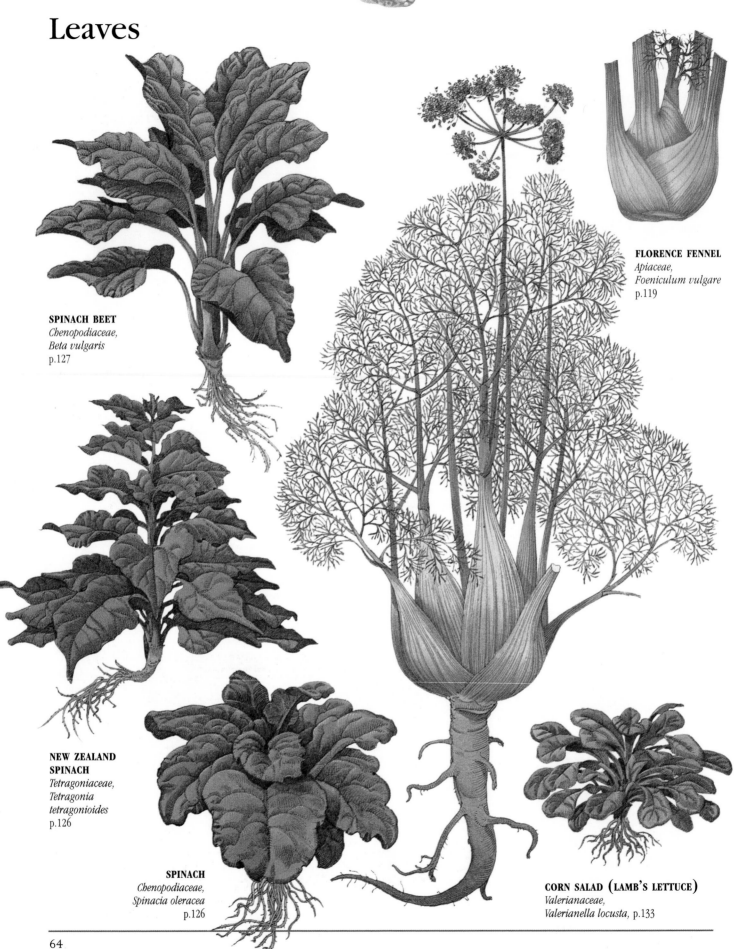

SPINACH BEET
Chenopodiaceae,
Beta vulgaris
p.127

NEW ZEALAND
SPINACH
Tetragoniaceae,
Tetragonia
tetragonioides
p.126

SPINACH
Chenopodiaceae,
Spinacia oleracea
p.126

FLORENCE FENNEL
Apiaceae,
Foeniculum vulgare
p.119

CORN SALAD (LAMB'S LETTUCE)
Valerianaceae,
Valerianella locusta, p.133

CABBAGES
Brassicaceae,
Brassica oleracea, pp.96-102

RED CABBAGE

WHITE CABBAGE

KALE
p.102

SAVOY CABBAGE

CONICAL-HEARTED CABBAGE

BRUSSELS SPROUTS
p.100

COLLARDS
p.102

CRESSES
Brassicaceae
p.105

ROUND-HEARTED CABBAGE

WATERCRESS
Nasturtium officinale

CRESS
Lepidium sativum

LAND CRESS
Barbarea verna

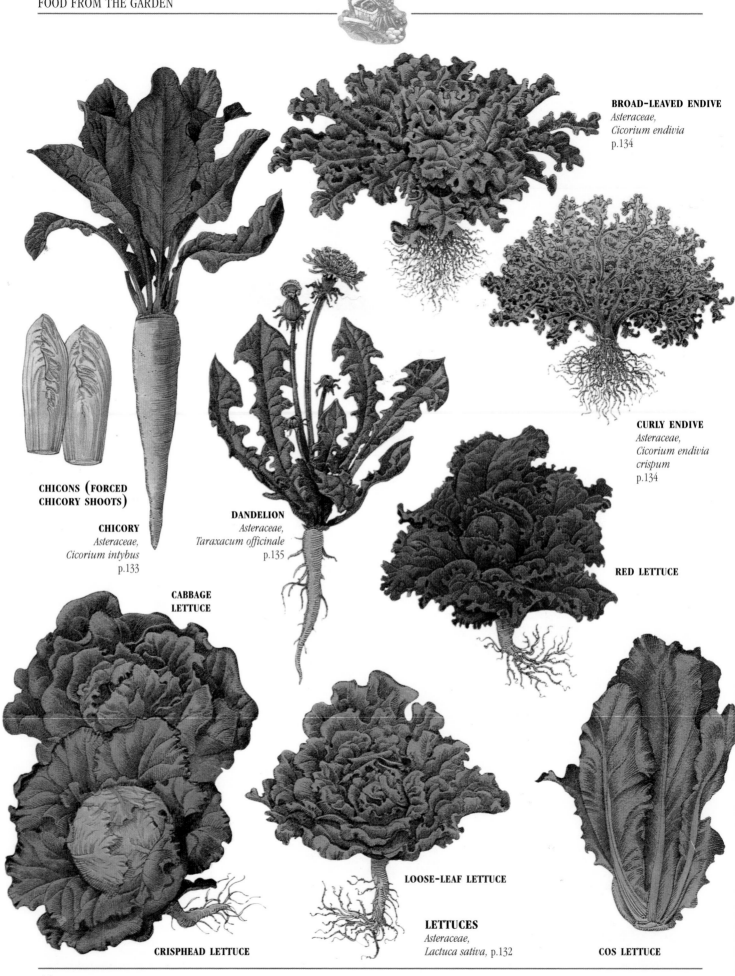

BROAD-LEAVED ENDIVE
Asteraceae,
Cicorium endivia
p.134

CURLY ENDIVE
Asteraceae,
Cicorium endivia
crispum
p.134

CHICONS (FORCED
CHICORY SHOOTS)

CHICORY
Asteraceae,
Cicorium intybus
p.133

DANDELION
Asteraceae,
Taraxacum officinale
p.135

RED LETTUCE

CABBAGE
LETTUCE

LOOSE-LEAF LETTUCE

LETTUCES
Asteraceae,
Lactuca sativa, p.132

CRISPHEAD LETTUCE

COS LETTUCE

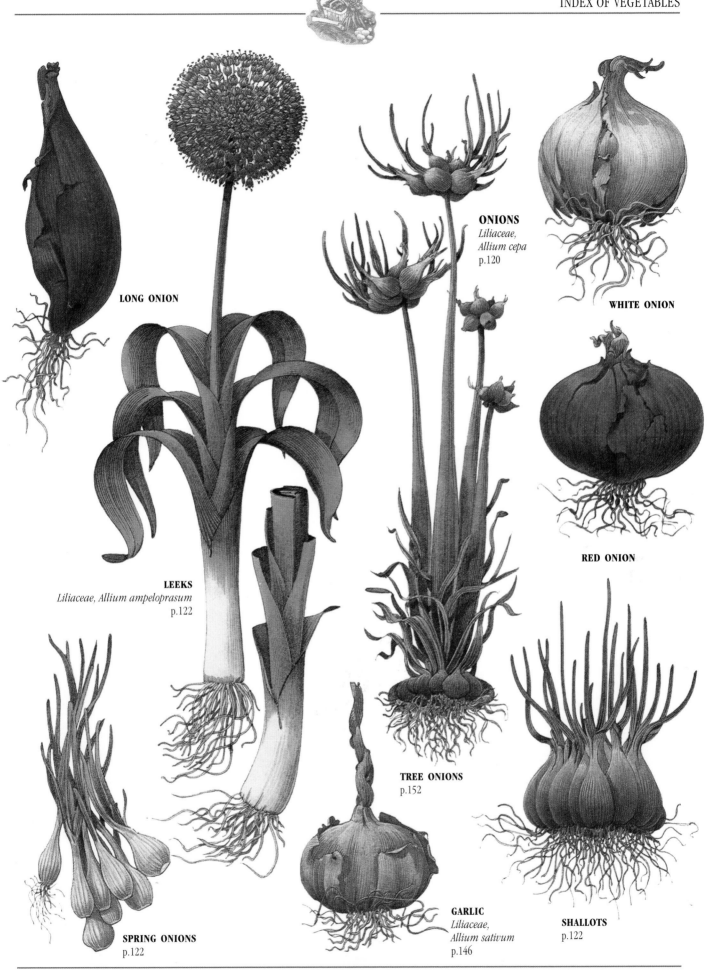

LONG ONION

ONIONS
Liliaceae,
Allium cepa
p.120

WHITE ONION

RED ONION

LEEKS
Liliaceae, Allium ampeloprasum
p.122

TREE ONIONS
p.152

SHALLOTS
p.122

SPRING ONIONS
p.122

GARLIC
Liliaceae,
Allium sativum
p.146

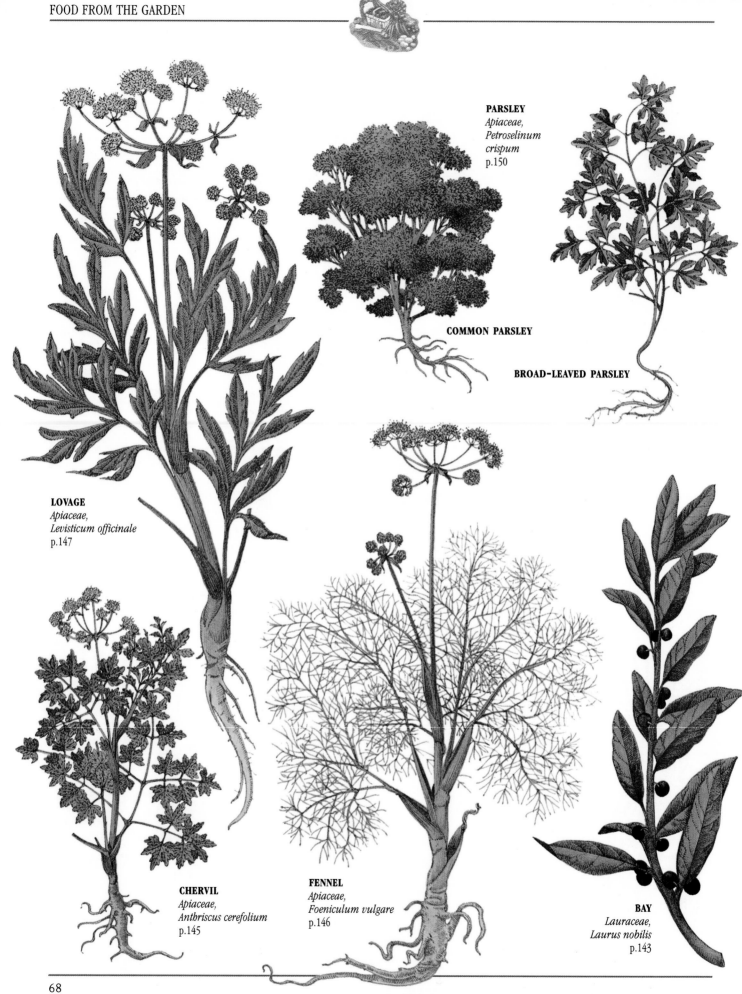

PARSLEY
Apiaceae,
Petroselinum
crispum
p.150

COMMON PARSLEY

BROAD-LEAVED PARSLEY

LOVAGE
Apiaceae,
Levisticum officinale
p.147

CHERVIL
Apiaceae,
Anthriscus cerefolium
p.145

FENNEL
Apiaceae,
Foeniculum vulgare
p.146

BAY
Lauraceae,
Laurus nobilis
p.143

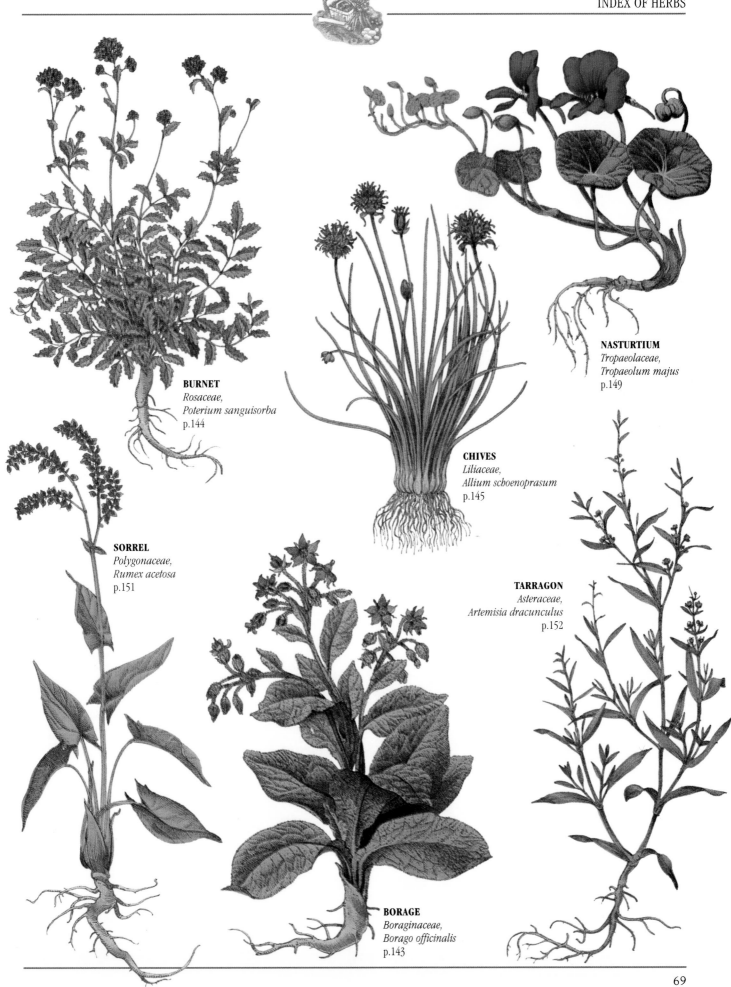

BURNET
Rosaceae,
Poterium sanguisorba
p.144

NASTURTIUM
Tropaeolaceae,
Tropaeolum majus
p.149

CHIVES
Liliaceae,
Allium schoenoprasum
p.145

SORREL
Polygonaceae,
Rumex acetosa
p.151

TARRAGON
Asteraceae,
Artemisia dracunculus
p.152

BORAGE
Boraginaceae,
Borago officinalis
p.143

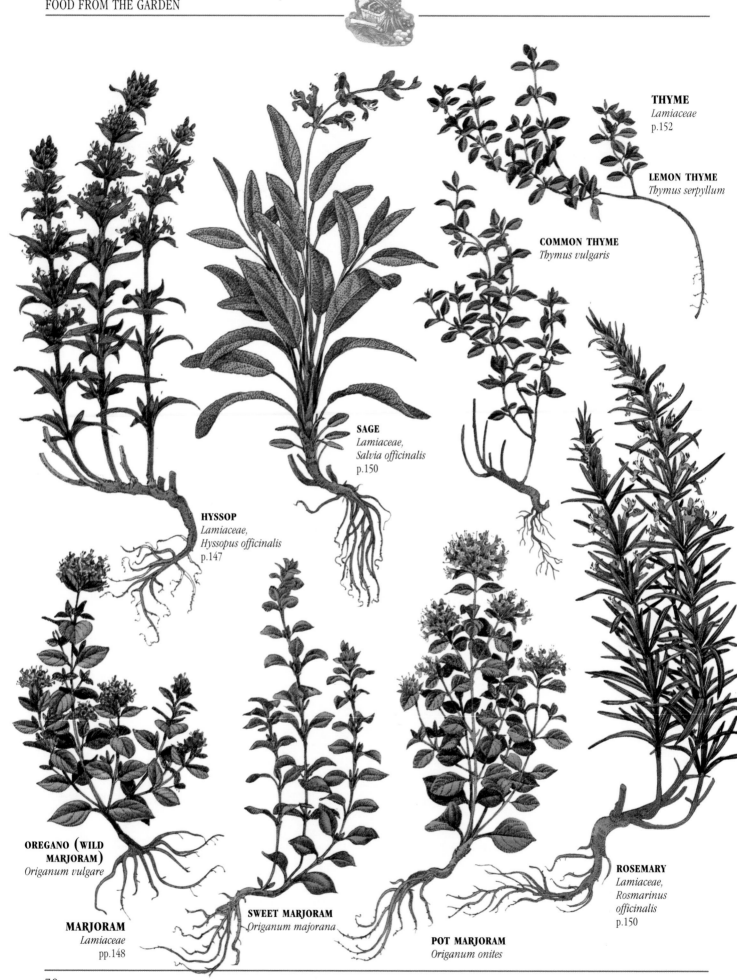

THYME
Lamiaceae
p.152

LEMON THYME
Thymus serpyllum

COMMON THYME
Thymus vulgaris

SAGE
Lamiaceae,
Salvia officinalis
p.150

HYSSOP
Lamiaceae,
Hyssopus officinalis
p.147

OREGANO (WILD
MARJORAM)
Origanum vulgare

MARJORAM
Lamiaceae
pp.148

SWEET MARJORAM
Origanum majorana

POT MARJORAM
Origanum onites

ROSEMARY
Lamiaceae,
Rosmarinus
officinalis
p.150

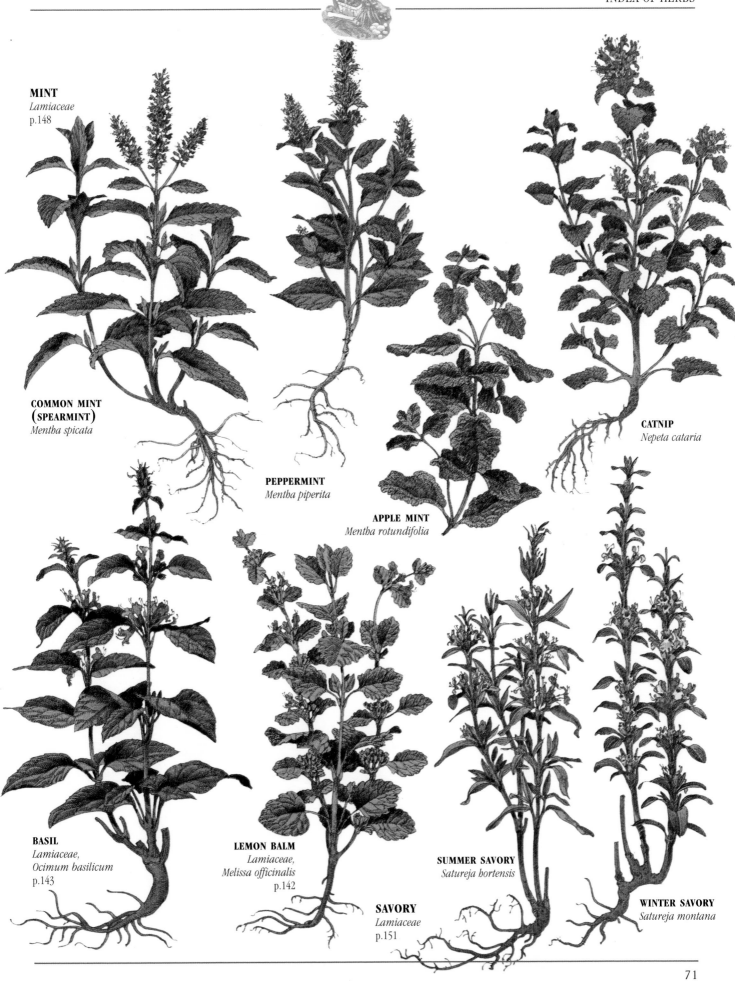

MINT
Lamiaceae
p.148

**COMMON MINT
(SPEARMINT)**
Mentha spicata

PEPPERMINT
Mentha piperita

APPLE MINT
Mentha rotundifolia

CATNIP
Nepeta cataria

BASIL
*Lamiaceae,
Ocimum basilicum*
p.143

LEMON BALM
*Lamiaceae,
Melissa officinalis*
p.142

SAVORY
Lamiaceae
p.151

SUMMER SAVORY
Satureja hortensis

WINTER SAVORY
Satureja montana

Flowers and Vegetable Fruits

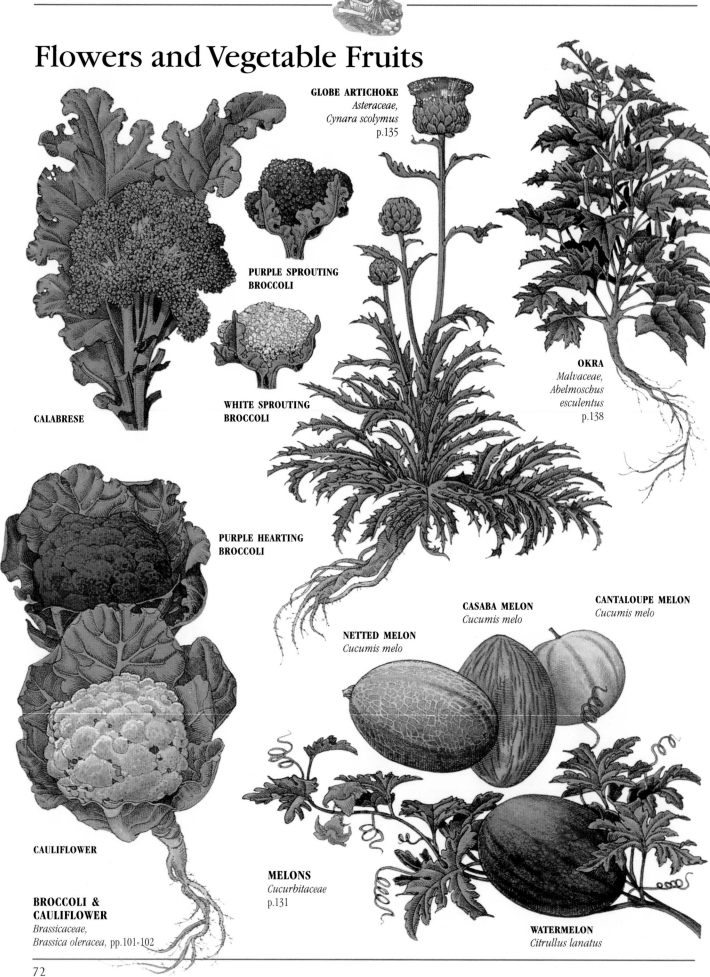

GLOBE ARTICHOKE
*Asteraceae,
Cynara scolymus*
p.135

**PURPLE SPROUTING
BROCCOLI**

**WHITE SPROUTING
BROCCOLI**

CALABRESE

OKRA
*Malvaceae,
Abelmoschus
esculentus*
p.138

**PURPLE HEARTING
BROCCOLI**

CAULIFLOWER

**BROCCOLI &
CAULIFLOWER**
*Brassicaceae,
Brassica oleracea*, pp.101-102

NETTED MELON
Cucumis melo

CASABA MELON
Cucumis melo

CANTALOUPE MELON
Cucumis melo

MELONS
Cucurbitaceae
p.131

WATERMELON
Citrullus lanatus

PEAR TOMATO & YELLOW TOMATO

TOMATOES
Solanaceae,
Lycopersicon
lycopersicum
p.111

WHITE
EGGPLANT

PEPPER
Solanaceae,
Capsicum
annuum
p.113

EGGPLANT
Solanaceae,
Solanum melongena
var. esculentum
p.113

CHILI PEPPER
Capsicum annuum

CONTINENTAL
TOMATO

GHERKIN & RIDGE
CUCUMBER

SPAGHETTI SQUASH

ZUCCHINI

MARROW
Cucurbita pepo

CUSHAW SQUASH
Cucurbita mixta

PUMPKIN
Cucurbita pepo

CUSTARD
SQUASH
Cucurbita pepo
var. melopepo

CROOKNECK
SQUASH
Cucurbita moschata

CUCUMBER

CUCUMBERS
Cucurbitaceae,
Cucumis sativus
p.128

SQUASHES
Cucurbitaceae
p.130

HUBBARD SQUASH
Cucurbita maxima

Seeds and Pods

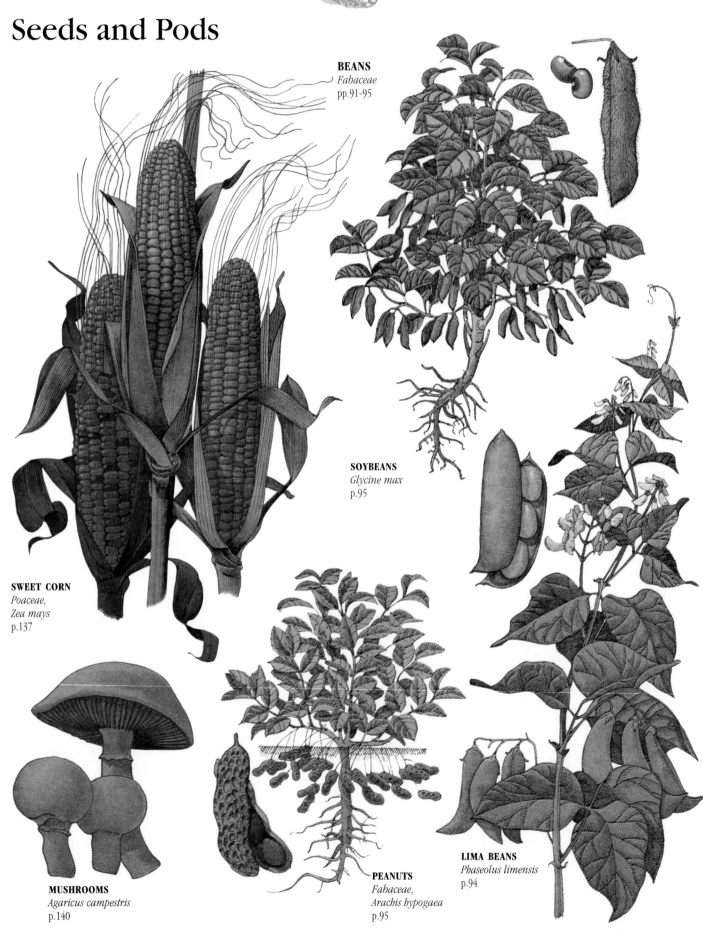

BEANS
Fabaceae
pp.91-95

SOYBEANS
Glycine max
p.95

SWEET CORN
Poaceae,
Zea mays
p.137

MUSHROOMS
Agaricus campestris
p.140

PEANUTS
Fabaceae,
Arachis hypogaea
p.95

LIMA BEANS
Phaseolus limensis
p.94

GREEN BEANS
Phaseolus vulgaris
p.94

RUNNER BEANS
Phaseolus vulgaris
p.92

FAVA BEANS
Vicia faba
p.91

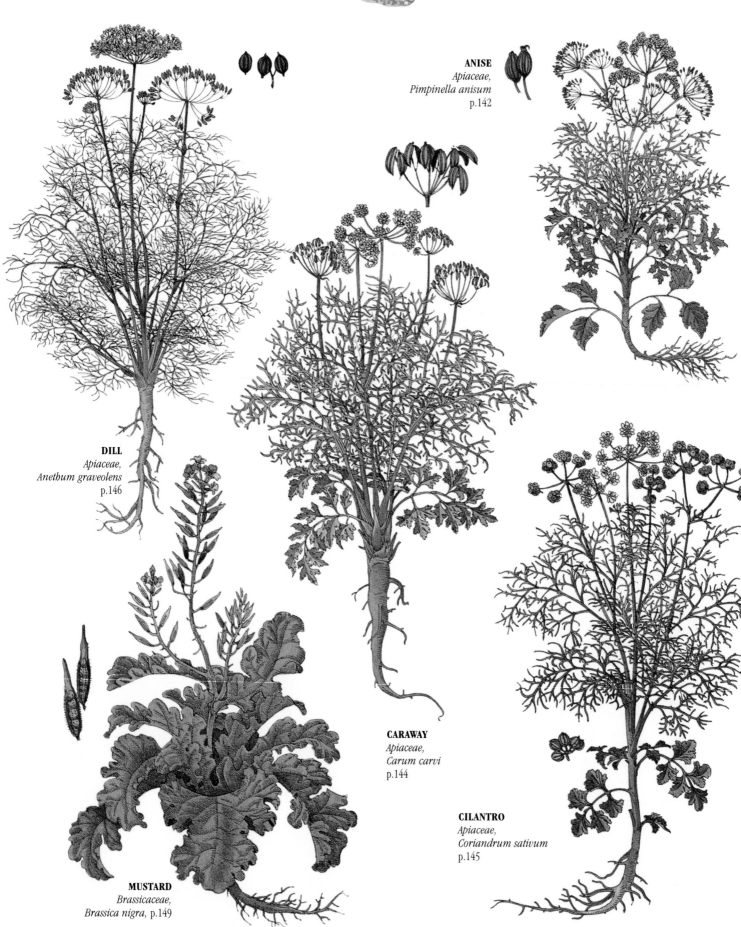

ANISE
Apiaceae,
Pimpinella anisum
p.142

DILL
Apiaceae,
Anethum graveolens
p.146

CARAWAY
Apiaceae,
Carum carvi
p.144

CILANTRO
Apiaceae,
Coriandrum sativum
p.145

MUSTARD
Brassicaceae,
Brassica nigra, p.149

PEAS
Fabaceae,
Pisum sativum
pp.88-90

SNOW PEAS

PURPLE PODDED
PEAS

LENTILS
Fabaceae,
Lens culinaris
p.90

GARDEN PEAS

ASPARAGUS PEAS
Fabaceae,
Lotus tetragonolobus
p.90

Fruits

PEARS
Rosaceae,
Pyrus communis, p.156

'RED BARTLETT' PEAR

'WILLIAM'S BON
CHRETIEN' PEAR

'CONFERENCE' PEAR

'DOYENNE DU
COMICE' PEAR

'ABATE' PEAR

MEDLARS
Rosaceae,
Mespilus germanica
p.160

QUINCES
Rosaceae,
Cydonia oblonga
p.160

'RED DELICIOUS' APPLE

'GRANNY SMITH' APPLE

'GOLDEN DELICIOUS' APPLE

APPLES
Rosaceae,
Malus pumila, p.154

'COX'S ORANGE PIPPIN' APPLE

'BRAMLEY' APPLE

'ALLINGTON PIPPIN' APPLE

'RUSSET' APPLE

'JONATHAN' APPLE

PLUMS
Rosaceae,
Prunus domestica
p.159

GREENGAGES
Prunus insititia

APRICOTS
Rosaceae,
Prunus armeniaca
p.158

DAMSONS
Prunus insititia
p.159

PEACHES
Rosaceae,
Prunus persica, p.158

NECTARINES

MORELLO CHERRIES
Prunus cerasus

CHERRIES
Rosaceae
p.157

SWEET CHERRIES
Prunus avium

OLIVES
Oleaceae,
Olea europaea, p.172

AMERICAN RED GRAPES

GRAPES
Vitaceae,
Vitis vinifera
p.173

WHITE SEEDLESS GRAPES

**EUROPEAN
RED GRAPES**

BLACK GRAPES

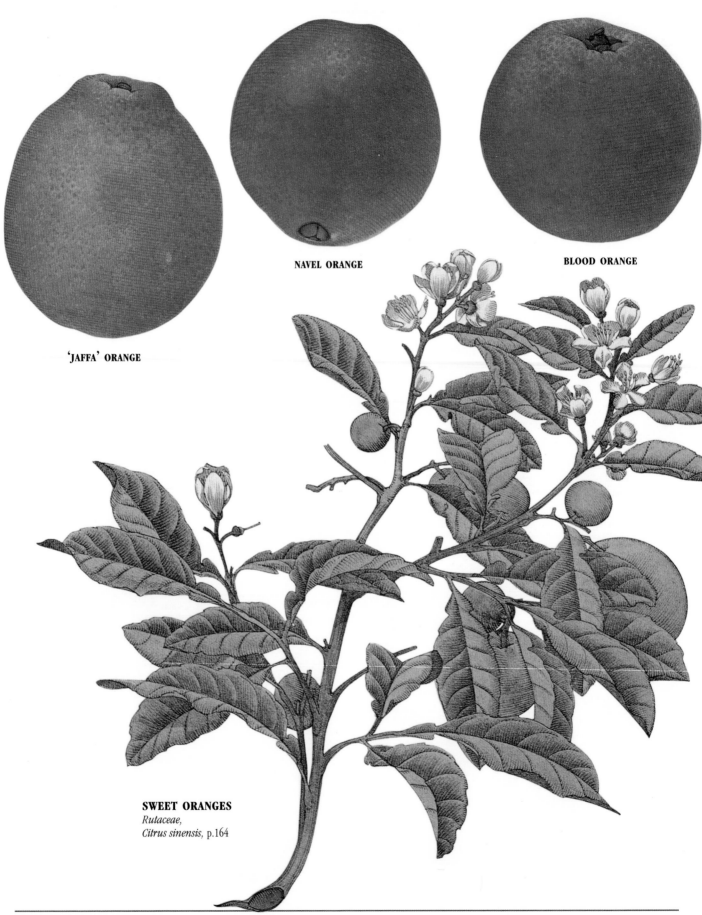

'JAFFA' ORANGE

NAVEL ORANGE

BLOOD ORANGE

SWEET ORANGES
Rutaceae,
Citrus sinensis, p.164

TANGERINE

MANDARIN ORANGES
Rutaceae,
Citrus reticulata
p.165

CLEMENTINE

KUMQUAT
Rutaceae,
Fortunella margarita, p.165

SEVILLE ORANGE
Rutaceae,
Citrus aurantium, p.164

GRAPEFRUIT
Rutaceae,
Citrus × paradisi, p.166

LEMONS
Rutaceae,
Citrus limon, p.166

LIME
Rutaceae,
Citrus aurantiifolia, p.166

LOGANBERRIES
Rosaceae,
Rubus ursinus var. loganobaccus
p.161

BLACKBERRIES
Rosaceae,
Rubus macropetalus
p.161

RASPBERRIES
Rosaceae,
Rubus idaeus
p.160

STRAWBERRIES
Rosaceae,
Fragaria × Ananassa, p.162

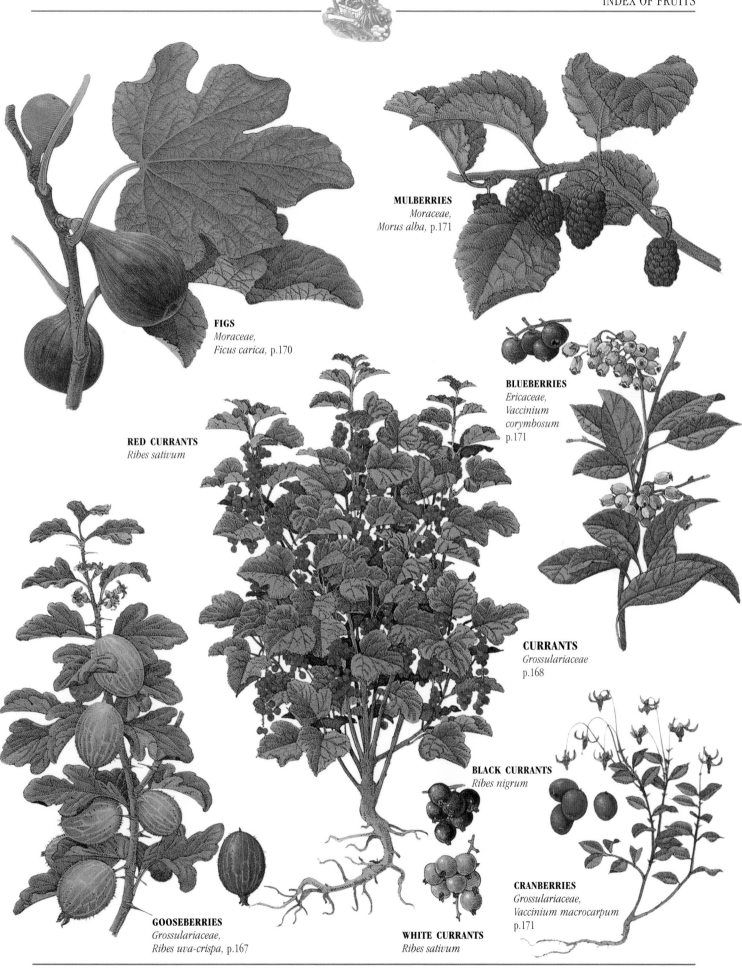

MULBERRIES
Moraceae,
Morus alba, p.171

FIGS
Moraceae,
Ficus carica, p.170

BLUEBERRIES
Ericaceae,
Vaccinium
corymbosum
p.171

RED CURRANTS
Ribes sativum

CURRANTS
Grossulariaceae
p.168

BLACK CURRANTS
Ribes nigrum

GOOSEBERRIES
Grossulariaceae,
Ribes uva-crispa, p.167

WHITE CURRANTS
Ribes sativum

CRANBERRIES
Grossulariaceae,
Vaccinium macrocarpum
p.171

Green Manure Crops

GREEN MANURE
p.262

COW PEA
Vigna unguiculata

VETCH
Vicia sp.

RYE
Secale cereale

ANNUAL LUPIN
Lupinus angustifolius

CROTALARIA
Crotalaria usaramoensis

CLOVER
Trifolium sp.

COMFREY
Symphytum officinale

ALFALFA
Medicago sativa

The Cultivation
of Vegetables

Containing the sowing, growing, and harvesting instructions for
members of the families Fabaceae, Brassicaceae, Solanaceae,
Apiaceae, Liliaceae, Chenopodiaceae, Cucurbitaceae, Asteraceae,
Poaceae, Malvaceae, and Polygonaceae.

Fabaceae

Peas, fava beans, runner beans, green beans, Lima beans, soybeans, and peanuts are all members of the *Fabaceae* (formerly *Leguminosae*). For those who wish to grow as much of their own food as they can in a garden, this family is surely the most useful of them all. It provides more protein than any other. It is hard to see how a vegan, or for that matter any person who aims to be completely self-sufficient without much meat, can subsist in a healthy state without the *Fabaceae*.

The other useful thing about the *Fabaceae* is their nitrogen-fixing ability. Organic gardeners who don't like spending their money on expensive nitrogenous fertilizers (which make the soil lazy about fixing its own nitrogen) find that peas, beans, and the clovers are the answer. For the *Fabaceae* are the plants which, *par excellence*, fix nitrogen in the nodules on their roots. Pull out any healthy leguminous plant and examine its roots. You should find small pimples or nodules. If you were to cut these open and examine them with a powerful microscope, you would see bacteria. These live symbiotically with the plant. The plant feeds them with everything they need except nitrogen: they fix nitrogen from the air (combining it with oxygen to form nitrates), and this they use themselves and also feed to the host plant.

If you grow any leguminous plant, and dig it into the soil when it is lush and green (at the flowering stage), it will rot down very quickly, providing its own nitrogen to feed the putrefactive bacteria, and this nitrogen will then be released into the soil. It is worth growing clover for this very purpose. If you put leguminous plants on the compost pile, they will have the same beneficial effect. If you have a lawn, remember that if you put nitrates on it, you will encourage the grasses but suppress the clover. If you put on phosphate you will encourage the clovers at the expense of the grasses.

Leguminous plants should account for at least a quarter of your acreage each year and there is nothing wrong with having far more than that. They are not acid-loving plants, so if your soil is acidic, give it lime. They also like phosphate and potash. But in good garden soil that has been well manured or composted over the years, and in which any serious lack of lime, phosphate, or potash has been corrected, you can grow peas and beans without putting anything on at all.

Peas

GARDEN PEAS
The first fresh peas of the summer eaten raw are one of the great rewards of growing your own vegetables. And later in the season, of course you can cook them and dry them. Whatever you do, they are a great source of nourishment. Dwarf peas are a good idea for a small garden.

Soil and climate
Peas are not too fussy as regards soil; light soil will give you an early crop, heavy a late one. Rich loam is best, and any soil can be turned into this by constant composting. As for climate, peas are not a tropical crop and will grow well in cool climates, with plenty of moisture, but too much rain when they are ripening will give them mildew. In hot latitudes they generally have to be grown in the spring or fall, to avoid the very hot part of the summer. As small plants they are frost-hardy, therefore in climates where frosts are not too intense they can be sown in the fall for a quick start in the spring. They will not grow fast and produce flowers and pods, however, until the arrival of spring and warmer weather.

Soil treatment
Peas need deeply cultivated ground. If you are trying to grow them in land that has previously been gardened inorganically you should try to spread 7 to 10 hundredweight (350 to 500 kg) of manure or compost on every 100 square yards

DRILLS FOR PEA SEED
Use the flat blade of a draw hoe to make broad drills about 2 inches (5 cm) deep and 4 inches (10 cm) wide in the soil.

SOWING PEA SEED
Sow evenly, leaving an inch or two between seeds. If necessary you can keep mice away by dipping the seed in kerosene* before planting.

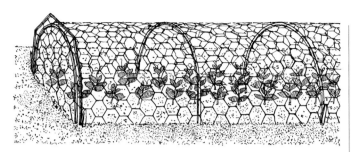

PROTECTING PEAS FROM BIRDS
Wire-netting pea-guards, which you can easily make yourself, will protect seeds and seedlings from attack by birds. So will mini-greenhouses (*see p.111*) such as you use for deep beds; but you should cover them with wire rather than with plastic.

(84 sq m). Put this on the land the fall before, and possibly 25 lb (11 kg) of slag or ground rock phosphate per 100 square yards (84 sq m) and 10 or 12 lb (4.5 to 5.4 kg) of wood ash. Peas don't like acidic soil; if the pH is about 6.5, that is all right. If it is below this, lime it; a quarter of a pound (100 g) per square yard (1 sq m) is about right.

If your soil is not yet sufficiently fertile and you cannot bring in enough compost or manure from outside, you can still grow excellent peas over trenches taken out the previous year and filled during the winter with kitchen garbage and other material that will readily decompose, such as old newspaper. The organic gardener's aim, though, should be to raise the whole of his garden to a high level of fertility, so that such piecemeal treatments as this are unnecessary.

Propagation
I make broad drills with the flat of the hoe, about 2 inches (5 cm) deep and 4 inches (10 cm) wide. I then sprinkle the seed in evenly, so there is an inch or two between each seed.

I then rake the soil back into the trench from each side and bang down firmly with the back of the rake—or, if the land is puffy and dry, I tread it with my boots. A good soaking of the drill, if the soil is dry, will then start them growing. If you use the deep-bed method (*see p.44*), allow 3 inches (8 cm) between plants all ways. You leave this distance in the deep bed because you are not sowing in rows, of course, but in clumps.

Many people speed up germination by soaking the seed, for as long as forty-eight hours, before they plant it. It should be remembered that all these seeds that are large and edible, like peas and beans, are a standing invitation to rodents and birds, and so the sooner they start to grow, the less time there is for them to be eaten by something. Birds may have to be kept away by thin black threads, or, better still, inverted wire-netting pea-guards. And if you are troubled by mice, dip the seed into kerosene* just before planting. The mice don't like the smell.

Now peas take about four months to grow to maturity: perhaps three-and-a-half if you plant early varieties or if you like your peas very young like I do. Sow them successively, every two weeks from March to July (sow earlies in July), and you will get fresh peas all summer.

Care while growing
All but the smallest dwarf peas are better if they have sticks to grow up. Any fine branches with some twigs left on them will do for this. Hazel trimmings make ideal pea sticks. If you need a hedge between your garden and the next one, use hazel. It will give you nuts as well as pea sticks. If you just can't find pea sticks then use wire netting. Get the coarsest mesh you can (it is cheaper)—say, 3 feet (90 cm) wide—and make an inverted "V" of it so that a row of peas climbs up each side. This method has the advantage that many of the peas hang down inside the wire where the birds can't get at them. If the wire is wide-gauge, you will be able to get your hand in to

BUILDING WIRE PEA FRAMES
You can build a "fence" of wire netting for peas to climb up, or you can build an inverted "V" shape and train a row of peas up each side. The peas will dangle into the middle where the birds can't get them. Use wide-gauge netting—it is cheaper and you can get your hands through the mesh quite easily.

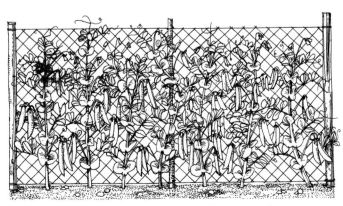

TRAINING WITH PEA STICKS
Any branch with a few twigs left on it will make a pea stick. Hazel branches are especially good, as they will provide you with nuts, too. Cut them to a length of about 4 feet (1.2 m), sharpen the thick end, and drive well into the ground beside each plant.

pick the peas; otherwise you can put your hand down through the gap in the top. There are plenty of dwarf pea varieties nowadays, which are supposed to need no support at all. They are worth growing in a small garden, but the yield is low and unless you take precautions (*see p.54*) slugs will attack the peas near the ground.

Peas don't like drought, and watering in dry weather always pays in more peas, but remember that soil rich in humus retains water more efficiently.

Pests and diseases

PEA AND BEAN WEEVIL This creature is the color of soil, falls off the plant and feigns death when you disturb it, and is nocturnal; it hides under clods of soil during the day. No-digging gardeners suffer from it a lot because the compost with which they have to cover their ground gives it splendid cover. It nibbles around the edges of young pea leaves and often eats out the growing centers. Dusting the plants with lime*, while the dew is on them, is a deterrent, or you can do the same with soot*. If you have neither, spray the young plants and the surrounding ground with quassia* spray, or nicotine*.

PEA MOTH This is a small brown moth that lays eggs on young pea pods. The larvae bore in and eat the peas. If you dig, or cultivate, the soil frequently, but very shallowly, during the winter you can get rid of these pests, for the birds (chiefly robins and starlings) will come along and eat the pupae—thereby breaking the moth's life cycle.

PEA THRIPS These tiny browny-black insects make minute holes in the leaves. The plants become yellow and shrivel up. A thorough drenching with soapy water will get rid of them.

MILDEW In very damp weather, pea leaves and pods may go white with mildew, and then rot. Sticking the peas well, so that they can climb high, helps prevent this. Don't water the foliage of peas in hot muggy weather. Spraying with Bordeaux mixture* sometimes works. Otherwise there's not much you can do about it, but it is not disastrous.

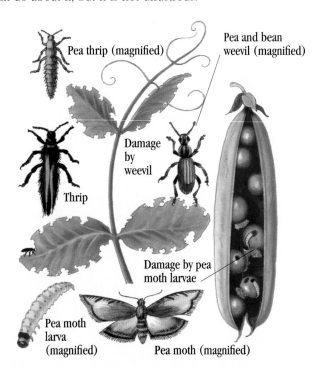

Pea thrip (magnified)

Pea and bean weevil (magnified)

Thrip

Damage by weevil

Damage by pea moth larvae

Pea moth larva (magnified)

Pea moth (magnified)

Harvesting

Always use both your hands to pick peas! Put the basket on the ground, and hold the vine with one hand and the pod with the other.

Very young peas taste quite exquisite raw and contain high doses of vitamins A, B, and C. They are very sweet because they contain sugar. A few hours after the peas are picked this sugar turns to starch, which is why store-bought peas taste dull and dried peas completely different. If you pick peas and freeze them immediately, you can preserve this sugar, which is why frozen peas don't taste too bad.

I like to eat fresh peas all summer and then enjoy dried peas, rather than frozen peas, during the winter, so that I come to the first fresh peas in May or June with a fresh palate and enjoy what is then an exquisite gastronomic experience. The palate jaded by "fresh" peas all year round never has this great sensation.

As fresh peas grow older and tougher on the vine, you have to boil them. When your peas get too tough to be perfect boiled, leave them on the vines and just let them go on getting tougher. Wait until they are completely ripe, as hard as bullets; then pull the vines out and hang them up in the wind but out of the rain.

When the vines are thoroughly dry, thresh the peas out of them; either rub the vines hard between your hands, or bash them over the back of a chair. Put the peas away, thoroughly dry, inside covered containers. When you want some in the winter, soak the dried peas in water for a day or two. Then boil them with salt until they are soft, and eat with boiled bacon. A plate full of peas and bacon, in December, and you are fit to go out and dig for a few hours.

Pea pods make the basis of a good soup. Boil them well and press them through a sieve.

SNOW PEAS

These are also called sugar peas. Cultivate them just like ordinary peas. The difference is that you harvest and eat the pods with the young peas inside them, because they lack the hard membrane that lines the ordinary pea pod. Start picking and eating the pods as soon as they are about 2 inches (5 cm) long and when the peas inside are tiny flat bumps. You then have a long picking season because you can go on picking until the peas inside are quite big. Personally I prefer ordinary peas, but snow peas are nonetheless worth growing and eating.

ASPARAGUS PEAS

These are not true peas, but you can treat them the same way, although you must plant them later—say, in April—and then, if you live in a cold place, protect them with cloches. Support them just like peas. Cook the complete pods when they are about an inch long. They are quite delicious.

LENTILS

Lentils are closely related to peas and are excellent for drying. However, they are low-yielding and are really only worth growing if you have space to spare after allowing for your staples. They like the same climatic conditions as peas, and do best on sandy loam. Propagate them and care for them exactly as though they were garden peas. When the plants are well ripened, pull them out and hang them up in a shed. Thresh when required.

Fava beans

For the self-supporting gardener, fava beans are one of the most important crops. They really will feed you and your family right through the year, and if you have dried fava beans and potatoes, you will not starve. The old English bean was the "longpod," and this is still the best bean to grow if you really want food that will keep you in high-protein vegetable nourishment right through the winter as well as the summer (unless your climate and conditions enable you to get a good yield with soybeans).

All the other beans, like runner beans, green beans, and dwarf beans, came from the Americas, especially the hot parts of South America. They are all very frost-tender. The good old longpod fava bean, however, can stand up to a fierce winter and get away early in the spring. It stands up straight and tall, needs no support, and produces a heavy crop of fine, big kidney-shaped seeds, which can be either cooked and eaten fresh, or dried and kept for the winter.

Tic beans, horse beans, and cattle beans, which are all grown by farmers to provide high protein grain for feeding animals in the winter, are varieties of the same plant. Their seeds are smaller and white, but they are heavy cropping. They are more liable to get the dreaded chocolate spot than fava beans and they are said not to be edible before Christmas. But then they are said not to be fit for human consumption yet I eat them freely every winter.

The ordinary longpod fava bean, however, is the best thing for the gardener; but if you can get a handful of tic beans from a farmer, why not experiment with them and see what happens?

Soil and climate
Fava beans like strong soil, even heavy clay, but compost-rich soil suits them no matter what the original soil was—clay or sand. Their behavior in different climates is very similar to that of peas (*see Peas*). If you can plant out your peas in the fall, then you can do the same with your fava beans, for they are rather more hardy than peas.

Soil treatment
Beans don't like too much acid; like peas, they find a pH of 6.5 ideal. Potash does them a lot of good, so if you have a limited supply of wood ashes, put it on your fava bean patch at a rate of about 4 oz (100 g) to 2 yards of row. Comfrey too, dug in as a green manure, is good, both for the potash that it contains and for its capacity to hold water.

Dig the soil deep and well, digging in ashes and comfrey leaves if you have them, and as much manure or compost as you can spare. I like to plant fava beans after main-crop potatoes, so the soil is already full of manure that was put in for the spuds, and it has been well worked. Lime, then, is only necessary if the pH is much below 6.5.

Propagation
It is far and away better, if you live south of the heavy snow line, to sow your fava beans in the fall—in, say, October or November. If the birds get them, or it is too cold where you are, sow them as early as you can in the spring—in February if the ground is not frozen then. It is best to soak the seeds in cold water for twenty-four hours before planting them; this softens them up and gives them a head start over the birds.

Take out drills about 3 inches (8 cm) deep with the hoe, drills about 2 feet (60 cm) apart, and put the seeds in 6 inches (15 cm) apart. Or—and here I think is a very good tip—sow them in rows 6 feet (1.8 m) apart and, later, sow green or dwarf beans in between the rows. Fava beans make a fine nurse-crop for these more tender plants, keeping the wind off them. Instead of digging drills you can put out a garden line and make a hole with a trowel for each seed. If you use the deep-bed method (*see p.44*), leave 4 inches (10 cm) between plants in all directions.

INTERCROPPING
Tough, tall fava beans make an excellent nurse-crop for smaller plants like green beans. Plant the fava beans in rows 6 feet (1.8 m) apart in fall or early spring. When the weather warms up in early summer, fill the spaces between the rows with low-growing green beans.

Care while growing
As the young beans grow, it is a good idea to earth them up a little with the hoe. Keep them clear of weeds, of course. In windy and exposed positions, it is worth driving in a stake at the corners of the rows, and running a string from stake to stake around each row, to prevent the beans from being blown over. In most gardens, though, this is not necessary. Any sort of mulching between the plants is valuable.

Pests and diseases

CHOCOLATE SPOT This looks exactly like its name, and if you get it there is nothing you can do. If you get it early, it will lower your yield considerably, but a late attack is not so bad. To guard against it you need plenty of potash in your soil. If you keep getting it in fall-sown beans, you must give up fall sowing and sow your beans in the spring instead, because these are less liable to attack.

BEAN RUST You are not likely to get this. The symptoms are small white spots on leaves and stems in the spring. Spray with diluted Bordeaux mixture* (*see p.51*), and burn all your bean straw after harvesting to destroy the spores.

BLACK FLY OR APHID If you sow spring beans you are very likely to get this, and in fact unlikely not to get it. It does not trouble fall-sown beans very often. The aphids can only pierce the skin of tender young growing points and the winter beans are generally grown enough by the time the aphids are around. If aphids do attack you will find them clustered on the tips. If the beans have already grown high enough, pick these tips off; this will deny the fly its food. You can cook and eat the tips; they are tender and juicy. If you get a really bad attack, spray the plants hard with soft soap and kerosene* solution. Bees love bean flowers, so it is important not to spray with anything that will harm bees. Pyrethrum sprayed at night will kill the aphids and not harm the bees in the morning.

PEA AND BEAN WEEVIL (*See Peas*).

BEAN MILDEW Spray with Bordeaux mixture*.

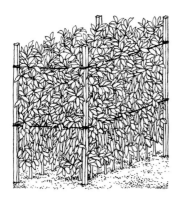

SUPPORTING FAVA BEANS
If your fava bean patch is exposed to wind, support the plants with strings run between stakes, which are driven in at the ends of the rows.

BANISHING BLACK FLY
Black fly or aphids on your fava beans will almost certainly cluster on the tips. If the beans have grown high enough, simply pick the tips off.

Harvesting and storing

The tips of growing fava beans, nipped off in the spring to thwart black fly, are one of the first and most tasty fresh greens of the spring. Soon after eating these, you can start pulling the very small pods and cook them as they are. Later, the pods get too tough for this, so you split them open, remove the beans from their silky beds, and cook the seeds. When the seeds get too tough for this, let them dry on the plant, and harvest by pulling out the whole plant. Then hang it in an airy but dry place. Shuck the seeds out when they are dry and store them for the winter. Soak them for at least twenty-four hours (twice that long is not too much) before cooking and then boil them well. Eaten either with butter or with bacon, they will give you strength to face the winter.

Runner Beans

The runner bean was brought to Europe from North America in the seventeenth century by people who thought it was beautiful rather than nutritious. The fact that it is both makes it ideal for the small-scale vegetable garden.

Soil and climate

The runner bean is not frost-hardy and it prefers a warm, sunny climate, although this is not essential. In warmish climates, it will survive the winter, underground, and grow up again in the spring as a perennial. In cold climates you can get a crop by sowing in peat* pots indoors and planting out after the last frost. The runner bean needs plenty of moisture at its roots, and its flowers will not set without an occasional shower of rain, or spray from a hose. It will grow in most soils but likes rich ones; it benefits from plenty of humus and plenty of moisture. And it does not like acidic soils. 6.5 pH is ideal, so lime if necessary.

Soil treatment

The classic method is to take out a deep trench in the fall or winter and fill it with manure or compost, or else spend the winter filling it with kitchen refuse and anything else organic you can find. In the spring, cover the trench with soil and plant on that. The compost, or whatever it was, will have subsided as it rotted and so there will be a shallow depression for the water to collect and sink into, and runners like plenty of water. If you don't dig a trench, you must still dig deeply and put in plenty of compost.

SOWING RUNNER BEANS
To get as many plants as possible into the space available, sow seeds 3 inches (8 cm) deep, 10 inches (25 cm) apart in two rows 1 foot (30 cm) apart. Stagger the seeds in the rows. You can speed germination by soaking the seed in water before planting, although you should not do this if you suspect halo blight.

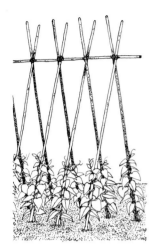

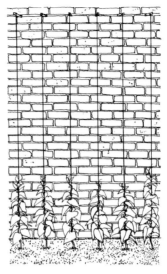

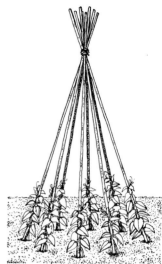

STAKING RUNNER BEANS
Each runner bean plant must have its own stake, anywhere between 7 feet (2 m) and 12 feet (3.5 m) high. With two rows; you can use the crossed pole method, where pairs of poles are tied together to form forks near their tops and the whole row is made secure with a pole laid through the forks and tied down. If you want your beans against a wall, fix wires close to the wall by attaching them to long nails top and bottom. The wigwam method is excellent, even in a tub or large barrel. Sow eight to twelve seeds in a circle; when the plants come up, give them each a pole and tie them all together near their tops.

Propagation

If you want early runner beans, sow in peat* pots in the greenhouse, or in a sunny window, during early April. A temperature of about 55°F (13°C) is fine. Most people just sow them outdoors *in situ* during May after the last frost. I draw two drills a foot (30 cm) apart and sow the seeds 3 inches (8 cm) deep, 10 inches (25 cm) apart in the rows and staggered. If you use the deep-bed method (*see p.106*), you must still plant in a row so that all your plants receive plenty of light. Therefore, plant no closer.

Care while growing

Weed them, of course, water them in dry weather, and before they are many inches high, stake them with stakes at least 7 feet (2 m) high. They will climb as high as 12 feet (3.5 m) if you give them long enough stakes, and personally I like them to do it. The more beans, the better, and you can always stand on a box to pick them. Put in stakes when two true leaves are well opened.

There are several methods of training runner beans. As long as you have plenty of space—enough for two rows of plants—you can use bamboo or bean sticks (like pea sticks, only longer) to build a row of crossed poles, with their apexes in between the rows. Tie them together where they meet and strengthen by tying canes along the top. If you are short of space you can plant your beans in a circle and build a wigwam of poles around the circle. (This is better in my opinion than using dwarf varieties in a small space.)

Another method is to plant the seeds along the bottom of a wall and train the plants up wires against the wall. I love to see a really high screen of beautiful runner beans, sited so as not to shade anything that must have sun (plenty of plants, like lettuces, grow well in shade) and screening some "unpleasaunce" in the garden.

If the flowers are out in a dry period, spray them lightly with water—preferably water that is not too cold. This helps the flowers to set.

Pests and diseases

With good organic soil you are unlikely to get trouble, but you might just have one of the four varieties below.

BEAN DISEASE This is a fungal disease that causes black spots to appear on the pods of runner and green beans; later on, the spots develop reddish outlines. At the first sign of this disease, spray with Bordeaux mixture*, but if the disease gets a strong hold, root out the affected plants and burn them. Never save seed if you have had an attack of bean disease.

HALO BLIGHT Caused by bacteria, this results in semitransparent spots surrounded by a yellow halo on leaves. Spray with Bordeaux mixture*. Do not save seed for next year, and if you have any doubt about your seed do not soak it before planting.

MOSAIC DISEASE This shows itself as yellow blotches on the leaves. It lives in clover, so do not plant runner or green beans in soil where old clover has been dug in. If you do get it, pull up the plant and burn it.

MEXICAN BEAN BEETLE This is a brown spotted beetle a little bigger than a ladybug. If your beans are prone to attack, you will find they will attack your main crop more than your early crop. So put in your main crop as early as you can. If you are attacked, pick off and kill any beetles you see.

Harvesting and storing

Pick runners, like peas, with both hands. Hold the vine in one hand and pull the pod with the other. Harvest on the "pick and pick again" principle. Keep picking them when they are young and tender, and suffer them not to get old and haggard on the vine. If you keep picking, they will keep coming—they are the most generous of crops.

If you can't eat them all, salt them (*see p.308*). But remember, only salt them when they are young and tender.

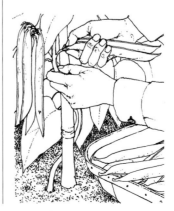

PICKING RUNNER BEANS
Pick beans and peas with two hands. If you pick with one hand, you can do lasting damage to the vine. Pick them while they are young, and you will be encouraging more to grow. Don't ever leave them to get old on the vine: if there are too many for you to eat all at once, salt them. Frozen runner beans don't taste as good as salted ones.

Green Beans

Green beans are not nearly as hardy as fava beans. When fully ripened and dried they are haricots and form a rich source of winter protein.

Soil and climate
Plant when the soil has warmed up in the summer. They prefer lightish soil, or soil that has been well-improved by compost, and a pH of about 6.5.

Soil treatment
Don't lime for them if your soil is not too acidic. The more humus you can incorporate when digging the soil, the better.

Propagation
When sowing in drills, have the rows 2 feet (60 cm) apart and sow 1 foot (30 cm) apart in the drills—deep-bed method four to 6 inches (10–15 cm) apart (see p.44). It is worth sowing two seeds in each station and removing the weaker of the two plants after they germinate. If you want early beans, start them off in seed boxes in your greenhouse.

Care while growing
Keep the bed well weeded and the soil loose.

Pests and diseases
CUTWORM Cutworms can be kept away by placing a 3-inch (8-cm) cardboard collar around the stem of the plant (see p.98). Bend the cardboard so that it is half an inch (1 cm) from the stem all the way around. Allow one inch (2.5 cm) below ground and 2 inches (5 cm) above. Alternatively, place a ring of wood ash around each plant.
WIREWORM If you are troubled by wireworms, try to trap them during the winter by burying cut pieces of potato 6 inches (15 cm) deep at intervals of about a yard. Mark them with sticks, carefully dig them up each evening, and destroy the wireworms that you will find there.

Harvesting and storing
Like all beans, green beans are grown for two purposes: for the green pods with immature beans inside and for the ripened beans that can be dried into haricots. To dry beans, you just let them ripen, hang the vines upside-down in a shed, and thresh them when you want them. To harvest, pick the beans by hand. They can be stored green in salt.

Lima Beans

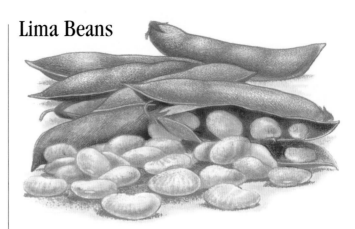

These are tropical American beans which have been adapted for growth in warmish temperate climates. They can be cooked and eaten when green, or dried for winter storage. There are bush and climbing varieties.

Soil and climate
Unless they are started off under glass, they need three months of pretty warm days and nights. The seed needs warm soil to germinate, so don't plant until two or three weeks after the last frost. And bear in mind that the first fall frost will cut them down. If you have this sort of climate, they are worth growing because they are very heavy-cropping. Limas like lightish soil but will grow in any soil except heavy clay. Atypically for beans, they prefer a slightly acidic soil; a pH of 6 is about right.

Soil treatment
Limas should follow a well-manured crop such as potatoes or celery. Simply dig the soil fairly deeply and, if you can spare it, mulch with compost.

Propagation
Sow the seed about 3 feet (90 cm) apart for bush varieties and 8 inches (20 cm) apart for climbers. The former should be in rows 30 inches (75 cm) apart; the latter should be in one row. For the deep-bed method (see p.44) allow 1 foot (30 cm) between bushes, or 6 inches (15 cm) between climbers, which should still be planted in one row. In colder climates, plant indoors in peat* or paper pots and plant out in warm weather.

Care while growing
Mulching is very valuable, and the beans must also be kept well watered.

Pests and diseases
Lima beans are pretty tough. If they do suffer, it will be from something that attacks runner or green beans (see Runner Beans and Green Beans).

Harvesting and storing
For eating green, harvest on the "pick and pick again" principle, once the beans are swelling in the pod. Don't pick them too late because, like runner beans, they get tough. If you want to dry them for what are called "butter beans," leave the pods on the plant until the plants are dry. Pick the beans by hand, or thresh by walking on the plants.

Soybeans

You can eat soybeans green in the pods, or dry them. Either way, they are very high in protein. The beans can be crushed for their oil, and the flour that is left can be added to the flour of cereals to make a high-protein bread.

Soil and climate
Soybeans grow well only where it is warm. They don't mind slightly acidic soils, like high organic matter, and will grow in quite moist conditions.

Soil treatment
Soil with plenty of humus in it just needs a light forking. Otherwise, dig thoroughly and lime for a pH of 6.5.

Propagation
Sow them outdoors in early summer; a good rule is to sow when the apple trees are in full bloom. Sow an inch (2.5 cm) deep and 3 inches (8 cm) apart in the rows—deep-bed method (*see p.44*) 4 inches (10 cm) apart. Where the beans have not been grown before, the seed should be inoculated with nitrogen-fixing bacteria, because it is likely that the right bacteria do not exist in the soil.

INOCULATING SOYBEAN SEED
Where soybeans have not been grown before, the soil may not contain the right nitrogen-fixing bacteria. Prepare seeds by stirring them up with water in a bowl. Add nitrogen-fixing bacteria to the water-coated seeds, making sure each seed is thoroughly covered with the bacteria. Careful inoculation will increase your yield by up to a third—and improve your soil as a bonus.

Care while growing
Hand-weed rigorously, and mulch with compost if you can.

Pests and diseases
Soybeans are very hardy, but they can suffer from various fungus diseases (*see Runner Beans*). These can be prevented by proper crop rotation.

Harvesting and storing
Pick soybeans green and eat them whole, or wait for them to ripen, in which case steam or boil the pods for a few minutes before shelling them. Otherwise, pull the plants and hang them up to dry.

Peanuts

Peanuts, also called groundnuts or monkey nuts, are very rich in the vitamins A, B, and E. They grow extensively in the Southern states of the US but can only be grown in colder regions with glass protection at each end of their season. As they are quite cheap to buy and as there are so many other things we really need our glass for, they are hardly worth growing in cool climates.

Soil and climate
Peanuts need a warm growing season of over four months; five is ideal. They like sandy soil and, unlike most legumes, they like acidic soil—a pH of 5 is about right.

Soil treatment
Dig the soil deeply and incorporate plenty of compost. Never lime for peanuts.

Propagation
You can plant peanuts, shells and all, or shell them and plant the nuts. Plant shells 8 inches (20 cm) apart, nuts 4 inches (10 cm) apart. For the deep-bed method (*see p.44*) allow 4 inches (10 cm) and 3 inches (8 cm), respectively. In warm climates, plant 4 inches (10 cm) deep, but in cool climates make it only one-and-a-half inches (4 cm). To give them the longest possible growing season in cool climates, they should be planted at about the time of the last probable frost. You may need to start them off under glass, if you live in a very cold place. Sow them in rows 30 inches (75 cm) apart.

Care while growing
The yellow flowers are the staminate ones; the productive pistillate flowers are inconspicuous, and after being fertilized they bury themselves in the ground and develop into peanuts. Raise the soil in a circle around the plant so that the fruits forming at the ends of their stems can easily bury themselves. Peanuts will only ripen below ground.

Pests and diseases
Peanuts don't seem to suffer from much at all.

Harvesting and storing
In a warm climate, pull the vines when the leaves turn yellow and hang them in a dry airy place. In cooler climates, leave them until after the first frosts—the nuts will continue to ripen underground even after the leaves have frosted away. Before eating them, roast your peanuts in their shells for 20 minutes in a 300°F (150°C) oven and leave them to cool—a vital part of the peanut roasting process.

Brassicaceae

Cabbages, Brussels sprouts, cauliflowers, broccoli, kale, kohlrabi, rutabagas, turnips, seakale, cresses, and radishes all belong to the *Brassicaceae* (formerly *Cruciferae*), which is one of the most important families, for it includes the genus *Brassica*, the cabbage tribe. This contains a great variety of plants that have been bred by humankind to a profusion of different forms, most of which are very good to eat. The reason for the peculiar succulence of the brassicas is that nearly all the cultivated members of it are descended from the sea cabbage, and this gives them certain important characteristics. One is that they share with desert plants the ability to make do on very little fresh water; another is that they are adapted to store what water they can get. It is this last fact that makes them so succulent. They guard the water they get under a waxy, waterproof cuticle.

Another characteristic of the brassicas is that they are biennials: that means they store food in themselves during their first year of life and then flower and go to seed in their second. The stored food and energy of the first year's growth is available to us and our animals all winter.

Cabbages

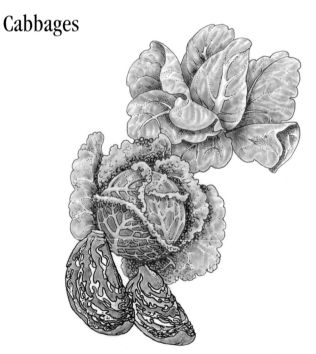

COMMON CABBAGES

You can grow cabbages all year in mild climates, and in climates with freezing winters you can easily store them the winter through in a shed or basement. And if they are organically grown, and not overcooked, they are a delicious vegetable and you need never get tired of them.

They come with round or conical hearts, but this makes no difference to the way you grow them. Winter main-crop cabbages are very high-yielding: it is not unusual to get, on a field scale, 40

Seed-bed for brassicas

There are spring cabbages, summer cabbages, and summer cauliflowers, but you can take it that most of your brassicas will be for winter use. So you will find yourself, around early spring in temperate areas, establishing a seed-bed. This might be an area—depending on the size of your garden—as big as a table top. Work it to a very fine tilth, score parallel lines 6 inches (15 cm) apart with the corner of a hoe, lightly sprinkle seed along the rows, then cover the seeds with fine compost or soil, firming with the side of the rake. Plant a row each of cabbage, red cabbage, Brussels sprouts, winter cauliflower, sprouting broccoli (including calabrese), and, for good measure, leeks. I know the latter are not brassicas, but they go in there just the same. You must keep this seed-bed well watered, and when the plants are about 5 inches (13 cm) high, plant them out in their permanent beds, or if you are trying to get two crops, their holding-beds. In cold climates you must sow these seeds in seed boxes (flats) indoors, and plant them out later.

tons per acre (100 metric tons per hectare). On a garden scale, you can figure on getting from a pound to a pound and a half (500–700 g) of cabbages per foot (30 cm) of row. So they are a good crop to grow, even if you only have a small garden.

Soil and climate

Cabbages will grow almost anywhere, but in hot, dry areas they can only be grown in the fall and winter. They will stand winter frosts down to 20°F (−7°C): below this temperature, it is better to store them. They are greedy plants and like good soil, with plenty of organic matter in it and plenty of nitrogen and lime.

Soil treatment

Unlike the other *brassicas*, cabbages like deeply dug ground with plenty of humus worked into it. If they follow the *Fabaceae* (pea and bean family) they will not need lime. If they don't follow the *Fabaceae,* they may well fare better if you do add a generous helping of lime.

Propagation

If you want cabbages year-round, you have to divide them into three groups: winter, spring, and summer.

SPRING CABBAGE Sow seed in the seed-bed (*see above*) in midsummer in cooler climates and late summer in warmer ones. Plant out into a permanent bed in early fall 18 inches (45 cm) apart or 12 inches (30 cm) in the deep bed (*see p.44*). Don't fertilize too heavily with nitrogen before the winter. Instead, give them a boost when the spring arrives. These plantings will keep you going all through the late spring and early summer if you live in a cool climate.

SUMMER CABBAGE Cabbages are apt to be forgotten in summer, for there are so many other things to eat at this time, but they are excellent for eating raw in salads. You can grow them quite easily as long as your summers are not too hot and dry. Choose a fast-growing summer variety and sow in your seed-bed (*see left*) in early spring, or, in cold areas, sow indoors in late winter. Plant out when they are tiny, about two inches (5 cm) high, in very good soil, and keep them well-watered. Plant in staggered rows 18 inches (45 cm) apart with 18 inches (45 cm) between rows.

WINTER CABBAGE These will form by far the greater bulk of your cabbage plantings and will be sown in the brassica seed-bed (*see left*) in early spring, or indoors in flats or peat* pots in cold climates. When they are about 5 inches (13 cm) tall, you can either plant them straight out in rows 2 feet (60 cm) apart—15 inches (38 cm) in the deep bed—with 20 inches (50 cm) between cabbages, or you can double-crop—that is, take two crops of different vegetables from the same bed in quick succession. To do this you must plant them out firmly in a holding-bed, a piece of the garden set aside for them, with each plant about 6 inches (15 cm) from its neighbors. Then, when ground becomes available as you harvest your early potatoes or peas and beans during the summer, you can plant out your cabbages and any other *brassicas* that are in the holding-bed. This double transplanting does not seem to do them much harm.

Planting out

Plant out cabbages and all *brassicas* firmly. Make a hole with a dibber, put the plant in at the same depth as it was in the holding-bed, and firm the soil around it with either the dibber, your hand, or your boot. Swilling *brassica* roots in a bucket of thin mud with a handful of lime in it before planting out helps them a lot. This brings the roots into instant contact with the waiting soil. I knew an old gardener who dipped his plants in a paste of half soil and half cow dung with a handful of soot in it; he grew magnificent cabbages.

Care while growing

Cabbages must suffer no check. They must have ample water, ample nitrogen, and no weed competition. If you are going to the extravagance of using some organic high-nitrogen manure like blood meal, meat meal, cottonseed meal, or chicken or rabbit manure, then the *brassica* crops are good ones to put it on. Use it as a top-dressing when they begin to grow. If the plants are checked—say, by cabbage root fly—urge them on with a dressing of this kind. You may save them. Don't put nitrogen on just before the winter; it drives them on too fast, making them sappy and susceptible to frost damage. Earth up the stems as the plants grow.

Pests and diseases

Alas, these are plenty and virulent. But you may, if you are a good organic gardener and lucky, avoid them all.

CLUBROOT One of the most troublesome things in the garden, but many people live all their lives and never see it. Your garden either has it or it hasn't. Beware, though, if it hasn't got it, because it can get it: by your buying in infected plants; your bringing in manure from a contaminated source; you can even bring it in on your boots, after visiting a neighbor's garden that has it. Don't put the stems of bought cabbages on your compost pile unless you have inspected them first and made absolutely sure they have no clubroot.

When you have got clubroot you will find lumps or malformations on the roots of your wilting cabbages. You can get this with all the *brassicas*. Cut a few of your root swellings open. If there is a maggot inside one, what you have probably got is cabbage gall weevil, not clubroot. Rejoice. At least that is preventable. But you can, of course, be plagued by both.

Clubroot is caused by microscopic spores of a fungus that can lie dormant in the soil for up to seven years. The disease can be eradicated if the land is rested completely from cruciferous plants for seven years, and that means no cruciferous weeds, either—so no shepherd's purse or charlock. The disease thrives in acidic soil, so lime helps to reduce it. If you can get the pH up to 7 you may get rid of it. But many gardeners have to live with clubroot (I have done so for several decades) and just grow *brassica* crops in spite of it. Nonorganic gardeners dip the roots of their plants in calamine* at the planting-out stage. Calamine is a highly poisonous mercuric compound. The mercury is persistent in the soil and over the years inevitably builds up to serious proportions. Furthermore, the treatment is only occasionally effective. I fear that the plants are often infected invisibly at the seed-bed stage in which case nothing will cure them.

Preventive measures are: strict rotation so that cruciferous plants don't recur more often than once in four years; liming; burning of all affected roots; putting half a mothball (camphor) down each hole before planting; putting a half-inch (1-cm) length of rhubarb stem down each hole before planting; putting an equal mixture of wood ashes and crushed eggshells down each hole. I have not had complete success with any of these, but they may help depending on your particular circumstances.

Another line of attack, which is being researched by the Henry Doubleday Association in the UK, is to douse the land that is not being planted with brassicas with water in which brassica plants have been boiled. The effect of this is to wake

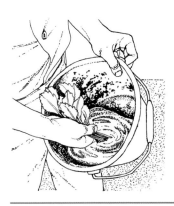

SWILLING, DIBBING AND FIRMING
Prepare cabbages for planting by swilling the roots in a bucket of thin mud mixed with a handful of lime. Remember that cabbages should be planted firmly. Use a dibber to make a hole to the same depth as the plant was growing in the holding-bed. Then pack the soil around the plant and heel in firmly with your boot.

the sleeping spores by fooling them into thinking that *brassicas* have been planted. But there are no *brassicas* and the awakened spores, being unable to go dormant again, die.

Yet another approach, which is worth trying, is to sprinkle affected ground with 65 lb (30 kg) of quicklime per 100 sq yd (84 sq m) and then leave the ground brassica-free for at least five years.

CABBAGE ROOT FLY This attacks cabbages and cauliflowers but is less likely to go for Brussels sprouts or broccoli. If your plants wilt and you pull them out and cut into the roots and stems and find maggots, those are cabbage root fly maggots. When plants are badly affected their leaves appear bluish, with yellow edges. The fly, which looks like a house fly, lays its eggs on the top of the ground near the plants. The larvae hatch out, dig down through the soil, and then burrow up into the stem. Once there, nothing will shift them completely and they can kill the plant. Poisons don't help because they kill predators but on the whole tend to miss the maggots.

Small squares of tarred felt put like collars around each plant can obstruct the maggots. Either slit a 5-inch (13-cm) square piece of tarred felt from one side to the middle and slip each plant into the slit, or else fold the felt in half, snip a "V" out of the middle, and thread the plant through the resulting hole. The flies lay their eggs on the felt and the maggots can't get down into the earth. A smear of kerosene* on the felt is a good idea.

If plants do become infected, I hate to say it but a teaspoonful of nitrate of soda, or some other high-inorganic-nitrogen substance, works wonders. It not only helps the plant to start growing quickly and make new roots, but it also seems to disperse the maggots. Banking the soil up around the stems of affected plants also seems to help them; the plants can put out new and healthier roots. Kerosene* just sprinkled on the ground around each plant, once a week until they are large and healthy, also acts as a deterrent. Burn all infected roots

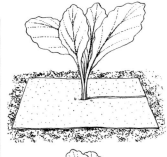

A TARRED COLLAR
Slit a 5-inch (13-cm) square of tarred felt from one side to the middle and slip it around the plant. A smear of kerosene or grease on the felt is also a good idea. The cabbage root fly will lay its eggs on the felt, but the maggots will not be able to get down into the soil to burrow up inside the plant stem.

A SEED-PACKET COLLAR
An old seed packet, torn at both ends and placed over your cabbage plant, is effective protection against the destructive cutworm. Alternatively, surround each plant with a ring of wood ash.

after the plants are lifted and fork the soil over frequently in winter to allow the birds to help themselves to the pupae that are lying dormant in the soil.

CABBAGE GALL WEEVIL These sometimes attack plants in the seed-bed, and you will see small galls on the roots when you come to transplant. If there's only one gall, cut it open and kill the maggot. If there are more, burn the plant.

CUTWORM These minute worms frequently nip small plants off at ground level. Keep them away with a ring of wood ash or by placing a cardboard collar around each plant. A simple collar can be made by tearing both ends from an old seed packet.

CABBAGE WHITE BUTTERFLY The caterpillars of these can completely ruin a stand of cabbages if allowed to go unchecked. The best way to get rid of them on a small scale is to pick

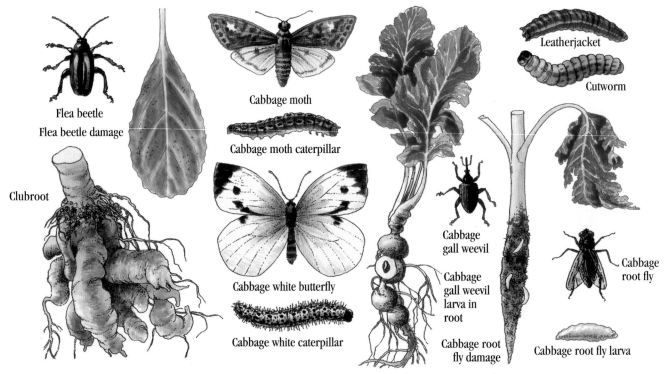

Flea beetle

Flea beetle damage

Clubroot

Cabbage moth

Cabbage moth caterpillar

Cabbage white butterfly

Cabbage white caterpillar

Leatherjacket

Cutworm

Cabbage gall weevil

Cabbage gall weevil larva in root

Cabbage root fly damage

Cabbage root fly

Cabbage root fly larva

them off carefully. Another possible remedy is to soak with soapy water.

CABBAGE MOTH Pyrethrum or derris spraying will kill these larvae, which eat the hearts of cabbages and whose droppings can cause mold.

LEATHERJACKETS These are the gray-brown legless larvae of the cranefly. They sometimes eat the roots of brassica seedlings in late spring, causing the plants to wilt and die. All you can do is dig the ground very thoroughly and frequently in early spring so that the birds can eat the larvae.

Harvesting and storing

When you have cut a cabbage, pull the root out immediately; if you leave it in, it will encourage disease. If the plants are healthy, you can bash the stems with a heavy mallet or sledge-hammer, or else run the garden roller over them. The object is to crush them, so that they can be put on the compost pile or buried in a trench over which you will plant next year's runner beans.

Cabbages can be stored by putting them on straw in a frostproof shed or basement and covering them with more straw. In mild climates, just leave them growing until you want them: 20°F (–7°C) won't hurt them.

HARVESTING CABBAGES
Cut your cabbages at the top of the stem with a sharp knife. Remember to pull both the stem and the root from the ground.

BASHING CABBAGE STEMS
Bash the uprooted cabbage stems with a mallet. The crushed stems can be left to rot for compost or buried in a trench.

SAVOYS

These are the hardiest cabbages, and for late winter and early spring use, they are the most valuable. Treat them like winter cabbages, but don't eat them until the winter is well advanced and most other vegetables are gone. They fill a gap in the early spring.

RED CABBAGES

These need an extra-long growing season. Sow seed in a seed-bed in early fall in drills 6 inches (15 cm) apart. As the seedlings appear, thin them in the seed-bed. Plant out in spring 24 inches (60 cm) apart, and make sure the soil is firm, otherwise the cabbages will not develop large and compact heads. Cut red cabbages in the fall, and remember that although you can eat them raw, if you cook them they need far longer than ordinary cabbages—up to two hours.

Chinese Cabbages

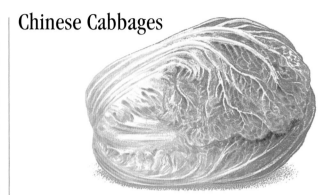

There are two kinds of Chinese cabbage—pe-tsai and pak-choi. Pe-tsai comes to a head; pak-choi doesn't and you just eat the leaves.

Soil and climate

Chinese cabbage is not so winter-hardy as cabbage, but nevertheless it does not do well in too much heat. It does not like acidic soil.

Soil treatment

They like plenty of humus. A 4-inch (10-cm) covering of compost on the soil forked in before planting is ideal.

Propagation

Sow Chinese cabbage seed in situ in late summer or even later if you have no winter frost. Either broadcast and single later or sow thinly in rows.

Care while growing

Chinese cabbages need plenty of water. Mulching when the plants have grown to 6 inches (15 cm) helps to conserve moisture. Tying with raffia at top and bottom also helps to conserve water. Thin to about 9 inches (25 cm) apart. If the plants grow big and crowded, uproot half and eat them. They suffer very little from pests or diseases; what they do have will be something that afflicts cabbages (*see Cabbages*).

TYING A CHINESE CABBAGE
You must never allow a Chinese cabbage to go without water. When it has grown to about 6 inches (15 cm), a good mulching will help to conserve moisture. But as soon as the heart begins to form, it is an excellent idea to tie the leaves together top and bottom with strips of raffia. This will keep the plant sufficiently moist and at the same time blanch the inner leaves. Later on, thin the plants to about 9 inches (25 cm) apart; if they still grow crowded, uproot half and eat them.

Harvesting

Uproot them and eat them, either in salads or as cooked greens, as soon as they have a good heart. This can be as soon as ten weeks after planting.

Brussels Sprouts

In my view, Brussels sprouts are the tastiest of the brassicas, and they will stand through the winter in temperate climates, allowing you fresh sprouts right through to the spring.

Soil and climate
Sprouts grown in countries that have no frost are tasteless, but where there is frost they make a noble standby for late winter and spring. Sprouts grow well in any good soil.

Soil treatment
Deep cultivation and plenty of manure or compost are the rule. They need lime if the soil is acidic. The traditional way to grow them is in very firm soil. Deep-bed gardeners can transplant them into soft deep beds (*see p.44*) by planting them deeper than usual and pressing down the soil around them with one hand before and during planting.

Propagation
Traditionally, seeds are sown in an outdoor seed-bed in early spring. But you can get better results by sowing indoors in seed boxes (flats) from midwinter onward. Prick them out into

frames if you sowed them early, then when they are about 5 inches (13 cm) tall plant them in a holding-bed and then again into their permanent quarters, where they should be 3 feet (90 cm) apart in rows 3 feet (90 cm) apart. Like other brassicas, they seem to benefit from transplanting. Deep-bed gardeners should allow 20 inches (50 cm) between plants.

Care while growing
Brussels sprouts gain a lot from being earthed up while they are growing, and mulching is also good for them. Like all other brassicas, they don't like weed competition. Brussels sprouts grow very tall, so in very windy situations in exposed places, it may be necessary to stake them, but in most places a good earthing up will provide sufficient support. It is important to strip the lower leaves off when they begin to turn yellow.

Pests and diseases
Brussels sprouts are prone to all the diseases that afflict cabbages (*see Cabbages*).

Harvesting and storing
Seed sown in midwinter, indoors, will give sprouts as early as September, but these will not have the flavor of the later ones that have the benefit of a touch of frost. Like all vegetables, other than roots, they can be picked just as soon as they are ready. Pick the bottom ones first, then pick upward along the stems as more ripen, and finally eat the tops of the plants. If you have chickens, hang the denuded plants upside down in the chicken run. You can go on eating fresh sprouts in mild climates right into the spring, hence the classic idea of a British garden in February is of a bare and untidy mud patch, with a sprinkling of snow on it and a few dozen tattered Brussels sprouts, naked as to their lower parts, bravely leaning against the freezing wind, sleet, or hail.

In countries of intense cold or deep snow, you can harvest the sprouts by pulling the plants out of the ground before the worst weather comes, and store them by heeling them into soil or sand in a basement or storeroom. If it is cold enough they will keep for months like this.

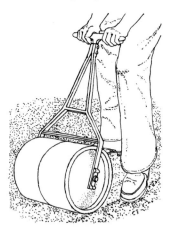

ROLLING THE BED
Sprouts need firm soil or they will grow loose-leaved. Prepare the bed for planting by stamping on it or rolling with a heavy garden roller.

EARTHING UP
Deep cultivation is essential for sprouts. At regular intervals, earth up around the base of each plant with a hoe.

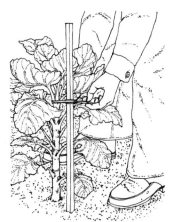

STAKE SUPPORTS
Sprouts can grow very tall, so it's a good idea to stake the stem of each plant—especially if it is growing in a windy position.

PICKING SPROUTS
When the sprouts have grown to the right size, pick first from the bottom of the stem, then work upward to the top of the plant.

Cauliflowers

EARLY AND MAIN-CROP CAULIFLOWERS

To develop cauliflowers, and also broccoli, man has taken the basic biennial cabbage plant, which naturally flowers in its second year of growth, and bred it to flower in its first. Cauliflowers have heads made up of tightly bunched white or purple flowers; the purple ones, sometimes called purple hearting broccoli, turn green when cooked. When you grow cauliflowers, remember that you are asking biennial plants to get through the whole of their life-cycle—growth, storage of nourishment, and flowering—all in one short season.

Soil and climate

Cauliflowers do best in temperate climates. They prefer heavy, moist soil with plenty of humus. They simply won't grow in poor soil, or in bad conditions.

Soil treatment

They need very firm soil, so don't pull out the pea or bean plants that may precede the cauliflowers in the bed, because this will loosen the soil. Hoe them off instead, leaving the roots in the ground. Then roll or tramp. Like all brassicas, cauliflowers don't like acid, so you must lime as necessary. Fork on a good dressing of fish manure two weeks before planting. They also need some potash.

Propagation

You can get very early cauliflowers by sowing seed in mid-winter, indoors, and planting out as soon as the ground has

PLANTING OUT CAULIFLOWER

Young cauliflower plants can be removed from the seed box as soon as they have grown three true leaves in addition to the original two seed leaves. But check that the plant isn't "blind"—meaning that it has failed to develop a bud in the center. If it is blind, then it won't be of any use to you—without the bud, your cauli just won't flower.

warmed up after the winter—probably in the middle of spring. With luck you will be eating them by midsummer.

For your main crop, sow seed in your brassica seed-bed (*see p.96*) in early spring. Sow a quick-maturing variety so that you can begin to harvest in late summer, alongside a slower variety that can be harvested in fall and early winter. Plant out as soon as the plants have three true leaves as well as the two original seed leaves. If you are double-cropping, plant out in your holding-bed and move them to their final position after peas or beans in midsummer. Examine the plants when you take them out of the seed-bed. If they are "blind," meaning they have no tiny bud in the middle, throw them away. They won't make curds, as the flowers are called. For the final planting-out, allow 2 feet (60 cm) between rows with 20 inches (50 cm) between plants. Allow 15 inches (40 cm) between plants if you use the deep-bed method (*see p.44*).

Care while growing

Do plenty of hoeing. Top-dress the growing plants with high nitrogen if you have it, but if your ground is really organic, with plenty of humus in it, a mulch of compost will do very well. Don't let your cauliflowers dry out because they must keep moving.

PROTECTING THE CURDS

Sunlight striking cauliflower curds can cause not only discoloration, but sometimes even a bad taste, so you need to protect them from the sun. Cover them by bending or breaking some of the outer leaves of the plant, and tying these in position over the plant with string.

If you don't want the trouble of blanching your cauliflowers, try growing purple ones. They last longer in the ground than the white-headed variety and need no blanching. The heads are deep purple on top and turn green when cooked; the flavor is like a mild broccoli.

Pests and diseases

Caulis share pests and diseases with cabbages (*see Cabbages*).

Harvesting

Harvest your cauliflowers as soon as they develop solid curds. The first should appear in late summer. If you wait, the curds will loosen and deteriorate. Cut well below the head if you want to eat the cauliflower immediately. If you pull them up by the roots you can store them in a cold basement for up to a month.

WINTER CAULIFLOWERS

Winter cauliflower is also known as self-protecting broccoli, but it looks and behaves like cauliflower, except that it is hardy and comes to harvest from midwinter onward. Sow in late spring and treat like main-crop cauliflower.

Broccoli

PURPLE AND WHITE SPROUTING BROCCOLI
The broccolis are easier to grow than cauliflowers. The great virtue of the purple and white sprouting varieties is that they are winter-hardy and can be harvested from late winter on, when kale and sprouts will be your only other greens.

Soil and climate
Good soil is not essential and they will grow in any but the very coldest climates.

Soil treatment
Give them very firm ground; even grassland from which you have just stripped the sod will do. Sprinkle with lime.

Propagation
Sow broccoli in your *brassica* seed-bed (*see p.96*) in spring and plant it out when you have room, preferably after peas and beans. Let it wait in the holding-bed a month or two if necessary. Allow 18 inches (45 cm) between plants and 30 inches (75 cm) between rows. For the deep-bed method (*see p.44*), allow 18 inches (45 cm) all ways.

Care while growing
Mulch between the rows in summer. Mulch with straw in winter and stake the plants if they grow tall.

Pests and diseases
Broccoli can develop a mild case of clubroot. It does not suffer badly from pests.

Harvesting
Pick, and pick again, from the little flowering shoots as these become available in late winter. Keep picking right through spring and even into summer.

CALABRESE
Calabrese is a broccoli with green sprouts. It has more flavor than the other varieties, but the plants are less hardy. Sow it and plant it out along with the broccolis. Start picking it when the green flowerheads appear, until the first frost.

Kale

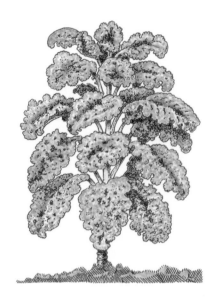

Kale is very winter-hardy and is often the last of the winter *brassicas* left standing. There are many varieties, both crinkly- and smooth-leaved, including collards. Kale is a non-hearting cabbage plant. All you get is the green leaves, and these are much better after a frost. Although they don't have the same delicacy of flavor as other *brassicas*, they are very nutritious and rich in vitamins. Cooked kale, provided it is only lightly cooked, has twice as much vitamin C as the equivalent weight of orange juice.

Soil and climate
Grow it wherever there are frosts. Any soil will do, but it crops best on rich soil.

Soil treatment
Kale likes fertile soil, which need not be especially firm.

Propagation
Grow kale for eating in your *brassica* seed-bed (*see p.96*) and plant it out, when you have room, 20 inches (50 cm) apart in rows 30 inches (75 cm) apart. If you use the deep-bed method (*see p.44*), allow 15 inches (40 cm) between plants in all directions.

Pests and diseases
Kale has a strong built-in resistance to clubroot. You can protect it from cabbage root fly and cabbage white butterfly by spraying with nicotine* in the fall. Kale is very tough, but all the same, it can suffer from any of the cabbage pests and diseases (*see Cabbages*).

Harvesting
Harvest from January onward. Pick leaves and side-shoots, but always leave some on the plant. Your crop will last you till May if you are very lucky. If you have a surfeit, kale makes a fine feed for hens, rabbits, goats, pigs, or any other domestic animals that are not carnivores.

Rutabagas & Turnips

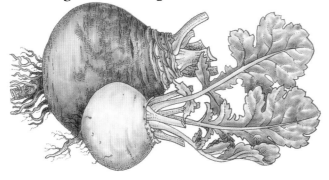

Rutabagas and turnips are both brassicas in which the first year's nourishment is stored in the root instead of, like the other brassicas, in the stem or the leaves. Rutabagas are orange whereas turnips are white, and rutabagas have their leaves coming out of a neck on top of the root, whereas turnip leaves grow directly from the root. Turnips will not stand severe frost, but rutabagas are a lot more hardy.

Turnips will come to harvest between 60 and 80 days after sowing. Rutabagas take about a month longer. Both can be sown late in the summer. They therefore make a good "catch crop"—a crop put in late after you have cleared the ground of something else. This is another way of getting two crops from the same plot in one year. When you are choosing what variety of turnip to plant, don't overlook the fact that some varieties can do double duty by producing both edible leaves and roots. In some varieties the foliage can be used for greens a month after seeding.

Soil and climate
They do best in a cool and damp climate. In hot weather they become hard and fibrous and are likely to go to seed. If you live in a hot climate, you must sow either very early in the spring so that they can be harvested when very young and tender, before the hot weather of the summer, or late in the fall when they will grow happily into the winter and come to full maturity. Light fertile loam is ideal, but they will grow in most soils. They like neutral or slightly alkaline soil like all brassicas, so lime if your soil is acidic.

Soil treatment
Cultivate deeply. Like all root crops, turnips and rutabagas like a very fine tilth. If you get a lot of rain in your area, grow your turnips and rutabagas on ridges. You can encourage their capacity for fast growing by manuring a year in advance.

Propagation
In cool temperate climates, turnips for picking and eating young should be sown in late spring and then, if you are a turnip lover, twice more at monthly intervals. Sow main crop turnips for storing in late summer. Even early fall is not too late to get a good crop of "turnip tops," which are even tastier than spinach and contain lots of iron. Sow rutabagas in early summer. The same sowing will provide young sweet rutabagas for eating in late summer and main crop for storage. Sow both turnips and rutabagas thinly in shallow drills where they are to grow. An ounce (28 g) of turnip or rutabaga seed will sow 250 feet (75 m) of row.

THINNING THE SEEDLINGS
Turnip or rutabaga plants shouldn't be crowded together. Start thinning them out, using a hoe, when they are still quite small. Leave about 9 inches (23 cm) between plants. If you're using the deep-bed method, a distance of about 6 inches (15 cm) between plants will be enough.

Care while growing
When the plants are still tiny, thin them out with the hoe so as to leave one plant about every 9 inches (23 cm)—deep-bed method, one plant every 6 inches (15 cm). Leave a shorter distance for successional summer sowings that are to be eaten very young, and a greater distance for the winter main crop, which is intended for storing.

Pests and diseases
Turnips and rutabagas are subject to most of the pests and diseases that afflict cabbages and the same remedies can be applied (see Cabbages).

FLEA BEETLE When they are very young, turnips and rutabagas may get flea beetle (see p.98). This shows as tiny holes on the leaves. A good shower of rain should cure it, or a good hosing with water if there is no rain. If this doesn't work, either derris or pyrethrum dust will kill them.

BORON DEFICIENCY Turnips and rutabagas are usually the first vegetables to suffer from boron deficiency. The core of your turnip or rutabaga will develop grayish-brown areas that will eventually rot and stink. A minimal amount of boron dissolved in water and added to the soil is sufficient to correct this deficiency.

BORON DEFICIENCY
Turnips and rutabagas are good indicators of boron deficiency in your soil, since they are generally the first vegetables to suffer. The core of the turnip or rutabaga will turn a grayish-brown color and begin to rot and stink—sometimes becoming completely hollow in the center. An ounce (28 g) of boron is sufficient to restore a quarter of an acre (1,000 sq m) of land. Dissolve it in enough water to cover this area.

Harvesting and storing
The early successionally sown crop should be pulled during the summer when they are not more than 3 inches (8 cm) in diameter and are then at their sweetest. Main-crop turnips should be harvested before the first very hard frost and put in either a root store or a clamp (see p.110). Rutabagas in all but the severest climates can be left out in the ground until they are wanted. So, eat your turnips before your rutabagas.

Kohlrabi

This strange-looking plant is merely a cabbage in which all the nutrients are stored in a swollen stem instead of in tight-packed leaves.

Soil and climate
Kohlrabi likes the same conditions as other brassicas but is even more dependent on moist soil; drought makes them hard and woody.

Propagation
It is better not to transplant kohlrabi, but to sow the seed out where the plants will grow. Sow thinly in two or three successional sowings between April and June.

Care while growing
Thin the plants you want to eat in the summer to 6 inches (15 cm) apart—deep-bed method, 4 inches (10 cm). Those you want to store through the winter, thin to 10 inches (25 cm).

Pests and diseases
Kohlrabi can suffer from the pests and diseases that afflict cabbages (*see Cabbages*).

Harvesting and storing
Pick the plants very young and tender—about 2 to 3 inches (6 cm) across—and eat them raw or cooked. Store them as shown below.

STORING KOHLRABI
Pack kohlrabi in an unheated shed or basement between layers of straw.

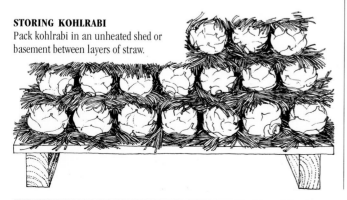

Radishes

SUMMER RADISHES
Radishes grow in three to four weeks, are rich in iron and vitamin C, and are excellent for adding bite and crispness to salads. They are good for growing in odd vacant corners, and they do well in windowboxes as well. Winter radishes are larger and can be black, white, red, or red and white.

Soil and climate
Radishes like good, rich, damp soil and a cool, moist climate. Since they grow fast and are eaten quickly, it does not matter if they are grown in beds not reserved for *Brassicaceae*, for they don't have time to develop diseases. In hot countries they can be grown only as a winter crop. In cooler climates they can be grown in spring, summer, and fall.

Soil treatment
Like most *Brassicaceae*, they don't like acidic soil, so you should lime if it seems necessary.

Propagation
Just sprinkle the large black seeds thinly in shallow drills and cover them, or else broadcast and rake in. Sow very few at a time, but sow often—even once every two weeks—so you have fresh tender radishes whenever you want them. The seeds will keep for five years, so don't throw them away. If you want early radishes, you can sprinkle them among other crops that you are forcing in a hot-bed, or in a deep bed covered with transparent plastic or glass. In the deep bed (*see p.44*) sow 1 inch (2.5 cm) apart in each direction.

Pests and diseases
FLEA BEETLE These pests are the only hazard. If heavy rain does not wash them away, give them a good hosing. If this fails, dust with derris or pyrethrum.

Harvesting
Just pull, wash and eat. If you have too many, pull them out anyway. Don't let them grow up hard and woody, or go to seed.

WINTER RADISHES
White radishes should be sown between late spring and midsummer; others toward the end of the summer. They will all be ready for harvest at the end of the fall. White ones must be dug and stored in peat. The others can be left in the ground until required during the winter.

Seakale

Seakale is a perennial whose young shoots should preferably be harvested in spring, but if you wish, it can be forced for eating fresh in winter.

Soil and climate
Seakale likes rich, deep, well-manured loamy soil and a cool, damp climate. Don't try to grow it anywhere hot and arid.

Soil treatment
Dig deeply—at least two spits—and incorporate plenty of rich manure into the soil.

Propagation
Seakale can be started from root cuttings, called thongs, or from seed. The former method is preferable, because plants started from root cuttings begin to yield the second year, a year earlier than seedlings. However it is said that a new race should be raised from seed from time to time. Get your thongs from a seed merchant or a fellow gardener. They are just bits of root about 4 inches (10 cm) long. Plant them 6 inches (15 cm) deep and 30 inches (75 cm) from each other in late winter—deep bed 15 inches (38 cm) apart. If you plant from seed, sow in shallow drills in March.

Care while growing
If you sow seed, thin to 4 inches (10 cm) apart and transplant to 30 inches (75 cm) apart the following spring.

Keep well weeded. You cannot eat green seakale because it is bitter. Therefore the plants must be blanched—that is, deprived of light completely so that they turn white. You can do this by covering them in situ with pails, boxes, or overturned flowerpots with the drainage holes blocked. If you want fresh seakale during the winter, you can force its growth. Either spread hot manure over the blanching covers so as to provide heat, or take the roots from their outdoor bed in the fall and plant them in loam in a hot-bed, or warmed frame, or even in a warm basement. Keep your seakale warm—the soil should be 55 to 60°F (13–16°C)—and dark, and you will get a good winter crop.

Pests and diseases
Small seedlings are occasionally attacked by flea beetle (*see Turnips*); otherwise they are not prone to attack.

Harvesting
Cut shoots when they are about a foot (30 cm) high in spring, unless you have forced the plants for a winter harvest. Like all perennials that are harvested for food, seakale must be treated with respect. After you have taken your just dues, let it grow up into the sunshine, green and strong, and build itself up for next year.

Cresses

WATERCRESS
If your garden has a corner that is persistently damp, watercress is the ideal crop. It has the distinctive hot flavor of the *Brassicaceae*.

Soil and climate
It does best in cool climates, but will grow perfectly well in a warm one, especially if it is standing in cold flowing water.

Propagation
It is possible to create a bed next to a flowing stream. Flood the bed by admitting water from the stream after sowing the watercress. You can grow it from seed, either planting the seed in the wet mud just above the water or sowing it indoors, in potting mix, in earthenware pots, which should be kept in a tray into which water flows constantly. You can bring it to maturity like this or else plant it out in a stream or damp bed. Another method is to buy really fresh commercial watercress from the store, put it in a plastic bag with some water, take it home, and plant it.

Care while growing
Pinch out the top shoots to make the plants bushy. If a plant flowers, cut it back.

Pests and diseases
Never grow watercress in water to which sheep or cattle have access. If you do, you might just get liver fluke.

Harvesting
Pick out side-shoots. The more you pick, the more grow.

CRESS
Like mustard (*see p.149*), cress is eaten in the seedling stage, although if you are growing them together remember that cress takes a few days longer than mustard to germinate. Grow it on damp burlap or a damp peat* bed. Sow it thickly throughout spring and summer.

LAND CRESS
Also known as American cress, this is a relatively hardy salad plant, which should be pulled after about seven weeks of growth. Sow successionally through the summer for several months' salad supply. Sow half an inch (1.5 cm) apart and later thin to about 6 inches (15 cm) between plants. Find a fairly shady site that will not dry out, and protect the crop under glass as the weather becomes colder.

Solanaceae

Potatoes, tomatoes, peppers, and eggplants are all members of the *Solanaceae*. There is something a little exotic about this family, for it includes such dark and midnight subjects as deadly nightshade and tobacco, as well as such luscious tropical annuals as green peppers and chili peppers.

But there is nothing exotic about the potato. Even that great farmer and writer of the early nineteenth century, William Cobbett, termed it "the lazy root," for he thought it would supplant wheat, the cultivation and after treatment of which he considered to be the nursery of English virtues.

The other important member of the family is the tomato, which is so closely related to the potato that a hybrid has been that which has inferior potatoes on its roots and inferior tomatoes on its stems. Potatoes and tomatoes, like green and red peppers, came from tropical south and central America.

Most of the edible *Solanaceae* come from this area and they therefore require very rich, damp, and fertile soil, as similar to the rich leafmold of the tropical jungle as possible. Furthermore, none of the food-bearing *Solanaceae* are frost-hardy, which means, if you live in a cool climate, you must either start them off indoors, or not plant them until all danger of frost is past.

The *Solanaceae* have several pests and diseases in common and it is therefore advisable to grow them all in the same bed, or in the same part of the rotation. In this way your land is given a rest from solanaceous plants for the full cycle of four years, and there is no chance for disease to build up or for pests to accumulate. Certain eelworms, for example, can multiply to frightening proportions if tomatoes and potatoes are grown too often on the same land. Never touch any solanaceous plants when your fingers have been in contact with tobacco, because tobacco is a member of the *Solanaceae* and frequently contains virus disease.

One of the great values of most plants of this family is that they are rich in vitamin C. Potatoes are the richest source for most inhabitants of temperate climates; chili peppers are the richest source in many parts of the tropics. The reason why Indians eat hot curry is not to cool them down, but to provide themselves with vitamin C. All in all life would be much poorer were it not for this tribe of strange, soft-stemmed, potash-hungry, tropical-looking plants.

Potatoes

The potato is one of the few plants on which a person could live if he could get nothing else; and, unlike the others, it requires very simple preparation: no threshing, winnowing, grinding, or any of the jobs that make grain consumption a difficult technical operation.

Self-sufficiency from the garden in temperate climates is unthinkable without the spud, and I would recommend anybody, except those with the tiniest of plots, to devote at least a quarter of his land to it, and preferably as much as a third. Being a member of the family *Solanaceae*, it provides the soil with a rest from those families that are more commonly represented in our gardens. Without the potato break, we would find ourselves growing brassicas, for example, far too frequently on the same ground.

Soil and climate
Never lime for potatoes. They thrive in acidic soil: anything over a pH of 4.6. Scab, which makes them unsightly but doesn't really do them much harm, thrives in alkaline conditions but is killed by acidity. Potash is essential for good potatoes (but if you put on plenty of manure or compost, you will have enough of that) and so is phosphate. Nitrogen is not so important, although a nitrogen shortage (unlikely in a good organic garden) will lower your yield.

Unfortunately, the potato did not originally evolve for the climates of the northern hemisphere. It evolved in the Andes, and the wild potato is a mountain plant, although tropical. Its provenance makes it very frost-tender; the least touch of frost will damage its foliage and halt its growth.

Soil treatment
It is well worth digging the soil deeply the previous fall, and incorporating a heavy ration of manure or compost while you're at it; 8 cwt (400 kg) per 100 sq yd (84 sq m) is about right. Another excellent thing to do is to broadcast some green manure crop, such as rye, the previous fall after your root break. If you do this you should leave the crop undisturbed until a month or two before you want to plant your potatoes—unless, that is, your green manure is clover, in which case you should dig it in in the fall. In any case, dig the green manure crop well into the ground and at the same time dig in compost or manure. Or, and this works perfectly well, you can, if you have been short of time in the winter or if the weather has not enabled you to dig, actually dig the green manure crop when you plant the potatoes. Throwing any available compost or manure into the bottom of the furrow, plant the potatoes on top of this and fill in with the green manure.

GREEN MANURING
Plant your potatoes where a green manure crop like winter rye has been growing. A month before planting, dig the green manure crop into the ground along with compost or manure.

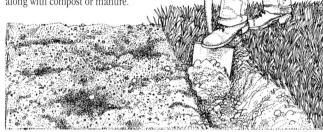

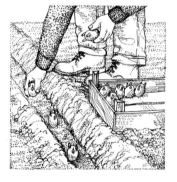

SOWING EARLY POTATOES
Make a trench 5 inches (13 cm) deep with a hoe, put in some manure or compost if you have it and put the seed potatoes in, rose-end up, about a foot (30 cm) apart.

COVERING EARLY POTATOES
Three to 4 inches (8 to 10 cm) of soil is usually enough covering for the early seed potatoes that you have planted. You will be earthing them up later on anyway.

Propagation

I know of nobody who grows potatoes from actual seed, although potatoes set seed in little green fruits that look just like small tomatoes. It is better to use sets, which are, in fact, just potatoes, although they are called "seed." If you plant a potato it will grow into a potato plant that produces between six and a dozen more potatoes. (The actual potatoes, by the way, are not *roots*—they are swollen underground *stems*.)

Potatoes grown in temperate climates near sea level are heir to certain diseases, which are the price they pay for growing in the wrong place. Among these are certain virus diseases that are transmitted by aphids. If you plant potato "seed" you will probably get a good crop of potatoes. But if you plant them where aphids abound, and you plant the new generation of sets from them the next year, the crop is likely to be slightly less. If you go on for a third year, and a fourth year, the crop will diminish even further. This is because there is a build-up, with every generation, of the virus diseases introduced by aphids.

The remedy is to get your "seed" from people who grow potatoes in places where there are no aphids. In practice, "seed" potatoes must be grown above a certain altitude, or else on some windswept sea island where aphids wouldn't have a chance. The specialty seed growers carefully "rogue" the potato plants as they grow (that is, pull out any weak or diseased potatoes) and protect them from infection.

The tubers that they lift are subsequently certified by the government agricultural authorities of the country concerned as being disease-free seed and fit for consumption.

All this does not mean that you cannot keep and plant your own tubers. Most people do, and you can even buy "once-grown" or "twice-grown" seed from your neighbors. And if you have land at over 800 feet (240 m) in the northeastern US, or on a sea-girt island, you can probably grow "seed" forever, both for yourself and to trade for other goods with your neighbors.

Seed potatoes should, ideally, be about 1½ ounces (40 g) in weight. You can cut larger tubers in half, provided you leave some "eyes" (small shoots) on each half, but I don't like doing this, as it can let in disease. Ideally, seed should be "chitted" before being planted. That is, it should be spread out, one spud thick, in a cool place, and in diffused light. Don't allow frost to get to it (frost will immediately rot spuds) and keep it out of hot sunlight. If the place is too hot and dark, long gangly shoots will grow off the spuds and tend to break off before you plant them. (If you can plant them without breaking these shoots off, though, the potatoes will grow very well.)

So the best thing to do with your seed potatoes is to lay them in chitting boxes in midwinter. These will stack one on top of the other and admit light and air to the spuds, and can be carried conveniently out to the garden for planting.

EARLIES " Earlies" are potatoes that grow quickly and can be eaten straight from the ground. They are not for storing. Plant them as early as you can, but remember that frost will kill them once they appear above the ground, unless they are protected with cloches or a thick covering of straw or compost. If they get frosted, you may be able to save them by hosing the frost off with warm water.

MAIN CROP Your store of "main crop" potatoes will go a long way toward keeping you alive during the winter. Plant them in late spring.

Chitting is well-nigh essential for early potatoes, but if you don't get around to chitting for your main crop, never mind—plant them just the same. You will still get a crop—it will just be later, that's all. And never plant any diseased tuber, or one that looks defective in any way. You will simply be spreading disease among your own crops, as well as those of your neighbors.

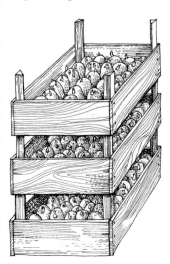

CHITTING SEED POTATOES
Place seed potatoes in single layers in chitting boxes. Put the seeds in "rose-end" up—the end with the most eyes. Protect from frost and direct sunlight. Before planting, rub off all but three sprouts at the "rose-end."

USING A POTATO PLANTER
If your soil is light, loamy, or sandy, you can save yourself some toil by using a potato planter. Ram it down into well-dug ground with your foot, drop a potato into the cup, then close the cup by pushing the handles of the planter together. Withdraw the planter, and the potato will be left buried in the ground. The method isn't quite as good for the potato as simple trenching, but it is easier and quicker. The potato planter is useless for sowing in heavy soil or clay, but it is ideal for the deep-bed method.

Don't put early potatoes in too deep: if they have 4 inches (10 cm) of soil over them when you have finished, that is usually enough. If the land has been dug before—that is, if you are not digging it for the first time since the previous fall—just make a furrow with the corner of a hoe, about 5 inches (13 cm) deep, put the spuds in, and cover with about 4 inches (10 cm) of soil. You will earth them up well enough later, and do not want the crop to grow inconveniently deep in the ground. If you have light, loamy, or sandy land, you would do well to get a potato planter, which is also the ideal thing for the deep-bed method (*see p.44*).

For early potatoes, have the drills about 2 feet (60 cm) apart, but have them 30 inches (75 cm) for main crop. Put earlies in a foot (30 cm) apart in the rows: main crop about 15 inches (38 cm). Remember, main-crop plants have much longer to grow and produce much bigger and heavier crops.

Now there are other methods of planting potatoes. One excellent one is to plant the potatoes on compost, cover them with more compost, and then a thick mulch of straw or spoiled hay. Or you can use leaves or leafmold in this way with good results. If you grow early potatoes with this method, you can gently remove some of the mulch, take a few spuds, and let the plant go on growing to produce some more. All these mulch-cover methods do great good in that they enrich the soil for other crops after the potatoes are finished. As you rotate your potato crop around your garden, the whole property becomes enriched.

PLANTING ON COMPOST
Put a good layer of compost in the furrow, and plant the potatoes on top. Cover them with compost, then mulch with straw.

HARVESTING FROM COMPOST
Lift some of the mulch, pull a few potatoes, and replace the mulch. The plant will go on to produce the main crop.

A very effective method, which has the advantage that it can be done in a small space (even on a patio), is to grow potatoes in a barrel. Fill the bottom of a barrel with a thin layer of soil and plant a single "seed" potato in it. Keep adding more soil as the plant grows upward and you will find that more and more tubers will form in the new soil. Finally the green plant will be sprouting out of the top of the barrel. Wait for the plant to flower and then simply empty the barrel out. You will find a huge number of potatoes in it.

You can work the same principle to even better effect by laying an old car, truck, or tractor tire on its side, filling it with soil, and planting one or more potato sets in it. When the plants have grown, but before they flower, add another tire and fill it with soil. Allow the plants to continue growing. Keep adding tires until the plants reach about 4 feet (1.2 m). Then harvest by dismantling the whole structure. This is better than the barrel method because the plants have plenty of light throughout their growth.

GROWING POTATOES IN BINS
Growing potatoes in bins is particularly useful if your space is limited—even a patio will do. Take an old garbage can, and fill about a sixth of it with soil. Plant one or more potato sets. When the plants have grown, but before they flower, put another layer of soil on top. Continue building up layers of soil as the plants appear, until they reach about 4 feet (1.2 m). When the potatoes are ready for harvesting, simply empty out the bin and you'll find you have a surprisingly heavy crop.

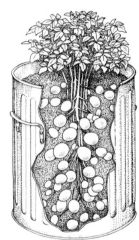

If you plant in a deep bed you should get an enormous crop. You can plant 18 inches (45 cm) deep. And in the very soft earth of the deep bed you can plant with a potato planter. Leave a foot (30 cm) between potatoes.

Care while growing
Potatoes need a lot of room under the ground, and they will turn green if exposed for more than a day or two to the light, in which case they become bitter and poisonous. This is because they produce a toxin called solanin. It is usual therefore to earth them up—that is, to draw or throw soil up around the plants so as to protect the growing tubers from the light and give them plenty of room for growth and expansion. Of course people who grow beneath a mulch don't have to do this, but they do have to make sure that there is plenty of mulch to cover the potatoes completely. Potatoes do not like weed competition, and in the very rich, deeply cultivated soil that they grow best in, weeds grow at an amazing rate. When you ridge up, you must be sure to kill the weeds. When weeds sprout up on the ridges between the potatoes, you must either hoe them out or pull them by hand. Throw them down in the furrows to rot and they will help by forming a mulch.

One tip about earthing up potatoes: for some reason the plants stand upright at night and in the early morning, but sprawl helplessly during the heat of the day. Potatoes are far

EARTHING UP POTATO PLANTS
Draw up soil around the plants with a hoe, covering any exposed tubers and giving them room for further growth. It's best to do this at night or in the early morning when the plants are standing upright.

easier to earth up early in the morning when they are standing up like guardsmen on parade. Like real guardsmen, when the sun gets hot they are inclined to faint. You may have to earth up several times; the final one should be thorough, the ridges patted down with the back of the space and made steep and even, for in this way they defy the spores of potato blight should this disease strike (as it very likely will).

When the tops of the main crop meet over the rows, they will suppress weeds and, after the final earthing up, you can relax for a while.

Pests and diseases

POTATO BLIGHT When the potato first came to Europe, blight did not affect it. In cool, damp climates, people living on peaty acidic soils—where the potato grew better than any other food crop—became entirely dependent on it. In Ireland, particularly, it became the mainstay of the poorer country people, to the exclusion of almost anything else. Then, in the middle of the nineteenth century, the blight struck. In one year it spread right through Ireland, blasted the tops of the growing crop, and later rotted the potatoes in their clamps, turning them into a slimy mass. Millions of people died.

No cure was found for blight until somebody noticed that potatoes growing downwind from copper smelting plants in South Wales did not get blight. So could copper prevent this dreaded disease? A mixture of copper sulfate and lime was tried—similar to the mixture already being used by the vignerons of Bordeaux against mildew on their grapes. It was found that if the foliage was sprayed with this at "blight times"—when the temperature and humidity of the air were above a certain point—the foliage was protected from the drifting spores of the blight. So now, to avoid blight I spray, very thoroughly above and below the leaves, with Bordeaux mixture*, and I do it about once every two weeks throughout the hot and humid weather of the summer. If you are in a dry windy area you may not get blight. Ask your neighbors. You can buy a commercial spray or else mix up your own Bordeaux mixture* (*see p.51*).

And what if you do get blight? You will know by black patches that appear on the leaves, and thereafter develop borders of white powdery stuff which is, in fact, the spores of the fungus that causes the disease. You cannot cure it by spraying then, although you may protect healthy plants from its spread. But do not despair. Unless the attack is a very early one the spores will not spread down to your tubers, and if you have earthed up well, spores that are washed down by the rain will not sink into the earth and come in direct contact with the tubers. You must cut the haulms (foliage) off with a very sharp blade (sharp so as not to drag the potatoes out of the ground) and burn them. It is sad for an organic gardener to have to say burn anything, but—yes—burn them. Then leave your tubers undisturbed in the ground for at least three weeks after you have removed the haulms. If you lift them immediately they will come into contact with billions of spores on the surface of the soil. If you leave them be the spores will be washed down the steep sides of the ridges into the furrows where they will sink harmlessly into the soil below. Leave the spuds for as long as possible. In the moderate climate where I live I often don't lift them until I need them to cook—even after Christmas sometimes. They are safer there in the ground than they are if I lift them.

WART DISEASE This is becoming less common as it is becoming compulsory, under EC regulations in Europe at least, to grow only immune varieties. The disease manifests itself by wartish growths that can cover the surface of the potato. Burn all such spuds. I've grown wart-free potatoes for a lifetime, but when it does infest your ground, you should plant only immune varieties. Otherwise, don't grow potatoes for six years on that land and hope the disease will die out. 65 pounds (30 kg) of quicklime* per 100 sq yd (84 sq m) of infected land are said to kill it.

SCAB You will probably get this if you grow spuds in very alkaline soil or in soil that has been recently limed. It is not serious. If you want to sell potatoes it matters, for they don't look nice. If you just want to eat them, don't worry about it; simply peel the scab off. But plenty of manure or compost will prevent scab, so organic gardens simply shouldn't have it.

POTATO ROOT EELWORM This arrived in Europe from its home in South America before World War I and has been with us ever since. It attacks chiefly the monoculturists who grow potatoes on the same soil year after year—or at any rate too frequently. Don't grow spuds too often on the same soil. If you get it really badly you will have to give up growing potatoes there for at least ten years, although it is said that if you grow several crops of *Tagetes minuta* on the land, and compost it, or dig it in as green manure, it will suppress eelworm. And, if you grow a crop of *Tagetes minuta* the year before planting potatoes, it will fool the eelworm cysts, by its secretions, into remaining dormant during the tenure of the potato crop.

COLORADO BEETLE This is yellow with four black stripes on its back. It hibernates deep in the soil and emerges in early summer to lay its eggs on potato foliage. The grubs then eat the leaves and can easily destroy a whole crop. Potatoes

SPRAYING FOR BLIGHT
During hot and humid weather, you can protect your potato crop against blight by spraying over and under the leaves every two weeks or so with Bordeaux mixture*. If some of your crop is affected in spite of this, continue spraying the healthy plants, so that the disease is prevented from spreading.

Leaf blight   Eelworm damage

Scab

Tuber blight   Colorado beetle   Wart disease

grown on a very large scale are the most susceptible. If you do see a beetle on the leaves, squash it, and immediately notify the authorities. The grubs can be sprayed with derris, pyrethrum, or, best of all, nicotine*. Deep dig in the winter to expose the beetles to attack by birds.

The other diseases of the potato (and there are over a hundred of them) should not be a problem provided you use only clean, healthy seed and grow on heavily manured or composted ground, preferably not more than once every four years. Don't suffer any "volunteers" to exist; that is, plants that have grown up from potatoes that you have inadvertently left in the ground. They will only cause a build-up of disease.

Harvesting and storing
You can harvest any time after the plants have flowered. Dig potatoes carefully with a fork, taking great pains not to spear any, and if you do spear any, eat those first, for if you store them with the others they may cause rot. You can scrape and eat early potatoes immediately: just dig them as you want them

half an hour before a meal. Earlies have a lot of their carbohydrates in the form of sugar, because they are still busy growing and must have their energy in a still soluble form.

Main-crop potatoes, however, have ceased to grow, and the sugar has all turned into starch, which is really what potatoes are. So lift your main-crop potatoes as late as you like but before the very hard frost sets in, and preferably in dry weather. By then the tops will have wilted and dried. Leave the spuds lying on top of the ground for a day or two for the skins to "set," or harden, and the spuds to dry. Don't leave for longer, because potatoes left too long in the light will grow green and become bitter and poisonous, but two days won't hurt. If you have a lot of potatoes—say, a ton (1,000 kg) or more—you can clamp them. That is, pile them in a steep-sided heap, cover with straw or dry bracken, and then cover with soil. The colder your winters, the thicker the covering of straw you will require. In places with very cold winters you cannot clamp at all because the spuds will become frosted. Leave small chimneys of straw sticking out on top of the ridge of the clamp every two yards or so, and build straw-filled tunnels at similar intervals around the base. Beware, a thousand times beware, of rats. If they make their homes in your potato clamp, it's goodbye to your potatoes.

If you have less than a ton (1,000 kg), or live in a very cold climate, store your potatoes indoors. The requirements are: they should be in complete darkness; they should be ventilated; they should be as cold as possible but not subjected to frost, which rots them. So, a plastic or metal garbage can with a few ventilation holes knocked in the top and bottom will do, or else wooden crates, or barrels, but again, with ventilation. And in fact your potatoes will come to no harm if you just leave them in a pile in a completely dark corner of a frost-proof basement or shed. Sacks are no good, except for certain open-weave synthetic fiber sacks; burlap or canvas will rot, and so will paper.

The reason for the old-fashioned "root cellar" in the northern US is very hard winters. In most of Europe the clamp is the traditional way of storing potatoes in large quantities, and on the whole it is the method of storing I prefer.

DIGGING AND CLAMPING
Harvest your early potatoes at any time after the plants have flowered. Late potatoes can be left in until the plants have died down. Dig potatoes out carefully with a fork, making sure you don't spear any. If you do, don't store them because they will very likely cause rot. If your crop is large—say, over a ton (1,000 kg)—it can be stored in a clamp (*right*). Pile your potatoes steeply on a bed of straw, cover with more straw, and mound over with soil. Ventilation is important, so make small chimneys of straw every two yards along the top of the clamp, and insert straw tunnels at the same intervals at ground level.

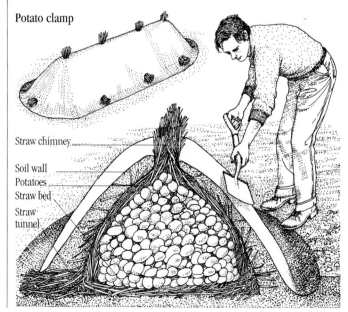

Potato clamp

Straw chimney

Soil wall
Potatoes
Straw bed
Straw tunnel

Tomatoes

Like the potato, the tomato is a native of tropical America. It is a perennial, but in temperate climates, where it is only half-hardy, it is grown as an annual. The tomato has enormous value for the self-sufficient gardener, for not only does it improve any dish to which it is added, it is also a very rich source of a whole range of vitamins and, most important, these do not seem to be damaged a great deal by cooking or canning. If you grow enough tomatoes in the summer to have them canned (or frozen) all winter, you will not suffer from vitamin deficiency.

Soil and climate
To grow tomatoes outdoors, you must have at least three-and-a-half months of warm weather with plenty of sunshine. If you don't live in this sort of climate, you must start them off indoors and plant out in the summer. If the summer turns out too cold or cloudy to bring them to ripeness, they can be ripened indoors or else made into green tomato chutney. In cool or cold climates, they grow well in greenhouses, and are far and away the most valuable greenhouse crop. But remember that, unlike cucumbers, tomatoes do not like a lot of humidity.

Tomatoes do well in any rich soil. In light soil they will give an earlier crop than they do in heavy soil. On the other hand, they grow well in heavy clay that has had several years of compost application.

Soil treatment
For each seedling, I like to dig a hole about a foot (30 cm) deep and as wide across, and fill it nearly to the top with compost, as though I were planting an apple tree. Then I fill the hole up with soil and, when the time comes, plant out in that. It is best to do this about six weeks before planting out. In fact, it is a good idea to prepare the stations at the same time as you sow the seed indoors. However you manage it, tomatoes need rich soil, plentifully endowed with rich muck or well-rotted compost. As the compost rots and settles, the ground sinks a little, which helps the tomatoes retain water.

Propagation
Except in very hot climates, sow the seed indoors in seed boxes during spring. In all but the coldest climates, an unheated greenhouse will do; a temperature of 70°F (21°C) is ideal. Sow thinly in either commercial seed-starting mix or a mix that you make yourself (see p.47). Cover the seed boxes with newspaper during the night, but in the day make sure they are in full

sunlight. Two or three weeks after sowing, prick the tiny plants out 3 inches (8 cm) apart in larger seed boxes or, better still, peat* pots. Again, use commercial potting mix or your own mixture. Don't water too much; keep the soil slightly on the dry side—just dry-to-moist. And always give them all the sun there is.

After a month, start gently hardening the plants off. Put them outside in the sun in the day but indoors at night, or else move them to cold frames and keep the covers on at night but off in the day. At the beginning of summer they should be sufficiently hardened off for planting out in their stations. If you have cloches, plant your tomatoes out two weeks earlier and keep them covered for that period.

PLANTING OUT SEEDLINGS
Avoid disturbing the soil around your tomato seedlings. Two weeks before planting out, cut squares around each plant in the seed box, so as to keep the soil intact when it comes to planting.

PINCHING OUT SIDE-SHOOTS
A straggly or untidy tomato plant may not set any fruit. With your fingers, pinch out the little shoots that emerge at the point where the leaf stalks meet the main stem.

Planting out
You must provide tomatoes with adequate vertical support, because by nature they are trailing plants. The best way is to use stakes, at least 5 feet (1.5 m) tall. Sink them about a foot (30 cm) into the earth. Position the stakes when you plant out the tomatoes, but don't damage the root clusters. Plant the tomatoes quite deeply so that the lowest leaves are just above the ground. Tomatoes tend to put out adventitious roots from their stems and this should be encouraged. If you have any long straggly plants, you can make them stronger by laying a length of the stem horizontally in the ground; the stem will send out new roots.

Spacing depends on what sort of plants you intend to grow. In cooler climates, plants should be kept small, and 2 feet (60 cm) apart in rows 3 feet (90 cm) apart is about right. In warmer climates, they can grow larger, so more space should be allowed. In hot climates you can let them sprawl, and then plants should be 4 feet (1.2 m) apart. If you use the deep-bed method (see p.44), allow 2 feet (60 cm) between plants.

A method that is worth trying in a small garden is to plant out leaving only a foot (30 cm) between rows. Then stop the plants when they have set one truss only and allow no side-shoots to develop. This sounds ruthless, but you should get more ripe tomatoes than with usual methods.

When planting out, take great care to disturb the soil around the roots as little as possible. If you are using peat* pots, just soak the plants and plant the peat pots as they are.

If you use seed boxes, cut the soil in squares around each plant down to the bottom of the tray with a knife. Do this two weeks before you plant out, and try to retain that soil intact when you plant.

RING CULTURE Ring culture is another way of growing tomato plants from seedlings. It is best practiced in the greenhouse, though it can be done outdoors. The method is worthwhile if you are short of soil or short of space, or if your soil is disease-ridden.

Two weeks before you want to plant your seedlings, stand rings of plastic 9 inches (23 cm) in diameter and 9 inches (23 cm) high on a bed of clean gravel. Fill the rings with commercial potting mix or your own mixture (*see p.47*). Two days before planting, water the gravel and the rings with water in which a complete organic compost or manure has been steeped—a thick soup, in fact, and lace it if you can with a little fish meal.

When you plant the seedlings, water the rings with ordinary water, and continue watering through the rings only for the next ten days. After that, when the roots have reached the gravel, water the gravel only, and ensure that it is permanently moist. Once a week, give the gravel a good dousing with your organic soup. Otherwise treat like ordinary tomatoes.

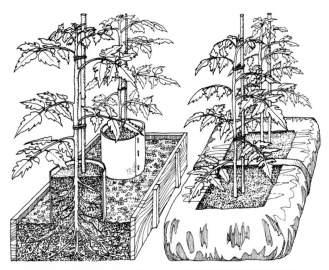

THE RING CULTURE METHOD
Stand rings of plastic on a bed of clean gravel, fill with potting mix, and plant seedlings. Feed the plants with organic compost or manure steeped in water. After ten days, water the gravel only.

PLANTING IN GROW BAGS
Plant four seedlings into a commercially prepared grow bag or in an old fertilizer bag filled with peat*. Take care with watering since the bags won't drain and the plants may become waterlogged.

PEAT BAGS This is a space-saving method that works indoors and outdoors, and is especially good for people who have just a patio or a balcony. Buy a specially prepared bag or simply fill an old fertilizer bag with peat*. Plant four seedlings in each bag and water carefully; there is no facility for drainage, so the plants can easily get waterlogged.

Care while growing

Tie the tomato plants loosely to their stakes with soft string and keep tying as they climb. Don't tie too tightly or you will cut the stems. An excellent alternative is to drop a tube of wire netting, about 15 inches (38 cm) in diameter, over each plant. The plants will climb inside the tubes.

Pinch out the little shoots that spring up at the base of each leaf stalk; otherwise you will get an untidy straggling plant that probably won't set any fruit. And don't let your plants get too high.

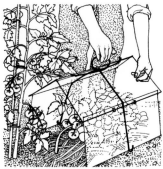

KEEPING TOMATO PLANTS LOW
Four trusses on each staked plant are enough. To stop them from growing higher, simply break off the tops above the fourth truss.

FALL RIPENING
When the nights draw in, take the plants off their stakes and lay them on straw under cloches. Tomatoes must be warm to ripen.

Tomatoes do not want too much water but they want some; if the ground dries right out, the fruit will crack. The very best thing to water the plants with is liquid manure. (Make it by half-filling a barrel or tank with farmyard muck and topping up with water.) Remember that tomatoes need warm roots, so nip the bottom leaves off and train the plants as upright as possible so that the sun can get to the soil around the roots. In fall, when the nights begin to draw in, take the plants off their stakes, lay them down horizontally on straw, and cover them with cloches. This certainly helps to ripen the fruit.

Pests and diseases

BLIGHT Outdoor tomatoes are just as susceptible to potato blight as potatoes are, so spray your tomatoes with Bordeaux mixture* (*see p.51*). Spray once every two weeks during the warm summer weather, and if it pours with rain just after you have sprayed, spray again.

CUTWORM These pests bite plants off just above the ground. Protect the plants with small collars of cardboard (*see p.98*) or sprinkle wood ash around them.

Harvesting and storing

Pick the fruit gently with the stalks on and take great care not to damage the skin. Red tomatoes must be eaten fresh, or must be canned or frozen immediately. (Tomatoes for cooking can be stored in a freezer.)

Green tomatoes, or tomatoes that are not quite ripe, can be covered with cloth or paper and kept in a cool place until they ripen. Keep them in the dark, never in the sun. A time-honored method is to lay a sheet of soft felt in the bottom of a drawer in a cool room, lay a layer of tomatoes on top, making sure none of them are touching each other, lay another piece of felt on the tomatoes, then more tomatoes, and so on. Lay the greenest at the bottom and the ripest on top. Be sure the tomatoes are all healthy or you may end up with a drawer full of mold. Green and ripe tomatoes can be stored as chutney (*see p.318*).

Peppers

Green peppers, red peppers, and chili peppers are all capsicums. In their native South America they are perennials, but we grow them, like tomatoes, as annuals.

Soil and climate
They are slightly hardier than tomatoes. You can grow them outdoors in warmish temperate climates, but they are better started off under glass, and better still if they do all their growing under glass. They need at least 65°F (19°C) when they are flowering or they won't set fruit.

Soil treatment
They prefer light soil and benefit from compost.

Propagation
You can buy seed, but I think it is much better to buy some ripe red peppers of the kind you like best, break them open, and take the seed out. Sow the seed indoors at least six weeks before the last expected frost. Sow a few seeds in each pot and when they are about 5 inches (13 cm) tall, thin to the strongest one. Plant outside about three weeks after the last expected frost (two weeks earlier if you have warmed the ground with cloches) in beds prepared as if for tomatoes (*see Tomatoes*). Like tomatoes, plant them deeply.

Care while growing
Treat just like tomatoes but give them more water while they are young. Always water the roots, never the peppers; if they get too wet, they are liable to rot. Mulch heavily.

Pests and diseases
ANTHRACNOSE As long as you plant your peppers well away from your beans, they will not suffer from anthracnose. If they do get it, they will go bad. Burn them.
CUTWORM Protect your seedlings with cardboard collars (*see p.98*) when planting out.

Harvesting and storing
Cut them off (don't break them) with an inch (2.5 cm) of stem on each fruit. If you have more than you can eat fresh, hang the vines up in a dry, windy place to dry. You may have to finish the drying process by hanging them over mild heat indoors. You can then just drape them, decoratively, in your kitchen or storeroom until you want them in winter.

Eggplants

Even the most dedicated flower gardener has to appreciate the eggplant. As well as their luscious fruit, they have luxuriant purple flowers and large velvety leaves. They are not high in nutrition, but they make up for this with their unique flavor.

Soil and climate
In frost-free areas, the eggplant plant will grow as a perennial bush, but where there is the slightest touch of frost it must be grown as a tender annual. It needs a hot summer and deep rich soil with plenty of moisture, but it does not thrive in wet weather.

Soil treatment
Dig plenty of manure or compost into your soil. Eggplants like a pH of about 6.

Propagation
Sow the seed indoors about ten weeks before you plant out. Soak the seed overnight and then plant each seed in a peat* pot filled with good potting mix. If you have no peat* pots, sow an inch (2.5 cm) apart in seed boxes filled with potting compost. When the seedlings are 2 inches (5 cm) high, plant out into even richer potting mix 4 inches (10 cm) apart in seed boxes or in a cold frame.

When your plants are about ten weeks old, and the ground outdoors is warm to the hand, plant the peat* pots out 3 feet (90 cm) apart—18 inches (45 cm) apart if you have a deep bed (*see p.44*). Take great care not to damage the roots.

Care while growing
Until the warm weather comes, keep cloches over them if you can spare them, and if you have a deep bed, use mini-greenhouses. Keep them well watered—with manure water if possible—but don't overwater.

Pests and diseases
FLEA BEETLE These pests may attack when the plants are young. The leaves are quickly eaten away if they are not checked. Use derris dust to get rid of them.
MOULD The plants may get moldy in damp climates. The answer is to reduce the humidity in the air, so that the mold dries up. If your plants suffer much, try in the future to use fungus-resistant strains.

Harvesting
Cut them off—don't pull them—as soon as they have that lovely unmistakable bloom and before they are fully grown. The plants will then continue to fruit.

Apiaceae

Carrots, parsnips, celery, celeriac, Hamburg parsley, and Florence fennel belong to the *Apiaceae* family (formerly the *Umbelliferae*). Members of this family also include several herbs such as caraway, angelica, and parsley.

Umbelliferous plants have numerous tiny flowers borne on radiating stems like umbrella ribs. They are a decorative family: the foliage of carrots is very attractive and will look good among your ornamental shrubs. Many members of the family are good to eat (beware the poisonous hemlock, though), and very many are eaten by animals. Cow parsley, for example, is well worth gathering for feeding to rabbits.

A feature that all members of the *Apiaceae* share is that their seed is very slow to germinate. So do not despair if you sow some *Apiaceae* seed and the plants take ages to show their heads. Just sow a few radish seeds along with the others; the radishes will be up in no time and will show you where the rows of your *Apiaceae* are.

The members of the *Apiaceae* family are closely related to all sorts of interesting plants, wild and cultivated, including such things as ginseng, whose ground-up roots are said to "relieve mental exhaustion," and sarsaparilla, which is used to make old-fashioned root beer.

Carrots

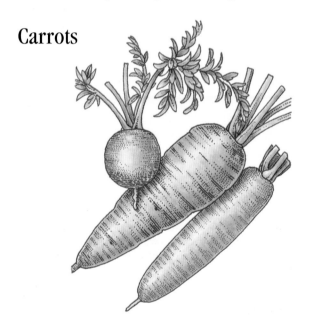

Like so many valuable food plants, the carrot is a biennial, and stores in its first year what it is going to spend in its second in the form of seed. We thwart its aims by gobbling it up in the first year before it has time to grow to maturity. Carrots have been bred to be either long and slow-maturing but heavy-cropping, or short, stubby and quick-maturing but lighter-cropping.

The most important constituent of carrots is carotene, which the human body converts to vitamin A. No other vegetable or fruit contains comparable quantities of this vitamin, which, among its other virtues, improves your eyesight; hence the parental exhortation to generations of children: "Finish up your carrots and you will be able to see in the dark."

Soil and climate
Carrots are a cold-climate crop. They can be sown very early in the spring in temperate climates, or in the fall or winter in subtropical ones. Carrots prefer to follow a crop that has been manured the previous year. A sandy loam is ideal for them. Heavy clay is not good for them, but if that is the soil you are blessed with, you can improve it enormously by copious and constant manuring or composting. Two pails of compost and two of leafmold applied to every square yard will convert even heavy clay into suitable soil for carrot-growing. They like deep soil, particularly the heavy-cropping long-rooted maincrop varieties.

Soil treatment
Do not apply fresh manure just before sowing carrots because it makes them tough, watery, and inclined to fork. If the soil is acidic, it should be limed, although carrots will flourish in a pH as low as 6. Like all root crops, they like both phosphate and potash; plenty of manure or compost should supply this, but be sure to apply manure at least six months before the carrots are planted. Rock phosphate and wood ashes are also worthwhile. The land should be dug deeply and raked down to a fine tilth.

Propagation
Draw little furrows about half an inch (1 cm) deep if you live in a moist climate but an inch (2.5 cm) deep in a drier one. Sprinkle the tiny seeds fairly thickly—four or five to an inch (2.5 cm)—as some of them don't germinate. With the deep-bed method (*see p.44*), sow 2 inches (5 cm) apart each way. Pelleted seed (seed that has been coated with fertilizer so that each seed forms a little pellet) can be used to good effect with

DREDGING CARROT SEEDS
Since carrot seeds are hardly visible, it is difficult to scatter them sparsely. Coat the seeds by shaking them up in their packet with a spoonful of slaked lime or ground limestone.

GERMINATING CARROT SEEDS
Carrot seeds need moisture if they are to germinate properly. Two days before planting, encourage them by placing them between two sheets of wet paper towel. But watch for mold.

carrots. Sow it with a precision drill, far more thickly than you think you need to, as germination is even poorer than in conventional sowing. Cover the seed lightly with fine soil or, better still, with fine dry compost. In dry weather, soak the furrows well. Don't worry if nothing happens for a bit. Carrots take a long time to come up.

Try interplanting carrots with onions row by row. This is said to deter both carrot and onion fly, for the scent of the one masks the scent of the other.

Care while growing

You can just leave early carrots as they are in the ground, which will be very overcrowded, and pull them for what gardeners call "bunching." They are tiny like this but they taste very sweet.

Main-crop carrots, which you want for the winter, you will have to thin, and here your problems start. For as soon as you bruise a few carrots, and disturb the soil around their roots, you attract the carrot fly, which is said to be able to smell a bruised carrot for up to six miles. In areas where carrot fly is very bad, it is often best to do your thinning only on a wet day, preferably in light rain. Then, after pulling the thinnings, carefully step the ground down around the remaining carrots. Thin to 1½ inches (4 cm) between plants first; later on thin to 3 inches (8 cm) apart. For a deep bed (see p.44), thin once to 2 inches (5 cm). You can eat the thinnings.

Don't hoe near carrots. It is not good to loosen the soil and even worse to cut the carrots. You can hoe between the rows, but hand-weed only in the rows. Try not to let the carrot bed dry out. If you have to water the soil, give it a very thorough soaking; you want the water to go deep down and pull the carrots downward with it. Just watering the surface is no good at all.

Pests and diseases

CARROT FLY Carrot flies lay eggs on carrots; the larvae burrow into the root and spoil the crop. The carrot fly looks much like a small housefly; still, it is not the fly itself you are likely to notice, but the leaves of your carrots turning dark red as a result of the damage to the roots. The fly can be kept away

with a dressing of soot, or you can mix an ounce (30 cc) of kerosene* in a gallon (4.5 l) of water and sprinkle that on, shaking it up well as you do so. Alternatively, mix a pint (0.6 l) of kerosene* with a bushel of sand and sprinkle that on at the base of the plants. If the carrot flies are bad, you may have to repeat the dressing every two weeks, and after every rain in the case of soot. If you have suffered from a very bad attack, dig the bed thoroughly in late fall, so that birds have a chance of getting at pupae in the soil. In an organic garden, you will have lots of beetles, and these may well eat up to half the carrot fly eggs before they hatch.

CARROT DISEASE This can be bad in inorganic gardens but is unlikely to worry the good organic gardener. Brown spots appear on the roots and ultimately tiny red spores come to the surface of the soil; these are the spores of the mycelium that causes the disease. Burn all diseased roots and sprinkle the diseased soil with two parts of sulfur mixed with one part of lime and don't plant carrots there again for at least five years.

Harvesting and storing

If you pull carrots out of the rows at random you will attract carrot fly. So when you pick early carrots for eating fresh in summer, start at one end of the row. Main-crop carrots for winter storing can be left in the ground until well into the winter. In cold climates, lift them before the ground gets too hard and store them, not letting them touch each other, and twisting off the leaves first. Pull your carrots as early as possible if you have had a bad attack of carrot fly. The emerging larvae are then unable to pupate and produce a new generation of flies. If you do leave the carrots in the ground too long in wet weather, the roots are inclined to split; make sure that when you lift the carrots, you take care of the roots. Eat any damaged in lifting; don't store them with the others. And remember that if you wash carrots before storing, they will inevitably go totally rotten.

Store in a well-ventilated, cool place; just above freezing suits them best. Do not store year after year in the same root cellar because disease will gradually build up. It is best to store them in sand or peat*. You can use a variety of containers: a garbage can with plenty of holes punched into it to let in the air; a barrel; a dark corner of a cold shed (but beware of rats and mice); or even a box sunk in the ground outdoors, covered with a lid, some straw on top of that and then some soil. If you have a very large number, you can clamp them (see *Potatoes*).

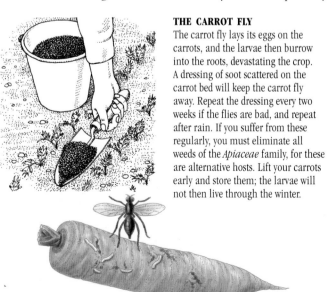

THE CARROT FLY
The carrot fly lays its eggs on the carrots, and the larvae then burrow into the roots, devastating the crop. A dressing of soot scattered on the carrot bed will keep the carrot fly away. Repeat the dressing every two weeks if the flies are bad, and repeat after rain. If you suffer from these regularly, you must eliminate all weeds of the *Apiaceae* family, for these are alternative hosts. Lift your carrots early and store them; the larvae will not then live through the winter.

STORING THE CARROT CROP
When harvesting your carrots, be careful not to damage the roots. If you do, then don't store with undamaged carrots. It is best to store in a cool but well-ventilated place. An old barrel makes a good container. Place the carrots so that they don't touch each other, and build them up in layers of sand or peat*. Make sure the barrel is ventilated—drill holes if necessary. Don't store carrots year after year in the same place because you may get a gradual accumulation of disease.

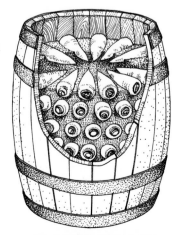

Parsnips

Parsnips are biennials like all good root crops and are even slower-growing than carrots. They are a good crop to grow in dry soil, because they are capable of forcing their food-storing taproots 2 feet (60 cm) down into the soil in their search for water.

Soil and climate
Parsnips will grow in fairly poor soil; they are so slow-growing that they do not need very rich conditions. On the other hand, in good soil they will grow better, more quickly, and produce more tender roots. And, of course, like every plant they flourish best in soil in which there is a high content of organic matter. They like soil about neutral: pH about 6.5. Very heavy soil is not good for them because it makes them fork. Stones and too much fresh manure also make them fork. A cold climate suits them best: without frost, they don't develop their full flavor.

Soil treatment
The deeper you dig, the better; for a really heavy crop dig in very well rotted manure or compost at least 18 inches (45 cm) deep—any less and your parsnips will fork.

Propagation
Traditionally, parsnip seed is the first of the year to be planted outdoors (not counting shallots, which are not a seed anyway). They were, and often are, sown in late winter—February in a temperate climate. However, in common with many other gardeners, I find it better to sow them later—well into the spring. Parsnips sown late are smaller, sweeter, and less woody, and they keep better. But, unless your garden really is an old-established organic garden in which the soil is largely humus, you should give late-sown parsnips a dressing of fish meal, bone meal, or some other organic fertilizer high in phosphate.

Again breaking with tradition, I like to sow parsnip seeds sparsely, but continuously, in drills, and thin the plants to about 10 inches (25 cm) apart when they grow up. With the parsnip seed I sow radish seed. The radishes grow much more quickly than the parsnips and show you where the rows are so that you can side-hoe (the radishes "declare themselves," as gardeners used to say). The radishes also keep the crust of the soil broken, thereby giving the parsnips a better chance, and the leaves of the radishes shelter the young parsnip shoots from the sun.

THINNING PARSNIPS
Sow parsnip seed thinly in long furrows 1 inch (2.5 cm) deep. When the plants declare themselves twenty to thirty days later, thin them to about 10 inches (25 cm) apart. Hoe frequently, and mulch if you can and provide plenty of water.

The drills should be about 1½ inches (4 cm) deep. After sowing the seed, push the soil back with your boot and walk along the row to firm it. Better still, cover the seed with fine compost and then firm it.

Care while growing
Young parsnips need plenty of moisture. Hoe from time to time, and mulch with compost if you have it.

Pests and diseases
CELERY LEAF MINER If you see tunnels mined in the leaves of your parsnips, look for the maggots, which will be living in blisters on the leaves, and squash them. To guard against this pest, spray with an ounce (30 cc) of kerosene* to a gallon (4.5 l) of water.

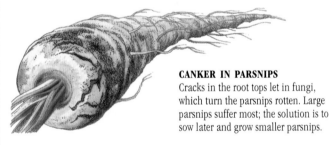

CANKER IN PARSNIPS
Cracks in the root tops let in fungi, which turn the parsnips rotten. Large parsnips suffer most; the solution is to sow later and grow smaller parsnips.

CANKER This is very common. The tops of the parsnip roots go rotten and brown. The worst attacks of canker occur in acidic soil and in soil that contains too much fresh manure. So, if your parsnips suffer badly, lime before sowing and refrain from adding fresh manure. A late crop is less likely to get canker than an early one.

RUST FUNGUS This appears as a rusty mold on the crown of parsnip plants. Mix two parts of lime with one part of sulfur* and sprinkle this on the soil around the plants. Don't grow parsnips on that bed for at least five years.

Harvesting and storing
Parsnips are completely frost-hardy but they don't like alternate freezing and thawing, so don't just leave them in the ground until you want them. Dig them up carefully and store in soil or sand in a very cold place. The very best thing is to make a pile outdoors. Do this with alternate layers of soil and parsnips—cover the whole pile with straw as an insulator, and cover this with patted earth to stop the straw from blowing away.

Celery

Celery, like parsnips, benefits from frost. In my view it should be eaten only in winter, when it is the most delicious vegetable available. During the rest of the year, it is tasteless and insipid, because it has not had the benefit of frost.

Soil and climate

Organic soil, such as peat* or soil rich in humus, is best for celery. Above all it needs constant moisture. It was originally a marsh or streamside plant, and it suffers badly if it dries out. A high water table is desirable, but if you don't have that, you need plenty of humus in the soil and you must water frequently if the weather is dry. Celery stands fairly acidic soil and does not need lime. Grow it in any climate where there is frost.

Soil treatment

I like to take out trenches about a foot (30 cm) deep and 15 inches (40 cm) wide, and dig plenty of compost or peat into the bottom. I do this in spring.

Propagation

Prepare a seed box by filling it with either a mixture of three parts sifted loam, one part of leafmold and one part of sharp sand, or with commercial potting mix. I prefer to do this in late winter but early spring is not too late. After the soil has been well soaked, sow the celery seeds sparsely and give them a light covering of soil.

Place the seed box indoors at a temperature of about 60°F (16°C) with either glass or old newspaper over the seed box. If you use glass, wipe off the underside twice a day to prevent moisture from dripping onto the seedlings. Keep the plants near the panes of the greenhouse or window so they don't get drawn sideways. Keep the soil just damp at all times; it is best to water with a fine spray, or you can stand the seed box in an inch (2.5 cm) of water and let the seedlings soak it up.

The plants will produce seed leaves before forming true leaves. As soon as the first pair of true leaves has appeared, prick out the plants into another box, which should contain three parts of loam, one part of leafmold, and half a part of rotted manure. Put the plants in carefully, 2 inches (5 cm) apart, and continue to spray them with water. Gradually harden them off by admitting more air, until late spring, when they can be put outside. Never let young celery plants dry out or your sin will be brought home to you months later when they suddenly run to seed before they are ready.

Although mature celery benefits from frost, the young plants will be damaged by it. So don't plant them out until you are sure there won't be another frost. Plant them out a foot (30 cm) apart—deep-bed method (*see p.44*) 6 inches (15 cm) apart—in the bottom of the trench you have already prepared for them.

TRENCHING FOR CELERY
Dig trenches for celery, a foot (30 cm) deep and 15 inches (38 cm) wide. Work in 3 inches (8 cm) of manure, and cover it with 3 inches (8 cm) of topsoil.

PLANTING OUT SEEDLINGS
Plant out the seedlings a foot (30 cm) apart in the prepared trenches. Water the seedlings regularly until they are established, and continue to do so if there is no rain.

EARTHING UP AND TYING
In late summer, gather up the celery leaves and stems in a bunch. Tie the tops together, pack soil as tightly as you can around the plants, and remove the ties.

EARTHING UP AGAIN
Two or three weeks after the first earthing up, repeat the process; bank up the soil around the celery plants until only the leaves are still left showing.

If you have two or more rows of celery, plant them 3½ feet (105 cm) apart, because when you come to earth them up, you will need the space. Sow lettuces, radishes, and other quick-growing catch-crops between the rows. Harvest these before you need the soil to earth up the celery. Keep them well watered, especially for the first two weeks, if there is no rain.

Care while growing

There are several ways to earth up celery. If you have no help, tie the tops of the plants together, and pack the soil around the plants as tightly as you can, but without getting too much earth inside them. Fill the trench level in this way, then remove the ties on the tops of the plants. This should be done in late summer. Two or three weeks later, earth up again, using more lime to thwart slugs, and bank the soil well up around the plants. A further earthing up may be necessary in another few weeks. If you have enough peat*, use it in the later earthings up, but lay slates or tiles on the slopes of the bank to stop it from washing or blowing away.

The purpose of all this earthing up is to keep the stalks away from light. Like potatoes, they become bitter as they turn green from exposure to light, so the higher you keep them earthed up, the more crisp white celery you will have to eat. You can wrap the celery in collars of paper or plastic sheet before it is earthed up to prevent soil from getting inside the plants, but this method attracts earthworms and slugs.

Pests and diseases

LEAF MINER This is very common. It occurs when the maggots of the celery fly begin to mine tunnels into the leaves of the celery plant. Pick off any affected leaves and burn them. To control the disease, spray liquid manure* over the plants once a week. The smell deters the flies from laying their eggs.

LEAF SPOT Also known as "celery blight," leaf spot can destroy your celery if it is not quickly checked. The disease, which is spread through the seeds, will cause small yellowish brown spots to appear on the leaves. Spray immediately with fungicide or the whole plant will become affected. And only sow seeds that have been dipped in formalin*.

DAMPING-OFF DISEASE Young celery plants will suffer damping-off if they get too much water or too little air. The main symptom is a watery soft rot. Wipe off condensation if you're growing seedlings under glass, and make sure the seedlings are properly aired.

Harvesting and storing

Pull celery whenever you want to eat it, and if you are interested in flavor, do not start eating it until there has been a frost. Thereafter try to make it last until well into the winter. It is a very good idea to protect part of a row with cloches as soon as the really heavy frosts set in. This will keep the celery good until late in the winter. (So as not to waste cloche space, plant a double row of celery in the same trench.) If you haven't got cloches, you can use straw or bracken at night, but take it off on warmer days.

SELF-BLANCHING CELERY

To my taste, self-blanching celery is not as good as celery, but it is easier to grow. You raise it from seed in the same way as celery, plant it on the flat in late spring or early summer, and it is ready to eat in late summer. It won't stand frost at all.

Celeriac

The most delicious part of a stick of celery, in my opinion, is the crunchy base—the heart, as it were, of the celery. With celeriac you grow all "heart" and no stem. The plant consists mostly of a bulbous base, or swollen stem, with only small green shoots, which you can't eat, above it. Grow it exactly as you grow celery.

Soil and climate

Celeriac needs rich and mellow soil that has been well-manured. It grows best in a cool, moist climate.

Soil treatment

The deep-bed method (*see p.44*) is ideal for celeriac, but, whether you use it or not, dig deeply and incorporate plenty of manure or compost.

Propagation

Sow indoors in late winter or outdoors in a nursery bed at the beginning of spring. Plant out in early summer.

Care while growing

Celeriac should be watered frequently and kept free from weeds. When you hoe, draw soil away from the plants. Don't earth up as you would for celery.

Pests and diseases

CELERY LEAF MINER Like celery, celeriac can be attacked by leaf miner, though usually to a lesser degree. Simply pick off affected leaves or spray the plants with liquid manure*.

Harvesting and storing

You can begin to harvest celeriac in the late fall. In a very cold climate, store celeriac in a root cellar, but if your winters are milder, leave them in the ground and harvest them as you want them.

Hamburg Parsley

Hamburg parsley or "turnip-rooted" parsley grows as a root vegetable and can therefore be stored. It is not just an herb for flavoring things, although the leaves taste very similar to ordinary parsley; it can also be eaten raw or cooked like celeriac, which it resembles.

Soil and climate
You can get a good crop of Hamburg parsley wherever ordinary parsley will grow, namely, in moderate climates. The more sun the plants get, the better.

Soil treatment
Hamburg parsley tolerates poorer soil than most root crops, but dig deeply and work in plenty of well-rotted manure.

Propagation
Like all the *Apiaceae*, the seed takes a long time to germinate. Soak the seed before planting and sow sparsely in drills either in fall or early spring. A dressing of a high-phosphate fertilizer such as fish meal or bone meal is useful.

Care while growing
When the plants come up, you should thin them out to about 4 inches (10 cm) apart, either in the rows or the deep bed (*see p.44*). Hoe the plants. They don't need to be watered much unless it is a particularly dry summer.

Pests and diseases
CANKER It is possible that the canker that can attack ordinary parsley may also attack Hamburg parsley. It gives a rusty appearance to the stems and causes the roots to decay. To prevent it, do not water too much. If you do get it, burn all your diseased plants.

Harvesting and storing
The leaves can be picked off and used as an herb, but the roots should be pulled as late as possible, because—and this is unusual—the largest roots taste the best. But don't leave the plant in the ground after the first frost. Store it in peat* or sand, in wooden crates or garbage cans in a root cellar or other similar cold storeroom.

Florence Fennel

Unlike ordinary fennel, which is used only as an herb (*see p.146*), Florence fennel can be eaten on its own because the leaf-stalks swell at the base of the leaves to form large "heads." Sliced raw, these can be added to salads. The stems can be cooked like celery, and the leaves and seeds can be used for flavoring. It is well worth growing for its unique taste, which combines the flavors of aniseed and licorice.

Soil and climate
Florence fennel will grow as a perennial only in hot climates, but it can be grown as an annual nearly anywhere. If you want really tender and delicious stems, grow it in the richest ground you have.

Soil treatment
Prepare the ground as for celery, digging deeply and making sure you incorporate a lot of manure.

Propagation
Sow seeds thinly in shallow drills, either in the late fall or during early spring.

Care while growing
Florence fennel needs very little attention. Thin to 6 inches (15 cm) apart in the rows or deep beds (*see p.44*) and water when required. It is worth earthing up the heads so that the plants retain moisture.

Pests and diseases
Florence fennel is happily disease-free, as well as also being highly resistant to pests.

Harvesting
Cut the heads when they are about 2 inches (5 cm) across. The stems above them should be harvested before they get too old and stringy and stripped of their outer skin.

Liliaceae

Onions, leeks and asparagus are all members of the *Liliaceae*, or lily family.

As I have discussed elsewhere (*see p.57*), the main subdivisions of the plants that provide us with nearly all our food are the two great classes: the monocotyledons (monocots for short) and the dicotyledons (dicots for short). Most of our vegetables are dicots. That is, they have two seed leaves—the first leaves they make—while the monocots have one. But the important difference between the two classes is nothing so trivial: it is that they have entirely different ways of growing. The dicots grow outward from the edges of their leaves. The monocot grow from the bases of their leaves, which means that they push their leaves up and out from the bottom.

The members of the lily family are monocots, as you can easily see by looking at their leaves. These don't have the network of veins that dicots have, but instead have parallel veins—each vein starting at the base of the leaf. Onions and leeks make use of this particular form of leaf growth to store nourishment in hard swollen bulbs, which are nothing more than many leaf bases compressed together to form a bulb. Asparagus is not so instantly recognizable as a monocot, but it is one nonetheless. The shoots, which are the edible part, grow from a "rhizome"—a horizontal stem that remains underground. The attractive, fernlike branches that sprout as the shoots grow taller are like leaves and these grow up from their bases like the leaves of the other monocots. The rhizome takes nourishment from the leaves in one year and uses it to produce the next year's shoots.

Humans, and other sapient animals, have always made use of the way plants store up in their first year's growth what they are going to use for flowering and fruiting in their second, and, although we don't eat lily bulbs, we do eat onions, leeks, and asparagus.

Onions

COMMON ONIONS

With careful growing, harvesting, and storing, there should be no part of the year in which your kitchen lacks that most indispensable ingredient, the onion. But you may well feel confused by the amount of conflicting advice that is available. Onions have been grown for centuries, and it sometimes seems as if each grower has his own special technique. In fact, the right timing and method depend largely on where you live.

Soil and climate

Onions need good rich soil. Sandy loam, peat*, and silt are all fine, but onions don't like clay, sand, or gravel. They grow successfully in widely different climates, although they prefer cool weather while they go about developing their leaves, followed by very much hotter weather during the period when they make their bulbs.

Soil treatment

Onions have very shallow roots and grow quickly, so they need plenty of nourishment in the top 4 inches (10 cm) of soil. Muck the onion bed well the previous fall with well-rotted manure or, even better, with a large amount of thoroughly rotted compost. They like plenty of potash and phosphate but not too much nitrogen. It is useful to add any of the following to your soil: wood ash, ground rock phosphate, soot, seaweed meal, a sprinkling of salt. The soil should have a pH of 6. If it is lower, then add lime.

Before planting out, firm the ground by treading or rolling—preferably both. And the soil must be dry, whether you are sowing seed or transplanting.

Propagation

If your neighbor is a successful onion-grower, it's a good idea to ask him for advice. There are four possibilities.

LATE SUMMER SOWING The idea of this is to get the onions to form bulbs by the early spring, before hotter weather causes them to bolt, and then allow them to mature through the summer. Sow the seed thinly in shallow drills, cover with half an inch (1.5 cm) of compost, and firm the ground. If the winter is particularly hard, put cloches out during the worst of it. In the spring, thin out the onions to about 6 inches (15 cm) apart. The thinnings can be used in salad.

WINTER SOWING In very frosty areas, it is best to sow onion seeds indoors in midwinter, for planting out in the spring as soon as the ground is dry enough. Sow seed thinly in seed boxes filled with either a commercial potting mix or a mixture of three parts sifted loam, one part leafmold, one part fine compost, and a sprinkling of sand. Keep moist but not wet, and cover with glass or paper. When the seedlings show, remove the covering and keep the seed box at about 65°F (19°C) near a window. When the second leaf is about half an inch (1.5 cm) long, prick the seedlings out into another box so that each plant is 2 inches (5 cm) away from the next. Use the same soil mix for the pricking-out box, but add one part of well-rotted manure. Harden the plants off gradually until they are in the open air, in a sheltered place, by the last frost. Plant the seedlings out in the spring. It is best to leave their permanent bed rough until the last moment so the soil can dry out. Before planting, rake it down as fine as powder and step it down firmly.

SPRING SOWING This is only good where there are cool, damp summers, and you won't be able to store the bulbs. Sow out of doors as you would onions sown in late summer and thin them out to 4 inches (10 cm) apart when they are big enough for the thinnings to be used as salad onions.

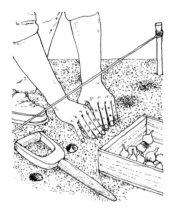

PLANTING ONION SETS
To grow onions from sets, it is essential to press the soil very firmly around each set. Make holes 6 inches (15 cm) apart; press the sets into the holes. Contrary to the usual advice (which is to leave the tops just showing), I suggest that you bury the sets completely, so that they are out of the reach of birds.

ONION SETS If you prefer them to seed, onion sets grow best in temperate climates where they should be planted in the spring. Make dibber holes every 6 inches (15 cm)—deep-bed method, 4 inches (10 cm)—along a line and push the sets into them, pressing down the soil around each set to hold it firm. I bury the sets completely—so that the topknot is just below the surface where the birds can't pull it out.

Care while growing
The most important thing is to keep your onions well weeded. In their later stages, they benefit from a mulch and this can be done with uprooted weeds. If your onions flower, pinch out the stems while they are still small.

PICKING OUT FLOWER STEMS
If necessary, pinch out the flower stems while they are still quite small. If you don't do this, the plants will "bolt," that is to say, they will produce flower heads. These in turn prevent the bulbs from forming properly. When you are picking out the flower stems, take care not to loosen the bulbs.

Pests and diseases
ONION FLY The maggots of the onion fly are one of the nastiest pests we have to suffer, as they can stop onions from growing altogether. The maggots eat into the bulbs of seedlings. Spring-sown onions are the worst hit, but onions grown from sets aren't likely to be affected. To deter onion flies and their maggots, dust your rows of onions with flowers of sulfur* or soot, or sprinkle with an ounce of kerosene* to a gallon of water. Dust regularly, particularly when you thin the plants.

DOWNY MILDEW This occurs particularly during wet seasons, and causes grayish or purple streaks on leaves. If you find it, dust with Bordeaux powder*.

EELWORM These microscopic worms will cause the tops of your onions to wilt. Burn all affected plants and don't grow onions or allow chickweed, which also harbors them, to grow on that land for six years.

NECK ROT This disease attacks onions in storage. A gray mold forms on the onion skins and later the centers turn brown. Prevent it by drying your onions off well after harvesting and storing in a cool airy place.

ONION SMUT Onion smut shows as black blisters on stems and bulbs. If you do get it in your garden, water the rows with a solution made from a pint (0.5 l) of formalin* and four gallons (18 l) of water when you sow. However, you are unlikely to get onion smut.

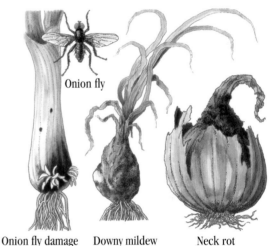

Onion fly

Onion fly damage   Downy mildew   Neck rot

Harvesting and storing
It is well worth bending over the tops of your onions when they will grow no more. This will start them ripening. In a hot, dry fall, ease the onions out of the ground and leave them a week or two in the sun to dry. But don't damage the skin or you'll let in neck rot. In wet places, lay the onions on wire netting after harvesting in order to keep them off the ground. But put them under cover if it's rainy. It is vital to dry onions well. When they have dried, the best thing to do is string them. Otherwise, put them in layers in some cool, airy place. They must not suffer severe frost, but it is better for them to be cool than hot. If you hang a string by your stove, use them fast before they rot.

BENDING THE TOPS
When the tips of the leaves start turning yellow, bend over and break the necks of the onions. This starts the ripening process. At the same time, loosen the onions with a fork to start them drying, but take care not to damage the skins. A few days later, ease them out of the ground and leave them in the sun to finish drying out.

It is vital to dry onions well. When they have dried, the best thing to do is string them. Otherwise, put them in layers in some cool, airy place. They must not suffer severe frost, but it is better for them to be cool than hot. If you hang a string by your stove, use them fast before they rot.

STRINGING ONIONS

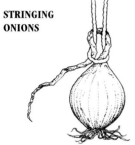

1 Knot together the ends of a 3- foot (90-cm) length of string and hang the loop from a hook. Weave the first onion through the loop.

2 Use the leaves of the second onion to weave in and out of the string. The weaving must be tight and the second onion should finally rest on the first.

3 One by one, add onions to the original two, weaving first from the left, then from the right. As the bunch grows, check to make sure it is well balanced. When you finish, hang up the string in a cool, dry, airy place and the onions should keep until early summer. Remember that all onions for stringing need long, dry leaves.

SPRING ONIONS
To fill the gap after the last of your stored onions have gone rotten—if you haven't planted spring onions specially—buy bunches of green onions and plant them out 3 inches (8 cm) apart. They will quickly produce small bulbs. Alternatively, sow any onion seed, or the special green onion varieties in late summer, and pull them in the spring. But, of course, if you have sown onions outdoors in late summer, you will have spring onions anyway as a result of thinning them.

PICKLING ONIONS
Pickling onions are basically ordinary onions grown close together and in poor soil so that they stay small and mature early. Sow the onion seed thinly in the spring. Don't thin them. Pull them when the tops wither.

SHALLOTS
In England, it is traditional to plant shallots on the shortest day and to pull them on the longest, but they will grow if you plant them any time before early spring. Prepare the ground in the same way as for onions, and plant the shallots as you would onion sets, about 6 inches (15 cm) apart. When you harvest, hang them in a string bag to store.

Leeks

Cawl, the great soup that is the Welsh national dish, has leeks for its heart and soul—and not for nothing have the Welsh made this their national emblem. If you wish to grow only one vegetable of the *Liliaceae* family, begin with the leek. It will not let you down.

During the dreary hungry gap when all else fails, which stretches from late winter through to the middle of spring, the stalwart leek is there to relieve you from a diet of salted this and frozen that.

Soil and climate
Leeks like rich loam, but they can, and often do, put up with practically anything. Still, for leeks that you can be proud of, give them plenty of manure and plenty of compost. They need moist but well-drained soil, and they like a high pH—between 6 and 8. They are temperate climate plants but will grow in any climate except a tropical one. In my view, though, leeks grown in particularly dry weather don't seem to have the flavor of those grown under cloudy skies.

Soil treatment
For really fine leeks, treat your soil as you would for onions (*see Onions*). It is common to follow early potatoes with leeks—forming a part of the legume break in our recommended rotation (although they are not of course legumes). In this case, the heavy manuring the potatoes have had will be perfect, though the leeks will probably want some lime.

However, I generally plant leeks with the brassicas because they are then sharing the only bed that does not need digging up until late the following spring. While leeks are very closely related to onions, they do not fit easily into the onion bed, for the onions are strung and hung up in a cool shed before we even start to eat the leeks.

In hard ground, trench for leeks, digging one spit deep and mixing in plenty of compost or well-rotted manure.

Propagation
In very cold climates, sow seed indoors in late winter and keep at about 60°F (16° C). For summer leeks you should do this anyway, but I think it is a pity to eat leeks in the summer— "the fruits of the earth in their season" is what suited Adam

and Eve before they tasted of the wrong fruit—and it is nice to come to leeks around Christmas with an unjaded palate. For winter leeks, in all but the coldest climates sow fairly thickly along the drills in the brassica seed-bed in early spring. Do not throw the leftover seeds away after sowing; each quarter-ounce (7 g) holds about a thousand seeds, and they keep for around four years. Plant out in the garden when they are 4 inches (10 cm) high.

It is common advice to snip an inch off the tops of the plants and at the same time snip the roots to about half their length. Then simply drop each plant into a hole made with a dibber and pour a little water in. This works perfectly well but, since I prefer not to mutilate plants more than I have to, I plant them as I do cabbages. Simply make a hole with your dibber, pour a little water in, and push the unmutilated leek down into the mud. I suggest you try half a row each way and see which grows the best. Plant them 6 inches (15 cm) apart—deep-bed method 4 inches (10 cm) (*see p.44*)—in rows wide enough to work between—say 16 inches (40 cm).

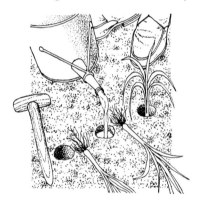

PLANTING LEEKS
Using a long dibber, make holes 8 inches (20 cm) deep and 6 inches (15 cm) apart, in rows wide enough apart to allow space for maneuvering—say, 16 inches (40 cm). Pour a little water into each hole, and push the leeks down into the mud, roots first. To snip an inch off the top and the longer roots beforehand is a matter of personal preference.

Care while growing
Never let leeks go short of water. Hoe them and mulch if you can. Earth them up every now and then as they grow, in order to blanch them.

Pests and diseases
Leeks are said to suffer from all the same pests and diseases as onions, but I have never known a leek to suffer from anything—except somebody digging it out of the ground and eating it and that, surely, is a glorious death.

Harvesting and storing
When digging up leeks, avoid cutting off too much of the foliage because the leeks' prime food value consists of the vitamin A to be found in the leaves. So, as well as eating the stems, try and make use of the leaves, in soups and so on: they taste very savory.

In freezing climates, leeks can be dug up before the first severe frost and heeled into soil in a basement. In less severe climates they should be earthed up nearly to the tops of the plants. In temperate climates, leave them in the ground if possible until at least Christmas, and spare them even after that until late winter when the Brussels sprouts begin to look a sorry sight and you are tired of broccoli and kale. Then dig them up as you need them. However, if you wish to clear the bed for something else, it is perfectly all right to dig all your leeks up and heel them into the ground in a short row out of the way and near the kitchen.

Asparagus

If you ignore the common associations with luxury and decadence, then asparagus is in fact an excellent vegetable to grow, for it gives you a fresh bite of green stuff in the spring. It can be cut and cut again for a period of six to eight weeks, and it is impossible to conceive of anyone ever getting tired of so exquisite a taste. On the other hand, an asparagus bed takes up a lot of space, especially since you have to wait for three years from the time of sowing for your first taste.

Soil and climate
Asparagus came from the seaside and can put up with salt. It likes a mild, moist summer and a cold enough winter to make it go to sleep for half the year. Only a very severe frost will harm it after it has died down for the winter, but it is a good idea to cover the bed with straw if the winter is frosty.

The plant flourishes in a light, well-drained loam and it will grow well in sandy land if it has been well-mucked and composted and is not allowed to dry out. The soil should have a pH of 6.5, which may mean you have to add lime. It is possible to artificially create soil that is suited to asparagus—heavy clay, for instance, can be properly modified by adding plenty of compost and sand—and it is well worth doing this if you can, as asparagus is a perennial that will go on feeding you for years.

Soil treatment
The bed must be entirely free from perennial weeds, because once the roots of these are thoroughly intertwined with the roots of the asparagus, which spread out as far as 5 feet (1.5 m) you will never get them free. So the fall before you intend to plant, fork the planned bed over and over again and remove every last inch of couch grass root, ground elder, or convolvulus.

Then, if your land needs it, fork in lime and also if necessary rock phosphate or wood ash or some other form of potash, but if you have enough compost you needn't bother with this. Half a pound (200 g) of fish meal and half a pound (200 g) of ash per square yard is good insurance.

The old-fashioned method of preparing the bed, and one that I think can't be beaten, was to take out a trench 5 feet (1.5 m) wide and one foot (30 cm) deep, placing the topsoil to one side separately. Put 6 inches (15 cm) of good stable manure in the trench, 6 inches (15 cm) of rotted sod on top of this, and another few inches of well-rotted manure or compost. Replace the topsoil on this and you will have a bed for three rows of plants. An alternative is just to dig plenty of manure or compost into the soil in the fall and plant in that, in either single rows or rows about 4½ feet (1.4 m) apart.

Propagation

Asparagus can be grown from seed. Collect your own seed by hanging up some of the female ferns when they are quite ripe, letting them dry, and then rubbing the seed out with your fingers. But if you grow them from seed you won't get any asparagus to eat for three years. If you can't wait that long, buy two- or three-year-old crowns from a nursery. Even one-year-old crowns save you some waiting time, they are cheaper than older plants and transplant more easily.

If you are sowing seed, do it either indoors in seed boxes or outdoors in a seed-bed, sowing in early spring and later thinning to 3 inches (8 cm) apart.

Whichever method you choose, when the plants are ready for their final bedding out, take out a trench or trenches 9 inches (25 cm) deep and a foot (30 cm) wide. Make a cushion of fine soil in the bottom, slightly convex in section, and lay the plants 2 feet (60 cm) apart in the rows—deep-bed method a foot (30 cm) apart (*see p.44*). Never let asparagus crowns dry out. If you buy crowns from a nursery, keep them moist until you put them in the ground, then give them a good soaking. Cover immediately with fine soil and compost.

Care while growing

Asparagus benefits enormously from heavy mulching. I like to mulch with seaweed, but otherwise mulch with any organic material that is nonacidic—don't, for instance, use pine needles or oak leafmold unless you mix thoroughly with lime first. If you use sawdust or anything very hard to break down, put on some high-nitrogen material, like blood meal. Don't hoe too deeply or you'll damage the asparagus roots. Your mulch is the best weed suppressor.

Many people cut the ferns down in fall as soon as they turn yellow, but I prefer to leave them to die down naturally and return their goodness to the plants.

Pests and diseases

ASPARAGUS BEETLE Use your fingers to pick off any beetles that appear on the asparagus shoots, and kill them. Do it early in the morning when the beetles can't fly. Otherwise dust with derris powder when the dew is on them.

ASPARAGUS RUST If you live in a very humid area, your asparagus may be affected by this fungus, so plant a rust-free variety. If you still get it, spray with Bordeaux mixture*.

Harvesting and storing

Don't touch the plants for three years if you grew them from seed, or for two years if they grew from roots. Then cut the shoots before they begin to open as you want them. Cut for six weeks after they begin to shoot the first year, and thereafter for two months. Midsummer day is the last day you should let yourself cut asparagus. From a five-year-old bed sporting two healthy plants, you will probably find that you can cut enough asparagus for one person to have one helping a week throughout the cutting season.

Reckon on ten years as the lifetime of a bed, and plant again in time to avoid a dearth after that. A good tip, when you scrap an old bed, is to take the plants out carefully at the end of fall and plant them on a hot-bed. You'll benefit by getting asparagus a month earlier than usual.

Asparagus can be canned or frozen (*see pp.208 and 209*). My personal prejudice is against doing either because the fierce pleasure of eating fresh asparagus in the spring—surely one of the heights of gastronomic experience—is lost if the palate is jaded by having munched away at canned or frozen stuff the rest of the year.

TRENCHING FOR ASPARAGUS
Dig a trench 9 inches (25 cm) deep and a foot (30 cm) wide. Leave the bottom slightly convex, so that it will hold water, and cover it with a layer of fine soil.

PLANTING THE CROWNS
Set out the asparagus plants on the layer of fine soil, 2 feet (60 cm) apart. Lay them with the roots spread out carefully so they can absorb all available moisture.

MULCHING THE PLANTS
Seaweed or fish meal is ideal for heavy mulching; otherwise use any nonacidic organic material. When the ferns turn yellow in fall, let them die naturally.

HARVESTING THE CROP
Three years from sowing or two from planting is the time to harvest your asparagus. Cut the shoots for not more than six weeks the first year, and two months subsequently.

Chenopodiaceae

Beets, spinach, seakale beet or Swiss chard, and spinach beet are the edible members of the *Chenopodiaceae* family. This very distinctive family originally came from the seashore, and its members share with the cabbage tribe the characteristic that their leaves have a tough, cutinous surface that is designed to limit transpiration (the escape of water from the plant) and thus preserve the moisture that the plants win so precariously from their salty surroundings. Seashore plants share with desert plants the need to conserve moisture, for their salty environment tends to draw it out of them by osmosis.

The beet family also has the peculiarity of producing its seed in little fruits that remain intact until they germinate in the ground. What we plant as the "seed" of beet and spinach is in fact a small fruit containing four or five seeds, each of which grows into a plant. Thus you find that when you plant these fruits, you get plants coming up in clusters. The clusters should be thinned to leave one plant from each for the best beet or spinach.

The family includes sugar beet, which is grown for sugar, of course (the roots can be up to 21 percent sugar), and mangolds, or "cattle-beets," which are grown specifically for feeding to cattle and other stock. The beet family is characterized by the fact that the swollen roots that we grow them for display rings when you cut them across. These rings are alternately storage tissue and conveying tissue. It is the storage tissue that contains the nutrients that the beet stores up in its first summer, so that it can leap ahead quickly in its second summer and produce seed before it dies. The conveying tissue transfers the nutrients from the roots to the rest of the plant.

Beets and spinach can send their roots down 10 feet (3 m) or more into the soil. They also occupy the soil very fully, filling it with a mass of fibrous rootlets. This has a benign effect, breaking up the soil and loosening it, so that when the roots rot, they leave passages for water and air far down into the subsoil.

It is possible now to get fragmented seed of the *Chenopodiaceae*—where the fruitlets have been broken—or to get pelleted seed. Each of these makes it possible to sow singly, either by hand or with a precision drill, which saves thinning later. But the expense is really only justified if you are growing on a market-garden scale.

Beets

The western culinary imagination never seems to get much beyond boiling beets for hours and then soaking them in vinegar. But we have only to look to Russia and to the delicious borscht to see just what can be done with this sadly underused vegetable.

Soil and climate
Beets are really a cold-climate crop; in hot countries, they must be grown in the winter, early spring, or fall. Beets like well-drained soil, with plenty of humus, but not fresh manure. They won't grow at all if the ground is too acidic, and need a pH of about 6.5.

Soil treatment
In my suggested four-course rotation (*see p.181*), beets should come in the root break. The land should by then have been heavily manured three years before for the potatoes, limed two years before for the *Fabaceae*, and probably well-mulched with compost one year before for the brassicas. The soil should be well-dug and without too many stones.

Propagation
The main crop of beets for storing should be sown about three weeks before the date of your usual last frost. But you can go on sowing successively until midsummer. It's worth soaking the seed for a day or two before sowing. Sow the seed thinly three-quarters of an inch (2 cm) deep in drills a foot (30 cm) apart. When the plants appear, first single each cluster, then thin out to 3 inches (8 cm) apart for small beets and 9 inches (25 cm) apart for large beets for winter storing—deep-bed method (*see p.44*), 4 inches apart (10 cm). You can eat the baby thinnings.

Care while growing
Hoe several times to suppress weeds until the shiny leaves of the beet start doing the work themselves. Beets grown in dry conditions become hard and woody and they can often bolt. Mulching and watering should prevent this.

Pests and diseases
LEAF MINER The larvae of the beet fly will bore through the leaves. Pull off the affected leaves and burn them.
BEET BEETLE Beets may become infested with tiny black beetles. Water the plants with nicotine* water.

Harvesting and storing
The tops of beets can be eaten as well as the roots, but if you're going to store beets, wring the tops off—don't cut them since it makes them bleed. And avoid bruising.

By far the best way to store beets is to lay them gently in moist sand without allowing them to touch each other. If you lay them in the open, they will shrivel up.

Spinach

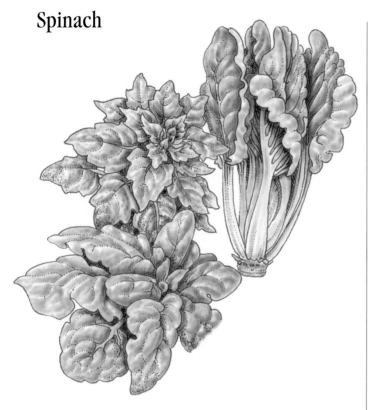

Spinach in reasonable quantities is good for you, but if Popeye had eaten a quarter of the spinach we saw him eat in the cartoons, he would have died of oxalic acid poisoning. If you like spinach, you can have it year-round with careful planning. In hot climates or even in more temperate ones, New Zealand spinach (which belongs to the *Tetragoniaceae* family) can be grown in the summer.

Soil and climate
High temperatures during the first couple of months of its growth will cause spinach to bolt to seed, so it is really a winter crop in hot climates. It likes good rich loam, and should be kept damp, but it will grow in most soils if there is enough organic matter present. It isn't a good idea to plant in soil where fresh manure has recently been applied.

Soil treatment
Spinach will go in odd corners as a catch crop, but it doesn't like acidic soil, so lime if necessary to bring the pH to between 6 and 6.5. If the soil is over 6.7, spinach will be one of the first plants to show manganese deficiency, since manganese gets locked up by too much lime. The ground should be well dug; alternatively, use a good layer of compost.

Propagation
In cool climates, the prickly seeded variety of spinach is best in the winter and the smooth-seeded variety in summer. In hot climates the smooth-seeded variety should be planted in winter. Even in pretty cold climates you can sow smooth-seeded spinach in winter (though not, of course, where the ground is frozen) and successively thereafter—say, once a month—until late summer. In wet winters it is a good idea to

sow spinach on raised ridges for better drainage. In spring and summer, sow on the flat. Sow three-quarters of an inch (2 cm) deep and, when the plants declare themselves, thin to 4 inches (10 cm) in rows a foot (30 cm) apart. Allow 3 inches (8 cm) in both directions between thinned plants in the deep bed (*see p.44*), and take care not to step on the bed when thinning.

Care while growing
Hoe and mulch if you can to keep down weeds. Water only if the weather is very dry; if the soil is allowed to dry out, the plants will bolt.

Pests and diseases
MOLD Spinach is virtually free from pests and diseases in good organic gardens, but in muggy, damp weather it can get moldy. This mold manifests itself as yellow patches on the leaves and gray mold on their undersides. If it appears, the best thing to do is scrap it and plant some more. If you plant some every month (a short row, of course), you won't have to go long without it. If it bolts, then the only place for it is the compost pile.

Harvesting
Simply pluck the leaves from your spinach as you need them. In fact, if you want the plant to go on bearing, you should pluck the outer leaves fairly often. Spinach tastes best if you simply rinse it quickly and put it, still wet, straight into a pan with a close-fitting lid. Don't add any more water; just leave it to simmer for five minutes or so.

HARVESTING SPINACH
You need a lot of spinach before you have enough for one helping. The secret is to have sown enough plants: as long as you spread the plucking over several plants, the more often you pluck the leaves, the better. Pick young leaves from the outside, taking care not to denude any one plant.

NEW ZEALAND SPINACH
New Zealand spinach is not in fact a member of the *Chenopodiaceae* family but it is similar enough to warrant talking about here. New Zealand spinach doesn't have the high oxalic content of true spinach, so its nutritional value is more available. It is less frost-hardy than true spinach and it should be grown in the summer. In very hot climates it will stand up to heat far better than ordinary spinach, but it does need protection from the sun.

Don't sow until all danger of frost is past. Grow New Zealand spinach in rows 4 feet (1.2 m) apart in good soil, or closer together in poor soil. When sown directly into a deep bed, it will grow particularly well. Soak the seeds in water for twenty-four hours before sowing; otherwise their hard cases make them slow to germinate. Plant three seeds to each station and later pull out the two weaker plants. Otherwise treat New Zealand spinach just as you would treat true spinach.

Swiss Chard

Swiss chard or seakale beet is just a beetless beet, as it were: it's a beet that puts down deep narrow roots instead of making one swollen root. It is an excellent crop for your garden, since it sends its tough roots 3 feet (90 cm) down into the subsoil and draws up what is good down there. Both the leaves and the midribs of the leaves can be eaten; you should cut the midribs up before cooking them, and they need cooking longer than the leaves.

Soil and climate
Swiss chard will grow in most climates except the very hottest and in any soil that is not waterlogged.

Soil treatment
Swiss chard, like the other beet crops, needs a pH of about 6.5, so lime if necessary. A small amount of well-rotted compost or manure is a good idea.

Propagation
Soak the seed as you would beet seed (see Beets). Sow seeds an inch (2.5 cm) deep and 3 inches (8 cm) apart—deep-bed method (see p.44) also 3 inches (8 cm) apart. The plants need room, so make the rows 18 inches (45 cm) apart. The seed should be sown two or three weeks before the last expected frost, though in milder climates you can sow in late summer for harvesting and eating in winter and spring.

Care while growing
Swiss chard needs little attention, though it will probably be worthwhile to mulch it.

Pests and diseases
Swiss chard is hardy and resistant to pests and diseases.

Harvesting
When the leaves are 7 inches (18 cm) long, start breaking the outer ones off and eating them. As the leaves get bigger, tear the thin leaf off the midribs.

RUBY CHARD
Ruby chard is exactly like Swiss chard except that its leaves and stems are deep red in color. It is said to thrive in heavy soils better than its rivals.

Spinach Beet

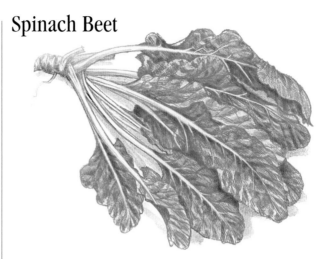

Spinach beet is a beetless beet, meaning that it does not make a swollen root as beets do. It is also known as "perpetual spinach" because you can get a year's supply of leaves from only two sowings, instead of having to sow successively through the year, as with spinach. You can eat the leaves and the plant will go on to produce more. Spinach beet is hardier than spinach; it is unlikely to bolt in summer, yet can withstand frost. It tastes similar to spinach, but contains less oxalic acid.

Soil and climate
A cool moist climate is best for spinach beet, and it likes good deep soil. It grows very well, like the rest of the deep-rooting beet family, in deep beds (see p.44).

Soil treatment
Dig deeply and add as much compost or manure as you can spare. You don't have to worry about forking roots with spinach beet, so there is no danger of adding too much fresh manure as there is with many root crops.

Propagation
If you sow in spring and again in midsummer, you can have leaves to eat throughout the year. Sow seeds an inch (2.5 cm) apart in rows 18 inches (45 cm) apart. When the seedlings are well established, thin to leave 6 inches (15 cm) between plants. If you have a deep bed (see p.44), allow 6 inches (15 cm) between plants in all directions.

Care while growing
Keep the ground clear of weeds and pick off any flower stems that appear. Your crop will benefit from mulching.

Pests and diseases
Spinach beet is not greatly affected by pests or diseases, but watch out for slugs (see p.54) in fall.

Harvesting
Pull the leaves off the plants carefully by twisting them downward. Pick from the outside, leaving newer, younger leaves to go on growing. Never denude a plant altogether. Don't allow any leaves to become large and old, for this will stop the plant from producing more. If they grow too old for eating, pull them off and put them on the compost pile.

Cucurbitaceae

Cucumbers, squashes, zucchini, pumpkins, and melons belong to the *Cucurbitaceae*, a family that has evolved to live in extreme climatic conditions.

Nothing is more fascinating in working with nature than observing how plants have evolved to fill nooks and crannies left in the complex ecosystem of the larger and grander species. Thus in the huge tropical rain forests, where mighty trees strive against each other to reach the light, you will find soft, apparently defenseless fast-growing creepers using their mighty rivals to support themselves, making use of speed in growing and flexibility of habit to carry on a kind of guerrilla existence down below.

Other members of the *Cucurbitaceae* are adapted to deserts, and these again make use of speed of growth, sacrificing strength and rigidity and all sorts of other virtues to this end. They shoot away quickly from a seed that has been lying dormant perhaps for

years and store away the water of a flash rainstorm in quick-growing fruit. The Tsava melons of the Kalahari and Namib deserts of Africa are prime examples of this. As soon as it rains, these spring up all over the formerly waterless and barren deserts, and the San people, and other desert dwellers, are able to leave the water holes to which they have been confined and roam where they will—secure in the knowledge that they will find water wherever they go, in the Tsava that lie all around. Meanwhile, the Tsava benefit from their depredations, for as animals and men eat their fruit and suck in their water, the seeds get dispersed, to lie dormant perhaps for years again until the next rain.

Melons and cucumbers seem to be made to comfort people in hot dry climates—in Persia (present-day Iran), a dish of sliced cucumber in vinegar is often offered to the thirsty guest.

Cucumbers

In temperate climates, nearly all the cucumbers that have smooth edible skins can only be grown in greenhouses (*see p.80*). There is one smooth-skinned strain*, optimistically called "Burpless," that is hardy and can be grown outdoors, but otherwise the methods described on this page and the next apply only to ridge cucumbers. Ridge, or outdoor, cucumbers are not fully hardy, but can be grown with success in temperate regions as long as all risk of frost is avoided. They are much easier to grow than frame cucumbers, and very prolific in favorable conditions.

Soil and climate
Cucumbers like soil that is nearly all compost or well-rotted manure. They will not stand wet feet, although they like plenty of moisture all through their growing period. Ridge or outdoor cucumbers can be grown in most parts of Europe and North America: they are fast-growing and complete their life during the heat of the summer. Although they are easily injured by frost, they mature fast enough to be unaffected by winter weather.

Soil treatment
The soil needs deep digging to ensure adequate drainage, and a large quantity of ripe manure or compost. Half manure and

half soil is ideal. Dig it in a foot (30 cm) down in each station. Like tomatoes, cucumbers must have full exposure to the sun. The two crops like much the same soil, so it is a good idea to alternate cucumbers with tomatoes in a sunny bed up against a south wall or fence. Remember that cucumbers are good climbers, and take up far less room and do better if they are allowed to climb. If you can train them up a fence or a trellis on a wall, so much the better.

Propagation
You can sow cucumber seeds outdoors in their stations during the first week of May, with glass jars inverted over them for protection. Remove the jars when the plants get too big for them. Cloches are even more useful, because they can be left on longer and can be improvised with transparent plastic and wire.

SOWING SEED INDOORS
To get early cucumbers, start them off indoors in peat* pots or soil blocks. Sow two seeds on edge in each pot or block. Do not press the soil down; cucumbers are that rare thing, a vegetable that dislikes firm soil. Water them and keep them warm, but out of direct sunlight. You can then transplant them, at about the time of the last expected hard frost, without disturbing the roots. Sow more seed outdoors at the same time.

The alternative is to start your cucumbers indoors in peat* pots or soil blocks. Then plant them out, long after the last possible frost, in their prepared stations. If your land is heavy and wet, it is best to plant them on ridges or heaps, because if you plant them on the flat in badly drained land, they are likely to die from damping off.

If you are not letting them climb, they can do with 6 feet (1.8 m) of space all around them; 4 feet (1.2 m) is the absolute minimum. If you are planting them in a deep bed (*see p.44*), allow 2 feet (60 cm) each way, or else stagger them among other crops. I sometimes plant mine right on top of an old compost pile. They love it. When you plant them out, sow some more seed outdoors as well—this will give you a second crop just when your first is running out.

Care while growing
Cucumbers must have water all the time: many people sink a flowerpot into the ground near each plant and pour water straight into this so that the water quickly reaches the roots. Keep them well weeded.

TRAINING CUCUMBERS
Cucumbers thrive if encouraged to climb. Train them up a fence or trellis (*left*); when they reach the top, pinch out each growing point (*below*).

When they have six or seven true leaves—not seed leaves—it is best to pinch out the growing points to make them branch and straggle. Do not remove the male flowers from ridge cucumbers. Do this only with smooth-skinned cucumbers— the ones that you can only grow in the greenhouse. Keep the fruit off the ground by placing a bit of slate, plastic sheet, tile, or glass under each one.

Pests and diseases
MILDEW OR BLIGHT This can develop in very hot and muggy conditions. It produces white powdery patches on leaves and stems. Avoid by planting resistant varieties.
CUCUMBER BEETLE These are yellow and black striped beetles. The adults attack the leaves, and the larvae the stems and roots. Repel them with nicotine spray*.
CUCUMBER MOSAIC VIRUS Leaves become mottled and shriveled. Pull and burn affected plants immediately.

Harvesting
Pick and eat your cucumbers as soon as they are ready. Above all, don't leave any to grow old on the vines.

PICKLING CUCUMBERS
Treat pickles in exactly the same way as ridge cucumbers. They don't need quite as much space between plants as cucumbers do; 2 feet (60 cm) is about right. Pick them when they are only 2 inches (5 cm) long.

Pumpkins

Pumpkins have much in common with squashes, but the two can be distinguished botanically: pumpkins have soft rinds and hard stalks, squashes hard rinds and soft stalks.

Soil and climate
Pumpkins like humus if they can get it, but they will grow on unmanured ground as long as it is well drained. They need plenty of water.

Propagation
You can sow pumpkin seed outdoors, under polythene cloches or inverted jelly jars in spring, or else without protection in early summer. You can also sow seed indoors in peat* pots or seed boxes shortly before the last frost, and plant the seedlings out at the start of the hot weather. Allow 4 feet (1.2 m) between plants, or 30 inches (75 cm) if you use a deep bed (*see p.44*).

Care while growing
Let each side-shoot grow a male flower—a flower without a pumpkin attached to it. Then, when the next female flower—a flower with a tiny green pumpkin—appears, cut the shoot short just above the female flower. This will encourage the growth of several smallish pumpkins instead of one enormous one. Place upturned saucers under your pumpkins to prevent them from suffering from rot (*see Squashes*).

Harvesting
Color is no indication of ripeness. It is best to wait until the first frost before cutting off the pumpkins. Leave about 2 inches (5 cm) of stalk on each one.

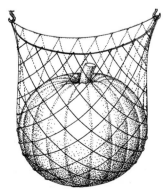

STORING PUMPKINS
Pumpkins need to be stored at a warmer temperature than any other vegetable: 50–60°F (10–16°C) is ideal. Never hang them up by their stalks, as eventually these will shrivel up, and the pumpkins will drop and bruise. By far the best way of storing them is to hang them in nets in an airy place.

Squashes & Zucchini

There is a bewildering variety of squashes, and zucchini are simply young squashes. The best thing to do is to try several different ones, see which you like, and then plant one good one for eating fresh and another that is good for storing. But bear in mind that the huge wheelbarrow-size squashes that praise the Lord at harvest festivals in English churches are better for that purpose than for any other.

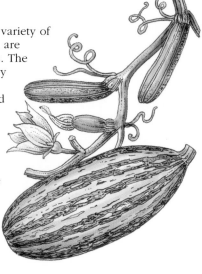

Soil and climate

The best place to grow a squash is on a compost pile. They will not grow very well on unmanured ground and like as much humus as they can get. They don't like poorly drained land, but they do need plenty of moisture during their short, quick growing season. Work in plenty of compost or manure, and lime if the pH is below 6.

Propagation

In warm climates, sow the seed straight outside in the bed at the beginning of summer. In countries with shorter summers you can sow them inside in peat pots or seed boxes two weeks before the last frost and plant them out toward the beginning of summer. Otherwise, sow the seed outdoors in situ, under cloches or inverted jelly jars, and remove the cloches when the warm weather begins. Allow 4 feet (1.2 m) between stations—30 inches (75 cm) for a deep bed (*see p.44*). Sow two, or even three, seeds, 2 inches (5 cm) deep in each station, and when they declare themselves, remove the weakest plants, leaving only one. It is said to be best to sow the seeds on edge and not lying flat. I find they grow whatever I do.

POLLINATING THE FLOWERS
Dust a little pollen from the male flower into the open female flower. To tell them apart, look for a squashlike swelling, directly behind the female flower; this is absent in the male.

Care while growing

Never let them go short of water. Mulching is very good for them. Though insects pollinate some flowers, it is important to pollinate by hand as well. Trailing varieties must be trained up fences or a wigwam of sticks.

TRAINING UP TRIPODS
If trailing varieties of squash are allowed to grow along the ground, they take up a great deal of room; the shoots can be several yards long. To save space, train them to run vertically. Grow them up trellises or chicken wire; alternatively, train them up tripods. Tie three poles, 7 feet (2 m) long, together at the top, and train one plant up each pole. When the shoots reach about 5 feet (1.5 m) high, pinch out the growing points.

Pests and diseases

MILDEW White patches caused by lack of moisture in the soil, and a high degree of humidity in the air, appear on leaves. The solution is to water them more.

VINE BORER This pest hollows out the squash stems; the leaves go limp and die. Burn affected stems and prevent the pest spreading by earthing up the remaining ones.

SUPPORTING SQUASHES
As the squashes appear and grow to their full size, there is a danger of rot coming up from the soil and affecting them. So keep the squashes just off the soil, by laying a piece of slate, plastic sheet, tile, wood, or glass under each one.

Harvesting and storing

Pick zucchini when they are between 4 and 6 inches (10–15 cm) long. If you leave them to mature, they will turn into squashes. Keep picking to make more grow. Don't harvest until the frost is really threatening. Cut the stems off several inches from the vegetables; don't break them off, as the wound lets in rot, and be certain not to bruise them. Store like pumpkins (*see Pumpkins*).

Melons

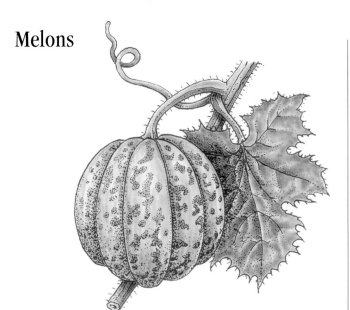

There are three main types of melons: the true cantaloupe, which comes from Europe; the netted melon; and a group that includes honeydews and casabas. My own preference is perhaps for the cantaloupe, but I have never tasted a melon— as long as it was ripe and freshly picked—that was not a memorable experience.

Soil and climate
Wherever you receive four months of summer, which culminates at melon-ripening time with days of 80°F (27°C) and nights of not less than 50°F (10°C), you can grow melons if the soil is right.

They like lightish soil with plenty of humus, not heavy clay, and they like it alkaline: a pH over 7 is best. You will probably have to lime for them.

Soil treatment
Unless your soil is already half manure or compost, dig in plenty, enough to give you a covering of at least 4 inches (10 cm) before you work it in. Or else dig out "hills" or stations, spaced about 4 feet (1.2 m) apart, digging to one spit (a spade's depth) deep and several spits square. Dump in a big forkful of manure at each hill, and then cover this with soil again so that each station forms a shallow mound.

Propagation
In hot climates, just sow the seeds two weeks after the last frost, edge-upward, six to a station, and an inch-and-a-half (4 cm) deep; keep them well watered. If you have a deep bed (*see p.44*), you should sow cantaloupes 18 inches (45 cm) apart; they will do better if you intercrop them with other plants. Thin to two or three plants in a station when the seedlings are established.

In cool climates you must sow indoors in late spring or else outdoors toward the beginning of summer under cloches or upturned glass jars. If you sow them indoors, don't transfer them outside until all frosts are past and summer has definitely begun.

A method of getting them off to a flying start is to shoot the seeds first, by putting them between wet paper towels in a warm place until they begin to sprout. Do this about a week before you would normally sow the seeds, indoors or out. Don't let them dry out, but don't drown them.

Growing melons in a cool climate is a race against time. Fruit that sets after the middle of summer should ripen before the frost kills it off.

Care while growing
Treat just like outdoor cucumbers. As soon as the little melons are as big as your fist, balance them on a glass jar or an old tin can to keep them off the ground. They are more likely to ripen like this.

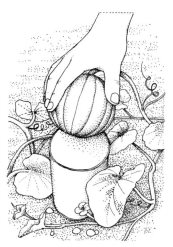

PROTECTING MELONS
You should care for your melons in the same way as for outdoor cucumbers. They need plenty of water and must be kept weed-free. When the little melons have grown to about the size of your fist, balance them on an old tin can to keep them off the ground. This will keep out rot and also makes them more likely to ripen.

Pests and diseases
CUTWORM These pests eat through the stalks of young seedlings. If you get them in your garden, put paper or cardboard collars around the small plants when you plant them out.

ANTHRACNOSE This is a fungus disease that causes brown spots on the leaves and ultimately causes the melons to go moldy. You can avoid it—along with some other fungus diseases—if you don't grow cucurbitaceous plants more than once on the same ground in four years.

BOTRYTIS, OR GRAY MOLD Very wet conditions may bring this on. Although the plants need constant moisture, there is no need to soak the ground. If botrytis strikes, all you can do is to destroy all affected fruits and vegetation.

Harvesting
Melons generally begin to crack around the stems when ripe, and the fruit will break easily from the stem. Tapping helps when you have had experience: a ripe melon makes a unique hollow sound. Some experts get on their hands and knees and sniff the melons to see if they are ripe. You don't store melons; you just pick them and eat them.

WATERMELONS
These need really warm weather for at least four months and a terrific amount of space because the vines straggle over large areas. Unless you have both of these, and sandy or very light soil, don't consider them. But if you have these conditions, go ahead and grow them—there is nothing so refreshing on a hot day. When you think a watermelon is ripe, knock it with your knuckles and heed Mark Twain's advice: a ripe melon says "punk," an unripe one says "pink" or "pank."

Asteraceae

Lettuce, chicory, endive, salsify, scorzonera, dandelions, globe artichokes, cardoons, Jerusalem artichokes, and Chinese artichokes are all members of the *Asteraceae* (formerly the *Compositae*).

The *Compositae* derive their name from the fact that their flowers, which look just like single flowers, are in fact clusters of many small flowers packed together and cunningly disguised as single flowers. The family contains two important groups, which are best described as the salad group and the thistle group. The salad group—lettuce, chicory, endive, salsify, scorzonera, and dandelions—are fast-growing, soft-stemmed plants, which gardeners should usually treat as annuals. They have white milky sap in their stems and a slightly bitter taste. This is the family from which most of the ingredients that make up the basis of good salads come.

The thistle group embraces a lot of the world's thistles, of which globe artichokes and cardoons are of especial interest to gardeners. Closely related to these are a number of other plants that look very different, but to a botanist are quite similar; these include Jerusalem artichokes, Chinese artichokes, and sunflowers. The vegetables in this group generally have to be cooked, but it is surprising what you can eat if you are hungry. Not long ago I was slashing down spear thistles in my meadows when somebody came along and told me that I could eat them. She proceeded, somewhat painfully, to peel the stalk of one of them (a young one) and yes, you could indeed eat them. You would have to be very hungry to make a meal of them though—unless you found a better way of getting the prickles off.

Lettuces

Lettuces have been cultivated for such a long time that several distinct and firmly fixed varieties have developed. The three common types are cabbage lettuce, cos lettuce, and butterhead lettuce. The cabbage variety is green on the outside with crisp, white leaves that form a closed heart; the cos has tall green leaves and forms a loose, elongated head; and the butterhead has tender, green leaves in a flattened, soft head.

With careful planting and selection of varieties, you should be able to grow lettuce for a large part of the year, at least in mild climates. For the purposes of cultivation, lettuce falls into three categories: winter lettuce, spring lettuce, and summer

lettuce. Winter varieties are bred to grow through mild winters. They do especially well if they are covered with cloches. Spring varieties are very fast-growing so that they can come to harvest in early summer. Summer lettuces grow big and lush and form the vast bulk of the lettuce crop. Lettuces are excellent for small gardens and windowboxes, and grow well indoors too.

Soil and climate
Lettuces like cool moist conditions. They will grow well in shade, and are inclined to "bolt" or run too quickly to seed in hot sun. Thus they do best in cooler and moister climates, and should only be grown in winter in hot regions.

To grow lettuces well you need good rich soil. The ground should be well-drained but humus-rich to retain water. Lettuces will not grow well in heavy ground, so if you have, for example, clay soil, you must temper this for some years with plenty of manure or compost. The deep-bed method (*see* p.44) is ideal for lettuces.

Soil treatment
The best plan is to give the lettuce bed a heavy dressing of really well-rotted manure or compost: a pound (500 g) to the square foot (900 sq cm) is not too much. The soil should be pH 6 or 7, so lime if necessary.

Propagation
You can sow lettuce seed directly in the bed, or in a seed-bed or seed boxes for transplanting. Seed will only germinate in fairly cool, moist conditions, so in very hot countries it is a good idea to put the seed between two sheets of wet paper towel and keep it in a refrigerator for five days before planting. Allow 10 inches (25 cm) between plants and 1 foot (30 cm) between rows—deep-bed (*see* p.106), 8 inches (20 cm) all around.

Winter lettuce should be sown outdoors in early fall. Spring lettuce can be started indoors in seed-boxes (or peat* pots) in late winter, or else sown out of doors in fall and allowed to stay more or less dormant during the winter, protected by cloches or even some straw or leaves. Summer lettuce is best sown direct outdoors, and sown successfully right through the summer. Lettuces are also a good crop for windowboxes or indoor culture.

Care while growing
Lettuces should be hoed, and watered if necessary. Mulching is also beneficial. Shade the plants if there is a very hot sun, and in winter protect them from heavy frost.

Pests and diseases
CUTWORM Cutworms sometimes gnaw into the stems of seedlings near the ground. If your lettuces suffer badly from this, place collars around the seedlings when you plant them out. This will also discourage slugs, who love to eat lettuces.
LETTUCE ROT In some gardens there is a rot that comes from the soil and may attack the lettuces, spreading through the plants. This can be prevented by a layer of sand on top of the ground around each lettuce. With proper rotation, however, this should not be a problem.

PREVENTING LETTUCE ROT
Lettuce rot comes from the soil and spreads through the plant, via the lowest leaves that are touching the soil. Avoid it by spreading a layer of clean sand over the soil around each lettuce. Also, never plant lettuces in the same place two years running.

Harvesting
Lettuces will not store, and lettuces that have been stuffed inside a refrigerator for days are worthless. So pull them when you want them—making sure that the roots come out with the lettuces. Don't let them grow to seed (unless you want seed), but pull them before they have a chance to bolt, and give them to your poultry or put them on your compost pile when they become overripe.

CELTUCE
Celtuce or stem lettuce is grown for its thick stems rather than its leaves. It needs soil with lots of manure or compost. Sow successively in shallow drills from spring to midsummer, and thin the seedlings to about 12 inches (30 cm) apart. Water the plants well, as they tend to get tough if allowed to dry out. Otherwise treat them as you would lettuce. The stems will be ready for cutting three months after sowing. You can eat the leaves, too; these should be harvested as they form.

CORN SALAD OR LAMB'S LETTUCE
In my view, corn salad, or lamb's lettuce, which is a member of the family *Valerianaceae*, is rather tasteless, but its virtue is that it provides salad during the winter. It grows wild in cornfields, and this gives it an extra hardiness when it is cultivated in gardens. Sow it in early fall and treat exactly as you would lettuce. When the seedlings have three leaves, thin them to 6 inches (15 cm) apart. If the winter gets very hard, cover the plants with a mulch of leaves until early spring, when you can begin picking again. Harvest a few leaves from each plant as you need them.

Chicory

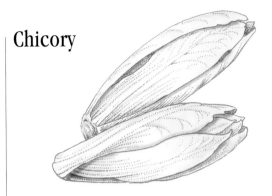

Chicory produces green leaves that are eaten as salad in summer, and, more importantly, shoots that are forced indoors to provide winter salad. Witloof is the best variety for winter forcing.

Soil and climate
Chicory prefers a coolish climate, but will grow virtually anywhere. Rich soil with a pH of 6–7 is best.

Soil treatment
Dig the bed at least two spits (spade-depths) deep, so that the long, straight roots will come out easily when you need to dig them up in the fall. Chicory grows well without mature compost or manure, but if you have some to spare it is worth digging it in well, especially in deep beds.

Propagation
Grow chicory from seed sown half an inch (1 cm) deep and 3 inches (8 cm) apart in rows 2 feet (60 cm) apart, or, if you have a deep bed (*see p.44*), in stations 6 inches (15 cm) apart in both directions. Sow successively through spring and summer for salad; in June for winter forcing.

Care while growing
Weed your chicory bed and keep the soil loose. If you sowed chicory for forcing, thin them to 6 inches (15 cm) apart and eat the thinnings as salad. Chicory suffers very little from pests and diseases.

Harvesting and storing
Pick leaves for summer salad as you want them. Dig your roots for forcing after the first hard frost, and force them as described below.

FORCING CHICORY
After the first hard frost, dig up a few chicory roots for forcing. Cut off the tops to within an inch (2.5 cm) of the crown. Plant them in a pot, or box of soil in a dark basement, with the temperature not less than 50°F (10°C). Shortly, new sprouts, or chicons, will grow; if you break them off carefully, a second crop will follow. Never pick them until you need them—even an hour in the light makes them droop.

Endives

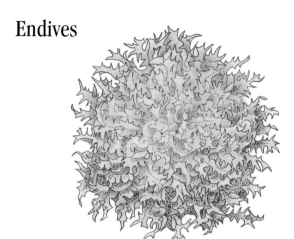

Endive is one of the many minor salad plants that can be eaten either raw or cooked. It has more flavor than, but lacks the delicious crispness, of lettuce. Curly endive comes to harvest in late summer; broad-leaved, or Batavian, endive is picked in fall or winter.

Soil and climate
Endives will grow in practically any soil. A neutral pH between 6 and 7 is best, and the more humus in the soil, the better. Endives prefer a cool moist climate to a hot dry one.

Propagation
Sow curly endive seeds thinly in shallow drills at the beginning of summer. Make two more sowings at three-week intervals. Sow broad-leaved endive in late summer. Thin the seedlings when they appear, to 9 inches (23 cm) apart or 6 inches (15 cm) in deep beds (see p.44).

Care while growing
Endives don't like too much sun, so shade them if necessary and keep them moist. In cooler climates, this shouldn't be necessary. Three or four months after sowing, start blanching by covering the plants with something that will keep out the light. Whitewashed cloches are ideal. Alternatively, you can pull them up and plant them in earth in seed boxes and put them in a dark place.

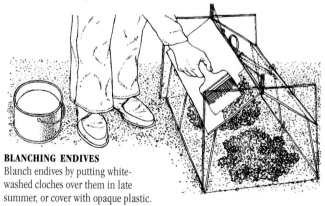

BLANCHING ENDIVES
Blanch endives by putting white-washed cloches over them in late summer, or cover with opaque plastic.

Harvesting
Simply eat endives once they are blanched; this will be about three weeks after you covered them.

Salsify

Salsify or "vegetable oyster" is grown mainly for its long roots, though the leaves may also be eaten. There are in fact two kinds—true salsify, and Spanish salsify, which is also known as scolymus—but the differences are minimal.

Soil and climate
Salsify likes deep, rich loam. If you have to grow it in heavy clay, take out a trench a foot (30 cm) wide and 18 inches (45 cm) deep and fill it with well-rotted manure.

Soil treatment
A bed dug deeply with well-rotted manure or compost is best. Fresh manure will cause the salsify root to fork. The soil should have a neutral pH, between 6 and 7.

Propagation
Sow seed in early spring an inch (2.5 cm) deep and 2 inches (5 cm) apart in rows about a foot (30 cm) apart. In a cold climate, you can sow it anything up to a month before the last frost, but you must cover it with glass. Thin to 4 inches (10 cm) when the plants appear. Sow closer and thin to 3 inches (8 cm) in a deep bed (see p.44).

Care while growing
Keep the salsify weeded, and mulch in fall before hard weather sets in. It rarely suffers from pests or diseases.

Harvesting and storing
The roots should be allowed to grow to 1½ inches (4 cm) in diameter and 8 inches (20 cm) long before you harvest them. They are improved by frost—even quite a hard frost—so you can leave them in the ground quite late. But in very cold climates, harvest them in the fall and store them in damp sand in a cool basement. Since salsify is a biennial, it will go to flower and seed in the spring of its second year. If you still have some in the ground at this stage, cut the flower stalks before they get too hard; you will find they taste very good if you eat them like asparagus.

SCORZONERA
Very similar to salsify, scorzonera should be grown in the same way. One minor difference is that you can, if you want, treat it as a biennial, digging up and eating the roots in their second year of growth.

Dandelions

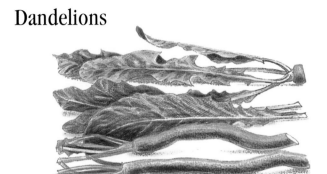

The wild dandelion has been tamed and improved to make a very useful vegetable. The leaves can be used, sparingly, in salads and are especially useful for salads early in the year before the first lettuces are ready; mulched over, the plants will survive the winter and grow away fast in the spring. Cooked dandelion leaves make an excellent vegetable, better tasting and far more vitamin-rich than spinach. The roots may be dried, ground, and used as a substitute for coffee. The coffee tastes quite good, but doesn't give you the lift that caffeine does. We might all be a lot healthier if we went over to it. The flowers make fine wine, but it is sensible to eat the leaves of your cultivated dandelions and gather flowers from wild dandelions.

Dandelions are perennial plants; if you look after them they will last for years.

Soil and climate
Dandelions thrive in any soil and in any climate except those that are very hot.

Soil treatment
Dig well and incorporate compost or manure.

Propagation
Dandelions grow easily from seed that can be bought from seed catalogs. Sow successively from the middle of spring until midsummer. Sow thinly in rows 18 inches (45 cm) apart and thin to a foot (30 cm) apart in the rows when the leaves are 2 inches (5 cm) long. On the deep bed (see p.44), broadcast and subsequently thin to about a foot (30 cm) apart each way.

Care while growing
Water if the bed dries out, and keep it well weeded. Cover the plants with a light mulch in cold winters. Pick off any flowering shoots (use wild dandelion flowers for wine).

Pests and diseases
Cultivated dandelions are closely related to their wild ancestors and are therefore very resistant to disease. Keep the slugs away though (see p.54).

Harvesting
Dandelions are perennials so you must not cut too many leaves off during the first summer of their lives, because the roots gain strength from the leaves. Cut them hard the second year. You can dig dandelion roots up in the fall and force them to grow shoots in the same way you can force chicory (see p.133).

Globe Artichokes

Eaten as it should be—that is, when still young and tender—the globe artichoke is, in my view, supreme among vegetables. But more than that, it is as beautiful a plant as you are likely to have in your garden. A thistle *par excellence*, I've actually seen a globe artichoke grow to a height of 10 feet (3 m). You will, however, need a fair amount of space to grow globe artichokes, so they are better left out of the very small garden. On the other hand, they are decorative enough with their fernlike, grayish leaves not to be grown only in the vegetable garden. They are not related either to Jerusalem or to Chinese artichokes.

Soil and climate
Low-lying black alluvial soil is ideal for globe artichokes. It should be moist but not waterlogged. If you don't have this—and there is a good chance you won't—any rich, moist soil will do. They are not really winter-hardy in cool temperate climates, since hard frosts cut the leaves right down. Even so, the roots will survive and the plants will shoot up in the following spring. Some protection, such as straw or leaves, helps them to survive the winter.

Soil treatment
The bed for your globe artichokes should be dug deeply. Work in large amounts of organic material. The pH should be around 6.5, so test the soil.

Propagation
Globe artichokes can be grown from seed and it doesn't take as long to get heads from them this way as many people seem to think. Sow the seed in a hot-bed in late winter, plant out in spring, and you should be eating artichokes in early fall. You can also sow seeds in their permanent position in the spring, but you will have to wait to harvest blooms until the next year.

A popular alternative to sowing seed is to grow the artichokes from suckers or offsets. If you uncover the old plants at the roots in the spring or fall, according to your climate, you will find a number of small shoots getting ready to grow. Cut some of these out carefully, taking with each shoot a "heel," which is a bit of the mother plant. But don't take so much as to harm the mother plant. Plant these suckers straight into the ground at about the same depth they were before. Do this in early spring in cold climates or in fall in hot ones. They should give you heads by the following summer.

Spacings vary according to variety and the kind of soil the plants are to grow in—in very rich soil plant them farther away from each other because they are likely to grow much bigger. Generally, 4 feet (1.2 m) between plants is about right. Make it 5 feet (1.5 m) in a deep bed (see p.44), because the soil will be rich.

You can have good heads to eat for six months of the year in cooler climates if you protect some old plants very well in the winter. These will give you blooms in late spring and early summer. If you planted good suckers in early spring, these will give you a crop in late summer. And you'll get heads in the fall from suckers planted, say, six weeks after the first planting. In very hot climates you should get most of your crop in the winter and spring.

Since globe artichoke plants tend to lose vigor after a few years (though I have had good crops from an eight-year-old plant), try replacing a quarter of your total crop every year with new plants. That is, each fall dig out the oldest quarter of the crop, and replace them in the spring with new plants. But take the suckers from the old plants before scrapping them and plant them in sand or soil indoors. In the spring these can be used for replanting.

Care while growing

Heavy mulching with compost or manure is always a good idea with globe artichokes. And where the winters are cold, it is best to cut the plants down to the ground in the fall and to pile hay, straw, or leaves over them. But if you do this, uncover the plants on mild days to let them dry out. In summer droughts, soak the ground around the plants regularly and thoroughly.

Pests and diseases

BOTRYTIS This causes a gray mold on leaves and stalks and may attack plants in very warm wet seasons. If it does, remove and burn all affected plants.

ARTICHOKE LEAF SPOT In hot, muggy weather, leaves may go brown and die. Use a weak solution of Bordeaux mixture*.

Harvesting

Ignorance of the following rule makes artichokes less popular than they should be: harvest them when they are very young! Don't wait until they are huge prickly things, as hard as wood and as sharp as needles. If you cut them when they are still tight, green, and small, you can eat practically the whole thing. If they are too old, only the bottom tips of the leaves and the heart will be edible. Simply cut through the stalk about an inch below the globe.

HARVESTING GLOBES
If you harvest your globe artichokes while they are still very young, you can eat the whole head, instead of just the heart and the base of the inner leaves. Harvest the globes by cutting through the stalk about 1 inch (2.5 cm) below the globe.

Cardoons

Cardoons are thistles that are very closely related to globe artichokes. They have been specifically bred for their stems, which should be eaten blanched. They taste delicious but take up a lot of space.

Soil and climate

Although strictly speaking perennials, cardoons are always grown as annuals, so they are not as fussy about soil as globe artichokes are. Cardoons grow in a wide range of climates, although they don't like it too wet.

Soil treatment

Dig holes about 1 foot (30 cm) across and 3 feet (90 cm) apart, and fill these with compost. Or you can dig out trenches as for celery (see Celery).

Propagation

Sow three or four cardoon seeds in each hole or at 3-foot (90-cm) intervals along the trench in the spring. Alternatively, sow in peat* pots a little earlier and plant out toward the end of spring. Pull out all but the strongest plants when they appear.

Care while growing

Cardoons should be kept watered and weeded, and, since they need blanching, they should be earthed up like celery (see Celery). But before earthing up you should wrap the plants in straw, or put a length of drainpipe over them to protect them. They are rarely affected by pests or diseases.

BLANCHING CARDOONS
About three weeks before harvesting, bunch up the cardoon plants and tie them together. Then wrap them completely with straw, or anything else that will keep out the light. Leave the tips of the leaves showing. When the blanching process is complete, you will have cardoons all through the fall and winter.

Harvesting

You can begin to harvest your cardoons in fall and continue well into the winter. Three weeks before you intend to harvest a batch, blanch the plants, which may be 3 feet (90 cm) tall. Gather them up and tie them together, then wrap each one with straw.

Jerusalem Artichokes

It is most unfortunate that the Jerusalem artichoke was so named, since people constantly mix it up with the globe artichoke. Strangely, they are members of the same family, but only a botanist could see any resemblance between them. The Jerusalem is in fact more closely related to the sunflower; the plant looks very similar except that it has small flowers and tubers on its roots. The tubers are pleasant to eat and are especially good for diabetics because they contain a special form of sugar and no starch.

Soil and climate
Jerusalem artichokes grow best in light or sandy soil. They do very poorly in boulder clay. In light land they will grow like weeds if you let them—as high as 7 feet (2 m)—and they will smother any plant that tries to compete with them. They grow in practically any climate.

Soil treatment
If you have to grow them in heavy soil, dig it well, make sure it is free of perennial weeds, and incorporate as much manure or compost as you can. Sandy soil is little trouble, although the more manure, the bigger the crop.

Propagation
Simply dig a hole with a trowel and plant the tubers 6 inches (15 cm) deep. I put them in in late winter. Even a tiny scrap of a tuber will produce a plant. Plant 18 inches (45 cm) apart each way—deep-bed method (see p.44), 15 inches (38 cm). They make a smother crop.

Once you have had a crop of Jerusalem artichokes it is very difficult to get rid of them. They will come up again year after year unless you hoe them out constantly.

Care while growing
In light land you don't need to do anything. In heavy land hoe between them because Jerusalem artichokes are not vigorous enough to beat weeds. Alternatively, mulch heavily. Pests and diseases rarely affect them.

Harvesting and storing
Dig them up in late fall, or else leave them in the ground until you want them. In climates with hard frost, dig them up after the tops have died back and store them. The tops are fine for mulch, and can be woven as a windbreak.

CHINESE ARTICHOKES
Strictly speaking a member of the *Lamiaceae* family, the Chinese artichoke is also grown for its tubers, in exactly the same way as the Jerusalem artichoke. Regular watering and fertilizing with soluble manure will add extra flesh to the tubers, which should be lifted in fall when the leaves die.

Sweet Corn

Sweet corn is a member of the *Poaceae*, or grass family; this includes all the world's cereal crops and a lot of other species besides.

The plants, which I have seen as tall as 12 feet (3.6 m), send a mass of fibrous roots deep into the soil. This takes a lot out of the soil, but when in due course the plants are returned in the form of compost they put most of the goodness back again. There are small varieties bred for gardeners that only grow to 4 feet (1.2 m). These are useful in a small garden because they don't cast so much shade.

Soil and climate
Sweet corn likes deep, well-drained, humus-enriched loam. Clay is too cold for it in northern climates; it must have an early start, as it needs four months to come to maturity. It will grow in light sandy soil, but only if there is plenty of humus in it. Hungry old gravels and sands just won't grow it at all. It needs good soil.

As for climate, sweet corn prefers four months of hot weather without much cloud cover. However, you can grow it in fairly cloudy countries, if you start it early enough.

Soil treatment
Sweet corn needs plenty of humus thoroughly mixed into the soil (not just dumped on top at the last minute) because the roots go deep as well as spreading wide. A couple of inches (5 cm) of well-rotted manure dug well in a spit (a spade's depth) deep is ideal. Alternatively, plant sweet corn after a heavily manured main potato crop. Soil must be neutral: pH 6.5 to 7.

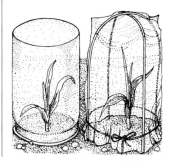

PLANTING SWEET CORN
So that the roots are not disturbed by transplanting, start sweet corn off outdoors under protection. An overturned jelly jar makes an admirable cloche; alternatively, improvise one out of polythene and wire. Remove the cloches before the plants become too big.

Propagation

It is better to sow sweet corn in wide blocks instead of in long thin lines. This is because it is wind-pollinated and in a thin line some plants may get missed. To give it a flying start, sow it outside two weeks before the last probable frost under cloches, overturned jars, or plastic umbrellas. Remove these, of course, before the plants get too big for them. Or better still, especially in cool climates, start it off indoors in peat* pots, soil blocks, or even small flowerpots. Sweet corn doesn't take to being transplanted but this doesn't mean it can't be done. In the cool climate where I live, I like to sow it in peat pots in the greenhouse in early spring and transplant it—pots and all—a month, or six weeks, later.

Sow the seed or transplant the plants about a foot (30 cm) apart each way, in blocks or in the deep bed (see p.44).

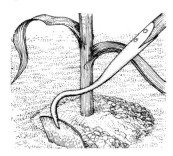

EARTHING UP SWEET CORN
If you intend to earth up your sweet corn stalks while they are growing, sow the seed 18 inches (45 cm) apart instead of 12 inches (30 cm) apart. Pulling up the soil around the plants in this way gives them support while they mature and causes them to put out more roots higher up.

Care while growing

Sweet corn doesn't like to go short of water. Mulching does it nothing but good. Earthing up is beneficial too, because the plant will put out more roots higher up its stem.

Pests and diseases

EARWORM These bore into the tips of the ears of corn. If you see them when you are picking the ears, destroy them.
SMUT Smut is a fungus that causes large gray boils to appear on the kernels. Burn the affected plants and don't leave rotting sweet corn on the ground; bury it or compost it. Otherwise it may develop smut.

HARVESTING SWEET CORN
Pick the corn by jerking the cobs sharply downward and breaking them off; if you cut them off you risk damaging the plant.

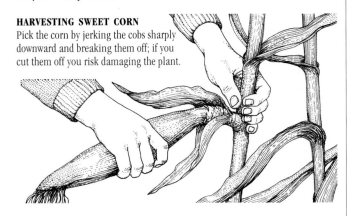

Harvesting

The ears are ready to pick as soon as the white, silky tassels go brown; otherwise, test for ripeness by opening the husk and pressing your fingernail into a grain. If it is firm but still slightly milky it is ready. Rush the corn to the saucepan! The moment you pick it, the sugar starts turning to starch and the flavor is lost.

Okra

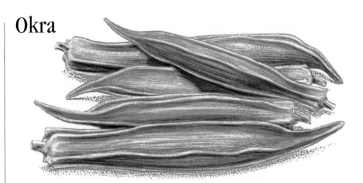

Okra, familiarly known as "lady's fingers," is a tropical plant of the *Malvaceae*, or mallow family, whose most renowned member is the cotton plant. The pods of the okra plant make the most delicious vegetable with a very subtle and distinctive taste. They are much used in Indian curries. When the seeds are well developed they can be shelled and cooked like peas. The whole plant is extremely attractive with large yellow and red flowers. Three or four plants will keep a family well supplied with okra.

Soil and climate

Okra can be grown in greenhouses in cool climates. Outdoors it needs a lot of summer sun, and it is not much good trying to grow it in countries with cool cloudy summers. But where outdoor tomatoes really thrive and crop reliably, okra can be grown. It likes a light soil with plenty of humus but not too much fresh manure, since this will produce too much leaf and not enough fruit.

Soil treatment

Okra grows especially well by the deep bed method (see p.44) and in cooler climates can be grown under portable deep-bed mini-greenhouses. Otherwise cultivate deeply and work in some well-rotted compost. The soil should have a pH between 6 and 7.

Propagation

Okra can be started indoors, but only in peat* pots because it doesn't like being transplanted. If you sow the seed outdoors, wait until the soil is thoroughly warm. You can help here by warming the soil yourself under a mini-greenhouse or under cloches (see p.48). Dwarf varieties should be sown 30 inches (75 cm) apart; larger varieties can be sown up to 4 feet (1 m) apart.

Care while growing

Okra should be watered occasionally, but not swamped.

Pests and diseases

CATERPILLARS Pick caterpillars off and step on them.

Harvesting and storing

You can harvest about two months after sowing. Harvest when the okra is still quite young, a few days after the flowers have fallen. Pick pods every other day whether you need them or not, so that the plants keep producing more. Pods can be frozen or canned, and in Italy I have seen them laid out on a rack in the sun and dried. They keep well like this, but I prefer them fresh. Keep picking them as long as they grow, which can be right up to the first frost.

Rhubarb

Rhubarb is a vegetable because we eat its stems, not its fruit. It is thought of as fruit merely because our whim is to eat it as a dessert, like most other fruit. These days there is so much frozen fruit, as well as fruit from abroad, that there is no longer an endless gap between the last of the stored apples and the ripening of the raspberries. In the old days that gap was filled with rhubarb. But rhubarb is still well worth growing, for it is a good fruit substitute. Its stems contain oxalic acid, which scours pans clean and sets your teeth on edge.

Soil and climate
Rhubarb likes a cold climate (it comes from Mongolia) and is no good at all in a hot one. Unless it enjoys frost in the winter it does not have the dormant period that it needs, and its stalks, instead of being red and edible, are green and inedible. It likes quite acidic soil, so don't give it lime, but otherwise it will grow in any well-drained soil, and it seems to thrive in that milieu of nettles, old rusty cans, and broken bottles at the end of many old country gardens.

Soil treatment
Put rhubarb in a part of the garden devoted to perennials because, properly treated, it will continue to grow and yield for years. Clear its bed of perennial weeds, dig it deeply, and put plenty of manure on it. It pays to dig a deep pit, discard the subsoil, and fill in with manure and topsoil.

Propagation
Rhubarb seldom breeds true with seed, and so the usual method is to use divided roots. Commercial growers generally dig up their beds every four years, divide the roots, and replant on fresh ground. You can either buy root cuttings or get them from a neighbor who is in the process of dividing his rhubarb. Just plant the bits of root the right way up 3 feet (90 cm) apart, and up the plants will come. Nothing can stop them.

PLANTING RHUBARB CROWNS
It is possible to raise rhubarb from seed, but this is not the most reliable method of growing it. It is best to get hold of some rooted crowns. Dig a deep hole, fill it with compost, put back the topsoil, and plant the roots the right way up and 3 feet (90 cm) apart. They are sure to grow.

Care while growing
Plentiful mulching is good for rhubarb. In the winter, when it dies down, you can bury it deeply in a mulch of manure, leafmold, compost, or what you will. As long as it is provided with ample organic matter in this way, you need not dig it up every four years: it will last almost indefinitely.

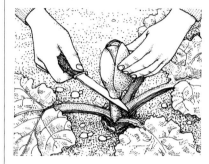

CUTTING OFF FLOWERS
Flowering rhubarb will not produce succulent juicy stems. The flower stalks divert all the nourishment away from the plant; cut them off when they appear.

In the spring draw the mulch away from around the plants to let the sun warm the soil. Then, when the plants begin to grow well, you can cover them with old pails and in the winter, cover the pails with fresh long-strawed manure, so that the heat from the manure will force the rhubarb on, and you will get stems to eat early in the spring.

You can cover the crowns with oil drums, painted black to absorb the heat of the sun, open at the bottom end, and with a 6-inch- (15-cm-) diameter hole cut in the top. The oil drums should then be pressed firmly into the ground around the plants; they should be adequately weighed down to prevent them from blowing over.

Pests and diseases
RHUBARB CURCULIO This is only found in North America. It is a rust-colored beetle about an inch (2.5 cm) long. It bores into every part of the rhubarb plant, but can easily be picked off. The beetle lives in dock plants, so suffer not docks to exist near rhubarb.

FORCING RHUBARB
Cover each plant with an old bucket, and when winter comes, insulate the bucket with long-strawed manure. If you lift two-year-old roots in late fall and force them indoors, you can have rhubarb to eat through the winter. Otherwise, start forcing the plants in the same way outdoors in very late winter, and you will reap the benefits in early summer.

Harvesting
Spare the plants altogether for their first year, and thereafter only harvest the big, thick stalks: let the thinner ones grow on to nourish the plants. Never take more than half the stems of a plant in one year. Don't cut the stems, as this lets in rot; break them by pulling them back from the plant, then forcing them downward an inch or two. This does not hurt the crown. Stop harvesting altogether in July.

You can make jam with rhubarb (*see p.312*) but the best thing you can do with it is to make wine (*see p.326*).

Mushrooms

Mushrooms, which are fungi and not vegetables at all, are an obvious choice for the self-sufficient gardener who has space to spare indoors. Mushrooms have a higher mineral content than meat (twice as high as any other vegetable), and contain more protein than any other vegetable except for certain types of beans. Another good thing about growing mushrooms is that the compost you need for growing them can all end up in your garden outside.

Climate
In warm weather you can grow mushrooms outdoors or indoors without artificial heating, using the method I will describe. In the winter, keep the temperature over 60°F (16°C). Never leave mushrooms in direct sunlight.

Soil treatment
To grow mushrooms you need boxes that ideally should be 2.5 feet (75 cm) long, 9 inches (25 cm) wide, and 9 inches (25 cm) deep.

You can buy suitable compost and this is really the best thing to do for growing small quantities of mushrooms. However, to make enough compost for 60 square feet (6 sq m) is not difficult. Get four bales of wheat straw (no other straw will do) and shake it out into layers, soaking it thoroughly with water. Leave it for a day or two, but throw on more water from time to time, because it must be saturated. You should also have: 7 pounds (3 kg) of gypsum (from a home improvement store), 28 lb (12.7 kg) of poultry manure, and 14 lb (6.3 kg) of mushroom compost activator.

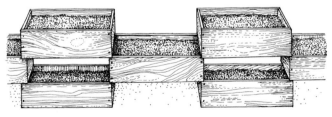

STACKING MUSHROOMS IN BOXES
Allow at least 6 inches (15 cm) between the top of one box and the bottom of another. There should also

be perhaps a dozen half-inch (1.5-cm) holes in the bottom of each box. I like cedarwood boxes best, but you can use fiberglass trays.

When the straw is thoroughly wet, spread some out 12 inches (30 cm) deep over an area 5 feet (1.5 m) square. Shake over this layer a trowelful each of the poultry manure, gypsum, and activator. Add another foot (30 cm) of straw and on this another sprinkling of the other goodies, until all the materials have been used up. The pile should be about 6 feet (1.8 m) high. If it is outdoors, cover it with an old carpet, paper, or plastic.

By the fourth day the temperature of the pile should be 160°F (71°C). Leave it another two days, then turn it so the outsides are in the middle. If any part of the pile appears dry at this turning, sprinkle water on it, just enough to moisten it but not enough to wash away the special ingredients. When you turn the pile, shake out the straw thoroughly and rebuild very carefully. The success of your crop depends on this care.

After another six days, turn again. Be even more sparing with water, but if there are any dry patches or gray patches, sprinkle them lightly. Then, after four more days, turn yet again. If the compost appears too damp, apply more gypsum. Six days later the compost will be ready for the boxes.

Propagation
When it is ready for use, the compost should be fairly dry and springy; it should consist of short pieces of rotted straw but should not be sticky. Fill each box, tamping the compost down well with a brick, until the final topping-off is level with the top of the box.

By now you will have bought some spawn. There is "manure" spawn, which comes in lumps that you break into small pieces, and "grain" spawn, which you simply scatter on the compost. I suggest that beginners use manure spawn, because it is easy to use and reliable.

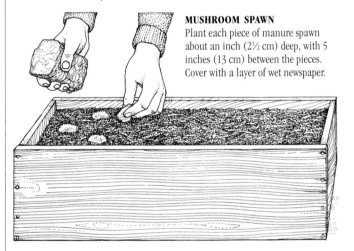

MUSHROOM SPAWN
Plant each piece of manure spawn about an inch (2½ cm) deep, with 5 inches (13 cm) between the pieces. Cover with a layer of wet newspaper.

Care while growing
During the next week or two, do not let the temperature fall below 60°F (16°C); 70°F (21°C) is even better. On the other hand, beware of overheating; 90°F (32°C) may kill the spawn. After three weeks you should see the white threads of the mycelium growing in the compost. At this point you must apply "casing." Mix some well-moistened horticultural peat with the same bulk of freshly sterilized loam (the loam should be from permanent grassland). Put an inch-and-a-half (4-cm) layer of mixed peat* and loam on top of the compost and press it down gently. Mushrooms should appear about three weeks later. Give them a little water. Keep the temperature between 60°F (16°C) and 64°F (18°C).

Harvesting
When you harvest mushrooms, twist them out. When the crop seems over, try to persuade it to go on cropping a little longer by watering it with a weak salt solution. Eventually dump the spent compost on your compost pile, wash the boxes with formaldehyde solution*, and put the boxes out to weather for several weeks before you use them again.

The Cultivation of Herbs

Containing the sowing, growing, and harvesting
instructions for the many useful herbs that can be nurtured
in the kitchen garden.

Angelica
BIENNIAL

Angelica takes up a lot of space; the plants can reach 6 feet (1.8 m) high and are quite imposing. If your space for herbs is in any way limited, this is one you can think of doing without. The leaf stalks can be candied or crystallized, and the roots and stems can be cooked with stewed fruit to provide natural sweetness.

Soil
Angelica is best grown at the back of the herb garden, in deep rich soil and partial shade.

Propagation and after-care
The seed does not keep very long; to make sure of good results I pick the seed fresh and ripe in the fall, seal it up in an airtight container, and sow it early in the spring an inch (2.5 cm) deep in moist soil. The seeds will take a long time to come up. Seedlings should be given 6 inches (15 cm) of space toward the end of the first year, 2 feet (60 cm) in the second, and anything up to 5 feet (1.5 m) after that. Angelica usually flowers in its second year, so strictly speaking it is biennial. However, sometimes it does not flower until its fourth or fifth year. After it has flowered, the plant will die.

Harvesting
If you want to harvest the leaves, cut them in early summer when the oils are strongest. As well as eating the leaves as a vegetable, you can dry them very successfully. Leaf stalks for candying should be picked at the same time as the leaves. As for roots, dig them up in the second fall, because they become too woody after that.

Anise
ANNUAL

Anise seed can be baked into bread and cake, and used to flavor cheeses, puddings, candies, and cordials with its delicate licorice scent. An ounce (28 g) of seed in half a pint (300 ml) of brandy, allowed to stand in the sun for two weeks, makes a fortifying drink.

Soil
Anise likes warm, well-drained soil, and a sunny position.

Propagation and after-care
Sow seeds in spring in situ, thinning when the plants are established to 8 inches (20 cm) apart. Take care when thinning, because the herb is easily damaged. The more sun the seeds get, the more quickly they will mature.

Harvesting
You should be able to harvest in midsummer, when the seed heads have turned gray-brown. Cut the stalks, tie them in bunches, and hang them up to dry them out. Thresh them when they are thoroughly dried. Save some of the seed to sow the following spring.

Balm
PERENNIAL

Balm, or lemon balm as it is sometimes called, adds a subtle flavor to fruit salads or cooked fruit and is good when added to poultry stuffing. Its pleasant smell recommends it to makers of *potpourri* and the scent lasts for a very long time. If you have it in your garden it will attract bees, which is a good thing because they will pollinate your vegetables.

Soil
Balm likes shady places and rich moist soil, but it needs a little sun to prevent it from getting stringy and blanched.

Propagation and after-care
Sow seed in spring or early summer indoors or in a cold frame. It will take three or four weeks to germinate. Plant out when the seedlings are 4 inches (10 cm) high. Alternatively, sow seed outdoors in midsummer, then lift and replace the seedlings early the following summer.

If you have an existing clump or can buy or beg one, divide it up and plant the portions in the fall or spring. Balm divides easily into clumps. There is no difficulty in looking after it.

Harvesting
Harvest some leaves just before the buds flower, and then cut the plants right down in the fall and cover them with compost or leafmold.

Balm bruises easily, so be careful when picking and don't expect too much during the first year's growth. Dry it in a dark airy room and store in sealed jars in the dark.

Basil

ANNUAL

In cool climates basil must be sown every year, because frost will kill it. In warm climates you may be able to turn it into a perennial by cutting it right back in the fall, so that it shoots up in the spring. Basil grows very well in containers indoors.

Basil leaves have a strong flavor and used in large enough quantities will dominate even garlic. In France, many cooks steep basil leaves in olive oil and keep this for dressing salads.

Soil

Basil needs dry, light, well-drained soil. A sunny but sheltered position is what it likes best.

Propagation and after-care

Sow seed indoors in early summer. Wait until the soil is warm before planting out the seedlings, 8 inches (20 cm) apart in rows a foot (30 cm) apart. Water the plants well, to keep the leaves succulent.

Harvesting

Pick off leaves as soon as they unfurl and use them fresh. Cut the plants down for drying in late summer or early fall; basil takes longer to dry than most herbs.

Bay

PERENNIAL

Bay has a hundred uses in the kitchen, and because it is evergreen there is no storage problem. Freshly dried leaves to put with pickled herrings, with stews, casseroles and soups, should always be available.

Soil and climate

Bay will do well on any average soil. It likes some sun, but needs sheltering from harsh winds. Bay is susceptible to frost, so in cold climates you should grow it in tubs that can be moved indoors in winter. Add compost occasionally, and some bone meal or other material that contains phosphate.

Propagation and after-care

You can buy a young tree and plant it in the winter, or you can propagate it easily from hardwood cuttings or half-ripened shoots.

Harvesting

Pick leaves fresh all year round. You must dry them before you can eat them. Dry them in layers in a warm shady place. Never dry them in full sun. If the leaves begin to curl, press them gently under a board. After two weeks of drying, put them into airtight containers, preferably glass jars, because the leaves exude oil.

Borage

ANNUAL

Both the flowers and the leaves of borage are used in many different cool drinks, as they contain viscous juices that actually make the drinks cooler. You can sprinkle the blue flowers over salads, or use them for a tisane. The plant is very decorative.

Soil

Borage will grow on any piece of spare ground, but it likes sun, and prefers well-drained loamy soil.

Propagation and after-care

Borage can only be propagated from seed. Sow the seed in spring, in drills 1 inch (2.5 cm) deep and 3 feet (90 cm) apart. Cover the seed well with soil. The plant will self-sow.

Harvesting

Eight weeks after sowing, begin cutting the young leaves and keep cutting from then on. Pick the flowers when they appear. You may get two flowerings in one season. Dry the herb quickly at a low temperature.

Burnet
PERENNIAL

Use fresh young burnet leaves chopped up in salads or as a flavoring in sauces. Add the leaves to cream cheese, where they enhance the cool taste. Dried leaves are well worth adding to vinegar, and they can also be used to make a fragrant tea.

Soil and climate
A dry light well-limed soil suits burnet best. The plants need full sun in order to flourish. But burnet is hardy and will do well in most climates.

Propagation and after-care
Sow the seed in early spring, and later on thin the seedlings to a foot (30 cm) apart. It is a good thing to sow seed each year for a continual supply of fresh young leaves. If you want leaves specifically for drying rather than just fresh, you can propagate burnet plants by division.

Harvesting
Pick the young leaves frequently, use them fresh or dry them carefully.

Caper
PERENNIAL

The flower buds of this herb are pickled in vinegar a few hours after being picked, and then become what we know as capers. These are used to much effect in rice dishes, salads, stuffings, and sauces for meat and sea food. Caper grows wild in Mediterranean climates where it flourishes, but it is a difficult herb to grow in temperate climates (where nasturtium may be considered an acceptable substitute).

Soil
Caper does best on poor dry soils; the plant needs full sun and grows well on slopes.

Propagation and after-care
In subtropical areas, grow capers from cuttings or division, planting out the established bush into a well-drained mixture of gravel and sand. When you plant the bush, sprinkle enough water to set it, and thereafter hardly water it at all. You can grow caper successfully in rock gardens, if you simply drop the seeds with a little sand into crevices between rocks. In temperate climates try growing caper under glass, in a well-drained sandy loam, planting out the cuttings in early spring. It also makes an attractive pot plant on a sunny windowsill, but in these circumstances it is unlikely to produce enough buds for culinary use.

Harvesting
Pick off the flower buds as soon as they are fully developed. Leave them in the dark for a few hours before pickling them.

Caraway
BIENNIAL

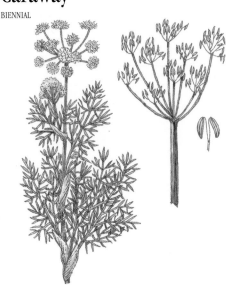

Caraway seeds have long been used in cakes, breads, cheeses, sweets, and sauces. Ground seeds can also be added to rich meats such as roast pork or to spicy stews like goulash. You can use the leaves of the plant in salads, and the roots can be cooked and served as a vegetable.

Soil and climate
Caraway is adaptable and will accept most soils, as long as they are not too wet, but it prefers clay loam and a sheltered location. It is winter-hardy and is best suited to a cool climate.

Propagation and after-care
Sow seed as soon as it ripens on an existing plant; alternatively, sow bought seed in late spring. Thin seedlings to a foot (30 cm) apart and keep them weed-free. Then leave them until the following year, when they will flower and seed. Caraway plants need protection from wind, so that the seed heads don't shatter before the seed is ripe.

Harvesting
When the seed turns brown, snip off the flowerheads and dry the seed in an airy place before threshing.

Chervil

BIENNIAL

Chervil is a most important herb, a top priority if you are only choosing to grow a few. It is a substitute for parsley but its leaves have a far finer flavor; it is the basis of French cookery with *fines herbes*, the fundamental ingredient of a magnificent soup; it is a fine constituent of salads, one of the very best flavorings in the world for omelets, and it takes its place proudly in many a noble sauce. The habit of boiling chervil is a barbaric one; it must be added to cooked dishes at the last moment so that its delicate flavor can emerge unimpaired.

Soil

Chervil will grow in any soil except heavy clay or wet ground. It needs some shade in summer but full daylight in winter, so ideally grow it in the partial shade of a deciduous tree.

Propagation and after-care

You should sow some seed in the spring for summer use, and then some more in high summer for cutting in winter. Many chervil lovers sow successionally all through the summer. Chervil does not take to being transplanted, so sow it where you mean it to stay, in drills 10 inches (25 cm) apart, thinning later to about 8 inches (20 cm) between plants. From then on it will self-sow quite rapidly. I often cloche a summer sowing; alternatively, chervil grows well indoors in containers.

Harvesting

You can eat chervil from six to eight weeks after sowing. Cut the leaves off with scissors before the plant flowers. Chervil is tricky to dry, because it needs a constant low temperature, but luckily you can get it fresh all year.

Chives

PERENNIAL

Chives are mini-onions and like onions are members of the *Liliaceae*, but you eat the leaves of chives and not the bulbs. They are perennial, easy to grow, and you can go on and on forever snipping the grasslike tops and flavoring all sorts of food with them.

Soil

Chives will grow in most conditions, but they will do best on good soil with plenty of humus and they prefer a warm, shady position. They will grow well in containers indoors. They like a pH of 6 or 7.

Propagation and after-care

You can sow seed in the spring, but you will get quicker and better results if you plant seedlings or mature plants. You can buy clumps or bum them from a neighbor. Simply divide the clumps up and plant them. The spring or summer is the best time for this. You must keep them moist so it is best to plant them near a pond or water tank, or even a faucet. The plants die down in the winter but you can keep some going for winter use by planting them in a container indoors and putting it on the kitchen windowsill. Every three years or so dig up your chives and replant in fresh soil.

Harvesting

Chives are ready for cutting about five weeks after the seeds were sown. Just clip the "grass" off as you need it to within 2 inches (5 cm) of the ground. You can clip the tips of the leaves as much as you like without damaging the plants because like all the *Liliaceae*, chives are monocotyledons (*see p.56*). Thus clipping the tips off has no effect whatever on the growing point down below. The more you cut them the better they will be.

Cilantro/Coriander

ANNUAL

Don't be put off by cilantro's intense smell, because it is a staple of Mexican cooking, and its seed, called coriander, is essential to Indian cooking: you can use the seeds crushed or whole in curries and mixtures for stuffing vegetables like squash, tomatoes and peppers. If you coat coriander seeds with sugar you can add them to your homemade marmalade, or your children can eat them as sweets.

Soil

Rich soil suits cilantro best. It also needs a sunny, well-drained site.

Propagation and after-care

Sow the seed in late spring in drills 12 inches (30 cm) apart; later thin to 6 inches (15 cm). The plants will very probably reach a height of 2 feet (60 cm) or more.

Harvesting

When the seeds begin to turn brown, cut the plants near the ground and hang them up to dry. Thresh the seeds when they are thoroughly dried and store them in jars. Never use partially dried coriander seeds; they have a very bitter taste.

Dill
ANNUAL

Dill seeds are mildly soporific and are much stronger than the herb derived from the leaves. They are traditionally used in the making of dill pickles. The slightly bitter taste of the seeds is absent from the leaves, which bring out the taste of fish or chicken.

Soil
Dill accepts almost any soil as long as it is well-drained. It must have sun but should not be allowed to dry out.

Propagation and after-care
Sow seeds flat on the bed in the spring, pressing them slightly into the soil. Sow successively all through spring and summer for a continuous supply of dill leaves. Thin the plants to 9 inches (23 cm) in rows a foot (30 cm) apart. As long as you keep them well watered, the plants will grow fast, producing great numbers of leaves before flowering. Very dry weather and inadequate watering will cause them to flower before the leaves are fully grown. Fennel is a bad neighbor for dill as cross-pollination can often take place.

Harvesting
You can start cutting the leaves when the plant is about 8 inches (20 cm) tall and keep on cutting right through to late fall. The best time to cut for drying is just before the plant flowers. If you want to use the seeds for pickling, cut them when both flowers and seeds are on the head. Seeds you want to use for flavoring or for sowing the following spring should be left on the plant rather longer, until they go brown. Dry the seed heads before threshing them. The drying temperature must not rise above blood heat.

Fennel
PERENNIAL

Fennel looks very like dill, but has a quite different, stronger flavor. The leaves are much used for flavoring oily fish such as mackerel or herring, and should make part of the stuffing for "a pike with a pudding in its belly." You can use them raw in salads as well. The seeds are nice to chew and can be added to liqueurs.

Soil
Fennel grows well in any garden soil provided it is not acidic, too heavy, or too wet. It prefers rich chalk soil and a sunny location.

Propagation and after-care
Sow the seed in fall for a crop the following year. Sow three seeds in a station and leave 18 inches (45 cm) between stations. If you want seeds and not leaves, sow in early spring under glass. Another approach is to treat fennel as a biennial by digging up roots in the fall and storing them through the winter indoors in sand. The following spring, divide the roots and plant 12 inches (30 cm) apart in rows 15 inches (38 cm) apart.

Harvesting
Cut leaves through the summer; harvest the seeds when they are still green and dry them out of the sun in thin layers, moving them as they sweat. Drying fennel leaves can be done if you use great care and a low temperature; it is best to use them fresh.

Garlic
PERENNIAL

Garlic can be added to almost any dish. It can be eaten cooked or raw, and it can even be chewed by itself. So grow plenty and use it with abandon.

Soil and climate
Garlic is a southern European plant, but it will grow in cooler temperate regions. It needs the same sort of good rich soil as onions need, with plenty of manure or compost incorporated. Plant it where it will get plenty of sun.

Propagation and after-care
Buy garlic bulbs, from the farmer's market or supermarket if they are cheaper there than at the seed merchant. Pick off the individual cloves and plant them. You can plant them in the fall, or in the early spring. The sharp end is the top end of the clove—plant each one in a hole deep enough to leave the top just covered with soil. Plant 4 inches (10 cm) apart in rows as close together as you can manage, or 4 inches (10 cm) in all directions in a deep bed (see p.44). Keep the cloves weeded. They don't want too much water.

Harvesting
Fork the garlic out of the ground when the stems dry up and dry them out for a few days in the sun if possible, or under cover in some place where the rain won't reach them. Drying is essential if you want to store garlic. Tie the heads into bunches and hang them up in an airy, cool, dry place; use them as you need them, but keep some to plant the following year.

Horseradish

PERENNIAL

The roots of horseradish make a hot-tasting herb. Either grate the roots and use them as they are, moistened a little with vinegar, or make a sauce by mixing them with oil and vinegar or grated apples and cream. Horseradish goes well with roast beef, cold meats, and smoked fish.

Soil and climate

Horseradish likes deep, rich soil and will grow in any climate that is not too hot. In hot climates, horseradish must be grown in shade.

Propagation and after-care

Just plant 3-inch (8-cm) pieces of root, about as thick as your finger. Contrary to normal practice, I prefer to put them in nearly horizontal and only 2 inches (5 cm) below the surface. You can plant horseradish any time of the year, and once you have it, you have it forever. The problem is how to stop it from spreading across the garden. You can confine it inside slates or tiles dug deeply and vertically into the soil. Another method is to set a 12-inch (30-cm) land drain pipe into the soil on its end, fill it with loam and compost, and plant a piece of root in it. The plant will grow very well, produce clean, tender roots, and be very easy to harvest. And it won't spread. If you don't confine the roots you must dig it out of the ground where it is not wanted.

Harvesting

All parts of the root are edible. Just dig them up and grate them. In cold climates you can store the roots like carrots, in a container of moist sand.

Hyssop

PERENNIAL

Hyssop is a member of the *Lamiaceae* (mint) family and has a pungent and rather bitter taste. The leaves and the ends of the stalks contain the flavor and will go with a variety of dishes. Hyssop is a good plant for encouraging bees into the garden, where they do a great deal of good by pollinating vegetables, especially beans.

Soil and climate

Hyssop prefers chalky soil, well-drained and containing plenty of lime. The plant thrives in warm weather, but will also manage to withstand winter in cool temperate climates.

Propagation and after-care

You can sow seed in drills a quarter-inch (0.5 cm) deep and transplant the seedlings in midsummer to the open bed when they are about 6 inches (15 cm) high. Plant them in rows 2 feet (60 cm) apart.

Harvesting

Once the plants are mature, about 18 inches (45 cm) high, cut back the tops frequently so that the leaves are always young and tender. Cut leaves and stalks for drying shortly before the plants flower.

Lovage

PERENNIAL

All parts of lovage except for the roots can be used in cooking. The bottoms of the stems can be blanched and eaten like celery. The leaves have a strong, yeasty, celerylike flavor as well, which means they can be used to flavor soups and casseroles when celery is not available. The seeds taste the same as the rest of the plant but the flavor is more concentrated.

Soil

Lovage is a hardy herb and likes rich, damp soil and a shady site.

Propagation and after-care

Plant seeds in midsummer, in drills an inch (2.5 cm) deep. Transplant the seedlings in fall or spring to positions 2 feet (60 cm) apart. By the time the seedlings are four years old they will have reached their full size and should be spaced about 4 feet (1.2 m) apart. Lovage grows immensely tall; one large plant will be enough to keep a family adequately supplied through the year.

Harvesting

If you want the very large, aromatic leaves for flavoring, water the plants especially well. If they have enough water you will be able to take plentiful cuttings at least three times a year. If you only want leaves, don't allow the plants to flower and seed. Lovage can be dried successfully in a cool oven, at a temperature of less than 200°F (100°C), with the door left a little ajar.

Marjoram (Pot)

PERENNIAL

Pot marjoram is the only type of marjoram that is truly winter-hardy in cool temperate climates. It is a plant that tends to sprawl, throwing out long flowering stems.

Soil

Pot marjoram prefers dry, light soil, with a modicum of sun.

Propagation and after-care

You can grow it from cuttings established under glass and planted out in the spring, or by putting in bits of root in spring or fall. Keep it moist until it is well established. The alternative is to sow seed in spring, in drills half an inch (1 cm) deep and 8 inches (20 cm) apart. Thin to 12 inches (30 cm) apart when the seedlings are big enough to handle.

Harvesting

Harvest leaves and stems in late summer. Pot marjoram dies down in winter, but it is a good idea to pot it and bring it indoors each winter. If you do this the plant will grow through the winter and may well last years longer than it would if you left it outside. Seeds for sowing next year ripen in late summer or early fall.

Marjoram (Sweet)

ANNUAL

Sweet marjoram is the only annual of the three marjorams; it has a delicate aromatic flavor, and goes well with game and poultry stuffings.

Soil

Sweet marjoram needs medium-rich soil, with a neutral pH; it wants a good helping of compost and a warm, sheltered spot.

Propagation and after-care

Sow seeds in pots under glass in early spring. Plant out in early summer 12 inches (30 cm) apart. A combination of warmth and humidity is vital to the good growth of the seedlings while they are still young.

Harvesting

Pick leaves and stems toward the end of summer, before the buds open. Use them fresh or dry in thin layers in the dark and you will get a strong-smelling green herb.

Mint

PERENNIAL

As well as common mint (also known as spearmint), you can grow apple mint, which combines in one plant the flavors of apple and mint; Bowles mint, which is the best type of mint for mint sauce; or peppermint, used to best advantage in peppermint tea. All these mints are slightly and subtly different, but you grow them all in the same way.

Soil

Mint likes moist soil—next to a stream is ideal. It needs sunlight to make it grow with full flavor, although it will stand partial shade.

Propagation and after-care

The best way of establishing mint is to get some roots from somebody who is being overrun by it. In the spring, lay them horizontally in shallow drills 3 inches (8 cm) deep. Don't harvest much mint that first summer. In the fall, cut the plant right down and cover the roots with compost. If you are overrun by it, simply hoe it out.

If you want to force some mint for using in winter, dig up some roots in the fall, plant them in a seed box in good potting mix, and keep them indoors or in a greenhouse under slight heat, say 60°F (16°C). Mint grows well in containers indoors.

Harvesting

Cut fresh leaves whenever you want them. If you want mint for drying, harvest it in midsummer just before it flowers, but don't cut it after a shower of rain; wet leaves will just turn black and go moldy. Peppermint leaves for tea should be dried and stored whole.

Mustard

ANNUAL

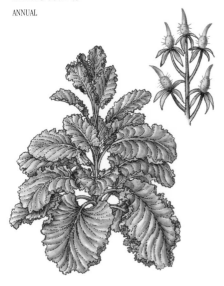

Mustard is grown extensively by gardeners for digging in as a green manure crop, just before it flowers. It grows quickly, makes a bulky crop, and deters the potato-loving eelworm. Mustard can be grown in the herb garden for seed, however, and it is this that makes the mustard that goes in mustard pots. The seeds are ground very finely and the resulting powder kept dry until it is needed, for mixing with water or vinegar. Seeds can be used whole for pickling or for adding to casseroles. Young mustard shoots cut two or three weeks after sowing form the mustard ingredient of the traditional British salad, mustard and cress.

Soil
The seed needs good rich soil, with a pH no less than 6.

Propagation and after-care
The culture of mustard for seed is very easy. Sow in early spring. Broadcasting very thinly will do, but it is better to sow thinly in rows 2 feet (60 cm) apart and thin to 9 inches (23 cm) when the seedlings are established.

Harvesting
Pull the plants out of the ground before the pods are fully ripened, when they are a yellow-brown color. Hang them up in bunches to dry, and thresh the seeds out when the pods are well dried. Grind with a mortar and pestle.

Nasturtium

ANNUAL

Nasturtium is a great asset in the organic garden, because it seems to keep pests away from other plants, especially peas, beans, and soft fruit. People who love pepper but who find it upsets them should turn joyously to nasturtium, for it is an excellent substitute. The leaves spice up salads and add taste to a bland cream cheese spread. You can use the flowers and seeds in salads, and you can pickle the seeds while they are still young and green to use them like capers.

Soil
Nasturtium is an easygoing plant and will grow anywhere, given plenty of sun and light, sandy soil. Poor soil is best if you want a good crop of flowers; but if leaves are your priority, add plenty of compost to the soil.

Propagation and after-care
Sow the seeds *in situ* in late spring. Water them sparingly. The seedlings need little attention. Nasturtium will also adjust quite admirably to being grown in containers.

Harvesting
Cut the leaves in midsummer, just before the plants flower. Chop and dry them, before shredding and storing. The nasturtium flowers do not dry well and are best eaten fresh.

Oregano

PERENNIAL

Oregano, or wild marjoram, is a favorite ingredient in Italian cooking. Its strong spicy flavor suits strong-tasting, oily dishes; if you use it in more delicate dishes, use it in moderation.

Soil
Oregano prefers chalky or gravelly soil, and a warm, dry location. Hillsides are ideal locations.

Propagation and after-care
Sow seed in early spring, thinning later to between 8 and 12 inches (20–30 cm). The final distance between mature plants should be 20 inches (50 cm). Hoe the seedlings well. Like pot marjoram, you can grow oregano from cuttings. It is slow to grow, and needs a hot spell to bring it on really strongly.

Harvesting
Pick the oregano leaves and stems in late summer. Seeds for sowing ripen in early fall. Use fresh or else dry in thin layers in the dark.

Parsley
BIENNIAL

Parsley will enhance almost any dish you care to mention, from the blandest poultry to the spiciest sausage. Its great virtue is that it never overpowers the natural taste of food, just brings it out more fully. Broad-leaved, or French parsley, which is grown in the same way, is more substantial and can be used as an ingredient in salads.

Soil
Many people think that parsley is difficult to grow, but I find that as long as it is given rich enough soil, with plenty of humus, this is not the case. The soil needs to be well worked so that the roots can penetrate deeply. Parsley thrives in containers, but again the soil must be rich and well drained.

Propagation and after-care
You can grow parsley from seed, but the seed is extremely slow to germinate. (A good tip to speed germination is to put the seed between two layers of wet paper towels in your refrigerator for about two weeks.) Sow seed in spring, and exercise patience. Put the seeds in drills half an inch (1 cm) deep; later thin to 3 inches (8 cm) and eventually, when the plants are mature, to 8 inches (20 cm).

You can sow in late summer, for winter forcing. In the winter put a cloche or two over some of your parsley patch. Parsley usually goes to seed in the second year, so you should sow it fresh every year to ensure succession.

Harvesting
Pick a few leaves at a time from each plant. If you want bunches, you can pick off whole plants close to the soil, once the stem is 8 inches (20 cm) high. For drying you should pick leaves during the summer and dry them quickly. Parsley is the only herb to need a very high drying temperature—between 100 and 200°F (39–93°C). Dry it in an oven with the door open.

Rosemary
PERENNIAL

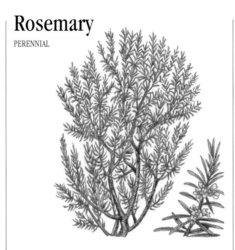

This woody shrub originates from the dry, chalky hills of southern France. It is very ornamental and can grow to more than 5 feet (1.5 m) so it is useful grown in rows to divide vegetable beds. It goes best with rich meats, such as lamb, mutton, or pork. Its piney flavor is pleasant but pervasive, so exercise some restraint.

Soil
Light, sandy, rather dry soil suits rosemary best. It needs plenty of lime, shelter, and a southern exposure.

Propagation and after-care
Sow seeds 6 inches (15 cm) apart in shallow drills in spring. When seedlings are a few inches high, transplant them to a holding-bed, leaving 6 inches (15 cm) between plants. When they are well established, plant out 3 feet (90 cm) apart. Seeds do not always germinate, so taking cuttings—before or after flowering—is more efficient. Cuttings should be 6 inches (15 cm) long. Remove the lower leaves and bury two-thirds of their length in sandy soil in a shady position. By fall they will be ready for planting out. Protect them during their first winter by cutting them back to half their length in late summer; this enables the new shoots to harden off before the onset of cold weather. Then mulch with leafmold and cover securely with burlap.

Harvesting
Pick sprigs in small quantities from the second year onward. You can do this at any time of the year, but late summer is best for drying. You can use rosemary flowers for flavoring as well as stalks and leaves. Pick the flowers just before they reach full bloom.

Sage
PERENNIAL

Sage is strong-tasting stuff—too strong to mingle well with other herbs—but it goes well with spicy sausages, fresh garden peas, or as a flavoring for cream cheese. For cooking use narrow-leaved sage; for drying, broad-leaved. A mature bush is about 2 feet (60 cm) high and is both a useful and an attractive plant to grow in a small garden.

Soil
Sage likes well-drained chalky soil, so lime well if the ground is at all acidic. It does not like damp ground nor too much water.

Propagation and after-care
Narrow-leaved sage can be grown from seed sown in late spring. Transplant seedlings 15 to 20 inches (38–50 cm) apart in early summer.

Broad-leaved sage is always grown from cuttings. Take cuttings with a heel of stem on them, plant out in spring, and water well at first. Sage will last for several years but it is just as well to establish a new bush from time to time.

Harvesting
If you want leaves rich in oils, it is best to wait until the second year before harvesting. Cut narrow-leaved sage in early fall. Broad-leaved sage will not flower in temperate climates; it should be cut in midsummer and again a month later to stop it from going woody. The leaves are tough and take longer to dry than most herbs.

Savory (Summer)

ANNUAL

Summer savory is an annual and tender in cold climates. It can be used fresh or dried. In spite of its strong aromatic smell, it has a more delicate flavor than winter savory. You don't need to grow large quantities, as it grows fast and you only need a little at a time.

Soil and climate

Summer savory will accept poor chalky soil, but thrives on rich humid soil as long as it has not been freshly manured or composted. It will grow in all but the coldest climates.

Propagation and after-care

Sow in late spring in rows 1 foot (30 cm) apart, and thin seedlings to 6 inches (15 cm). It is said that the seed should lie just on top of the soil to germinate, but I find it germinates quite well just below the surface where it is less likely to be eaten by birds. Work the soil well before sowing and keep it damp afterward. Summer savory will often seed itself and shoot up again in the fall.

Harvesting

You should be able to cut summer savory twice from the one sowing; once in summer and again in the fall. Cut shoots just before the flowers open. Harvest the seeds for sowing next year when they go brown. To dry summer savory, lay it on frames, cover with a fine-meshed net, and place in a dark cupboard with a low temperature.

Savory (Winter)

PERENNIAL

Winter savory is more hardy than summer savory. It grows 1 foot (30 cm) high and is bushy, making it an ideal plant for filling the low gaps in garden hedges. Winter savory's strong flavor makes it a good accompaniment for baked fish or lamb.

Soil

Winter savory grows well on poor soil and likes well-drained chalky land. It needs plenty of sun.

Propagation and after-care

Sow seed 12 to 15 inches (30–38 cm) apart in drills in late spring. Don't cover the seeds because they need light to germinate. You can also propagate by planting out cuttings 2 feet (60 cm) apart in the spring.

Harvesting

You can cut shoots in the second year from early summer onward. As with most herbs, harvest before flowering so that you get the maximum content of volatile oil; this also stops the stalks from going woody. Winter savory leaves become very hard when dried, so you should grow the herb indoors during the winter and pick it fresh.

Sorrel

PERENNIAL

Sorrel has a refreshingly acidic taste. It is a close relative of the dock and looks rather like it. It can go raw into salad, and is very good cooked with spinach, omelets, veal, or fish. Sorrel and lettuce soup can be quite exquisite.

Soil

Sorrel likes light, rich soil in a sheltered place, with plenty of sun, but it will grow very adequately in the shade.

Propagation and after-care

You can sow seed in spring and thin the seedlings out later to 6 inches (15 cm) apart. Alternatively you can propagate by dividing roots in spring or fall. When the plant flowers in early summer, cut it back before it goes to seed.

Harvesting

You can start harvesting four months after thinning, or whenever a plant has formed five strong leaves. Cut the leaves with a knife or pull them straight off the plants; cook with them in an enameled pot because an iron one will turn them black. You can dry leaves in the dark and store them in airtight jars.

Tarragon

PERENNIAL

Tarragon is traditional with chicken, good with fish, and excellent in soups; and tarragon vinegar is an excellent salad dressing. There are in fact two varieties, which are often confused: Russian and French tarragon. Russian tarragon is the tougher and the taller of the two plants; French tarragon is stronger-flavored and needs to be checked in its summer growth to stop it from becoming too bushy in the winter.

Soil
Tarragon does not like "wet feet," so good drainage is vital. Try to plant it on a slope so that the roots never get waterlogged. Tarragon likes being exposed to the elements, and puts up with fairly poor soil; it does not even mind stony ground.

Propagation and after-care
It is best to buy young plants or divide mature ones, planting them out to 2 feet (60 cm) apart, after the last hard frost. Every four years transplant cuttings so that you have plants with a full flavor. Do this in spring or fall. You can grow tarragon in pots that you bring indoors in the winter, or cut the outdoor plants right down every fall and cover them well with compost or other litter.

Harvesting
Pick fresh leaves all through the growing period; this will encourage new ones to grow. If you want to dry them, cut the plants down to just above the ground before they flower. You may manage to cut three times during the growing season of an established plant. Dry in the dark at a fairly low temperature.

Thyme

PERENNIAL

This hardy perennial is native to southern Europe. Common thyme has a sharp bittersweet taste. Shoots, leaves, and flowers can all be used—fresh or dried—in soups, stews, and meat dishes of all kinds. Less hardy than common thyme, lemon thyme has a beautiful scent and taste. The leaves are delicious, chopped fine and sprinkled sparingly, on salads or meat. Otherwise lemon thyme is mainly used for flavoring. It is a good plant to grow if you have bees; it gives honey a delicious fragrance, but bees will only collect the nectar in hot weather.

Soil
Thyme likes light, well-drained soil that has been well limed. It does best in a sunny position, and is excellent in rock gardens.

Propagation and after-care
If you grow thyme from seed, sow it in late spring in drills a quarter-inch (0.5 cm) deep and 2 feet (60 cm) apart. It is more usual to propagate by division from an established plant, or by cuttings taken in early summer. Keep the beds well watered and weed-free. Cut back a little before the winter and in subsequent springs cut the shrubs well back to encourage new growth. Lemon thyme trails and in exposed positions should be protected during the winter with straw or leafmold.

Harvesting
Cut once in the first year, but from the second year onward you can cut twice. Cut early if you want to, but flowers can be used with leaves, so you can cut during the flowering period. Cut off shoots about 6 inches (15 cm) long, rather than stems from the base of the plant.

Tree Onions

PERENNIAL

Tree onions are delightfully pungent, and can be used for pickling as well as in stews, or chopped up raw in salads. Also known as Egyptian onions, they differ from other onions in that the onions grow at the top of the stems. The parent bulb stays in the ground to produce another crop the next year, although if you want you can eat the underground bulbs as well as the ones that form on the flower stems.

Soil
Tree onions like a sunny and well-drained spot. They should be started off with a heavy mulch of either compost or well-rotted manure.

Propagation and after-care
You can plant bulbs in fall and spring. Plant them in clumps, 6 inches (15 cm) apart in rows 18 inches (45 cm) apart. Mulch from time to time with compost. The stems may grow as tall as 5 feet (1.5 m), so when the little onions begin to form, use sticks to support the weight of the plants.

Harvesting
Pick the bulblets from the top of the plants as and when you need them.

The Cultivation of Fruits

Containing the planting, growing, and harvesting instructions for members of the families Rosaceae, Rutaceae, Grossulariaceae, Moraceae, Ericaceae, Oleaceae, and Vitaceae.

Rosaceae

Apples, pears, quinces, cherries, peaches, nectarines, apricots, plums, damsons, raspberries, blackberries, and strawberries all belong to the useful and beautiful family of the *Rosaceae*. It is a huge family that includes agrimony, burnet, mountain ash, 500 species of hawthorn, and, of course, the mighty rose.

Most of the fruits grown in temperate climates belong to this family, which splits into several subdivisions. Among them are plants that have stone fruits, like cherries and plums; those that have berries, like strawberries and raspberries; and those that have what botanists call pomes, like apples and pears.

All the species are insect-pollinated, which is why they have such enticing flowers. They also depend on birds and animals to scatter their seed—suitably manured—which is why they have attractive and edible fruits. And so, with the help of other living things, the cycle renews itself, and the *Rosaceae* continue to enhance our lives.

Apples

Apples are far and away the most important hard fruit crop of temperate climates. If you grow early and late varieties and a variety bred for keeping, you should have apples to eat throughout the year. The gap will come in the summer when you should have plenty of soft fruit.

Soil and climate
Apples prefer a good, deep, well-drained loam, though they will do well on a heavy loam. They do not thrive in gravel, very sandy soil, heavy stubborn clay, or shallow soil above chalk or limestone. But if you have unsuitable soil, you can always dig a big pit where you want to plant a tree and bring in some good topsoil from outside.

In places where peaches, outdoor grapes, figs, apricots, citrus fruit, and such things grow well and freely outdoors, it is better not to grow apples. The apple is a cold-climate tree and does better for a period of winter dormancy. It doesn't mind very cold winters (certain varieties will even grow in Alaska), but it doesn't like late frosts once it is in blossom. Late frosts are generally the sort that creep over the land on a still, clear night. Therefore, take care not to plant apples in frost pockets—those places where cold, frosty air gets trapped after it has flowed down from high ground. The floors of valleys and dips in the sides of hills—especially if they contain some obstruction, such as a thick hedge—are likely to be frost pockets. If your land is not flat, plant your apple trees fairly high on the side of a hill, or on a gentle rise, where cold air will not linger. But don't plant them where it is too windy.

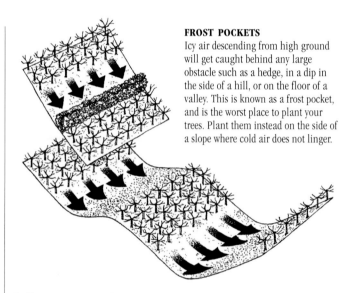

FROST POCKETS
Icy air descending from high ground will get caught behind any large obstacle such as a hedge, in a dip in the side of a hill, or on the floor of a valley. This is known as a frost pocket, and is the worst place to plant your trees. Plant them instead on the side of a slope where cold air does not linger.

Soil treatment
It is a good thing to clear-cultivate land—thoroughly dig it over—before you plant fruit trees on it. Ideally, after clear-cultivating you should grow a crop or two of green manure (*see* p.43) and dig, plow, or rototill this into the soil. But you may be in too much of a hurry to do this—I always am—in which case simply clear-cultivating is perfectly adequate. It improves drainage and kills perennial weeds. Firm the soil well after digging by rolling or treading it, then leave it for two weeks to settle. Make absolutely sure the land is well drained.

Soil should be around neutral (about pH 7) for apples. If your soil is acidic, lime it, but not excessively.

Propagation
Most varieties of fruit tree will not breed true from seed. To establish new varieties you have to grow trees from seed (indeed there is no other way), but once you have found a good variety, the only way to reproduce it faithfully is by vegetative rather than sexual reproduction. In other words, you use hard-wood cuttings instead of seed.

Most apple trees are now grown on dwarfing rootstocks. The different stocks are distinguished by the letter M (for Malling) with a number after it. The most dwarfing rootstock is M9. It produces early maturing trees, large good fruit, and very dwarf trees, but it only grows well on good soil. M26 and MM106 are good semi-dwarfing rootstocks, and M25 is a very good rootstock for large trees. M2 and M111 are good for growing large trees on poor soil.

You can plant seeds to grow your own rootstocks and cut your own "scions," which are healthy fruiting twigs of the current season's growth, usually about 18 inches (45 cm) long. You can then join the two together by grafting or budding.

Plant standard apple trees 16 feet (5 m) apart. You can grow large trees in a circular deep bed (see p.110); goblet or dwarf varieties thrive in an ordinary deep bed, 6 feet (1.8 m) apart, with other plants growing in between the trees.

Care while growing

Maintain mulch around the tree at all times. For the first four years of the tree's life, keep the ground around it free of grass. But the very best thing you can do for the young trees is to keep the ground clear-cultivated all summer and then sow a winter green manure crop in the fall. A mixture of half winter rye and half winter vetch is ideal. Rototill, or dig this in shallowly, in the spring.

PRUNING There are two main forms of pruning: winter pruning and summer pruning. They are quite different and have different purposes.

Winter pruning, which is principally to shape the tree, encourages growth but may delay fruiting; the more you prune a tree in winter the faster it will grow. But a tree putting all its energy into growing can't produce fruit. So once a tree has reached its adult size (usually after about four years for standards), restrict winter pruning to a minimum. Summer pruning, which consists of shortening the current year's growth, helps to stop the tree from growing too fast or too big, and encourages earlier fruiting.

Pests and diseases

My belief is that a thorough spraying with a proprietary winter wash* (*see p.51*) in late winter, well before the buds open, is all the spraying you should need to do. But apart from spraying, there are other things you ought to do.

Be hygienic. Do not leave prunings, dead dropped fruit, or other rubbish lying on the ground. Burn all prunings. Leave fallen leaves to be dragged down by the worms unless they have mildew on them, in which case burn them. Don't leave diseased or cankered trees; pull them out and burn them.

If you have a lot of trouble with pests, wrap a band of paper or cloth covered in grease around the trunk of each tree. Any pests that walk up the trunks will get stuck.

If you have hens, keep them under your fruit trees, because they eat a lot of harmful grubs. In midsummer, carefully examine all your trees, remove any deformed or diseased fruit and put it on your compost pile.

MILDEW If your trees suffer from either downy or powdery mildew, which causes a whitish down on the leaves, then you should burn all the leaves when they drop in the fall.

CODLING MOTHS Codling moths lay their eggs on the blossoms and eventually the caterpillars burrow into the fruit. The solution is to wrap corrugated paper or old burlap around the trunks and major branches in midsummer. The caterpillars will take refuge in these to pupate, and when they do, you can burn them in the fall.

SCAB Scab is a fungus that makes brown patches on fruit. As long as the scabs are small, they are not important. Winter washing* and careful hygiene are the only cures.

APPLE SAWFLY In late summer, yellowish maggots tunnel into the fruit, sometimes leaving them completely inedible and covered in ribbonlike scars. In late summer, hang glass jars, covered with wire gauze, from branches on the sunny side of your tree to trap maggots. Fill the jars with water mixed with sugar, honey, treacle, or molasses.

WOOLLY APHID OR AMERICAN BLIGHT Woolly aphid attacks apples and leaves, causing growths that look like cotton batting on the leaves. Painting such patches with denatured alcohol* will kill the grubs. You can also grow buckwheat near your fruit trees. This will attract hoverflies, which eat the aphids.

APPLE-BLOSSOM WEEVIL Apple-blossom weevils lay their eggs in the blossoms, which commonly causes the blossoms to turn brown and die. The adult weevils eat the leaves. If you get these, put on the burlap or paper trap for codling moths a month early. It will then trap both pests.

CANKER Canker mainly attacks tress in wet climates. Rot develops on branches or trunks. Prune off the affected branches and the affected parts of trunks down to the clean wood and paint the wounds.

Harvesting and storing

Late apples are best stored in a temperature of 40°F (4°C). Frost and excessively high temperatures are fatal. Ventilation must be good but not too vigorous. Throw water on the floor if the air seems too dry. Thick walls and stone, dirt, or tiled floors are better than attics. Either lay the fruits out in a single layer so they are not touching, or or better still, wrap each fruit in newspaper or oiled wraps.

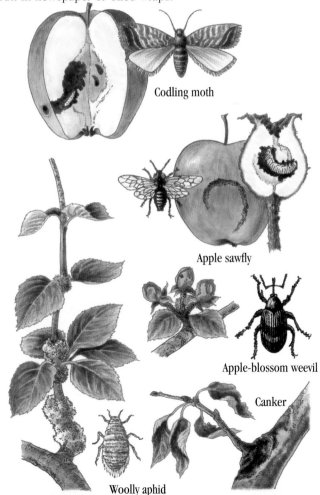

Codling moth

Apple sawfly

Apple-blossom weevil

Canker

Woolly aphid

Pears

If you have space to spare after putting in three apple trees, a pear tree is a good fourth choice, but remember that most varieties need a partner nearby for pollination. The culture of pear trees is very similar to that of apple trees (*see Apples*), although pears are a bit more fussy and they need extra care and attention.

Soil and climate
Pears suffer more from frosts than apples do, because they blossom earlier and the frost can kill or severely injure the blossoms. They also need a dormant period in order to fruit. They prefer heavy soil, but it must be well drained.

Soil treatment
Before planting any fruit tree, you should clear-cultivate the soil (dig it over thoroughly), and pears are no exception to this rule. Soil should be around neutral, pH 6.5 to 7.5.

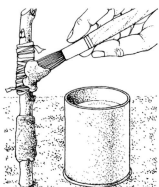

"DOUBLE WORKING" PEARS
Pears are generally planted on quince rootstocks (the quince is closely related to the pear, but hardier and smaller). However, some varieties of pear will not take on quince rootstock and must first be grafted on to a compatible pear variety, which is itself grafted on to the quince.

Propagation
Pears will not breed true from seed. To produce trees that will fruit well and are also hardy and vigorous requires grafting (*see p.176*). The difference between apples and pears is that pears sometimes have to be "double worked."

East Malling Research Station is a worldwide source of pear rootstock. Malling Quince A is most commonly used. Malling Quince C is the best rootstock if you want dwarf trees. Pears are often self-sterile and have to be planted with mutually fertilizing varieties. Plant pear trees in the way described on *p.176*. They can also be grown in a circular deep bed, or six feet (1.8 m) apart in an ordinary deep bed as long as they are kept small.

Care while growing
Except that pears can bear heavier pruning than apples without being stimulated into rampant growth, the pruning procedure for apples and pears is identical (*see Apples*). Tip-bearing pears should be treated like tip-bearing apples.

If a pear tree ceases to produce new growth—and this can happen in a tree that is still very much alive—cut back into two- or even three-year-old wood in order to stimulate new growth.

Fireblight

Leaf blister mite

Pests and diseases
Pears can get all the apple diseases and the same steps should be taken (*see Apples*). There are also some pests and diseases that are peculiar to pears:

FIREBLIGHT Fireblight must be tackled as soon as it is discovered. It attacks at blossom time, causing the blooms to blacken and shrivel, and subsequently every part of the tree blackens as though it has been on fire. Cut out all affected parts at least six inches (15 cm) back from the site of infection with a sterilized knife and burn them immediately. Several varieties of pear are resistant to fireblight.

LEAF BLISTER MITE These tiny mites attack leaves in spring, causing green or red blisters to appear. Pick off and burn the leaves immediately.

PHYTOPHTHORA ROT This is a disease caused by a fungus. Brown patches appear on the skin and the flesh rots. Burn all rotten fruit and spray with Burgundy mixture*.

Harvesting and storing
Pick pears a little before they are completely ripe, as soon as they come off the tree easily when you lift them away. Take exaggerated precautions not to bruise them. Store them like apples as near 30°F (−1°C) as possible, but before you eat them bring them into room temperature and wait for them to ripen. Eat them when they are slightly soft. There is one day in the life of every pear when it is perfect, and with pears, perfect is perfect.

Cherries

It is only really worth planting a cherry tree if your garden or orchard fulfills two conditions. First, there must be ample space to spare after allowing for vegetables, soft fruit, and staple tree fruit—apples, pears and plums; a cherry tree can cover an enormous area of ground, often about 500 square feet (45 sq m). Second, your garden must be relatively free of birds. If it isn't, the birds will eat the cherries, in which case the best thing to do is grow your cherries against a wall and hang a net over them.

There are two kinds of cherries: sweet and sour. Generally speaking, sweet cherries are for eating fresh, and sour cherries are for cooking, canning, and jam-making. Sour cherries have the advantages that they are less attractive to birds and can be grown anywhere in the garden, while sweet cherries need a sunny position or a south-facing wall.

Soil and climate
Sweet cherries thrive on lightish well-drained loam. They even do quite well in gravelly soil, although they send their roots deep and need a good depth of soil beneath them. Sour cherries will do better in clay than sweet cherries will, but they also prefer light deep soil. Both sorts prefer a pH of 6 or 7, but will tolerate more lime than apples, so a pH of 8 will do. They will grow in temperate climates and there are even sour varieties that will fruit in very severe climates. The blossoms of most varieties, however, are frost-tender and should not be grown in frost pockets (see p.154).

Soil treatment
Clear-cultivate the soil (that is, dig it thoroughly).

Propagation
Cherry scions are mostly grafted on wild cherry rootstock. Malling 12/1 is the most common. The simplest thing is to buy the cherry tree you want, already grafted, but if you want to do your own grafting, the appropriate methods are described on p. 176. As nearly all cherries are not self-fertile, it is a good idea to have two varieties grafted on one tree. Choose varieties that flower at the same time. Plant the trees just like apple trees (see p.176). In an orchard they should be 45 feet (13 m) apart. If cherries grow in a border up against a wall, it can be dug as a deep bed (see p.44). Otherwise cherry trees are too large to grow in a deep bed.

Care while growing
Prune cherry trees as illustrated below. It is an advantage to apply material high in nitrogen—about an ounce (28 g) for each year of the tree's growth until it is five years old. Simply sprinkle it on the ground near the base of the tree. Thereafter apply five ounces (140 g) per year. One ounce (28 g) is found in 1 pound (500 g) of cottonseed meal or a half pound (225 g) of blood meal.

Keep the soil bare under cherry trees for the first five years, but don't dig deeply. Hoeing or mulching is sufficient. After the fifth year, clear all weeds away, plant some daffodils, tulips and crocuses around the tree, grass the land down, and leave it. The other alternative is to run chickens under your cherry tree. If you do this make sure you have enough chickens to produce about 25 pounds (11 kg) of manure in a year.

Pests and diseases
BLACK CHERRY APHID These aphids cause severe leaf curl, which is sometimes accompanied by black patches on the leaves. If your cherry trees are badly affected, spray with tar wash or Burgundy mixture* (see p.51).
SILVER LEAF DISEASE If left unchecked, silver leaf disease may kill the tree. It is caused by a fungus that lives on dead wood, so you won't get it as long as you prune well in early summer and cover all wounds with paint.

Harvesting
Harvest sweet cherries when they are quite ripe and eat them immediately. With sour cherries, pull the fruit off, leaving the stalks; otherwise you will tear the tree.

PRUNING A CHERRY TREE
Start with a "maiden" tree. In the spring, shorten all its branches by 6 inches (15 cm). The next spring, cut out all main branches but five. A year later, prune all but two secondary branches on each main branch. Every spring thereafter, cut out all dead or inward-pointing branches.

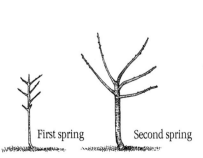

First spring   Second spring   Third spring   Fourth spring

Peaches & Apricots

Peach and apricot trees are very similar and should be grown in the same way; they share the same pests and diseases. Nectarines differ from peaches only because they have smooth skins; botanically they are identical. A peach or apricot is only worthwhile in a cool climate if you already have more than enough apples, pears, and plums. In warmer, but not subtropical, climates they can be treated as a staple. They can be grown in greenhouses.

Soil and climate

Peaches and apricots will grow in sand, or very sandy or gravelly soil, provided there is plenty of humus in it. They like a hot summer and a fairly cold winter. Ideally the winter temperature should go below 40°F (4°C) for some weeks to give them a dormant period, but it should not get too cold. Peach and apricot trees must have a sunny position and must not be grown in frost pockets (*see p.154*). Land sloping down to a lake, river, or estuary is fine. In cool temperate climates they are a very uncertain crop to grow outdoors, but fan-training them up south-facing walls can be successful. If you have to grow them in the open, strangely, a north-facing slope is better than a south-facing one. This is because they won't come into flower so soon on a north-facing slope and will therefore miss the last frosts.

Soil treatment

Dig the soil well and dig in plenty of humus, but not humus too rich in nitrogen. Too much nitrogen makes peach trees rampant, sappy, and more susceptible to frost damage. Peat* and leafmold are very good. A pH of 6 or over is ideal.

Propagation

Plant peach trees in the early spring, except in very mild climates, because cold weather could injure them in their first year. Choose a variety that is known to be suitable for your area (ask a specialty nursery), and plant the trees as you would apple trees (*see p.176*). Peaches can be grown in a circular deep bed. You can buy peach trees ready grafted, or you can do your own grafting (*see p.176*). St. Julien A is a good root stock if you want a small tree; Brompton is best for large trees. Special hardy varieties of peach are now bred that do not need grafting.

Care while growing

The fruit only grows on the previous year's wood and it is wise to remember this when pruning. When you plant a sapling, cut the tree back to about 2 feet (60 cm) above the ground, cutting just above a branch. Prune it hard again in the early summer; cut back all branches to within an inch (2.5 cm) of the trunk (not flush with it). New branches will sprout that first summer beside the stubs of the old ones. Rub off all of them except three, which will form the framework, or "scaffold," of the tree. Do this as soon as the tiny branches show themselves.

The aim now is either to let the most upright of the new branches go upward and make a trunk, or, better still, to let all three grow up and away from each other and form an upside-down tripod. All your subsequent pruning, which must be done each year in early summer, should maintain this shape. Cut out all inward-pointing shoots and cut back all shoots that have died at the tip, until you reach clean white wood with no brown in the middle. Protect all wounds meticulously with tree paint.

In cold climates, give all peach trees nitrogen in the very early spring, about an ounce (28 g) for every year of the tree's growth. This controlled amount of nitrogen enables the tree to grow and fruit vigorously in the summer but to stop growing long before the freezing winter, when new, sappy wood would suffer from frost. Give dressings of compost or manure, in late fall.

Fruit should be thinned so as to give one fruit every 9 inches (25 cm) of wood. This is best done in two stages: toward midsummer, thin to 4 inches (10 cm) apart and then, about four weeks later, when the fruit is the size of a walnut, thin to 9 inches (25 cm).

Peach leaf curl

Pests and diseases

PEACH LEAF CURL This is very common in Europe. The leaves curl and crinkle. Spray with Bordeaux mixture* (*see p.105*) in midwinter and again a month later. Spray once more in the fall just before leaf fall.

LEAF SPOT This is a bacterial disease that causes brown spots on the leaves, and it can be serious. If a tree gets it, give it plenty of manure and it should get over it.

Harvesting and storing

When peaches have turned yellow and are slightly soft to gentle pressure, it is time to pick. Turn the fruit slightly and it will come off. It can be stored for up to two weeks in a cool basement, or frozen (*see p.306*) or canned (*see p.308*). Apricots should be picked and eaten when soft and ripe, or they can be picked a little earlier when still firm, and then dried. To dry them, split the fruit in two and remove the stones. Leave them in trays in the sun, split side up, for up to three days.

Plums & Damsons

Plums and damsons are nice easy crops to grow compared with apples, pears, and peaches. They are fairly hardy, don't get many diseases, and yield very heavily in some years.

Soil and climate
Plums like deep soil, and will flourish in deep loam or clay as long as they are well drained, but they do not thrive in dry, shallow soil at all. Damsons are slightly more tolerant of shallow soil than plums. Plums flower early and are therefore susceptible to spring frosts, so don't plant them in a frost pocket (*see p.154*). Like other temperate climate fruits, plums need to lie dormant through a cold winter.

Soil treatment
A neutral soil is best, around pH 7, so lime if your soil is acidic. Clear-cultivate (thoroughly dig) the land before planting plums, and then, ideally, grow a crop, or even two crops, of green manure. Dig or rototill these into the soil. The land must be well drained. If it is not, fill the bottom foot (30 cm) of the hole you dig for each tree with stones, and bury a line of drain pipes to lead the water away to a ditch or lower piece of ground.

Propagation
Plums and damsons should always be grafted (*see p.176*), and nearly always will be if you buy from a nursery. "Myrobalan B" is a good rootstock for large, heavy-cropping trees that will tolerate clay. "St. Julien A" and "Common Plum" are best for small trees. Plant plum trees as you would apple trees (*see p.176*). Plums are not self-pollinating, so you must plant at least two, and preferably several, compatible varieties. You must get advice from a nursery on this.

Allow 24 feet (7 m) between standard trees if they are planted on "Myrobalan" stock and, say, 15 feet (4.5 m) between trees planted on semi-dwarfing stock such as St. Julien. Plums can be planted in the circular deep bed. Plant plum trees in early winter; but in areas with exceptionally cold winters, plant in early spring.

Care while growing
Plums benefit from quite rich feeding. It is an advantage to have hens or other poultry running under them. Otherwise apply heavy dressings of compost, or stable or cow manure.
PRUNING Plums can be pruned to form all the tree shapes described on p. 177. Prune when you first plant the tree, and thereafter confine pruning to early summer only, because silver leaf disease may develop if you prune in winter.

In some years plum trees bear a considerable weight of fruit, and because their branches tend to be quite slender, those that carry a lot of fruit may need support. There are two ways of doing this. You can build a T-shaped wooden scaffold, which should be firmly rooted in the ground next to the trunk and secured to it with a plastic strap. Ropes from the top of the "T" can be tied around the drooping branches. The other solution is to use a forked branch as a support. Protect the branch with burlap to save it from chafing.

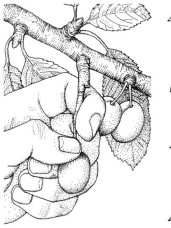
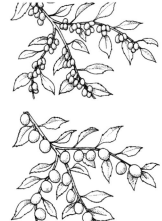

THINNING PLUMS
If your crop is allowed to become too heavy on the tree, the plums may be small and tasteless. Therefore you should thin them when the plums reach about half their final size. Don't pick off the stalk when you pinch off the fruit. Leave at least 2 or 3 inches (5–8 cm) between remaining plums.

Pests and diseases
Plums suffer from the same pests and diseases as apples (*see Apples*), as well as a few of their own.
SILVER LEAF DISEASE The symptom of this is silvering of the leaves, but the disease attacks and can kill the whole tree. It is caused by a fungus that grows in dead wood. As long as you rigorously prune out all dead wood in early summer, burn the prunings, and cover the wounds with paint, your trees won't suffer from silver leaf.
BACTERIAL BLIGHT This shows first as black streaks on the young shoots. Later on, black spots appear on leaves and fruits, which become inedible. There is no cure for this, beyond the pruning and burning of all diseased wood. Some varieties are more resistant to this than others. "Myrobalan" rootstock confers a degree of immunity.
HEART ROT Leaving sawn-off stumps of branches on a tree can cause heart rot; the stumps heal slowly, so bacteria can get in and kill the wood under the bark. You won't get it if you cut all branches flush with the trunk.

Harvesting and storing
For jam or jelly, or for canning (which suits plums admirably), pick the fruit as soon as the bloom appears on their skins, but before they get soft. For eating fresh, pick them when quite ripe, which is when they give a little and come easily off the tree. In hot, dry climates, plums to be turned into prunes can be left on the tree until they are quite dry and ready to be shaken off. They should then be dried in the sun on trays. In damp climates, they can be dried artificially.

Quinces

Quinces are so closely related to apples and pears that the latter are often grafted on to quince stock, because quince stock is hardy and produces small trees. Quinces are not grown as much as they should be; they have a very special and delicate flavor and quince jelly is one of the world's great gastronomic experiences.

Soil and climate
Quinces will grow in any soil or climate that apples will (*see Apples*), although they are a little more tender. They prefer a warm summer and a fairly cold winter. Heavy soil suits them best, but it must be well drained.

Soil treatment
Dig the land thoroughly, and if you are not in a hurry, grow and dig in one or two crops of green manure. The soil should be neutral, pH 7. Quinces don't like too much nitrogen but need phosphate and potash.

Propagation
If you don't buy a seedling from a nursery, the best way to propagate is from cuttings made from the suckers that quinces put out every year. In the fall, cut lengths about 9 inches (23 cm) long, and bury two-thirds of their length in sandy soil. After a year, move these to their permanent positions.

Care while growing
You can prune quinces to all the tree shapes (*see p.177*) or you can leave them strictly alone, in which case you will get a spreading bush shape. Quinces are not prone to being attacked by pests and diseases.

Harvesting and storing
You can leave the fruit on the tree until after the first hard frost. Then make jelly (*see p.313*) right away, or if you don't have time to make jelly immediately you can store the quinces in cool moist conditions for up to three months.

MEDLARS
Medlars are hardier than quinces and can therefore cope with colder conditions. They do best if they are grafted (*see p.176*) on to thorn, pear or quince rootstock. Otherwise treat them like quinces. The fruit is unusual in that its five seeds are visible and it is only edible—and it is actually very good to eat—when it is half rotten.

Raspberries

Raspberries are one of the best soft fruit crops the self-sufficient gardener can grow. They are hardy, and will stand neglect, although they shouldn't have to. They are easy to grow and heavy-yielding.

Soil and climate
They prefer the soil to be slightly acidic, so do not lime under any circumstances. Lime can cause chlorosis (yellowing of the leaves). They do need good soil though, so if your soil is light and sandy, put in plenty of manure. Raspberries prefer sun, but if you have a garden where sun is at a premium, grow your raspberries in a shady area. They will stand colder climates than most other fruits.

Soil treatment
In the fall, dig a trench two spits deep and fill it with soil mixed with compost or manure. They need a lot of potash, so incorporate wood ashes with the soil if you have any; otherwise mix in some other potash fertilizer. They have both shallow and deep roots, and need a lot of humus.

If you only want one row, you have no problem: but the roots spread far and wide, so if you want more than one row then have them quite far apart: 6 feet (1.8 m) is usual in commercial gardens but 4 feet (1.2 m) will do if you are trying to save space.

PROPAGATING RASPBERRIES
Like strawberries, raspberries propagate by "walking." Raspberries "walk" by pushing out roots that send up suckers to form new plants. Just let your plants send up suckers, cut off the roots connecting them to the parent plant with your spade, then lift the suckers and replant them.

Propagation
I strongly advise you to buy raspberry stock that is certified disease-free. Such plants will give higher yields and last far longer than the plants your neighbor offers you when he has to get rid of his suckers in the fall. The certified plants you get will consist of one cane, or whip, with a heel of root attached to it. Plant roots a foot (30 cm) apart in rows 4 feet (1.2 m) apart. Put the root down about 3 inches (8 cm), cover with soil, and firm well. Immediately cut the cane down to 9 inches (23 cm) above the ground.

As long as you start with disease-free stock, there is no reason why you should not then multiply your own raspberry plants in subsequent years. Like strawberries, raspberries "walk," but they do it in a totally different way. In the deep bed (*see p.44*), raspberries should be planted in three rows with 18 inches (45 cm) between the rows. Their shallow roots make intercropping inadvisable. Don't plant raspberries where raspberries have been before.

Don't plant them immediately after potatoes or tomatoes either, for these plants get some of the same diseases.

Care while growing

Don't let them fruit the first summer: remove the blossoms, otherwise the plant will be weakened by fruiting. By the second summer they should bear well. Keep weeds down near the plant by heavy mulching—say, within a foot (30 cm) of them. Lawn cuttings, leaves, or compost are all good. Hoe between the rows. Don't allow grass or weeds to establish themselves; raspberries will not flourish in grass. So be sure that the mulch is thick enough every spring. The raspberry

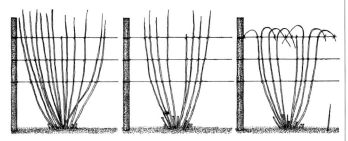

PRUNING RASPBERRY CANES
After cutting out all the old wood, thin the canes, leaving only the best six or eight to fruit the next summer. When these grow over the top wire, shorten them to 6 inches (15 cm) above it; or else bend them over in an inverted "U" shape and tie them to the wire.

rows are a good repository for wood ashes. Training is simple but necessary. You must have a fence, with three wires, the top one 5 feet (1.5 m) from the ground, the others at regular intervals below it. Tie the canes to these. Some people have three pairs of wires and simply shove the canes in between each pair. This works but individual tying is better.

PRUNING In the fall, after the leaves have died off, cut off all the canes that have fruited close to the ground and prune as shown above.

Remember that raspberries act like biennials, although actually of course they are perennials. The wood made in one year fruits the next year and then dies down. So cut out the wood that has fruited every year and keep the wood that grew that year, because that will fruit the next.

Pests and diseases

There are several virus and fungoid diseases that raspberries get. If you see any discoloration or other sign of disease, cut out and burn the affected part.

MOSAIC DISEASE This is the worst of various virus diseases and makes the leaves curl and show red and yellow mottling. Completely dig out the bushes that have this and burn them. If you don't, aphids will spread the virus to other plants.

IRON DEFICIENCY If you see yellowing between the veins of the leaves, suspect iron deficiency. This is especially likely if you have very alkaline soil.

Harvesting and storing

Eat as many as you can ripe and raw with cream. Store the rest; they freeze well (*see p.306*) and can well (*see p.308*). When rain falls on ripe fruit, pick the fruit immediately after the rain stops and can or freeze it; if you don't, the raspberries will go moldy. Don't leave moldy fruit on canes, because the mold will spread to the others.

Blackberries

In most temperate parts of the world, wild blackberries grow nearly everywhere and it is fun hunting for them. Nevertheless, for a regular supply it is worth keeping a few bushes.

Soil and climate

There are several species of blackberry, and cultivated varieties have been developed from them that will grow happily in every climate from the very coldest temperate region to the subtropics. They prefer rich, well-drained soil (pH 7), and a sheltered site.

Propagation

You can propagate blackberries from cuttings, from suckers, by layering, or by division of roots—digging up a piece of plant with roots on it, and replanting. The simplest method of all is to propagate from tip cuttings—cut the tip off a cane, push it into the ground, and it will root. Wrap all planting material in moss or wet newspaper and store it in a plastic bag until you need it.

If you want to grow blackberries from seeds you must "stratify" them; this means that over the winter you must keep the seed in a box full of sand at a warm room temperature for three months, then store them at 40°F (4°C) for another three months.

Plant cuttings, layers, roots or seedlings in late fall or early spring. Allow 6 feet (1.8 m) between the bushes. It is a good idea to plant along a fence, and dig the bed to form a deep bed (*see p.44*).

Care while growing

Blackberries fruit on last year's wood, so prune in winter by cutting all wood that has just fruited unless you have "Himalaya" or "Evergreen" varieties; these fruit for several years on the same wood and therefore it should not be cut out so ruthlessly. As a general rule, leave about ten strong newly grown canes to fruit the following year. They are very greedy plants and need rich mulching to grow and fruit well.

Pests and diseases

ORANGE RUST This shows up as bright orange spores under the leaves. Look for these if your plants give out spindly shoots with narrow leaves. Root out and burn infested bushes.

Harvesting and storing

Blackberries are ready for picking when they almost fall off the bush into your hand. Put them in shallow boxes and store in a refrigerator, or freeze (*see p.306*) for eating in winter.

LOGANBERRIES

Grow loganberry bushes in a sheltered place; although they flower later than blackberries, severe spring frost will damage the canes. Plant the bushes 10 feet (3 m) apart. Unlike blackberries, loganberries only fruit in fall for a two- to three-week period.

Strawberries

Strawberries are fun to grow, if a little awkward. Most gardeners would agree with the remark "Doubtless God could have made a better berry but doubtless God didn't."

Strawberries are a "walking" plant, because they are perennials that don't have an elaborate root system. Therefore they exhaust the ground on which they grow within a year or two. To escape from it and find fresh ground, they send out runners that meander over the ground until they find somewhere to send down roots.

STRAWBERRIES IN BARRELS
Strawberries grow well in pots and tubs of all kinds. A barrel makes an ideal container. Drill several staggered rows of holes three inches (8 cm) wide and 15 inches (38 cm) apart. Drill the rows at eight-inch (20-cm) intervals. Drill several holes in the base and put a layer of gravel in the bottom. Then insert into the center a vertical wire mesh tube four inches (10 cm) in diameter. Fill it with gravel. Then fill the barrel with potting mix up to the first row of holes. Set one plant next to each hole, with the crown emerging. Repeat all the way up the barrel, watering each layer as you go. Finally, set four or five plants in a circle at the very top.

There are several varieties of what are called "remontant" or "perpetual" strawberries. These fruit later than ordinary strawberries and continue fruiting into late fall. It is a very good idea to plant a few, so as to give yourself a treat in the cold weather. If you force ordinary strawberries in the spring under cloches, plastic tunnels, or mini-greenhouses and have remontants as well, you can have strawberries from early summer to late fall.

Soil and climate

Strawberries are a woodland plant, and you should bear this in mind when choosing a site for them and looking after them. It means that they tolerate shade, although they fruit far better in sun; they like plenty of humus (they will grow in almost pure leafmold as they do in the wild); and they don't object to fairly acidic conditions. They do better on light soil than clay, but granted plenty of humus they will thrive in any well-drained place. They are a temperate-climate crop and develop a far better flavor in a cold climate than a hot one. It is best to move on to totally fresh ground every three years with new plants.

Soil treatment

Dig the land one spit deep, incorporating plenty of compost or any well-rotted organic manure. Strawberries do well on the no-digging system (*see p.245*) as long as the bed has had enough compost put on it. They are also potash-hungry, so if you have wood ashes to spare, use them on your strawberry patch. Farmyard manure can be rich in potash.

ENCOURAGING RUNNERS
Start with disease-free strawberries from a reputable source. From then on you can propagate from runners. Every year you should remove the blossoms from a proportion of your healthy plants, so that they are encouraged to send out plenty of strong runners.

Propagation

The first time you plant strawberries, get virus-free stock, from a reputable source, certified healthy. Unless you want to grow new varieties of strawberry, in which case you should grow them from seed, the best thing to do is to multiply them from runners. There are a few varieties that do not make runners, and these are multiplied by dividing up the crowns themselves.

Most varieties of strawberry will make runners that will root themselves whatever you do, but you can encourage them by removing the blossoms from a few of your plants. You have merely to sever the runners from the main plant, dig out the little mini-plant on the end of it, and transplant it. But an even surer way of doing it is to bury small pots of soil in the ground near the parent plants and peg the ends of runners down on these pots. When the runners have rooted properly, sever them from the parent, dig up the pots, and transplant to their new positions. In this way you can establish a new strawberry bed every year and scrap one every year, after it has fruited for three seasons. Every fall you will have a newly-planted bed, a year-old bed, a two-year-old bed, and a three-year-old bed, the last of which will be ready for digging up. Always plant your new beds as far from the old ones as you can, to hinder the spread of disease.

You can plant or transplant strawberries at any time of the year (if the winters are mild enough) but it is traditional to plant in late summer, as you can then harvest a crop the next year. In regions with dry summers, plant in early spring. Plant 15 inches (38 cm) apart with 30 inches (75 cm) between rows. Plant so that the crown is at ground level but the roots are spread out widely and downward. Water the

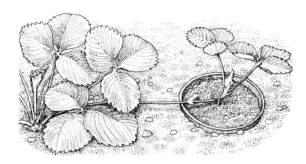

NEW STRAWBERRY PLANTS FROM OLD
Bury pots of soil in the ground near the parent strawberry plants, and peg down the ends of runners on top of the pots. Eventually you will be able to sever the old plants from the new plants, dig up the pots, and then transplant them to their permanent positions in your garden.

new plants well. Strawberries do very well on the deep bed (*see p.44*). Plant and space them as for a conventional bed.

Care while growing

It is very easy for a strawberry bed to become infested with weeds. The plants straggle relentlessly and make most methods of weeding very difficult. Hoe for as long as you can hoe and then weed by hand. If you have planted between the end of one summer and the beginning of the next, let the crop fruit in the year after that but not before: during the plants' first summer, pick off the flowers.

Prick over the ground with a fork in the spring and, as the crop begins to spread, put plenty of straw under the straggling stems. This suppresses weeds and keeps the fruit clean and healthy. But keep an eye out for slugs.

If you suffer much from birds, you will *have* to use a net. You can either have a net low over the strawberries, in which

PROTECTING THE PLANTS
When the fruit begins to form, put a good mulch of straw under the plants. This keeps weeds down and keeps the fruit clean and disease-free. If birds are a nuisance, make a net. Set up posts and invert a glass jar over each one, before putting the netting over the framework; the jars stop the netting from catching.

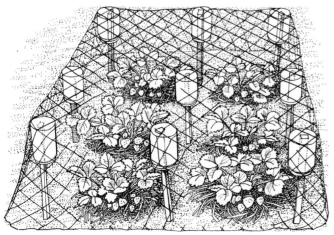

case you will have to remove it every time you want to pick a strawberry, or else a fruit cage, which is expensive unless you make it yourself.

Pests and diseases

Don't try to chase your strawberries on with nitrogen, because it makes them soft and open to disease.

POWDERY MILDEW This white powder will make strawberries turn a dull brown color. Spraying with sulfur* at regular intervals can help.

APHIDS These are a menace because they spread virus diseases, principally strawberry crinkle and strawberry yellow edge, both of which show in the leaves and weaken the plant. To prevent it, spray the plant centers hard in April with a nicotine spray* or with derris. Don't use the nicotine when the berries are nearly ripe. Remove any stunted or discolored plants and burn them; these diseases are incurable.

Strawberry beetle

Gray mold

Powdery mildew

STRAWBERRY BEETLE This little pest feeds on strawberry flesh. Keep the bed well weeded, and it will be discouraged from settling near your strawberries.

GRAY MOLD This is also called botrytis. It appears first as a gray spot on the flowers and then on the strawberries themselves, where it grows to form a gray fur that rots the fruit. Dust with flowers of sulfur* at the very first sign.

ROT If berries rot after rain, remove them to the compost pile. Pick all ripe berries immediately after rain.

Harvesting

Pull the fruits off the plant with their stems intact. Leave the stems on until just before eating; when the stems are removed, vitamins and other nutrients are lost. Store them in the shade for a few hours, or in a refrigerator for a day or two. Strawberries can be frozen, but go soft when thawed.

After you have harvested your crop, remove the straw from under the stems and clear the bed of dead leaves, surplus runners, and weeds.

Rutaceae

Oranges, tangerines, kumquats, lemons, limes, and grapefruit are all members of the *Rutaceae*. Because it includes the genus *Citrus*, the *Rutaceae* family is as important to people who live in the subtropics as the *Rosaceae* family is to people who live in temperate climates. Citrus plants are very aromatic, broad-leaved evergreens.

Citrus fruits grown in the tropics do not taste as good as those grown in what is known as a Mediterranean climate. At the other extreme, they can't stand frost, although oranges can bear marginally lower temperatures than lemons, which are damaged and sometimes killed at temperatures below 26°F (–3°C). This means that citrus fruits growing out doors tend to be limited to the Mediterranean seaboard in Europe; to Florida, southern California, and part of Arizona in North America; and to South Africa, subtropical South America, and Australia. But this does not prevent citrus from being a viable greenhouse crop: in the 18th century, conservatories known as orangeries were common among the wealthy in England.

My own feeling is that if I only had the space under glass to grow one citrus tree, I would grow a lemon. One orange tree provides only a small proportion of the fruit needed by a family through the year, whereas one lemon tree would fill a family's requirements.

Oranges

What the apple is to temperate regions, the orange is to the subtropics. It is heavy-yielding, delicious, will keep well, and has the enormous advantage that it can just be allowed to hang on the tree, for as long as six months. It is a rich and reliable source of vitamin C. In temperate climates, oranges must be grown under glass. They can be grown in tubs, which must be brought indoors in the winter, but the yield from trees grown like this is fairly low.

Soil and climate
Orange trees can stand winter frosts as low as 20°F (–7°C) but fruit and young growth are injured at temperatures below 25°F (–4°C). Oranges like lightish land: sandy loam is ideal; heavy clay is unsuitable. Deeply drained soil is necessary, for they will not thrive on a high water table. Slightly acidic soil is best for them: they will tolerate a pH anywhere between 5 and 7, although they prefer it to be around pH 6.

Soil treatment
Make sure the site is well drained. Dig deeply, and incorporate phosphatic material and potash into the soil. Rock phosphate, granite dust, wood ashes, compost, or farmyard manure all make a reserve for the roots to draw on in times to come.

Propagation
Nearly all orange trees are grafted on rootstocks, because the best fruiting varieties are not the most hardy and vigorous. It really is best to buy them ready-grafted, because grafting oranges is a delicate process, but if you want to graft your own, the techniques are described on p.176. When you buy your trees, you should take note of the rootstocks, as these will affect the type of fruit that your trees produce. The most common rootstocks are listed below:

TRIFOLIATE This is best for most gardens. It is very hardy, can put up with cold better than most other varieties, and is a dwarfing stock.

CLEOPATRA This is the best rootstock for both tangerines and small oranges.

ROUGH LEMON This rootstock thrives on sandy soil. It produces fruit early, but the trees are rather short-lived.

SWEET ORANGE Good in well-drained sand, this rootstock is useless in clay, where it gets foot-rot. It produces juicy, smallish fruit.

SOUR ORANGE Strange as it may seem, the sour orange rootstock is good for sweet orange fruiting stock, because it is hardy and disease-resistant.

There is a huge selection of fruiting stocks available. They are all either sweet for eating, or sour for making marmalade. The most common sweet varieties are "Jaffa," which are large and juicy, "Valencia," which are good to eat and have a long fruiting season, and "Washington Navel," which is the best one for hot, dry climates like the southwestern US.

You can plant orange trees at any time of the year as you would apple trees (*see p. 176*). Good nurseries send the trees out with their roots "balled": that is, wrapped in burlap with soil inside around the roots. Plant orange trees with extreme care so as not to disturb the soil around the roots.

Place the roots, wrapping and all, in the hole; pour some topsoil around the ball, then carefully withdraw the wrapping. A big tree should be 25 feet (7.6 m) from its neighbors: one on a dwarfing stock such as Trifoliate, 20 feet (6 m). Water well after planting and make sure the tree is well watered for two weeks. After that, continue to water regularly—about once a week, depending on the soil.

A modification of the deep-bed method may be used for oranges and all other citrus fruits. Deep-dig a circle for each tree. The diameter of the circle should correspond to the dripline—that is, where the branch extremities of the adult tree are expected to be. Keep the circle of soil raised, heavily mulched, and don't step on it.

PLANTING ORANGE TREES
Your orange tree should arrive from the nursery with its roots already "balled"; that is to say, with a ball of soil wrapped around the roots with burlap. Place the tree in the hole prepared for it with the wrapping still around the roots. Pour some topsoil into the hole before gently removing the burlap.

Care while growing
In regions with high rainfall, some watering in dry periods may be necessary for the first three years; after this, none is needed except in cases of real drought. In dry areas, where there is little rainfall, trees need a good soaking every two or three weeks; this means 20 to 30 gallons (90–140 l) per tree. More water than this may wash the nutrients down out of reach of the roots. Watering "little and often" encourages foot-rot.

You should also feed the soil by mulching heavily with organic material once a year. If low-nitrogen material is used, such as hay or straw, some source of more concentrated nitrogen—blood meal or cottonseed meal—should be added to help rot the material down. If rotted compost is used, nothing need be added.

Pruning is minimal with orange trees. Trees should come from the nursery already pruned so as to leave a suitable "scaffold" of four or five branches. Small sprouts that come from the trunk under this scaffold should be rubbed out by hand when they are tiny. Old weary trees can be stimulated into new life by pruning some of the old wood away; choose wood in the center of the tree, which does not get much sun. Cut out any frost-damaged branches, but not until the summer after the frost. It is important not to stimulate trees into

RUBBING OUT SHOOTS
You will usually receive your tree with a good scaffold of four or five branches already established; it is therefore unlikely to need much pruning. If you notice any new shoots emerging from the trunk, rub them out by hand while they are still very small.

excessively rank growth by cutting out too much wood. Sometimes upper branches grow so long that the lower growth is shaded. You cannot remedy this by pruning. But in a group of several trees, the solution is to take out one or two, so that more light reaches the rest.

Pests and diseases
The many pests that trouble orange trees in inorganic orchards are seldom present in organically managed ones. Eelworm, for example, never becomes a serious problem in an orchard planted on organically rich soil, because predators thrive on unsprayed trees.

FOOT-ROT In long periods of wet weather, orange trees are susceptible to foot-rot, which rots the bark near the soil line and in extreme cases can kill the tree. You can prevent this by observing a few simple rules: keep the mulch at least a foot (30 cm) away from the trunk of the tree; keep that circle free of fallen leaves and debris; don't water right up against the trunk, and don't water too *often*; always keep the junction of trunk and roots clear of soil.

Harvesting and storing
The delightful thing about oranges is that you can leave them on the tree and just pick them when you want them. Pull tight-skinned oranges off with a twist: loose-skinned ones should be snipped off with a little stalk left on them. They can be stored under refrigeration—at 30°F (–1°C) with a humidity of 80 or 90 percent—but you are unlikely to need to do this, because oranges have a very long harvesting season. And remember that a green orange is not necessarily unripe. Orange-colored oranges will sometimes turn green again when the weather gets warmer. They still taste the same.

TANGERINES, MANDARINS, AND SATSUMAS
Tangerines, mandarins, and satsumas are all classified as *Citrus nobilis*. Tangerines have a deeper-colored skin than mandarins and the name "satsuma" was originally applied to a particular variety of tangerine. The terminology has now become confused and the names "mandarin" and "satsuma" are often used to apply to the whole group. The fruits are in general smaller than ordinary oranges, the skins are looser, and the sections separate more easily. The advantage is that the trees are smaller and more hardy than orange trees and are therefore suitable for small gardens, roofs, and patios. Cultivate the trees as you would orange trees, bearing in mind that most varieties are not as productive as sweet orange trees.

KUMQUATS
A kumquat tree is an attractive proposition, particularly in a small garden, and they can be grown on roofs and patios in tubs. Kumquats belong to the *Fortunella* genus, but this is so closely related to *Citrus* that crosses between kumquats and oranges can be made. Certainly the orange-colored kumquats look exactly like tiny oranges. The fruits are rarely bigger than one and a half inches (4 cm) in diameter, but are very juicy and good to eat; also, the peel is spicy and makes splendid marmalade or candied peel. Kumquat trees are very decorative and rarely grow taller than 10 or 12 feet (3–3.5 m), and their other advantage is that they are hardier than virtually any other citrus fruit (especially if grafted on to Trifoliate rootstock). You grow them in exactly the same way as oranges.

Lemons & Limes

Apart from ordinary lemons, you can also grow the Meyer lemon, which is a hybrid particularly suitable for small gardens. It is hardy—sufficiently so to survive temperatures of 15°F (–9°C)—and quite small. Outdoors it makes a bush about 6 feet (1.8 m) tall. It grows well in tubs, on roofs, and on patios. Limes are used in much the same way as lemons, but contain more acid and more sugar.

MEYER LEMON BUSHES
This hardy little lemon hybrid will flourish, given a sheltered spot, full sunshine, and plenty of compost. Flowers, immature fruit, and ripe fruit are all to be found on a thriving bush at one and the same time.

Soil and climate
Lemon trees are slightly more tender than orange trees and prefer heavy soil. As they fruit all year, the crop can be badly damaged by winter frost. This also applies to limes, which are less hardy still. Lemons and limes are very much a subtropical fruit. They will tolerate most soils, provided that the water table is below the depth of their roots, which go down no more than 4 feet (1.2 m). You should incorporate plenty of phosphatic material into the soil.

Propagation
Buy lemons and limes already grafted. Plant them as you would any other tree (*see p.176*). The most usual rootstocks are the same as for oranges. You can plant lemons in a circular deep bed.

Care while growing
Lemons need a little more pruning than oranges, enough to stop them from straggling and becoming vulnerable to bad weather. Shorten any outward-straggling branches to inward-pointing buds so as to keep the tree compact. You can do this at any time of the year. Limes do not need any pruning. If your trees are thriving but not bearing, protect them from the wind and feed them a lot of extra compost; this extra attention should make all the difference.

Harvesting
Both lemons and limes bear year-round in suitable climates, so just pick them when you want them.

Grapefruit

Grapefruit evolved in the West Indies as a sport, or mutation, of the shaddock, which is a coarse and rather unattractive fruit, but the grapefruit, as we all know, is delicious. It is also a rich source of vitamin C.

Soil and climate
Grapefruit must have deep, well-drained soil and like it to be slightly acidic: a pH of 6 is best. As for climate, they can stand as much cold as oranges, 20°F (–7°C), but they need more heat to ripen perfect fruit. In temperate climates, grapefruit must be grown under glass.

Soil treatment
Well-drained soil is most essential. Deep digging—four spits deep if possible—is important, and you should incorporate some phosphate and potash into the soil. Compost or manure buried below the roots can only do good.

Propagation
Grapefruit are generally grafted on to sour orange rootstock, although on poor sandy soil it is better to use lemon. Plant the young trees (*see p.176*) at any time of the year; because they are evergreens, one time is as good as another. You must plant them very carefully, as you must other evergreens (*see Oranges*). Plant trees 25 feet (7.6 m) from their neighbors. You can plant them in a circular deep bed.

Care while growing
Grapefruit need plenty of water. In high-rainfall areas they need watering for the first three years and then probably not at all. In dry areas they need a good soaking—say, 25 gallons (100 l) per tree every three weeks. Don't put water actually on the trunk. Heavy mulching can only do good, provided you keep the mulch 2 feet (60 cm) away from the tree. Prune them in exactly the same way as oranges; they suffer from the same pests and diseases (*see Oranges*).

Harvesting and storing
Grapefruit will stay happily on the tree for months, but when the fruits begin to turn yellow, test the occasional one so that you know when to pick them. When they are just right, pick them, wipe them with a clean damp rag, let them sit in a cool place in a breeze for a few days, then put them in the refrigerator.

Grossulariaceae

Black currants, red currants, white currants, and gooseberries are members of the family *Grossulariaceae*. They belong to the important genus *Ribes*, all of whose members are shrubs that display familiar small round berries. Currants and gooseberries are exceptionally hardy and are cultivated almost as far north as the Arctic circle. They are very popular in Europe, but less so in North America, because they can be alternative hosts to white pine blister rust and are for this reason prohibited in several states and countries. Personally I would rather have black currants and gooseberries and prohibit white pines, because I think they are both magnificent fruits, and black currants are probably the best source of winter vitamin C available to mankind. White currants, which are actually more yellow than white, have a fine, distinctive flavor when eaten raw. Red currants are grown primarily for making into red currant jelly, though they are good eaten raw or cooked.

Gooseberries

Gooseberry bushes are good plants to grow in smallish gardens because they yield a lot of fruit from a small area. They can be trained as cordons (*see p.177*), in which case they take up hardly any space at all.

Soil and climate
Gooseberries will thrive in almost any soil but have a slight preference for heavy soils. They like a cool climate, and are very tolerant of shade. They can therefore be planted in places where there is too much shade for most plants.

Soil treatment
Dig deeply and incorporate manure or compost in the top spit, over quite a wide area, because the roots are shallow but spread a long way laterally. A pH of 6 to 8 is suitable for them. Incorporate some lime if the pH is less than 6.

Propagation
Plant new bushes during fall or winter. Bush plants should be 5 feet (1.5 m) apart and cordons a foot (30 cm) apart in the row. In a deep bed (*see p.44*), gooseberries should be planted 4 feet (1.2 m) apart in a line down the middle of the bed.

Care while growing
When the bushes are two or three years old, cut half the length off each leader to a suitable bud. If the plant is droopy, cut to an upward-pointing bud: if it is upright, cut to an outward-pointing bud. Cut all lateral growths back to within three inches (8 cm) of the stem. In each subsequent year, cut out a good proportion of the old wood.

Every summer, shorten all laterals, keeping about five leaves on each. At that time you can examine the bushes for mildew, and cut out any shoots that are infected. Gooseberry bushes should be grown on a "leg," a short main stem. You must keep the ground under and between the bushes clear of weeds. Don't dig, for fear of injuring the shallow roots, but hoe, scuffle, or rototill very shallowly.

Pests and diseases
AMERICAN GOOSEBERRY MILDEW The first symptom is a white felt that covers the young leaves and shoots. The berries themselves acquire a brownish covering. The best prevention is not to give the bushes too much nitrogen. If you do get it, pick off and burn all affected shoots, and spray, in midsummer, with a mixture of half a pound (228 g) of soft soap, 1 pound (500 g) of washing soda*, and 5 gallons (23 l) of water. You can spray with this again in the spring when the bushes flower and once again when the fruit is set.

GOOSEBERRY SAWFLY These are small caterpillars with green and black spotted bodies and a yellow tail. They produce three generations in a season and can strip your bushes of leaves. Spray hard with derris, pyrethrum, or quassia*.

RED SPIDER MITE The tiny red mites cluster on gooseberry leaves, causing them to turn bronze with a white area underneath. Ultimately the leaves will dry up and die. The answer is to knock them off the bush with a jet of water.

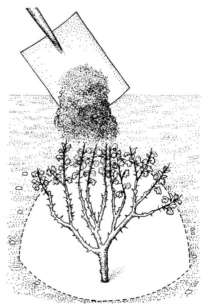

"MOUNDING" GOOSEBERRIES
Cut an old bush back in early spring to within 12 inches (30 cm) of the soil. This encourages new shoots to grow. Then in midsummer build up a mound of soil and compost around the bush, so that only the tips of the canes are visible. By fall the canes will have put out roots. You then gently remove the soil, cut out the canes with the strongest roots. and transplant them.

Harvesting
Strip the fruit off by pulling the branches through a hand protected by a thick leather glove. The fruit falls off and can be caught in a sheet. It can then be separated from the leaves and other flotsam that get stripped off by rolling the whole lot down a board. The fruit rolls, the rest does not. If you don't eat them fresh, can them or make jam.

Currants

BLACK CURRANTS

Black currants are one of the best and most reliable sources of vitamin C in cold, moist climates. Alaska is not too far north to find them growing, and they thrive in Scotland and Sweden. They are hardy and easy to grow, store well, and make all sorts of delicious preserves and wines. They are heavy-yielding and do not take up too much room. You do not have to wait too long to start picking, either. In my view, of all fruits, either "hard" or "soft," black currants are the most rewarding to grow.

Soil and climate

A fertile heavy clay-loam with plenty of organic matter in it is perfect for black currants, but you can grow them on practically any soil if you add enough compost or farmyard manure. I have grown them with great success on heavy boulder clay and on sand, but with both I had to mulch heavily every year with organic material. A great advantage of black currants is that they are hardy enough to be planted in frost pockets. They like a cool and moist climate, because hot winds dry out their leaves. But they can be grown in hot dry countries as long as they have some shade, such as the north-facing wall of a house. You can also intercrop with apple trees in an orchard, although in this case make sure that the bushes are not starved of moisture as well as being protected from heat.

Soil treatment

Black currants are shallow-rooted. Nevertheless, prepare the ground by digging deeply, because they benefit from soil that is well drained and aerated. Also incorporate plenty of organic material before planting. Dig in ground rock phosphate if you can get some cheaply, hoof and horn, or anything else that is going to last a long time and release nutrients slowly. I always give black currants plenty of manure, but I don't use well-rotted compost, because I reserve this for the things that really cannot do without it. For all my soft fruit, including black currants, I use long-strawed stable or cow-shed manure.

Make sure the ground is free of perennial weeds: once the bushes are in the soil, it will be hard to destroy any weeds that are left.

Propagation

To start off it is best to buy bushes from a reliable nursery so that you are sure they are healthy. After that, you can multiply your own stock for the rest of your life, because black currants

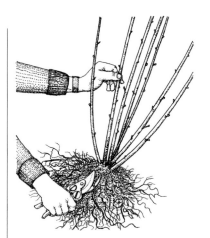

TRIMMING BACK ROOTS

When you are planting your black currant bushes, the roots should be wet. Spread them out well over the shallow holes you have dug in readiness, and cut back first any roots that are broken or torn. Then trim back any very thick roots, but leave all the fine, fibrous ones intact.

grow very easily from cuttings. Because currant buds start growing very early in spring, plant the bushes in late winter; if your winters are not harsh, plant in fall, so the roots can get established before the ground freezes.

When you plant your new bushes, dig wide shallow holes 4 feet (1.2 m) apart. If the roots of the bushes are dry when you get them, soak them in water for several hours before planting. Spread the roots carefully, first snipping off any very long or broken ones. If you use the deep-bed method (*see p.44*), plant a row of bushes along the middle of the deep bed at intervals of 4 feet (1.2 m), preferably alternating currants with gooseberries. Use the space at the edges of the bed to grow annual vegetables. As soon as you have planted the bushes, snip off all the branches to outward-pointing buds, leaving at least three or four buds on every shoot.

When you come to propagate from cuttings you must use the current year's wood. Black currants fruit on the previous year's wood, so it is not expedient to cut too much new wood off the bushes. But when you are pruning older bushes, you will inevitably cut out a certain amount of old wood on which some new wood has sprouted.

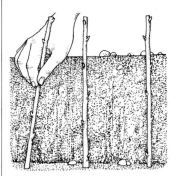

PROPAGATING FROM CUTTINGS

Prune off cuttings of new wood from 8 to 12 inches (20–30 cm) long, and in the fall, plant them deeply in good light soil with two buds above ground. Keep them from drying out, and protect them with straw mulch; plant out the following spring.

Care while growing

Prune the bushes annually in early winter. The thing to remember is that they fruit only on the previous year's wood, so you cannot expect any fruit the first year. Therefore, preserve all new wood (which is yellow or light brown) every year, if you possibly can, so that it can fruit the following year, but cut out all the wood that has already fruited. You can tell which is the older wood because it will still have the little stalks of the berries on it.

Mulch with plenty of manure, and wood ash when you have it, and keep the ground clear of weeds.

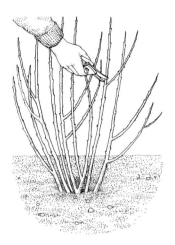

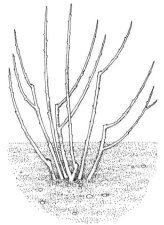

PRUNING BLACK CURRANTS
Every year in early winter, cut out as much old wood that has already

fruited as possible, while preserving the new. Cut off the old wood just above a good new low-growing shoot.

Pests and diseases

LEAFSPOT FUNGUS This distressing disease can cause all the black currant leaves to turn brown and drop off in midsummer. Rake up all affected leaves and burn them or put them in a hot compost pile.

CURRANT MAGGOT The black currants themselves are sometimes attacked by maggots. This is more common in North America than in Europe. Currants that ripen before their time should be examined and any with maggots destroyed.

BIG BUD This very common disease causes the new buds of the plants to swell unduly in midsummer. Simply pick off all such swollen buds and burn them.

REVERSION The big bud mite carries the reversion virus. The leaves of the bushes change shape and look rather like nettle leaves. The bushes flower earlier and the flowers are brighter than usual, but the crop is poor and dies fast. There is no cure for reversion, so the moment you notice it, you should root up the bush and burn it.

CURRANT SHOOT BORER/CURRANT CORE BORER Apply a winter wash* in January with a tar-oil spray to prevent these pests; the spray will also keep off aphids. If you do see a cane's leaves wilting at the tip, cut the branch back until you find the tunnel, and kill the borer.

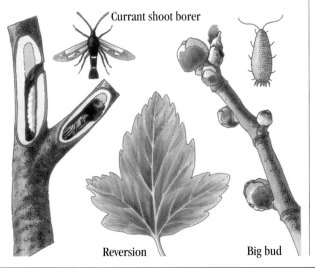

Currant shoot borer

Reversion   Big bud

CORAL SPOT/DIEBACK These two fungus diseases are caused by too much nitrogen. Cut back any wood that seems to be dying, or that shows the distinctive red spots of coral spot on the branches. Cut right back to sound white wood, and burn the affected branches. Then stop feeding the bushes

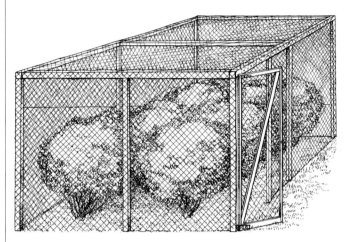

PROTECTING BLACK CURRANTS
If birds are likely to strip you of your entire black currant crop, you must

protect the bushes. An excellent way of doing this is with a fruit cage of wire mesh supported on a frame.

with high-nitrogen manure such as stable manure; mulch instead with waste vegetable matter, spoiled hay or straw, and a little well-rotted compost.

Harvesting and storing

You can just leave currants on the bushes if there are no birds; likewise, if you grow them in a fruit cage there is no hurry to pick. But don't leave them too long, or they will fall off the bush. Currants freeze well, can well, and make fine wine, jelly or jam. They are one of gardening's greatest rewards eaten raw with cream.

RED AND WHITE CURRANTS

You should treat red and white currants in exactly the same way as black currants, but there is one important difference. The fruit on red and white currant bushes is borne on two- or three-year-old wood. This means that you prune for the first time when the bush is two years old, by cutting out all the wood except seven or eight good shoots.

Each year after that, cut out all new shoots, except for three or four that suit your plan for the shape of the bush. In the third year and every year after that, cut the oldest shoots right back to the ground.

The aim is to have a few one-year-old, a few two-year-old, and a few three-year-old branches on every bush, with plenty of short fruiting spurs on each branch. The other important thing is a good shape—open in the middle, not too spread-eagled, and yet not too bunched up.

Prune the fruiting spurs as you would on an apple tree (*see p.155*), because the fruit is borne on spurs like apple spurs. The principle is to snip back side-shoots to one or two buds to encourage spur-making.

Bush trees should be trained on "short legs" (main stems a few inches high), but red and white currants are also excellent for cordon training or espaliers (*see p.177*).

Moraceae

Figs and mulberries belong to the family *Moraceae*, whose other members include: hemp; hops; the rubber trees of Southeast Asia and their diminutive, the popular household rubber plant; and a number of tropical and semitropical trees with exotic-sounding names like the breadfruit tree, the snakewood tree, and the trumpet tree. Figs and mulberries are unusual members of the family in that they thrive in temperate climates. All they need is plenty of sun. And figs do better on poor soil than on rich soil, where in order to make them fruit, their roots must be confined artificially. Figs and mulberries are both delicate fruits that do not travel or store well. They should therefore be eaten fresh from the trees; otherwise, figs must be dried or canned, and mulberries must be made into jam or wine. Both trees are attractive and long-lived and grow to about 30 feet (9 m) high.

Figs

Figs are a Mediterranean fruit that was said, in ancient Greece, to be the food of the philosophers. Whether this is so or not, they are quite an experience to eat. They will also grow in much colder climates than is generally thought, as long as they get lots of sun and plenty of water.

Soil and climate
In temperate climates, figs will flourish on the worst soil you have, provided it is well drained and in full sun. They grow very well against a south-facing wall and will tolerate clay, lime-rich soil, sandy soil, or rubble.

Soil treatment
Figs like plenty of humus, so you can mix compost with their earth. Give them a little lime as well. In heavy clay, poor gravel, or sandy soil, you will have no problems; this is the sort of soil found in the warm countries where the fig is native. But in all other soils it is best to confine the roots. This can be done by growing the trees in a concrete box, or in any other sturdy receptacle, buried in the ground. They will also grow in barrels or huge pots, indoors or on a patio. Allow for drainage from the box or container.

Propagation
Figs will grow from suckers, cuttings, or layers. To grow them from cuttings, cut lengths of ripe wood about a foot (30 cm) long from an existing tree in late fall. Plant these cuttings in a shallow trench of good light loam, so that they come out of the ground at an angle of 45 degrees. Leave one growing point only above the surface. Plant the cuttings at 9-inch (22-cm) intervals.

Cover them with loose soil during the winter, so that they are completely buried. In spring, scrape away the surface soil and expose the cuttings, cover them with cloches, and water them whenever the soil is dry. They must not dry out. When the weather has really warmed up, remove the cloches, mulch well, and keep them well-watered until the fall. Then plant out the cuttings in their final position, taking great care not to damage the roots.

If an old tree throws up suckers from its roots, you can dig these out in late fall, keeping the roots intact, and plant them in their permanent position. You can also layer a low branch by pegging it down to the soil. Once it has rooted, transplant it.

Care while growing
Cut out a branch from time to time to keep the tree open, if it seems to be overcrowded. And in early summer each year, nip off the first half-inch (1 cm) of all the leading branches to make them bush out instead of allowing them to grow long and straggly. When the fruit begins to swell, water copiously. Two or 3 gallons (9–14 l) a day are in order if the weather is dry.

Pests and diseases
COTTON ROOT ROT Figs get this disease if they are planted after cotton. It is incurable; trees wilt and die.
SOURING If disease-carrying insects get into the open end of the fruit, the fruit will shrivel and taste sour. Pull off any diseased or shriveled fruit and put on the compost pile.

Harvesting and storing
Eat your figs straight from the tree when they are ripe. Any that you can't manage to eat should be dried. This can be done in hot sun, on racks, or in a drying box.

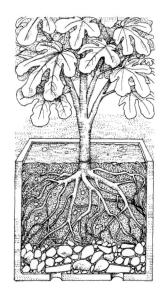

CONFINING FIG TREE ROOTS
If you plant a fig tree in good soil, it will grow well and get very large, but it may not set any fruit for as much as half a century. This is because the roots spread so much farther than the top of the tree that a severe imbalance is caused: nourishment at the root tips never reaches the leaves, so branches straggle and growth is weak. The solution is to confine the roots. Grow the tree in a concrete box buried in the ground. Allow for drainage from the box by making one or more drainage holes in the bottom. Shield the holes well with tiles or broken crockery, so that water can get out but the roots stay in.

Miscellaneous

Mulberries

The name mulberry in fact refers to a multitude of fruits, from a white or red mulberry tree 50 or 60 feet (15–18 m) tall, right through to a white mulberry shrub grown to feed silkworms. The white mulberry grown so freely in the mountains of Persia (present-day Iran) is an insipid fruit, but the wine-red mulberry grown in Europe and North America is a splendid fruit and deserves to be cultivated a lot more.

Soil and climate
Mulberries will grow in any garden soil with a neutral pH. Most varieties are very hardy in temperate climates, apart from the black mulberry which only grows in hot regions.

Soil treatment
Dig deeply and incorporate compost or manure.

Propagation
If you can get a tree from a nursery, just plant it as you would an apple tree (see p.176). Allow it plenty of room to grow; trees should be about 30 feet (9 m) apart. They can be planted in circular deep beds. After you have planted one or two, the trees will proliferate, because birds drop seeds far and wide; otherwise you can propagate from cuttings.

Care while growing
There is nothing difficult about growing mulberries. Just give the trees a good mulching now and again. They are rarely attacked by pests or diseases. When the trees are established, sow grass around them, because this will facilitate harvesting.

Harvesting and storing
Mulberries are highly perishable, so eat them when they are ripe. From a commercial point of view this is a disadvantage; the fruit does not keep for any time at all and must be eaten very quickly. Wait for the fruit to fall to the grass below the tree and gather it immediately. If the tree is situated so grass cannot be grown beneath it, spread hay or straw on the ground during the fruiting season. A word of warning: mulberry juice stains very badly, so wear old clothes when harvesting.

Mulberries and cream are delicious; mulberry wine (see p.326) can be superb. Birds adore mulberries; if you grow them near cherries they will eat the mulberries and leave the cherries; if you grow them in or near a chicken run, the great weight of fruit that a mature tree produces every summer will fall to the ground and feed the hens, and you will get all you want, too.

Blueberries

Blueberries are the fruit for those who have sandy, acidic, waterlogged soils in cold climates. "Blueberry" is often misused as a collective name for several species of the *Ericaceae* or heath family, which includes such fruits as bilberries and cranberries. All these edible fruits grow wild, in cold mountain climates where no other fruit will grow. Only the blueberry proper can be cultivated with success, however, and there are several improved cultivars.

The bushy shrub has attractive white or pinkish flowers and brilliant fall leaf color. It can grow as high as 15 feet (4.5 m). The bushes are slow to mature; after three years they will probably provide you with at least some fruit, but it may take as long as eight years before they bear a full crop. Mature bushes bear very heavily.

Soil and climate
Wild blueberries grow on very acidic soils with a high water table. They do not possess root hairs, so they cannot suck moisture from damp soil particles as other plants can. They therefore need water within reach of their roots. Also, they cannot absorb nitrates and must therefore have their nitrogen in the form of ammonia. This means they must have acidic soil because ammonia-forming bacteria cannot live in anything else.

Ideally they should be planted in light loamy soil with plenty of humus and some sand, and the pH should not be above 5; 4.5 is ideal. They must have a cold climate with at least 100 nights at a temperature as low as 40°F (4°C), but they should be planted in full sunlight.

Soil treatment
Blueberries must have plenty of organic material. They will not grow in purely mineral soils, no matter how much artificial fertilizer is put into it. If the pH is above 5 you should lower it by digging in plenty of leafmold, sawdust, or peat* some months before you intend to plant.

Propagation
Blueberries do not root easily and it is better to buy plants from a nursery. Plant them in spring six feet (1.8 m) apart in rows 8 feet (2.5 m) apart, in shallow holes that have been filled with an equal mixture of topsoil and organic matter. After planting, mulch heavily with sawdust, and cut half the length off each branch. Blueberries will grow from layers as well. Nick the underside of each branch before pegging it down for layering.

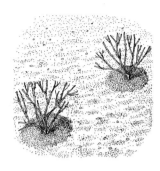

PLANTING BLUEBERRY BUSHES
Immediately after the bushes are planted, give a 4- to 6-inch (10–15-cm) mulch of sawdust (*above left*).

At the same time, cut all the branches back by half (*above right*); this gives the roots a chance to catch up with the top growth.

Care while growing

Keep the soil constantly moist under the mulch during the first year. For the first four years, don't allow the bushes to fruit at all. Strip off all flower clusters. From the fifth year on, remove all fruiting buds except one for every 3 inches (7 cm) of branch. Cut out some of the main branches, aiming to leave one for every year of the tree's age. Cut out all small weak laterals every summer. The bushes do not reach full maturity until they are ten to fifteen years old. From then on they will yield as much as 30 pints (17 liters) per year. When strong new shoots grow up above the top of the bush, cut them to the level of the bush to encourage the growth of laterals. Every year the trees must be heavily mulched with organic material. Don't let any lime or sea-sand come near them.

Pests and diseases

TENT CATERPILLARS These pests are the most harmful insects to attack blueberries. They spin tents of silk over the leaves; either pick off the eggs during the winter or remove caterpillars and eggs in the spring.

CANKER This causes reddish-brown wounds on the stem that kill the buds nearby, and in severe cases can girdle the trunk and kill the whole cane. Canker can be prevented by growing the blueberries in an airy place, by keeping the bush open by pruning, and by immediately removing any cankered material.

HARVESTING BLUEBERRIES
Leave the fruit on the bushes until it has become really soft. Then test each one by rolling it gently between thumb and finger; the ripe berries will come off easily and the unripe ones will stay on.

Harvesting and storing

Let the fruit stay on the bushes until it really begins to soften, which will be about ten days after it turns blue. This is when the sugar content is at its highest, and consequently when the flavor is strongest and sweetest. If you pick the fruit any earlier, they will be rather tasteless. Then roll the berries gently so that the ripe berries come off and the unripe ones stay on. Store in a refrigerator, or freeze (*see p.306*).

Olives

Not only can a man live on olives, bread, and wine alone (and many a man has), but from this fruit is expressed the best edible oil in the world. Olive trees belong to the *Oleaceae* family, and have stunningly beautiful flowers.

Soil and climate

The olive will thrive in practically any soil; it grows in Mediterranean countries where there is no true topsoil at all. But as to climate it is very specific. It needs a cold winter—around 45 to 50°F (7–10°C)—but never below 10°F (–12°C), because this will kill it; even 18°C (–8°C) will do it some damage. Although they don't suffer from late frost, they need a hot summer; it can scarcely be too hot. If you are not between latitudes 30° and 45°, either north or south of the equator, it is not much good trying to grow olives; nor can they grow above 2,500 feet (800 m).

Propagation

The easiest thing to do is to buy a sapling, and plant it like any other tree (*see p.176*). Otherwise olives are best propagated from cuttings in a mist propagator (*see p.49*). It is best to use softwood cuttings of the current season's growth. Take the cuttings in early fall. Small cuttings should be planted vertically, larger ones horizontally below the soil.

Care while growing

In the first three years after planting, the tree should be shaped to make four or five good strong branches for the scaffold. Cut out all other branches, crossing branches, and branches that grow inward. Let the new laterals on the main scaffold branches grow. By the fifth or sixth year the tree should begin to fruit. If in any one year the tree bears a terrific lot of fruit, thin it; otherwise it will strain itself and not give any fruit next year. In countries with very dry summers, irrigate plentifully during fruiting.

Pests and diseases

OLIVE KNOT This causes swellings on any part of the tree. Cut out such swellings and paint the wounds with tree paint.

SPLIT PIT Heavy watering after a drought when the fruit is swelling causes the stones inside the fruit to crack, ruining the fruit. Keep watering regularly while the tree is fruiting and you won't get it.

Harvesting and storing

Pick the biggest olives by hand from the tree in fall and use them for pickling (*see p.310*). Fruit from which you wish to press oil should be left on the tree until late in the winter, when it will be quite shriveled. You then beat the branches with poles and catch the olives on tarps spread on the ground below the trees.

Grapes

"Without wine all joyless goes the feast," sang the poet, and certainly since ancient times the vine has had a notable effect on the development of civilization and culture.

Like the olive, the vine, which belongs to the family *Vitaceae*, grows out of the subsoil. There is a theory that the early Mediterranean mercantile civilizations came about because the overcropping of wheat, and the grazing of goats, caused the topsoil to waste away in those countries. The inhabitants were forced to farm their subsoil, which they did with such crops as vines and olives. They were then forced to trade wine and oil for wheat. This meant they had to become potters (because they had to make *amphorae* to carry wine and oil), shipbuilders, sailors, and merchants. This in turn sped up their industrial and mercantile development.

Some variety of grape is native to nearly every temperate region of the world, and to several subtropical ones as well. Grapes of the Mediterranean species, *Vitis vinifera*, will grow and ripen to wine status in southern England and Wales only with difficulty, and will thrive in North America only in California and Arizona. Americans are lucky in having two native species that will grow in cooler climates: *V. labrusca*, also known as the fox grape or Concord, and *V. rotundifolia*, the Muscadine or southern fox grape. In Britain, *V. labrusca* will grow much better than *V. vinifera*.

Soil and climate

Vines grow well on poor, dry, stony soil. They will grow on limestone soil, and certain varieties will even flourish on chalk, although this is not ideal.

Stony soils on slopes make good vineyards. Many of the best French vintages come from alluvial gravel terraces. I have grown grapes successfully on soil composed largely of decayed fossil seashells. Rich clay soil is bad for grapes, causing them to lose their fruit or ripen it too late. It is fortunate for humankind that the vine thrives on soil that is little good for anything else.

The climate most suitable for grapes is the Mediterranean type. The winter must be cold enough to give them a dormant period, but not so far below freezing as to harm their dormant vines. Most varieties can take temperatures as low as 27°F (−3°C) or even 17°F (−8°C). In cases where temperatures are lower than this, the pliant vines can be bent down and covered with soil to protect them from the elements.

But more important than winter temperatures are the warmth and sunshine that grape vines must have in the summer, both for the fertilization of the flowers in midsummer, and for the ripening of the fruit in late summer. Dessert grapes do not need as long a ripening period as wine varieties; grapes that are pleasant to eat may still not contain enough sugar to make good wine. Late spring frosts are not a problem, because the vines start growing late enough to miss them.

Soil treatment

Clear the soil completely of perennial weeds; incorporate rock phosphate and potash, and dig deeply. If the pH is much below 6, lime the soil to bring it to about 7. Good drainage is absolutely essential.

Propagation

You can, of course, buy year-old plants from a nursery. But most vines are grown from cuttings, although it's often hard to stop them from growing from seeds, which rarely produce strong, heavy-yielding vines. If you have existing vines, make cuttings by separating your winter prunings into two bundles: the ripe, reddish-brown wood and the tender new wood. Tie the ripe wood in bundles, marking the top end with a tiny scratch, label the bundles with the variety, and bury them in moist sand. Feed the new wood to rabbits or goats, or put it on the compost pile. Take the bundles out in March and select the pieces that are about as thick as pencils; make cuttings by chopping them into foot-long (30-cm) lengths, with a bud near the bottom of each. The best cuttings are made from canes with about three or four buds to the foot. Make a long, deep nick with a spade in the sandiest soil you have and plant the cuttings the right way up. The top bud should be just above soil level. Step the cuttings in hard.

During the summer, most of these cuttings will root, and by the following spring, they will be ready to replant. Most experts tell you to dig a wide hole for each cutting and spread the roots carefully over a mound of soil. I suggest that you simply snip off all the roots of each new plant to about 2 inches (5 cm) so that it looks like a shaving brush, then make a hole with a crowbar, about 6 inches (15 cm) deep, drop the plant in, and stamp the soil down firmly. I know this works because I have done it in England and seen it done in Italy. You will get excellent results this way because the new vine is forced to put out plenty of new fine roots.

GRAFTING Most European vines are grafted on to American rootstocks, because *Vitis vinifera* cultivars, which Europeans prefer, cannot be grown on their own roots; they are attacked by an aphid called *phylloxera**. American rootstocks have a high degree of immunity to this insect. In Britain this does not apply, because it is perfectly possible to grow *Vitis vinifera* on its own roots: there is no *phylloxera** in this country as yet.

Grafting grapes is quite simple and should be done in winter. Wood of the rootstock should be cut to one-foot (30-cm) lengths with three or four buds on each. The scions should be cut to 2- or 3-inch (5–8-cm) lengths with one bud. Cut the scion and the stock as you would for any other grafting (*see p.172*), and tie them together with raffia or tape. Cover the joint with wax.

When this process is complete bury them shallowly in layers in moist clean sand. Put the box containing them in some place where the temperature does not fall much below 70°F (21°C): a heated greenhouse is ideal. As soon as warm weather comes, plant them out at a slant in a holding-bed, with one bud of the scion just above the soil.

TAKING GRAPE CUTTINGS
In winter, tie ripe prunings in bundles and bury them in damp sand. Take them out in the spring and chop the best into sections a foot (30 cm) long. The best cuttings have three or four buds per foot.

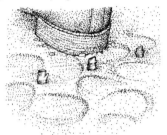

PROPAGATING FROM CUTTINGS
Take a spade and make a long, deep nick in sandy soil. Plant the cuttings, leaving the top bud just above soil level. Step them in hard. Most of the cuttings will root and by the next spring will be ready to plant out.

Soon after midsummer, scrape the soil away and cut off any roots that have grown from the scion with a sharp knife. Do this again at the same time the next year. Do not allow the scion to put down roots.

Plant out stocks and scions in the vineyard in the second or third year. Plant them with the joint just above the ground, but then heap some soil over the joint to cover it. After a year, hoe the soil away, since the joint will now be strong enough not to need this protection.

If you wish to change the scion of an unsatisfactory vine, you can try approach grafting. This is a very simple method. Plant a cutting of the desired scion in a pot. When it has taken, place the pot near the growing vine and slice off a short piece of bark with a little wood from the stems of both vine and scion. Put the two cut faces together, and bind and wax them. When the graft has taken, cut off the scion plant below the graft and the rootstock plant above it.

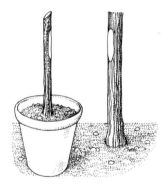

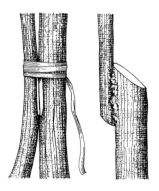

APPROACH GRAFTING
You can improve the quality of a vine by changing the scion. Plant the new scion in a pot near the vine. Chop off

a little slice of wood from both vine and scion (*above left*). Put the two cut faces together, and bind and wax as usual (*above right*).

Care while growing
For the first three or four years it is most important to keep the ground beneath and between vines free of weeds. At first you can do this by deep digging or plowing. Then, as the roots spread, shallower cultivation is better, because this will not damage them. A rototiller is useful, but shallow scuffling with a hoe will do as well. Heavy green mulching is also effective: comfrey or alfalfa are good for this. Moderate feeding with manure or compost from time to time is beneficial.

PRUNING Training and pruning are subjects of labyrinthine complexity and endless argument: only the benign fermented juice of the grape itself serves to prevent such arguments from becoming vitriolic. The best thing to do, I suggest, is to copy your grape-growing neighbors. But as a general rule, the colder your climate is, the smaller you should keep your vines. In Italy you may find great straggling vines growing up elm trees. In Britain you must keep outdoor vines very small indeed, because the climate will certainly not allow you to grow many ripe grapes otherwise.

The thing to remember when pruning vines is that grapes only grow on this year's shoots, sprouting from last year's wood. Old wood will not fruit, and neither will new shoots springing from two or three-year-old wood. Therefore there must be just enough of the last year's wood to produce the current year's fruiting spurs. And it is these fruiting spurs that will send out new fruiting spurs next year. You can keep some of the present year's canes free of fruit, by stripping young fruit off them, and use them as the next year's base for new fruiting canes. But this method is expedient only in climates where grapes grow freely.

GUYOT METHOD In practice, in cold climates, you will probably need to use the Guyot method, which works as follows. Plant the vines 4 feet (1.2 m) apart in rows 6 feet (1.8 m) apart. Erect a two-wire fence along each row with the bottom wire 15 inches (38 cm) from the ground and the top wire a foot (30 cm) higher. Set a light stake 4 feet (1.2 m) long and tie it to both horizontal wires.

In the third winter after planting, cut all the canes except two down close to the ground. Tie the two remaining canes to the upright stake and pinch them off when they get a few inches taller than the stake. Do not allow them to fruit, and pinch the laterals off when they are a few inches long.

The following winter, cut one of the two vertical canes right off (it was only spare), bend the other one over, and tie it along the bottom wire. Come summer it will send out fruiting branches. When they are long enough, tie these to the top wire. Prune any that are not going to bear and snip off the ends of the fruiting branches, leaving four to five leaves above the flowering bunches.

Now new shoots will come from the stool (stem) of the plant. Keep two of them and cut off all the others. Cut the tips off when they are taller than the stake—say, 5 feet (1.5 m) high. The next winter, cut off the horizontal that bore the fruiting branches, bend down the better of the two vertical

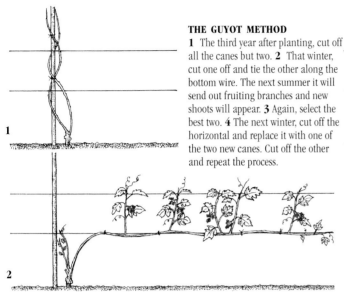

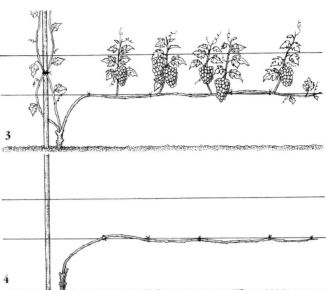

THE GUYOT METHOD
1 The third year after planting, cut off all the canes but two. **2** That winter, cut one off and tie the other along the bottom wire. The next summer it will send out fruiting branches and new shoots will appear. **3** Again, select the best two. **4** The next winter, cut off the horizontal and replace it with one of the two new canes. Cut off the other and repeat the process.

canes to take its place, and cut the other cane right off. Next year, repeat the process. In this way, every summer you always have one horizontal cane bearing fruiting wood, and two of the current year's canes being kept in reserve to fruit the following year.

If you are training vines up walls—one of the best ways of growing them—you can practice exactly the same method in a modified but more extensive form (*see below*).

It is a good idea to grow vines on south-facing walls if you can: they are more decorative than any ornamental creeper and far more useful.

Pests and diseases
POWDERY MILDEW OR OIDIUM This very common complaint originated in North America. A fine dusty film forms over the vine. To prevent it, dust with sulfur* every three weeks from the flowering stage until the grapes start to ripen.
DOWNY MILDEW This causes a much thicker layer of white down than powdery mildew. To prevent it, spray with Bordeaux mixture* (*see p.51*) every three weeks. You will not get the disease under cloches or in greenhouses, because it is spread by droplets of rain.
BLACK SPOT OR ANTHRACNOSE This can appear after periods of wet weather. It causes well-defined black spots on the leaves.

TRAINING UP WALLS
A modification of the Guyot method works well. Instead of cutting the vine right back each year, let it establish a framework of old wood and then allow horizontal branches to develop as if the top of the old wood were at ground level. If the wall is high, plant two vines or more; let the permanent wood grow tall on some and keep it short on others. Vines fruit at their extremities, so if you try to make one vine cover the whole wall, you will only get fruit at the top.

Routine spraying for downy mildew should prevent it. If it does not, increase the strength of the mixture to 1 pound (500 g) of copper sulfate*, 14 ounces (400 g) of lime, and 6 gallons (27 l) of water.
VINE MITE This produces blisters on the tops of the leaves. Sulfur dusting* for powdery mildew will also control this.
BIRDS It is quite possible to lose your entire grape crop to the birds. If you suffer from them badly, you must enclose your vines with netting.
WASPS Wasps can decimate a crop of grapes. Prepare a bait made of some sweet stuff, include a few squashed grapes, and mix some poison in with it. Track down and destroy nests.

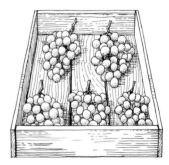

STORING GRAPES
Spread out the bunches of grapes in single layers as far as possible, and leave them after picking until the stems begin to shrivel (*above left*). Then store them in shallow trays and keep them in a cool, slightly humid place (*right*).

Harvesting and storing
Leave the fruit on the vines until they are fully ripe, because the riper they get, the sweeter they taste and the better wine they make. They are ripe when the stem of the bunch begins to turn brown.

Snip the bunches from the vines with pruners. Spread out the bunches in single layers and leave at 50°F (10°C) until the stems begin to shrivel. Then store in shallow trays in a cool, slightly humid basement or storeroom at 40°F (4°C). Grapes will keep fresh for several months when stored in this way. For instructions on making wine, see p.326.

Caring for Fruit Trees

Planting

All fruit trees are planted in the same way. If your climate allows, it is best to plant during the winter months, when the sap is not moving around the tree. Normally you would buy three-year-old trees to plant from a nursery, but get the nursery to prune them before they deliver them.

If you take enormous care with planting, you can have an almost "instant orchard" by planting even seven-year-old trees. But these trees would be much more expensive, and you really need to know what you are doing when you plant them. You would have to put a bag around the root ball to keep the soil in, dig right below and all around the roots, plant with immense care, and keep watered for a month. So I would recommend that anyone inexperienced in orchard growing buy three-year-old trees.

Grafting

If you buy trees from a nursery they will already be grafted: cuttings from the fruit tree that you think you are buying will have been grafted onto another kind of tree. The latter will be some hardy, near-wild variety: for example, it will be a crab if the fruit tree is an apple. Thus you have the advantage of a hardy variety for the all-important root and trunk, and a highly bred, high-yielding variety for the fruit. Very few amateur gardeners do much grafting, but there is no reason why they shouldn't, since it is easy enough.

It is no good grafting onto an old, diseased tree, or one that is prone to, or has had, canker (rot in the bark or wood). A very useful exercise is the top-grafting of old, established fruit trees that are of a poor variety, or are neglected, badly pruned, and in need of reviving. The growing tree you graft onto is called the stock, and the tree you graft on top of it is called the scion. Scions can be made from winter cuttings. Heel in the cuttings (bury them in a cool place) after you have cut them off an existing healthy young tree of the type you want, just as if they were ordinary cuttings. Then, in spring, cut all the branches of the old tree you wish to revive down to about a foot from their point of union with the trunk, for top-grafting. Trim the edges of the saw cut with a super-sharp knife, and go about grafting your scions onto each branch.

There are several methods of grafting, according to what kind of branch you are grafting on, but the principle is always the same, and involves bringing the cambium (under-bark) layers of stock and scion into close contact. It is in this layer just under the bark that growth and union of tissue start.

Apples and pears are easily grafted. In Europe, where silverleaf is a problem, grafting plums is much more difficult because it lets in the disease, so don't graft plums unless you have to. You can, by the way, graft pears onto hawthorn trees, and get pears! If we had the time and energy we could do this all along our hedges.

PLANTING A TREE

When planting out a tree or a bush, put yourself in its place. Consider the shock to the roots, accept that the tree is delicate, and treat it accordingly. Start by digging a hole much bigger than the root ball of the tree.

Drive a stake into the bottom of the hole before you put the tree in. You train the tree up the stake. Then put the tree in and prune off any broken roots or very long ones.

You should only transplant the tree when it is dormant; but even so you can minimize the shock. Put a heap of rich loam in the middle of the hole and spread the roots around it. Make sure you plant the tree at the same depth as it was before. Sift in more loam around the roots with your fingers, and rub the soil gently into them. Continue filling the hole until the roots are in close contact with the soil.

As the tree grows, it will need a good supply of nutrients below it. So the soil under the tree and all around it must be firm; If the soil caves away under the roots and leaves a cavity, the tree will die. You should firm each layer of soil as you plant, making sure it is broken up finely. When you have installed the roots to your satisfaction (and the tree's), throw more soil in on top and stamp gently but firmly.

Do not stamp heavily—this will tear delicate roots. When the hole is completely filled in, and the soil heaped up a little, you can stamp harder. The stake ensures that no movement disturbs the roots of the tree once growth begins.

A tree must have moisture after it has been replanted. So water it well, and then put a good thick mulch of organic matter on the soil around the tree to conserve the moisture.

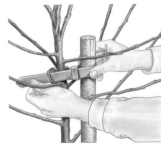

Tie the tree to the stake with a plastic strap and buckle. Do not overtighten. Regularly check the strap and loosen it as the trunk grows and thickens.

TREE SHAPES

Train your young fruit trees into a variety of decorative shapes. This can save space, and in some cases can considerably increase yields.

Fans

Train a "maiden" (a single-stemmed, one-year-old tree) along a wall or fence, with the help of canes tied to wires 6 inches (15 cm) apart (above).

Cordons

Train a young fruit tree up a fence at an acute angle, and limit it to one stem and no long laterals (right).

WHIP GRAFTING

This is a form of grafting that is used when the stock and the scion are approximately the same size. The stock is the branch onto which you graft the scion; the scion is a shoot that you have cut in winter, and then heeled in a cool place until needed for grafting.

Prepare the scion by making a cut just behind a bud at the lower end of the scion so that it slopes away to nothing at the base. The cut might be 2 inches (5 cm) long. Near the top of this cut, make another small one upward, without removing any wood, so that a small tongue is formed. Cut the tip off the scion, leaving from three to five buds. Now make cuts on top of the stock branch to correspond with those you have made in the scion.

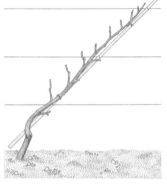

Fit scion to stock, slipping one tongue down behind the other. The two cambium layers must be in contact with each other.

Tie the two parts together with raffia (or garden tape) and cover the whole joint with grafting wax.

Espaliers

Stretch horizontal wires 12 inches (30 cm) apart between posts. Train the central stem vertically upward and the lateral shoots at 90°, tying them to canes fastened to the wires.

Dwarf pyramids

The advantages of dwarf trees are that they take up less space than full-size stock, but their fruit yields are as heavy. Restrict the growth of a young tree to 7 feet (2 m). Keep side shoots short. Dwarf trees fruit earlier, but do not live as long as full-size stock.

BUDDING

This method of grafting is much used by rose-growers, although it can also be done with fruit trees. In summer, select a strong healthy scion about 12 inches (30 cm) long and put it in water.

Cut a T-shaped slit along the back of your stock.

Peel back the two flaps of bark formed by the cut.

Take your scion out of water and slice out a shield-shaped piece of bark that contains a bud within a leaf axil.

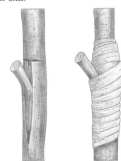

Insert the shield into the T-shaped cut. Remove any of the shield sticking out above the T-shaped cut; put back the flaps on each side. Bind with raffia or tape after insertion. As the bud grows, you can cut off any stock above the bud-graft.

Vegetables through the Year

Exactly the same principle of crop rotation applies to the garden as to field crops, but in the garden there are two main factors to consider: you want the biggest possible gap (at least three years) between brassica crops to prevent clubroot disease from building up, and the biggest possible gap between potato crops to guard against nematodes. You should also take into account that potatoes don't like freshly limed ground, which makes them scabby, whereas beans and peas do like lime. Brassicas prefer limed ground, but after the lime has been in it a few months. The root crops don't like land too freshly mucked or manured.

You can cater to the needs of all these plants if you adopt a four-year rotation something like this:

Manure the land heavily and sow potatoes. After the potatoes are lifted, lime the land heavily, and the next year sow peas and beans. Once the peas and beans are lifted, set out brassicas immediately from their seed bed or their "holding bed" (see below). The brassicas will all have been eaten by the next spring, and it will be time to put in what I call mixed crops. These will be onions, tomatoes, lettuce, radishes, corn, and all of the gourd tribe (zucchini, squash, pumpkins, cucumbers). Follow these with root crops such as carrots, parsnips, beets and celery. (Mixed crops and root crops can be very interchangeable.) Don't include turnips or rutabagas, which suffer from clubroot and therefore must go in the brassica rotation if you aren't already growing them on a field scale, which suits them better. Then back to spuds again, which is where we started.

This suggested rotation will suit a garden in a temperate climate with a fairly open winter. (Snow doesn't hurt unless it is extremely deep, but intense frost stops you from having anything growing outside in the winter at all.) Probably no one would stick to this (or any) rotation slavishly. I know that there are idiosyncrasies in it, but I also know that it works. For example, I cram the brassica break in after the peas and beans, and clear the land of brassicas the subsequent spring: this may be crowding things a bit, but two main crops are being produced in one year. To do this (and personally, I find it a very good thing to do), you must sow your brassica seed in a seed bed, preferably not on any of your four main growing plots at all but in a fifth plot, which is for other things such as perennials. Then you must plant out the little

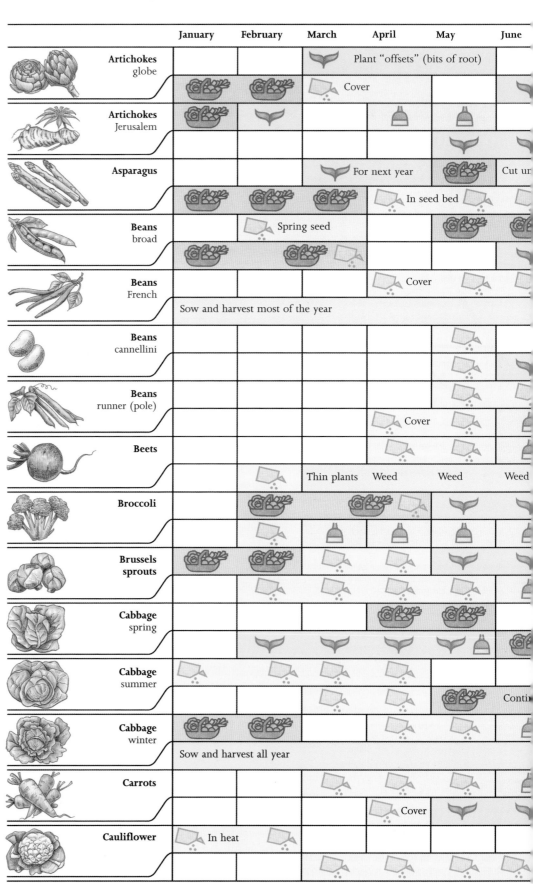

	August	September	October	November	December	
Harvest	Harvest	Harvest			Protect with straw	**Celery and Celeriac**
	Earth up		Earth up	Harvest	Harvest	
	Harvest	Harvest	Harvest			**Cucumber**
			Cut fern			
Plant out			Hoe		Harvest	**Kale**
Clear		Winter seed		Harvest	Harvest	
Plant out	Hoe	Hoe		Harvest	Harvest	**Leeks**
Harvest	Harvest	Harvest				
		Sow under glass				**Lettuce**
		Harvest	Harvest			
Hoe	Harvest	Harvest				**Corn**
Harvest	Harvest	Harvest				
Harvest	Harvest	Harvest				**Squash, Zucchini, and Pumpkin**
Hoe	Hoe	Harvest	Harvest	Clamp		
Harvest	Sow	Harvest	Harvest			**Onions**
Hoe	Hoe	Harvest	Harvest			
Plant out		Harvest	Harvest	Harvest		**Parsnips**
Harvest	Harvest	Harvest	Harvest			
Sow				Sow		**Peas**
Harvest	Plant out	Plant out				
	Spray	Harvest	Harvest			**Potatoes**
Harvest	Harvest	Harvest				
sow and harvest		Harvest				**Radishes**
Hoe				Harvest	Harvest	
						Spinach
Sow Hoe	Weed		Harvest	Harvest		
Hoe	Harvest	Harvest				**Tomatoes**
Harvest	Harvest	Sow	Harvest	Harvest		
Hoe	Hoe	Harvest	Harvest			**Turnips and Rutabagas**

plants from your crowded seed bed to a holding bed. This is a piece of clean, good land, in which these small brassica plants can find room to grow and develop, for it will be late in the summer before many of them can go in after the just-harvested peas and beans, and it would be fatal to leave them crammed in their original seed bed until that late. So cramming five main crops into four years requires a holding bed as well as a seed bed. We can then look upon such quick-growing things as lettuces, radishes, and early peas (which are actually best sown late) as catch crops, ready to be dropped in wherever there is a spare bit of ground.

Perhaps you think that radishes are brassicas and therefore should only go in the brassica break? Well, we pull and eat ours so young that they don't have time to get and perpetuate clubroot. But don't leave them in to get too old and go to seed, or they will spread this rather nasty disease. Provided you keep brassica crops three years away from each other, you won't have much trouble.

Climate is all-important, and for the seasonal plans on the following pages, I have taken as the norm a mild climate, which will support brassicas outdoors all winter but will not allow us to grow subtropical or even Mediterranean plants outdoors at all. In a climate with no winter frosts, we could get three or four crops a year, provided we had enough rain or enough irrigation. In climates too cold for winter greens to survive outside, we would have to devote the summer to one plot of brassicas for storage during the winter.

A vegetable calendar
The chart shows sowing, planting out, hoeing, and harvesting times for vegetables that grow in a temperate climate. Ask your neighbors for local advice; the climate where you live could make as much as a month's difference.

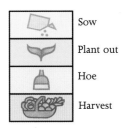

	Sow
	Plant out
	Hoe
	Harvest

Winter

Winter is a time for building and repairing, felling timber and converting it, laying hedges, digging drains and ditches, building fences and stone walls. If the soil in the garden is heavy clay, it is best to keep off it as much as possible, because digging or working such soil in winter only does harm. On lighter land, the same inhibition does not apply. In cold climates, the land may be deep under snow anyway, and all the crops that have been harvested will be safe in a clamp (*see p.298*) or root cellar, or stored in jars or bottles, crocks, and barrels. Good husbandmen and women should start the winter feeling that their labors have secured them a store of good and varied food to keep them and their families through the dark months, and to provide hospitality for friends. So winter is also a time for feasting.

Greenhouse and perennials

In the greenhouse, it is time to clear winter lettuce, and the enriched soil that grew tomatoes last year goes out to the garden, with fresh soil barrowed in and mixed with compost. Tomato and cucumber seed are sown in the heat of the greenhouse. Hot beds can be built up in the cold frames. Seakale should be ready for harvesting. Mature compost is emptied on to the land intended for potatoes. Any remaining compost then goes into an empty bin to aerate it, and a new compost pile is begun. Perennial plants protected from the winter cold by straw and seaweed are resting, preparing for their spurt of growth in the spring.

Plot A

This plot will have been very heavily mucked after the potatoes were lifted last fall. A small proportion of it may well be winter-sown broad beans this year if the winter is mild. The rest will go under winter rye or another winter green crop, which will stop the loss of nitrogen, and keep it ready to dig in as early as the land is dry enough to work in the spring. The plot was limed last fall after the potatoes were lifted, and this will benefit the peas and beans that are to follow and also the brassica crop that will come after them. A small part of this bed will have been planted with spring cabbage plants last fall, and there will be a bed of leeks, which will be ready to pull.

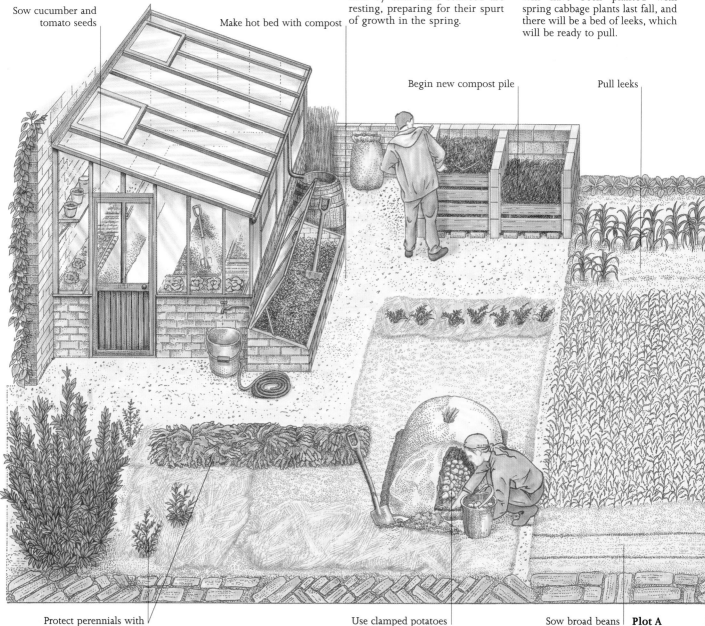

Sow cucumber and tomato seeds

Make hot bed with compost

Begin new compost pile

Pull leeks

Protect perennials with straw and seaweed

Use clamped potatoes

Sow broad beans | **Plot A**

Plot B

This plot should be full of big brassica plants: Brussels sprouts, hearting broccoli ("winter cauliflower"), big hard-hearted winter cabbage, kale, red cabbage, and any other brassica plant that can weather the winter. There may well be a few rows of rutabagas, if these haven't already been harvested and stored. Turnips must be in the clamp or root cellar by now, because they can't stand the winter as rutabagas can. This plot will provide most of the greenstuff during the winter, helped by the leeks in Plot A. In temperate climates, this helps to avoid much complicated canning and preserving. Shallots can be planted out, as this plot becomes the "miscellaneous" break next summer.

Plot C

This plot is under green manure such as rye or some other winter crop. Last year it bore the miscellaneous, short-lived crops. As soon as the land is dry enough to work, the green manure can be forked into the ground, so that it can begin to rot down. There is no hurry because this plot is going to be "roots" this year, and most of these will not have to be planted out very early.

Plot D

This plot is fallow, or else under green manure, although if the roots were harvested late last year, there may not have been time to sow any green manure. It is time to barrow out compost or muck for the future crop of potatoes. If barrowing is done in heavy frost, it is easier to push the barrow. It also does the ground less damage. There may be a row of celery left undug, and this can be remedied as winter progresses.

Fruit plot

Fruit trees only need spraying with dormant oil if pests have afflicted them badly. After the middle of February, fruit trees, gooseberries, and other bushes are pruned. The currants may well have been pruned in the fall. All prunings should be burned. Muck or compost is barrowed and dumped around trees and bushes, and the ground between soft fruit bushes is forked lightly.

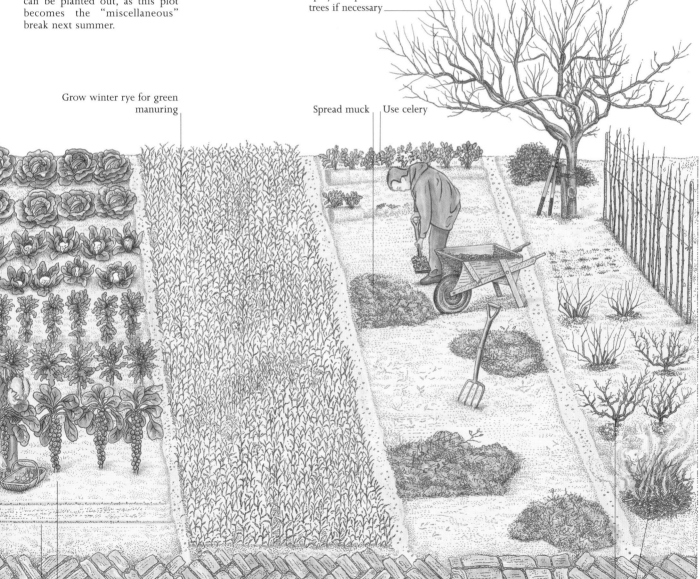

Spray and prune fruit trees if necessary

Grow winter rye for green manuring

Spread muck   Use celery

lot B   Use brassicas
Plant shallots   **Plot C**   **Plot D**   Prune fruit bushes late in the season   **Fruit Plot**
                                                                                                    Burn prunings

Spring

There is so much to do in spring that it is difficult to get going fast enough. For a start, the green manure crops are turned in (a rototiller is helpful), the seed beds prepared, and seed sown. But it is no good being in too much of a hurry to sow seeds, because they can't grow in half-frozen ground, and wet ground is cold ground. It is better to sow a week or two later, in dry, warm soil, than earlier, in wet, cold soil. Some things, like parsnips, need a very long growing season, and can be put in early. Some others are best started off early, but under glass. Cloches are a great help at this time of year, to warm the soil for early sowing. In March I have a big sheet of transparent plastic over February-planted early potatoes. The soil under it feels warm to the touch, while the soil outside is freezing.

Greenhouse and perennials

In a heated greenhouse, corn is sown in peat* pots and green peppers in seed boxes. As the tomato and cucumber plants become big enough, they can be planted out in pots or greenhouse soil. Cucumbers can be sown in the hot bed. In the herb garden, lift, divide, and replant perennial herbs such as mint, sage, and thyme if they need it. The seaweed covering should be removed from the asparagus bed, and then put in the compost pile. Blanch seakale and force it to grow under cover, as you would rhubard at this time. Globe artichokes should be progressing well. Seeds are sown in the seed bed ready for planting out later: onion, broccoli, cabbage, kale, Brussels sprouts, cauliflower, and leeks. Lettuce can also be sown in the seed bed if space is tight in the main garden and lettuce plants are wanted ready for replanting later when there is room.

Plot A

The leeks are cleared and eaten as the spring advances. The winter-sown broad beans will be growing well, but if there aren't enough of them, spring-sown varieties may be planted early in the season, when early peas will also go in. After this, peas will be sown in succession as the year advances. However many are grown, there will never be enough! Early turnips, soybeans, kohlrabi, Hamburg parsley, and rutabagas should go in this plot, which will be brassicas next winter. The row of spring cabbage will do for fresh greens, and will get eaten as spring advances. Plant lima beans two or three weeks after the last frost.

Sow corn and green peppers in peat* pots and seed boxes

Sow cucumbers in hot bed

Eat last leeks
Harvest spring cabbage
Sow peas

Divide and replant perennial herbs

Remove covering from asparagus

Force seakale and rhubarb

Sow brassicas and onions in seed bed

Plot A Plant out early turnips, rutabagas, soybeans, kohlrabi, and Hamburg parsley

Plot B

Spring is more of a hungry gap than winter, but the late hardy brassicas, together with the leeks, tide things over. The brassicas are nearly finished, but a few Brussels sprouts may still be standing, with some kale, some sprouting broccoli, and perhaps a few hearting broccoli. As the plants are finished, they must be pulled out, the stems smashed with an ax and then put on the compost heap. The shallots should be growing well.

Plot C

By now the winter rye sown last year as a green manure crop should be dug in, to make way for the roots to be sown later in the year. The only root crop sown early on is parsnip, but as spring progresses, onion seed and carrots are sown in the bed. It is time to plant out onion sets and fall-sown onions. As spring turns into early summer, more and more crops go into this root break bed.

Plot D

A row of early potatoes could be growing under cloches or transparent plastic. These will have been planted toward the end of February in mild climates, or late March in severer ones. The main crop won't go in until mid-April. The earlies get planted shallowly, but the main crop ones go in deep furrows, both with ample muck compost. They are ridged up as they grow.

Fruit plot

Prune gooseberries early in the season. In mild climates, some people set out strawberry plants in March or April. The ground around soft fruit such as gooseberries, raspberries, and currants should be kept hoed and cultivated to prevent grass from growing. Insect pests are to be avoided, and something must be done about them if they attack. Grease bands put around fruit trees will catch crawlies climbing up. It is important not to spray insecticides on flowering trees, since they kill the beneficent bee.

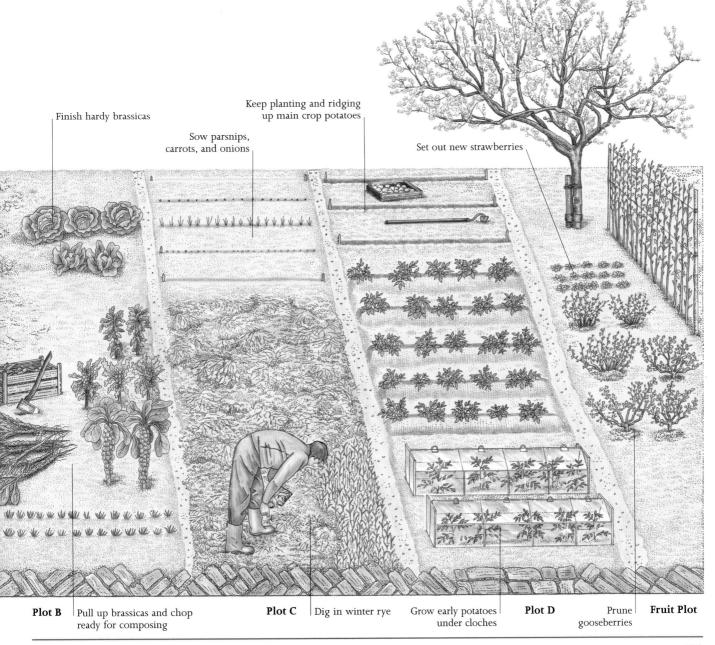

Finish hardy brassicas

Sow parsnips, carrots, and onions

Keep planting and ridging up main crop potatoes

Set out new strawberries

Plot B | Pull up brassicas and chop ready for composing

Plot C | Dig in winter rye

Grow early potatoes under cloches

Plot D | Prune gooseberries

Fruit Plot

Early Summer

Successional planting must go on unabated with many crops during April, May, and June. A constant supply of fresh peas, lettuces, radishes, and French beans can be maintained by planting these short-lived plants little and often. Fresh young turnips should be available all summer, too. Hoeing should never be neglected during the early summer, since this is the time when the weeds are scrambling to get a foothold along with everything else. If they are allowed to get away with it, the crops will be miserable or nonexistent. Onions and carrots must be meticulously hand-weeded. If some radish seed is sown along with the parsnips, radishes will be clearly visible before the slow-growing parsnips have declared themselves, and the planting can be side-hoed with safety.

Greenhouse and perennials

Asparagus can be cut and eaten until the end of June, when it must be abandoned and allowed to grow. Herbs will thrive on frequent pickings. Artichokes are growing fast. The seed bed is kept weeded, and if flea beetles appear on brassica seedlings, they can be dusted with pyrethrum. The ventilation in the greenhouse must be carefully adjusted. The top glass should be lightly shaded with whitewash. A good airing is vital during the day, but cold air must be kept out at night. The air is kept humid by spraying the floor and plants. Tomato plants are fed with water in which muck has been soaked, and as small cucumbers begin to develop, they too are fed. Brassica plants are pricked out into a holding bed. The lids on cucumber frames should be propped open. Forcing of rhubarb and seakale continues.

Plot A

Peas are sown in succession and given sticks to twine around as they need it. More turnips and rutabagas can be sown. May, or June in later districts, is the time to sow out French and runner beans on previously prepared well-composted beds. These need regular weeding and watering; all these legumes require frequent watering in a dry season. It is time to harvest broad beans, and if there had been any signs of aphids earlier, the tops of the broad beans should have been snapped off immediately and cooked. As soon as they are finished, cut them down and sow French beans in their place.

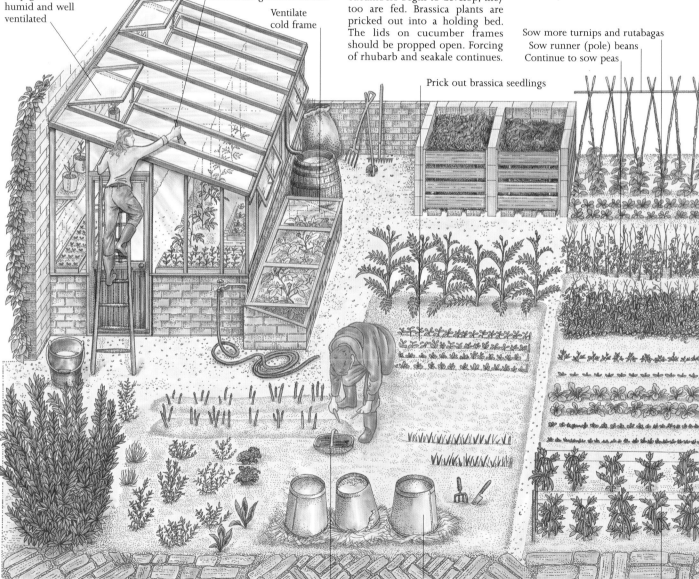

Keep greenhouse humid and well ventilated

Whitewash greenhouse roof

Ventilate cold frame

Prick out brassica seedlings

Sow more turnips and rutabagas
Sow runner (pole) beans
Continue to sow peas

Cut asparagus until the end of June

Continue to force seakale and rhubarb

Plot A Harvest broad beans

Plot B

Now cleared of last winter's brassicas, this plot becomes the new miscellaneous bed for growing crops such as outdoor tomatoes, zucchini, pumpkins, squashes, melons, radishes, lettuce, ridge cucumbers, spinach, spinach beet, sweet corn, Chinese cabbage, and salsify. As all these things— some of them reared in the greenhouse or cold frame—become ready and the weather is warm enough, they are planted out, and should be watered and tended. A good mulch of well-rotted muck or compost, if it can be spared, will do them all good. It revives the soil, and shouldn't make next year's roots "fork" too much if put on well in advance.

Plot C

Onions in the root break plot should be growing well and will need weeding and thinning. The carrots should be thinned if they are wanted for winter storing but not if intended for summer eating. The wily carrot fly must be avoided. Carrots should be thinned when it is raining, if possible; otherwise, the tops should be protected with floating row covers. Parsnips are thinned and weeded. Endive, beet, and Swiss chard are sown. Celery should be planted out before the end of May in a previously prepared celery trench, and never allowed to dry out at all. You can also sow Florence fennel at this point. Prepare the ground as you would for celery; dig deeply and incorporate lots of manure.

Plot D

The potatoes already planted should be earthed up as they grow. Very early morning, or late evening, is the best time to do this, because the leaves lie down and sprawl during the day and make earthing up difficult. Turnips can be sown to come up in the brassica break when the early potatoes are out. The trick of planting leeks after spuds have been lifted can only be done if the spuds are early ones. Earlies are being eaten by June, so leeks can be transplanted into the ground when it is clear.

Fruit plot

Nets go over strawberries, straw underneath them, and birds must be kept off other soft fruit, too. Soft fruit such as gooseberries can now be picked, starting with the hard ones for cooking, so as to give the younger ones a chance. Insects and various blights must be kept at bay. The ground between soft fruit bushes is hoed, and a mulch of compost or anything else put on. This is vital on light land.

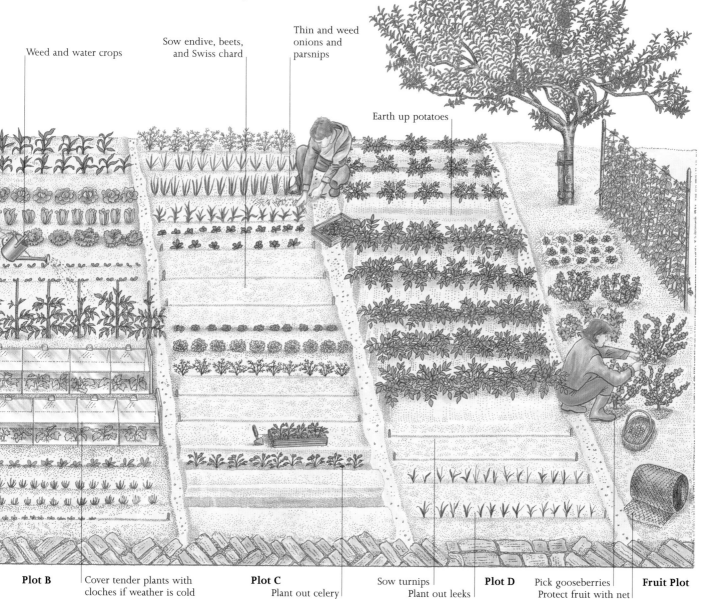

Weed and water crops

Sow endive, beets, and Swiss chard

Thin and weed onions and parsnips

Earth up potatoes

Plot B | Cover tender plants with cloches if weather is cold

Plot C | Plant out celery

Sow turnips | Plant out leeks

Plot D | Pick gooseberries | Protect fruit with net

Fruit Plot

185

Late Summer

Earlier labor will now start bearing fruit in earnest. There is almost an *embarras de richesse* of harvest, and it is time to think of giving away, or trading, the surplus of many crops. The surplus of French or runner (pole) beans can be stored in salt, and the cannellini beans and peas prepared for dry storage. As fast as peas and beans are harvested and cleared, the space is filled with well-grown brassica plants. Fitting the main brassica crop in as a catch crop after the peas and beans have been cleared is made possible by the use of the holding bed, which comes into its own this season. Brassicas seem to benefit from the twice planting-out. Hand-weeding must go on incessantly, for weeds that are too big to hoe must be pulled out before they have time to seed: one year's seeding is seven years' weeding.

Greenhouse and perennials

With the lid now taken off the cold frames, the cucumbers will run riot. Tomatoes, cucumbers, and peppers in the greenhouse will be bearing, and will want watering and feeding. They now need plenty of ventilation. In the seed bed, early spring cabbage seed can be sown. The herb and asparagus beds are kept weeded, and the rhubarb needs to be regularly pulled. Soon the flowers of globe artichokes will be eaten; they should not be neglected, because uncut plants will not produce any more. However, it is fun to leave a few to burst out in brilliant blue flowers and add to the scenery.

Plot A

The peas and beans are watered if they need it, and the flowers of runner (pole) beans sprayed with water every evening, to help the flowers set. Peas, French beans, and runner beans galore are ready to be picked. So are the turnips and kohlrabi. As each row passes its best, it must be ruthlessly cleared out of the way, and the space planted up with well-grown brassica plants from the holding bed. When the runner beans begin to yield, they must be picked and picked again and never allowed to get old and tough. A great many are salted for the dark days of the winter. The true country person always bears the winter in mind; it is easy enough to get plenty to eat in July.

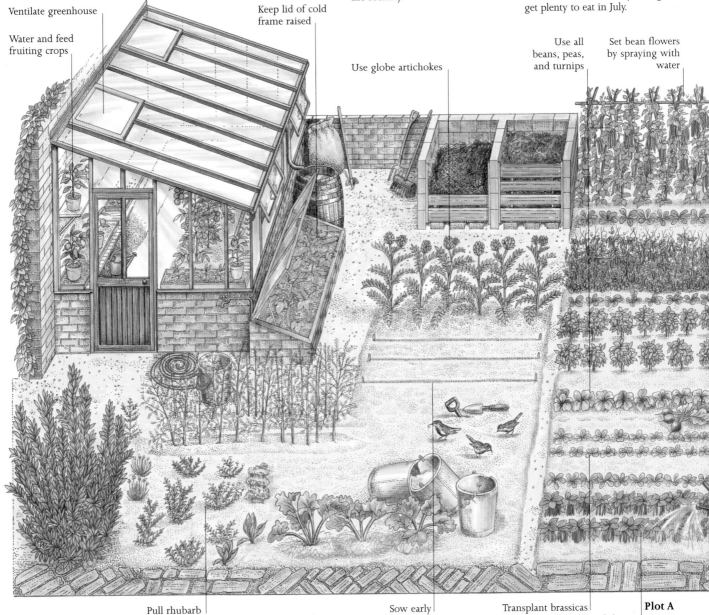

Ventilate greenhouse

Water and feed fruiting crops

Keep lid of cold frame raised

Use globe artichokes

Use all beans, peas, and turnips

Set bean flowers by spraying with water

Pull rhubarb

Sow early spring cabbage

Transplant brassicas
Water French beans

Plot A

Plot B

Any straggling vines of melons, pumpkins, and squashes must be cropped. The tomatoes must be staked, side-shoots picked out, and the plants stopped when they have four trusses. They must be well-watered if it is dry. In damp climates, it is a good idea to lay the tomatoes down at the end of August and put cloches over them so that more of them may ripen. Outdoor cucumbers are stopped before they get out of hand, and they must be picked hard and continuously so as not to get too big and bitter. All male flowers must be picked off. Lettuce should be eaten when ready, and not allowed to go to seed.Successional plantings of both lettuce and radishes continue. Corn is now high, in a block to facilitate wind pollination. The shallots can now be harvested.

Plot C

There is little to do now but hoe all the root crops, keep the weeds down, and kill any slugs lurking in the vegetables. In fact, this is far and away the best time of the year to clear all the weeds in the garden. Celery can be earthed up and sprayed with a Bordeaux mixture*. Start harvesting the onion tribe now.

Plot D

By now the early potatoes are gradually being eaten, and the second batch started on if there are any. The main crop must not be lifted yet, but can be sprayed twice with Bordeaux mixture*, if blight is feared. Warm, muggy weather is the enemy. The main crop must be well earthed up, but when the tops meet across the furrows, it won't be possible or necessary to hoe any more, though the big annual weeds should still be hauled out. Turnips and leeks should be establishing themselves.

Fruit plot

Cut any superfluous suckers from the base of raspberry plants. Thin immature apples where they are too thick on the tree (the "June drop" may have done this naturally) and summer-prune fruit trees, particularly cordons and trained trees. Eat plums and soft fruit while birds are eating the cherries. Eat mulberries as soon as they are ripe. I think August is the time to plant a new strawberry bed, so root the strawberry runners in small sunken pots. Keep on hoeing between soft fruits to keep the grass down and give the birds a chance to eat creepies.

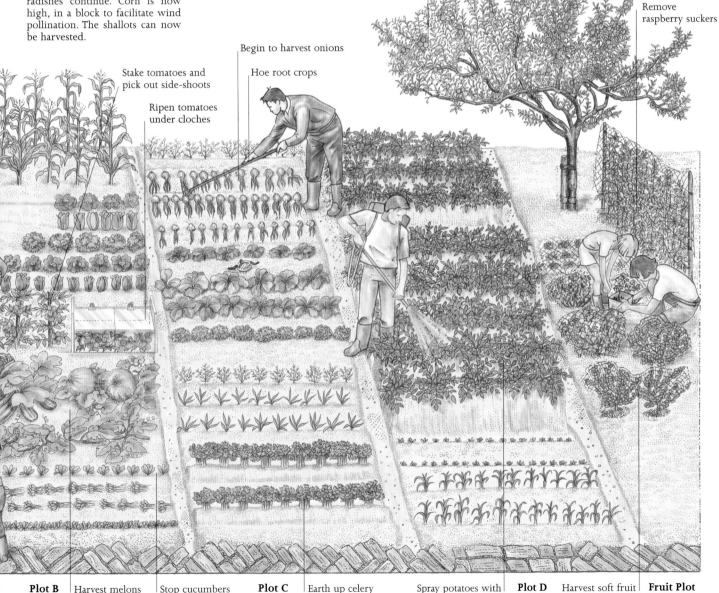

Thin apple crop

Remove raspberry suckers

Begin to harvest onions

Hoe root crops

Stake tomatoes and pick out side-shoots

Ripen tomatoes under cloches

Plot B | Harvest melons and cucumbers | Stop cucumbers from spreading | **Plot C** | Earth up celery | Spray potatoes with Bordeaux mixture* | **Plot D** | Harvest soft fruit | **Fruit Plot**

Fall

Fall is the season of mists and mellow fruitfulness, according to Keats. It is also the real harvest time, when all the main crops have to be gathered in and stored for the winter. The good gardener will try to broadcast green manure seed wherever beds are left empty, although on very heavy soil, old-fashioned gardeners are fond of leaving it "turned up rough" after digging so that frost can get at it. Use annual weeds as a green manure if you like.

After the first frost has touched celery and parsnips, it is time to start eating them, and time to think of parsnip wine for Christmas (or the Christmas after next, as purists would have it).

Greenhouse and perennials

Frames and greenhouse can be sown with winter lettuce, spring cabbage, and summer cauliflower. The last two will be planted out next spring. Asparagus ferns are cut down and composted, thus defying the asparagus beetle. Potatoes may be clamped near the house or put in the root cellar (or anywhere cold, dark, and frost-proof). Globe artichokes are cut as long as there are any left. Then they are abandoned, except for a covering of straw, as they die down, to protect them against frost. It is a good idea now to cover the asparagus bed with seaweed, or manure, or both. Plant the seakale in loam in a hot bed, or warmed frame, or even in a warm cellar. Keep it warm and dark. All perennial crops need lavish manuring.

Plot A

Now it is time to clear away all the peas and beans, even the cannellini beans, soybeans, and any others intended for harvesting and drying for the winter. Pull the Hamburg parsley after the first frost. This bed will hold winter and spring brassicas, planted late perhaps, but none the worse for that, since they have been growing away happily in their holding bed. The cabbages will benefit from the residual lime left by the peas and beans and the residue of the heavy manuring given to the previous potatoes. When all weeds are suppressed it is a good idea to mulch the brassicas with compost, but slugs must be kept down.

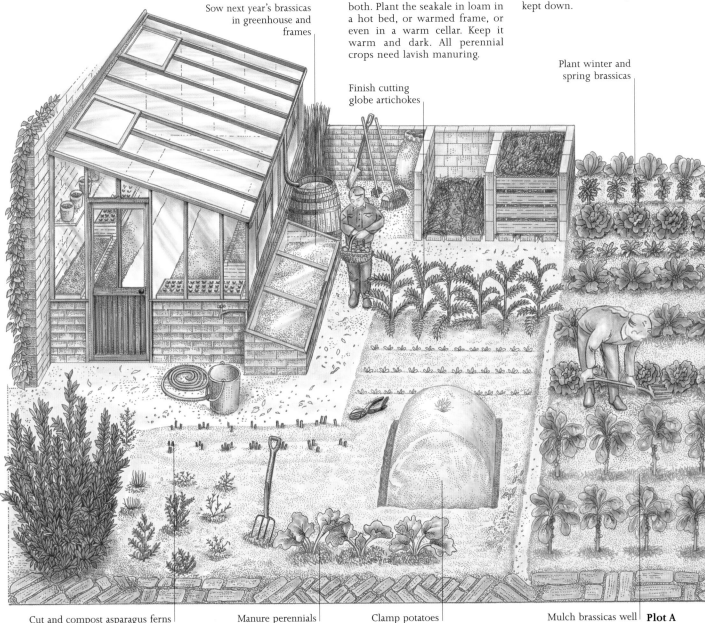

Sow next year's brassicas in greenhouse and frames

Finish cutting globe artichokes

Plant winter and spring brassicas

Cut and compost asparagus ferns   Manure perennials   Clamp potatoes   Mulch brassicas well   **Plot A**

Plot B

All the plants in this bed (which are plants with a short growing season) will have been harvested. After the bed has been cleared, it should be lightly forked over, and winter rye planted for green manure. Unfortunately, it is not much good trying a clover for this, since it is too late in the year; only a winter-growing crop such as rye will work.

Plot C

Parsnips can stay in the ground indefinitely. Once earthed up, celery will also survive much of the winter. The rest of the roots are lifted in September and put safely in store. Red beets need lifting carefully, because the roots bleed when damaged. As the land is cleared, rye can be sown in it at least up until the end of September. This bed will be potatoes next year, and manuring potatoes can now begin.

Plot D

Lift the main potato crop quite late, just before the first frosts are expected. This way the tubers will harden in the ground and keep better, and if blight is present there is less chance of spores being on the ground's surface to infect the tubers when they are lifted. The spuds should lie drying out on the surface for a day or two, while their skins set. Then they are clamped or stored away. The leeks are earthed up to be a great winter standby. This plot will be the pea and bean break next year, so broad beans are planted in October, or September if you have hard winters.

Fruit plot

Runners are cut away from the strawberries, and the ground is cleared and given a good top-dressing of muck or compost. All fruit is harvested as it becomes ripe, then apples, pears, and quinces are stored in a cool (not frosty) place, so that they don't touch each other. The old fruiting canes of raspberries are cut out, leaving the young wood, and currants are pruned in November or December. New fruit trees can be planted in November if the ground is not too wet. As tree leaves fall, take them up and compost them, because they harbor troublesome pests.

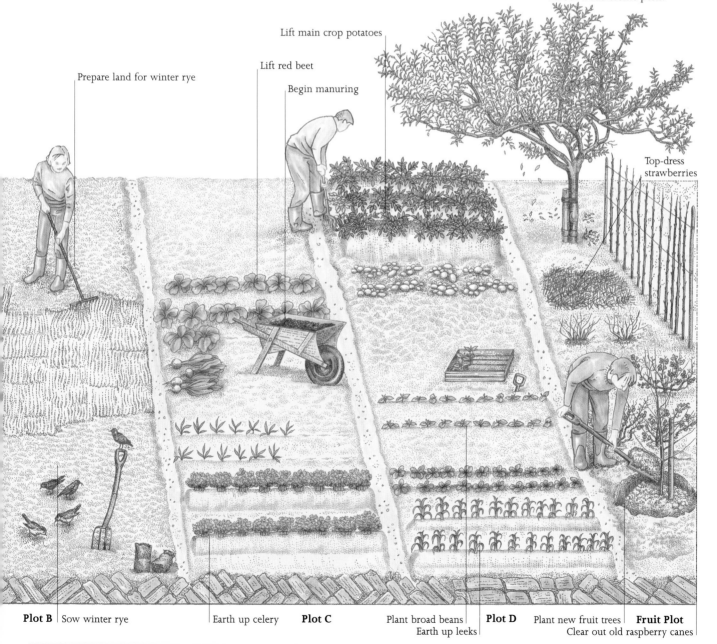

Lift main crop potatoes

Lift red beet

Begin manuring

Prepare land for winter rye

Top-dress strawberries

| **Plot B** | Sow winter rye | | Earth up celery | **Plot C** | | Plant broad beans | **Plot D** | Plant new fruit trees | **Fruit Plot** |

Earth up leeks

Clear out old raspberry canes

The Greenhouse

A greenhouse can be a very basic thing; it can consist of a 3-foot (90-cm) high foundation of brick, concrete or stone, a wooden framework containing the glass (heavy glass is best), a door, and four ventilators (two at each end of the building, one high up and another low down). Inside, you need staging for standing seed boxes on, and you should be able to remove this so that in the summer you can plant tomatoes in its place.

Unheated greenhouses

In countries where grapes and tomatoes will grow reliably outdoors, I personally would not bother to have a greenhouse, but would spend the money on other things. But in cooler climates even an unheated greenhouse is enormously useful for starting off things like celery seed, sweet corn, early summer cabbage, and anything else you wish to get off to a flying start outside as soon as the frosts are over. You can also use it during the summer for growing that magnificent plant, the tomato. Tomatoes are a most desirable crop for the self-supporter. They are expensive to buy, but easy to grow; they can well, and having a store of them makes all the difference between some possibly pretty dull food in the winter and la dolce vita. A couple of dozen large Mason jars filled with fine red tomatoes on the shelves come fall are a fine sight and give us hope for the future.

And in summer your cold greenhouse may nurture such luxury crops as eggplant, melons, green peppers (which turn into red ones if you leave them long enough), and, of course, cucumbers. The cucumbers you grow inside a greenhouse taste much better than frame or ridge cucumbers grown outdoors. And you can have lettuce almost year-round if you grow it in a greenhouse. In spite of this, a cold greenhouse will not help you much in the winter, except by bringing along some early cabbage or some winter lettuce, or something that is pretty hardy anyway, because the temperature inside the greenhouse, when there is no winter sun, may go well below freezing. So do not expect any marvels. Remember the limitations.

Heated greenhouses

If you can just manage—by hook or by crook, by oil or electricity, or wood-burning or natural gas—to keep the temperature of the air in your greenhouse above freezing all winter, and your greenhouse is big enough, you can have peaches, pears, nectarines, grapes, and most Mediterranean-climate fruits every year in any climate.

If you want to heat your greenhouse, you can have water pipes running through it. The pipes should slope gently up from the boiler as far as they go, since the hot water will tend to rise and the cold to sink back to the boiler. At the highest point of the pipes there must be a bleeder valve to let out air or steam that may collect. If the masonry inside the greenhouse is painted black, heat is absorbed during the day and let out during the night to allay the frost.

The self-supporter will like the idea of heating his greenhouse without buying fuel. This can be done possibly by harnessing an all-purpose furnace (see p.387) or by water or wind-generated electricity (see p.342–345). Solar heating, properly used, has always been adequate to heat greenhouses in the warmer months of the year.

Greenhouse temperatures

In the winter the temperature should be about 40°F (4°C) at night. The sun should bring this to about 50°F (10°C) on bright days. The day temperature should not be allowed to get too high, but it must not be kept down by admitting freezing air into the place, since this will inevitably kill tender plants. So cool the air by letting the boiler fire go out, but get it going again in the afternoon.

A LEAN-TO GREENHOUSE
This greenhouse is a practical way of getting such things as melons, peppers, grapes, and tomatoes off to a flying start in a temperate climate.

In this way the temperature can be kept up at night. During the daytime in winter, have the leeward top ventilator open. Then, as spring gets into its stride, open both top ventilators a little more. Eventually, open one of the bottom ones as well, but arrange for the cold air coming in through this to go over the hot pipes. In spring and summer, sprinkle water on the floor occasionally to keep the air humid. It helps if you can arrange for the water from the roof to go into an adjoining rain barrel.

Greenhouse soil

Greenhouse space, whether heated or not, is expensive, and it is therefore not practical to fill your greenhouse with any old soil. The better the soil in the greenhouse, the better use you will be making of this expensive space.

Upper ventilator

Black wall to absorb heat during the day and release it at night

Water kept at greenhouse temperature

Lower ventilator

If you mix very good compost, good topsoil, and sharp sand in equal parts, and add a scattering of ground rock phosphate and a little lime, you will have a very good soil for your greenhouse. You can put this soil in raised beds, or straight onto the existing soil of the greenhouse. The more you rotate crops inside the greenhouse, the better, but if you are driven to growing the same crop year after year, then you may have to remove the old, or spent, soil and replace it with new soil. Tomatoes particularly can suffer from disease if grown too many years in a row on the same soil.

Greenhouse crops

As to what to grow in the greenhouse, we are all guided in this by what we can grow and what we want. A cold greenhouse enables you to grow a slightly greater range, more reliably than you could outdoors. A hothouse enables you to grow practically anything that can be grown on earth. For my part the main uses of the greenhouse are growing winter lettuce and other salad crops; seed sowing in flats or seed boxes in the early spring of celery, tomatoes, peppers, melons, eggplant, sweet corn, okra, and cucumbers; and my best greenhouse crop is tomatoes, which go on all throughout the summer.

I know you are supposed to be able to grow tomatoes outdoors even in a cool climate, but you can't really. A tiny greenhouse, however, will produce a really impressive tonnage of ripe red tomatoes that can be eaten fresh until you are sick of tomatoes. Then they can be canned to provide marvelous food and flavoring right through the year. You simply cannot have too many tomatoes.

As for cucumbers, ridge and frame varieties can be grown outdoors, but there is no reason why you should not grow a few in the tomato greenhouse, too. The conditions are not ideal for them, though: the true cucumber house is much hotter and more humid than the good tomato house. My advice is to keep your house to suit tomatoes and let the cucumbers take their chances and do the best they can.

And then there is no harm, when you live too far north to grow grapes reliably outdoors, in having a big old vine growing up the back (north) wall of the greenhouse, trained under the roof so as to get the benefit of the sun without shading the precious tomato plants. A fan-trained peach tree, too, is a pleasing luxury in a fairly large greenhouse. And in countries with very cold winters it is quite useful to sow the seeds of temperate things like brassicas in the greenhouse in the very early spring.

Whatever you do, don't overcrowd your greenhouse. It is far better to grow plenty of one really useful crop, like tomatoes, in the summer, and another really useful crop, like lettuces, in the winter than to fill your greenhouse with innumerable exotic fruits and vegetables. Make all the use you can of hotbeds under cold frames, cloches, jelly jars and sheets of transparent plastic and the like, in your outdoor plots (*see* pp.48–49).

"People say to us sometimes, 'Why do you have cross-breeds and mixed-up strains

in your animals and poultry?'"... For us the all-around animal [is one that is]

not too highly specialized, not too developed away from the wild creature,

not too finicky and highly strung, not too productive.

People come and stay with us and sometimes express horror at me when I kill

an animal. 'How could you do it?' I always ask them what they had for dinner the

day before, and if they say 'meat' I know I can treat their scruples with contempt.

I do not like killing animals; but having decided, after a great deal of thought,

that it is right to kill animals, I do it without worrying myself about it [and]

aiming at least for a professional standard in paunching and plucking and

cleaning and butchering, and at doing the thing in a workmanlike manner.

To connive at the killing of animals while being too lily-livered to kill them

yourself is despicable. We could not have eggs unless we kept birds, and if we did

not kill off the surplus birds, we would very soon be overrun."

JOHN SEYMOUR FAT OF THE LAND 1976

CHAPTER THREE

FOOD
FROM
ANIMALS

The Living Farmyard

Just as I advise against monoculture when it comes to planting crops, so I would urge you not to specialize in one animal, but to keep a wide variety. This is the only way to make the best use of your land's resources and to take advantage of the natural ways in which your animals help each other. Your cows will eat your long grass, and then your horses, sheep, and geese can crop your short grass. After that, your pigs will eat the roots, and at the same time plow the field ready for sowing with grain, which all the animals, especially the hens, can eat. Pigs, of course, thrive on whey, and skim milk from butter-making, and cow's milk can nourish orphan foals or lambs. Your different animals will protect each other from disease as well, for organisms that cause disease in one species die when eaten by another.

COWS, HORSES, SHEEP, AND GOATS

Ruminants—cows, sheep, and goats—are the animals best equipped to turn that basic substance, grass, into food in the form of meat and milk. Horses, I hope, will not be exploited for meat or milk, but for their unique ability to turn greenstuff into power. These animals divide up the available food very efficiently among themselves, and in so doing they work to each other's benefit. A lot of horses kept on a pasture with no other animals will not thrive; with other animals, they will. It has been said that if you can keep 20 cows on a given piece of pasture, you can keep 20 cows and 20 sheep just as well. Cows will eat the long, coarser grass, and the sheep and horses will clean up after them by nibbling what they leave close to the ground. Goats, which are browsers rather than grazers, fill a useful niche because they will eat bark, leaves, brambles, and bushes, and if you want your land deforested, they will do that as well.

GEESE

Geese will compete directly with the ruminants for grass, but, like the ruminants, though less efficiently, they will turn grass into food in the form of meat. At the same time they will improve your pasture. It is well worth keeping a few, for the more you diversify your grazing species, the better.

DUCKS
Your ducks will eat a lot of food that will otherwise give you no benefit: water plants and aquatic creatures. And they will patrol your garden and eat that unmitigated nuisance, the slug.

PIGS
The pig is a magnificent animal and really the pioneer on your holding. He will eat anything, and in his efforts to find food he will plow land, clear undergrowth, and devour all surpluses, even your dishwashing water. As William Cobbett wrote in his *Cottage Economy*: "In short, without hogs, farming could not go on; and it never has gone on in any country in the world. The hogs are the great stay of the whole concern. They are much in small space; they make no show, as flocks and herds do; but without them, cultivation of the land would be a poor, a miserably barren concern."

CHICKENS
Chickens are essentially graminivorous, or at least they prefer to live on seed. They will pick up all spilled grain in your harvest fields, eat the "tail corn"—the grains that are too small to grind—and eat weed seeds. They will follow the pig, when that splendid animal is rooting away in the ground, and snap up any worms, wireworms, leatherjackets, or whatever else the pig turns up. And they will keep the rats away by pecking up spilled seed from corn cribs.

The Cow

There are four classes of cows: dairy cows, beef cows, dual-purpose cows, and just cows. Fifty years ago there were some magnificent dual-purpose breeds in Europe and the Americas, but economic circumstances caused them to die out as the pure dairy and pure beef animals took over. This is sad, from the point of view of the self-supporter, and from every other point of view, in fact, because beef should be a by-product of the dairy herd and not an end in itself.

One cow produces one calf every year, and she's got to do that if she is to give milk. If she is a beef cow, all she can do is suckle this one calf—unless she has twins, of course—until it is old enough to be weaned. But if she is a dual-purpose cow, she can have a good beef calf, provide him with enough milk, and provide you with enough milk as well. And if she is a pure dairy cow, she will have a calf each year and provide enough milk for it and more than enough for you; however, the calf won't be a very good one for beef.

Now, half the calves you have are likely to be male, and, of the other half that are female, only half will be needed as replacements for the dairy herd. Therefore, ultimately you will be forced, whatever you do, either to sell the three-quarters that are not wanted for beef, or to kill them for beef yourself. Otherwise, your cattle population will build up on your piece of land until there is no room for you or anyone else.

What breed?

But we can and do eat dairy cattle. The Holstein is one example. These cattle are large, bony, and give an awful lot of poor milk, meaning milk low in butterfat. They are hardy and their calves, although from dairy animals, give good beef.

At the opposite end of the scale there are the Channel Island breeds. Of these, the Jersey makes the best family cow. They are small and don't give as much milk as the Friesian, but it is the richest milk there is. Their calves make poor beef and are practically unsalable, but they are good to eat all the same—I've had them.

If you can get a good old-fashioned dual-purpose breed, I would say get it every time. The Danish Red is fine, the old Red Poll is, too, or the dual-purpose Shorthorn. From these you will get good milk and good beef. But there is no cow more tractable, or indeed lovable, than the little Jersey, and if you want a friend as well as a milk supply, I strongly recommend her.

Buying your cow

How do you get a cow in the first place? It can be difficult. You see, if a person who owns a herd of cows wishes to sell one of them, you can be sure of one thing: it is the worst cow in his herd. It may just be that a farmer wants to sell a cow or two because he has too many, and wishes to reduce his herd, but even if he does it for this reason, and his herd is a good one, you can still be sure that the ones he culls will be the worst in the herd. Generally speaking, if a farmer sells a cow, it is because there is something wrong with her.

However, there are a few legitimate reasons for putting livestock up for sale. One is that farmer really is just selling up (as many are). His whole herd will be put up for auction and the good cows sold along with the bad. Another is that the person (maybe a fellow self-supporter) has reared one or more heifer calves with the object of selling them "down calving." This means the cow has just calved and is therefore (another cowman's term) "in full profit"—in other words, giving a lot of milk. In this case you can buy a cow that has just calved for the first time, and she is just as likely to be a good cow as any other cow you might buy. The person selling her is not selling her because she is bad, but because he has bred her up especially to sell.

There is one disadvantage to buying a first-calver—at least there is if you are new to cows. You will both be

BROWN SWISS
Noted for longevity and the ability to produce large amounts of milk, which is admired by cheesemakers because of its high percentage of protein and fat.

THE FRIESIAN
The archetypal dairy cow. Big, heavy-yielding, hardy, and, given the right bull, will produce fine beef calves.

THE JERSEY
The classic family cow. Affectionate, hardy, with the richest milk in the world, but not so good for beef.

learners. She will be nervous and flighty, and may kick. You will be the same. She will have tiny teats, and you may not get along very well. So if you are a learner, consider buying a sweet old cow with teats like champagne bottles, kind eyes, and a placid nature. What does it matter if she is not the world champion milker? What does it matter if she only has three good "quarters"? (Each teat draws milk from one quarter of the udder.) Provided her owner is honest, and says she is healthy, and the cow doesn't kick, she will probably be fine.

Here are a few points to consider when you buy a cow:

1 Feel the udder very carefully, and if there are any hard lumps in it, don't buy her, because it probably means that she has, or has had and is likely to get again, very bad mastitis. (Mastitis is an extremely common complaint. One or more teats gets blocked, and the milk you get is useless). But if you are getting a cow very cheaply because she has a "blind quarter" (one quarter of her udder with no milk in it), then that is a different matter, as long as you know about it.

2 Make sure she is TT (tuberculosis tested), and has also been tested, and found free from, a disease called brucellosis. In many countries both these tests are obligatory, and it is illegal to sell milk from cows found infected with either. In any case, it is foolish. For more information on these diseases and testing procedures, contact your local extension or your state's department of agriculture.

3 If the cow is "in milk"—in other words, has any milk in her udders—try milking her (*see* p.198). Try each teat fairly carefully. Make sure she doesn't kick when you milk her and handle her, although, of course, common sense will tell you that, because you are a stranger, and because maybe she has been carted to some strange, new place, she will be more than usually nervous.

Also make sure she has some milk in each quarter. If you are buying her from her home, ask the seller if you can milk her right out (saving the seller the trouble!) and then you will really know how much milk she gives.

4 Look at her teeth—they will tell you how old she is (*see* p.201).

5 See that she is quiet and tame enough to let you put your arms around her neck and stroke her behind the ears.

6 Make sure she has that indefinable but nevertheless very real "bloom of health" about her.

7 If you are a real beginner, you may want to contact your local extension for advice on finding a suitable cow. Then enlist the help of some kindly cow-loving neighbor who is willing to go with you and advise you. If the neighbor is really into cows, do what he says.

Now, having gotten your cow, get her home and make her comfortable. Spoil her a little. Tie her up in your cowshed, give her some good hay, some oats or barley meal or cow-cake: give her time to calm down. Then, in the evening, milk her.

Feeding

"Agriculturalists" work out the feeding of cows by saying that a cow needs a certain amount of food for her "maintenance ration" and a certain amount more for her "production ration." That is, we work out what it will take to maintain the cow healthily if she is giving no milk, and then add some according to how much milk she is giving.

Maintenance ration

Twenty pounds (9 kg) a day of good hay will maintain a large cow during the winter. Twelve pounds (5.5 kg) would maintain a small cow like a Jersey. If you feed a cow nothing but fair-quality hay for her maintenance ration, she will need 3,700 pounds (1,675 kg) of hay for the winter if she is a big girl like a Friesian, or 2,300 pounds (1,050 kg) of hay if she is a Jersey. Now, if you want to feed other things besides hay for maintenance, the hay equivalents are given on the following page.

THE RED POLL
A good old-fashioned dual-purpose cow, producing plenty of good milk and good beef, too.

THE HEREFORD
Recognized all over the world as a fine beef animal. Good for crossing with other breeds for beef.

A ton of fairly good hay is equivalent to:

¾ *ton of very good hay*

4 tons of kale or other greens

5 tons of mangels

3 tons of fodder beet

Production ration

To give "maintenance plus one gallon," the winter's ration should increase to: 5,000 pounds (2,270 kg) for a Friesian and 3,700 pounds (1,675 kg) for a Jersey. The daily ration therefore goes up to 27 pounds (13 kg) hay or its equivalent for a Friesian and 20 pounds (9 kg) for a Jersey.

Now you can figure that if you feed 3½ pounds (1.6 kg) of a mixed "concentrate" ration for each gallon (4 liters) that the cow produces over the first gallon, that will do. And the concentrate could be:

2 parts barley (rolled)

I part oats (rolled)

I part beans (broken or kibbled)

To each ton of concentrates you can add if required:

20 lb (9.0 kg) limestone

20 lb (9.0 kg) steamed bone meal

20 lb (9.0 kg) salt

Cows kept naturally on organically farmed pastures and hay are unlikely to suffer from mineral deficiencies, but if you ever did get "grass staggers" or hypomagnasemia, or any other diseases that your vet told you were due to mineral deficiency, then you would have to add the missing element either to the diet of the cows or to the land. Seaweed meal is an excellent source of all minerals. You can just dump some seaweed on your pasture from time to time, and allow the cows to nibble it and lick it. They will not suffer from mineral deficiency if they do this.

All this means that if, in an average winter situation, you feed your cows, say, 30 pounds (13.5 kg) of kale or other greens a day and 12 pounds (5.5 kg) of hay for her maintenance plus one gallon, and, say, 3½ pounds (1.5 kg) of the above suggested "concentrate" for her production ration for every gallon over the first, you will not go far

wrong. But use what food you've got. Use common sense and watch the milk bucket. If the milk goes down, feed more and you should be all right.

Summer feeding

In the summer, if you have plenty of good grass, grass alone should give maintenance plus up to 5 gallons (18 liters). A cow yielding over this would have to have 3½ pounds (1.5 kg) concentrate per gallon over 5 gallons, but I hope you wouldn't try to keep such a cow. You don't want a ridiculous amount of milk, and very high yielders need a vet in almost constant attendance and have to be cared for like invalids. But grass varies enormously in value, and, if you suddenly find her milk yield dropping off, give her a little concentrate (even a pound or two) and see what happens.

Stockmanship is a matter of constant observation and common sense. Look at your animals: learn what the "bloom of health" means. Watch their condition. Are they getting fatter or thinner? Watch their milk yield; watch how hungry they seem to be. The "stockman's eye" may not be given to everyone, but it can usually be acquired.

Milking

Milk your cow twice a day, ideally at 12-hour intervals. Wash the cow's udder and teats in warmish water. The more you massage the udder in doing so, the better. Clean the rear end of the cow generally so that no dung or dirt will fall into your pail. Then thoroughly wash your own hands and dry them well with a towel. Give the cow something tasty to eat. Sit down beside her on a stool and grasp the two front teats in your hands. Or, if you are an absolute beginner, grasp one teat with one hand. Common sense will tell you how hard to squeeze. Next, keep holding on with your thumb and finger, and squeeze the teat, successively bringing in your other fingers, so as to expel the milk downward out of the teat. Release the teat and repeat the operation (*see below*). It sounds easy, but it is difficult, and it takes a week to learn to milk.

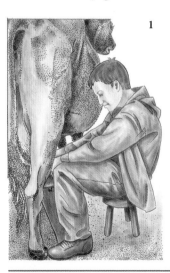

MILKING A COW
Sit down on the right side of the cow(**1**), grip the bucket at an angle between your knees and grasp the two front teats in your hands. To milk, squeeze high up the top of the teat with the thumb and index finger (**2**) to stop the milk from going back up to the "bag," as farmers call the udder. Then bringing in your middle (**3**), ring (**4**) and little fingers (**5**), squeeze progressively downward to expel the milk. If you can, practice on a dummy teat to get the necessary rhythmic motion. It is also much better to begin on an old cow who is used to being milked and who won't mind if you fumble.

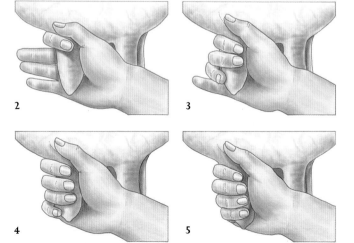

Housing

The modern milking shed is a concrete-floored building arranged so that the cow can be tied up to a vertical post. This has a ring on it that can slide up and down so that the cow can lie down if she likes. She is supposed to dung in the "dunging passage," and you are supposed to clean it every day.

But in my view all this is bowing down too far to the great god "hygiene." If you keep your cow in a house for all or part of the time and throw in plenty of dry straw, bracken, or other bedding every day, the dung will slowly build up and you will have the most magnificent muck. Your local dairy inspector will probably excommunicate you if you milk cows in such a house, and you would certainly not be allowed to sell milk or any milk product in any so-called civilized country; but in fact the milk you get from a cow milked on "deep litter" will be as clean as any milk in the world, provided you observe the other rules of hygiene. We milked our cows for eight years like this, cleaning the muck out about once a year, and the cows were indoors at night in the winter. Our milk, butter, and cheese were perfect.

A refinement is to have a house for milking the cow or cows and another house for them to sleep, eat, and rest in. This can be cleaned out regularly, or it can be strawed every day and the dung left for months. It will be warmer and more pleasant for the cows than the milking stall and they can be left free.

As to when to house: our cows only come into the cow shed to be milked, and to finish their hay. Winter and summer, night and day, they are out in the field except for an hour morning and evening when they come in to be milked and to eat. In the summer they don't want to come in. They want to stay out and eat grass. We don't feed them in the summer—except maybe a pound or two of rolled barley to make them contented. If there is plenty of grass, grass is enough for them. We don't go for very high yielders, nor should any self-supporter.

In the winter they come in eagerly because the grass is of little value and they are hungry. In bad weather I would prefer to leave them in all night and only turn them out in the daytime, and then, when the weather is really foul, keep them in some days, too. But to do this you would need an awful lot of straw in reserve. In really cold climates cows have to be housed all winter. Do what your neighbors do. But don't keep them in half the winter and then turn them out.

When you do turn them out in the spring, be careful about it. Wait for good weather, and only push them out for short periods at first. Too much grass may upset their stomachs if they are not used to it, and sudden exposure to weather can give cattle a chill. And if you can keep cows out all winter—that is, if any of your neighbors do—it is far less trouble.

Mating

A small cow might be mated at 15 months, a large cow at 20 months. A cow will only take the bull, or the artificial inseminator, when she is "bulling," or in heat. This condition occurs at intervals of 21 days in a non-pregnant heifer or cow, and continues each time for about 18 hours. You must watch for signs of bulling and then get the cow to a bull or have her artificially inseminated immediately, certainly by the next day, at the latest.

Signs of bulling are: she mounts other cattle or other cattle mount her; she stands around mooing and looking amorous; she swells slightly at the vulva; she will let you put all your weight on her back and apparently enjoy it. It may be a good thing to miss the first bulling period after calving, to give the cow a rest, but don't miss the second.

TEACHING A CALF TO SUCK

If you try to milk a cow in competition with a calf, the calf will win and you will lose. Many people therefore milk the cow themselves and feed the calf out of a bucket. To teach a calf to suck, put two fingers, slightly apart, in the calf's mouth. Get him to suck them, then lower your fingers and his nose down into the milk. He may start to choke, or he may find that he likes it and start to suck avidly. If he sucks, after a time gently remove your fingers and he will just suck the milk. You will need great patience.

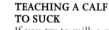

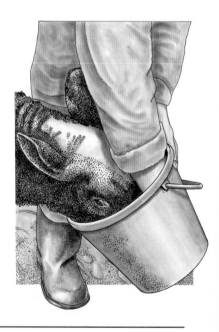

If there is a bull running with the cows, there is no problem. He knows what to do and when to do it. But if there is no bull, you will just have to use your eyes, that is all. Then you may take her to a neighbor's bull, or bring him to her. Alternatively, you can artificially inseminate your cow. Your local extension will give you advice about AI procedures and sources.

Calving

Leave her alone, out of doors, and you will probably find her one day licking a little calf that has just been born quite easily and naturally. Outdoor cows very seldom have trouble with calving. But watch the two for a few hours, until you are quite sure that the calf has gotten up and sucked. If the calf doesn't suck within an hour, be worried. Get it up and hold it to the teat and make it suck, and if necessary tie the cow up.

Cows calve up in the bare mountains in winter and rear their calves perfectly happily in the snow. As long as the calf runs out with the cow, and the cow has enough to eat, and the weather isn't too awful, he is all right. But as soon as you bring him indoors—and if you want the cow's milk, you will have to—you have upset the ordinary workings of nature, and you must keep the calf warm and out of drafts. He must suck from his mother for at least three days, because this first milk contains colostrum, a mixture of chemicals, organisms, and antibodies that are essential for the health—nay, survival—of the calf.

Then you can either take the calf away from the cow, and keep him out of earshot, if possible, or at least in a separate building, or you can keep him close to the cow's head so she can see him while you milk her. The easiest way for you to get your milk is to take the calf away and milk his mother yourself; she, after perhaps a night of bellowing for her calf, accepts the situation. She is not human, has a very short memory, and soon accepts you as her calf substitute. I have had a wet shirt many times because I couldn't stop a cow from licking me while I milked her!

Meanwhile, what do you feed the calf on? Well, if you have enough milk, feed the calf on the following mixture: the mother's milk at a rate of 10 percent of weight of calf (if the calf weighs 50 pounds [23 kg], give him 5 pounds [2 kg] of milk), plus added warm water (one part water to three parts milk). Feed him this mixture twice a day out of a bucket (*see illustrations opposite*) and serve it at blood heat.

After about a week or two, see that the calf has some top-quality hay to nibble if he feels like it. After a month, try hull with "cake," rolled barley, or other concentrates, and always have clean water available for him. After four months, wean him off milk altogether and feed him 4 pounds (1.8 kg) hay and 3 pounds (1.4 kg) concentrates, or let him out on a little clean grazing. By six months he should be getting 6 pounds (2.7 kg) hay and 3 pounds (1.4 kg) concentrates, unless by then he is on good clean grazing.

Calves can be subject to serious diseases. To some extent, good care can help prevent some of them. Prior to calving,

A COW'S TEETH REVEAL HER AGE
A mature cow has 32 teeth, of which eight are incisors. All eight are on the lower jaw and munch against a hard layer of palate called the dental pad. Within a month of birth, a calf has grown eight temporary incisors. These will slowly be replaced, until at age five the mature cow has eight permanent incisors. Age can therefore be determined by the number of temporary and permanent incisors present in a cow's jaw. The age of cows over five can be gauged by the wear on their teeth (by the age of 12, only stumps remain), and by the roughness of their horns. But beware cattle dealers who sandpaper cows' horns to make them look young.

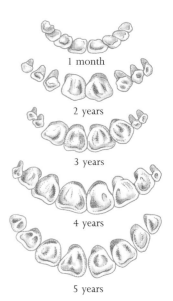

1 month

2 years

3 years

4 years

5 years

for example, outdoor cows should be moved to a fresh pasture (one not previously grazed by cattle), if possible. Still, it's always best to check with a veterinarian to find out which vaccines are recommended for calves and cows in your area.

There are other ways of rearing small calves and still getting some milk for yourself. If you are very lucky, you can find another cow who already has her own calf at heel, and fool her into thinking she has had twins. Then you can turn her, her calf, and your new calf all out together to pasture. This is the ideal solution, because the new calf is absolutely no more trouble and will thrive exceedingly. But such cows are rare. So another solution is to select a foster mother, tie her up twice a day, and force her to give milk to the new calf as well as her own. Many cows are pretty complacent about this; others will fight it. If yours fights, you may have to tie her legs up to stop her from hurting the calf. To get a young calf to suck a cow, put two fingers in his mouth and gently lead him up to the teat. Don't try to heave him forward from behind—that's useless.

Another way of getting milk for yourself and keeping the calf happy is to take some milk from the mother and let the calf suck the rest. Or you can let the calf run with his mother during the day, keep him away at night, and milk the cow the next morning. There are many ways you can play this game.

The whole subject of cows may seem to the beginner to be very complicated. Well, it is complicated, and there is absolutely no substitute for making friends with a knowledgeable neighbor and asking for help and advice. As for diseases of cows, these are many and various, and if your cows suffer from disease, you must send for the vet. But cows that are not unnaturally heavy yielders, and those that are kept as naturally as possible (not overfed but not underfed, and allowed out as much as climate permits) will very seldom get sick.

Beef

Before you kill any cattle, make sure you have plans for storing and using all the meat. This means emptying your chest freezers to ensure you have enough space: even the meat from a small bullock or heifer—less than half a ton in weight—will fill up an entire average-sized freezer, so beware. Talk to friends and fellow self-supporters: would they like some beef? Do any of them have experience killing cattle? By distributing some of your beef *largesse*, you can add substantially to your "credit" with self-supporters.

Sadly, today, big business has taken over many of the traditional small local slaughterhouses, and this has greatly pushed up the price of having your animals slaughtered. You will only consider killing your own beast as a last resort or in an emergency. Nevertheless, we should all know how these essentials of life are managed.

In practice, you should ask around for information about the best and most convenient meat processing plant. The smaller the place, and the closer to you, the better. Use a place recommended by other self-supporters—somewhere where you can be on first-name terms with the operators. Take some time to find out about their skills and problems; it will pay dividends in how well they hang and butcher your beast.

A beef animal will put on weight (and meat) very efficiently for its first three years of life. But most self-supporters will tend to have their animals killed somewhat younger than this, for a number of reasons—the most important of which is that a very large animal takes up a lot of space, both in the field or cowshed and in the freezer. Kill an animal younger than six months and you get very tender meat—but very little of it.

You can, of course, rear and sell your beef animals for cash at a livestock market, but in an age of polluted and unreliable foodstuffs, it seems crazy to let go of large quantities of meat you know to be wholesome. And you will find you pay at least twice as much for your meat as you get for an animal you sell, so you soon discover who makes the money out of farming.

Make your enquiries about slaughter well ahead of time, and make doubly sure you have all the paperwork that the processing plant requires. This will vary from state to state; always check with your state department of agriculture. If you do not have the right documentation, you will be stuck—and it can take weeks for the paperwork to be sorted out. Do not be tempted to believe that logic has anything to do with all this—in the end, it is simplest to jump through all the bureaucratic hoops.

About 10 days after the animal has gone to slaughter, the butcher will contact you to ask how you want the carcass cut up. You will need to do a little homework here—is it to be T-bone steaks, sirloin tips, ground round, or hamburger? Everyone has their preferences, but I would always get plenty of good-quality hamburger and some nice large roasts on the bone, and keep the ground round (on the legs) for braising.

So, paperwork and rules apart, here is the lowdown on how you can deal with your own meat if you really have to. I know of no other place where you will find simple instructions on butchery.

Slaughtering cattle

Before killing a cow, you should really starve it for 12 hours, but it's not the end of the world if you don't. Bring the animal quietly to where you are going to kill it. Then either shoot it with a small-bore rifle (which almost always means a .22) or with a humane killer. If you shoot it, it never knows anything is going to happen to it. Shoot just above the point at which imaginary lines from alternate eyes and horns cross.

The cow will fall immediately and lie on its side. Beware—all animals have violent death throes, and those hooves can be dangerous if you get in their way. Once it has fallen, stand under its chin with one of your legs pushing the chin up to stretch the head upward, and the other leg in front of and against the forelegs. If the animal starts to lash out with its forelegs now, it cannot hurt you.

With the throat thus stretched, stick a pointed knife through the skin at the breastbone and make a cut 12 inches (30 cm) long to expose the windpipe. Then stick your knife right back to the breastbone, pointing it at an angle of about 45 degrees toward the back of the animal. Make a deep cut forward as long as your other incision. Your knife will now be along one side of the windpipe. This cut will sever several main veins and arteries and the animal will bleed. If you have a block and tackle, you should haul the animal up by the hind legs at this juncture to assist bleeding. Catch the blood and, if you don't like black pudding, add it to the pigs' mash.

Skinning cattle

Skinning is the most difficult part of the whole process, and you will wish you had seen an expert on the job. Lower the animal to the ground to skin it.

Skin the head first. You can do this with it lying flat on the ground, but it makes it easier if you cut through the nostrils, push a hook through the hole, and haul the head just off the floor with the block and tackle. Slit the head down the back, from the poll to one nostril by way of the eye, and simply skin away until you have skinned it. I am not going to pretend this is an easy job, or a very pleasant one, but there is a lot of very good meat on the head and you can't just throw it away.

When you've skinned it, grab the lower jaw and stick your knife in the neck close to the head. Cut just behind the jaws first, then disjoint the atlas bone, the top bone of the vertebral column, and take the head off. Lay the carcass straight on its back with some wedges. Sever the tendons of the forelegs, cutting from the back, just below the dew claws. Slit the hide of the leg from this point to just above the knee. Skin the shank.

BEEF CUTS

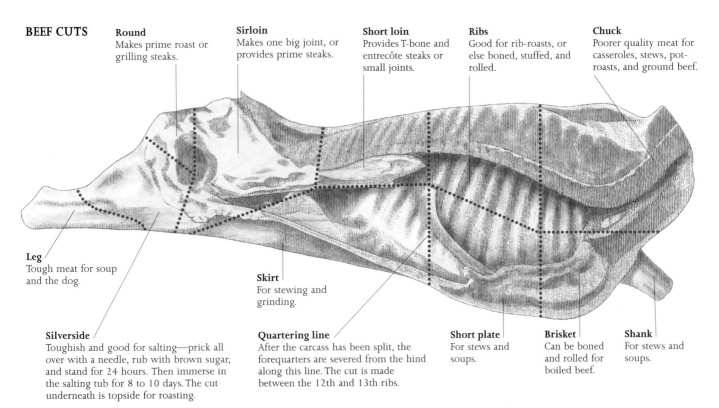

Round
Makes prime roast or grilling steaks.

Sirloin
Makes one big joint, or provides prime steaks.

Short loin
Provides T-bone and entrecôte steaks or small joints.

Ribs
Good for rib-roasts, or else boned, stuffed, and rolled.

Chuck
Poorer quality meat for casseroles, stews, pot-roasts, and ground beef.

Leg
Tough meat for soup and the dog.

Skirt
For stewing and grinding.

Silverside
Toughish and good for salting—prick all over with a needle, rub with brown sugar, and stand for 24 hours. Then immerse in the salting tub for 8 to 10 days. The cut underneath is topside for roasting.

Quartering line
After the carcass has been split, the forequarters are severed from the hind along this line. The cut is made between the 12th and 13th ribs.

Short plate
For stews and soups.

Brisket
Can be boned and rolled for boiled beef.

Shank
For stews and soups.

Cut through the lower joint or, if you can't find it, saw through the bone. Skin all the legs out to the midline of the body. Slit the skin right down the belly, and haul as much of the skin off as you can. Use a sharp, round-pointed knife for this and incline the blade slightly so the edge is against the skin and not the meat. Hold the skin as taut as you can while you use the knife. Skin both sides as far as you can.

Open the belly now, putting the knife in just behind the breastbone and protecting the knife with the hand so you don't pierce the paunch. Slit the abdominal wall right down the center line to the cod or udder. Don't puncture the paunch! Then cut along the breastbone and saw along its center. Saw through the pelvic bone at the other end. Cut the tendons of the hindlegs and the hock-bone, make loops of the tendons, and push the ends of your gambrel (which is a wooden or steel spreader) through them. Haul the hindquarters clear of the ground with the tackle. Slit the hide along the underside of the tail, sever the tail near the rump, and haul the tail out of its skin for ox-tail soup.

Gutting an ox
With a pointed knife, cut all the way around the rectum (bung) to separate it from the rest of the animal. After it is free, tie a piece of binder twine around it, tightly, so that nothing can fall out of it. Then cut it free from the backbone. Now haul the beast up fairly high and pull the rectum and other guts forward and downward so they flop out. Cut the liver out carefully, and remove the gallbladder from it. Hang the liver on a hook, wash it, and hang it up in the meat safe. Pull out the paunch, or guts and stomach,

and all the innards, and let it flop into a tub or basin. You can clean the stomach thoroughly by putting it in brine, and then use it for tripe. The intestines make good sausage skins (don't eat the reticulum or "bible" stomach—it looks like the leaves of a book inside). Haul the carcass clear off the ground now. Cut out the diaphragm (the wall between chest cavity and abdomen). Heave out the heart and lungs, and hang them up. The lungs (lights) are for the dogs, but the heart is for you. Rip the hide right off the shoulders and fling a few buckets of cold water into the carcass.

Go to bed after a hefty meal of fried liver; only the offal is fit to eat at this stage. In the morning, split the carcass right down the backbone with a cleaver if you have faith in yourself, or a saw if you don't. Wash the two halves of the carcass well with tepid water and trim to make it look tidy.

At this point I would strongly advise you to enlist the aid of a butcher. Jointing is a complicated process, and there is no substitute for watching an expert do it. After all, you want to make the best use of the animal you have spent all that time fattening for this moment. And you can't really improve upon the recognized butcher's cuts.

Salting beef
The traditional salting tub has a loose, round board with holes in it beneath the meat, and another on top of the meat. You can put a stone on the top board to keep the meat down, but never use a metal weight. To make your brine, boil salted water and allow to cool. Test the brine for strength; if a potato will not float in it, add salt until it does. Pickle the tongue by spicing the brine with herbs, cloves, lemon, onions, and soaking the tongue in it for six days.

Goats

Goats are called "desert-makers" in some dry regions because they destroy what scrub there is and prevent more from growing. But where the goat is controlled, it can fill a place in a mixed ecology, and if you want to discourage reforestation it has a very useful part to play. In cut-over woodland, for example, the goat can go ahead of the other animals as a pioneer, suppress the brambles and briars, prevent the trees from coming back, and prepare the way, perhaps, for the pig to come and complete the process of clearing the old forest for agriculture.

Goats will thrive in deciduous woodland (perhaps one to an acre), and give plenty of milk, but they will, have no doubt of it, prevent any regeneration of trees. In coniferous woodland, goats will find very little sustenance, but on heather or gorse-covered mountainsides they will thrive, and there is no doubt that a mixture of goats and sheep in such situations would make better use of the grazing than sheep alone. Goats, concentrated enough, will clear land of many weeds, and they will eat vegetation unsuitable for sheep and leave the grass for the sheep.

For the self-supporting farmer, the goat can quite easily be the perfect dairy animal. For the person with only a garden, the goat may be the only possible dairy animal. This is because goats are very efficient at converting roughage into milk and meat. Goat's milk is not only as good as cow's milk, in many respects it is better. For people who are allergic to cow's milk it is absolutely ideal. For babies it is very good. It makes magnificent cheese because its fat globules are much smaller than those of cow's milk and therefore do not rise so quickly and get lost in the whey. It is harder to make into butter, because the cream does not rise within a reasonable time, but with a separator, butter can be made and is excellent. On the other hand, milking goats takes more labor per gallon of milk than milking cows, however you do it, and so does herding, or fencing, goats.

Fencing and tethering

Restraining goats is the goat-keeper's chief problem, and we all know goat-keepers who also try to be gardeners and who, year after year, moan that the goats have yet again broken into the garden and in a few hours completely ruined it. Young fruit trees that have taken years to grow are killed and the vegetables absolutely ravaged. But this annual experience has no effect whatsoever on the beliefs of true goat-keepers. Next year, they tell themselves, they will win the battle to keep goats out of the garden. What they forget is that the goats have 24 hours a day to plan to get into the garden, and the keepers don't.

Three strands of electric fence, with three wires at 15 inches (40 cm), 27 inches (70 cm), and 40 inches (1 m) above ground level, will restrain goats, and so will a 4-foot (1.2-m) high fence of chain link with a support wire at 4½ feet (1.4 m) and another support wire lower down. Wire netting will hardly deter goats at all.

Tethering is the other answer. If you can picket-tether goats along road shoulders, on commons, and so on, and thus use grazing where you could use no grazing before, you must be winning. But it is unfair to tether any animal unless you move it frequently; above all, don't keep putting it back on the place where it has been tethered before, except after a long interval. Goats, like sheep, soon become infested with internal parasites if they are confined too long on the same ground. By tethering you are denying the animal the right to range and search for clean, parasite-free pasture. Picket-tethering is very labor-intensive, but for the goat-keeper with a couple of goats and plenty of time, it is an obvious way to get free pasture.

Another form of tethering is the running tether. A wire is stretched between two posts, and the tether can run along the wire. This is an obvious way of strip-grazing a field, and also a good way of getting rid of weeds that other animals will not touch.

TOGGENBURG
A fairly small Swiss goat. Yields well and can live on grass.

NUBIAN
Gives very rich milk, but in relatively low quantities.

SAANEN
A large goat of Swiss origin. Capable of high yields, if given good grazing.

Feeding

A kid should have a quart (1 liter) of milk a day for at least two months, but as he gets older, some of this may be skim milk. A reasonable doe should give from 3 to 6 pints (1.5 to 3 liters) of milk a day. In the winter a doe in milk should have about 2 pounds (1 kg) a day of very good hay (you should be able to raise this—about 750 pounds or 340 kg a year—on a quarter of an acre), one or two pounds (0.5–1 kg) of roots or other succulents, and one or two pounds (0.5–0.9 kg) of grain, depending on milk yield. Goats should have salt licks available. It is a mistake to think that goats will give a lot of milk on grazing alone: milking goats need good feeding. They will, for example, thrive on the silage you can make by scaling grass clippings in fertilizer bags (see pp.266–269). As for the grain you feed to your goats, a good mixture, such as you might feed to dairy cows, is fine, or you can buy "cake," or "dairy nuts" from a merchant (and pay for it, too). All debris from the market garden or vegetable garden can go to goats, but it is better to crush, or split, tough brassica stems first. Feed them their concentrates individually, or they rob each other.

Housing

Goats are not as winter-hardy as cows and cannot be left out all the time in North American winters and expected to give any milk. They don't like cold and they hate rain. High-yielding goats (which personally I would avoid) need very high feeding and warm housing, but medium-yielding ones must have shelter from the rain, and an airy but fairly draft-proof shed to sleep in at nights. Giving them a table to lie on, with low sides to exclude draft, is a good idea, and if they are lying in a fierce down-draft of cold air, adjust the ventilation until they are not. Maybe a board roof over the table to stop down-drafts would be a good idea.

Otherwise, you can treat milking goats much the same as you treat cows. Dry them off eight weeks before kidding. But a goat may milk for two or three years after kidding without kidding again.

Rearing orphans

One possible good use for goats is rearing orphans of many kinds. Goats are excellent for suckling other animals: calves thrive better on goat's milk than they do on their mother's, and it would be reasonable, if you kept cows, but had some wilderness or waste land on which cows could not thrive, to keep a flock of goats on the bad land and use them for suckling the calves so that you can milk their mothers. Goat milk is very digestible, and pretty good milk anyway, and orphan piglets, for example, which don't take very kindly to cow's milk, will thrive on goat's milk. Calves will suck straight from the nanny. Lambs will, too, but don't let them—they may damage her teats and give her mastitis. Milk her yourself and bucket-feed the lambs. Milk the nanny and feed the milk to piglets through a bottle.

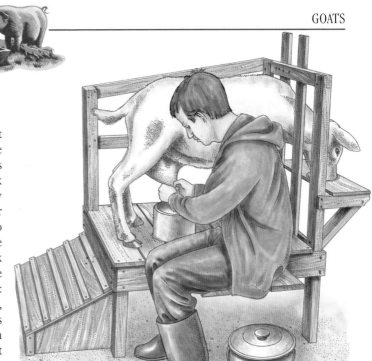

MILKING A GOAT
You can milk a goat that is standing on the ground, just as you would milk a cow (see p.198). But because goats are so much smaller, a stand helps. Coax her into position with some hay or grain.

You can rear foals on goats. The suggestion has been made that a suitable person could make a living, or at least half a living, by running a goat-orphanage—not for orphan goats but for other animals. Neighbors soon get to know such things, and orphan lambs are a dime a dozen in the lambing season in sheep districts, and very often a sow has too many piglets.

Billy kids

Kids come whether you want them or not, and in the end you have to find something to do with them. What you can do is castrate them and then eat them. The most humane way to castrate a goat or anything else is to use rubber rings, put on with an "Elastrator," which you can buy from any agricultural supplier.

A billy becomes very male at three months, whereas a lamb does not develop specific male characteristics until about six months. Therefore, many of us who produce fat lamb don't bother to castrate, but male goat kids should be castrated unless you intend to eat them before three months, or they will become strong-tasting. In my opinion, a goat wether (castrated billy goat) tastes as good as any mutton, particularly if you lard it well, or marinate it in oil and vinegar, or oil and wine, for it is short of fat compared to sheep. Up to six months old, it lends itself very well to roasting with various herbs or spicy sauces. If the billy goat has not been castrated, the meat has a strong gamey taste, and it is best to marinate it for three days in wine and vinegar and then curry it. Cooked in this way it is delicious. As a general rule, though, it is better to castrate if you are going to eat it.

Pigs

The pig fits so well into the self-supporter's economy that the animal almost seems designed with that in mind. It is probably the most omnivorous animal in the world and will thrive on practically anything. It is even more omnivorous than man, because a pig can eat and digest grass, while we cannot. A pig will not thrive on grass alone, but it can make it a substantial part of its diet. And it will convert virtually anything that you grow or produce on the farm into good meat. Throw any vegetable matter, of whatever kind, to a pig, and he will either eat it—converting it within hours to good meat and the best compost in the world—or he will tread it into the ground, dung on it, and turn it into compost that way. Put a pig on rough grassland, or scrubland, that you wish to bring into cultivation, and he will plow it for you, and root it up for you, and manure it for you, and at the same time extract sustenance from it to live and grow on.

Feeding

Self-supporters should aim to produce all the food they need to feed the pigs on their farm. Barley meal, corn meal, potatoes, Jerusalem artichokes, carrots, fodder beets, parsnips, turnips, or rutabagas—these are all crops that may be grown to feed pigs; and if supplemented with skim milk or whey they make a pretty good diet. I have fattened pigs very successfully on boiled potatoes and skimmed milk. I have fattened them on raw carrots and separated milk. Wheat "offals," such as bran and middlings, are good too, but there is no doubt that either barley meal or corn meal have no peers when it comes to fattening pigs. Even then, they must have a "protein supplement," which may well be whey or separated milk, though any other high protein food will do: meat meal or fish meal, cooked meat or fish, bean meal, or any other high-protein grain. Soy is excellent for fattening pigs. If pigs are outdoors, they don't want mineral supplements. If your pigs get some fresh greens, some milk by-products, and some scraps, they don't want or need vitamin supplements.

Let sows run out over plenty of land, and in summer they will get nearly half their sustenance from grass, if they are not in milk. Keep sows or growing pigs on artichokes, or a field of potatoes, or where potatoes have been harvested, or on another crop, and they will get half their food from that.

But for milking sows, or sows in late pregnancy, animal protein is absolutely essential, as it is the only source of vitamin B12. A good rule for rations is that breeding sows, outdoors on grass and with access to scraps, surplus vegetables, and so on, will need 2 pounds (1 kg) a day of concentrate such as barley meal and some protein, but 6 pounds (3 kg) a day when they farrow. If they are indoors or having concentrates only, you can double these amounts. When the baby pigs are three weeks old or so, you can start "creep feeding" them: that is, allowing them through fence holes too small for the sow, where they can eat concentrates unrestricted.

Fattening pigs can be given as much as they can eat until they reach about 100 pounds (45 kg) in weight (half grown), after which their ration should be restricted or they will get too fat. Restrict them to what they will finish in a quarter of an hour. If they take longer than that, give them less the next day; if they wolf it all in five minutes and squeal for more, increase their ration. Feed them like this twice a day. Do not restrict their intake of roots and vegetables—only of concentrates. Watch your pigs constantly, and if they look too thin, or too hungry, feed them more.

I have kept pigs successfully for over 30 years with nothing more elaborate than some rolled barley, skim milk, maybe in a pinch some fish meal, some bran, plenty of roots and vegetables, and whatever else there is to give away.

The pig bucket

Now I must touch on the high art of the pig bucket. For the man with a thousand sows it is irrelevant, but for the self-supporting family, fattening a pig or two in the yard to kill, or with one or two dear old breeding sows who become almost part of the family themselves, the pig bucket is very relevant indeed.

DUROC
A breed of hogs with origins in the eastern United States and in the Corn Belt. Compact, attractive color, and good for fleshing out.

GLOUCESTER OLD SPOT
A fine and beautiful English breed evolved originally for living in apple orchards and woodlands. It is hardy, prolific, and a fine baconer.

WESSEX SADDLEBACK
Also known as the British Saddleback, this English breed is an ancestor of the American Hampshire.

WELSH
A popular commercial breed in Great Britain because it's white, long, and lean. It is a reasonable outdoor breed.

PIG HOUSING

A pig house should be very strong, either movable or else easily dismantled and reerected, and, if possible, constructed at little or no cost. Mine are made of scrap corrugated iron nailed to bush timber. Walls and roof can be double iron sheets with insulation (old paper bags or bracken, for example) stuffed in between. When piglets are three weeks old, make a gap in the fencing that is too small for the sow but large enough for the piglets to get through and "creep feed" on concentrates.

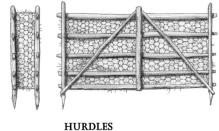

HURDLES
Two hurdles lashed together with straw in between, and covered.

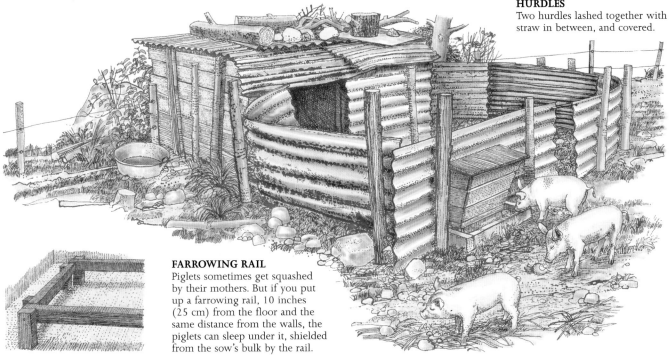

FARROWING RAIL
Piglets sometimes get squashed by their mothers. But if you put up a farrowing rail, 10 inches (25 cm) from the floor and the same distance from the walls, the piglets can sleep under it, shielded from the sow's bulk by the rail.

Nothing should be wasted on the self-sufficient holding. The garbage truck should never have to visit. Under the kitchen sink there should be a bucket, and into it should go all the household scraps except such as are earmarked for the dog or the cats. When you do the dishes, develop the "pig bucket technique." This means scraping all scraps first into the sacred bucket; then dribble (rather than run) hot water from the faucet over each plate and dish so that the water carries all grease and other nutriments into a bowl (helped by a brush). Throw this rich and concentrated dishwater into the pig bucket. Finish washing the dishes any way you like and let that water run down the sink. The concentrated dishwater from the first wash is excellent food, and should not be wasted on any account.

Housing and farrowing

Except when sows are actually farrowing (giving birth to a litter) or have recently farrowed, they can live very rough. If they have plenty of straw or bracken and are kept dry, with no through drafts, and if possible with well-insulated walls and roof in cold climates, they will do very well. Several sows together are, generally speaking, much happier than one sow alone.

However, when a sow farrows, she must have a hut to herself. It needs to be big enough for her to turn around in comfort. If you like, you can have a farrowing rail, which prevents the sow from lying on the piglets (we kept six sows for eight years and only lost two piglets during all that time from crushing). The books say the sow should have no litter when she farrows. All I can say is we give our sows access to litter, and they carry as much as they want of it indoors and make an elaborate nest. What they don't want they throw out.

It is delightful to watch a sow making her nest, and there is no doubt that she is most unlikely to have any trouble if she is able to go through all her rituals before farrowing, and is then left alone in peace to farrow, with no other pigs jostling her, and no overanxious owner fussing over her like an old hen. Sows eating their piglets, or lying on them, are generally products of an artificially organized system. If you break the chain of instinct here, you do so at your own risk.

The period when the sow wants a boar occurs at 21-day intervals, as in the cow. I do not like to put a gilt, or young female pig, to the boar until she is nearly a year old. The boar can be of a different breed, since pigs interbreed well.

Getting a sow "in pig"

If you keep six sows or more, you can afford the keep of a boar, so you can buy one and let him run with the sows. If you have fewer sows, you can take a sow to a neighbor's boar when she needs it. Gestation will be about 115 days, and litters can vary from six to 20 piglets: 10 is about the average, but we often had 12 (and reared them all) with monotonous regularity when we kept sows outdoors. You can, if you prefer, buy weaners (piglets from eight to 12 weeks old) from neighbors to fatten. If you do buy weaners, you won't have to have a sow at all. We often bought and fattened three weaners, sold one and ate two, and the one we sold paid for the two we ate.

Slaughterhouse or do-it-yourself

First, check out the situation with regard to local slaughterhouses. It is simplest to have the pig slaughtered, scraped and split into two halves. You can then butcher the carcass yourself for joints, pork, hams, and bacon (*see opposite*). Remember that many modern slaughterhouses will only process relatively small pigs. If your pig is a large baconer, you may have to look farther afield to find a suitable slaughterhouse.

Before all the regulations came in, the traditional way to kill a pig was to stick it in the throat, but I don't recommend this. Although I see nothing wrong with killing animals for meat, I see everything wrong with making them suffer in any way. If we kill an animal, we should do so instantaneously, and the animal should have no inkling that anything nasty is about to happen to it.

Were a pig to be killed in situ, I would use food to lure the pig into the place where he was going to be killed, and then, when he was interested in the food, shoot him in the head—either with a humane killer (captive bolt pistol) or a .22 rifle. Immediately after the pig had dropped, you would stick it, squatting squarely in front of the recumbent pig while someone else held it on its back, stick the knife just in front of the breastbone, and when you felt the bone, let the knife slip forward to go under it. Then the knife would be pushed in a couple of inches and sliced forward with the point of the knife toward the head. This severs the artery. Then you need to look out: a nervous reaction occurs. The pig appears to come to life and thrashes around, so great care is needed not to be cut by its hooves.

Scraping

If you are going to scrape your pig yourself, you must scald him, and this is a ticklish operation. You can either dip your animal right into a hot water tub, or you can lay him on the floor or a scraping bench, and baste him with hot water. Not having a tub big enough to immerse a whole hog in, we lay the pig on its side and slowly and carefully pour hot water over a small part of him. The water should be 150°F (65°C) when it comes from the bucket (so it should be slightly hotter when it goes into it). Keep pouring gently, and from time to time try some bristle with the thumb and forefinger. When the bristle begins to lift, scrape—and scrape furiously. It is better not to use a knife. A sharpened hoe head or metal pot lid is sharp enough. Off comes the bristle, off also comes the outermost skin of the pig, and no matter what color your pig started off as, he will become white as snow.

Keep working until the pig is absolutely clean. Put the legs right into the bucket of hot water; then take out and pull the horny toes off with a hook. You really need two or three helping hands to scrape a big hog, with someone to bring on the hot water and another to fetch the home-brewed beer (vital on such an occasion). The head is difficult: you might set fire to some straw with denatured alcohol, hold the head over the flame to singe it, and scrub with a wire brush. When finished, douse the pig with cold water to get rid of all the loose skin, bristles, and any blood.

If you dip him, leave him in water at 145°F (63°C) for five minutes and then haul him out and scrape him. You can only do this if you know your water is going to stay at this temperature (pretty well exactly). If it is a few degrees too cold, it won't loosen the bristles.

CARVING YOUR PIG CARCASS

It's a good idea to butcher your own pig (that is, cut up the carcass), even if local regulations forbid home slaughter (actually killing the animal yourself). You need to gut and clean your carcass before jointing (*see p.211*). Home butchery is important because it's the only way to make sure the joints are exactly how you want them. To make good bacon and ham, it is far better to cut up the meat yourself. You will need strong beams and an easily washable floor to do the job. Use a block and tackle to lift the carcass.

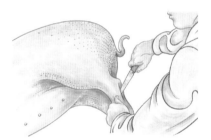

1 Cut vertical slits on each side of the tendons of the hind legs in order to insert the gambrel.

2 Split the breastbone. First, cut down to the bone with a knife, then saw through it.

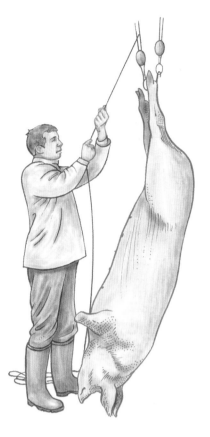

3 Sling the pig up on the gambrel.

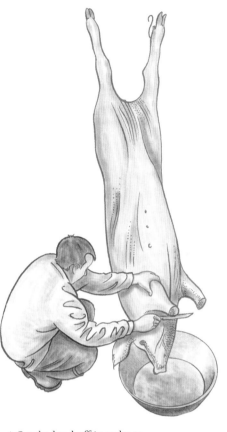

4 Cut the head off in order to sever the windpipe and gullet.

5 Cut around and tie off the rectum to prevent it from leaking.

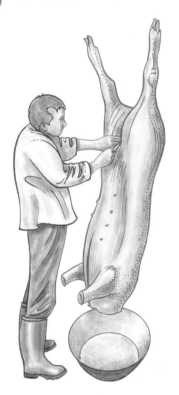

6 Slit along the line of the abdomen without cutting the guts. Have a large receptacle on the floor.

7 Haul out the innards. Keep the pluck (heart, pancreas, and lungs) separate. Throw a bucket of cold water inside the carcass.

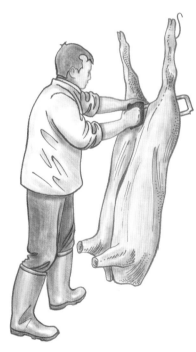

8 Saw down the backbone so as to cut the pig completely in half. Leave him to hang in an airy place overnight.

Hanging your pig

An inch or two above its foot on the back of the hind leg is a tendon. Cut down each side of this with a vertical slit through the skin and raise the tendon out with your fingers. Don't cut the leg above the hock as beginners do; this is barbarous and spoils good meat. Insert each cod of your gambrel through the two tendons in the legs.

Now, don't haul that pig off the ground until you have sawn through the breastbone or sternum! Cut down to the breastbone with a clean knife, then split it, right down the middle, with a saw. If you try to do this after you have hung up the pig, all the guts will come flopping out and make the operation very difficult. Now lay on to the fall of that tackle and heave away! Up goes your pig. Cut off the head just behind the ears, at the first spinal bone (the atlas), and you shouldn't have to use the saw. Put the head into brine.

EDIBLE PARTS OF A PIG

Pigs' feet
Pigs' feet can be cooked up for brawn, or boiled separately and eaten with vegetables.

Ham
The ham makes a huge joint of prime roast pork, or it can be salted and smoked to make a cured ham.

Back
A large pig's back can be cured as bacon. On a smaller pig it may go for chops. On a large baconer it can be cut into good roasting joints.

Belly
A baconer's belly can be salted whole for bacon. The thin end is sometimes pickled in brine. The thick end makes prime bacon. On a porker the belly makes chops.

Spare ribs
The spare ribs can be roasting joints or cut into chops. The shoulder can make a joint, or it can be cured to make second-rate bacon.

Picnic
The picnic can be roasted, or cut up for sausage meat.

Jowl
The jowl is used for sausage meat.

Before you have hauled the pig up too high, cut all the way around the bung (the anus) to sever it from the pig, but do not pierce the rectum. Tie a string around it to prevent the excrement from coming out. Now, haul the pig up farther, to a convenient height, and score a tight cut right down from between the hams (haunches or hind legs) to the stick-cut in the throat. Don't cut through the abdominal wall! Cut right down it, keeping the guts back from the knife with your hand. You don't want to pierce the guts or stomach. Cut through the H-bone that joins the two hams, if necessary, with the saw, but don't cut the bladder. Then, gently haul out the rectum, the penis if it's male, the bladder, and all the guts, and flop the whole works out into a basin. The penis and rectum can be thrown away, or used for the dogs, but the rest is all edible or useful stuff.

Guts and brawn

Do not waste the guts. They need to be washed well, after which you should turn the intestines inside out. You can do this by inverting them on a smooth piece of bamboo or other wood. Then scrape their mucus lining off with the back of a knife against a board. Get them very clean and transparent. Lay them down in dry salt and they will come in handy, in due course, for sausage skins. The bladder can be filled through a funnel with melted lard, which will harden again and keep for months.

The stomach is edible, as are the intestines; together they are called "chitlings" or "chitterlings" and are quite good. Turn the stomach inside out, wash it, and put it down in dry salt until you want it. Now rescue the liver, which you can eat the same night, and peel out the gallbladder, which you can throw away. The heart should come away with the lights (lungs), and this is called the "pluck." Hang it on a hook. Carefully remove the caul—a beautiful filmy membrane that adheres to the stomach—and throw this over the pluck. The lungs are a treat for the dogs, while you can eat the heart. Throw several buckets of cold water inside and outside the carcass, prop the belly open with some sticks that are pointed at both ends, eat some fried liver, finish the home-brew, and go to bed.

In the morning the carcass should be "set" (stiff) if the weather is cold enough, and you can split it right down the backbone. A butcher does this with a cleaver; if you are a beginner, you may want to do it with a saw. Take each half off, lay it on the table, and cut it up, as shown opposite.

Don't waste the head or the feet, for they make excellent brawn, or pork-cheese. Put the bones, skin, and all into a pan (with the bits of skin in a muslin bag so you can draw them out after all the goodness has been extracted) and boil and boil. Let it cool, break it into small pieces, boil again and add salt, pepper, and as many spices (marjoram, coriander, allspice, cloves, caraway) as your taste buds can take. Boil it again, and pour into containers such as jello molds. The fat will rise to the top and form a protective covering, and the brawn will keep a long time. Eat sliced cold. To deep-freeze, pour straight into plastic bags.

JOINTING A PIG

This pig is a baconer, because it's too large for eating entirely as fresh pork. Therefore, most of it will be cured and preserved as bacon, ham, sausages, and so on. You will, of course, take a joint or two to eat as fresh pork, and if you have a chest freezer, this may be a larger proportion. Remember, a baconer is a fat animal, and his meat is not as suitable for eating fresh as that of a little porker.

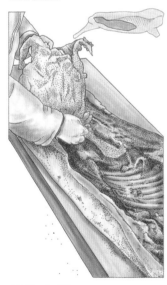

1 Split the carcass right down the backbone. A butcher might use a cleaver all the way, but amateurs will probably do better with a saw.

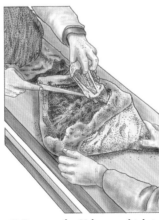

2 The leaf fat comes away very easily. It makes the best and purest lard. Next, take out the kidneys.

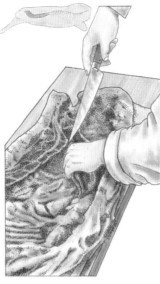

3 The tenderloin lies inside the backbone. It is delicious wrapped in the "caul," stuffed and roasted. The caul is a white, fatty membrane that supports the intestines.

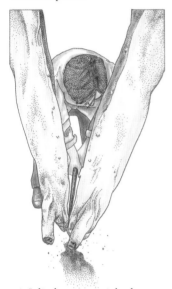

4 Cut the flesh of the ham using a saw.

5 Remove the H-bone, which is one half of a ball-and-socket joint, to leave a clean, uncut joint.

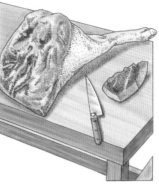

6 The ham must be trimmed so that a clean surface is left for the salt to penetrate. Work salt into every crevice.

7 This foot is being cut off at the hock joint. You can saw the shank off below this joint to leave a cleaner surface for salting.

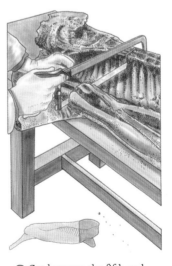

8 Cut between the fifth and sixth ribs to part the shoulder from the side, or flitch. The shoulders can be salted whole, or else boned and used for sausages.

9 Next saw off the chine, or backbone, and joint it.

10 Leave the ribs in the salted flitch. I like to cut them out later and use them for soup. The rest of the side is salted for bacon.

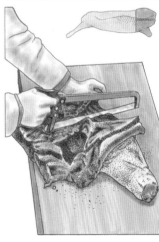

11 Salt the whole shoulder, or you can halve it, roasting the top and salting the bottom.

SALTING PIG MEAT

Most of a big pig should be turned into bacon and ham, for there is no better way of preserving large quantities of meat. The ham is the thick part of the pig's hind leg—the rump, in fact. Bacon is the side of the pig. The shoulder can be cured, too, or used for joints or sausage meat. But by far the most valuable parts of the pig are the two hams. There are two main methods of salting pig meat—dry curing and brine curing.

Dry curing

The first essential for dry curing to be effective is to guard against damage by blowflies. Even though your weather must already be cool, it is important to cover meat carefully with cloth or muslin. More important still, avoid loose pieces of meat, fat, or cavities that will provide perfect hiding places for maggots. Check all curing meat regularly. The easy way to make ham and bacon is by simply rubbing salt and sugar into the meat, then burying it in salt, then leaving bacon sides for two weeks in the salt, and hams for three. It is better to do it more scientifically, because you save salt and the meat is not so salty when you eat it. I get over the problem of excess salt by slicing my bacon first, then soaking the thin slices for ten minutes or so in warm water before frying them.

The proper way to do it, if you are going to be more scientific and efficient about it, is to use the following mixture for every 100 pounds (45 kg) of meat:

8 lb (3.6 kg) salt
2 lb (0.9 kg) sugar

Prepare this mixture with extreme care. Take half of it and put the rest aside. Use the half you have taken to rub the meat very thoroughly all over, rind-sides as well. Stuff salt hard into the holes where the bones come out in the hams and shoulders, and into any cavities. Success lies in getting salt into the meat quickly: it's a race between salt and bacteria. If the latter win, you may lose a lot of valuable meat. Unless the weather is too warm—36°F (2°C) is an ideal temperature, but don't let the meat freeze—if you follow these instructions the bacteria won't win.

Cover all surfaces with the salt and leave on a salting tray, or a shelf. If you use a box there must be holes in it to allow the "pickle"—juice drawn out of the meat by the salt—to drain away. Make sure all the joints are carefully packed on top of each other. Be careful when you do this first salting to put roughly the right amounts of salt on each piece: not too much on the thinner bacon sides but plenty on the thick hams.

After three days, give another good rubbing with half the remainder of the salt (a quarter of the whole). Put the pig meat back in a different order to ensure even distribution of the salt all around. After another week, haul out again and rub well with the last of the salt mixture. Put it back. Now leave it in the salt for two days per pound

for big joints such as hams and 1½ days per pound for small joints and bacon. If you say that roughly a big side of bacon should cure for two weeks and a large ham for three weeks, you won't be far wrong.

Take the joints out at the allotted time, scrub them lightly with warm water to get the loose salt off, string them, and hang them up for a week or two in a cool, dry place. Then either smoke them or don't smoke them, as the mood strikes you. Unsmoked or "green" ham and bacon taste very good, although personally I like them smoked. It's really all a matter of taste. (*See also recipes on p.315*)

Brine curing

For every 100 pounds (45.0 kg) meat you should mix:

8 lb (3.6 kg) salt
2 lb (0.9 kg) sugar
6 gal (22.7 l) boiled but cooled water

In theory, thicker joints, like hams, should have a stronger brine—the above mixture with 4½ gallons (20.4 liters) of water—and the thinner joints, like bacon and bath-chaps, which are the jowls of the pig, should have the mixture in 7 gallons (27.3 liters) of water. Put the meat in the brine, make sure there are no air pockets, put a scrubbed board on top and a big stone on top of this to keep the meat down (don't use an iron weight), and leave in the brine for four days per pound of each big joint. Thus you ought to weigh each joint before putting it in, and pull each one out at its appointed date. Bacon and small joints should only be left for two days per pound. After four or five days, turn the joints around in the brine, and again every so often. If, in hot weather, the brine becomes "ropy" (viscous when you drip it off your hand), haul the meat out, scrub it in clean water, and put into fresh brine.

When you have hauled the meat out of the brine, wash it in fresh water, hang it up for a week in a cool dry place to dry, then, if you want to, smoke it. You can eat it "green," i.e., not smoked at all. It should keep indefinitely, but use small joints and bacon sides before hams. Hams improve with maturing: I have kept them for two years and they have been delicious. Bacon is best eaten within a few months.

Cured hams and shoulders should be carefully wrapped in wax paper and then sewn up in muslin bags and hung in a fairly cool, dry place, preferably at a constant temperature. If you paint the outside of the muslin bags with a thick paste of lime and water, so much the better. Like this, they will keep for a year or two and improve all the time in flavor until they are delectable. Bacon can be hung up "naked" but should then be used within a few months. Light turns bacon rancid, so keep it in the dark. Keep flies and other creepies off all cured meat. Some country people wrap hams and bacon well, then bury them in bran, oats, or wood ashes, which are said to keep them moist and improve the flavor.

Sheep

Sheep have a great advantage for the lone self-supporter without a chest freezer. In the wintertime, a family can get through a fat lamb or a small sheep without it going bad. It is not that it keeps better than other meat, but just that the animal is smaller and you can eat it more quickly. However, I have kept mutton for a month, and in a climate where the day temperatures rose to over 100°F (39°C) in the shade. But the days were dry and the nights were cold. At night I hung mutton outside, in a tree—though out of reach of four legged prowlers—and then, very early in the morning, brought it in and wrapped it in several thicknesses of newspaper to keep out the heat. The mutton was perfectly edible. You could do this in any climate where the nights are cold enough and the days are not muggy; and you could do it with any meat.

Sheep have two other advantages: they provide wool, and in various parts of the world they provide milk, too. I have milked sheep, very often, and it's a very fiddly job. The milk tastes no better, and no worse, than cow's or goat's milk.

The chief disadvantage to keeping sheep on a very small scale is the problem of getting them tupped (mated). It doesn't pay to provide grazing for a ram if you have fewer than, say, half a dozen sheep. If you buy a ram to serve your sheep, you pay quite a high price for him, and when you sell him after he has served them, or next year, say, you only get "scrap price," i.e., very little. And if you eat him you will find him very tough. I have eaten a three-year-old ram, and I know. So tupping is a problem with very small flocks of sheep.

Broadly, there are two quite sensible things you can do. You can keep some pet ewes and take them to a kindly farmer's ram to get them tupped in the fall, or you might be able to borrow a ram. If you put a chest-pad on the ram with some marking fluid on it, or—in the old-fashioned way—rub some *reddle* (any colored earth or dry coloring matter) on the ram's chest, you can see when all your ewes are served and then return the ram. Homesteaders in hill-sheep countries, such as Great Britain, can buy "store" lambs. Most hill farmers cannot fatten their lambs off in their first summer sufficiently to get them ready to sell, and so they sell them as "stores." If you buy, say, 20 store lambs in the fall, and keep them either on good winter grass or on rape, turnips, or other winter fodder crops, maybe allowing five lambs to the acre, you will probably find that you not only get your sheep meat for nothing, but you also make a profit, too.

You can achieve this by killing one whenever you want some lamb to eat, and setting the fat lambs you haven't killed in the very early spring. If you also feed the store lambs a little concentrate (say, 1 pound or 0.5 kg a day of crushed barley and oats, or alternatively 2 pounds or 1 kg a day of corn and hay) they will fatten very readily.

Feeding

Sheep do well on pasture that has not had sheep on it for six months or so, because such pasture is free from sheep parasites. Five sheep will eat as much grass as a bullock, so an acre of good grass in the summer will easily support five sheep, but the stocking rate should be very considerably less in the winter, because the grass doesn't grow. Sheep are very good for grass in the wintertime—they "clean it up" after cows have been grazing on it all summer, because they graze much closer than cows. Sometimes you can fold sheep to great advantage on a catch crop of winter greens, turnip, rape, or hardy greens. This would be put in after a crop harvested fairly early in the summer. But you may decide you want this fodder for your cows.

During the winter the pregnant ewes need surprisingly little food, and if you have even a little grass they should make do on that. In very cold climates, of course, they need hay, and possibly grain, as well. People in very cold countries often winter ewes indoors and feed them entirely on hay, grain, and possibly roots.

DORSET HORN
A uniquely useful breed because it can lamb twice a year.

BORDER LEICESTER
A classic English sheep, a prolific breeder, and good for mutton and wool.

SOUTHDOWN
A very small sheep, and therefore useful for the small self-supporting family.

LAMBING

The shepherd should not have to interfere at all, but if there is too long a delay in a birth, the lamb or the ewe may die, so it may become necessary to lend a hand.

1 Lay the ewe on her back, and preferably prop her up with a large bale of straw.

2 Wash your hands and the ewe's hindquarters very well. Lubricate your hand and her vulva with mineral oil or obstetric lubricant.

3 If you see the forefeet, but the ewe cannot give birth after an hour, tie a soft cord around the feet and pull gently when she strains.

4 If you can't see anything, introduce the hand carefully while the ewe is not straining.

5 If the presentation is normal, grab the forelegs and pull the lamb out carefully.

6 Pull more and more strongly while the ewe is straining, but don't pull when she isn't.

7 As the lamb's body appears, support it with your free arm. When it is half out, twist slightly to relieve the pressure.

8 Make sure the new lamb's nostrils are free of mucus, and leave it for the mother to lick.

ABNORMAL PRESENTATIONS

There can be many abnormal presentations. The shepherd must feel with his hand to find which one he is dealing with. In the case of twins both trying to get out together, he must gently push one back. Sometimes with a single lamb he must push the lamb back and adjust the limbs or the head. The whole thing is a matter of common sense and sympathy for lamb and mother. The lamb or lambs must be positioned so the head is not backward and the limbs are not doubled up.

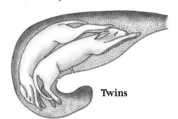

Twins

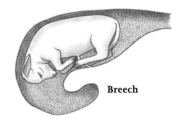

Breech

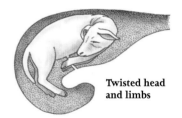

Twisted head and limbs

If you feed sheep, and they have no grass, a ewe will need about 4 pounds (2 kg) hay daily if there is nothing else, or, say, ½ pound to 1 pound (0.25–0.5 kg) a day, plus 15–20 pounds (6.8–9.0 kg) of roots. They will live on this without any corn or concentrates at all. They must not be too fat when they lamb, or else they will have lambing difficulties, but also they must not be half-starved.

In the spring, as soon as the ewes have lambed, put them on the best grass you have, and preferably on clean grass: that is, grass that has not had sheep on it for some time. The grass is very nourishing at this time of the year, and the lambs should thrive and grow quickly. Within four months, most of them will be fat enough either to eat or to sell to the butcher as "fat lamb."

Mating

In cold climates, sheep are generally mated in the fall. If you have a flock of ewes, it is best to cull them before mating: that is, pull any out that are so old that their teeth are gone. A full-mouth ewe, which has eight incisor teeth up, is four years old and should already have had three lambs. She may go for another year or two, or she may not, depending on the state of wear of her teeth.

Before putting the ram in with the ewes, you should flush the flock. This means keeping them on very poor pasture for a few weeks, then putting them on very good pasture. Then put the ram in. All the ewes will take the ram then in fairly quick succession, and you will not have a very drawn-out lambing season. A ram can serve up to 60 ewes in the tupping season. The gestation period is 147 days. Some people try to get ewes to lamb very early so as to catch the early lamb market, but unless you intend to lamb indoors, and with very high feeding, I would not recommend this. I like to see lambs coming in late February or March, and I find the later ones soon catch up with the poor little half-frozen winter lambs and pass them.

Lambing

Watch them carefully when they start to lamb. Leave them alone to get on with it: they generally can. But if a ewe is in labor for more than an hour and obviously cannot deliver her lamb, give her help. Get the ewe into a small pen where you can catch her. Lay her down (if she is not already down, *see opposite*). Wash your hands using mineral oil or obstetric lubricant. If the lamb's forefeet are just showing, work them gently out, only pulling when the ewe strains. The feet are very slippery, so put a soft cord around them—a scarf or a necktie will do—and haul gently when the ewe strains: haul slightly downward.

If you are not winning, insert your hand very gently into the vagina, feeling along the forelegs, and make sure that the head is not bent backward. If it is, push the lamb back gently and try to pull the head forward. The lamb should then come out.

You can get your hand right inside and feel around for abnormal presentations, but it is difficult because the uterus exerts great pressure on your hand. Still, if you only have a few ewes, and they are healthy, the chances are that you will have to do nothing with them at all.

Switching lambs

If a single lamb dies and you have another ewe with twins, it is a good thing to give one of the twins to the bereaved ewe. Put the bereaved ewe in a small pen, rub the twin lamb with the dead body of her lamb, and try to see if she will accept the new lamb. If she won't, skin the dead lamb, keeping the skin rather like a jersey, and pull the skin over the live lamb. Almost invariably the foster mother ewe will accept him. The advantage of this is that the mother of the twins feeds one lamb much better than she would do two, while the bereaved ewe does not get mastitis and have trouble drying up her milk. The mothers are happy, the twins are happy, and so are you.

Orphan lambs

Orphan lambs are one answer for the self-supporter. Farmers will often let you have orphans for nothing, or nearly nothing, and you can bring them up on the bottle, with a teat on it. You can give them warm cow's milk, diluted with water at first, later straight. Goat's milk is better than cow's milk, but don't let them suck the goat direct—milk her and feed from the bottle. Keep the lambs warm. They will grow up thinking they are humans.

Shearing

I start shearing at the beginning of July, but people farther south start earlier. So see what your neighbors do. Most people don't shear the new lambs, but only the ram, the ewes, and any wethers (castrated males) left over from the previous year.

If you shear by hand (*see also illustrations on p.216*) you will find it much easier to sit the sheep up on a bench or a large box. Hold her with her back toward you and practice holding her firmly with your knees, thus leaving your hands free. Clip the wool off her tummy. Then clip up the throat and take blow after blow (a blow is the shearer's term for one row of wool clipped) down the left side of the neck, shoulder, flank, and right down as far as you can get it, rolling the sheep around as you clip. When you can get no farther on that side, roll the sheep over and start down the right side, hoping to meet the shorn part from the other side as you roll the sheep that way. The last part involves laying the sheep down to clip the wool near the tail. The sheep should then leap away leaving her fleece in one entire blanket.

Lay the fleece, body-side down, on a clean sheet or floor and cut away any bits of dunged wool. Fold the edges over toward the middle, roll up from the head end, twist the tail end into a rope, and wrap around the tight bundle and tuck the rope under itself. If the wool is for sale, pack the fleeces tight into a big sack. Put the dunged bits in a separate sack and mark it "dag" (for preparation of wool for spinning *see p.368*).

Some hand shearing tips

If people tell you hand shearing is easy, you can tell them they lie. It is back-breaking, hand shears make your wrist ache, and it is extremely difficult. Keep your shears sharp and cut as close to the sheep as you can without nicking her. If you do nick her, dab some wound dressing on the cut. Beware of her teats. Of course mechanical clippers make the job much quicker, but it is still very hard work. But shearing is fun: if several of you are doing it, there is a great sense of camaraderie, and you have a sense of achievement when you get good at it. At first it seems impossibly difficult, but just persevere and don't give up. You'll win in the end.

Sheep disease

Except on mountains, sheep suffer from a bright green blowfly that "strikes" (lays eggs on) them, particularly on any dunged parts. It is good practice to cut this wool off them before shearing. This is called "clatting" or "dagging." But if about two weeks after shearing, you either spray or dip your sheep in some commercial sheep dip, you will protect them from fly strike for at least two or three months: in fact, probably until the cold weather comes and does away with the flies. If you don't protect them, they will get struck and the maggots will eat right into the sheep and eventually kill them in the most unpleasant manner possible.

In some parts of North America, liver fluke is a serious problem. Sheep that graze in wet places can pick up these worms from a certain minute freshwater snail. The worms live in the bile ducts of the sheep's liver. Draining land, and keeping sheep away from wet places, can help avoid the problem. If you see worms wriggling around in the liver of a sheep you kill, consult your veterinarian to discuss treatment options for your remaining animals.

SHEEP SHEARING

Sheep should be shorn in the summer when the weather is warm enough.

1 Grab the sheep by the wool on her flanks, not by the wool on her back. Pick her up and sit her down on her rump for ease of handling.

2 Clip all the wool of her stomach down as far as the udder. Take great care to avoid cutting the udder on a ewe, or the penis on a ram or wether.

3 Open the wool up her throat and start shearing around the left side of her neck and head.

4 Go down the left side of the shoulder and flank as far as you can reach in that position. If you can hold the sheep with your knees, your hands will be free. Hold her skin tight with your left hand. Shear as close to it as you can get with the other.

5 Roll the sheep over and clip down her right side. The fleece should come right off her body, except at the hindquarters.

6 Lay the sheep flat on the ground and put your left foot over her to hold her between your legs. Finish taking the fleece off the hindquarters.

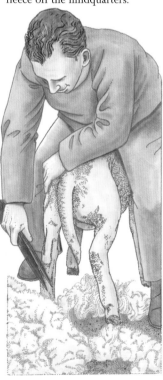

7 Trim her tail and hind legs separately for appearance. Keep the wool from these parts separate from the main fleece.

ROLLING A FLEECE

To roll the fleece, lay it body side down on a clean surface. Pick out any thorns, straw, etc. Turn the sides inward and begin to roll tightly from the neck end. Twist the neck end into a rope. Tie it around the fleece and tuck it under itself.

DIPPING SHEEP

About two weeks after shearing, the sheep should either be dipped or sprayed with a commercial mixture. Dipping is better because it really soaks in. This is for various purposes. In areas where scab is present it is often compulsory, but in most places it is necessary to guard against "strike" (see p.215) or blowfly maggot infestation. It also kills keds and other parasites.

Another disease to which sheep are especially prone is foot rot. It is a common problem where sheep graze in damp lowlands. To protect against foot rot, trim the feet occasionally (it's better to use sharp pincers than rely on a knife) to remove excess horn. But if your sheep have foot rot, the best cure of all is to walk them through a foot bath of a 10–20 percent solution of zinc sulfate.

To kill a sheep for mutton and lamb
You stick a sheep by shoving the knife into the side of the neck as close to the backbone and the head as you can get it. Keep the sharp edge away from the backbone and pull the knife out toward the throat. This cuts all the veins and arteries in the neck and the windpipe, too. But I would never, ever do this until I had stunned or killed the sheep with either a .22 bullet, a humane killer, or, in want of these, a blow on the head from the back of an ax.

Skinning
With the sheep on the ground or on a bench, slice a narrow strip of skin off the front of the forelegs and the back of the hind legs. Grasp the foreleg between your knees and raise this strip of skin off, right down into the brisket (chest). Keep the knife edge against the skin rather than the meat, so as not to cut the latter.

JOINTING A SHEEP
There are a vast number of ways of cutting up any carcass, but whichever way you follow, you still end up with meat. So it doesn't really matter much which way you do it, provided you do it neatly and cleanly.

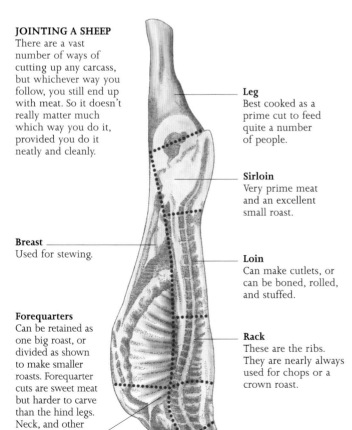

Leg
Best cooked as a prime cut to feed quite a number of people.

Sirloin
Very prime meat and an excellent small roast.

Breast
Used for stewing.

Loin
Can make cutlets, or can be boned, rolled, and stuffed.

Forequarters
Can be retained as one big roast, or divided as shown to make smaller roasts. Forequarter cuts are sweet meat but harder to carve than the hind legs. Neck, and other odd bits, go for stew or soup.

Rack
These are the ribs. They are nearly always used for chops or a crown roast.

Hold the strip of skin tight away from the leg with the left hand. Do the same with the hind legs (along the back of them) as far as the anus. Then skin out the legs, still holding each leg in turn between your knees. Don't tear or cut the meat. Cut the feet off at the lowest joint, and raise the tendons of the hind legs for sticking the hook through. Pull the flap of skin you have raised between the hind legs off the carcass as far as it will go.

Fisting
Now "fist" the skin away from the belly. (Fisting is the forcing of your fist in between skin and the carcass.) Use the knife as little as possible. Keep your hand washed when you fist, and don't soil the meat. Cleanliness is essential in all butchery operations. When you are fisting a sheep skin off, make sure that you leave the "fell," or thin, tough membrane, on the meat and don't take it off on the skin. On the skin it is a nuisance; on the meat it is a useful protection. Fist the skin off both the rear end and the brisket as far as you can. Then insert the hook and hoist the sheep up.

Slit the skin right down the belly, and then fist the skin off the sheep as high and low as you can. It will stick on the rump—fist here from below as well as above. Try to avoid using the knife as much as possible. If it's a nice fat lamb the skin will come off easily, but if it's a skinny old ewe, or a tough old ram, you've got problems. Free the skin with the knife from anus and tail. Then you can often pull the skin right off the sheep, down toward the shoulders, like taking a jersey off.

Finally, use the knife to take the skin off face and head. Then cut the head off at the atlas bone—this is right next to the skull.

Disemboweling
Cut around the anus. Pull several inches of the rectum out, tie a string around it, and drop it back. Now rip the belly right down as you would do with an ox or pig (see p.209). Protect the knifepoint with your finger to stop it from piercing the guts or paunch. Pull the rectum down with the rest of the guts. Take the bladder out without spilling its contents, and carefully hoist out the paunch and guts and other innards.

Carefully haul the liver free, and then haul the whole mass up and out of the sheep. You will have to cut the gullet to do this, and you should tie the gullet above the cut so the food doesn't drop out. Remove the liver carefully, and drop the guts into a big bowl. You can clean the guts and use all but the third stomach for tripe.

Cut down the breastbone. With a lamb, you can do this with a knife; with an older sheep, you may have to use a saw. Pull the pluck (heart and lungs) out and hang them up. Finally, wash the carcass down with cold water and go to bed.

The next morning, early, split the carcass and cut it up. You can use the small intestine for sausage casings.

Poultry

CHICKENS

All hens should be allowed access to the great outdoors, except in the winter in very cold climates. Not only is it inhumane to keep chickens indoors all the time, it leads to all the diseases that commercial flocks of poultry now suffer from. Some poultry-keepers go to such extremes of cruelty as keeping hens shut up in wire cages all their lives. Sunshine is the best source of vitamin D for poultry, as it is for us. Hens evolved to scratch the earth for their living, and to deny them the right to do this is cruel. They can get up to a quarter of their food and all their protein from freshly growing grass and derive great benefit from running in woods and wild places. They crave, and badly need, dust-baths to wallow in and fluff up their feathers to get rid of the mites. In well over 20 years of keeping hens running outdoors, I have yet to find what poultry disease is, with the exception of blackhead in turkeys. Our old hens go on laying year after year until I get fed up with seeing them, and put them in the pot.

Feeding

Hens running free outdoors on good grass will do very well in the summertime if you just throw them some grain. In the winter they will need a protein supplement. You can buy this from a feed store, or feed them fish meal, meat meal, soy meal, other bean meal, or fish offal. I would recommend soy meal most of all, because soy is the best-balanced of any vegetable protein.

CHICKEN BREEDS

Old-fashioned broody hens are hard to find because commercial breeders breed hybrids for egg production and nothing else. So you will have to search for those marvelous traditional breeds that can live outdoors, lay plenty of eggs, go broody and hatch their eggs, rear their chicks, and make good table birds as well. The Rhode Island Red is a good dual-purpose hen, meaning it is a good layer and a good table bird. The various Plymouth Rock and Wyandotte fowl are also popular and good for both eggs and meat. British homesteaders like the dual-purpose Light Sussex, an Old English breed, or the Cuckoo Maran, which is very hardy and lays large, deep-brown, very high quality eggs, though not in prolific quantities.

So if you live in a region where soybeans can be grown successfully, the problem of your protein supplement is easily solved. But soy must be cooked, because it contains a substance which, when raw, is slightly poisonous. Sunflowers are good, too, particularly if you can husk the seed and grind it, but they're quite good just fed as they are. You can also feed the hens lupin seed (either ground or whole), rapeseed (but not too much of it), linseed, peanuts or cottonseed (but this must be cooked first), crushed or ground peas or beans, alfalfa, or alfalfa meal. These all contain protein.

From 10 days old onward, all chickens should have access to fresh vegetables, and after all, this is one thing we can grow. So give them plenty of vegetables whether they run out on grass or not. My method of feeding hens is to let them run outdoors, give them a handful each of whatever high-protein meat or grain I have in the morning, and scatter a handful each of whole grain in the evening. Wheat is best, or kibbled corn. Barley is very good, but it should be knocked around until the awns (spikes) are broken off. An equally good method is to let the chickens eat both protein and grain from self-feed containers. These should be placed out of the reach of rats.

If you allow hens to run outdoors, or to have access to a good variety of foods, they will balance their own rations and not eat more than they need anyway. But if hens are confined indoors, you can balance their rations like this:

Laying mash

110 lb (50 kg) *wheat meat*
110 lb (50 kg) *corn meal (preferably yellow corn)*
110 lb (50 kg) *other gram meal (oats or barley or rye)*
110 lb (50 kg) *fish meal*
30 lb (13.5 kg) *dried milk*
20 lb (9.0 kg) *ground seashells*
5 lb (2.3 kg) *salt*
Give them free access to this, and a handful each of whole grains to scratch out of their straw or litter.

Cuckoo Maran   Rhode Island Red   Light Sussex   Barred Plymouth Rock   Columbian Wyandotte

COOPS

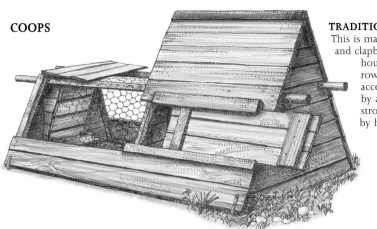

TRADITIONAL COOP

This is made of sawn timber and clapboard. It has a night-house with perches, a row of nesting boxes accessible from outside by a door, and a run. It is strong but easily movable by handles at each end.

BROODY COOP

Individual sitting hens need a broody coop. It must have a rat-proof floor and slats in front to confine the hen, if needed, but admit her chicks.

HOMEMADE COOP

The homesteader should try to make his coop for nothing, and used fertilizer bags are free. We made this ark for nearly nothing. Thatch would work as well, and would look better.

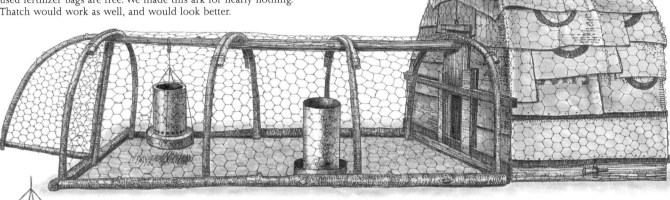

SELF-FEED HOPPER

You can buy galvanized hoppers, but you can make them yourself, for free, by hanging up an old oil drum, bashing holes around its base to let the hens peck food out, and hanging the cut-off base of a larger oil drum underneath to catch spilled food. Hang above rat-reach.

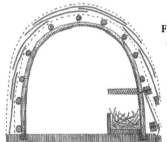

FERTILIZER-BAG COOP

A layer of chicken wire over the overlapping bags keeps them from flapping. The bags can be supported underneath by closely spaced horizontal rods of hazel, willow, etc. An inspection door for nesting boxes can be made by hanging up fertilizer bags weighted with a heavy batten across their bottoms.

Fattening mash for roosters or capons

Barley meal is the best fattener for any poultry, but can be replaced by boiled potatoes. Skim milk is also ideal. Feed the mash freely:

330 lb (150 kg) barley meal
110 lb (50 kg) wheat meat
55 lb (25kg) fish or meat meal
30 lb (13.5 kg) dried milk; plus some ground seashells and salt

Little chick mash

30 lb (13.5 kg) meal (preferably a mixture of wheat, corn, and oats)
12 lb (5 5 kg) fish meal or meat meal
12 lb (5.5 kg) alfalfa meal
2 lb (1 kg) ground seashells
1 lb (0.5 kg) cod-liver oil
1 lb (0.5 kg) salt; plus a "scratch" of finely cracked cereals

If you give them plenty of milk (skim is nearly as good) you can forget all but a little of the cod-liver oil, the alfalfa meal, and half, if not all, the fish meal or meat meal. If you have food that is free to you, or a by-product of something else, it is better to use that (even if the books say it is not perfect) than something you have to pay for. I am a great believer in making the best of what is available.

Free range

If hens run completely free range, it is often better to keep them in their houses until noon. They generally lay their eggs before that time, so you get the eggs before you let them out, instead of losing them in the bushes, where the rats get them. Hens will do a pasture good if they are not too concentrated on it, and if their houses or coops are moved from time to time over the pasture.

The chicken is a woodland bird, and hens always thrive in woodland (if foxes don't get them). They can also be run very advantageously on stubble (land from which cereals have just been harvested). Keep them out of the garden or you will rue the day.

Limited grass

If you have fresh grassland, it is a great advantage if you can divide it into two (a strip each side of a line of hen houses, for example), and let the hens run on each strip in turn. As soon as they have really eaten the grass down one strip, let them run on the other. In the summer, when the grass grows so quickly they can't cope with it, let them run on one strip long enough to let you cut the other strip for hay. Or alternate hens with sheep, goats, cows, or geese. Poultry will eat any grass provided it is kept short, but ideally it should be of the tender varieties, like timothy or the meadow grasses. There can be clover with it, although the hens will provide enough nitrogen in their droppings.

The Balfour method

This is suitable for the backyard poultry-keeper or the person who only has a small or limited yard. You have a pen around your henhouse in which you dump plenty of straw, bracken, or whatever vegetation you can get. In addition, you have two (or three if you have the space) pens that are grassed down, and that can be approached by the hens from the straw yard. The hens will scratch in the straw yard and so satisfy their scratching instincts and spare the grass. Now let the hens run into one of the grass pens. Change them into another pen after, say, two or three weeks. They will get a bite of grass from this, and the grass in the first pen will be rested and have a chance to grow. The straw yard will provide half a ton of good manure a year from each hen. The old backyard poultry yard, which is a wilderness of scratched bare earth, coarse clumps of nettles, rat holes, and old tin cans, is not a good place to keep hens or anything else.

Housing

The ordinary commercially produced hen house, provided it is mobile, works perfectly well. If used in the Balfour or limited grassland methods described above, it doesn't even have to be mobile, unless you intend to move it from time to time into another field. Utter simplicity is fine for a henhouse. Hens need shelter from rain and wind, some insulation in very cold climates, and perches to sit on. Make sure the perches are not right up against the roof, and are placed so their droppings have a clear fall to the floor. The nesting boxes should be dark, designed to discourage hens from roosting in them, and roofed so hens don't leave droppings in them. You should be able to reach in and get the eggs easily.

There are patented nesting boxes that allow the eggs to fall down to another compartment. I think these are a very good idea; they prevent the eggs from getting dirty.

We have movable hen coops (*as illustrated*), with an enclosed sleeping area and a chicken wire open run. They hold 25 hens each and cost nothing but a handful of nails, some old wire netting, and some free plastic fertilizer bags.

In countries that have heavy snow in the winter, the birds will have to be kept in during the snow period. It is not a bad idea to confine some birds in a house in which there is electric light if you want eggs in the depth of winter. Give the birds, say, 12 hours of light and they will think it is summertime and lay a lot of eggs; otherwise they will stop laying as soon as the days get really short.

Rearing chickens

It is always a good idea to keep a rooster among your hens, and not just to wake you up in the morning. The hens will lay just as many eggs without a rooster but the eggs won't be fertile. Also, if each batch of hens has a cockerel to marshal them and keep them together outdoors, they fare better and are less likely to come to harm.

If you leave a hen alone, and she isn't caught by a fox, coyote, owl, or other predator, she will wander off into the bushes and wander back again in a few weeks with a dozen little chicks clucking at her heels. These chicks, being utterly naturally reared, will be the healthiest little chicks you will ever see. Alternatively, you can watch your hens for broodiness. You can tell when a hen is broody by the way she squats tight on her eggs and makes a broody clucking noise when you try to lift her off. Help her by enclosing her in a broody coop (a little house with slats in front of it that baby chicks can get through and the mother can't). Give her nice soft hay or something as a nest, and put a dozen fertile eggs under her. (They can be any kind of poultry egg you like). See that she always has water and food: she will eat very little. Let her out once a day for a short walk, but get her in within half an hour or the eggs will get cold. Eggs should hatch out in 21 days from the start of brooding. As soon as the chicks are a few days old, you can let the hen out, and she will lead them around and teach them how to look for food. This is by far the best way to raise poultry, and beats any incubator.

If you are just starting with hens, you can either order "day-old chicks" or "point-of-lay pullets," which are young females just about to lay. When chickens are only a day old, they don't need to eat and can be packed into cartons and sent around the country with impunity. A day or two older and they would die.

Keep such pullets as you need for your dock replacements and fatten the cocks for the table. Feed all little chicks on a fairly rich diet of high protein and finely ground meal. For the first few days, add minced hard-boiled eggs and milk by-products to their ration. Wheat meat mixed with milk is also a perfect food.

Always make sure that chickens have access to enough lime, in the form perhaps of ground seashells, and to insoluble grit like crushed flint. Hens running outdoors are not so dependent on artificial supplies.

KILLING AND PREPARING A CHICKEN

Grab the legs with your left hand, and the neck with your right hand so that it protrudes through the two middle fingers and the head is cupped in the palm. Push your right hand downward and turn it so the chicken's head bends backward. Stop as soon as you feel the backbone break, or you will pull the head off.

PLUCKING

Start plucking the chicken as soon as it is dead, while it is still warm; once it gets cold, the feathers are much harder to get out. Be very careful not to tear the skin.

DRAWING

1 Slip the knife under the skin at the bottom of the neck and cut up to the head.

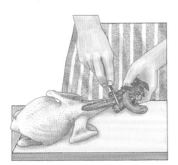

2 Sever the neckbone at the bottom end with pruning shears or a sharp knife.

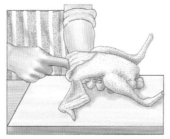

3 Remove the neckbone. Insert the index finger of your right hand, move it around inside, and sever all the innards.

4 Cut between the vent and the tail, being careful not to sever the rectum.

5 Cut all the way around the vent so that you can separate it from the body.

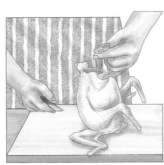

6 Carefully draw the vent, with the guts still attached, out from the tail end.

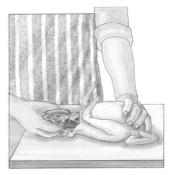

7 The gizzard, lungs, and heart will follow the guts.

8 Remove the crop from the neck end of the bird.

TRUSSING

If you put the bird in the oven and cooked it, it would taste just the same as if you trussed it. But do a neat and professional job— it is worth trussing properly.

1 Thread a large darning needle, force the chicken's legs forward, and shove the needle and thread through the body, low down.

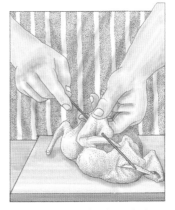

2 Push the needle through the wing and bring it across the skin at the neck.

3 Push through the other wing and tie the ends of the thread together.

4 Rethread the needle and pass over the leg, below the end of the breastbone, and around the other leg.

5 Cross the thread behind the hocks and tie around the rump.

Cockerels should weigh 2–3 pounds (1–1.5 kg) at eight to 12 weeks, and are called "broilers." Birds or table breeds should, at 12 or 14 weeks, weigh more—3–4 pounds (1.5–1.8 kg)—and are called "fryers." After this you may call them "roasters." At six or nine months old they are called "stewing fowl"; so are old hens culled from your laying flock. An old hen can make good eating.

Good laying hens should have bright eyes, large, red, healthy-looking combs and wattles, wide-apart pelvic bones (fairly loose so eggs can get out) and a white, large, moist vent. If they have the opposite, wring their necks. They won't lay you many eggs and you should certainty not breed from them. Don't stop hens from going broody. Finally, it goes without saying that eggs are much better eaten fresh, and it is quite possible to have new-laid eggs throughout the year. If you want to store eggs, clean them first and drop them into water-glass (sodium silicate solution).

GEESE

These are most excellent birds for the self-supporter. They are hardy, tough, self-reliant grazers and they make good mothers. The best way to start breeding geese is to buy eggs from somebody and put them under a broody hen. A hen will sit on five or six goose eggs and hatch them, but you want to make sure that she hasn't been sitting too long when you put the goose eggs under her, for goose eggs take longer to hatch than hens' eggs do (up to 30 days or even more).

During the last week of the sitting, take the eggs out from under the hen every day and wet them with lukewarm water (goose mothers get wet but hen foster mothers don't). On the day when the eggs start to pip, wet them well. Some people remove the first goslings that hatch so that the foster mother doesn't think she's done her job, and then they replace them when the last egg has hatched. I've never bothered and always had good results.

Feed the goslings well for the first two or three weeks on bread soaked in whole milk (or skim milk). If they are fairly safe where they are, let the hen run around with them. If you fear they will get lost, confine the hen in a broody coop. I prefer the hen to run loose. When the young birds no longer need the foster mother, she will leave them and start laying again.

If you start reducing the goslings' food after three weeks, they will live on grass. As adults, they don't need any food except grass, but it is a good idea to chuck them some corn in January and February when you want to feed the goose up a bit to get her to lay well. Three weeks before you intend to kill them (generally around Christmas), you should confine them, and feed them liberally with barley meal, corn meal, and milk if you have it to spare. They will fatten on this, and one of them will provide the best Christmas dinner in the world.

Geese pair for life, so I prefer to keep one goose and one gander together as a breeding pair, though many people keep a gander to two or three geese. They lay early: in February or March. If you leave them alone they will sit on a dozen or more of their own eggs and hatch them with no trouble at all, but if you are greedy you can keep stealing their eggs and putting them under broody hens. But hens aren't always broody as early in the year as that.

Geese are fierce and strong birds. They make good "watchdogs" to alert you to unexpected visitors, human or otherwise, and they can even help protect smaller poultry from predators. But they are still vulnerable to enemies. Two of these are rats and foxes. Rats will pull goose eggs out from under a sitting hen or goose, and they will kill baby geese whenever they get a chance. Foxes will snatch a sitting goose off her eggs whenever they can. If there are foxes in the area you must confine sitting geese in a fox-proof place. For advice on dealing with rats, foxes, and other poultry predators, ask your state department of natural resources or your local extension.

When the time comes to kill a goose (or turkey, for that matter), grab the bird by its legs with both hands. Keep the back of the bird away from you. Lower the head to the floor, and get someone else to lay a broomstick across the neck just behind the head. Stand on both ends of the broomstick, and pull the legs upward until you feel the neck break. If you hold the tips of the wings as well as the two legs, the bird will not flap after it is dead. Then treat as with a chicken (*see* p.221).

DUCKS

To say that ducks don't need water is nonsense. Ducks do need water and cannot possibly be happy without it. It is inhumane to keep animals in conditions grossly different from the ones their species has evolved to live in. So give them access to water, but keep your ducklings away from it for their first week or two, until they have the natural protection of oil on their feathers. You must give them drinking water, however.

Swimming water for ducks is better if it is flowing, and renews itself. A stagnant pond is less healthy. Many eggs get laid in the water, or on the edge, and if the water is dirty, the eggs, which have porous shells, can absorb pathogens and be dangerous to eat. So don't eat eggs that have been lying in filthy water, no matter how much you superficially clean them. If there is no natural water on your farm, my advice is not to keep ducks. You can, of course, create an artificial pond, either out of concrete, puddled clay, or plastic sheeting buried in the ground, but if you do, make sure the water is renewable and does not become stale and stagnant.

One drake will look after half a dozen ducks and enjoy it, but ducks make rotten mothers. If you let them hatch their own eggs, you must confine them in a broody coop, or they will kill the little ducklings by dragging them all over the place. Hens are much better duck-mothers than ducks are. Duck eggs hatch in 28 days and the baby ducks need careful feeding. Up to 10 weeks, feed them as much barley or other meal as they will eat.

Add milk if you have it. Feed ducks about the same as you would hens when you are not fattening them. The duck is not a grazing bird to the extent that the goose is, but ducks will get quite a lot of food if they have access to water, or mud, or are allowed to roam around. They are partly carnivorous, and eat slugs, snails, frogs, worms, and insects. Don't let breeding ducks get too fat, or they will produce infertile eggs. They like a mash in the morning of such things as boiled vegetables, flaked corn, pea or bean meal, wheat meat, and a little barley meat. Give them about half a handful each for breakfast, and half a handful of grain in the evening. If you find they get fat, give them less. If you find they get thin, give them more.

There are ducks (such as the Indian Runner) with very little meat on them that lay plenty of eggs, and table ducks (such as the Aylesbury) with plenty of meat but not many eggs. Then there's the Muscovy, a heavy, hardy, and far too intelligent bird that's good to eat but has dark flesh.

Kill your young ducks at exactly 10 weeks. They are full of bristles before and after that time. They won't put on weight afterward anyway. At 10 weeks they are easy to pluck and are at their prime. You can, of course, eat old ducks if you want to, but they are tougher and much fattier.

Housing for ducks can be extremely simple, but this does not mean that it should be tumbledown. Ducks like a dry, but well-ventilated house. If it's mobile, so much the better, because otherwise the immediate surroundings get messy. Make it fox- and rat-proof.

TURKEYS

Compared to other poultry, these are very delicate birds. If they associate in any way with chickens, they get a fatal disease called blackhead, unless you medicate their water or food. If you want to have them without medicating them, you must keep them well away from all chickens.

You must even be careful about walking from the hen run to the turkey run without changing your boots and disinfecting yourself. It's hardly worth it. Turkeys do not seem to me to be a very suitable bird for the self-supporter, unless he wants to trade them. In this case he can rear them intensively in incubators and brooders, or buy them reared from another breeder.

PIGEONS

Squabs are a delicious dish. They are young pigeons killed at about four and a half weeks. The parent birds are sometimes reared intensively, in a special house with a wire run or "fly" for the birds to flap around in. Kept like this, the birds should be fed on grain, with some peas included, since they must have some protein. A pair of pigeons might eat a hundred pounds (45 kg) of grain a year and raise up to 14 squabs a year, so if you had a dozen pairs, you would be eating squabs until you were sick of them. If they are confined in this manner, you must give them grit, as well as water for drinking and bathing in, and you must attend to hygiene by having some sort of litter on the floor that you can change.

Personally, I would object strongly to keeping pigeons like that and would always let them fly free. Have a pigeon loft, get a few pairs of adult pigeons (already mated) from somebody else, and before letting them loose, keep them for three weeks in some sort of cage in the loft, where they can see out (this is important). Then let them out, toss them a little grain every day, and let them get on with it. Kept like this, they are no work and little expense, and in fact do very little damage to crops, although you hope they eat your neighbor's and not yours. If he shoots a few, well, that won't break you. Harvest the squabs when the underside of the wing is fully feathered. Kill, pluck, draw, and truss, as if they were chickens (see p.221).

AYLESBURY DRAKE
The best British table breed. It is large, heavy, and very hardy, and its ducklings grow exceptionally fast.

EMBDEN GANDER
The Embden is a good table breed. Its feathers and down are pure white and ideal for stuffing pillows and eiderdowns.

WHITE TURKEY
These can grow up to 38 pounds (17 kg). There is a small, quick-maturing form of this breed called the Beltsville White.

Rabbits

Rabbits are a very good stock for the self-supporting family to keep. They can be fed largely on weeds that would otherwise be wasted, and they make excellent meals. New Zealand Whites are a good breed to have because they are good meat and their skins are very beautiful when cured. Californians are also excellent. Such medium breeds tend to be more economical than very large rabbits (like Flemish Giants), which eat an awful lot and don't produce much more meat. If you get two does and a buck, these should provide you with up to 200 pounds (90 kg) of meat a year.

Shelter

In the summer, rabbits will feed themselves perfectly well on grass alone, if you either move them around on grassland in small portable shelters, or else let them run loose in adequate fenced paddocks. The wire netting of the paddocks should be dug 6 inches (15 cm) into the ground to prevent them from burrowing; if you have foxes, you have problems. You can keep rabbits in hutches year-round. They can stand cold but not wet, and they don't like too much heat but need a cozy nest box.

Breeding

You can leave young rabbits on the mother for eight weeks, at which age they are ready to be killed. If you do this, you should remove the mother six weeks after she has given birth and put her to the buck. After she has been served, return her to her young. Remove the young when they are eight weeks old and the doe will give birth again 17 days after the litter has been removed, gestation being about 30 days. If you keep some young for breeding replacements, you must separate does and bucks at three months.

Sexing rabbits is easy enough. Lay the rabbit on its back, head toward you: press your fingers gently on each side of where its equipment seems to be, and this will force out and expose the relevant part. It will appear as an orifice in the female and a slight rounded protrusion in the male. When a rabbit the size of a New Zealand White is ready for mating, she weighs 8 lb (3.5 kg): don't keep her until she gets much heavier or she will fail to conceive. Always take the doe to the buck, never the buck to the doe, or there will be fighting, and always put a doe by herself when she is going to kindle. A doe should rear from seven to nine rabbits a litter, so if the litters are over 12, it is best to remove and kill a few, or else foster them on another doe that has just kindled with a smaller litter. If you do this, rub the young with the new doe's dung and urine before you give them to her, to confuse her sense of smell.

Feeding

Rabbits will eat any greens or edible roots. They like a supplement of meal: any kind of ground grain will do, but a pregnant doe should not have more than 4 ounces (115 g) of meal a day or she will get fat. Assuming that rabbits are not on grass and that you are not giving them a great quantity of greenstuff, feeding should then be on the order of 3 ounces (85 g) of concentrates a day for rabbits over eight weeks old, plus as much hay as they want. Then, 18 days after mating, the doe should be given no more hay but fed on concentrates. She should have these until her eight-week-old litter is removed from her, and at this time will eat up to 8 ounces (225 g) a day. Young rabbits can have meal when they are two weeks old.

Killing

To kill a rabbit, hold it by its hind legs, in your left hand; grab its head in your right hand and twist it backward. At the same time, force your hand downward to stretch its neck. The neck breaks and death is instantaneous. Before the carcass has cooled, nick the hind legs just above the foot joint and hang up on two hooks. Make a light cut just above the hock joint on the inside of each rear leg and cut up to the vent (anus). Peel the skin off the rear legs and rip it off the body. Gut by cutting down the belly and removing everything except the liver and kidneys (this is called hulking). Remove the gallbladder from the liver.

FLEMISH GIANT
These are rather too large and unwieldy for meat production, but they are useful for crossbreeding.

CALIFORNIAN
A good meat rabbit weighing up to 10 pounds (4.5 kg). It is healthy and easy to rear.

NEW ZEALAND WHITE
Another good meat rabbit, and popular with breeders for its fur, which dyes well.

Bees & Honey

Bees will provide you with all the sugar you need, and as a self-supporter you shouldn't need much. A little sugar (or, preferably, honey) improves beer, and sugar is necessary if you want to make "country wines" (which I discuss on pp.326–329), but otherwise the part that sugar plays in the diet is wholly deleterious. It is such an accessible source of energy that we satisfy our energy requirements too easily, and are not induced to turn to coarser foods, whose valuable constituents are less concentrated and less refined. The ideal quantity of refined sugar in the diet is: none.

Honey will do anything that sugar can do and do it much better (but you should never give honey to a child under the age of 12 months because of the danger of infant botulism, a very serious form of food poisoning). Not only is honey a healthier food, for beekeepers it is also free. It is sweeter than sugar, so if you use it for cooking or wine-making purposes, use about two-thirds as much as you would sugar. The flavor of honey depends upon the flower visited and nectar gathered by the bee. If you live in a citrus area, you may have the delicate taste of orange blossom. In grassland, clover honey may be produced. In some areas farmers with apple orchards or citrus groves will pay you to bring your hives to them at pollination time. The rent-a-hive business means you are being paid twice: once for your bees as pollinators, and again for their honey. Beekeeping is really a way of getting something for nothing. It is a way of farming with no land, or at least with other people's land. You can keep bees in the suburbs of the city, or even in the center of the city, and they will make plenty of excellent honey.

The medieval skep

The medieval method of keeping bees was in the straw skep. You braided straw or other fibers into ropes and twisted the ropes into a spiral, lashing each turn to the next, until you formed a conical skep. You placed this in a cavity left in a wall, to protect it from being blown over or soaked by rain. In the fall, if you wanted the honey, you either destroyed the bees you had in the skep by burning a piece of sulfur under them, or you could save the bees by turning their skep upside down and standing another empty skep on top of it. The bees in the inverted skep could crawl up into the upper skep.

More sensibly, you could stand an empty skep on top of a full one, with a hole connecting them, and the bees would climb up. When they had done so, you removed the old skep, which was full of honey and comb. If you dug this comb out, you could wring the honey out of it by putting it in some sort of strainer (muslin would do), squeezing it, and letting it drip.

If you can get the skep-inversion method to work without killing the bees, it is a good way of keeping them. You need no equipment except some straw, a bee veil, gloves, and a smoker. You get nothing like so much honey as you do out of a modern hive, but then you could keep a dozen skeps with practically no expenditure, whereas a modern hive, even at its most basic, is a fairly costly item. When hundreds of people kept bees in skeps, and probably every farm had half a dozen or more, there were a great many more bees in the countryside, and swarms were much more common than they are now in a new millennium. It was easy to find them and not so necessary to conserve the bees you had.

Langstroth's method

In 1851, a Philadelphian named Langstroth discovered the key secret about bees, which was what he called the "bee space." This is the exact distance between two vertical planes on which bees build their honeycomb without filling the space in between, leaving themselves enough room to creep through. This discovery made possible an entirely different method of keeping bees, and turned beekeeping from a hunting activity into a farming one.

The method Langstroth developed was to hang vertical sheets of wax the correct distance apart. Instead of building their comb in a random fashion, the bees would build it on these sheets of wax. Then, with the invention of the queen excluder, which is a metal sheet with holes just big enough for the workers but not the queen to get through, the queen was kept down below in a special chamber (the brood chamber) so that she could not lay eggs in the cells above, which as a result were full of clean honey with no grubs in them. You could then remove the frames, as the vertical sheets of wax were called, with their honey, extract the honey without killing any of the bees or bee larvae, and replace the emptied frames for the bees to build up and fill once more.

The modern hive

Langstroth's discovery has affected the construction of the modern hive. This has a base to raise it, and an alighting board, with a narrow slit for the bees to enter. On top of the base is the brood chamber, with its vertically slung "deep" or "brood" frames. These wooden frames have foundation inside them, like canvas inside a picture frame. The foundation is sheets of wax that have been embossed by a machine with exactly the pattern made by comb-making bees. Above the brood chamber is a super, which is shallower. The queen excluder divides the two chambers. You may have two or three supers, all complete with frames fitted with foundation one on top of the other. On the very top is a roof.

The roof has a bee-escape in it, through which bees can get out but not in. There should also be a clearer-board, a board with a bee-valve to let bees through one way but not the other. Then you should have a bee veil, gloves, a smoker, and an extractor, which you may be able to borrow. The extractor is a centrifuge. You put your sections full of honey into it and spin them around at high speed, which flings the honey out of the comb onto the sides of the extractor. It then dribbles down and can be drawn off.

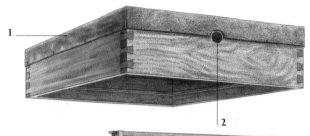

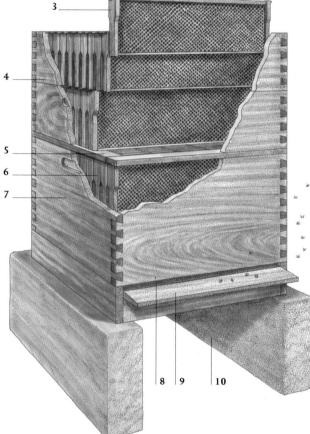

THE HIVE

1 Waterproof roof
2 Ventilator and bee-escape
3 Shallow honey frame
4 Super
5 Queen excluder

6 Deep brood frame
7 Brood chamber
8 Entrance
9 Alighting board
10 Base blocks

THE SKEP

The original beehive, or skep, is made of twisted straw or rope sewn together into a conical shape with straw. If you use a skep your honey will be full of brood, or immature bees, because the queen can lay eggs in every cell. There is no queen excluder as there is in a modern hive. You can strain the brood out, but you kill a lot of bees. It is also impossible for the bee inspector to check a skep to see whether your bees have any diseases.

COLLECTING HONEY

Take the honey-loaded super out and bang, shake, and brush the bees out of it. Or else insert a clearing board the day before under the super, or supers, from which you wish to extract honey. The supers will then be free of bees when you want to take them out.

FEEDING

If you take all the honey from a beehive in the late fall, you will have to feed the bees sugar or syrup. The feeder allows the bees to lick the syrup without drowning.

ROBBING

Smoke, which is best applied with a special "smoker," calms bees and makes them fill with honey and sting less readily. Use a screwdriver to break the top super off.

DECAPPING

To remove the honey, cut the wax capping from the comb with a hot knife. Use two knives—heat one while you use the other.

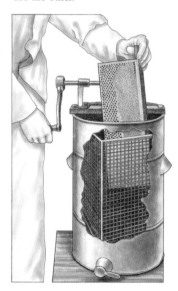

EXTRACTING

Put the decapped frames in the extractor. Spin fast until the honey is all out of one side, turn the frames around, and spin again.

THE HONEY TANK

This is useful if you have a large number of bees. Pour the extracted honey carefully through the strainer and let it settle before drawing it off into jars or containers.

Capturing a swarm

If you are lucky enough to come across a swarm, what you will find will be a cluster of bees about the size of a football hanging onto a tree, or something similar. If it is a tree, you just hold a big, empty cardboard box under the swarm, give the branch a sharp jerk, and the swarm will fall *kerplomp* into the box. When this happens, turn the box upside down, put a stick under one side to keep it just off the ground, and leave it until evening. This is to let the scouts, out searching for a new home, come back to the swarm. Some ruthless people simply take the swarm away immediately. Swarming bees are unlikely to sting you, since they are loaded with honey and don't like stinging in this condition, but I'm not going to say they will never sting you.

To get a swarm into your hive, lay a white sheet in front of the hive, sloping up to the entrance, and dump the swarm out onto the sheet. They should all crawl up into the hive. Make sure the queen, who is bigger and longer than the others, crawls into the hive, too: without her you won't have any bees.

Bees in a colony

The fine South African scientist Marais proved conclusively that a colony of bees, for all practical purposes, is one individual. Apart from the queen, the separate bees are more like cells of an organism than like individuals. One colony mates with another and produces a swarm, the bee equivalent of a child. The queen lays the eggs, and exerts a strong hold over the rest of the colony; kill her and if the workers can't rear another queen quickly enough from an existing grub, the colony will just die. The drones are as expendable as spermatozoa. Each one tries to mate with a young queen of another colony; whether mating is successful or not, the drone is killed by the workers, because he is of no further use. There are about 20,000 workers in a mature colony, and they spend their lives working: gathering nectar, building cells for storing the honey, feeding the queen, nursing the young bees, ventilating and cleaning the nest, guarding it, and generally doing everything that needs to be done. If a worker stings you, she dies. Her death is unimportant, for she is not an individual, but merely a cell. Her sacrifice means nothing.

The organism survives at the expense of the individual, so if you capture a swarm, you can just leave the bees to get on with it, and they will establish themselves. Remember also the adage:

A swarm of bees in May is worth a load of hay,
A swarm of bees in June is worth a silver spoon,
A swarm of bees in July is not worth a fly.

This means that you won't reap much honey from a swarm of bees in July. But all the same, don't turn your nose up at it: hive it, and it will establish itself and give you honey the following year.

Buying and feeding a nucleus

If you can't find swarms, you can buy nuclei of bees from other beekeepers or dealers, who are fairly common in most parts of the United States; then just follow the instructions on the box. If you do this, you should feed the nucleus for a while. You can do this by giving them two parts sugar to one part water in a feeder, which you can buy and put in your hive on top of the brood chamber. In the case of a nucleus, don't use a super: confine them in one brood chamber until that is full of honey and grubs before adding any supers on top.

Registration and inspection

However you acquire your bees, keep in mind that some states require you to register your hives and have them inspected yearly. Check with your state's department of agriculture for more information.

Gathering the honey

As the frames get built up and filled with honey, and the brood chambers below with bee grubs, you may add a super, then a second super, and you may decide to take some honey. To do this, take out one super, insert the clearer-board under it, and replace it. The next day, go and remove the super, which should be full of honey but empty of bees. Put the frames in the extractor and spin the honey out of them. You must first cut the capping off the combs with a hot knife. Each frame should be turned once to extract both sides. Then put the empty frames back in the super and return it to the bees so that they can start building on it again. Always work quietly and calmly when you work with bees. There is no substitute for joining a local beekeepers' group, or for making friends with a knowledgeable beekeeper and learning from him or her.

You should leave at least 35 pounds (16 kg) of honey in the hive for the winter. I rob my bees only once, in early August. After that I leave them alone, with one empty super, and they make enough honey to last through the winter. My one hive gives me 20–40 pounds (9–18 kg). The later honey in our case is heather honey, which I could not extract anyway, because it will not come out in the extractor: it has to be pressed out. People who take all the honey from their bees have to feed them heavily all winter on syrup or candy. In fact, some commercial honey is little more than sugar turned into honey by the bees. The honey you buy from small beekeepers, on the other hand, is generally flower honey and is much better as a result.

Wax

The cappings you cut off the combs are beeswax, which is a very valuable substance: it makes polish and candles (the best in the world), and is good for waxing leatherwork and other purposes. Gentle heat melts the wax, and it will run down a slope for you to collect, minus most of its impurities, in a container. The heat can be supplied by the sun, shining through a glass pane into an inclined box.

"French peasants do not 'garden,' although they eat the best and most varied vegetables in the world. They grow their own vegetables on a field scale—a row of this down the field and half a row of that. And why not? A quarter of the labor. Up to now we have had a lot of pioneering work to do… but when only the routine, recurring work of stockmanship, cultivating, harvesting and that is left to do, I believe that we could manage our little holding on somewhat the above lines with not very many hours of work a week. And, after all, if a family can grow all its food 'for free' off a piece of land that is no more than that family's fair share of the land surface of its country, and have some produce left over for other people, and still have time to do other work, it is in a very sound position and nobody can say that it is not pulling its weight."

JOHN SEYMOUR FAT OF THE LAND 1976

CHAPTER FOUR

FOOD
FROM THE
FIELDS

Clearing Land

Unless your farm is big and you plan to run a proportion of it on the "dog and walking stick" principle, one of your first priorities will be to see if you can gain any extra usable land by clearing overgrown wood and bush land. Such land is worth clearing as long as it is not on a ridiculously steep slope, or irretrievably boggy, or covered in boulders. Clearing land is hard but rewarding work, although it can be extremely expensive and time-consuming.

Send in the pigs and goats

Your pig is your best pioneer. If you concentrate pigs in bush land, they will clear it for you with no effort on your part at all. They won't, of course, remove trees, but all brambles, gorse, and undergrowth generally will yield to their snouts and they will manure the land at the same time. If there are any stubborn areas of thicket, try throwing some grain into them and the pigs will soon root them out.

Goats will kill small trees, and big ones, too, if they are concentrated, by barking them, and they will prevent trees from coming back. They will not, of course, get the trees out, any more than pigs will. You will have to do that.

Clearing woodland

It is essential to have a gasoline-powered chainsaw for this work (of course you could rent a mechanical excavator, which is another consideration of cost against time, plus the backbreaking "slashing" of usable timber when the wood is green). A chainsaw is a lethal, noisy monster and you'll have to learn to use this with great care. (Courses in chainsaw safety are available, and you should ask your supplier about this.) First cut off all light branches that are no good for firewood, then cut logs from timber that might serve as good firewood (this includes sections of large roots when the stumps are pulled out). Take all this away to your woodshed for cutting up and splitting later. You can then get a few helpers—kids often love this job—to take all the brashings (small branches) to make a bonfire (if local regulations allow burning). Build the bonfire in a corner somewhere where the flames will do no harm and you can then leave it for a couple of months until a cold, dry winter day makes a good bonfire party.

If you leave the tree stumps reasonably high, say at about 2 or 3 feet (50 cm–1 m), this will make it much easier to lever them out. A good digger driver can clear a big area in a day at a reasonable cost. Have the stumps piled up in a corner for burning a few months later when they have dried out.

It is cheaper to haul stumps out with a tree-jack or monkey-winch. You might rent or borrow one of these, or buy one if you had a lot of land to clear, but they are expensive. There are many varieties of them. Alternatively, you can dig stumps out with spade and mattock, but this is very laborious.

HAND TOOLS
If you don't have pigs or machines to clear your land, you can do it by hand, but you need the right tools, especially a chainsaw (*opposite page*).

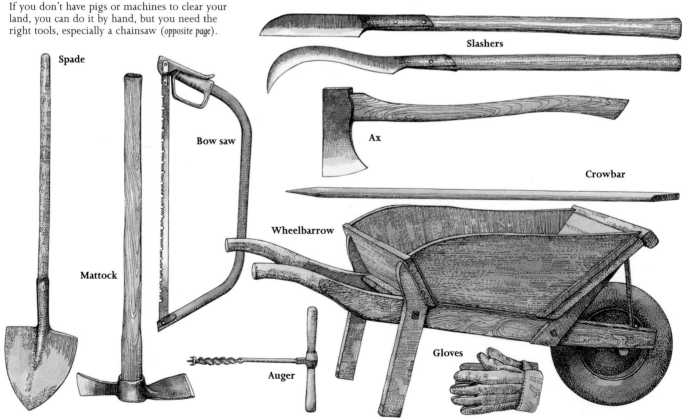

Spade

Slashers

Bow saw

Ax

Mattock

Crowbar

Wheelbarrow

Auger

Gloves

If you have many stumps, it might be worth renting a stump grinder to level them. A slower removal method is to drill large holes as deep as possible into the stump, then fill the holes with sugar, buttermilk, or dried milk powder to encourage decomposition. Another option is to pile charcoal briquettes on and around the stump to burn it out; check with your local fire department first to make sure burning is allowed.

Gorse, broom, and brambles

Areas covered with gorse, broom, and brambles can be cleared very effectively with a bow saw and a sharp scythe. Make sure you have a good pair of leather gloves and you can remove gorse fairly quickly with a small bow saw. A chain saw is noisy and will quickly blunt when cutting gorse close to the ground (which is what you want to do). Your scythe will easily cut brambles if it is sharp and you always pull away from the roots.

Cutting thorny brambles from a distance with a scythe is very effective: use a pitchfork to pile them up in a heap for burning. Once you have cleared an area, you may need to pass over it with your scythe once or twice every year for a few years afterward to keep down the prickly shoots that are reemerging.

Removing rocks

Rocks can be very obstructive, particularly on boulder-clay or glacial till in which boulders have been deposited by the retreating ice in a completely random fashion. Again, a mechanical excavator can deal with these if they are not too big, hauling them out and dozing them to the side of the field.

You can lift quite large rocks, of several tons or more, with levers. Dig down around the rock, establish a secure fulcrum at one side of it—a railroad tie will do, or another rock—insert a long beam of wood or a steel girder (a length of railroad line is ideal) and raise that side of the rock a few inches. Now pack small rocks under the big rock, let the latter subside, and apply your lever to the other side. Do the same there. Continue to work your way around the rock, raising it again and again the few inches made possible by your lever and packing small stones under it each time you have gained a bit. You will eventually work your rock to a point above the surface of the surrounding ground. Once you have gotten a boulder out, you may be able to roll it to the side of the field, again using levers. If it is too big for this, you can try lighting a big fire under it, heating it through, and then throwing cold water on it. This should crack it.

Don't forget that clearance is not the only option. It is perfectly possible to renovate old woodland by judicious felling and replanting. You can then leave the old stumps to rot in situ. When the timber is more mature, the wood will make an ideal holding ground for pigs or poultry. Or consider if it would not be better to replant old woodland as new woodland and farm it as forest.

CHAINSAW

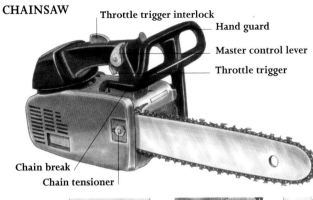

Throttle trigger interlock
Hand guard
Master control lever
Throttle trigger
Chain break
Chain tensioner

Tensioning Check if the chain tension is right by pulling with your thumb, and make sure the chain lubrication is filled up and working properly.

Sharpening With a file holder you leave the chain on the bar, and lock it with the hand guard. Always file from inside to outside with the cutter horizontal.

BURNING A STUMP

You can drill holes in a stump to help it start to rot away. For faster results, build a fire on top.

LEVERING UP A BOULDER

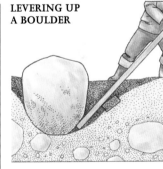

1 Use a rock or a chunk of wood as a fulcrum. Work a lever down beside the boulder.

2 Raise the boulder as far as possible. Prop up with stones. Take lever and fulcrum to the other side.

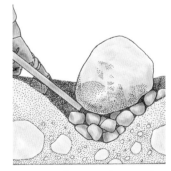

3 Repeat the process over and over, gaining a few inches each time. Once the boulder is out, roll or lever it off your field.

Draining Land

If you are lucky, your land will not need draining at all. Much land has porous subsoil and possibly rock through which water can percolate, perhaps has a gentle slope, and is obviously dry. But land with an impervious subsoil, very heavy land, land that is so level that water cannot run away from it, or land with springs running out in it may well need draining. Badly drained land is late land, meaning it will not produce plants early in the year. It is cold land, and it is hard to work. You cannot cultivate it when it is wet—particularly if it has clay in it. In short, it will not grow good crops.

You can tell wet land even in a dry summer by the plants growing in it. Such things as flag irises, sedges, rushes, and reeds all give away the fact that, although dry in the summer, it will be wet and waterlogged in the wintertime and should be drained.

Cutoff drains

Often, on sloping land, you can drain a field by digging a ditch along the contour above it (*see illustration*). The effect of this ditch is to cut off and take away the water that is percolating down from above. The rain that actually falls on the field is not enough to cause it to become waterlogged: it is the water that drains down from above that does the damage.

Springs

You can drain springs by connecting them by ditch or land drain (*see illustration*) to a stream that carries the water away.

You can tell where springs are by wet patches or by the presence of water-loving plants. If there is a large waterlogged area around the spring, common sense might tell you to make a larger hole around the mouth of your pipe and fill it with stones.

Land drains

Level land can be drained simply by lowering the water table. The water table is the level at which the surface of the underground water lies. It will be higher in the winter than it is in the summer, and in severe cases may be above the surface. You lower it by digging ditches, or putting in land drains, to take the water away. You can even do this with land below sea level, by pumping water from the deepest ditches up into the sea, or to raised-up rivers that carry it to the sea.

Obviously, heavy soils (soils with a high clay content) need more draining than light soils, but even sand, the lightest of all soils, can be waterlogged and will then grow nothing until it is drained. The heavier the soil is, the closer together your drains will need to be, for the less is the distance water can percolate. A very few drains will be enough to drain light or sandy soil. If you have had no experience, it will pay to get the advice of somebody who has: ask your neighbors for advice or consult your local extension office.

There are three main types of land drain: open ditches, underground drains, and mole drains. An open ditch is just what it says. You dig a ditch with battered (sloping) sides, or

THREE SITUATIONS WHERE YOU NEED DRAINS
A Water runs downhill through porous soil or rock before hitting an impervious layer. This forces it generally sideways to the surface, where it emerges as a spring.
B An impervious subsoil prevents rain from soaking in.
C Absolutely flat land has no slope to allow drainage.
The plants on the right are sure signs of wet land: (*left to right*) marsh orchid, marsh violet, yellow flag, marsh marigold, jointed rush, wood sedge, common rush, and cattail.

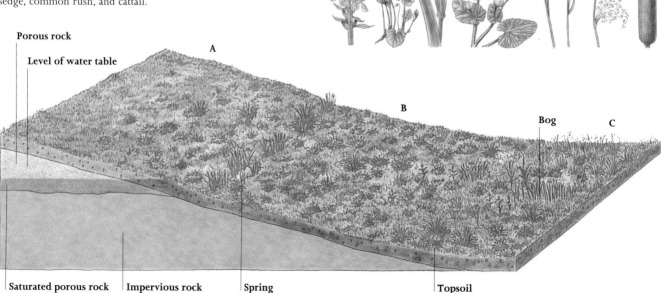

Porous rock

Level of water table

A

B

Bog

C

Saturated porous rock | Impervious rock | Spring

Topsoil

THE MOLE DRAINER
A torpedo-shaped steel object at the bottom of a narrow blade is dragged through the soil. The narrow slot made by the blade fills in, but the drain remains. The drain lasts much longer in clay than in soft, sandy soil.

THE CHISEL PLOW
The chisel plow, or subsoiler, cuts a series of deep, evenly spaced furrows in the soil. This works very well with heavy clay, where the furrows last and ensure free drainage.

THE USES OF DRAINS AND DITCHES
A cutoff ditch will intercept water draining downhill, and lead it around your field to a receiving ditch at the bottom. An underground drain can be used to drain a spring, and a series of underground drains—a herringbone pattern is ideal—can take sufficient water away to lower your water table. You want to get the water table at least 18 inches (45 cm) below the surface. Four feet (1.2 m) is ideal.

have it dug by machine. On light land (sandy soil) the slope needs to be much less steep than on heavy land because the latter supports itself better. Common sense will tell you how much to slope. If the sides fall in, it's too steep.

Depth is also a matter of reasoned judgment. If the ditch is deep enough to lower the water table sufficiently for the crops to grow happily, it is deep enough. You certainly don't want standing water in the soil at less than 18 inches (45 cm) from the surface. It's better if you can lower the water table to 4 feet (1.2 m).

If you have to dig the ditch by hand, you won't want it too deep. And remember that open ditches need a thorough clearing of scrub and weeds every year or two, and cleaning with a spade every five to 10 years. They also need fencing.

Underground drains are of many types. As long as they are deep enough not to be affected by deep plowing or cultivating, and their slope is continuous to the outfall so that they don't silt up in the dips, they will require no maintenance and should last for centuries. Mole drains do not last for more than five to 10 years—less in sandy land.

But draining is simple common sense. Imagine what is going on down there. Dig try-holes to find how deep the water table is and where the springs are. Arrange to drain that water away to the nearest stream or river or whatever, or even let it flow into wasteland below your land, and you will have well-drained, productive land.

Plastic drain pipe **Semicircular tile drain**

Stone culvert drain **Bush drain**

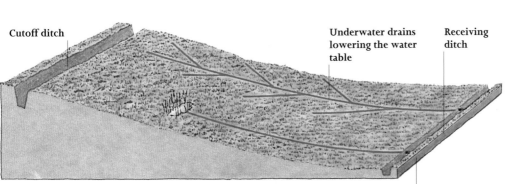

Cutoff ditch — Underwater drains lowering the water table — Receiving ditch — Underground drain capturing spring water

DRAINING A SPRING
Dig down to the spring. Lay a pipe or dig a ditch to carry the water away. If the spring covers a large area, fill in around your pipe with some stones.

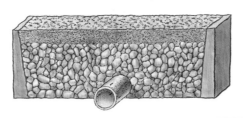

UNDERGROUND DRAINS
Stone culvert drains and tile drains are naturally porous. Plastic pipe drains have slits in them to let the water in. The Roman bush drain (simply bushes covered with earth) can be reinforced with a piece of perforated corrugated iron.

233

Irrigating Land

Wherever you live, your crops will benefit from irrigation, and in some countries they just won't grow without it. The luckiest cultivators are those who live in a hot, dry climate with plenty of water for irrigation. They have far better control over their husbandry than those who live in high-rainfall areas. They have no serious weed problems: they simply kill their weeds by withholding water from them when the land is fallow. They can drill their seed in dry dust before they water it, and then immediately flood the land to make the seed grow. They can give the crop exactly enough water for its needs throughout its growing time, and then withhold water when it comes to harvest, and thereby harvest in perfect conditions. They have it made.

But the rest of us can also use irrigation to advantage. It takes 27,200 gallons (103,000 liters) of water to apply a 1-inch (2.5-cm) depth of water to an acre (0.405 hectare). If there is no rain during the rainy season, it is nice to apply an inch (2.5 cm) a week during the period of hardest growth of the crop. In temperate climates with a fair rainfall, like most of northern Europe and the eastern United States, the addition of 2–6 inches (5–15 cm) during the growing season will probably be enough. In any case, the irrigator cuts his coat according to his cloth. Anything is better than nothing.

If you are lucky, you may be able to tap a stream above the land you wish to irrigate and lead the water down in a pipe, but unless your source is much higher than your land, you won't get much pressure. On the other hand, contrary to popular Western belief, you don't really need a lot of pressure: you only need the water. By the simple means of laying a hose on the ground and moving it around from time to time, as patch after patch gets flooded, you can do a great deal of good. You can do more good by letting water run down furrows between your rows of crops, moving the hose each time the water reaches the bottom of another furrow.

Sprinkle irrigation

Broadly, there are two types of irrigation: sprinkle irrigation and flood irrigation. Western farmers tend to go for the former. They use pumps and either "rainers,"

rotary sprinklers, or oscillating spray lines, all of which need considerable pressure to make them operate. This is fine if you can afford the equipment and fuel and have the water, which does not have to be above the field. But all this is expensive, and not really for the ordinary self-supporter. Personally, I could never see the point of squirting water up in the air at some expense just to have it fall down again, and have always practiced some form or other of flood irrigation.

Flood irrigation

In countries where irrigation is really understood—and these are the countries where it is really needed—flood irrigation is what is used. If you have a stream running next to a field, it is not difficult to get a little gasoline-powered pump and a hose, and to move the pump along the bank of the stream as one stretch of the field after another is irrigated. Alternatively, you may be lucky and have a stream at a higher level than the field.

Ideally, the land should be either terraced in perfectly level beds or, if the field has a natural gentle slope, leveled into gently sloping beds with bunds separating each bed from the next. (A bund is a small earth bank not more than a foot high.) You can grass these bunds, in which case they are permanent, or level them down each year and build them up again. If you are working with tractors you will probably level them, because it gives you more room to maneuver. At the head of all the sloping beds is a water channel. To irrigate, you build with a spade a little dam of earth about 1 foot (30 cm) high across this channel at the first bed, and break the bund that separates the channel from the bed with the spade. You sit there in the sunshine, watching the butterflies, until the water has meandered down the bed, covered all of it, and gotten to the bottom. If your bed is not properly leveled, and has no crop in it, you can use your spade to level it to spread the water evenly. On a hot day this is a delightful job.

Now you will have already built small dams level with each of the other beds. When the first bed is watered, you close the gap in its bund, break its dam down, break a hole in the bund of the second bed, and let the water run into there. And so you go on.

Of course, this presupposes that the water in your head-channel is higher than your beds. What if it is lower? Then you must do what many a Chinese or Egyptian does: just raise it a few inches. You can do this with a bucket, very laboriously, or a hundred other devices that ingenuity will lead you to. A small pump might be one of them, a tiny windmill another.

If your field is very steep, it is obvious that beds sloping down it will not do for flood irrigation. You will have to terrace it. This will involve stone (or at least turf) retaining walls and is a tremendous job. And if you have a very big field, you may need two or more head channels on different contours, because the water won't be able to meander down from the top of each bed to the bottom.

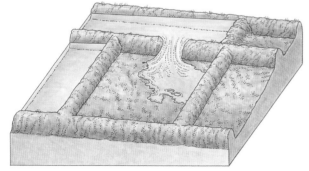

FLOOD IRRIGATION
Sloping beds with a water channel at the head are separated by earth. Make a dam across the channel at the first bed; break a hole in the bund separating the channel from the bed. Close the gap when flooded. Repeat when necessary.

Making Use of Woodland

The most useful trees for the self-supporter are, in order of importance: sweet chestnut (the best tree in the world for timber), oak, ash, and larch. In North America you would add hickory, sugar maple, and black cherry. If you have a saw bench capable of ripping down trees, then softwoods or any of the timber hardwoods are useful, too.

Hardwoods and softwoods

When considering timber for purposes other than fuel, you should look out for: a fairly quick rate of growth, hardness and resistance to rot, and what I will call "cleavability" or "splittability."

For very many farm uses it is better to cleave wood rather than rip-saw it (saw it along the grain). Cleaving is quicker, cheaper, the resulting wood is stronger, and lasts longer. Why? Because when you rip-saw you inevitably cut across some of the grain, or wood fibers. When you cleave, your cleavage always runs between the grain, which avoids "cross-graining" and leaves undamaged grain to resist the weather.

Sweet chestnut cleaves beautifully. It is fast-growing, straight, hard, and strong. It also resists rot better than any other tree. Oak cleaves well, too, but not as well as chestnut. The heart of oak is as hard, and lasts as long, but the white sapwood on the outside—most of a small tree—is useless. Oak is extremely slow-growing and needs good soil to grow at all. Ash, however, is tough and resilient, but will rot if put in the ground. It is straight, grows fast, and splits well.

Above the ground, but exposed to the weather, ash will last a long time if you apply a preservative every now and then. It makes good gates or hurdles. Larch is unusual in that it is a conifer but not an evergreen. It is very fast-growing and is the best of the conifers for lasting in the ground, as long as it is treated with preservative. All the other conifers, or softwoods, are hopeless in the ground if not treated with preservative, and even then they don't last many years.

Cherry and all other fruit woods are hard, and make fine firewood. They are good for making cog teeth in water mills, for example. Hickory is the best wood for tool handles. It doesn't grow in Europe (why, I don't know), and so is either imported or else replaced with ash, which is a pretty good substitute. Elm—alas, now being killed off by Dutch elm disease—is good for any purpose where you want a non-splittable wood, such as for wheel hubs, chopping blocks, and butcher's blocks. It is great under water. Maple and sycamore are good for turning on a lathe, and making treen (carved objects). Walnut is a king among fine woods, and fit to harvest in a mere 150 years, though 350 is better if you have the patience to wait for it!

Firewood

Trees are your most likely source of fuel. If you have even an acre or two of woodland, you will find that, with proper management, the trees in it will grow faster than you can cut them down for your fire. A piece of woodland is the most efficient solar heat collector in the world.

THE FORESTER'S ESSENTIAL TOOLS
Fell your tree with ax and saw. Use hammer and wedge, or club and froe, for splitting. Adze and draw-knife are for stripping and shaping.

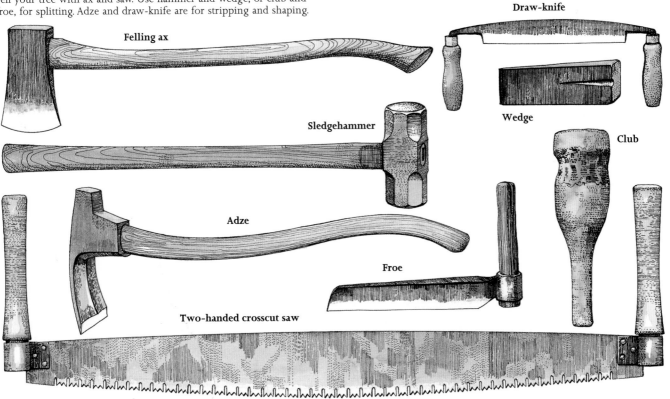

Draw-knife

Felling ax

Sledgehammer

Wedge

Club

Adze

Froe

Two-handed crosscut saw

Which tree to plant?

Ash is the best of all firewoods. ("Sere or green, it's fit for a queen!") The loppings of felled ash are excellent. It burns as well when newly cut as when mature. Oak, when seasoned, is a fine and long-burning firewood, but it grows far too slowly to be planted for this purpose. Silver birch is good for firewood, though not for much else. It burns very hot when seasoned, and it grows fast.

Conifers aren't much good for firewood. They spit a lot and burn very quickly, but in the frozen north, where there's nothing else, that's what people have to use. Birch is better as firewood, and it will grow farther north than any other tree. All the weed woods, like alder and pussy willow, are very sluggish when green, but can be burned when dry, though even then they don't burn well or give out prolonged heat. But what else is there to do with them? Any wood in the world will burn. But if you are planting trees especially for firewood, plant ash, and then coppice it.

Coppicing and planting

Coppicing means cutting down all your trees when they are about 9 inches (23 cm) in diameter, and then letting them grow again. They will "coppice" by putting up several shoots from each bole. Cut these down again in 12 years, and they will grow once more. This 12-yearly harvesting can go on for centuries, and help you harvest the greatest possible quantity of firewood from your woodlot.

Plant trees very close together and they will grow up straight and tall, reaching for the light: 5 feet by 5 feet (1.6 m x 1.6 m) is fine. When they become crowded, you thin them and get a small preliminary harvest. In winter, plant trees at least three years old. You can buy them from a nursery, or the Forestry Service, or you can grow them yourself from seed. Keep the grass and yard waste down every summer for three or four years, so the trees don't get smothered. Saw off low branches from the growing trees to achieve clean timber without knots. Feed with phosphate, potash, and lime if needed. A scythe is ideal for clearing around young trees.

In existing woodlands, uproot the weed trees (alder, pussy willow, thorn) to give the other trees a better chance. Wet land favors weed trees, so drain if you can. Keep out sheep, cattle, and goats to give seedlings a chance. Cut out undergrowth if you have time, or try running pigs in the wood for a limited period. They will clear and manure it, and they won't hurt established trees. They will also live for months in the autumn on acorns or beechnuts.

Seasoning wood

Stack the planks as they come out of the log, with billets of wood in between to let the air through. Kiln-drying is a quick way of seasoning, but time is better. Some wood, such as ash, can be laid in a stream for a few weeks to drive the sap out. This speeds seasoning, but some trees do take years to season. If you want woods for cabinetmaking, for example, there must not be any subsequent movement. But for rough work, gates, or even timbers for rough buildings, seasoning is not so important. Always remember to treat trees as a crop. Don't hesitate to cut mature trees when they are ripe, but always plant more trees than you cut down.

TREES TO PLANT
These trees are among the most useful that you could grow on your land: **1** Ash **2** Larch **3** Silver Birch **4** Elm **5** Walnut **6** Hybrid Chestnut **7** Shagbark Hickory **8** Oak.

1   2   3   4

FELLING A TREE
Use an ax to trim off roots and cut a face in the side of a tree.

A "face" is a forester's term for a deep V-shaped notch. Cut it in the side toward which you want the tree to fall. Now begin sawing from the other side, making your cut a few inches above the deepest part of the face. When the tree "sits on" your blade, so you can't move it, use your sledgehammer to drive a wedge in behind your saw. Keep sawing until you are close to the face.

The tree should feel like it is about to fall. Now pull out your saw, bang the wedge farther in, and over it goes. A jagged piece of wood, called the "sloven," will be left sticking up from the stump. Trim it off with your ax.

RIVING WITH WEDGE AND SLEDGEHAMMER
Wedges and a sledgehammer are the best tools for "riving," or splitting, large logs.

Use the sledgehammer to drive a wedge into the end grain of the log. Then drive more wedges into the resulting cleft until the log splits right down its length.

Never use an ax as a wedge. The handle will break.

RIVING WITH FROE AND CLUB
For riving smaller wood, the ideal tool is a froe. Whack the blade into the end grain with a club.

Or use a mallet. Now work the blade farther into the wood by levering sideways with the handle of the froe.

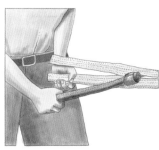

You won't get far before the wood splits down its length. This is much quicker than using wedges.

SAWING PLANKS
A pit saw is a time-honored tool for sawing logs into planks. One man stands on the log; the other is down a pit, dodging the sawdust. Band saws and circular saws are easier but more expensive.

SEASONING PLANKS
Stack planks as they leave the log with spacers to let air through. Leave for at least 18 months.

5   6   7   8

Hedging & Fencing

Domestic animals can be herded—that is, kept where they are supposed to be by human beings. But self-supporters will of necessity be busy people. Fences will not only relieve them or their spouse and children of the time-consuming task of herding, but will provide a useful tool for better land management. Without the fence you cannot enclose sheep or cattle on fodder crops; you cannot concentrate pigs on rooting; you cannot even keep goats and chickens out of your garden.

Quickthorn hedge

The most natural barrier you can build is a quickthorn hedge. "Quick" means alive, and such a hedge is established by planting thorn bushes close together in a long line. Ask your local extension which plants are best for your area. Seedling thorns, about 6 inches (15 cm) high, can be planted in two lines, staggered, 9 inches (23 cm) between rows, 18 inches (45 cm) between the plants in the rows.

You can buy the plants from nurseries or grow them yourself from seeds. But the hedge must be protected from stock for at least four years, and this is what makes a quickthorn hedge so difficult to establish. Animals, particularly sheep and even more particularly goats, will eat a young quickthorn hedge. Therefore, some other sort of fence—probably barbed wire—must be established on both sides of a new quickthorn hedge: an expensive business.

Laying a hedge

But once the quickthorn hedge is established, it is there, if you take care of it, for centuries. You maintain it by laying it—that is, every five years or so, cutting most of the bushes' trunks halfway through and breaking them over. The trunks are all laid the same way—always uphill. They are pushed down on top of each other, or intertwined where possible, and often held by "dead" stakes driven in at right angles to them. Sometimes the tops of these are pleached (intertwined) with hazel or willow wands twisted through like basketry. In due course the pleaching and the dead stakes rot and disappear, but the hedge puts out new growth and can be very stockproof.

The quickthorn hedge is a labor-intensive way of fencing, but labor is all it uses, and it lasts indefinitely. Also, it looks nice, gives shelter to birds and small animals, and serves as a windbreak (very important in windy regions). In days of old it supplied, with no extra work, wood for heating bread ovens and other purposes, to say nothing of the lovely berries. You can often restore old hedges to efficiency on a new farm by laying them, judiciously planting here and there an odd thorn bush to fill in a gap.

Dry-stone wall

If there is freestone (stone that cleaves out of the quarry easily in fairly even slabs) in your area, you probably already have dry-stone walls. "Dry" means no mortar. If you have dry-stone walls, you will need to maintain them. If you don't but you have the stone on your land, you can build some. It is backbreaking but costs nothing. You need tons of stone—much more than you think you are going to need—and a good hand and eye. Dig a level foundation trench first, then lay the stones carefully, breaking all joints, keeping sides vertical, and fitting the stones in as snugly as you can. Dry-stone walls can be quite stockproof. They are enormously costly in terms of labor and need repairing from time to time.

Stone-hedge

It is possible to build a cross between a wall and a hedge. You find these in areas where the natural stone is rounded or boulder-shaped, not the rectangular slabs that are found in limestone country. Two stone walls are built with a pronounced batter—that is, they lean inward toward each other. The gaps between the stones are filled in with turf, and the space between the two walls is filled with earth. A quickthorn hedge is then planted on top. After a year or two, grass, weeds, and scrub grow from the earth and the turf. The wall is quite green and not, to be quite frank, very stockproof. If you look at a hundred such hedges, I'll guarantee you'll find a discreet length of barbed wire or two, or even sheep-netting, along ninety of them. These wall-hedges aren't really much good unless you fortify them with barbed wire.

Wattle-hurdle

If you can get stakes from your own trees, a wattle-hurdle fence is free except for labor, and fairly quick to erect, but it doesn't last long. You drive sharpened stakes into the ground at intervals of 9 inches (23 cm) and pleach, or weave, pliable withies (willow branches), hazel branches, holly, ivy, blackberry, or other creepers between the stakes so as to make a continuous fence. The weaving material soon dries out, cracks, and gets rotten, and you have to ram more in. The stakes themselves, unless of chestnut or heart-of-oak or other resistant wood, rot after a few years and break off. Where stakes or posts are expensive or hard to come by, it is an extravagant form of fencing.

Post-and-rail

A post-and-rail fence is stronger and, unless you are able to grow your own wood, more economical. It consists of strong stakes, either of resistant wood or softwood treated with preservative, driven well into the ground, with rails of split timber nailed onto them. Abraham Lincoln, we are told, started his life as a "rail-splitter." The rails he split would have been for post-and-rail fences, for in his day that wonderful invention, wire, had not begun to encompass the world, and yet the new settlers heading west over North America had to have fences on a large scale. Today, we have the benefit of simple but highly effective post-hole diggers. Two people may be needed, but you can drive posts into what seems like extremely unlikely soil.

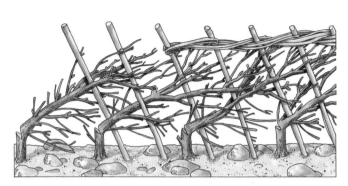

BUILDING OR REPAIRING A HEDGE

Cut stakes out of your hedge so as to leave strong bushes at intervals of about 12 inches (30 cm).

Wearing leather hedging gloves, bend each trunk over and half-cut through the trunk near the base with a billhook. Force the half-cut trunk down to nearly horizontal

and try to push the end under its neighbor to keep it in position. Be sure not to break it off. Take the stakes you have just cut and drive them in at right angles to the

trunks, and interweave them with the trunks. Intertwine the tops of the stakes with pliable growth (e.g., hazel or willow). The stakes will rot, but the living hedge will be secure.

OVERGROWN HEDGES

Tame a runaway hedge with a slasher (*left*). Clear the under-growth with a bagging hook (*above*), but also hold a stick, or you might lose a finger or thumb.

USING STONE

A well-maintained dry-stone wall is even more stockproof than an established hedge. You need stone that comes in even, flattish slabs. Dig down about 9 inches (23 cm) and make a level foundation trench. Lay the stones, neatly fitting them together. Make sure the sides are vertical and all joints are broken. If you have large, round stones on your land, you can make a stone hedge. Build two stone walls leaning toward each other, 12 inches (30 cm) apart. Plug the gaps between the stones with turf and the space between the walls with earth, and plant a hedge on top. To make it really stockproof, reinforce with barbed wire to ensure sheep don't walk straight over it, at least until the hedge is mature.

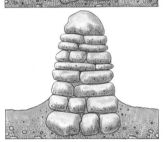

Steel wire

The invention of galvanized steel wire was the answer to the fencer's dream. It can be plain wire (often high-tensile), barbed wire, or netting. Plain wire is effective only if stretched. Barbed wire is more effective if it is stretched, but often a strand or two attached somewhat haphazardly to an old unlaid hedge is all there is between animals and somebody's valuable crop.

Netting is very effective but nowadays terribly expensive. Square-meshed netting is strongest for a permanent situation, but is awkward to move very often: diamond-meshed netting is much weaker but stands being repeatedly rolled up and moved, and is therefore ideal for enclosing sheep.

Stringing wire

If you buy a wire stretcher, you can see easily enough how to use it, but there are several very effective ways of improvising one. A tool often used in Africa consists of a forked stick 2 feet (60 cm) long, with a 6-inch (15-cm) nail fastened with staples along its length just below the

fork. The wire to be stretched is inserted under the nail and then wrapped twice around it for firmness. You then take up the slack by twisting the stick, using the fork as a handle.

Then you put the final tension on by turning the stick around the corner post, using the stick as a lever. You can get short lengths of wire tight enough like this, although if you are stretching extremely long lengths at a time, you will need a store-bought wire stretcher, unless you pull the wire taut with a tractor.

Stretching tips

If you stretch wires on a post on a cold winter day, you may well have to stretch them again on a hot day next summer. Heat makes metal expand. Often, in practice, you can apply strain to wire by hauling it sideways—out of the line of the fence—to, say, a suitable tree with another length of wire. This practice is frowned upon by farm managers but is often useful just the same, especially when you are trying to make a fence stockproof down in the depths of the woods on a pouring wet day.

Stretching and anchoring fences

If you can't get a wire stretcher, you can exert quite a bit of tension by using a post as a lever, or by using a block and tackle, or even by using a horse or a tractor. Many farmers use the tractor method. But do not strain wire too much. It breaks the galvanizing and takes the strength out of the wire. Always use common sense.

A stretched fence is only as good as its anchor posts. A wire strainer, such as you can purchase, or easier still borrow from a neighbor, can exert a pull of two tons, and this multiplied by the number of wires you have in your fence will pull any corner post out of the ground unless it is securely anchored.

You can anchor a fence with a kicking post, a post placed diagonally against the corner post in such a way as to take the strain. The kicking post itself is secured in the ground against a rock or short post. Alternatively, the strain can be taken by a wire stretched taut around a rock buried in the ground. A refinement of this, the box anchor, is the most efficient of all (*see illustration*).

Remember, if you anchor wire to any tree that is not fully mature, the tree will gradually lean over and the fence will slacken. It is bad practice to fasten wire to trees anyway: the staples and lengths of wire get swallowed up by the growing tree and ultimately break some poor person's saw blade. However, not that many of us are innocent in that respect.

Electric fencing

The electric fence provides marvelous control over stock and land, making possible a new level of efficiency in farming.

You can get battery fencers, which work off six-volt dry batteries or 12-volt accumulators, or mains fencers that work off the main electricity supply and will activate up to 20 miles (32 km) of fencing! One strand of hot wire will keep cattle in—it should be at hip height—and one wire 12 inches (30 cm) from the ground will keep pigs in if they are used to it. Until they are, use two wires. The wires needn't be strong, or stretched, just whipped around insulators carried on light stakes, and the whole thing can be put up or moved in minutes.

Hurdles

Except for electrified wire-netting, which is expensive and hard to come by, sheep won't respect an electric fence. So when we wish to keep sheep on fodder fields, we make hurdles (*see illustration*). It's cheaper than buying wire netting. Some wood that rives (splits) is necessary: ash or chestnut is fine. If you use ash you should treat it with preservative. To erect hurdles, drive a stake in at the point where the ends of two hurdles meet, and tie the hurdles to the stake with a loop of binder twine. To carry hurdles, put as many as you can manage together, shove a stake through them, and get your shoulder under the stake. A fold-pritch is the traditional implement for erecting hurdles, and you can hardly do the job without it.

You can make wattle-hurdles out of woven withies or other flexible timber. These are light, not very strong, and don't last long, but are good for windbreaks at lambing time. To make them, you place a piece of timber on the ground with holes drilled in it. Put the upright stakes of your hurdle in the holes and then weave the withies in. It is simply basketwork.

THE BOX ANCHOR

A fence is only really secure if its wires are stretched, which means they can be subjected to a pull of two tons. Half a dozen stretched wires will pull your corner posts straight out of the ground unless they have good anchors.

The box anchor is the best of all. Heavy soft wire (generally number 8 gauge) goes from the buried rocks to the second post. A cross-piece mortised in this supports the two corner-posts on which the wires are held.

TEN ANCHORS IN A FIELD

Every length of stretched wire fence needs an anchor, and one anchor can only take a strain in one direction. Thus each corner of your field will need two anchors, and you will need one on each side of the gate.

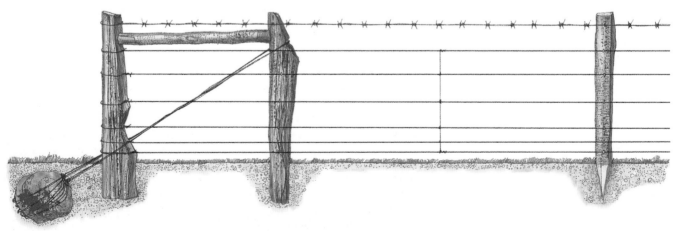

USING A POST RAMMER

Metal post rammers are popular with British homesteaders, since they are the simplest and easiest way to drive posts into light soils. First, you need to get the post embedded upright in the ground, and you might need someone to help you. Use a mallet to drive the pointed end of the post into the earth. Your goal needs to be accurate here, or you may split the timber. Once the post feels secure, drive the posts in with the post rammer. You just hold the heavy rammer at head height above the post and let go, so that the sheer force and weight of the hollow cylinder drives the post down into the earth. Quick and effective!

HURDLES

Hurdles are movable fences that you can easily make yourself from any wood that splits. Use mortises to join the horizontals to the pointed uprights. Be sure that the ends of the horizontals are tapered in such a way that they apply pressure up and down and not sideways; otherwise the uprights will split. You can drive thick nails through the joints to hold them, or else use wooden dowels. Nail the cross-braces. Drill all your nail holes or you will split the timber. To erect your hurdles, drive stakes into the ground and fasten the hurdles to them with string.

WATTLE-HURDLES

Wattle-hurdles can be made of split hazel or willow withies woven onto uprights. Put a balk of timber with appropriate holes drilled in it on the ground to hold the uprights while you are weaving.

POST-AND-RAIL FENCING

Strong uprights must be well tamped into the ground. Drive all nails all the way through and clench them.

A FARM GATE

A cattle-proof gate for a field or farmyard is best built of split ash or chestnut. Use bolts to join the four main timbers to make up the frame, and also bolt the hinges on. Use clenched 6-inch (15-cm) nails for the other joints.

Drill holes for the nails as well as the bolts, and pour preservative through all holes. If you have a forked timber, use the fork as the bottom hinge, but put a bolt through the throat to stop it from splitting. The diagonal timbers hold the thing in shape; fit as shown.

WIRE NETTING

Wire netting is often convenient but always expensive. Square-meshed, or pig, netting (right) makes an excellent permanent fence, and coupled with a strand of barbed wire is completely stockproof. Diamond-meshed, or sheep, netting (below) is weaker, but it can be rolled up and reerected, which is what you need for folding sheep.

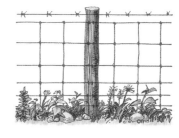

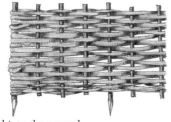

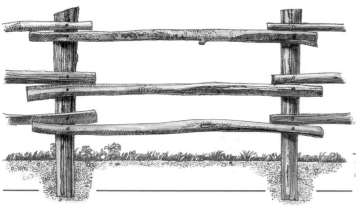

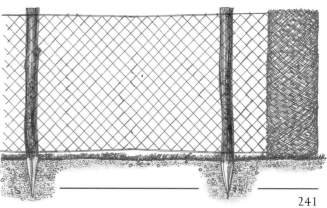

The Working Horse

There is great nobility about a working horse, and great beauty, too. If you want to plow your acre a day for month after month with a pair of horses, you will need big horses such as the Shire, Suffolk Punch, Clydesdale, or Percheron. If you have very little heavy farm work to do—just pulling a light pony-plow in already arable land, for example, or pulling a horse-hoe—then a light cob, or a large, sturdy pony, will do. They are fun to ride and drive, and make a pet, too.

Feeding

Horses, like other herbivorous animals, need to be fed often: they need a feed at least three times a day while they are working and must be given at least an hour to eat each meal. Also, they should have some hay to mumble at night if they are in the stable, or else be put out on grass. For working horses "good hay hath no fellow" as Bottom said in *A Midsummer Night's Dream*, but it must be good hay; dusty hay makes horses broken-winded, moldy hay upsets them, and too much clover hay, if too fresh, will cause them to scour (have diarrhea).

During the summer, when grass is good, working horses may be run on grass. They graze very close to the ground and should be put on pasture after cows have eaten off the long, lush grass, or else rationed severely as to how long they have on the pasture. Do not expect a horse to work hard, or get hard, on grass alone, for grass makes horses fat and soft. A horse on grass should have 6 pounds (2.7 kg) of oats a day for every half-day that he works.

In the winter, or when grass is short, a horse is best kept in a stable and could eat: 16 pounds (7.2 kg) of hay, 12 pounds (5.4 kg) of oats, and maybe some rutabagas or carrots or even fodder beet as well, while on medium work. A large horse on very heavy work might well have more oats: perhaps up to 20 pounds (9.0 kg) and the same of hay. But whatever you do, do not overfeed a horse, or you will kill him. A heavy horse doing only half a day's work should never get a whole day's ration. Hay will never hurt him, but grain will. A horse on a high ration, working hard and continuously, may be killed by a disease called hemoglobin urea (urinating blood) if you suddenly knock his work off but go on feeding him the same. The old practice was, on Friday night, to give a horse a bran mash (bran is coarse husk taken off wheat to leave white flour, and bran mash is bran soaked in water) instead of the corn feed, and then to feed nothing but plenty of good hay over the weekend: to keep up the corn ration while the horse was idle could be fatal. Similarly, it is not fair to expect a soft horse, that is, a horse that has lived for weeks out on grass, to do immediate heavy work. If you try to do this, he will sweat a lot, and puff and blow, and show signs of distress. Give him a little work each day, and feed a little more grain, and gradually harden him up.

Beans make a good feed for horses, but don't let them make up more than a sixth of the grain ration. It is very nice if you can get chaff (straw or hay cut up small by a chaff-cutter). Mix it with grain to make it last longer.

Foaling

Fillies can be put to the "horse" (horseman's word for stallion) at two years old (three might be better), and a colt can serve a mare when he is two years old. Pregnancy is slightly over eleven months. She should not work "in shafts" when far gone in pregnancy—the pressure of the shafts might harm her. A mare will probably have less trouble in foaling if she is kept working than if she is not, because she will be in harder condition. If the mare is out on grass in the winter, and not working, she should be given a small ration of hay and maybe a few oats (not more than 4 pounds or 1.8 kg a day), as well as winter grass. In summer, grass should be enough.

After foaling, a mare should not be asked to work for at least six weeks; suckling the foal is enough for her. The mare might do very light work after six weeks. But wait until four months, preferably six, before weaning the foal. Once the foal is weaned (taken away from his mother and kept out of earshot), the mother should be put into work immediately in order to dry off her milk. If you don't want to work the mare, you can leave the foal on as long as you like. If you do wean the foal he should be given, say, 4 pounds (1.8 kg) of oats a day and the same of hay.

Starting a foal

Colt foals should be castrated by a vet at about a year old, but this should never be done in the summer when flies are about, nor in frosty weather. A foal can be started (trained) at around two years old. But it is never too soon to get a halter on a foal (the first day is okay) to teach him to be led around. Foals have a great sense of humor and can be great fun. If you make a fuss over a foal and get him really tame, he is far less trouble to start. And the foal's feet should be lifted often, to accustom him to this necessary procedure.

To start him, get a bit into his mouth and drive him in front of you with a whip with long reins. After a few lessons, get a collar on him. When he gets used to this, hitch him to some not-too-heavy object like a log or a set of harrows and get him to pull. Then put him next to an older horse and get them both to pull, say, a plow. Wait until he is pretty calm before trying him in shafts.

Kindness, firmness, and common sense are the qualities needed for starting horses. It is absolutely essential that you should not be frightened of the horse, for if you are, the horse will sense it immediately and you will never start him. If you have great trouble, try keeping him away from other horses in a loose box (a room in which he is kept loose) for a week or so, and spend some time daily with him, talking to him, feeding him, handling him, and getting to know him. He will then get used to you.

Shoeing

If a horse is to be worked at all hard, he must be shod, perhaps every six weeks. The hooves grow under the shoes. If the latter have not worn too much they can be taken off, the feet trimmed, and the shoes nailed on again.

THE FULLY HARNESSED HORSE

The horse is now taken to the cart or implement and shut in. In other words, he is backed between the shafts and the tugs are hooked to the harness. Then the ridge chain that holds the shafts up is fastened, followed by the breeching chains. The tugs pull the implement or cart forward. The breeching chains hold it back if it tries to go too fast. A belly chain is passed from shaft to shaft under the horse's belly to prevent the shafts from skying if the cart or implement is backloaded.

See that all is well adjusted before you move off. The shafts must not pinch the horse, the breeching must indeed take the weight of the cart going downhill, and the tugs, not the ridge chain, must exert the forward pull on the shafts.

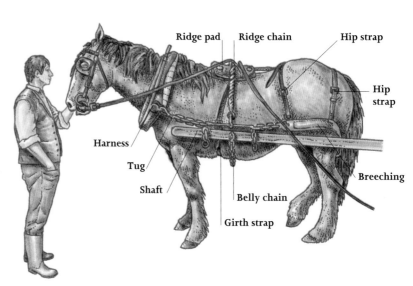

Ridge pad · Ridge chain · Hip strap · Hip strap · Breeching · Belly chain · Girth strap · Shaft · Tug · Harness

HARNESSING A HORSE

1 Use a halter to lead your horse for harnessing. Then take it off.

2 Have the collar in easy reach and the bridle hung on the crook of your left arm.

3 Hold the horse over his nose and fit the collar over his head upside down. Then strap the hames (the curved metal or wooden strips that take the strain) to the collar.

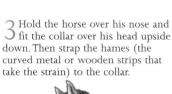

4 Tighten them at the top.

5 Slide on the bridle. To get the bit in the horse's mouth you may have to force his teeth apart by pushing your fingers in at the side. It takes practice.

6 Fit the saddle, or ridge pad, and tighten the girth, but not so much that the horse's wind is constricted. Sometimes the breeching will be kept fastened to the girth.

7 Here the breeching is being put on separately.

8 The crupper, a loop of leather that goes around the tail, must go on when the breeching is right back. It is then eased forward and strapped on to the saddle, if it is not already so strapped.

Horse & Tractor Power

There are three practical methods of powering instruments that have to be dragged over the land: farm tractors, garden tractors, and animals.

Farm tractors are large, enormously expensive (unless they are very old), cost a lot to maintain, and are unsuitable for small plots of land or gardens, because when twisting and turning in a small space, the wheels compact the soil to a damaging extent. I have sometimes been forced by circumstances to use a farm tractor in a garden and have always regretted it. A small, or garden, tractor is another matter altogether. It is light—lighter than a horse—and you can even pick it up if it is not too big. It does not compact the soil and is fairly cheap to buy and maintain. It will work in small corners and between row crops. It can often be adapted to many uses: one common type will mow grass, either by a reciprocating knife or a rotary knife; it will saw wood; drive all sorts of small barn machinery; rototill; plow (rather inefficiently and very slowly); row-crop cultivate; pull a small barrow; and scrape the snow off your paths. But many of these jobs you could do as quickly or quicker by hand, and compared with a large tractor or a horse, a garden tractor is extremely slow.

You can plow three acres a day with a small farm tractor or five with a large one, and it doesn't matter how rough the land is. With a horse, you can plow perhaps half an acre; with two horses, an acre. But one horse will only pull a small plow and work on arable land. To plow grassland, you need two horses. With a garden tractor it would take you days to plow an acre—and drive you mad with noise and boredom. It will rototill old grassland, but it will make pretty heavy weather of it.

Tractors have two major advantages. They are not eating or drinking when they are not being worked, and they do not use up your land in their search for food. But you do have to pay for their fuel, even though a garden tractor uses a tiny amount. On the other hand, a horse—the best example of animal power—can be fueled entirely from your land. Also, it can have another horse. It is unlikely that the tractor will ever be invented that can have another tractor. But a farm tractor is versatile. It will drive a really effective saw bench or any barn machinery (such as mills, chaff-cutters, and the like); it can be fitted with a powerful winch for hauling trees out, or down; it will pull a large trailer or cart; it will dig post-holes; and it will operate a digging arm that will dig ditches for you (but only just).

Maybe we can sum the whole complicated subject up by saying this: if you have only a garden, probably a garden cultivator will be valuable—at least if you don't want to do everything by hand, which you perfectly easily could do if you had the time. Don't think a garden cultivator is necessarily light work—some can be very hard to manage. If you have anything over 4 acres (1.6 hectares)—and like horses—a light horse might suit you very well. Once you have gotten your land broken up, either with pigs or with a borrowed farm tractor, a small horse will keep it that way, keep your land clean, and give you a lot of pleasure.

On the other hand, one of the larger garden tractors would do the work equally well, if not as pleasantly. A horse will eat the produce of an acre (0.4 hectare) of very good land in a year, or 2 to 3 acres (0.8–1.2 hectares) of poorer land. A horse doesn't waste an ounce of its food: what it doesn't convert into energy, it puts back into the land as manure. On a very small farm you might consider keeping a horse and buying in its hay and oats or corn. You are thus buying in fertility for your holding. If you have 10–15 acres (4–6 hectares) or over—and can pick up a cheap farm tractor in good condition (and know how to keep it going)—it might save you a lot of work, but two horses will do the job, though taking three times as long.

Oxen are very good draft animals. They are much slower than horses but exert a strong, steady pull. Some horses are inclined to "snatch" with a heavy load and break things—I have seen oxen sink to their knees in hauling a heavy wagon out of the sand or mud and exert tremendous traction. Oxen are growing into meat during their working lives: horses are depreciating in value, but oxen require two people to work them—horses, only one. So, two oxen will just about do the work of one horse—pull a very small single-furrow plow, a row crop cultivator, or a small cart. Four oxen will pull these things much better.

Mules are very hardy, particularly for hot and dry climates (they hate mud and constant wet). They walk fast, pull hard, and can live on worse food than a horse, but they will not exert so much traction as a heavy horse and are inclined to snatch, kick, bite, and generally misbehave.

Donkeys can exert some traction, but they walk very slowly. They can be used (as mules and ponies can) for carrying packs over ground too rough for a sled or a cart. One donkey won't pull very much at all—maybe a small row crop cultivator at best.

TRACTOR POWER
If you want mechanical power instead of horses, a rototiller is essential for any holding of more than 1 acre (0.4 hectares). There are two types, those that run on wheels and those that drag themselves forward by the action of their tines. Both do a good job, but the former, if big enough, is quicker and more powerful.

Preparing Land & Sowing

If you threw some seeds on grassland, or in a wood, all that would happen is that the birds would eat them. In order to sow seeds with any hope of success, you have to do two things: eliminate the competition of existing plants, and disturb the soil so that the seed can get into it. If possible, bury the seed—although, of course, not too deep.

The usual method of preparing grassland, or other land with an indigenous vegetation on it, is by plowing or digging. But if you have pigs, use them. They will do the job even better than a plow. If I plow old pasture to sow a grain crop, I plow it to turn it over as completely as possible, although it still stands up in ridges.

After that, I drag disc harrows up and down the furrows for two passes, so I don't knock the ridges back again. At this stage I would add any fertilizer, such as lime or phosphate, that the land might require. Then I would disc again across the furrows. The reason for using a disc harrow at this point is that it cuts the hard turf furrows of the old grassland to pieces—instead of dragging it out as a spike harrow would do.

A pass or two with the spike harrow works the land down to a fine seed bed. It must not be too fine for winter-sown grain, nor even for spring-sown if it is wheat or oats. Barley needs a much finer tilth than either. I then broadcast the seed (sow it by hand), but if I had a seed drill, I would drill it.

Remember: if you drill seed too deep, it will become exhausted before its shoots can get to the surface, and it will die. So the smaller the seed, the shallower it should be. About three times the diameter of the seed is far enough. I would then harrow once again. A pass with a roller completes the sowing process. With row crops, hoe between the rows when the seedlings are about 6 inches (15 cm) high and then the gate can be shut on the bed until harvest time.

No-plowing and no-digging

The no-plowing or no-digging theory is now very popular. Adherents of this theory claim that the land should never be plowed or dug because it is bad to invert the soil. Inverting the soil upsets the soil life, putting surface bacteria down so deep that they die, bringing deeper organisms to the surface where they die, too.

No-diggers and no-plowers have great success, provided they have very large quantities of compost or farmyard manure with which to mulch their land. The seeds are virtually sown under a covering of compost. My own experience shows that for bringing grassland into cultivation, either the plow or the pig's snout is essential. The next year, if you still wish to keep that land arable, you can often get away with cultivating only, or

even harrowing or other shallow cultivations. The idea of very heavy mulches of compost is fine—providing you can get the compost. But the land itself will never produce enough vegetable material to make enough compost to cover itself sufficiently deeply, and therefore you will have to bring vegetable matter in from outside.

Plowing

The plow that the Western world has used since Iron Age times has three main working elements: the coulter, the share, and the mold-board or breast. In Africa, Australia, and parts of North America, a similar plow, the disc plow, is much used. This is not to be confused with the disc harrow. It is a large, very dished steel disc, dragged through the soil at a certain angle. The angle is such that the leading edge of the disc acts as a coulter, the bottom edge acts as a share, and the belly of the disc acts as a mold-board. It is very good on trashy land.

Using the fixed-furrow plow

Now if you consider what happens when you actually take a fixed-furrow plow out into a field and begin to plow, you will realize that the operation is not as simple as you might think. Suppose you go into the middle of one side of the field and plow one furrow. Then what do you do? If you turn your horse or tractor around, face the other way and go back, you will either simply plow the slice you have plowed out back into its furrows so that you are back where you started from, or you will plow the other side of it and build up a ridge of two slices bundled up against each other, and under the ridge will be unplowed ground.

SOW THE SEED
Broadcasting is simply scattering the seed on the ground. A seed drill drops the seed down pipes so that it is buried and safe from birds.

USE PIGS OR A PLOW
For bringing grassland into cultivation, the pig's snout is unbeatable—and a pig manures the land as it digs it. If you don't have a pig, you need to plow.

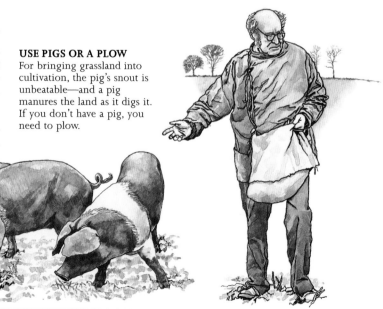

Making a ridge

The way to avoid the piece of unplowed ground is to plow your first furrow, then turn around and plow it back again with the piece of ground underneath it, too. Then turn around again and plow the next furrow up against the first two. You have then made a ridge. You then simply go around and around this ridge, every time plowing your furrow toward the ridge. It will be seen that, when you do this, you get farther and farther away from the ridge, and each time you have to go right around it. You soon find yourself having to travel a huge distance along the headland to get to where you are to start the furrows going back again. So what do you do then?

You go even farther along the headland, and plow out another "setting out" furrow, as the first furrow of a stetch of land is called, and make another ridge. (A stetch is the area of plowed land around a single ridge.) You then plow around that one. As soon as you come to the last furrow of the first stetch, you go back and travel on farther beyond your second stetch and set out a third stetch. And so on. The ridges are traditionally positioned 22 yards (20 m) apart.

It will be seen now that you will end up with a field with parallel furrows running down it, and in between each pair of furrows, parallel ridges. In other words, you have gathered the soil at the ridges and stolen it out of the furrows. If you go on doing this year after year, you will end up with the typical "ridge-and-furrow" land of parts of the English Midlands. On wettish, heavy land, this pattern of field has an advantage: the furrows, running up and down the slope, serve to carry the surface water away, and crops growing on the ridge part are well above the water table. In most parts of southern Europe and North America, though, it would be criminal thus to plow up and down the slopes, since it would lead to gully erosion.

Turnwrest plow

Now if you want a simple life, and don't want your soil gathered into ridges, there is another kind of plow that will suit your needs, and that is the turnwrest, or two-way plow. This has two plowing bodies, one in the ground and the other up in the air. One turns the furrow to the right, the other to the left. With this you simply plow one furrow, turn around, swing the two bodies over so they change places, and plow back again. And when you do this, both furrows are laid the same way. You avoid all the complications of setting out, "gathering up," and all the rest of it, and when you have finished your field is quite level, with no "lands" or stetches at all. Many tractor plows are of this type nowadays, and the famous Brabant plow, widely used in Europe and drawn by horses or oxen, is also a turnwrest. The Brabant is a marvelous instrument. I have a tiny, one-horse version, and it is worth its weight in gold.

Incidentally, the ancient belief in the necessity of turning the soil deeply enough to bury all rubbish completely is quickly becoming more and more discredited. Organic farmers, even in England and the eastern states of the US, now prefer to leave their compost or manure on top of the soil rather than plow it in. It is a fact that the enormous earthworm population in soil that has been organically farmed for some time drags all vegetable matter down into the soil without our help. Except for my potato field, I am tending more and more to leave manure on the surface and disturb the soil deeply as little as possible. But whatever their theories in this respect, practical growers find themselves forced, occasionally, to plow or to dig.

Sowing

There is no rule of thumb in farming, particularly when it comes to sowing seed. Examine the soil after every operation—remember the needs of the seed and the plant. If the seed is too shallow, the birds will get it, or it will dry out—that is, if the soil is dry and dusty on top. If it is too deep, it will use all its energy pushing its shoot up to the light and will die before the life-giving sun's rays can give it more energy. If the land is too wet, the seed will drown. If it is too sticky, the seed will not be able to push out its roots and shoots.

DISC HARROW
Sharp steel discs break up lumpy ground more effectively than spikes. You can create a fine tilth without dragging turf or rubble back up to the surface.

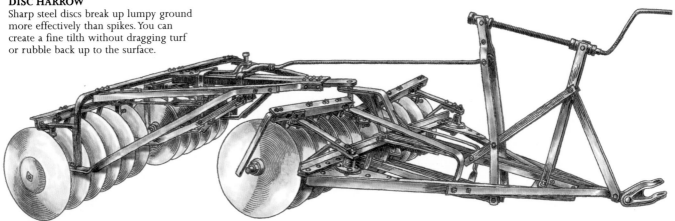

The plant itself needs open soil, which permits the air to circulate and the water to rise. Don't forget that temperature is most important for seed germination. I knew an old farmer in Suffolk, England, who used to drop his trousers in the spring and sit on his soil to see if it was warm enough to sow spring barley. He could sense the temperature, humidity, and so on with his bare backside more sensitively than he could with his hand. To drill his seed in too-cold ground was only to have it rot, or the birds get it, or the hardier weeds grow away from it and smother it. To plant it too late was to have a late and not very heavy crop of barley. To get it just right, he had to use his buttocks. He grew very good barley.

Hoeing

Having sown or planted your crop, you may have to "keep it clean," which is the farmer's way of saying suppress the weeds among it. Some crops don't need this because they grow quickly and densely, and smother the weeds by denying them light and soil space. You can often get away without hoeing cereals. But row crops do need hoeing.

There are two kinds of hoeing: hand-hoeing and mechanical hoeing. The hand-hoe is simply a blade on a stick with which you cut through the surface of the soil. The cutting can be either a pushing action with a Dutch hoe, or a pushing action with an ordinary hoe (*see* p.42). In either case, it is probably best to walk backward to avoid stepping on the weeds as you uproot them, thus leaving them exposed to wither and die. Walking forward would simply do the weeds a favor by pushing them back into the soil and transplanting them.

Mechanical hoeing is the pulling of mounted hoe blades along between the rows of the crop by animal or tractor power. This only cleans the ground between the rows. It cannot do it in between the plants, because no machine has yet been invented that can tell the difference between a weed and a crop plant. It takes the eye of man, or woman, to do that. Therefore, even if you horse- or tractor- hoe, you will still have to hand-hoe as well, at least once. And on that point I have neglected to mention another mechanical hoe, the wheel hoe, which is most useful for the food-producing garden: it's the equivalent of the horse-hoe in the fields. It usually has a single wheel at the front and the cutting blade behind it. You push it up and down between the rows. This means, of course, that you still have to hand-hoe in the rows between the plants.

There is another consideration about hoeing. Not only does it kill the weeds, but it also creates a mulch of loose earth. This mulch conserves the moisture in the land, for it breaks the capillary crevices up which water can creep to the surface. It is very nice to see loose, broken-up soil on the surface rather than a hard pavement. It is true that some crops—onions are one; brassica, or cabbage-tribe, plants are another—like firm soil, but once they have gotten their roots in, it is best to shake up the surface around them. This lets the rain and air in and stops the moisture from coming to the surface and evaporating too quickly. In Suffolk, old countrymen say: "a hoeing is as good as a shower of rain." Experience shows that it is, too, and you cannot hoe too much.

Weeds

Selective weed sprays, or preemergence wood sprays, are the agribusinessman's answer to weed suppression in row crops. We organic farmers don't use them, because we cannot believe that it is good to douse our soils year after year and decade after decade in what are, after all, nothing more nor less than poisons. Also, the hoe can do it not only just as well but much better.

Weeds have been defined as "plants in the wrong place." Wrong, that is, from the farmer's point of view. From their point of view, they might be in the right place. But do not become paranoid about them. Weed competition, it is true, can ruin a crop. The weeds are so much more vigorous, and fitted for their environment, than our artificially induced crops can be. But also, under other circumstances, they do no harm and often do good. Bare, naked soil, with no crop on it, should be anathema to the farmer. A good covering of weeds is as good as a crop of green manure.

Green manure is any crop that we plant merely in order to plow in again. A good crop of chick-weed, fat-hen, or many another annual weed, is just as good. And, in the summer when weeds are rampant no matter how many times we hoe, when you go along the rows and either hoe weeds out, or pull them up, and let them lie down between the crop rows to rot, you realize that they do a lot of good. They form a mulch, which covers the soil and stops the drying winds from getting at it, and eventually they rot and the earthworms drag them down and turn them into humus.

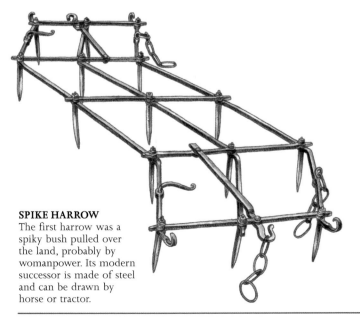

SPIKE HARROW
The first harrow was a spiky bush pulled over the land, probably by womanpower. Its modern successor is made of steel and can be drawn by horse or tractor.

Harvesting

The crown of the year is harvest time, and if you cannot enjoy that, you are unlikely to enjoy anything. You sweat and toil, along with friends and neighbors, to gather in and make secure the fruit of the year's labors. The work is hard, hot, sometimes boisterous, always fun, and each day of it should be rewarded with several pints of home-brewed beer or chilled homemade wine or hard cider.

All the cereals, with the exception of corn, are harvested in exactly the same way. When the crop is ripe, but not so ripe that it will shed its grain prematurely, the straw is cut. This may be done by scythe or combine. Sickling a field of grain is unbelievably tedious. A scythe used by a skilled man will cut two acres in a day, and if you can fit a cradle to it, it will dump the cut grain in sheaf-sized piles. Whet the blade at regular intervals with a rough stone, or hammer sharp as Alpine farmers do (*see pp.378–379*).

A horse- or tractor-drawn grass mower will cover a field fairly quickly, leaving cut grain all over the place. It must then be gathered into sheaves. A reaper-and-binder ties the sheaves for you, but it's a cumbersome machine and needs three horses to pull it for any length of time. If you are growing grain for home consumption, you should not need to grow much more than an acre. It is certainly not worth owning a reaper-and-binder to harvest such a small area, and it's hardly worth borrowing one, either.

Sheaf and stook

Sheaves are bundles of a size you can conveniently grab, tied around the middle either with string or with a fistful of the straw itself. To tie a sheaf with straw, rub both ends of the fistful to make it pliable, put it around the bundle gripped between your legs, twist the two ends together tightly, then tuck the twisted bit under the part around the sheaf. The reaper-and-binder, of course, ties its sheaves with string.

Then walk along the field and stand the sheaves up into six or eight stooks or traives. Take two sheaves and bang the heads together so that they lean into each other at an angle and do not fall down. Lean two or three more pairs against the first two. Leave them like that for a week or two so that the straw can dry out in the sun and wind, and the grain can become fully ripe.

Mow and rick

In wet climates the practice is then to form a mow (which is intermediate between a stook and a stack) or rick. To make a mow, stand about 20 sheaves up on their butts, leaning inward in a solid circle. Then start building another solid circle on top of the first one, starting from the middle. You can build in a spiral if you like. Lay the sheaves of this second layer closer to the horizontal, with the ears inward, toward the middle. To stop these sheaves from slipping, snatch a handful of straw from each sheaf and tuck it under the band (string or straw tie) of the next sheaf.

Keep working so that the center of the mow will be higher than the outside edges. Put layer after layer on like this, drawing each layer in a little so that the mow rises steeply to a point. It will then be crowned by, say, four sheaves with their ears upward, waving in the wind like flags. Very pretty. Any rain that blows into it will run downhill along the sloping straws and onto the ground.

But before the gales of winter blow up, you should get the grain out of the mows and into ricks or stacks, in your stackyard. When working on a fairly small scale, stacks are better circular.

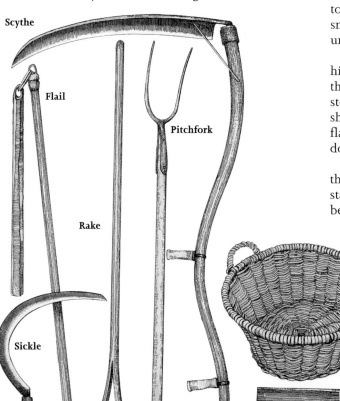

Scythe

Flail

Pitchfork

Rake

Sickle

Winnowing tray

Basket

Grain scoop

HAND TOOLS
Time-honored equipment works well and is adequate for the homesteader. Cutting with a scythe is old-fashioned, honest labor, and it is time-consuming, but it produces better grain than that cut and threshed with a combine. Also, in damp climates grain either has to be dried artificially, or stored hermetically while still moist, in a grain silo or sealed in a polyethylene bag.

Ricks

In ricks, you lay the sheaves horizontally, ears inward, layer after layer, always keeping your center firm and high. Work from the center out this time, and do not pull in as you did with the mow until the eaves are reached. Then pull inward sharply until the apex is reached. You must then thatch this rick (*see* p. 376), or provide it with a waterproof cover, just on top. Grain will keep well in such a rick for years, as long as the rats don't get into it. To keep rats away, you can build a raised platform on staddle stones.

Grain in the stook, mow, or rick is maturing naturally all the time, slowly ripening and drying out, and it is better grain than grain cut and threshed with a combine.

Threshing and winnowing

Next you must thresh your grain. This is the business of knocking the grain out of the ears. You can do this by bashing the ears on the back of a chair, putting them through a threshing drum, beating them with a flail, or driving horses or oxen over them.

A threshing drum is a revolving drum that knocks out the grain. A flail is two sticks linked together: the longer stick, which you hold, may be anything—ash or hickory is fine; the short stick, with which you wallop the grain, is often holly. The link that joins them can be leather, although eelskin was traditionally used for this, as it is very tough. (Eelskin is also excellent for "leather" hinges, by the way.) You try to lay the short stick flat on the ears of the grain.

After you have threshed (or knocked out) the grain, you must winnow it. Traditionally, this is done by throwing the grain, which is mixed up with chaff—broken pieces of ear and straw, thistle seeds, and so on—up into the air in a strong breeze. The light waste blows away, and the grain falls in a heap on the ground. Common sense suggests you do this on a clean floor, or else have a sheet of canvas or something similar on the floor to catch the grain. The chaff (the stuff that blows away) can be mixed with corn and fed to animals. Alternatively, a winnowing machine has a rotating fan that produces an artificial wind to winnow the grain. It also has a number of reciprocating sieves. These extract weed seeds, separate "tail" (small) grain from "head" (large) grain, and thoroughly clean the grain. They can be turned by hand or power.

Storing

When grain has been harvested naturally by the above means, it will keep indefinitely, so long as it is kept dry and away from vermin. You can store naturally dried grain in bins, on a grain floor, in sacks: anything will do, provided rats and mice and other creatures cannot get to it. The processes described above are just the same for wheat, barley, oats, rye, field beans, rice, buckwheat, sorghum, millet, linseed, rapeseed, and many other seed crops.

Harvesting by combine is another kettle of fish. Here the machine cuts the grain and threshes and winnows it in one operation, while moving around the field. It saves an awful lot of labor.

STOOKS
Get your sheaves into stooks quickly or the grain will sprout and rot. Rub two sheaves' heads together so they stick firmly and don't blow down.

MOW
After their initial drying in the stook, you can put your sheaves into a mow. It's quick to build, safe and waterproof.

A CIRCULAR STACK
Lay a base of sheaves with their butts outward, and build up, keeping the center high. Pull inward when you reach the eaves and let them overhang slightly so the rain runs off.

A THATCHED STACK
If your stack is outdoors, a thatch is the most effective protection you can give it. A good thatch will easily last the winter, whereas even strong plastic may tear in a gale. Thatching is described on pp.376–377.

Use rat-proof staddle stones to keep your circular corn stack off the ground, and you will keep out the damp as well as any rats.

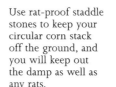

The Cereals

Cereals are the staff of life for most of us. Even our milk and our meat derive largely from them. They are grasses nurtured and bred by people so that their grain is large and nourishing. Except in parts of the tropics where such roots as tapioca and yams are the staple carbohydrate, and in wet, cold places where the potato plugs the gap, wheat, barley, oats, rye, rice, corn, and sorghum are what keep us all alive and kicking.

The cereals have all been bred from wild grasses, and bred so far away from their parent stocks that they are now distinct species. In fact, it is sometimes difficult to guess which wild grass a particular cereal is derived from, and, in some cases—corn, for example—the wild species is now probably extinct.

It was inevitable that the seeds of the grasses should become a humankind's staple food. After all, grass is the most widespread of plants, its seeds copious and nourishing and easily stored. When the Bushmen of the Kalahari find a hoard of grass seed in an ants' nest, stored there by the industrious insects for their future supplies, the Bushmen steal this seed, roast it on a hot stone, and eat it themselves. Our Stone Age ancestors no doubt did the same. And it is but a short step to harvesting the grass oneself and threshing the seed out of it. Then it was found that if you put some of the seed into the ground, in the right conditions, it would grow where you wanted it to. Agriculture was born—and with it civilization. This was made possible by people's ability to grow and store the food they had grown reliably.

Many self-supporters feel that grain growing is not for them: it requires expensive machinery, is difficult, and cannot be done effectively on a small scale. This is just not so. Anyone can grow grain, on no matter how small a scale, provided they can keep the birds off it. Harvesting can be done quite simply with the sickle or even an ordinary carving knife. Threshing can be done over the back of a chair, and winnowing outdoors in the wind. Grinding can be done with a coffee grinder or a small hand-mill. Baking can be done in any household oven. It is very satisfying to eat your own bread baked from grain you have grown and milled yourself, from your own seed.

When the Roman armies wanted to conquer Britain, they waited until harvest time, so that their soldiers could spread out over the country, reap the native wheat, take it back to camp, and make bread out of it. If the Roman legions could do it with such apparent nonchalance, there is no reason why we cannot do it, too.

It is fortunate that grasses are widespread: they grow in practically any climate our Earth affords, and therefore different cultures have been able to find, and adapt, one particular grass to suit each area. So if we live in the wet tropics, we may choose rice; the dry tropics, sorghum; temperate heavy lands, wheat; temperate dry and sandy lands, rye; cold and rainy lands, oats; temperate light land, barley; and so on. There is an improved grass for practically every area and climate in which the human race can survive.

Sorghum
Sorghum vulgare

Rice
Oryza sativa

Corn
Zea mays

Barley
Hordeum distichum

Rye
Secale cereale

Wheat
Triticum vulgare

Durum wheat
Triticum durum

Oats
Avena sativa

Wheat

Ever since our Stone Age ancestors found that they could bang the grass seeds collected by seed-collecting ants between two stones and eat them, we have used cereals for food, and in all those parts of the world where wheat will grow, wheat is the favorite.

Hard and soft wheat

Hard wheat grows only in fairly hot and dry climates, although there are some varieties that are fairly hard even if grown in a colder climate. It is much beloved by commercial bakers because it makes spongy bread, full of holes. It holds more water than soft wheat, and a sack of it therefore makes more bread. In temperate climates, soft wheat grows more readily and makes magnificent bread: a dense bread, perhaps, not full of huge holes, not half water and wind, but bread such as medieval battles were won on.

Sowing

Wheat grows best on heavy loam or even clay soil. You can grow it on light land, and you will get good-quality grain but a poor yield. It will also grow on very rich land, but it must have land in very good condition.

In temperate climates, wheat—and it will be one of the varieties called winter wheat—is often sown in the fall. Winter wheat grows quite fast in the fall, in the summer-warmed soil, then lies dormant throughout the winter, to shoot up quickly in the spring and make an early crop. In the northern United States and Canada, where the winter is too severe, spring wheat is grown, and this is planted in the spring. It needs a good hot summer to ripen it, and will come to harvest much later than winter wheat. If you can grow winter wheat, do so. You will get a heavier crop and an earlier harvest.

I prefer to put winter wheat in very early: even early in September, because it gets off to a quick start, beats the crows more effectively (crows love seed wheat and will eat the last seed if they get the chance), and makes plenty of growth before the frosts set in. Frost may destroy very young wheat by dislodging the soil around its roots. If the early-sown wheat is then "winter proud," as farmers say, meaning too long, graze it off with sheep. Graze it off either in November or in February or March. This will do the sheep good, and will also cause the wheat to tiller (put out several shoots), giving you a heavier crop. You can sow winter wheat in October and sometimes even in November. The later you sow winter wheat, the more seed you should use.

Spring wheat should be sown as early as you can get the land ready and you feel the soil is warm enough. I would say not before the beginning of March, although some people sow it in February. The earlier you sow it, the more you will lose to crows, who have little other food at that time of the year, and the longer it will take to get established. But wheat needs a long growing season, so the earlier you sow it, the better.

In other words, if you don't want a very late harvest, as always in farming, you have to find a compromise between tricky alternatives.

Wheat needs a fairly coarse seed bed—that is, it is better to have the soil in small clods rather than fine powder. For fall-sown wheat, the seed bed should be even coarser than for spring-sown. This is so that the clods will deflect the winter rain and prevent the seed from being washed out and the land becoming like chocolate pudding.

So plow, if you have to plow, shallowly, and then do not work your land down too fine. In other words, do not cultivate or harrow it too much. Aim at a field of clods about as big as a small child's fist. If you are planting wheat after old grassland, plow carefully so as to invert the sod as completely as you can, and then do not bring it up again. Disc the surface, if you have discs, or harrow it with a spring-tined harrow, or an ordinary harrow if you haven't got that. But do not harrow too much. Then drill or sow into that. The earlier you can plow the land before you put the wheat in, the better, so as to give the land a chance to settle.

You can either drill wheat, at a rate of about three bushels of seed to the acre, or else broadcast it at about four bushels to the acre. Whichever way you do it, it is a good thing to harrow it after seeding and also to roll it—that is, if you don't think the rolling will break down the clods too much. If it is wet, don't roll it. Discing is quite good after broadcasting seed, but only do it once: if you do it twice, you will bring the seed up again.

Care of growing crop

You can harrow wheat quite hard when it has started to come up but is not more than 6 inches (15 cm) tall. After you have harrowed it may look as if you have ruined it, but you haven't. You will have killed several weeds but not the wheat, and the harrowing does good by opening up the surface of the ground. If frosts look as if they have lifted the surface of the ground in the early spring, you can roll, preferably with a ring roller, but only if the ground is pretty dry.

Jethro Tull invented a seed drill and developed "horse-hoe husbandry." His idea was to drill wheat and other cereals in rows 12 inches (30 cm) apart (there was much experimentation with distances) and then keep the horse-hoe going up and down between the rows. Very good results were achieved. The practice has been discontinued because developments in husbandry have enabled the farmer to clean his land, meaning free it from weeds, more thoroughly. It is therefore not so necessary to weed the wheat. In any case, a good crop of wheat that "gets away" quickly will smother most weeds on reasonably clean land. Agribusinesses, of course, use selective weed poisons to kill weeds in wheat. I used them only once and have seldom had a crop of any cereal that has suffered badly from weed competition. Selective weed poisons are only necessary to cover up the effects of bad husbandry.

Milling Grain

Modern industrial grain milling is enormously complicated, and aims to remove everything but the pure starch from the flour that is ultimately used for bread. The milling of wholemeal, on the other hand, is very simple: all you do is grind the grain: nothing is taken out and nothing is put in. Wholewheat flour also has more of every beneficial thing, except pure starch (carbohydrate), than white flour has. And wholewheat bread is better for the digestion than white bread because it has roughage. Here is a percentage comparison:

	Protein	Fat	Carbohydrate	Calcium	Iron	Vitamin B1	Riboflavin	Nicotinic acid
White flour	2.3	0.2	15.6	4	0.2	0.01	0.01	0.2
Wholewheat	3.1	0.6	11.2	7	0.7	0.09	0.05	0.6

There are four types of mill for grinding grain. Two of them are of little use to the self-supporter: the hammer mill, which will smash anything up, even feathers, but does not make very good flour; and the roller mill, as used in huge industrial mills, where steel rollers roll against each other and the grain passes between. The other two types—the stone mill and the plate mill—are both suitable for anyone who wants to make their own bread.

Stone milling

The stone mill is one of the oldest and most basic types of mill. It consists of two stones, one of which turns on the other, which remains stationary. The grain is passed between the two, generally being dropped down a hole in the top, or runner stone. The art of milling with stones, and particularly that of millstone dressing—crafting the patterns of "furrows" (channels) and "lands" (raised grinding edges)—has all but died out. The sooner it is revived, the better. However, in response to the new demand for such devices, several firms have put miniature stone mills on the market, both hand- and electrically driven. These make very good flour, and they will grind very fine or coarsely as desired; the finer you grind, the longer it will take.

Plate milling

There are also some good hand-driven plate mills available. A steel plate with grooves cut in it revolves, generally vertically, against a stationary steel plate. Flour ground slowly with one of these seems just as good as stone-ground flour. If you have a tractor or a stationary engine, the ordinary barn plate mill found on nearly every conventional farm is quite satisfactory for grinding bread flour, provided you don't drive it too fast. If it goes too fast it heats the flour (you can feel it coming hot out of the spout). Heating the flour like this spoils the flavor.

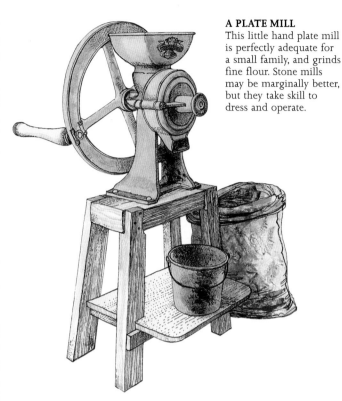

A PLATE MILL
This little hand plate mill is perfectly adequate for a small family, and grinds fine flour. Stone mills may be marginally better, but they take skill to dress and operate.

There is one thing to remember that makes the milling of all grain much easier. That is: dry the grain first. In a warm, dry climate this may not be necessary, but in a damp climate it makes a great difference. When you are nearly ready to grind your wheat, keep it in a jute bag over your stove, or furnace, or dry the day's supply on a tray over the stove, or in a warm oven: anything to get the grain quite dry. Don't cook it, of course. If you mill grain in larger quantities, a brick kiln is not a bad idea, and it is also useful for kilning malt (which I describe later in detail on p.321).

There is no reason why anybody, even somebody living in a 10th-floor apartment, shouldn't buy a small stone or plate mill and a sack of wheat from a friendly farmer, and grind his own flour and make his own bread. Do not believe it when people tell you to do so does not pay. Whenever we have kept accounts about bread-making, we have found it pays very well. You get your bread for considerably less than half of what you would pay at the store, and it is much better bread.

Bread made from freshly ground wheat and baked by home-baking methods is superb bread. You are not interested in trying to sell as much air and water as you can, as is the commercial baker. Your bread will be a lot denser than store-bought loaves, but well-leavened nevertheless, and, if your oven was hot enough, well-cooked. It will take far less of it to feed a hungry man than it takes of store-bought bread, and if you consistently eat your own good bread, you, and your family, will stay healthy and your visits to the dentist will be mere formalities. To see how wheat is harvested, see pp.248–249.

Oats & Rye

OATS

Oats will grow in a damper climate than wheat or barley, and on wetter and more acid land. Thus, it is a staple human food in Scotland, which led English author and philosopher Samuel Johnson to rib his friend Boswell about how in Scotland men lived on what in England was only thought fit to feed to horses. Boswell replied: "Yes—better men, better horses." In North America and Europe, oats tend to be grown in damper, colder places, and often on glacial drift, where the land may be heavy, acid, and not very well drained. Oats and potatoes have enabled people to live in areas where no other crop would have grown.

Sowing oats

In wetter areas, it is most usual to sow spring oats: in drier and warmer areas, winter oats are preferred and give a heavier yield and also are less attacked by frit fly, a common pest of oats. The only trouble with winter-sown oats is that it is likely to be eaten by birds. If it is possible to sow while other people are harvesting their spring-sown crops, it stands a better chance of survival because the birds are tempted by seeds dropped elsewhere. The cultivation of oats is exactly the same as that of wheat.

Harvesting oats

But whereas barley should be allowed to get completely ripe and dry before harvesting, oats should not. There should still be a bit of green in the straw. Oats are far better cut and tied into sheaves with sickle, scythe, reaper, or reaper-and-binder, than they are combined, for combining knocks out and wastes a lot of the grain. When cut and bound, oats should be stooked and then "churched" three times. Churching is the old farmers' way of saying that it should be left standing in the stook for at least three Sundays. The purpose of this is to dry the straw thoroughly, and any grass growing among it, and to dry the grain itself, so that the grain will not go moldy in the stack.

Many old-fashioned farmers, including me, feed oats to horses and cattle "in the sheaf." In other words, we do not thresh the grain out but simply throw animals complete sheaves. One per beast per day during the winter, plus grass, will keep bullocks and dry cows looking fine. The animals eat straw and all. Oat straw, whether threshed or not, is the best of all the straws for feeding: good oat straw is better feed than poor hay. But of course working horses should be fed on the grain alone. You will find more details about feeding horses on p.242.

Milling oats

The Scots, and other sensible people, mill oats thus: They kiln it—that is put it in a kiln (see p.321)—until it is quite dry. It must be completely dried, so they kiln it at quite a high temperature: this is the most important part of the operation. They then pass it between two millstones set at quite a distance apart.

This gently cracks the skin of the oats off. They then winnow it. This blows the skins away and leaves the grain. Finally, they pass it through the stones again, but this time set them closer to grind it roughly, not too fine. This is real oatmeal, and it makes the most delicious oatmeal cookies in the world.

There are two ways of making oatmeal, very different but both equally efficacious. One is sprinkle the meal into boiling water, stirring constantly, and the moment the oatmeal is thick enough for your taste, take it off the heat and eat it. The other is: do the above, but then put the closed pot in a hay-box and leave it overnight. (A hay-box is a box with hay in it.) You bury the pot in the hay when the oatmeal is boiling and, because of the insulation, it cooks all night. Eat it in the morning with milk or cream, and salt—never with sugar, which is a beastly habit, and not what oatmeal is about at all.

RYE

Rye is the grain crop for dry, cold countries with light, sandy soil. It will grow on much poorer, lighter land than the other cereals, and if you live on rough, heathy land, rye might be your best bet. It will thrive in colder winters than other cereals and tolerates acid conditions.

You might like to grow rye to mix with wheat for bread: a mixture of rye and wheat makes very good bread indeed. Rye alone makes a dense, dark, rather bitter bread; it's very nutritious and is eaten in pretty large quantities by the peoples of the Eastern Europe—and it seems to do them good.

Sowing rye

You can treat rye in exactly the same way as the other cereals (see p.252). If you plant it in the fall and it grows very quickly, which it often does, it is very advantageous to graze it off with sheep or cows in the winter, when other green feed is scarce. It will grow back again very quickly and still give you a good crop. It doesn't yield anything like as well as wheat, though, no matter what you do to it.

Rye is often used for grazing off with sheep and cattle only. A catch crop is sown, say, after potatoes have been lifted in the fall. This is grazed off green in the spring during the "hungry gap," when a green bite is very welcome. Then the land is plowed up and a spring crop put in. Its ability to grow well in the winter is thus utilized. One advantage of rye as a winter-sown crop is that it does not seem to be so palatable to birds as other grains. Wheat and oats both suffer badly from members of the crow family: rye seems to escape these thieving birds.

Harvesting rye

Rye ripens earlier than other grains. Cut it when it is completely ripe, and it will not shed much. The straw is good for bedding and is a very good thatching straw. In the past, I have grown rye specifically for thatching.

Barley

Barley has two principal purposes: one is feeding animals and the other is making beer. It doesn't make good bread because the protein in the grain is not in the form of gluten, as it is in wheat, but is soluble in water. It will not, therefore, hold the gases of yeast fermentation and so will not rise like wheat flour will.

You can mix barley flour with wheat flour, though—say, perhaps three to one wheat to barley—and make an interesting bread.

Barley will grow on much lighter and poorer soil than wheat, and it will also withstand a colder and wetter climate, although the best malting barley is generally grown in a fairly dry climate.

Sowing barley

An old saying goes: "Sow wheat in mud and barley in dust!" My neighbor says that the hired hands used to come to his old father and say: "Boss, we must get in the barley seed. The farmer over the valley is doing it."
"Can you see what horses he's using?" said the old man, who couldn't see very well.
"The roan and the gray gelding," they replied.
"Then don't sow the barley," said the farmer.
A few days later the same exchange took place, but when the farmer asked what horses his neighbor was using the men answered: "I can't see them in all the dust."
"Then sow the barley," said the farmer.

Don't take this too literally, but barley does need a much finer seed bed than wheat. There is such a thing as winter-sown barley, but most barley is spring-sown, for it has a much shorter growing season than wheat. It grows so quickly that barley will come to the sickle even if you plant it as late as May, but any time from the beginning of March onward is fine, just so long as the soil is warm and sufficiently dry.

As I explained before, a certain Suffolk farmer used to drop his trousers and sit on the land before he drilled his barley, to see if the land felt warm and dry enough.

Where I used to live we have a festival, in the town of Cardigan, called Barley Saturday. This is the last Saturday in April. We were all supposed to have our barley in by then, and to celebrate there was a splendid parade of stallions through the streets of Cardigan and the pubs stayed open all day.

Barley, particularly for malting for beer, should not have too much nitrogen, but needs plenty of phosphorus, potash and lime. I broadcast barley seed at the rate of four bushels, about 220 pounds (100 kg) to the acre. If I drilled it I would use less: three bushels, or 165 pounds (75 kg).

Drilling it would probably be better, but we haven't got a drill, and, in fact, we get very good results by broadcasting. Of course, after drilling or broadcasting, you harrow and roll just as you do for wheat. Excepting that the seed bed should be finer, the treatment is in fact exactly the same as for wheat, but one tends to sow barley on poorer ground.

Harvesting barley

Harvesting is the same as for wheat. If you harvest it with a combine, it must be thoroughly ripe. They say around here: wait until you think it is dead ripe and then forget all about it for two weeks. An old method of harvesting barley is to treat it like hay, which isn't tied into sheaves but left loose. You turn it around until it is quite dry, then cart it and stack it loose just like hay. You can then just fork it into the threshing machine.

If you do bind it into sheaves, leave it in the stook for at least a week. But however you cut it, do not do so until the ears have all bent over, the grains are hard and pale yellow and shed easily in your hand, and the straw is dry. You can then put it into mows and the straw can be fed to livestock. It is better for feeding than wheat straw, which is useless, but not so good as oats. It is no good for thatching, and not as good as wheat straw for litter or animal bedding.

The grain is the beer-grain *par excellence*, but most of the grain gets fed to pigs and cattle. It can be ground (best for pigs) or rolled (best for cattle). If you haven't got a mill, just soak it for 24 hours. If you want to eat it, try:

Barley soup
This is one of the self-supporter's staple meals, not just a soup. It's warm and nourishing. You can vary the vegetables according to what you've got. Add more carrots if you don't have a turnip, and so on. You need:

2 oz (56 g) washed husked barley
1 lb (0.5 kg) stewing mutton
2½ quarts (2.3 liters) water
1 teaspoon salt
3 or 4 carrots
2 or 3 leeks
3 or 4 onions
1 big turnip or
1 big rutabaga

Put everything in a stewing pot. Season slightly, cover, and simmer for three hours. Stir occasionally to make sure nothing is sticking to the bottom. Take out the meat at the end of the cooking time, remove the bones, and chop the meat into bite-sized lumps. Put them back in the soup. Add chopped parsley if you've got it.

Northumberland barley cakes
If you don't have a chest freezer, these will keep a lot longer than bread. They are like huge, thick biscuits and make a very good between-meal snack. Take:

1 lb (0.5 kg) barley flour
1 teaspoon salt
½ teaspoon bicarbonate of soda
¼ teaspoon cream of tartar
1¼ c (0.3 liters) buttermilk or skim milk

Throw all the ingredients in a mixing bowl and stir into a soft dough. Make this into balls and press them out until they are about 10 inches (25 cm) across and ¾ inch (2 cm) thick. Bake on a griddle until the cakes are brown on one side. Turn over and brown the other side. Serve up cold, cut in pieces and spread with butter.

Barley pastry
This is very light and crumbly and good for fruit pies and tarts, and for the dentist's nightmare and child's delight, molasses tart. Take any shortcrust pastry recipe, substitute barley flour for wholewheat flour and slightly reduce the amount of fat. For example, with 8 ounces (225 g) of barley flour, use 3 ounces (85 g) of fat instead of 4 ounces (115 g). Roll out and cook in the same way as you would pastry made with wheat flour.

Corn

Besides the potato, and that horrible stuff tobacco, the most important contribution the New World has made to the Old is corn. The first white settlers in America called it Indian corn, and this was shortened·to corn, and corn it now is. In England it is called maize, although gardeners also refer to it as sweet corn.

Corn is grown for several purposes. First, for harvesting when the grain is ripe and ready to be ground to make human or cattle food. Second, for harvesting before the ears are ripe, to be boiled, slathered with butter, and eaten as corn on the cob. The grain in the unripe cobs is still soft and high in sugar, because the sugar has not yet turned into starch for storage, but is still in soluble form so that it can move about the plant. Thirdly, corn is grown for feeding off green to cattle in the summertime, long before the grain is ripe, just as if it were grass. Fourthly, it is grown for making silage. This is done when the grain is at what is called the cheesy or "soft dough" stage. To make silage, the stems must be well cut up or crushed, in order that they can be sufficiently consolidated.

Corn will grow to the corn-on-the-cob stage in quite northerly latitudes, but it will not ripen into hard ripe grain (the grain is nearly as hard as flintstones) except in warmish climates. It is always planted in the spring and likes a warm, sunny summer, but not one that is too dry. It will stand considerable drought, and the hotter the sun, the better, but in dry climates it needs some rain or irrigation.

Sowing corn

Corn likes good but light soil: heavy clays are not suitable. It must be sown after the last danger of frost, since it is not at all frost-hardy. So plant one or two weeks after the last probable killing frost. You will need 35 pounds (16 kg) of seed for an acre, sown about 3 inches (13 cm) deep. Space between rows can be from 14 inches (35 cm) to 30 inches (75 cm): do what your neighbors do in this respect and you should be fine. There should be about nine plants to a square yard.

Care of crop

Birds are a terrible nuisance, particularly crows, and will, if allowed, dig up all your seed. Threads stretched about 4 feet (1.2 m) above the ground on posts hinder the crows (as they do you, too, when you want to hoe), and shooting the odd crow and strewing its feathers and itself over the land scares them off for a short time. Crows are a menace and there are far too many of them: the idea put about by crow-lovers that they are not after your seed but after leatherjackets is arrant nonsense, as the most cursory examination of a dead crow's gut will show.

Harvesting

Harvesting ripe cobs by hand, as the homesteader is most likely to do, is delightful work. You walk along the rows, in a line if there are several of you.

You then just rip out the ears and drop them in a sack slung over your shoulder. It's best to trample the straw down with your foot so you can see where you have been (the straw is as high as you are). When you get hungry, why not light a fire of dried corn straw, or sticks, throw some cobs on it, without removing their husks, and when the husks have burned off and the grain is slightly blackened, eat them? They are quite unlike the admittedly delicious sweet corn or corn on the cob and are food fit for a king—or at least a hungry harvester (who presumably has good teeth).

Corn in the garden

In cold latitudes you can grow corn for "sweet corn" in your garden. Plant it under cloches, or else plant it in peat pots indoors and then carefully plant out, pots and all, after the last frost. Or you can plant direct into the ground after the last frost, with two seeds in a station, stations 12 inches (30 cm) apart and 2 feet (60 cm) between rows. Plant in blocks rather than long thin lines because this helps pollination.

Corn likes well-manured ground. Water it if the weather is really dry. Pick it when the silk tassels on the ears go from gold to brown.

Cooking corn

Boil in the husks (at least I do) for perhaps a quarter of an hour. Eat it off the cob with salt and oodles of butter. This is food that I challenge anybody to get tired of. For years we Seymours ate tons of it. It was our staple diet for the whole fall. It is a crop that must be eaten as soon as possible after harvesting: if it is kept, the sugars begin to harden into starch and the fragrant elements of the succulent grains disappear.

Polenta or cornmeal mush

This can be made with ground corn or ground sorghum. It comes from northern Italy and is rather stodgy unless well buttered and cheesed after cooking, but it is quite delicious. You need for six people:

8 oz (228 g) cornmeal
2 teaspoons salt
2½ pints (1.4 liters) water
3 teaspoons grated cheese and butter

Boil the water in a large pan with salt. Then sprinkle in the cornmeal, stirring all the time to prevent lumps. Keep on stirring. After 30 minutes, it is so thick it is leaving the sides of the pan. Don't let it brown on the bottom. Stop cooking and spread it out on a dish. Cover it with blobs of butter and grated cheese, and push it under the broiler for a few minutes. It's very good by itself, and even better served up with fried spicy Italian sausages and plenty of tomato sauce.

Polenta gnocchi

Cook polenta as in the recipe above, but at the end of cooking, stir in two beaten eggs and some grated cheese, and, if you want to make it more exotic, add 4 oz (115 g) of chopped ham as well. Turn it all on to a flat wetted dish and spread it out so that it is about ¼ inch (1 cm) thick.

The next day, cut it into squares, lozenges, or circles about 1½ inches (4 cm) across. Lay these overlapping in a thickly buttered, ovenproof dish. Dot with more butter, heat in the oven or under the broiler, and serve sprinkled with more cheese.

Rice

Rice, before it is milled, is called "paddy" by English-speaking people in Asia. There are for practical purposes two kinds: "wet" rice that grows in water, and "upland" rice growing on open hillsides, but only in places with a very high rainfall, such as the Chin Hills of Burma. Wet (or ordinary) rice is grown on a large scale in the United States and in southern Europe, and there is no doubt that its cultivation could be extended to more northerly latitudes. It will grow and ripen in summer temperatures of over 68°F (20°C), but these must cover much of the four to five months that the crop takes to grow and ripen.

It might well be that some of the upland rice varieties would grow in northern latitudes. The reason why we in the northern latitudes do not attempt to cultivate them may be because we are congenital wheat-eaters and do very well without rice. The wheat-eating peoples of India have a strong sense of superiority over the rice-eaters and look upon rice as food fit only for invalids!

Sowing rice

The best way to grow rice on a small scale is to broadcast the seed on a dry seed bed when the ground has warmed up in the spring, rake it well in, and then flood the seed bed, but only just. As the shoots grow, always try to keep the water level below the tops of the plants. Rice survives in water by virtue of its hollow stem, which takes oxygen down to the rest of the plant.

When the plants are about 8 inches (20 cm) tall, pull them out in bunches and transplant them into shallow standing water in an irrigated field. Simply dab each plant into the soft mud 4 inches (10 cm) away from its neighbors. Billions of paddy plants are planted like this every year in India and China. Keep the paddy field flooded (never let it get dry) until about two weeks before you judge the grain ripe enough to harvest. Then drain the field and let the grain ripen in the dry field.

Harvesting rice

Harvest with a sickle; thresh as you would other grain; "hull" (separate grain from husk) by passing through a plate mill or stone mill with the plates or stones open enough to hull the grain without cracking it; and you are left with "brown rice," that magical food of the yin–yan adherents. It is in fact a good grain, very rich in starch but lower in protein and in several other qualities than wheat.

If you mill the brown rice more closely, you get pearled rice, which is generally and wrongly called polished rice. This is almost pure starch and a very incomplete foodstuff, even less nutritious than white wheat flour (which is saying a lot). A further process, called polishing, produces true polished rice which is what most of us buy at the store. If you live on practically nothing else but pearled or polished rice, you get beri-beri. So the sensible thing to do, if you live on rice, is to eat brown rice and not go to the trouble of removing the bran, which is the most nutritious part of it, and feeding it to the pigs.

Cooking rice

Unlike most other grains, rice does not need grinding before it is cooked. The Western way to cook your own home-milled rice is to wash the grain well in cold water and drain, then bring 2½ cups (0.6 liters) of water to the boil, add a teaspoonful of salt, and throw in 1 cup (170 g) of rice.

Bring this to the boil again and then allow it to simmer by reducing the heat. Cover the pan and simmer for 15 minutes. When the rice is tender, eat it. It will have absorbed all the water.

I personally use the Indian method. To do this, bring much more water than you really need to the boil, throw the rice in, bring to the boil again, allow to simmer until the grain is tender (but not reduced to that horrible rice pudding stuff), which will be in about a quarter of an hour, drain the water off by pouring through a strainer, toss the rice up a few times in the strainer to fluff it, and then eat it. Each grain will be separate if you do this properly and the rice will be perfect.

You can color and flavor rice very nicely by tossing a pinch of saffron into the rice while it is cooking. For brown rice, you need to allow at least 40 to 50 minutes of cooking time.

Wild rice

North American wild rice (*Zizania aquatica*) can be harvested when it is ripe, and dried in the hot sun or else "parched" by heating over a fire or kilning. This can then be boiled or steamed and eaten, preferably with meat. It is very nutritious but very laborious to harvest.

Risotto

This is usually made with rice, as the name implies, but it is very good made with whole millet or with pearl barley. You need:

1 measure grain (1 lb or 0.5 kg should feed 8 to 10 people)
2 measures hot water or good clear stock
a little oil, salt and pepper
a variety of firm vegetables, such as onions, green peppers, peas, carrots, etc.

Use a solid pan with a lid (earthenware is good). Slice the vegetables and lightly fry them in a little oil. Put them aside in a separate dish when they are soft and slightly brown. Put some more oil in the pan and dump in the dry grains. Stir them until they are well-oiled and start to change color.

Put the cooked vegetables back in the pan with half the hot water or stock. Season well. Turn the heat to low, or put the pan in a moderate oven, closely covered, for 15 to 30 minutes. Then add the rest of the broth, stir and cook another 15 to 30 minutes until all the liquid is absorbed, and the grains are soft and tender, but separate. Times vary with the hardness of the grain.

Rice griddle cakes

A good way of using up leftover boiled rice or rice pudding.

1¼ cups (0.3 liters) milk
4 oz (114 g) warm cooked rice
1 tablespoon melted butter or oil
2 eggs, separated
4 oz (115 g) wheat flour and a pinch of salt

Mix the milk, rice and salt. Add the egg yolks, the butter, and the flour, and then stiffly beaten egg whites. Heat a griddle and drop the mixture in spoonfuls onto it. Cook both sides.

Growing Crops for Oil

If you have a small piece of land not taken up with growing food, it is well worth planting some crop that will produce vegetable oil.

CANOLA
Canola will grow in temperate climates. You plant it like kale (*see* p.262) and harvest it when it is still fairly green. Pull the plant out of the ground, dry it in a stack, thresh it, and then crush the seeds to get the oil out. The residual "cake" can be fed to stock, but only in small quantities, since it can upset their stomachs.

FLAX
The seed of the flax plant is linseed, which is very rich in oil, and a good feed for livestock in itself. It is high in protein as well as in fat. If you crush the seed in a mill or scald it in hot water, you will have an excellent food for young calves, a good replacement for milk. This is good for most sick animals, and is fairly laxative. Linseed, mixed with wheat or mixed grain, makes a perfect ration for hens. Since you can grow half a ton to the acre, it is a crop well worth growing. It can be crushed for oil, but the oil is not very edible and is chiefly used in the manufacture of products such as soap, paint, and printer's ink.

I will deal with the production of flax for cloth and fiber on p.368.

SUNFLOWERS
Thirty-five percent of sunflower seed is edible oil, which is good for margarine and for cooking oil. Sow the seed one week before the last likely frost. Plant 12 inches (30 cm) apart in rows three feet (90 cm) apart. Harvest the crop when about half the yellow petals have fallen off the flowers. Cut so that you leave 12 inches (30 cm) of the stem on, and hang upside down in bunches under a roof.

To get the oil out, you will have to crush the seed. Or you can feed the seed directly to poultry at a rate of 1 ounce (28 g) to 2 ounces (56 g) a day, and it is very good for them. You needn't even take the seed from the flowers. Just give them the complete flowers. You can sprout sunflower seeds, then remove the husks and eat them.

POPPIES
In Great Britain, poppies can be grown for oil seed, as well as for more nefarious purposes, but if you try this in the US, where it is illegal, you will attract unwelcome attention from local law enforcement. Up to 50 gallons (180 liters) of oil can be obtained from an acre. It is good cooking oil, burns in lamps with a clear, smokeless flame, and the residual, "cake," after the oil has been removed, makes excellent stock feed.

In a temperate climate, sow the seed in a fine seed bed in April. Sow it fairly thinly—say, 3 inches (8 cm) apart in rows 12 inches (30 cm) apart. Harvest by going along with a sheet, laying it on the ground, and pouring the seed into the sheet. Go back about a week later and do it again.

PRESSING OIL
To obtain oil from crops, the seeds need to be cracked first and then wrapped in cloth to make what are known as "cheeses," which are cheese-shaped bundles. These cheeses are then piled into the press and clamped down. A handle is turned to provide the required pressure.

Or you can thresh the seed out in the barn with a flail. I grew two long rows of poppies once and harvested about a bushel of seed from it, but the kids ate all of it. Whether they got high on it I never found out. My kids seemed to be high most of the time anyway.

Olives and walnuts both make fine oil. You will find details about growing olives on p.172.

Extracting the oil
One primitive method used in hot climates to get the oil out of olives, oil-palm and other oleaginous fruits is to pile the fruit in hot sunlight on absorbent cloth. The oil exudes and is caught by the cloths, which are thereafter wrung out. The process sounds most unsanitary but is effective.

The other nontechnological method is pressing. Before pressing, the seed must be cracked in a mill (plate or stone), or with a mortar and pestle. The cracked seeds are then put in what cider-makers call "cheeses"—packs of crushed seeds wrapped in cloth. The cheeses are piled one on top of the other in a press. The whole pile is then pressed and the oil is exuded. If you don't have a press, rig one up with a car jack. If the cracked seeds are pressed cold, the oil is of better quality than if they are heated first, but there is slightly less of it. The pressed residue is good for stock feed.

Growing Root Crops

In Europe in the Middle Ages there was an annual holocaust of animals. It was impossible to feed all these extra animals during the winter, so most of them were killed in the fall and either eaten then or salted down. Salt meat was about all that medieval man had in the winter or, indeed, until the first lambs could be killed in the early summer. And milk, too, was in very short supply.

The introduction of the turnip changed all this. If a proportion of your land was put down to turnips, you could continue to feed and fatten animals all through the winter, and also keep up the milk yield of your cows. And the turnip was followed by all the other root crops.

With "roots" I am including all those crops known as fodder crops, such as kale, cow cabbages, and kohlrabi, as well as those crops of which the actual roots are the part of the plant that we grow to eat or to feed to our stock. This simplification is justified because all these crops can take the same place in our rotation, and serve the same purpose, which is, broadly, to feed our animals in the wintertime when there is very little grass. And we can eat some of the roots, too.

All these plants have this in common: they store up energy in the summer so they can lie dormant during the winter, and then release this energy early in the spring to flower and produce seed before other, annual, plants are able to do so. They are in fact biennials. We use them by making use of this stored nourishment for our winter feeding.

TURNIPS AND RUTABAGAS
Rutabagas are more nutritious than turnips, and I think they are the better crop to grow. They are also sweeter and pleasanter for you to eat. Rutabagas have a neck, are more frost-hardy than turnips, and store better, being less prone to disease. Turnips yield slightly more.

Both these closely related plants are members of the brassica family, and thus are liable to clubroot, a fungus disease sometimes called "finger-and-toe" in turnips and rutabagas. This is a killer and can reduce your yield very drastically or even to nothing. If your land is infected with it, don't grow turnips and rutabagas.

Sowing turnips and rutabagas
Turnips and rutabagas are sown quite late: rutabagas in May perhaps, and turnips about two weeks later. In very dry and warm areas, it is better to sow later still, for with early sowing in such areas, there is a tendency for "bolting" to occur. Bolting is when the plant skips a year, goes to seed at once, and becomes useless. But turnips and rutabagas are of most use in the wetter, colder areas.

The seeds are small and therefore want a fine seed bed. Get it by plowing in the fall and cross-plowing as early as you can in the spring. Or, if you can't plow in the fall, then plow for the first time as early as you can in the spring and plow again, or rototill, cultivate, and "pull your land about" with whatever tines or discs you may have or can borrow.

Then drill in rows, preferably with a precision drill. This will drop the seeds in one by one at a set interval. If you drill with such a drill at the rate of 1 pound (0.5 kg) an acre, this will be about right, but to do this you must use graded seed. You can buy such seed at a seed store: it is much more expensive than ordinary seed, which you can grow yourself, but because it goes much farther, it is cheaper in the end. In wet climates it is an advantage to sow on raised ridges, which can be made with a "double Tom" or ridging plow.

Singling
If you don't have a precision drill, then drill the seed in rows as thinly as you can and rely on "singling" when the crop has declared itself. Singling means cutting out with a hoe all the little seedlings except one every 9 inches (23 cm). You can't go along with a ruler, because the plants are at all kinds of intervals; you will end up with some closer than nine inches and some farther apart, but broadly speaking, it doesn't matter that much. This singling, of course, cuts out the weeds as well as the surplus plants. You will then have to hand-hoe at least once more, possibly twice, during the growth of the crop, to cut the weeds out in the rows, and you will save labor if you can horse-hoe, or tractor-hoe, several times as well.

Horse-hoeing is a very quick operation and does an enormous amount of good in a short time, but of course, in the end, you will always have to hand-hoe as well because the horse-hoe can't get the weeds between the plants in the rows.

Harvesting turnips and rutabagas
You can leave turnips and rutabagas out in the field until after Christmas if you like, except in areas that have deep snow or very heavy frost. You can feed the roots off to sheep by "folding"—moving the sheep over the crop—every day, giving them just enough to eat off in a day by confining them behind hurdles or wire netting. You will have to go along, however, either before the sheep have been at them, or afterward, and lift the turnips out of the ground with a light mattock. Otherwise the sheep leave half the roots in the ground and they are wasted.

You lift the crop by pulling by hand and twisting the tops off. Then you can clamp them, or you can put them in a root cellar.

MANGELS
Mangels are like huge beets, and crops of 50 tons of them to the acre are perfectly possible. Scientists say they are nearly all water. But experienced farmers answer to this is: "Yes—but what water!" For they know that the moment you start feeding mangels to cows, the yields of milk will go up.

Mangels are not suitable for humans to eat, but they make good wine. They are grown more in warmer, drier places than turnips are, but they are pretty hardy.

Sowing mangels

It is best, especially on heavy land, to plow for mangels the previous fall. You must then work the land down to a good seed bed in the spring, and then drill at the rate of 10 pounds (4.5 kg) of seed to the acre as near the first of April as you are able.

If it is a cold, wet season you may not be able to get a seed bed till May, but it is not much good sowing the crop after the end of May: better to sow turnips instead. Drill in rows about 22 inches (56 cm) apart and single out to about 10 inches (25 cm) apart in the rows. Then hoe and horse-hoe as for turnips.

Harvesting mangels

Lift in the fall before heavy frosts set in, top, and put in little heaps covered with their own leaves until you can cart and clamp. In the old days farmers used to slice the mangels in machines. Now we know that cattle can do it just as well with their teeth. Don't feed mangels too soon: not until after New Year's Day. They are slightly poisonous until mature.

FODDER BEET

Fodder beets are very similar to mangels, but smaller and far more nutritious. They are very high in protein, and are excellent for pigs, cows, or even horses. Personally I think they are a better crop. Sow and thin exactly like mangels, but thin to 8 inches (20 cm).

To harvest: break the taproots with a beet-lifter or break out with a fork before you pull. Top with a knife, put in small piles, cover with leaves against frost, and cart to clamp when ready.

CARROTS
Sowing carrots

Carrots need a fine seed bed just like turnips, and not too much fresh muck: it makes them fork. Carrots will not thrive on an acid soil, so you may have to lime. Sow them in rows 12 inches (30 cm) apart, or up to 18 inches (45 cm) if you intend to horse-hoe a lot, and sow the seed as thinly as you can. You should then be able to avoid singling, but the crop takes a great deal of labor in hand-weeding, since it grows very slowly—far slower than the weeds, in fact.

Harvesting carrots

In places with mild winters you can leave the crop in the ground until you want it, but if you fear hard frosts, lift it by easing out with a fork and then pulling. Twist the tops off; don't cut them. Then clamp or store in sand.

It is really too laborious a crop to grow for stock feeding, but it does make very good stock feed, particularly for pigs. You can fatten pigs on raw carrots and a very little high protein supplement as well, and they will live on just raw carrots. And, of course, they are an excellent human food: very rich in vitamin A.

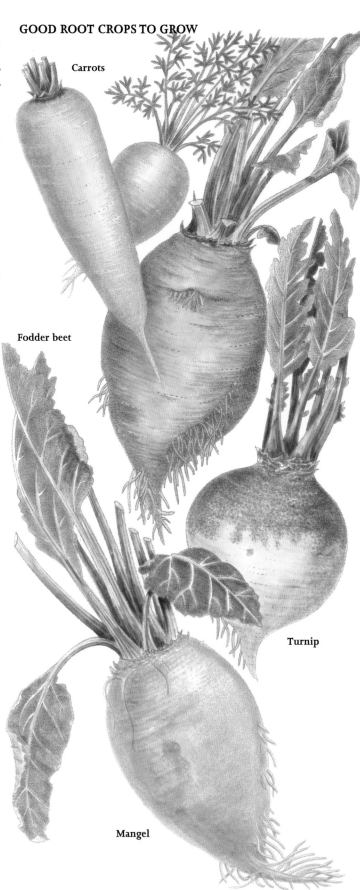

GOOD ROOT CROPS TO GROW

Carrots

Fodder beet

Turnip

Mangel

Cow cabbage

Kale

Kohlrabi

Field beans

White mustard

Jerusalem artichoke

Potatoes

KALE

The most common of the myriad kales are: marrowstem, thousand-headed, rape kale, and kohlrabi. There are lots of other curious kales around the world.

Sowing kale

Drill in rows about 20 inches (50 cm) apart, or broadcast, but drilling gives a better yield, and if you have a precision drill you save seed. Sow 2–4 lb (1–2 kg) of seed per acre. Drill most kales early in April, but drill marrowstem in May so that it doesn't get too woody. Thin and hoe in rows and you will get a heavier crop, especially of marrowstem kale. Kale likes plenty of manure.

Harvesting kale

You can fold kale off in the winter. It is more used for folding to cows than to sheep—it is a marvelous winter feed for milking cows. Let the cows onto it a strip at a time behind an electric fence. Or you can cut it with a sickle and cart it to feed to cows indoors. Use marrowstem first, and leave hardier kales until after the New Year. After you have cut or grazed off a field of kale, the pigs will enjoy digging up the roots. Or you can just plow in.

RAPE

Rape is like rutabaga but has no bulb forms. It is good for folding to sheep or dairy cows. It can be sown (generally broadcast, not drilled) in April for grazing off in August, or it can be sown as a catch crop after an early cereal harvest to be grazed off in the winter, but then it won't be a very heavy crop. Rape has too hot a taste for humans, so you can't eat it as a vegetable, although a little might flavor a stew.

COW CABBAGES

These are very similar to ordinary cabbages. Establish them like kale, or if you have plenty of labor, you can grow them in a seed bed and transplant them out by hand in the summer. This has the advantage that you can put them in after, say, peas or beans or early potatoes, and thus get two crops in a year: a big consideration for the self-supporter. You can get a very heavy crop, but remember that cow cabbages like good land and plenty of manure.

You can clamp cow cabbages, and they make splendid human food too, especially sauerkraut (see p.309). All the above brassica crops are subject to clubroot, and must not be grown too often on the same land.

MUSTARD

There are two species: *Brassica alba* and *Brassica juncea*, white and black mustard. They can be grown mixed with rape or grown alone for grazing off with sheep; or grown as a green manure to be plowed into the land; or harvested for seed, which you can grind, mix with a little white wheat flour, and moisten as required to produce the mustard that goes so well with sausages.

Remember that mustard is part of the cabbage tribe, though, and is therefore no good for resting the land from clubroot. I would never grow it as green manure for that reason. It is not frost-hardy.

Cleaning crops

It must be understood that all the aforementioned crops (except rape and mustard when these are broadcast and not drilled in rows) are cleaning crops, and thus of great value for your husbandry. Because they are grown in rows it is possible to horse-hoe and hand-hoe, and this gives an opportunity to get rid of weeds. So, although you may think that the growing of these row crops is very hard work, remember that it is hard work that benefits every other crop that you grow, and I would suggest that you grow a crop in every four years of your arable rotation.

POTATOES

Where potatoes grow well, they can be, with wheat, one of the mainstays of your diet, and if you have enough of them you will never starve. They are our best source of storable vitamin C, but most of this is in the skins, so don't peel them. You can even mash them without peeling them.

Seed potatoes

For practical purposes, and unless we are trying to produce a new variety and therefore wish to propagate from true seed, potatoes are always grown from potatoes. In other words, we simply plant the potatoes themselves. This is known as vegetative reproduction, and all the potatoes in the world from one variety are actually the same plant. They aren't just related to each other: they *are* each other.

We can keep our own "seed," therefore, from one year to the next, but there is a catch here. The potato is a plant from the high Andes, and grown at sea level in normal climates, it is heir to various insect-borne virus diseases. After we have planted our potato "seed" (tubers) year after year for several "generations," there will be a buildup of virus infections and our potatoes will lose vitality. Hence we must buy seed potatoes from people who grow it at high altitudes, or on windswept sea-islands, or in other places without the aphids that spread these diseases. An altitude of over 800 feet (245 m) is usually enough for growing seed potatoes: in India most seed comes from Himachayal Pradesh, from altitudes of over 6,000 feet (1,830 m).

The cost of seed potatoes now is enormous, and anybody who has land over 800 feet (245 m) would be well advised to use some of it for growing seed. In any case, many more of us ought to save the smallest of our tubers for "once-grown seed" or even "twice-grown seed." After we have carried on our own stock for three years, however, it will probably pay to import fresh seed from seed-growing areas rather than risk the spread of disease.

EARLY POTATOES

Potatoes that grow quickly and are eaten straight from the ground and not stored are called "early potatoes." To grow them you should chit, or sprout, them. They should be laid in shallow boxes, in weak light (not in total darkness, for that makes them put out weak, gangly sprouts) at a temperature between 40°F (4°C) and 50°F (10°C). A cold greenhouse is generally all right.

It is an advantage to give them artificial light to prolong their "day" to 16 hours out of the 24. This keeps the "chits" green and strong and less likely to break off when you plant the potatoes.

Planting early potatoes

Beware of planting too early, for potatoes are not frost-hardy, and if they appear above the ground before the last frost, it will nip them off. On a small scale you can guard against this to some extent by covering them with straw, or muck, or compost, or cloches. If they do get frosted one night, go out early in the morning and water or hose the frost off with cold water. This will actually often save them.

Plant earlies by digging trenches 9 inches (23 cm) deep and 2 feet (60 cm) apart, and putting any muck, compost, or green manure that you might have in the trenches. Plant the spuds on top a foot (30 cm) apart, and bury them.

Actually, you will get the earliest early new potatoes if you just lay the seed on the ground and then ridge earth over them—about 5 inches (13 cm) deep is ideal. You couldn't do this with main crop potatoes because they grow so large and numerous that they would burst out of the sides of the ridges and go green.

Potatoes go green if the light falls on them for more than a day or two, and they then become poisonous: green potatoes should never be eaten nor fed to stock. The fruit of the potato plant, and the leaves, are highly poisonous, being rich in prussic acid.

Potatoes are usually planted by dropping them straight on muck, then earthing them up. But more people are now plowing the muck in the previous fall. Twenty tons of muck per acre is not too much. And always remember that potatoes are potash-hungry.

Nonorganic farmers use "artificial" potash: organic ones use compost, seaweed, or a thick layer of freshly cut comfrey leaves. Plant the spuds on top of the comfrey; as the leaves rot, the potato plants help themselves to the potash that they contain.

Harvesting early potatoes

You might get a modest five tons to the acre of early potatoes, increasing the longer you leave them in the ground; but if they make part of your income, the earlier you lift them, the better.

When your crop is ready, you have the choice of either forking potatoes out, plowing them out, or lifting them with a potato-lifter.

MAIN CROP POTATOES

The potato plant has a limited growing season, and when this ends, it will stop growing. So it is best to let your main crop potatoes grow in the most favorable time of the year. This means the summer, and it is not advisable to plant them too early. Plant them in April and you should be fine.

Planting main crop potatoes

If you use bought seed, you can be a bit sparing with the amount: perhaps a ton an acre; where you are using your own seed, perhaps a ton and a half. Main crop potatoes should be planted 14 inches (35 cm) apart, in rows 28 inches (70 cm) apart if the seed averages 2½ ounces (70 g). If the seed is smaller, plant it closer: if it is bigger, plant it farther apart. You will get the same yield either way. If you plant by hand you can control this very accurately. Ideally seed potatoes should go through a 1¾-inch (5-cm) riddle and be stopped by a 1½-inch (4-cm) one. Anything that goes through the latter is a "chat," and goes to the pigs.

If you have a ridging plow, horse-drawn or tractor drawn, put the land up into ridges. Put muck or compost between the ridges if you have it, although it would be better if you had spread it on the land the previous fall. Plant your seed in the furrows by hand and, if you lack the skill or equipment to split the ridges—and it takes some skill—do not despair. Simply harrow or roll the ridges down flat. This will bury the potatoes. After about two weeks, take your ridging plow along again, and this time take it along what were, before you harrowed them flat, your ridges. So you make what were your ridges furrows, and what were your furrows ridges.

If you don't have a ridging plow, use an ordinary plow. Plow a furrow, plow another one next to it, and drop your potatoes in that. Plow another furrow, thus burying your potatoes, and plow another furrow and drop potatoes in that. In other words, plant every other furrow. Don't worry if your planted rows aren't exactly 28 inches (70 cm) apart. Potatoes know nothing of mathematics.

Care of main crop potatoes

Drag the ridger through once or twice more, whenever the weeds are getting established. This not only kills the weeds, it earths up the spuds, gives them more earth to grow in, and stops them from getting exposed and going green. If you haven't got a ridging plow, and are skillful, you can ridge up with a single-furrow plow.

Go through the potatoes with the hand-hoe at least once to kill the weeds in the rows, but after you have done this, and thus pulled down the ridges, ridge them up again. Up to 10 days after planting, you can harrow your potato field to great advantage to kill weed seedlings, but after that take care, because you might damage the delicate shoots of the potatoes. It's all a matter of common sense. You want to suppress the weeds and spare the spuds. When the potatoes meet over the rows, they will suppress the weeds for you and you can relax, but not completely, because of blight.

Blight

Blight is the disease that affected the Irish potato crop in 1846 and caused the deaths of 2 million people by killing their only source of food. You can be as organic as you like, but if it is a blight year, you will still get blight. However, if you do get blight, don't despair; you will still get a crop, since the virulent strain that starved the Irish has passed now. But your crop won't be such a big one.

You will know you have blight if you see dark green, water-soaked patches on the tips and margins of the leaves. If you see that, spray immediately, for although you cannot cure a blighted plant by spraying, you can at least prevent healthy plants from being infected. These patches soon turn dark brown and get bigger, and then you can see white mold on them.

Within two weeks, if you do nothing about it, your whole field will be blighted and the tops will simply die and turn slimy. The better you have earthed up your ridges, the fewer tubers will be affected, for the blight does not travel down inside the plant to the potatoes but is washed down into them by rain.

Commercial farmers spray the blighted tops with concentrated sulfuric acid, or else some of the newer chemicals. This burns them off and the blight spores do not get down to the potatoes. On my farm, I cut the tops off with a sharp sickle (it has to be sharp, or else you simply drag the spuds out of the ground when you cut) and burn them. Don't lift your spuds for at least two weeks, preferably longer, after the tops have been removed. This is so that they don't come in contact with blighted soil.

But, of course, you will never get blight, for you will have sprayed your "haulms" (tops) with Bordeaux or Burgundy mixture, or one of the modern equivalents, before the first blight spore settled on your field, won't you? To make a Bordeaux mixture, dissolve 4 pounds (1.8 kg) copper sulfate in 35 gallons (160 liters) of water in a barrel, or in plastic garbage cans. Then slowly slake 2 pounds (1 kg) freshly burned quicklime with water and make it into 6 gallons (23 liters) of "cream." Slowly pour the "cream" through a sieve into the copper sulfate solution. Make sure that all your copper has been precipitated by putting a polished knife blade in the liquid. If it comes out coated with a thin film of copper, you must add more lime.

Burgundy mixture is stronger and more drastic. It has 12½ pounds (5.7 kg) washing soda instead of lime. These mixtures must be used fresh, because they won't keep long. Spray with a fine spray very thoroughly. Soak the leaves above and below. All the spray does is prevent spores from getting in. Do it just before the haulms meet over the rows, and again perhaps a week later. An alternative is to dust with a copper lime dust when the dew is on.

Blight attacks vary in date: it strikes during warm, moist, muggy weather, and in some areas, agricultural departments issue blight warnings.

If you do get muggy weather when your potatoes are pretty well grown, spray for blight. You will get half as big a crop again as if you didn't. You can help prevent blight by not allowing "rogue" potatoes to grow: in other words, lift every single potato from your fields after harvest, for it is these rogues that are the repositories of blight. Pigs will do this job for you better than anything else in the world; they will enjoy doing it and they will fertilize the land, too.

Harvesting main crop potatoes

Harvest as late as you can before the first frosts, but try to do it in fine weather. Fork them out, plow them out, spin them out, or get them out with an elevator digger, but get them out. Leave them a day or half a day in the sun after lifting for the skins to set. Don't give them more than a day and a half or they will begin to go green.

Storing main crop potatoes

Clamping (see p.299) is fine. Stacking in a dark shed, or a dark root cellar, is okay. The advantage of clamping is that if there is blight or any other disease in your potatoes, you don't get a buildup of the organisms as you would in a permanent building. Do what your neighbors do.

In intensely cold winters, clamping may not be possible: no clamp will stop the frost, and potatoes cannot stand much frost or they will rot. But if they are too warm, they will sprout. If possible, they like it just above freezing.

JERUSALEM ARTICHOKES

Since a very few plants of these would give us more tubers than we would care to eat, they are seldom grown on a field scale, except by a few wise people who grow them to be dug up and eaten by pigs. They are wonderful for this purpose, and provided the pigs have enough of them, they will do very well on Jerusalem artichokes alone and a little skim milk or other concentrated food; ½ pound (0.2 kg) a day of "pig nuts," plus unrestricted rooting on artichokes, should be enough for a dry sow.

Sowing Jerusalem artichokes

Drop them in plow furrows 12 inches (30 cm) from each other; the furrows should be 3 feet (90 cm) apart. Put them in any time after Christmas, if the land is not frozen or too wet, and any time up to April. It doesn't much matter when, in fact. They won't grow until the warmer weather comes anyway, and then they will grow like mad.

They will smother every imaginable weed, and after the pigs have rooted them up, the land will be quite clean and well manured, too. But beware: pigs will never get the very last one, and next year you will have plenty of "rogues" or "volunteers." In fact, if you leave them, you will have as heavy a crop as you had the year before. I sometimes do, but never for more than two years running. They will grow in practically any soil and don't need special feeding, though they like potash. If you just put them into the ground and leave them, they will grow whatever you do.

BEANS

Beans can be distinguished from peas and the other legumes because they have a square, hollow stem instead of a round, solid one. There are hundreds of kinds and varieties of beans throughout the world. The various kinds of "runner" (pole) beans—scarlet runners, french beans, snap beans, and so on—are seldom grown on a field scale, so I will deal with them as garden vegetables (*see pp.87–140*).

FIELD BEANS

The crop that supplied most of the vegetable protein for the livestock of northern Europe and North America for centuries, and which should still do so today, is the field bean, tic bean, horse bean, or cattle bean: *Vicia faba*. This is a most valuable crop, and it is only neglected nowadays because vast quantities of cheap protein have flooded into the temperate zones from the developing world. As the people of the latter decide to use their own protein, which they sadly need, temperate-zone farmers will have to discover the good old field bean again.

It produces very high yields of very valuable grain, and it enriches the soil in two ways: it is a legume, and therefore takes nitrogen from the air, and it forms deep taproots that go down and bring up nutrients, and themselves rot down afterward to make magnificent humus. It is a most beneficial crop to grow, good for the land, and gives excellent yields of high-protein grain. As with other grains, there are two kinds of field bean—winter and spring—though farmers classify beans as "grain" or "corn."

Soil

Beans don't need added nitrogen, but they do benefit greatly from a good dressing of farmyard manure, plowed in as soon as possible after the previous crop has been harvested. In land already in good condition, they will grow without this. They need lime, though, as do all the legumes, and if your land needs, it you must apply it. They need potash very badly and phosphates to a lesser degree. Nonorganic farmers frequently apply 80 units of phosphorus and 60 units of potash, but we are more likely to rely on good farming and plenty of muck.

The seed bed need not be too fine, particularly for winter-sown beans. In fact, a coarse seed bed is better for the latter because the clods help to shelter the young plants from the wind throughout the winter. In very cold climates, you cannot grow winter beans, because very hard frost will kill them. You will get heavier crops from winter beans than from spring ones, less trouble from aphids, a common pest of the crop, but possibly more trouble from chocolate spot, a nasty fungus disease.

Sowing beans

You can sow with a drill, if you have one and it is adapted to handle a seed as big as the bean, or you can drop the seed in by hand behind the plow. Plow shallowly— 4 inches or (10 cm)—and drop the seed in every other furrow, allowing the next one you plow to cover them over. I find this method very satisfactory, since the seed is deep enough to defy the birds. Jays will play havoc with newly sown beans, simply pulling the young plants out of the ground.

Care of crop

By all means hoe beans. Horse-hoe or tractor-hoe between the rows and try, if you can, to hand-hoe at least once in the rows. Beans are a crop that can easily suffer from weeds.

Harvesting beans

Wait until the leaves have fallen off the plants and the hilum, or point of attachment of the pods to the plant, has turned black. Cut and tie the crop with a binder if you have one. If not, cut with a sickle and tie into sheaves. You have to use string for this because bean straw is difficult to tie with. Stook and leave in the stook until the crop feels perfectly dry (maybe a week or two). Then stack, and cover the stack immediately, either by thatching it or with a rick cover, or else stack it indoors. A bean stack without a cover will not keep the rain out, and if it gets wet inside, the beans will be no good to you.

Threshing beans

Do not thresh until the beans have been in the stack at least four months. Many farmers like to leave the stack until the next winter before they thresh it, because beans are better for stock after they are a year old. Thresh just as you would for wheat—that is, with a flail or in a threshing drum.

Feeding to animals

Grind or crack the beans before feeding. Mix them in as the protein part of your ration. Horses, cattle, pigs, sheep, and poultry all benefit from beans. Cattle will pick over the straw and eat some of it. What they leave makes marvelous litter (bedding) and subsequently splendid manure.

SOYBEANS

Soybeans are grown in vast acreages in China and the United States in the warmer latitudes. They don't work in the northern regions, and we must wait until a hardier variety is bred, if it can be, before we can grow them in these areas.

In climates where they can be grown, sow or drill them well after the last possible frost about an inch (2.5 cm) deep, 10 inches (25 cm) apart in the rows and with the rows 3 feet (90 cm) apart. Keep them well hoed, because they grow very slowly at first. Their maturing time can be anything from three to five months, depending on the climate. If you need to, you can extend the season by covering them with glass or plastic. If you pick them young, you can eat the pods whole. Otherwise, shell them for the three or four beans inside. The same instructions apply to lima beans.

Grass & Hay

By far the most important, and the most widespread, crop grown in the world is grass. Its ubiquitousness is amazing: it grows from the coldest tundra to the hottest tropics, from the wettest swampland to all but the driest desert. In areas where it only rains once every five or 10 years, grass will spring up within days of a rainstorm and an apparently barren and lifeless land will be green. This is why grass has been called "the forgiveness of nature."

All the cereals are, of course, grasses: just grasses that have been bred for heavy seed yields. Sugar cane is grass, and so is bamboo, but when farmers speak of grass, they means the grass that grows on land and provides grazing for their animals, and can be stored in the form of hay and silage.

Now the confusion here is that what the farmer calls "grass" is actually a mixture of all sorts of plants, as well as grass. Clover is the most obvious and important one, and most "grassland" supports a mixture of grass and clover, and very often clover predominates over grass. Therefore, whenever I write of "grass," I would ask the reader to know that I mean "grass and clover." Grass itself, too, is not just grass. There are many species of grass, and many varieties among the species, and it is of the utmost importance which species you grow.

Managing grassland

You can influence the makeup of the grass and clover species on your grassland by many means. For example, you can plow land up and reseed with a chosen mixture of grass and clover seeds. But these will not permanently govern the pasture. According to how you manage that grassland, some species will die out, others will flourish, and what the farmer calls "volunteer" grasses—wild grasses from outside—will come in and colonize. But essentially, the management of the grassland will decide what species will reign.

If you apply heavy dressings of nitrogen to grassland, you will encourage the grass at the expense of the clover. If you go on doing this long enough, you will eventually destroy the clover altogether. The reason for this is that normally the clover only survives because it has an unfair advantage over the grasses. This advantage is conferred by the fact that the clover has nodules containing nitrogen-fixing bacteria on its roots and can thus fix its own nitrogen. The grasses cannot. So in a nitrogen-poor pasture, the clovers tend to predominate. Apply a lot of nitrogen and the grasses leap ahead and smother the clover. Alternatively, if you put a lot of phosphate on land, you will encourage the clovers at the expense of the grass. Clover needs phosphate: grass nothing like so much. Clover-rich pasture is very good pasture and it also gives you free nitrogen.

If you constantly cut grassland for hay, year after year, and only graze the "aftermath" (what is left after you have cut the field for hay), you will encourage the coarse, large, vigorous grasses like perennial ryegrass and cocksfoot, and you will ultimately suppress the finer grasses and clover, because these tall coarse grasses will shade them out. On the other hand, if you graze grassland fairly hard, you will encourage clover and the short tender grasses at the expense of the tall coarse ones. If your land is acid you will get grasses like bent grass, Yorkshire fog, mat grass, and wavy hair grass that have poor feeding value. Lime that land heavily and put phosphate on it and you will, with the help of mechanical methods, too, and perhaps a bit of reseeding, get rid of these poor grasses and establish better ones. If land is wet and badly drained, you will get tussock grasses, rushes, and sedges. Drain it and lime it, and you will get rid of these. Vigorous and drastic harrowing improves grass. It is good to do it every year.

Topping off

People frequently ask me how they can get rid of tiresome weeds such as docks and thistles that often ruin grassland. Well, as with so many things in life, the motto is "prevention is better than cure." There are two vital things you should remember about docks and thistle: first, don't let them seed, and second, they hate being regularly cut down. The practice known as "topping off" deals with both and is most definitely an important grassland maintenance routine.

To top off a field you simply cut everything down frequently to a height of about 9 inches (23 cm). I do this with a scythe, and it makes a pleasant job on a breezy July day. Topping off is normally done in July, when thistles and docks are fully grown but have not yet set viable seed. You can buy or borrow special mowers for topping off, and over a period of time this will eliminate the large weeds and encourage tender, shorter grasses.

Improving old pasture

You may inherit grass in the form of permanent pasture that has been pasture since time immemorial. Often this is extremely productive, and it would be a crime to plow it up. But you can often improve it by such means as liming, phosphating, adding other elements that happen to be short, drastic harrowing (really ripping it to pieces with heavy spiked harrows), subsoiling, draining if necessary, heavy stocking and then complete resting, alternately grazing it and haying it for a season, and so on.

Now if you inherit a rough old piece of pasture, or pasture that, because of bad management in the past, is less than productive, the best thing to do may be to plow it up and reseed it.

THE BALANCED PASTURE
Some of these plants are almost certain to be found in a good pasture.
Left to right, top row: **1** Meadow fescue (*Festuca pratensis*);
2 Perennial rye-grass (*Lolium perenne*); **3** Cocksfoot (*Dactylis glomerata*);
4 Timothy (*Phleum pratense*); **5** Italian rye-grass (*Lolium multiflorum*).
Bottom row: **6** Burnet (*Sanguisorba officinalis*); **7** Alfalfa (*Medicago sativa*)
8 Red clover (*Trifolium pratense*); **9** Ribwort plantain (*Plantago lanceolata*).

One way to plow up is to "direct reseed it"—that is, plow it and work it down to a fine seed bed, sprinkle grass and clover seed on it, harrow it, roll it, and let it get on with it. You can do this, according to the climate in your locality, in spring, summer, or fall. What you need is cool, moist weather for the seed to germinate and the plants to get established. Or you can plow up, sow a "nurse crop" and sprinkle your grass seed in with it. The nurse crop can be any kind of grain or, in some cases, rape. When you harvest the grain you will be left with a good strong plant of grass and clover.

Seed mixture

As for what "seed mixture" to use when establishing either a temporary ley, which is grassland laid down for only a year or so, or permanent pasture, go to your neighbors and find out what they use. Be sure to get as varied a mixture as you can, and also include, no matter what your neighbors say about this, some deep-rooting herbs. Ribgrass, plantain, yarrow, alfalfa, and burnet are ideal deep-rooting herbs for your seed mixture. You can rely on them on to bring fertility up from down below, to feed your stock in droughts when the shallower-rooting grasses and clovers don't grow at all, and to provide stock with the minerals and vitality they need. On deep, lightish land, alfalfa by itself, or else mixed with grasses and clovers, is splendid, for it sends its roots deep down below. What if it does die out after a few years? It has done its good by bringing nutriments up from the subsoil and by opening and aerating the soil with its deep-searching roots.

HAY

Grass grows enormously vigorously in the first months of the summer, goes to seed if you don't eat it or cut it, then dies down and becomes pretty much useless.

In the winter, in northern climates, grass hardly grows at all. In more temperate climates, though, it may grow pretty well for 10 months of the year provided it is not allowed to go to seed.

Now, there are two ways of dealing with this vigorous summer spurt: you can crowd stock on the grass to eat it right down, or you can cut the grass and conserve it. The way to conserve it is to turn it into hay or into silage. You can then feed it to stock in the winter.

Hay is a more practical proposition for the average self-supporter. You should get two tons of good hay off an acre of good grass. The younger you cut grass for hay, the less you will have of it but the better it will be. Personally, I generally cut hay before my neighbors, have less, feed less, but the cattle do better on it. In France and in places where a very labor-intensive but highly productive peasant agriculture prevails, grass is cut very young, made into hay very quickly, and then the grass is cut again, maybe three or four times, during the season. The resulting hay is superb—better than any silage—but the labor requirement is high.

Haymaking

To make hay: cut the grass before, or just after, it reaches the flowering stage. If it has begun to go to seed you will get inferior hay. Then pull it around. Fluff it up and keep turning it. Let the wind get through it and the sun get at it. If you are very lucky it may be dry enough to bale, or, if you are making it loose, to cock, in three days. Then bale it or cock it and thank God. The chances are, in any uncertain climate, that you will get rain on it, which is always bad for it, and then you have the job of turning it again to get it dry again. In bad years you may have to go on doing this for weeks, and your hay will be practically useless for feed when you finally get it in.

HAYCOCKS AND TRIPODS

A haycock (far right) is a pile of hay, solid but loose enough to allow air to circulate. Another method of drying, which is particularly useful in wet climates, is the tripod. Take three light poles, say 6 ft (1.8 m) high each. Hold them together and tie a loop of string or cord very loosely around them near one end. Stand them up and make a tripod of them. Tie two or three strands of string or wire right around the tripod to hold the hay. Pile hay up around the sides, starting from a small circular base, keeping the outside walls as vertical as you can, and then bury the tripod completely with grass, rounding off the top nicely. Use bent tin to make air vents at ground level. There must be at least one on the windward side.

Haymaking hints

Even for small pieces of grass in the garden there will be opportunities to make useful hay. Each year we make a good hayshed full from our orchard,, and this is done totally by hand with scythe and fork. We learned a very useful trick from friends in Austria and that is how to carry a huge bundle of dry hay with using a doubled-up length of rope. You simply lay the rope out on the ground and pile your hay on top with a fork. When you have sufficient for a strong man to carry, you take the two loose ends of the rope over the top and put them through the loop, which is at the other side of the heap. When you pull on the free ends they tighten up the whole loop around your bundle and you sling it over your shoulder and march promptly to the hayshed. I will warn you now that haymaking like this is a scratchy and ticklish operation, since all the bugs in the world seem to love to rest in the new hay.

One of the pleasures of orchard haymaking is watching the chickens follow the scythe. The birds very quickly realize that under the newly cut swathe they will find a wonderfully varied selection of insect life. And by scything the orchard regularly you will, of course, keep all nasty weeds like nettles and docks well under control. You may even get two cuts of hay in a good year.

Cocking

A cock is a pointed-topped dome of hay that you build with a fork. It sheds most of the rain and allows a certain amount of in-cock drying, but if the grass is too green, or wet from rain, you may have to pull the cocks open again and spread the hay around to dry. Then, if rain threatens, throw it up in the cock again. If you are worried about too much moisture in hay that you have cocked, thrust your hand deep inside. If the hay in there is hot, or feels wet and clammy, you must spread that hay out and dry it again. You can only stack it when it is dry enough—that is, when it is no longer bright green and feels completely dry.

Baling

A bale is a compact block of hay that has been rammed tight and tied with string by a machine called a baler. You mustn't bale hay until you are sure it is dry enough. If you bale when it isn't dry it will heat in the bale and the hay will be spoiled. Once the hay is baled there is nothing you can do with it. Just get those bales inside as soon as you can: they will shed a certain amount of light rain. But once rain gets into them you have had it—spoiled hay.

A word here about the modern trend toward huge, round bales. These are fit for brutish giants and indeed can only be handled effectively by noisy diesel tractors with hydraulic lifting gear. We have found it is often difficult to buy in anything other than the big round bales these days because the old square balers are almost extinct. What you can do if this is the case in your area is to use your trailer sensibly to carry one bale at a time. Make sure, of course, it is well tied down in the trailer. When you get this home,

you have to have a setup where you (and a couple of strong friends) can roll it right into your hayshed. Once there you can pull out the miles of string used in its construction and feed it in the normal way.

Machines for hay

There is a great armory of machines, both tractor and animal-drawn, for dealing with hay. There are machines for tedding (fluffing up), windrowing (gathering together into long loose rows), turning (turning the windows over) and raking. But all you need if you don't have too much hay, or have enough labor, are some wooden handled rakes and some pitchforks. You can make the best hay in the world with just these. You can ted the hay with the pitchforks, rake it into windrows, then rake three or four windrows together, cock these with the forks, load the cocks on to a cart with the forks, and ultimately stack it. Haymaking in summer-wet climates is always a gamble; a triumph if you win, and something to put up with if you lose.

Tripoding

In wet climates the tripod is a useful means of drying wet hay. Grass that has only had maybe a couple of days of air drying can be tripoded, even if it looks quite green, for the air continues to get through it in the tripod. I have seen hay left on the tripods in bad weather for a month, but it does not necessarily make very good hay after that sort of treatment.

SILAGE

If you take grass, clover, alfalfa, crushed green corn, kale, or many other green things, and press them down tight in a heap from which you exclude the air, it will not go bad, as you might think, but will ferment into a food very nourishing to animals. In fact, good silage is as good as the very best of hay. And of course, because you can cut your green crop at any stage of growth, you can cut it young when its protein content is highest, so it makes good feed. Grass you can cut again and again during the season, instead of waiting until it is fully grown as most people do when they make hay.

Making silage

Silage making is not an easy option for the smallholder. You need a fair bit of fancy equipment to do the job well and it is almost impossible to do it in small quantities. Farmers use a special forage harvester that cuts and mashes up the grass, then blows it into another trailer pulled by another tractor.

Alternatively, the farmers use a machine to wrap the cut grass up in a great cocoon of plastic which is then sealed to keep out the air. You can do this yourself with cut grass, using fertilizer bags and sealing them with tape. It makes marvelous silage but is hardly an effective way to keep cows through the winter!

"Collecting wild food is part of our pleasure. If we go for a country walk we keep our eyes open for fungi. ...Wild mushrooms are becoming a very scarce bird... This is due to the use of chemicals on the land, the lack of horses, and probably most of all to the periodic plowing up of pastures and cropping and reseeding. The beneficent mycelium does not have time to establish itself. We are going to try this March to enspore our own piece of permanent pasture. The mushrooms grown on compost in sheds or dark cellars taste as much like real mushrooms as margarine tastes like butter.

Giant puffball is the easiest food in the world to prepare, for it cuts cleanly into lovely firm white slices which can be fried in butter; and then it is delicious. Parasol mushroom is another favorite of ours. It tastes similar to field mushroom, but is stronger-flavored and I think better. Champignon, or 'fairy ring' toadstools, are fine if you can find enough of them to make it worth cooking them, for they go down, as cooks say, 'to nothing.' "

JOHN SEYMOUR FAT OF THE LAND 1976

CHAPTER FIVE

FOOD

FROM THE

WILD

Game

Humans should be managers, not bandits. We have no right to slaughter animals just for fun, or to assuage our blood-lust. Nor do we have the right to endanger the stock of any species of animal. Yet we have a part to play in maintaining the balance of nature (and if we fail to play it, nature will very rightly shrug its shoulders and shake us off). And we can also supplement our diet with good food (wild meat is a far better source of protein than the meat of domesticated animals) as well as protect our crops. True husbandmen and women will accept their responsibility in this matter. They will also accept responsibility in the way they hunt game. It is unforgivable to wound an animal instead of killing it outright, so don't go shooting until you are a good shot. And never take a shot unless you are absolutely certain of a kill.

Guns

A shotgun is a smooth-bore tube that fires a charge of shot. Lead shot should never be used: it is a pollutant. Always buy cartridges using shot of other metals.

The sizes of shot are numbered according to the number of individual pellets it takes to make up an ounce (28 g): thus number 1 shot is very big (it is used, wrongly in my opinion, for roe deer), number 3 is about right for wild geese, number 5 for duck, and number 6 for pheasants, rabbits, and small game, while numbers 8 and 9 are used for snipe or woodcock.

Shotguns are graded according to the size of their bore (size of their barrel). The bore depends on the number of lead balls in a pound (0.5 kg) that exactly fit a barrel. Thus the barrel of a 12-bore takes 12 balls to fit it, making up a pound. The 12-bore is by far the most common size all over the world now and is a good all-purpose gun. Whatever the gun, it is all a matter of what people think is "sportsmanlike."

Cartridges are loaded with nitro-powder, which is smokeless and reliable, but some people load their own brass-cased cartridges (with an apparatus bought from a gun shop) and thus save a lot of money. Modern cartridges are fired by a percussion cap (small brass cap containing fulminite of mercury) pressed into the base of the cartridge.

A rifle has a series of spiral grooves cut down inside the barrel, and a single bullet of soft metal, or coated with soft metal. When the bullet is propelled out of the chamber of the gun into the barrel, the metal around it conforms to the shape of the spirals and this gives the bullet a spin. Without this spin the bullet will not travel accurately but will invariably veer off to one side or another. The ".22" is common all over the world and its ammunition is cheap, light, and small. The rifle is very effective up to several hundred yards. I have shot kudu, reed-buck, and various other big game with a .22, and have never once merely wounded an animal or failed to kill it; but then I would never use a .22 for such a purpose unless I was very close and quite sure of my target.

For larger game, however, larger rifles are really much better. Seven-millimeter is a very common size (the 7-mm Mauser has always been, in my opinion, the best small sports rifle in the world; the 6.5-mm Manlicher is as good ballistically but has an inferior magazine). The 9-mm is fine for thick-skinned game. I used a .404-inch bolt-action rifle in Africa; it gave me a certain sense of security when being charged by a buffalo, but by God, it kicked!

Rabbits as game

When they multiply, rabbits become an all-pervading menace, so that no forester can plant a tree without enormous expense on extermination and rabbit-proof fencing, and 25 percent of the crops in many areas might go down the rabbits' throats. In any case, they are also very good food. The most humane way of taking rabbits (along with hares, small deer or buck, or vermin such as foxes, crows and other marauders and birds) is to shoot them either with a shotgun or a .22. Very early in the morning is the best time to "walk up" rabbits with a shotgun, or to lie in wait for them with a .22.

Long-netting is perhaps the second-best way of killing rabbits. It is humane, quiet, cheap (no expenditure on cartridges), and, properly done, can be very efficient. You set up the net between the rabbits' grazing ground and their burrows in the daytime at your leisure. Keep it folded up out of the way where the rabbits can get underneath it, with a release string to let it drop when you pull it. You then go back at night, when the rabbits are out in the field grazing, and the net is between the grazing ground and the rabbit warren. You pull the string and down comes the net; your accomplice gets behind the rabbits and makes a noise; they all run off into the net and get tangled, whereupon you kill them. I have caught a dozen rabbits with one setting of a long net.

Ferreting

In Europe, a common good way of controlling rabbits is to hunt them with ferrets. (American homesteaders are denied this option, since the practice is illegal in the US.) You keep hunting ferrets in a hutch, keep them clean, feed them sparingly on fresh meat, and handle them often to keep them tame. Use deliberate, steady movements when handling them—they will sometimes bite your hand, thinking that you are giving them a piece of meat. Only a reliable ferret can be worked loose; an unreliable one may kill a rabbit down the hole and "lay up" with it.

A line ferret has a collar around its neck with a long line on it. The disadvantage of this is that the line may get snagged around a tree root far down a burrow, in which case you will have a lot of digging to do. We used to work them loose but keep one "liner" in reserve. If a ferret did lay up, we would send the liner down and then dig along the line and thus find the errant ferret.

Probably the best thing is just to use loose ferrets and trust to luck. The best way of recapturing a ferret if it lays

SKINNING A RABBIT

Once you have killed your rabbit you will need to prepare it for the pot. Before you skin it, you must "paunch" it (remove the guts). Skinning is not difficult; you will find the skin comes away from the flesh very easily. If the thought of preparing rabbit appalls you, just brace yourself and think of rabbit pie.

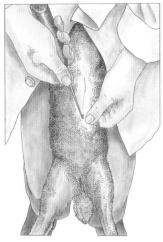

1 Hold the rabbit between your knees by its head, so that its tail hangs free and its belly faces upward. Cut a hole in its belly.

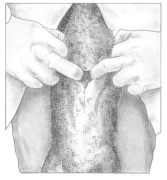

2 Pull the skin apart at the cut, and insert two fingers into the hole.

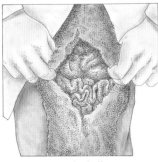

3 Prize open the belly to expose the guts and remove them. "Paunching" is now complete.

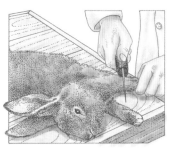

4 Cut off all four paws of the rabbit with a sharp knife.

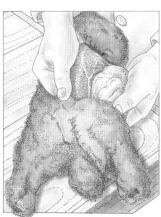

5 Separate the skin and fur from the flesh of the rabbit, at the belly.

6 Invert the skin and fur, so that the flesh of first one hind leg, then the other is exposed.

7 The hind quarters are now free from all skin and fur, and now is the moment to cut off the tail.

8 Hold the hind legs in one hand and pull the skin down to the front legs.

9 Expose the front legs and cut away the last tendon joined on to them.

10 Pull the skin over the rabbit's neck and cut off its head.

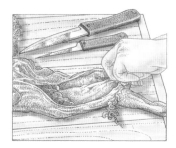

11 Split the hind legs from the belly and cut out the anal passage. Then place your knife in the rabbit's breast, and remove the "lights" and heart. You must remove the gall from the liver.

up is probably a box trap, with a dead rabbit inside it, and a trapdoor, so that when the ferret goes in, the door shuts behind it. Rabbits "bolted" by the ferret are best caught in purse nets. These are simply small bags of nets staked around the entrances to the holes.

Hanging game birds

Assuming you can legally shoot them, game birds such as pheasants, partridge, pigeon, and wild duck (I stopped shooting wild geese when I discovered that they mate for life) make fine delicacies. Most game should be "hung," that is, hung up in a cool, airy pantry for some time

before eating. Hang game birds up by the neck, not the feet as with tame birds. The reason for this is so the guts do not press against the meat of the breast. Do not gut the birds then. In the winter in a northern climate, it is all right to hang a pheasant, or a wild duck, for as much as 10 days. At the end of this period, pluck them and gut them.

Game birds hung up with their feathers on look pretty, but if you just want them to eat, it is quite a good plan to pluck them when you shoot them, there and then (if you are on your own land), because the feathers come out easily when the birds are still warm.

Fish & Sea Foods

The self-supporter ought to make the most of any opportunity he gets, and fish should figure at the forefront of his healthy, varied, natural diet. The "sport" of angling, in my opinion, is a complete waste of time. Catching fish, weighing them, and throwing them back does no one any good. Freshwater fish make wonderful food. People should be encouraged to take or farm freshwater fish for food. The methods I describe are not necessarily legal everywhere, but all I can say is that they ought to be.

FRESHWATER FISH

Trout Plenty of people catch trout with their bare hands by "tickling." You lean over a bank and very gently introduce your hand into a cavity underneath it, waggling your fingers in a tickling movement as you do so. When you feel a fish with the tips of your fingers, you just gently tickle its belly for a minute; then you grab it and throw it on the bank. "Groping" is another method: wade along in a shallow stream, walking upstream, and grope with your hand under rocks, grabbing any fish you find there. You might get bitten by an eel while you are doing it, though.

Pike "Snaring" was a method much used in when I was a boy. You have a wire snare hanging from a stick, and when you see a large pike hanging in the water, as pike do, you very carefully insert the snare in front of him and let it work slowly back to his point of balance. When you think it is there, you haul him out. If the wire does just touch him as you work it over him, he thinks it is a stick because it is going downstream.

Salmon You can "gaff" salmon. To gaff a salmon, first locate him; you will find him resting in a pool or under an overhanging tree. You then take the head of a gaff, which can be made from a big cod hook, out of your pocket. Cut a light stick from a bush, and lash the gaff on to the stick. You have a lanyard (light cord) running from the eye of the gaff to your wrist, where it is tied. You drag the gaff into the fish and then just let go of the stick. The line unwinds from the stick, which falls away, and you haul the fish in with the line. If you try to haul him in with the stick, he may well pull you in.

Eel Sensible people, among whom I include the Dutch and the Danes, account the eel the best fish there is, and indeed, if you have ever eaten well-smoked *gerookte paling* in the Netherlands, you must agree. You can take eels in "grigs" or "eel-hives": these are conical or square baskets made of osiers, wire netting, or small mesh fish netting on a frame, with an admission funnel like a very small lobster pot. Bait this with fresh fish or meat; whatever people say, eels don't like bad fish. Fresh meat or fresh chicken guts in a gunnysack, with the neck of the sack tied tight, and some stones inside it to sink it, will catch eels.

"Babbing" for eels is a good way of catching them. Get a bunch of worms as big as your fist, thread wool yarn through them, tie them in a bunch, and lower them into shallow water on the end of a string, which is tied to a stick. After a while, haul the "bab" gently out and eels may be found hanging to it, their teeth entangled in the yarn. Pull the bunch over your boat, or over the bank, and give it a shake. I have caught a hundred pounds of eels this way in an afternoon. I have not discussed conventional angling with rod and line, for this is done more as a sport than for food production, although good anglers can sometimes get a lot of food this way, too. But the fresh waters should be farmed for fish just as the land is farmed for crops and animals.

SEA FISH

From the viewpoint of the person who wishes to catch ocean fish, they fall into two groups; pelagic and demersal. The former swim freely through the seas, independent of the bottom. The latter are confined to the bottom of the seabed. Obviously the means of taking them are different.

Catching pelagic fish

Hooks and feathers Sometimes you can catch hundreds of pounds in a few hours when hooking for pelagic fish. Mackerel in particular can be caught productively in this way, though traditionally they were caught by a last. This was a piece of skin, about 2 inches (5 cm) long, cut from near the tail of a mackerel you had already caught. The method was to move along at about two knots, dragging the last on a hook astern. Then somebody discovered the "feathers." With this new invention you have perhaps a dozen hooks, on snoods (short branch lines), tied to a line with a weight on it. Each hook has a white or colored feather whipped to the shank (though almost anything will do—even scraps of white plastic or shiny tin). You lower the tackle from a stationary boat, find the depth at which the mackerel are biting, and plunge the feathers up and down with a motion of your arm.

Drift net Herring cannot be caught on a hook. Unlike mackerel, they don't hunt other fish, but live on plankton, so their mouths are too small for hooks. They are traditionally caught with a drift net. This fine net hangs down vertically in the water suspended from a float-line, which is a line with corks or plastic floats all along it. You can let it drop to any depth you like by hanging it on longer or shorter pendants. The whole net must have positive buoyancy. It will catch more at night, and a fine night is the best time for catching herring. "Shoot" (put into the water) the net from a boat and hang on to one end of it for an hour or two, letting boat and net drift with the tide. Cast off occasionally and row along the net, and lift a few yards of it to see if there are any fish. If a shoal hits the net, haul it in. Don't bother to try getting the fish out of the net yet; just pay the net down into the stern of the boat and go back to port. Then unload the net and shake the fish out into a piece of canvas laid on the beach. Drift nets will take any pelagic fish if the mesh is the right size: mackerel, salmon, sea trout, and many other fish are all taken in drift nets. But these nets can also snare and drown sharks, birds, and marine mammals, so never leave your net unattended.

Catching demersal fish

Trawl net Fish on the seabed can be taken by a trawl net. There are basically two kinds: the beam trawl and the otter trawl. The beam trawl is a net bag with its mouth held open by a beam that is supported on two "heads" like the runners of a sled. The otter trawl has two "otter boards" holding its mouth open: they swim through the water like kites, holding the trawl mouth open as they do so. For the self-supporter with a small boat, the beam is probably best, although many would dispute this.

You need considerable power to haul a trawl, particularly an otter trawl, which takes a certain minimum speed to keep the otter boards working. A small beam trawl can be hauled by sail alone, especially if you work downtide. Often the tide is enough to pull the net. Always trawl down-tide anyway, since the fish face up-tide. A small-meshed beam trawl also takes shrimp.

Tangle net This has very strong, thin, synthetic fiber. It is a very tight, large-meshed net that sinks to the bottom of the sea, where some of its width is supported by a submerged cork line and the rest just lies in a heap on the bottom. Anything that walks or swims near the bottom is taken by it, getting inextricably tangled, and then you have the lovely job of clearing the net! That is the disadvantage, for the net is hard to clear and always gets badly torn, so that you have to repair it. But it catches a lot of fish and will take crabs and lobster along with everything else.

Shore seine net This is another of the long wall nets. You keep one end of it on the beach, while the other end is taken out in a boat that goes around in a half-circle, coming back to the beach again. Both ends of the net are then pulled in, and any fish that were caught are dragged up on to the beach.

Long-line You can shoot this from a boat. The line can have any number of hooks on it, each one in a snood, and each one baited. Coil the line down carefully in a basket, or tin bath, or plastic tub. As you coil the line down, lay each hook in order over the side of the receptacle, next to the following hook in the line. The snoods are long enough to allow this. Bait each hook. Then go up-tide from where you wish to shoot the line, throw out one anchor, and let the line whip overboard as the tide drives it inexorably down-tide. The baited hooks should fly over one by one. Have a short piece of stick in your hand to help them do this if they are reluctant.

If you get in a "fangle," let the whole line go over; don't try to unfangle it or you will get a hook in your hand, as sure as fate. If you work carefully and keep cool, it should go over clear. When you get to the other end, throw over the other anchor and the buoy, and that is that. Come back the next day and haul against the tide, using oars or engine or the wind to carry the boat along at the right speed.

The size of hooks will depend entirely on the kind of fish you hope to catch.

HOOKS, LINES, AND SINKERS
1 Parlor pot, a type of lobster pot. **2** Bab, a tied bunch of worms for catching eels. **3** Feathers, weighted line with snoods. **4** Feather (detail). **5** Barbless hook, for removing hook from fish. **6** Last, a piece of shiny skin. **7** Lugworm bait. **8** Treble hook for pike. **9** Hook for cod. **10** Hook for dabs.

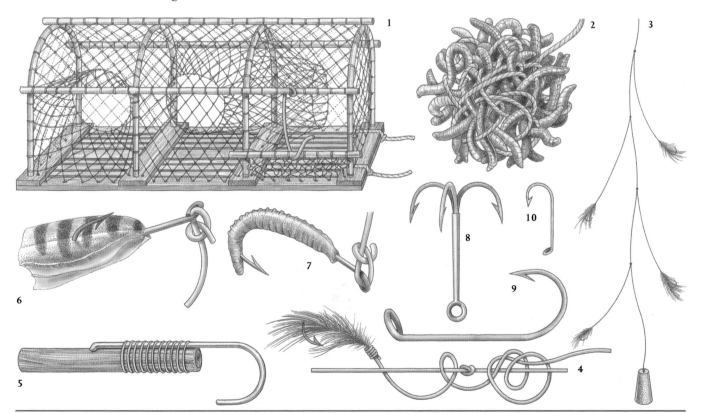

Hooks

Size 6 or 8 hooks are fine for dabs, plaice, and so on, while size 4/0 to 8/0 may be needed for conger eel, or large cod. Conger are likely to be caught on long-lines: I once helped catch half a ton in a night. Admittedly, there were 1,200 hooks. For such large fish it is good to have a swivel on each snood, so the hook can turn as the conger turns.

Getting a hook out of the throat of a large fish is very easy when you know how to do it. You need a small barbless hook securely attached to a handle. Get the hand-hook, as I call it, in the bite of the fish hook, and yank the fish hook out with the hand-hook, holding the snood firmly with your other hand so as to keep the two hooks engaged. You should carry a "priest" (small wooden club, traditionally of boxwood). It is so called because it administers the last rites, and is more humane than letting fish drown in air.

Hand-line Only once in a while is hand-lining for bottom fish productive. Those lines of hopefuls who lean endlessly on the rails of piers spend far more on bait and tackle than they take home in fish. Don't bother to hand-line unless you know there are fish there (ask a local). You can sometimes find a good mark for whiting, or codling, that makes hand-lining more than just a way of passing the time.

THE SEASHORE

You do not need a boat to benefit from the riches of the sea. A visit to the seashore provides ample opportunity to accumulate edible sea creatures of various sorts for a snack, if not a full meal. Indeed, someone without a boat may catch fish quite effectively with a beach long-line.

Go down to the bottom of a beach at low tide and lay a long-line (as described earlier) along the sand near the sea. As the tide comes back, demersal fish will follow the water, intent on helping themselves to such small beach animals as emerge from the sand to go about their business when it is covered. You will catch some fish, perhaps not many; you will be lucky to get a fish every 20 hooks, but after all, one fish is a meal and better than no fish at all. If you really want to practice this fishery effectively put down a lot of hooks; 100 is not too many.

The long-line must be anchored by a heavy weight at each end and should have a pennant (branch line) on it with a buoy on top to make it easy to recover. Remember here that the tide is not the same every day.

PLANTS AND CREATURES OF THE SEASHORE

1 Razor clam **2** Common whelk **3** Common limpet **4** Edible cockle **5** Common oyster **6** Common mussel **7** Common winkle **8** Edible crab **9** Lobster **10** Brown shrimp **11** Purple laver **12** Sea lettuce **13** Dulse

About the time of every full moon and about the time of every new moon there is a spring tide, when the water goes both higher and lower than in neap tides, which occur at half-moon periods. Even these spring tides vary: some come up much higher and go down much lower than others. So you may lay your line out at the bottom of the beach on one tide only to find that the tide does not go out far enough to uncover it the next day. If you have a buoy on a pennant you will be able to wade out and recover your line.

As for bait, on many beaches you will find the reliable lugworm. This can be dug out at low water with a spade or fork. There is a trick to this: lugworms throw up worm-shaped casts of sand. Do not dig under this. Instead, look for a small hole about a foot away from each cast. This is the worm's blowhole. Dig there, dig fast, throw the sand out quickly, and you will get your lugworm.

Other forms of bait are limpets, mussels, slices of herring or mackerel, whelks, and hermit crab tails. Limpets must be knocked off the rocks with a hammer by surprise; once you have warned them of your intentions they cling, well, like limpets, and you can only get them off by smashing them to pieces. Mussels are somewhat soft and some people tie them on to a hook with a piece of thread.

Shellfish

Mussels Pick these as low on the rocks as you can get at low tide, preferably below the lowest tide mark, although this is not always possible. They must be alive: if they are firmly closed it is a sign that they are. They must not be taken from water in which there can possibly be any pollution from sewage, since they are natural filters and will filter any bacteria out of the water and keep it in themselves. Advice commonly given is to cook them only long enough to make them open their shells. This is extremely dangerous. All mussels should be boiled or steamed for at least 20 minutes; otherwise, food poisoning can take place.

Cockles Rake these out of the sand with a steel rake. You quickly get good at spotting where they are under the sand, which somehow looks different: it is often grayer than the surrounding area. Then rake them into small hand-nets and wash the sand out of them in shallow water. It's much easier to harvest cockles on the sand flats when shallow water still lingers over the sand. Boil or steam them for 20 minutes.

Razor clam These betray themselves by squirting water out of the holes in the sand. They do this when you step on the sand nearby. They live very low down on the beach, right down where the sand is only uncovered at low spring tides. If you walk backward over the sand you will see the spurts of water after you have passed. The best way to get them is with a razor spear. This is a pointed iron rod with small barbs near the point. You push it gently down the hole and the razor clam closes on it and is pulled out.

Oysters You should only eat oysters raw if you are sure they are unpolluted. But they are delicious cooked and safer to eat then. To open an oyster, hold it in a cloth in your left hand and plunge a short stiff blade into the hinged end. You can cheat by popping them in a hot oven (400°F or 200°C) for not more than four minutes, but if you intend to eat them raw this is desecration.

Winkles These can be picked up in small rock pools at low tide. Boil them for a quarter of an hour in water. Pick them out with a pin, sprinkle them with vinegar, and eat with bread and butter. However, I think they are pretty dull.

Whelks Whelks are a deep-water shellfish and are caught in pots like lobster pots but smaller. Salt herring or mackerel make a good bait. Boil them for half an hour, or steam them. They taste a little like wet leather.

Lobsters and crabs These are normally caught in pots, which are cages with funnels into them so that the shellfish can get in but not out. The pots can be made of willow, steel mesh, or wire netting. A more sophisticated pot is the "parlor pot," which is longer, with an entrance hall at each end; the net funnels into the "parlor" which is in the middle. If you have to leave pots out for long because of bad weather, the parlor pot is good, because the lobsters, on finding themselves confined in the entrance halls, try to get out, get into the parlor, and wait there: the bait is not eaten and attracts more lobsters.

When trawling you may catch hermit crabs. Fishermen, if they don't want the tails for bait, normally throw them overboard. This is nonsense—the tails are delicious boiled. Spider crabs are also tasty.

Seaweed

Many seaweeds are edible, but there are two plants that are excellent to eat: laver weed (*Porphyra umbilicalis*) and samphire (*Salicornia europaea*). Laver weed has thin, translucent purple fronds and grows on rocks on the beach. To cook it you soak it for a few hours in fresh water, dry it in a slow oven, and powder it in a mortar. Then boil it for four hours, changing the water. Drain it and dry it and you have made laver bread, the stuff that the South Wales coal miners used to think was good for their chests. Eat it with bacon for breakfast. You can just wash laver weed well and boil it for several hours in water in a double saucepan. Beat this up with lemon or orange and a little butter or oil, and it makes a good sauce for mutton.

Other more delicate seaweeds, such as sea lettuce (*Ulva lactuca*) and dulse (*Rhodymenia palmata*) can be treated in the same way as laver weed.

The other really valuable seaweed, samphire, is not really a seaweed. It looks like a miniature cactus below high-tide mark, and can be eaten on the spot, raw, as is (provided the estuary is not polluted). Boil and serve like asparagus with butter; but if you eat it like this you must draw the flesh off between your teeth, leaving the rough fibers behind. Samphire also makes a most magnificent pickle: fill a jar with it, add peppercorns and grated horseradish; then pour in a boiling mixture of dry cider and vinegar in equal quantities, or else just vinegar.

Plants, Nuts, & Berries

There are innumerable wild foods that you can find growing in the woods, fields, and hedgerows, but my advice would always be: find out what the local people consider good to eat in your locality and eat that.

With fungi, you really must know which ones are safe, and for this you need either a knowledgeable friend or the advice of local people. Besides the common field mushroom, a few fungi that are delicious to eat and easy to identify are: shaggy mane (try it boiled lightly in milk), giant puffball, parasol, shaggy parasol, horse mushroom, porcini, boletus (several species), morel, and chanterelle.

An enormous number of "weeds" can be eaten; so can all kinds of seeds, and of course a great many wild fruits, berries, nuts, and fungi (see pp.280–281). More "weeds" can be eaten than are a positive pleasure to eat, but a few that are excellent are nettles, fat hen, and Good King Henry. Treat all three exactly as you would spinach: pick them in the spring when they are young and tender, cover with a lid, and boil briefly.

Some other wild substitutes for green vegetables are shepherd's purse, yarrow, ground elder, and lungwort. Common mallow can be pureed and turned into a good soup; chickweed can be cooked and eaten like spinach or used in salads; garlic mustard is a mild substitute for garlic. You will find many other varieties in your locality, and don't forget the dandelion—delicious raw in a salad. But use it sparingly.

Of the edible nuts, walnut is the king in temperate climates. After picking, leave the nuts for some weeks, until the husks come off easily, then dry them well. You can pick hazelnuts green when they are good to eat but won't keep, or you can pick them ripe and bury them, shells and all, in dry salt. In Europe, sweet chestnuts are magnificent food. Pick them when they ripen in fall. Take off the prickly covers and store the nuts in a dry place. Of course, the finest way to eat them is to roast them in the embers of a fire, but prick them first so they don't explode. Raw, they are bitter. Pureed, they taste marvelous, and turkey is unthinkable without chestnut stuffing. Beech nuts are tasty but fiddly to eat; better to crush them in a mill, put the pulp in cloth bags, and press it. It yields a fine oil. Ash keys make good relish; boil them well and pickle in vinegar.

Of the wild fruits, the elderberry is perhaps the most versatile. The berries can be used for cooking in a number of ways. Mixed with any other fruit, they improve the flavor; boiled in spiced vinegar they make an excellent relish or sauce that will keep well, if properly canned when hot. The berries also make an excellent wine, as do the flowers, which add flavor to cooked gooseberries and also gooseberry jam. If you find blueberries or bilberries in the wild, do not ignore them: they make a wonderful pie. And if you find cranberries you can preserve them, but their flavor is nowhere better captured than in a fresh cranberry sauce. Mulberries and rowan berries make very good jam. And do not forget juniper berries, which can impart an agreeably tart flavor to all savory dishes.

BIRCH SAP
Betula pendula

There are few people who realize that all around them are birch trees that can be the source of the most perfect country wine. Birch wine is made from the sap gathered in spring. Simply choose a good strong tree where the trunk is at least 12 inches (30 cm) in diameter. Using a cordless drill or brace and bit, drill a hole about 1 inch (2.5 cm) in diameter into the tree at a point where you can conveniently hang a bucket. The sap will flow into your bucket.

BLACKBERRY
Rubus fruticosus

For many households, the annual routine of blackberry gathering is an enjoyable signal that fall is near and the summer is almost gone. A walking stick with a good crook is useful for pulling down the higher berries, and even the smallest child can join in the fun. There are a thousand and one uses for the blackberry, from excellent wine to straightforward jam to a superb accompaniment to apples in pie.

CRAB APPLE
Malus sylvestris

Crab apples vie with sloes for the title of the bitterest of fruits. Some of this bitterness is caused by tannin, in which they are rich. One of their great uses is as an additive to tannin-poor wines. Mead, for example, ferments much better with a little crab apple juice added. But the best use is, of course, crabapple jelly, made by boiling and sieving through muslin.

ELDERBERRY
Sambucus nigra

The elderberry is one of the most versatile of wild fruits. Mixed with almost any other fruit, they greatly enhance the flavor, and boiled in spiced vinegar they make an excellent relish. Elderberry wine is one of the kings of country wines— it matures well and can almost pass for a claret after three or four years in the bottle.

ELDERFLOWER
Sambucus nigra

The secret of using elderflowers to make a delicious fruit cordial drink is never to put too many into your brew and always harvest on a fine, sunny day when the fragrance and nectar are at their height. I find I can reach even high blossoms (usually the best) by taking a garden hoe and pulling down the branches.

GORSE
Ulex europaeus

Few things can beat the spectacular show of color provided by gorse in full flower. On a hot spring day, the sight and smell are simply intoxicating. And it is with the flowers that we want to make what is probably the most enticing and delicate of country wines. It is a long and prickly job to collect sufficient flowers, but children love it, and what better thing could be found to pass the time on a fine sunny day?

HAZEL
Corylus avellana

Hazel is a moody tree that seems to grow like a weed in some places but can be completely impossible to grow in others. The nuts are a wonderful addition to a winter diet. You can use them in all kinds of ways. Nuts must be dry before you store them or they will rot.

OAK
Quercus robur

In their first flush of spring growth, the leaves of the mighty oak tree provide the raw material for a very fine country wine. The acorns that come later can be used to make a flour, but better by far to feed them to the pigs, for whom they will provide an excellent source of natural protein.

WILD PLUM
Prunus domestica

Wild plums are more common than you might think. Look out for their distinctive small white blossom in the hedgerows very early in the spring. Mark the spott and get back there in late summer to see how the crop is doing. Keep the location of your trees secret, for news travels fast and others will be eager to share your bounty.

SLOE
Prunus spinosa

Sloes make a marvelous fruit wine and are a magical addition to strong liquor. The invigorating color and flavor of sloe gin is something everyone should savor. Gather your sloes after the first frost. Take ½ pound (228 g) of sloes and prick them all over with a fork or pin. Each one must be pricked several times before being put into the gin. Half-fill a bottle with them; add an equal quantity of sugar, fill the bottle with gin, and in a few months you have a fine liqueur.

SWEET CHESTNUT
Castanea sativa

In most years the sweet chestnuts in northern Europe are too small to make good eating. But with the right varieties and a good season, the chestnuts will stand you in good stead. Far more people should grow sweet chestnuts, for the wood is also one of the best for furniture; it is stable and not liable to twist or shrink. Sweet chestnuts make the best stuffing you can get for that Thanksgiving turkey.

WALNUT
Juglans regia

For sheer volume of crop, you cannot beat a good walnut tree. The trees grow much better and faster than you might think. Plant from seed and grow on in pots before planting. Young trees are very easily damaged by frost, so avoid frost pockets and cover in cold weather: 15 years later you will begin to harvest. The nuts need to be separated from their green skins and well dried before you store them. Walnut oil is great for salads.

Mushrooms

There are few more remarkable sights in this world than to pass by a field or pasture that has been miraculously covered with perfect white field mushrooms. Sometimes, if the weather and soil make the right combination, you can find literally thousands of beautiful mushrooms.

The edible parts of fungi are the fruiting bodies that are produced very dramatically by huge spreading masses of mycelia, which draw their nutrients as parasites from roots and decaying vegetation. If you are new to mushroom picking, it is a good idea to learn from someone with more experience, since there are a huge range of excellent fungi to be found.

Where to look

You will always harvest your best specimens early in the morning. Fungi grow in a wide variety of places, but they will not tolerate chemical fertilizers or sprays. They say it will take 20 years for the horse mushroom to appear in grassland after the use of chemicals has been stopped, and I have found this to be true. In fact, the majority of edible fungi grow in the proximity of woodland and many have close symbiotic relationships with particular tree roots. But wild grassland does always produce an excellent crop of fungi every fall, and you will find each season's crop in places similar to the previous year's.

What to avoid

There is probably no need to warn you of the fly agaric, since this bright red and white spotted fungus is so well known. The most dangerous of all fungi is the deathcap (*Amanita phalloides*). A single death cap contains enough toxins to kill several people. Usually it grows in woodland, particularly with oak trees. It can vary in color, being similar in size to a field mushroom, but its characteristic features are white gills on the underside and a volval bag at the base. Any fungi growing from a volval bag are best left alone, for many are poisonous. A death cap has white spores, not brown like most edible mushrooms.

Another mushroom to avoid is the "yellow stainer," easily confused with field or horse mushrooms. It has the distinctive feature of turning bright yellow when bruised or cut. It also smells rather like disinfectant.

BAY BOLETUS
Boletus badius

Usually found in woodlands, this fungus is pale to brown in color. It has light yellow pores on the underside, and these stain blue if damaged, making the fungus easy to recognize. The flesh also stains a bluish color when cut and smells very mushroomy. The stalk has no frills but is smooth from base to cap. The flavor is very good and the season is a long one, from early summer to fall. You can store by slicing and drying or flash freezing. They taste fine raw when sliced and make great soup.

SHAGGY MANE
Coprinus cornatus

This is a very common but distinctive mushroom, and easy to identify with its egg-shaped, shaggy cap. It often grows on newly disturbed ground in large clusters. The cap is covered with beautiful white scales, and there is no veil on the stem when the cap opens to a bell shape with a dark black underside. These mushrooms need to be young and fresh to make good eating—and very good food they are too. Shaggy manes make a wonderful mushroom soup. These mushrooms do not store well, so again they are best used fresh.

GIANT PUFFBALL
Calvatia gigantea

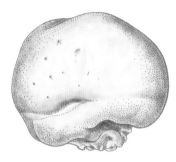

As its name suggests, the giant puffball can grow to a truly amazing size. I have seen them well over 18 inches (45 cm) across, which makes a major feast, but they can grow to over twice this size! The huge, white ball of a giant puffball is not hard to identify. They must be used young before the spores have time to develop and the insects have time to take their share. You have to slice them up like rump steak to cook them. By themselves they have little flavor, but fried quickly with a little bacon they are delicious.

HORSE MUSHROOM
Agaricus arvensis

This mushroom is a beauty and my personal favorite. You will only find it on old pasture that has been grazed by horses or cattle. Some of my earliest memories are of the excitement of finding these superb large fungi in early morning forays with my parents and then frying them up for breakfast. The horse mushroom has a slight aniseed smell and, unlike a field mushroom, does not shrivel up when cooked. Just beware you don't overindulge if you are lucky enough in these times of chemical farming to find a crop of these. The cap of the horse mushroom may be yellowy in color, but be careful not to confuse it with the "yellow stainer" fungus, which will make you sick.

CHANTERELLE
Cantharellus cibarius

These wonderful fungi are much beloved by the French and are usually found in woodland clearings. Seasoned mushroom hunters will keep their locations a close secret, since they tend to grow in the same places each year. These are fairly small mushrooms—up to 4 inches (10 cm) across but usually smaller—with a distinctive yellow color and a slight smell of apricots. The caps become like small fluted trumpets as they age, and the gills are heavy, irregular, and run down the stems. Chanterelles are best stored in good olive oil or in spiced alcohol. They taste delicious. Also delicious, but less common, is the winter chanterelle. This is a smaller and grayer version of the chanterelle that grows in woodland much later in the year.

ORANGE PEEL
Aleuria aurantia

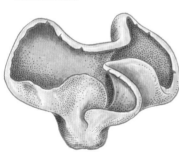

An extraordinary, brightly colored, and very striking fungus, you will find the orange peel quite commonly in large clumps in grassland and on bare earth from fall to early winter. The caps soon become wavy and are of fairly robust texture. Quite small—up to 2 inches (5 cm) across—the fungus is bright orange on top and a lighter shade on the velvety underside. These store well if dried.

PARASOL
Macrolepiota procera

Where the horse mushroom gives a blast of texture and flavor as befits the king of the fungi, the exquisite parasol is the most delicate and desirable queen. The mushroom is usually found in open fields and has large brown scales in a symmetrical pattern around a pronounced central bump. The cap can grow up to 10 inches (25 cm) across, and the gills are white. The stem is long and tough with a large ring around it. The parasol dries well for storage. You can make a delicious dish by dipping pieces of the parasol in batter and deep frying.

WOOD MUSHROOM
Agaricus silvicola

Only found in woodland, the wood mushroom is a more delicate version of its close relative, the horse mushroom. It does *not* grow out of a volval bag like the death cap, and its gills are pink to brown in color, not white. The flesh does not discolor when cut, and the smell is of a slight aniseed. The cap is a creamy-yellow color that darkens as it ages and is smaller than the horse mushroom, growing to only 4 inches (10 cm).

PORCINI
Boletus edulis

The porcini mushroom is also known as the "cep" mushroom and is a great prize for the mushroom hunter, since it has an unusual, nutty flavor. Found in woodland or sometimes in heather with dwarf willows, porcini can grow quite large—over 2 pounds (1 kg) in weight. When picking, cut the cap in half to check for maggots. These work their way up through the stems. You will recognize porcini because the cap looks just like freshly baked bread. The color darkens as the mushroom ages. The underside will have yellow pores, not gills. The stem is bulbous and solid white with brown, stripy flecks. It stores well if dried in thin slices.

THE PRINCE
Agaricus augustus

Resembling a stocky version of the parasol, the prince is a fine mushroom. It grows up to 10 inches (25 cm) wide and is found in woodland. The top is flecked with brownish scales. The gills are off-white when young, turning dark brown with age. The flesh is strong white, and smells of mushroom. The stem is very strong and often scaly with a large floppy ring under the cap—it is too tough to make good eating unless cooked in stews. It has a strong flavor and can be frozen or dried for excellent winter meals.

HONEY FUNGUS
Armillaria mellea

This yellowy-brown fungus is a tree-killer—but highly edible for humans! The active part of the fungus is a black, cordlike rhizomorph that covers huge areas under the soil and seeks out trees, which it destroys. It normally grows straight out from trees and stumps, usually in large clumps. The flesh is white and smells strong and sweet. The gills vary from off-white to brown and the stalks are tough, often fused together at the base and with a white cottonlike ring below the cap. The caps become tough if you dry them, so it's best to freeze.

FIELD MUSHROOM
Agaricus campestris

Undoubtedly the best-known of all mushrooms, before the days of chemical farming whole fields would be covered by the prolific field mushroom. To pick, get up early after a hot summer spell has been followed by rain. The silky white caps grow up to 4–5 inches (10–12 cm), the gills are pink, and the smell mushroomy. The ring around the stems is very fragile and often missing. Maggots can be a problem—check older specimens by cutting through the stems. I like to store by flash-freezing or drying.

"We kept blundering about trying to buy a cow. It is difficult buying a cow if you know nothing about it, and we don't want to be robbed. We went and looked at a herd of pedigree Jerseys and were offered one—a cull—at just the hundred and twenty guineas. And you can buy an awful lot of milk for a hundred and twenty guineas. And you can pay an awful lot of veterinary bills on a pedigree Jersey or a pedigree any other breed. We did have enough sense— or instinct—to steer away from overbred stock.

…When you learn to milk comfortably, which you do in about a week, it becomes a pleasant job. I look forward now to the morning and evening milking. There seems to me to be a friendliness between the cow and me. I put my head in her old flank and squirt away, and there is a nice smell, and a nice sound as the jets hiss into the frothing bucket, and I can think, and sum things up, and wonder what I am going to have for supper. In the winter it is dark and cold outside, but warm in the cowhouse, and the hurricane lantern throws fine shadows about the building. The whole job takes perhaps ten minutes—night and morning."

JOHN SEYMOUR FAT OF THE LAND 1976

CHAPTER SIX

IN THE
DAIRY

The Hayshed & Cowshed

THE HAYSHED

For all sorts of reasons, the hayshed has always been a rather romantic place. Of course, the hay itself embodies the bounty of the earth in spring. Good hay smells wonderful, and a full hayshed gives the self-supporter a marvelous gut feeling of satisfaction—looking forward to those long winter nights when the stock depends on hay for daily meals. Hay also feels good, and how many of us can remember an afternoon spent relaxing on this natural mattress? My own memories of the hayshed come in two parts. The first is the hot and sweaty time I spent as a teenager lugging heavy bales into those high corners under a hot roof. The ends of the compressed grass were rough, and the sweat would sting as it ran into the scratches. The second is of many gentle times relaxing with a friendly farm cat or, if luck was going my way, a nice young lady.

Hayshed hints

The hayshed must be functional, and it must be in the right place. Choose your location so as to minimize the distances the hay must be carried. I've tried to have the back of the shed opening onto a roadway for easy loading, while the front is only a few yards from the cowshed door. This is ideal. With a bit of extra cunning, you can also use one

wall of the shed to make the back of your compost pile.

It is important to make sure the hayshed is well-ventilated. Still, musty air is not going to improve your hay as it goes through the winter. Many farmers leave two or three walls open to the air. I have found that vertical wooden slats, with a couple of inches space between each, make excellent sides for a hayshed. The slats keep out most of the rain, which simply runs down them to the ground (if you had horizontal slats, this would not work).

Keep your construction cheap, strong, and simple. If you can find a source of whole pine trees (perhaps a local sawmill), then you can use these to make strong corner posts. Slap plenty of preservative onto the bottoms before you bury them 3 feet (1 m) deep in the earth. Get them accurately vertical before you ram back the earth. You can then saw off the tops to the exact heights you need. The roof is usually made of corrugated iron in any one of its modern manifestations. Now, if you can, find a source of offcuts from a sawmill to make your sides. Keep a big opening in one side, and if possible have this opening closest to your access road for easy loading. Your hayshed door must be large enough to allow easy access with a pitchfork full of hay. And it must be strong enough to withstand a good shaking by the wind.

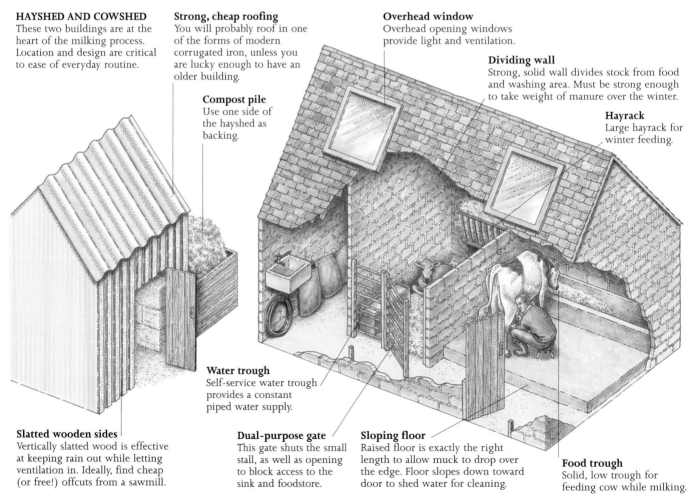

HAYSHED AND COWSHED
These two buildings are at the heart of the milking process. Location and design are critical to ease of everyday routine.

Strong, cheap roofing
You will probably roof in one of the forms of modern corrugated iron, unless you are lucky enough to have an older building.

Compost pile
Use one side of the hayshed as backing.

Overhead window
Overhead opening windows provide light and ventilation.

Dividing wall
Strong, solid wall divides stock from food and washing area. Must be strong enough to take weight of manure over the winter.

Hayrack
Large hayrack for winter feeding.

Slatted wooden sides
Vertically slatted wood is effective at keeping rain out while letting ventilation in. Ideally, find cheap (or free!) offcuts from a sawmill.

Water trough
Self-service water trough provides a constant piped water supply.

Dual-purpose gate
This gate shuts the small stall, as well as opening to block access to the sink and foodstore.

Sloping floor
Raised floor is exactly the right length to allow muck to drop over the edge. Floor slopes down toward door to shed water for cleaning.

Food trough
Solid, low trough for feeding cow while milking.

THE COWSHED

The modern cowshed is an extremely functional place, where each part is specifically designed for a particular purpose. Design and layout have evolved over many years of trial and error, so pay careful attention to the key points. In order to milk a cow efficiently, you must ensure various things: the cow must be contented, she must be fastened in a way that is secure without being too constricting, she must not be fretting for her calf and, last but not least, her back end must be in a place where manure will not splash onto you or into the fresh milk. Finally, you must have a milking area that can be easily cleaned.

These objectives are all achieved by careful layout. The cow is content because she has a big, strong manger of food in front of her nose. So the top end of your milking area must have a good feeding trough, just above floor level. We use a built-in concrete trough. Remember that anything that is not really robust will almost certainly be broken at some stage when the animal gets into a muddle over something. We use a built-in concrete trough that is 30 inches (76 cm) wide measured on the outside. Any food-bins, especially in the cowshed, should be securely latched in case the cow slips her tie.

The cow is fastened to a wall with a chain and ring that can slide up and down on a vertical steel rod. This allows the cow to move her head up and down easily even though she is firmly and closely attached to the wall. This way she cannot romp around, but she does not feel so restricted that she will panic. Her peace of mind is also much improved if she senses that her calf is close beside her—hence the need for a loose box adjacent to the milking area. This is where you can keep the calf while milking. The sensible width for a loosebox is about 5½ feet (165 cm), the length 9 feet (280 cm)—just big enough for a full-sized animal and plenty big enough for a calf.

To ensure that manure does not contaminate the milk (or the person milking), you have the milking area raised about 9 inches (22 cm) above the dunging passage at the rear of the animal. You must also make sure the length of the raised milking area is exactly correct (it is 5½ feet or 1.7 m measured from the outside edge of the feeding trough in our cowshed, and this works fine). Naturally, the floor must be sloping away from the head of the cow so that dirt and loose straw can be hosed away easily into the dunging passage. Make sure there is a convenient drain to take the waste water. Obviously, you must have a faucet and powerful hose close at hand to keep the cowshed clean. A modern power washer would be ideal, so make sure you have electric sockets within convenient reach. You will need a faucet and sink, too, for cleaning implements and equipment. And if you want to avoid feeding all the rats in the neighborhood, you will take steps to keep all foodstuffs (rolled barley, chicken food, and so on) in rat-proof, closed containers. We have found that old chest freezers are excellent for this purpose—and you can pick these up for next to nothing. I have found it convenient to keep all our animal food in the storage area of the cowshed, where there is water for mixing and a sink for cleaning. Don't forget that your loose box must have water (a small self-filling trough will do) and a good, large hayrack.

Toward a working dairy

The dairy is not where you milk cows, but where you process milk. Most homesteaders have to make do with the kitchen. We made butter, cheese, yogurt, and so on in our kitchen for 20 years, and pretty successfully, too. But it has to be said that it is a messy and difficult business doing dairy work in the kitchen, and a special room is a great convenience and luxury if you can create one.

The dairy should be as cool as possible and very airy. Working surfaces should be marble, slate, or dowels (round wooden rods). Ideally, the dairy should have a concrete or tiled floor with a drain for taking the water away. You must be able to swill it down with plenty of cold water and sweep the water out. Concrete rendering requires a very fine finish. Use four parts of sand to one of cement on the floor, and five to one on the walls. Smooth it off very carefully with a steel trowel. It is better not to whitewash or paint it. The ceiling should not have any cracks in it, or it will let down the dust.

Traditional dairies of the old farmhouse days were always on the north or east corner of the house—this is the coldest place, since it receives virtually no direct sunlight. Windows could open to let in plenty of air, but all ventilation would be protected by screens made of fine mesh wire small enough to keep out flies. Nowadays, screens for conventional windows can be bought at any home improvement store. Adjacent to the dairy would be a pantry; again with screened, ventilated windows facing north. This was where cheese and vegetables could be stored before the advent of refrigerators. Solid stone floors or heavy tiles also helped to keep the space cool. And there was always at least one door shutting off the whole area from the heated parts of the main house.

All your shelving in the dairy should be easy to wipe clean. Use either well-varnished wood or a modern synthetic surface as found on kitchen counters. Remember that any chipboard products are useless in the dairy: they absorb water and soon deteriorate.

There should be hot and cold water, with the hot preferably boiling, because sterilization is the most important thing. There should be a big sink and I prefer a draining board made with dowels. The water then drains straight down onto the floor through the gaps between the dowels, and the air comes up into the utensils.

The ideal dairy has the minimum of cupboards, refrigerators, and the like resting on the floor. This is so the whole floor can be hosed down and swept clean. Don't go to a lot of trouble to get milk, and then let it go bad because of lack of hygiene. Always avoid keeping anything in a dairy that is not absolutely needed, because everything catches or retains dust.

The Dairy

DAIRY EQUIPMENT

A cream separator or settling pans are a great advantage. Mount the separator on a strong bench. You will need a butter churn (any device for swishing cream around), and a butter worker (*see opposite*) or a flat clean table, ideally marble or slate for working butter. A cheese vat is a great labor-saving device. It is an oblong box, ideally lined with a stainless steel jacket. The milk inside the vat can be heated or cooled by running hot or cold water through the jacket. There should be a faucet at one end, and it should be easy to lift the vat so that the liquid whey that accumulates during cheese-making can be drained off.

You will also need a cheese press, a chessit, and a follower, unless you are going to make nothing but Stilton, which doesn't need pressing. The chessit is a cylinder open at the top and full of holes to let out the whey. The follower is a piston that goes down into it and presses the cheese. And the press itself is a complex combination of weights, levers, and gears that can put pressure on the follower, and therefore the cheese, inside the chessit.

Cheese presses are now hard to come by, but you can improvise. Drill holes in the bottom of an empty food can or an old saucepan. This is your chessit. Cut out a metal disk to fit inside it. This is your follower. Your pressing will have to be done with weights, which can be bricks, rocks, encyclopedias—anything that is heavy. Some of the small cheese presses you see for sale operate using a spring system and are very difficult to use. As the cheese is compressed, the pressure drops as the spring expands. The ideal press operates with weights and levers so that a constant pressure is maintained. We had a local carpenter make ours to a design we saw in the Netherlands (*see illustration*). It works perfectly.

Other requirements will be a dust-proof cupboard for keeping thermometers, an acidimeter, and a fly-proof safe for your butter and cream cheese. Hard cheese should not be stored in the dairy, because it is generally stored over long periods and it would get in the way.

Hygiene for dairy containers and utensils

1 Physically remove any cream, milk, dirt, and so on that may be adhering to the vessel, either inside or out, with hot or cold water and some sort of brush.

2 Scald the vessel inside with boiling water.

3 Rinse the vessel well with cold water to cool it down.

4 Turn the vessel upside down somewhere where it can drain and where the air can get into it.

5 Leave it upside down until you want it. Never wipe any dairy utensil with a cloth or rag, no matter how clean you think the cloth is.

Always clean dairy utensils the moment they are empty, but if you do have to leave them for some time before washing them, fill them with clean, cold water. Never leave utensils wet with milk. Remember, milk is the perfect food for calves, babies, and bacteria! The moment milk leaves the teat of the animal, bacteria attack it and it begins to go sour. If they are the wrong sort of bacteria, it will turn not sour but bad. Sour tastes nice, but sour. Bad tastes horrible. Enough bacteria of the sort that you need (chiefly *Bacillus lacticus*) will occur naturally in any dairy.

North window

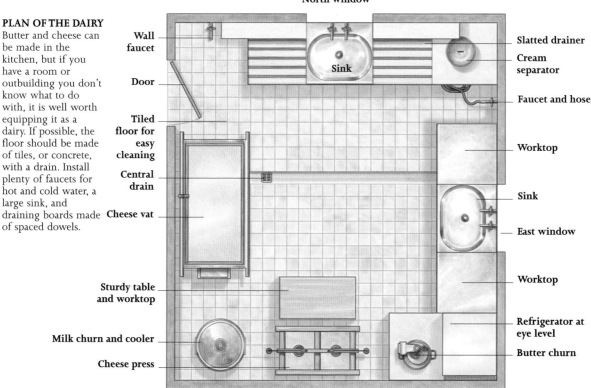

PLAN OF THE DAIRY
Butter and cheese can be made in the kitchen, but if you have a room or outbuilding you don't know what to do with, it is well worth equipping it as a dairy. If possible, the floor should be made of tiles, or concrete, with a drain. Install plenty of faucets for hot and cold water, a large sink, and draining boards made of spaced dowels.

Wall faucet

Door

Tiled floor for easy cleaning

Central drain

Cheese vat

Sturdy table and worktop

Milk churn and cooler

Cheese press

Sink

Slatted drainer

Cream separator

Faucet and hose

Worktop

Sink

East window

Worktop

Refrigerator at eye level

Butter churn

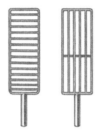

CHEESE VAT
Large, double-skinned tank that can be cooled or heated slowly and effectively by circulating water around the milk. Often mounted on wheels to make it easier to manage the heavy mass.

IN-CHURN COOLER
This device has long loops of piping that can be inserted into the milk churn and, when circulated with cold water, rapidly bring down the temperature of the fresh milk.

MILK CHURN
This large container is used for fresh milk and was once a common sight on the country roadside as it awaited its daily collection. it is now made from polypropylene and stainless steel.

CHEESE PRESS
A vital piece of equipment that must work perfectly in order to make good-quality cheese. Various designs are available; ours is cribbed from an excellent Dutch design.

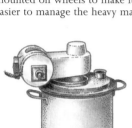

BUTTER CHURN
Large, strong container that can be turned around in order to shake cream into butter. Modern electric versions now make the task much easier, as well as managing smaller quantities.

CREAM SEPARATOR
This is basically a clever series of scoops designed to remove the rising cream from milk. Modern electric versions are smaller and neater than the traditional separator.

CURD CUTTERS
Curd knives are simply an array of knives or long blades that are used to cut curd into the correctly sized pieces for making cheese. They come in stainless steel or plastic.

RENNET
Enzymes removed from a calf's stomach and used to begin the process of making cheese from milk. Vegetarian rennet is available from some specialist suppliers.

SKIMMER
This is a simple tool for removing solids from the body or surface of milk. It is made of stainless steel and is about 4 inches (10 cm) wide.

THERMOMETER
The standard device for measuring temperature of liquids. It floats in a protective plastic cage. It needs to have a fairly large and sensitive scale up to 100°C (212°F).

CHESSIT
Stainless steel tube into which curd is placed to be pressed into cheese. Each different size has a correctly fitting "follower" that takes the pressure. Drainage holes allow liquid to escape.

MUSLIN
Fine cloth that is free of fluff. Used to strain soft cheese. Cheesecloth is sold in roughly 9-sq-ft (1-sq-m) units.

MOLD
These are shaped containers used to form cheeses. Modern plastic molds are designed specifically for different soft cheeses, such as Brie, Camembert, and ricotta.

COOKING PAN
Large, robust stainless vessel that can be put onto a burner to warm liquids. Other milking sundries include squat buckets and strainers made of aluminum or stainless steel.

STRAW MAT
Small mats are very useful for putting under freshly made cheese because they allow the cheese to "breathe." The straw mat must be kept clean and aired at all times.

SETTLING PAN
This is a stainless steel, shallow, wide-topped pan suitable for leaving cream to rise. A useful tip is to make a plywood top to keep out the flies and other aerial bugs.

Making Butter & Cream

CREAM

If you leave milk alone, the cream will rise to the surface and you can skim it off. You do this with a skimmer, which is a slightly dished metal disk with holes in it to let the milk run out but retain the cream. Or if you leave the milk in a shallow dish with a plug hole in the bottom, you can release the milk and leave the cream sticking to the dish. Then you simply scrape the cream off.

Alternatively, you can use a separator. This has a centrifuge that spins out the heavier milk, leaves the lighter cream and releases them through separate spouts. (Cream put through a separator is 35 percent butterfat (15 percent more than skimmed cream). Milk should be warm to separate.

The colder the milk is, the quicker the cream will rise to the surface. It is a very good thing to cool milk anyway, as soon as it comes from the cow. Cooling it slows down the action of the souring organisms. And, of course, the wider and shallower the pan that you settle the milk in, the faster the cream will rise to the surface.

Clotted cream

Leave fresh milk for 12 hours, then heat it to 187°F (92°C), and immediately allow it to cool. Leave for 24 hours, then skim. What you skim is clotted cream.

BUTTER

Butter is made by sloshing cream. But it will not work until the cream has "ripened": in other words, until lactic acid bacteria have converted some of the lactose, or milk sugar, into lactic acid.

Commercially, cream is pasteurized to kill all bacteria, lactic acid bacteria included, and then inoculated with a pure culture of bacteria. We can't, and don't want to be, so scientific, but we make equally good butter by keeping our cream until the oldest of it is at least 24 hours old. It can be kept twice as long as this if everything is clean enough. We add more cream to it at every milking, at a temperature of more or less 68°F (20°C). Then we make sure the last batch of cream has gone in at least 12 hours before we start churning it.

Churning

The best-known churn is simply a barrel in which the cream is turned over and over so it flops from one end to the other and bashes itself. But there are churns, like the blow churn, that have paddles that whirl around to beat the cream. You can make butter on a tiny scale by beating it with a wooden spoon or paddle, plunging a plunger up and down in a cylinder, or using an egg-beater. Anything, in fact, that gives the cream a good beating. If the cream is more or less at the right stage of acidity, and at the right temperature, it will "come," meaning suddenly turn into little butter globules, in as little as two or three minutes. If it hasn't come in 10 minutes, take its temperature, and if it is wrong, bring it to 68°F (20°C). Then try again.

It doesn't matter how sour the cream is when you churn it, provided it's not bad. Taste it. If it's bad, it's useless. When the butter has come, drain the buttermilk out. (If your cream has been kept right, it's the most delicious drink in the world.) Then you must wash the butter. Washing should be continued until every trace of cream or buttermilk or water has been removed.

Butter-worker

There is a fine thing called a butter-worker, which is a serrated wooden roller in a wooden trough. This squeezes the water out. Keep putting more cool, clean water on and squeezing until the water that you squeeze out is absolutely clean and clear, without a trace of milk in it. Traditionally, a wooden scoop was needed to dig out the butter from the butter-worker, after which it was formed into blocks, rolls, or rounds or pressed into storage dishes. Your butter is made when the last drop of water has been pressed or squeezed out of it. From now on, don't expose it to the light or the air too much, and if you keep it wrapped, it will last much longer.

If you don't have a butter-worker, don't despair. Do your washing and squeezing on a clean board with a "Scotch hand" or a wooden paddle. Very few beginners at butter-making ever wash the butter enough, and so their butter generally has a rancid taste, particularly after a week or so. Squeeze, squeeze, and squeeze again.

Salting

For salty butter, use brine for the last washing, or sprinkle dry salt onto the butter and work it in thoroughly. If you find the butter is too salty, wash some of the salt out. If you wash too much out, put some more back. It's as simple as that.

To keep butter, incorporate 2.5 percent of its own weight of salt into it, and follow this method: scald out an earthenware crock, tub, or barrel and dry it outside in the wind and sun. Throw a handful of butter into the vessel as hard as you can to drive the air out of the butter. Repeat, sprinkling more salt in after each layer and pummeling the butter down with your fist to drive out the air.

When your crock is full, or you have no more butter, cover the butter with a sprinkling of salt and some wax paper or other covering. It will keep for months. If it is too salty, simply wash some salt out before you eat it. It will be just as good as fresh butter. But remember that it must always be well washed in the first place.

Ghee

Ghee is a great Indian standby. Put butter in a pot and let it simmer gently over a slow stove for an hour. Skim off the scum. Pour the molten butter into a sterilized container, cover from the air, and it will keep for months. It won't taste like butter. It will taste like ghee. It's very good for cooking, and helps to give real curries that particular taste.

MAKING BUTTER

Butter is made by beating ripened cream. So a churn of some kind is essential. To shape the finished butter use two wooden paddles, called "Scotch hands," or, better still, an old-fashioned wooden butter mold.

1 I use a blow churn. Fill the churn with cream and turn the handle.

2 When the butter "comes," or coagulates, drain off the buttermilk.

3 Dump butter out on a clean draining board or on a butter-worker.

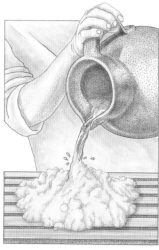

4 Wash the butter thoroughly by repeatedly mixing with cold water and squeezing.

5 Press the butter to remove all water and traces of buttermilk.

6 Add salt to taste, or if you want to keep the butter for a long time, add a lot.

7 Work the salt in well. You can always wash salt out again.

8 Shape the butter with wetted paddles. Take care to squeeze any remaining water out. The secret of making good butter is to wash and squeeze all milk and water out of it.

9 There are various churning molds and wooden blocks for the final shaping and imprinting of butter. With this mold, you pack the butter in tightly to fill in all the airholes.

10 Then it may even take two of you to force the butter out on to wax paper.

11 The butter can be patted into oblongs or put in a mold that impresses a design into the butter, such as thistles, cows, or wheat sheaves.

YOGURT

Yogurt is milk that has been soured by *Bacillus bulgaricum* instead of the more usual *Bacillus lacticus*. To make two pints (1 liter) of yogurt, put two pints of milk in a bowl. The bacteria need a warm climate. So if it's too cold for them, you should warm your milk to about blood heat. Stir in two tablespoons of a good live yogurt that you have bought at the store, and at this point mix in any fruit and nuts that you want for flavoring, though to my mind nothing beats a bowl of natural yogurt served up with a spoonful of honey.

Cover the mixture, and keep it at blood heat for two or three days. A good method of keeping it warm is to bury it in straw. When it has thickened, it is yogurt.

Take some out every day to use, and put the same amount of fresh milk back and so keep it going. But the milk should be very clean and fresh, the vessel should be sterile, and you must keep it covered. It may go bad after a while. If it does, start again.

Thick milk or curds and whey

If you leave clean milk alone in the summer, it will curdle, and become "curds and whey" such as Miss Muffett was eating when she had that unfortunate experience with the spider. Curds and whey are slightly sour and delicious to eat. Sprinkle cinnamon over the top, or a little salt.

ICE CREAM

I remember a strange experience I had in Oregon. While visiting friends, I was amazed by the terrific noise made during the night by tree frogs, so I set off into the woods to investigate. These frogs are tiny creatures, but they certainly make a loud racket.

After walking through the woods for 20 minutes or so, I saw lights up ahead. Houses are not common in these parts, where you can drive for three or four hours through woods without seeing a single home, so I went closer. The household was having a big party, and I soon found myself in the thick of it.

The hosts handed me an ice cream maker that was duly loaded up with a cream mixture, surrounded by salt and ice. It was then my job to look out for all the children in the place and ask each one to give the barrel a good shaking. In this way, the children were occupied for at least an hour shaking away happily, especially since there was the imminent prospect of fresh ice cream as a reward. Sure enough, as if by a miracle, the ice cream mixture set firm and we feasted on the results. It was the local way to keep the kids entertained while the adults had a ball—and very effective it was, too!

Ice cream: a history

Ice cream is said to have been invented by Catherine de Medici. It was made by placing a tin or pewter container inside another container, which was then filled with a mixture of ice and salt. Cream was then poured into the inner container and sugar and flavoring, such as fruit juice, liqueur, or even jam, added. The mixture was then stirred continuously with a spaddle, or revolving paddle, generally made of copper, and at the same time, the inner pot was turned by a handle. By keeping the mixture constantly on the move, the ingredients would not separate before congealing and no lumps would form. As the cream was churned, it also froze slowly to make the ice cream.

Ice cream made with cream is very different from the stuff you buy from fast food outlets and is really worth eating. Pure frozen cream is pointless. Ice cream should be sweet and fruity; egg white, gelatin, and even egg yolks can be used to enrich the texture.

William Cobbett, in his marvelous book *Cottage Economy*, described how to preserve ice from the winter right through the summer in a semi-subterranean ice house, insulated with a great thickness of straw, and with a provision for draining off the water from melting ice. Most large country homes and mansions had ice houses in their grounds. The ice would be collected from nearby frozen ponds, lakes, and rivers by cart and then buried in the ice house. This meant that ice cream and ice for cooling drinks was available year-round, particularly in the summer months.

To freeze ice cream with ice, you need a metal container, with a good cover on it for the ice cream and some means of stirring it when it is inside the container. This container must be buried in a larger container filled with the ice-and-salt mixture. The latter must be well insulated from the outside air.

To freeze ice cream in your refrigerator, set the fridge at its coldest and put the ice cream mixture in the freezer compartment. Open it up and stir it from time to time to prevent large ice crystals from forming. A chest freezer can be treated just like the freezer compartment of a fridge. Today, the widespread availability of fridges means that we all have the ability to freeze food—and make ice cream—very easily.

Strawberry ice cream
½ cup (115 g) sugar
1 pint (0.5 liter) water
1 lb (0.5 kg) strawberries
¾ pint (0.3 liter) cream or ½ pint (0.25 liter) whipping cream

Use the following method:
Make a syrup of the sugar and water.
Mash the strawberries and strain the seeds out, and when the syrup has cooled, pour it into the strawberry mash.
Add the cream as it is, or if you use whipping cream, beat it first and fold it in.
Then you have to freeze it. This can be done with a chest freezer, a refrigerator, or even with just ice.
If you do it with ice, you must mix the ice with salt, because salt makes the ice colder. Two pounds (0.9 kg) of ice to one (0.5 kg) of salt is about right.

Making Cheese

A pound (0.5 kg) of cheese has 2,000 calories of energy in it. Meat from the forequarters of an ox has a mere 1,100 calories. And cheese—or hard cheese, at any rate—is easy to store and, within certain limitations, improves with age. Cheese is made from milk whose acidity has been increased either by an additive, or by simply being left in the warm so that it does it itself. The extra acid causes the formation of curds and whey. Cheese is made from the curds. The whey is drained off and can be given to the pigs.

SOFT CHEESE

Soft cheese is made by allowing milk to curdle, either just naturally, which it does anyway in the summertime, or by adding rennet. Rennet is a chemical that occurs in the stomachs of calves and has the property of curdling milk Milk curdled with rennet is called junket. Milk that curdles naturally forms curds and whey. If you simply hang up some curds and whey in a muslin bag, the whey will drip out and the curds will turn to soft cheese. This is tasteless without flavoring, but seasoned with salt and herbs, or garlic, or chives, it is delicious. Eat it quickly because it won't keep long and is therefore no good for preserving the summer glut of milk for the winter.

Cream cheese and poor man's cheese

Cream cheese is simply soft cheese made with curdled cream instead of curdled milk. The result is smoother, richer, and more buttery.

Poor man's cheese got its name because it could be made from the milk of one cow. A lot of it was eaten in England in the Middle Ages. Warm some milk slowly in a pot and let it curdle. Leave the curds in the whey overnight and drain the whey off in the morning. Then cut up the curd, salt it, tie it up tightly in a linen cloth, and leave it all day to drip. Retie it more tightly in the evening and leave it to hang for a month. You can eat it at the end of the month and it will taste even better if you work some butter into the curd and leave it for three or four months to mature.

HARD CHEESE

Hard cheese is important as a method of preserving the summer flush of milk for the winter, and also as a very valuable source of protein and a marvelous food. Everyone needs cheese, and lacto-vegetarians can scarcely do without it. Hard cheese is difficult to make, and better cheese is made from the milk of many cows than from the milk of only one cow.

The reason for this is that, for bacteriological reasons, the best cheese is made from the milk from two milkings only: the evening's milking and the following morning's. If you have to save up more than those two milkings to get enough milk to make a cheese, you will almost certainly run into trouble with such things as overacidity and "off" flavors—the cheese will have a nasty taste.

CHEDDAR

If you make cheese on a fairly large scale—say, from the milk of six or seven cows—you should have certain equipment and do the job scientifically. On the next page I describe how to make hard cheese if you have approximately six gallons (23 liters) of milk from two milkings and don't feel the need to be too scientific. A marvelous cheddar cheese can be made in this way, but luck, as well as skill, and common sense come into it. If you don't make good cheese using the method overleaf, you will have to try using starters (*see p.292*).

Caerphilly

Once you have made cheddar successfully, you might enjoy trying to make other cheeses. Caerphilly originated as a semihard cheese made by the wives of South Wales coal miners, for their husbands to take down in the pit. It is an easy cheese to make, but will not keep as long as cheddar.

To make Caerphilly, strain the evening's milk into a vat and cool it if the weather is hot. The next morning, skim off the cream and add a starter to the milk at a rate of about 0.5 percent of the milk. Warm the cream of last night's milk and pour it in together with that morning's milk. The purpose of skimming last night's cream off and warming it up and putting it back again is that only in this way will you get it to mix back with the milk and enrich the cheese.

Heat the vat to 68°F (20°C). Measure the acidity with an acidimeter. When it reaches 0.18 percent, add a teaspoon of rennet extract to every six gallons (23 liters) of milk. About 45 minutes after renneting, the curd will be ready for cutting.

Cut both ways with the vertical knife but only one way with the horizontal knife. After cutting, leave for 10 minutes, gradually raising the temperature of the vat to 88°F (31°C): the "scalding." When this is complete, and there is 0.16 percent acidity, draw the whey off, scoop the curd into coarse cloths, and leave it in a dry vat to drain. After half an hour, cut the curd into 3-inch (8-cm) cubes, tie again in the cloths, and allow to drain for another half- hour.

Mill the curd (break it up into small pieces) and add 1 ounce salt (28 g) to every 3 pounds (1.5 kg) curd, mix well, and put it in cloth-lined chessits or molds. About 10 pounds (4.5 kg) of curd go into each chessit, and the chessits are traditionally fairly small and of flattish section, not the huge half-hundredweight cheddar ones. Two hours later, apply pressure of four hundredweight (200 kg). The next morning, take the cheeses out, turn and put on fresh cloths, put back in the press, and give them five hundredweight (250 kg). That afternoon, turn again, put on more clean cloths, and apply 15 hundredweight (750 kg) for the night. The next day take out and store it for a month at as near 65°F (19°C) as you can get, turning it two or three times a week and wiping it with a cloth dipped in salt water. After that, it is ready to eat.

Stilton

Properly made, this blue-molded cheese is one of the finest in existence. Factory-made, however, it's pretty boring. You need about 18 gallons (68 liters) of milk using the one- or two-curd system. Let the evening's milk curdle, and let the morning's milk do the same. Mix the two together and the rest of the process is the same. With the one-curd system, take the milk straight from the cow and put it in a tub or vat. Heat to about 85°F (30°C). Add a teaspoon of rennet extract for every six gallons (23 liters) of milk. Dilute the rennet with ½ pint (0.3 liter) of cold water before adding it to the milk.

After half an hour, try dragging the dairy thermometer upward through the curd. If it leaves a clean cut and no curd sticks to it, then it's ready for cutting. But don't cut it. Ladle it out into vessels lined with coarse cheesecloth, so the whey can drain through the cloth but not away completely (you've left the plug in the vessel or sink). About 4 gallons (16 liters) of curd should be ladled out in fairly thin slabs. After ladling, the curd should be left there soaking in its own whey for 30 minutes. Pull out the plugs and let the whey run away. Draw the corners of the cloth tighter around the curds. Replace the plugs and let the curds have a second draining for half an hour. If the curd feels soft, leave it longer in the whey; if it is firm, draw the plugs and drain the whey off. Now keep tightening the cloth around the curd—hauling one corner of the cloth around the other three corners and pulling tight. Each time you do this, you gently expel some whey. Do it five or six times. When the curd registers 0.18 percent acidity, turn it out of the cloths. Pile the bundles of curd up on top of each other, then cut into about 3-inch (8-cm) cubes.

Keep turning the pile every half hour until the acidity reaches 0.14 or 0.15 percent. This may take from two to four hours. If you haven't got an acidimeter, just go on until the curd is fairly solid but still moist and has a nice flaky look to it when it's cut. Now break the curd up into small pieces as for other cheeses, add an ounce (28 g) of salt to every three pounds (1.4 kg) of curd, and mix well. Place the curd in hoops or molds: 18 gallons (68 liters) of milk should produce about 26 lb (12 kg) of curd. Place it on a wooden board. By now the curd should be cool, not more than 65°F (19°C). Don't press, just let it sink down.

Take the cheese out and turn it twice during the first two hours, then once a day for seven days. When the cheese has shrunk away from the sides of the mold, take it out and scrape the surface of the cheese with a knife to smooth it. Then bandage it tightly with calico. Put it back in the hoop and mold. Take it out of the mold and rebandage it every day for three days. Then take it to the drying room, which should have a good draft and be about 60°F (16°C). Take the bandage off once or twice to help drying, and leave it off for a day. Then put it on again.

After 14 days, remove the cheese to a cellar, again about 60°F (16°C), but with not too much draft, and plenty of humidity. Leave it there for four months before eating it.

SEMISOFT CHEESE

For me *Pont-l'Eveque* is one of the best of the Continental cheeses. To make it, take 7 pints (3.5 liters) of 12-hour-old milk. Heat to 90°F (32°C) and add a teaspoonful of cheese-maker's rennet diluted with three times its own volume of water. Leave for half an hour to curdle. When the curd is firm enough (when it comes cleanly away from the side of the vat), cut it both ways with a curd knife.

Spread cheesecloth over a wooden draining rack and ladle the curd on to the cloth. Fold the corners of the cloth over the curd and gently squeeze. Progressively increase the pressure until you get a lot of the whey out. Place a mold, which is just a collar 1½ inches (4 cm) deep and about 6 inches (15 cm) square, on a straw mat on a draining board. After the curd has been draining for about an hour in the cloth, break the curd up and put it in the mold in three layers, with a layer of salt between each. Use two ounces (56 g) of salt for the seven pints (3.5 liters). Pack the curd well down and into the corners.

When the mold is full, turn it upside down onto another straw mat on another board. Both mats and boards should have been washed in boiling water. Repeat this turning process every 10 minutes for an hour. Turn the mold upside down again once a day for three days. Then take the cheese out of the mold and scrape the surface gently with a knife.

You can eat it there and then, but it is far better if you can keep it at a temperature of more or less 58°F (15°C) for two weeks, turning it on to a clean mat daily. The outside of the cheese will be covered with mold. Wrap the cheese in wax paper and keep for another month, turning it over each day. Before eating or selling, scrape the mold from the surface. The outside should then be quite firm, but the center should be soft and buttery and utterly delicious.

Starters

Starters are batches of milk rich in lactic acid bacteria; you can buy them or make them. Take a quart (liter) of milk from a healthy cow and allow it to get sour in a clean, well-ventilated dairy. Don't include the very first milk to come from the cow. See that the udder, and you, are washed thoroughly before milking. Strain the milk straight from the milking bucket into a sterilized container. Leave this fresh milk in the dairy for 24 hours. It is best if the temperature of the dairy is about 70°F (21°C). This quart of milk becomes almost a pure culture of *Bacillus lacticus*.

Put some fresh milk through your separator (don't worry if you don't have one). Heat this milk to exactly 185°F (85°C) and cool it quickly to 70°F (21°C). This pasteurizes it. Skim the top off the first quart of milk (give it to the cat). Pour the rest of the first quart into the new, now pasteurized, milk. This inoculated milk must be covered with a cloth and kept for 24 hours at about 70°F (21°C). This is then your starter. Add a pint (0.5 liter) of this every day to a new batch of pasteurized milk to keep the culture going for months.

MAKING A HARD CHEESE

1 Put the evening's milk in a settling pan and leave it overnight. In the morning, skim the cream off with a skimmer, put it in a separate pan, and heat it to 85°F (30°C). Pour it back into the milk and stir it in.

2 Now add the morning's milk and any *starter* if you have it—it "starts" the lactic acid bacteria working much more quickly and enables them to defy competition from unworthier organisms. Gently heat the milk to a temperature of 90°F (32°C).

3 Put one teaspoonful of rennet in a cupful of cold water and pour it in. Stir with your hand for about five minutes. As soon

as the milk begins to cling to your fingers, stop stirring.

4 Immediately start stroking the top of the milk with the skimmer. This stops the cream from rising to the surface. Stroke gently for about five minutes. After this, the curd should set enough to trap the cream.

5 When the curd feels firm to your hand (about 50 minutes after you have stopped stirring), cut it with curd knives or a long-bladed kitchen knife, into cubes about ¾ inch (2 cm) square.

6 Warm the milk—now "curds and whey"—extremely

slowly, to 100°F (38°C). If you don't have a cheese vat, the best way is to scoop a saucepanful of whey out, heat it, and pour it back again. As you do this, stir very gently with your hand.

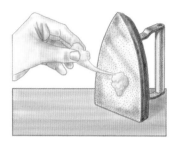

7 Pitching raises the acidity of the curd. You simply leave the curds to soak in the whey, and test every now and then for acidity. If you don't have an acidimeter, use the hot iron test. Take a bit of curd, touch it on hot iron so that it sticks, and draw it away. If the thread is less than half an inch (1 cm) long when it breaks, leave the stuff to go on pitching. When the thread breaks at about half an inch, the acidity is right (0.17 to 0.18), and you can drain off the whey.

8 A cheese-mill is two spiked rollers working against each other to break the curd up into small pieces. if you don't have a mill, you will have to do this by hand, which is a rather laborious task. To do this, break the curd up into small pieces (about the size of walnuts) with your fingers. Once separated, mix an ounce (28 g) of fine salt to every four pounds (1.8 kg) of curd and blend well.

9 Line the chessit with cheese-cloth, put your bits of curd into it, cover with the cloth, put on your follower, and apply pressure.

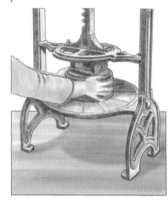

10 If you have a cheese press, apply pressure with this, or improvise. For the first six hours 20–30 lb (9.0–14 kg) of pressure is enough. Then pull the cheese out, wash the cheesecloth in warm water and wring it out, wrap again, and replace the cheese upside down. Put on half a hundredweight (25 kg) pressure. After a day, turn the cheese and replace it. After another day turn it and give it ½ ton pressure for 2 days, turning it once.

11 Paste the surface of the cheeses with flour and water, and then wrap with calico or clean cloth. Store at about 55–60°F (13–16°C). Turn every day for a week and thereafter about twice a week.

"After all these romantic yearnings for the fine and the primitive, we ended up with an *Aga* [a cast-iron, heat storage stove with big boiling and simmering plates]. It sits silent and brooding as though it has some atomic pile in its belly. It almost never goes out, it keeps the water beautifully and constantly hot, it will boil a kettle in a few moments at any time at all, night or day, it is marvelous for making bread and—an enormous economy—it is fine for boiling up potatoes for the pigs. Now, every night, we simply put a big iron pot full of spuds and water in the slow oven, and take it out in the morning when we make the early morning tea. The great objection to fattening pigs on potatoes—labor—is out. And any time of the winter or summer, our living kitchen is warm to go into, there is a fine hot cupboard for drying clothes, and the stove fairly economical with fuel, which of course we have to buy."

JOHN SEYMOUR FAT OF THE LAND 1976

CHAPTER SEVEN

IN THE
KITCHEN

The North-Facing Storeroom

While rearing, growing, and brewing are active and satisfying parts of self-sufficiency, good and effective storage has its own rewards, too, even if it might seem like a sedentary pursuit. Sadly, this is often only learned by bitter experience, as wonderful produce from the garden becomes useless fodder for the compost heap long before it can be eaten.

Pantries, larders, dairies, and cellars

For thousands of years, humans managed to live without refrigerators, freezers, tin cans, plastic wrapping, and all the other modern-day conveniences of consumerism. And it wasn't so long ago when houses were always built to include pantries, larders, dairies, and cellars—the storerooms. If you look at traditionally designed old farmhouses, you will see how carefully the builders took advantage of the lie of the land. All the old Northumbrian farmhouses were aligned east–west: the desire was simply to ensure that the front of the house faced due south and had the benefit of the sun's warmth throughout the day. All of the rooms (apart from the pantry and the dairy) faced south. The corridor and stairs were on the north side of the house, forming an insulating barrier against cold north winds.

If you are fortunate enough to have a house with a basement, then many of your storage problems will be eased. If you are building your own house, then think carefully how you could incorporate a cellar (at least part of which should be below ground level). A cellar keeps its cool and constant temperature by being under the earth. An old cellar will tend to be very damp and under-ventilated. You need to watch out for this and take steps to keep damp out of your stored produce. You may even want to increase ventilation by knocking a couple of holes through to the outside and putting in mesh to avoid flies and mice.

Self-supporters without an existing basement or cellar will have to improvise: and the north-facing storeroom is one way to solve the problem. If you cannot muster the resources to build such a space, then you can at least make do with the smaller and simpler device of a meat safe. My preference is to construct a storage area against the north wall of the house, or the east wall if there is no convenient north wall, to provide:

1 *a cool and even temperature*
2 *reasonable humidity that is not too dry and not too wet*
3 *security against rats and mice*
4 *good ventilation*
5 *fly-proof doors, walls and ceilings*
6 *no access for direct sunlight*

1 Temperature Good storage temperature should be cool, but without frost, and it should not change quickly. For wines, beers, jams, pickles, and all vegetables, this is the ideal. The underground cellar is the perfect answer as far as temperature is concerned, but it will suffer from lack of ventilation and may be difficult to protect from flies and rats. A north-facing storeroom or traditional pantry can avoid these problems, even though it may be warmer than we would like if the weather is hot.

2 Humidity If a place is too wet, then mold and fungus will thrive, string or muslin will rot, and paper will be worse than useless. On the other hand, if your storage is too dry, your vegetables will quickly shrivel up. For most purposes (in a northern climate), the ambient air humidity is reasonable enough. If there are sufficient vegetables in the store, then they will also create their own humidity as water slowly evaporates from them.

3 Security against pests Rats and mice get in through the tiniest of tiny holes, but they will also remorselessly gnaw away at wood, cement, or plastic when they scent the prospect of food. Plastic and wood will always be suspect materials at the base of doors, whereas aluminum sheeting is a good resistant material if you really want to keep the pests out. Hanging food from a rafter is useless protection against mice, but if you hang it from rings screwed into a flat, smooth ceiling then you will keep the little beasts at bay. Having cats, terriers, or hawks around will also disrupt rat or mice sorties.

4 Ventilation Screen mesh (and plenty of it) is essential. Make sure you have ventilation at top and bottom of the store or in line with the prevailing wind in order to keep a flow going through your store. Ventilation prevents mold and fungus, but it will tend to dry things out, so if the weather is very warm and windy, you may want to cover some of your vents.

5 Flies Unless you plan to store uncooked meats, it doesn't have to be perfectly fly-proof. My preference would be to have a special meat safe kept specifically for this purpose, and that would be perfectly fly-proof. Obviously, the more you discourage flies the better, and not just blowflies but also the moths that could lay eggs of vegetable-eating grubs on your produce. Cover individual items with muslin if you are worried about them.

6 Sunlight Direct sunlight not only creates unwanted warmth but can also discolor and dry out foodstuffs. Wines and beers should be kept out of the sun while they mature—hence the traditional use of brown glass bottles.

Other traditional cooling methods

Don't forget that you can keep things cool by standing them in water, in the shade, and covering with a cloth. The water will soak up into the cloth, which is then dried by the wind. As those of you who managed to get through a physics course in high school will know, water has a high latent heat of evaporation. Water cannot simply turn to water vapor without sucking in heat from its surroundings. So when the wind evaporates the water, it creates a significant cooling effect. The same principle applies when large trees are grown around city squares—the thousands of gallons of water that are evaporated every hour by the sun and wind cool down the air temperature.

BUILDING YOUR OWN

Your storeroom does not need to be enormous; even something just 6 feet (1.8 m) square will be extremely useful. Most importantly, it should not let in damp from the earth, so use a good-quality plastic membrane under your floor. Make sure you keep the edge of its base (where the door opens) well above ground level to deter pests and prevent flooding in heavy rain.

Your storeroom may or may not be a walk-in room, but either way, it is useful to have shelving that can be taken in or out as the need requires. All shelving should be easy to clean. Make sure any windows are weatherproof.

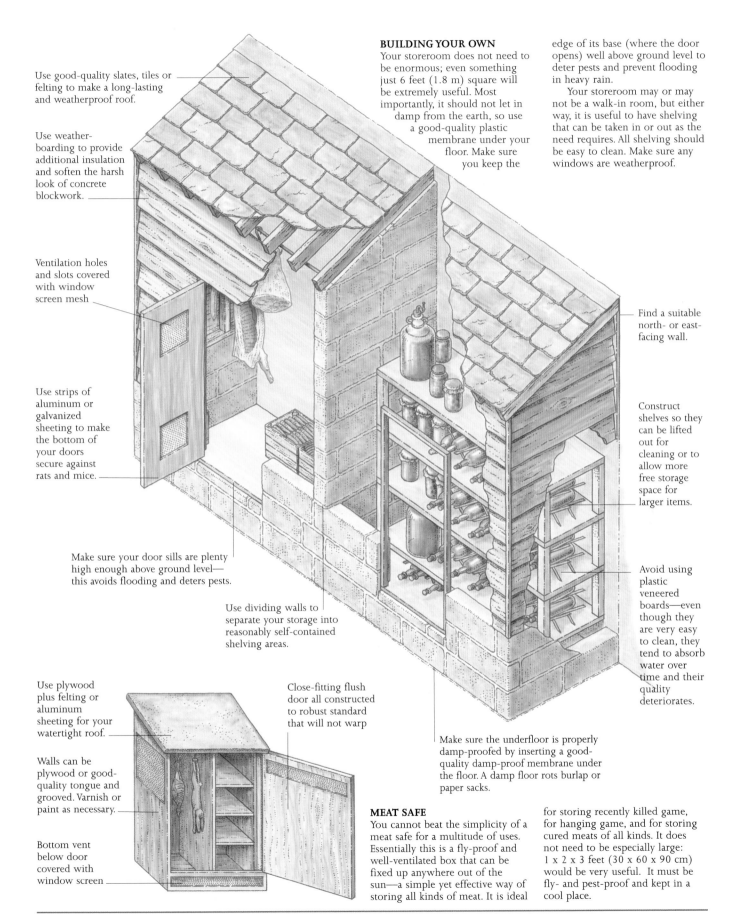

Use good-quality slates, tiles or felting to make a long-lasting and weatherproof roof.

Use weatherboarding to provide additional insulation and soften the harsh look of concrete blockwork.

Ventilation holes and slots covered with window screen mesh

Use strips of aluminum or galvanized sheeting to make the bottom of your doors secure against rats and mice.

Make sure your door sills are plenty high enough above ground level— this avoids flooding and deters pests.

Use dividing walls to separate your storage into reasonably self-contained shelving areas.

Find a suitable north- or east-facing wall.

Construct shelves so they can be lifted out for cleaning or to allow more free storage space for larger items.

Avoid using plastic veneered boards—even though they are very easy to clean, they tend to absorb water over time and their quality deteriorates.

Use plywood plus felting or aluminum sheeting for your watertight roof.

Walls can be plywood or good-quality tongue and grooved. Varnish or paint as necessary.

Bottom vent below door covered with window screen

Close-fitting flush door all constructed to robust standard that will not warp

Make sure the underfloor is properly damp-proofed by inserting a good-quality damp-proof membrane under the floor. A damp floor rots burlap or paper sacks.

MEAT SAFE

You cannot beat the simplicity of a meat safe for a multitude of uses. Essentially this is a fly-proof and well-ventilated box that can be fixed up anywhere out of the sun—a simple yet effective way of storing all kinds of meat. It is ideal for storing recently killed game, for hanging game, and for storing cured meats of all kinds. It does not need to be especially large: 1 x 2 x 3 feet (30 x 60 x 90 cm) would be very useful. It must be fly- and pest-proof and kept in a cool place.

Harvesting & Storing

Here are a few golden rules that I suggest you follow when it comes to harvesting your hard-won crops. Don't harvest more than you can process or store, or it will simply be wasted, unless, of course, you can give it away and improve your social credit ratings. Be extremely careful not to damage the crop when you pick it or dig it. You must never try to store substandard or damaged produce. Harvesting, processing, and storing are part of a seamless process, each dovetailing into the other and all useless without the others. In many ways, the excitement of the harvest is often tempered by the realities of processing and storage.

VEGETABLES

Clamping is the traditional way to store a variety of root crops. The problem for the smallholder is that this is not a very effective method for small quantities. Hence my suggestion that you try using an old freezer or two as a vegetable store. It can work surprisingly well, and it keeps out the rats. For beets and other roots, I have found burlap or sturdy paper sacks very good if kept in the confines of a good storeroom or cellar.

Beans and peas should be dried and stored away in great quantities every fall. When they are thoroughly dried, threshed, and winnowed, store them in crocks, barrels, bins, or other mouse-proof places. Mushrooms and most fungi dry out at an ideal temperature of 120°F (50°C), so crumble them afterward into a powder and store them in closed jars. The powder is marvelous for flavoring soups and stews. Sweet corn is excellent dried: it really is a thing worth having. Boil it well on the cob, dry the cobs in a slow oven overnight, cut the kernels off the cobs, and store them in closed jars. When you want to eat them, just boil them.

FRUIT

As a rule, the early-maturing varieties of apples and pears will not store well. So eat them as you pick them, and store only late-ripening varieties. Leave these on the trees as long as possible, and only pick them when they are so ripe that they come off if you lift them gently. Pick them and lay them carefully in a basket. Then spread them out gently in an airy place to let them dry overnight. The next day, store them in a dark, well-ventilated place at a temperature of 35–40°F (2–4°C). Pears like it very slightly warmer.

Ideally, each fruit should be wrapped individually in paper to isolate any molds or bacteria. Only perfect fruit can qualify for storing, so disqualify any with bruises, cuts, or missing stalks. If the floor is earth, stone, or concrete, you can throw water on it occasionally to keep the air moist. Storing fruit in a hot, dry attic is simply giving pigs a treat. Apples may well keep until spring. If you fear they won't keep long enough, you can happily dry them. Core them, slice thinly, string up the slices, and hang over a stove, or in a solar-heated dryer (see p.344), at 150°F (65°C) for five hours. When crisp and dry, put them into an airtight container and store in a cool place.

LIFTING POTATOES

Any damage to your potatoes or other root crops, especially carrots, will be multiplied twenty-fold by storage—roots are very easily bruised. Always sort the crop carefully into three piles: the first for storage (these are perfect and large); the second for more immediate consumption (these may be damaged or too small to store); and the third for the compost heap or burning (these are diseased, too small or too damaged to use). Remember that your crop must have time to dry out, preferably on a breezy day, before being put into storage. Also remember that the places you are going to store your crop must be scrupulously cleaned and dry—as must any straw.

DIGGING CARROTS

When digging carrots for storage, make sure your fork is well away from the roots. Put the fork right under and pull gently up with your hand grasping the foliage.

SELECTING CARROTS

Shake or brush the soil free, never wash in water, before you start selecting. Now sort your crop carefully into three piles: one to store, one to use, and one to dispose of.

STORING POTATOES

1 Use an old freezer for storing potatoes. First place a layer of clean dry straw across the base.

2 Dump in several baskets of dry undamaged tubers until you have a layer perhaps a foot (30 cm) deep. Then add a further layer of dry, clean straw.

3 Put in the next layer of spuds. Then put a final layer of straw over the top before closing down the lid onto a small shim to let in air but keep out rats.

CLAMPING

Clamping is a method of protecting root crops in the open, where diseases do not build up as they can in a cellar. But no clamp keeps out hard frost, so in very cold winters, you must store indoors.

1 When you pick potatoes for clamping you should let them dry for a few hours first. Prepare the clamp by putting a layer of straw on the ground.

2 Heap the potatoes (or other root crop) on top of the straw in the shape of a pyramid, so that when it is finished, rain will drain off.

3 Cover with a layer of straw or bracken. Allow a period for sweating before covering with earth.

4 Cover with a layer of earth 5–6 inches (13–15 cm) thick. Beat the earth flat with the back of a spade.

5 Make sure that bits of straw protrude from the clamp to admit some air to the crop inside.

STRINGING ONIONS

You can store onions on trays with slats, on polyethelene netting, or on a wooden stand. But the ideal way of keeping them is to string them up in a cool place with access to plenty of air. Before you store your onions, always remember to dry them thoroughly first, either by leaving them on the ground in the sun, or covered but in the wind if it is wet.

1 Make sure that all the onions you want to string have long stalks. Start by knotting four of them firmly together.

2 Add onions one by one to the original four. Twist their stalks and knot them tightly around string or binding twine.

3 Continue adding individual onions to the growing bunch, ensuring that each one is securely tied on, and that the bunch does not become too heavy.

4 Braid the knotted stalks around a long piece of string so that the onions hang evenly when you hold them up.

5 Hang the string up when you decide the your bunch is complete. The onions should keep indefinitely.

OTHER STORING METHODS

HANGING IN NETS

Squashes or pumpkins will keep best if hung in nets, although they can be stored on shelves, if turned occasionally.

STORING BEETS

Use dry sand so the roots don't touch, and keep safe from frost.

FLATBED STORING

Late-ripening apples last all winter if you keep them in a cool dark place, but be sure that they aren't touching each other. A storing bed (*see below*) is ideal for this. You could even wrap each one in paper also. Store onions on wire netting. If it rains they should be in the wind, but under cover.

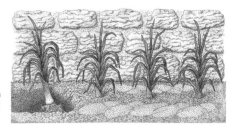

Apple storing bed

Wire-mesh onion drying bed

HEELING IN LEEKS

If you fear that your leeks, celery, and Jerusalem artichokes might be exposed to frost in the open, "heel" them into dry, sheltered ground near the house, where they will derive some protection from harsh weather. Otherwise they are generally best left in the ground until required.

Making Bread

There is white bread and wholemeal bread, and many gradations between the two. There is leavened bread and unleavened bread, and again many gradations. There is sourdough and soda bread, pita bread and flat bread, but the great thing for the self-supporter to remember is that whatever kind of bread you choose to make, and whatever kind of grain you make it from, the process is simple. It is also fun, and even the most ham-fisted cooks can take pleasure and pride in their efforts.

Undoubtedly the first breads were unleavened, and undoubtedly the first person who discovered yeast discovered it by accident. If you make a dough with flour and water without yeast or baking powder and then bake it, you will be left with something very like a brick. People got over this by rolling the dough out very thinly and cooking it that way. (In Baghdad to this day you will see bakers putting great sheets of thin dough—as big as small blankets—into enormous cylindrical ovens.) But no doubt one day someone mixed up some dough, didn't cook it immediately, and found the stuff began to ferment.

What had happened was that wild yeasts had gotten into it and were converting the sugar (in the flour) into alcohol and carbonic acid gas. The alcohol evaporated, but the carbon dioxide blew the glutinous dough up into bubbles. This unknown ancient took up the bubbling doughy mass and placed it upon his hot stone or maybe into a little hollowed-out stone oven and made what was the first leavened bread.

It was then found that bread could be made not in thin sheets but in thick loaves, and was still good to eat. Furthermore, it was discovered that leavened bread stays palatable longer than unleavened bread: good home-baked wholemeal bread can taste fine for five days or more, while unleavened bread tastes very dreary unless you eat it when it is still absolutely fresh.

Yeast

How long it took mankind (or womankind) to figure out the true nature of that lovely stuff yeast, we will never know. But certainly they must have found that if they were lucky enough to get a good strain of wild yeast in their dough, they could go on breeding it—simply by keeping a little raw dough back from each baking to mix in with the next batch of bread. The old pioneers in the Wild West were called "sourdoughs" because they made their bread thus. And even today, people out of reach of bakeries and yeast suppliers commonly make bread with sourdough.

If you live near a bakery, always buy your yeast fresh. It should be a creamy putty color, cool to the touch and easy to break, with a nice yeasty smell. Don't buy any that is crumbly or has dark patches. It will keep for a week to 10 days in a screwtop jar in the refrigerator. Or cut it into one-inch (2.5-cm) cubes and freeze it. Both yeast and bread freeze well. If you cannot obtain fresh yeast, you can still make a perfectly good bread with dried yeast.

This is widely available in packets, and it will keep for up to three months. But it is a good idea to test dried yeast if you have had it around for some time. Drop a few grains into a little warm liquid dough mix; if it is still "live," it will froth in under 10 minutes.

If you are using fresh yeast for any recipe specifying dried yeast, always double the quantity. Or halve it if the recipe asks for fresh yeast and you are using it dried.

Yeast flourishes in a warm atmosphere in temperatures between 48–95°F (9–35°C), but strong heat—over 140°F (60°C)—will kill it. Set your dough to rise in a warm place: on top of the stove, in the oven, or even under the quilt on the bed.

If you are brewing beer (*see pp.322–325*), you can use your beer yeast for your bread-making. Conversely, you can use your bread yeast in your beer-making. Neither is ideal because they are two different kinds of yeast, but we have done it often and we get surprisingly good beer and good bread.

Kneading

A word about kneading. Kneading is important because it releases the gluten and distributes the yeast right through the dough. Don't be afraid to treat your dough fiercely when you knead it. Push and pull it around until it seems to take on a life of its own, becoming silky and springy in your hands. Then leave it alone to prove, that is, to rest for a few hours until it has risen. When it has risen enough, it should jump back at the touch of a finger.

Keeping

If you don't have a freezer, keep bread in a dry, cool, well-ventilated bin. Don't put it in an airtight container or it will get moldy. Make sure the bread is cool before you stow it away or the steam in a warm loaf will make it turn soggy. Keep your flour in a dry, dark, cool cupboard.

There's much more to bread than white sliced or whole wheat. And we should all be thankful for that. Bread can be made from soy, rye, wheat, corn, sorghum, or oats. If you vary your grain, you vary your bread. It's as simple as that. Have it leavened or unleavened, plain or fancy, or try a mixture of flours.

Bread at its most basic, as we have just seen, is simply yeast, flour, salt, and water. Add milk, butter, eggs, sugar, honey, bananas, carrots, nuts, and currants and you will enrich your bread and change its taste and texture. Roll it in whole wheat grain, or poppy seed, sesame, dill, celery, caraway, sunflower, or aniseed, as you please. Brush it with milk; paint it with egg yolk. Shine a currant loaf with sugar syrup. Knot it, twist it, braid it. Experiment, and you will find that being your own baker is one of the great joys of the self-sufficient way of life.

On the following two pages, I describe some of the different flours and a variety of breads you can make in your own home—and how to make bread the traditional and tasty way.

Bread made with different flours

For people who grow rye, barley, oats, corn, rice, sorghum, and the rest, it is useful and interesting to try some breads made with these grains, or with them mixed with wheat flour. It must be remembered that of all the grains, only wheat has enough gluten to sustain the gas generated by the living yeast sufficiently to make fairly light, or risen, bread.

You can try a combination of two or three different flours, but it is usually worth adding some wheat flour. And always add salt. Oil, butter, lard, or margarine help to keep bread moist. Water absorption varies with the kind of flour. Here is a rundown of the different flours:

Wheat flour Wheat flour is rich in gluten, which makes the dough stretch and, as it cooks, fixes it firmly around the air bubbles caused by the leavening.

Rye flour Rye flour gives bread a nice sour taste, and can be used on its own, although a lighter bread will result if half or a third of the flour is wheat flour. Maslin, flour made from rye and wheat grown together and ground together, was the staple English flour of the Middle Ages. Only the rich ate pure wheaten bread.

Barley flour Barley flour alone makes very sweet-tasting bread. A proportion of one-third barley flour to two-thirds wheat produces good bread. If you toast the barley flour first, your bread will be extra-delicious.

Oatmeal Oatmeal is also sweet and makes a very chewy, damp bread, which fills you up very nicely. Use half oat and half wheat flour for a good balance.

Cornmeal Bread made from cornmeal has a crumbly texture. Try half cornmeal and half wheat flour.

Ground rice Ground rice bread is a lot better if the rice is mixed half and half with wheat flour.

Cooked brown rice Like the whole cooked grains of any other cereal, cooked brown rice can be mixed with wheat flour to make an unusual bread.

Sorghum By itself, sorghum (or millet) flour makes a dry bread. Add wheat flour and you will get nice crunchy bread.

Soy flour Soy flour, too, is better mixed with wheat. The soy flour adds a lot of nourishment.

Bread made without yeast

Unyeasted bread is really solid stuff, quite unlike yeasted bread, which is, after all, half full of nothing but air. To my mind, it can only be eaten cut very thin. Warm or even boiling water helps to start softening the starch in the flour. Kneading helps to release the gluten. If unyeasted dough is allowed to rest overnight, the bread you make will be lighter, because the starch will soften more and a little fermentation will begin. The carbon dioxide released will provide a few air holes.

I suggest the same proportions of whole wheat to other flours as with yeasted bread. Other ingredients need be nothing but salt and water, and perhaps oil to brush the tops of loaves. Knead well, and leave to prove overnight.

Unyeasted bread may need longer and slower cooking than yeasted bread. It will also need good teeth.

Standard wholemeal bread

I never measure my flour because what matters is getting the dough to the right consistency, and flour absorbs more or less water according to its fineness, quality, etc. But for people who must have exact quantities of everything, this is what Sam Mayall, an experienced English baker, who grows and mills his own wheat, uses:

2½ lb (1.1 kg) of wholemeal flour
1 oz (28 g) salt
½ oz (14 g) dried yeast
2 teaspoons soft brown sugar
1½ pints (0.7 liters) water

Put the flour and salt in a bowl. Put the yeast in another bowl, and add the sugar and some warm water. Leave in a warm place to rise.

When the yeast is fermenting well, add it to the flour and the rest of the water, and knead it until it is soft and silky in texture. Return it to the bowl and leave it to stand in a warm place until it has about doubled its size. Knead it again for a few minutes and mold into loaves. Place in warmed greased and floured pans, and, if it is soft wheat flour, leave it to rise for five minutes. If it is hard wheat flour, allow longer, up to 20 minutes. Put in the oven at 425°F (220°C) for 45 minutes.

Corn bread

Corn bread tastes good. It is crunchy and rather gritty and should have a nice brown crust. You will need:

1½ pints (0.7 liters) boiling water.
2 lb (0.9 kg) corn flour
2 teaspoons baking powder
3 eggs (optional)
½ pint (0.25 liters) buttermilk (optional)

Mix the meal with the baking powder and pour on the boiling water. Adding eggs and/or buttermilk improves the bread. Bake in a greased pan at 400°F (205°C) for about 40 minutes.

Sorghum bread

This is a rather dry bread, and only really worth making if sorghum is all you've got. Sorghum is much better mixed with wheat flour. You need:

12 oz (340 g) sorghum flour
1 teaspoon baking powder
1 teaspoon salt

Mix the ingredients and wet with warm water to make a stiffish dough. Bake for about 50 minutes at 350°F (175°C).

Oat bread

In those damp parts of the world where nothing else will grow, oat bread is common. It is heavy and sweet-tasting. To make it you will need the following ingredients:

1 lb (0.5 kg) rolled oats or oat flour
3 oz (84 g) sugar or honey
1 tablespoon salt
4 oz (114 g) butter
1 pint (0.5 liters) boiling water (use a little less
if you use honey)
1 oz (28 g) yeast or ½ oz (14 g) dried yeast

Mix the dry ingredients well, rub in the butter, and add the boiling water. Dissolve the yeast in a little tepid water. When it begins to froth, mix it well in with the other mixture. Leave to rise for a few hours. Then dump dough on a floured board and knead for about 10 minutes. Cut and shape into rounded, loaf-sized lumps, and allow for some expansion.

Put on a baking tray in a warm place and allow to expand for about an hour. Then put in the oven at 450°F (230°C) for 45 minutes. Test as usual by tapping the bottoms of the loaves to see if they are hollow. Stand to cool on a wire tray so that the air can circulate all around them.

MAKING BREAD

If you can boil an egg, you can bake bread. There is absolutely nothing difficult about it. To make six medium loaves, take 4½ pints (2.3 liters) of water, warmed to blood heat, 2 ounces (56 g) of salt, and the same amount of brown sugar, 1 tablespoon of fresh yeast (or half this amount of dried yeast). You can even use yeast from the bottom of your bee hive.

1 Put all the ingredients into a large mixing bowl. When the yeast has dissolved, pour in enough flour to make a fine, sticky mash. Stir this well with a wooden spoon.

2 The spoon should stand just about upright. Cover the dish with a cloth and leave it overnight in a warm place free from drafts.

3 Come morning, the yeast will have the dough spilling over with enthusiasm. Heap some dry flour on to a table and dump the dough into the middle of this.

4 Sprinkle dry flour on top of the dough, and it is ready for kneading. Start by mixing the dry flour with the wet dough.

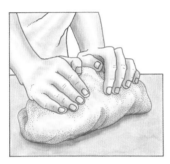

5 The goal is to make a fairly stiff dough, dry on the outside. You do this by pushing the dough away from you with the palms of your hands (*above*) and then pulling it toward you again (*below*). This is kneading, and it is a very sticky process. When the dough sticks to your hands (and it will), throw on some flour. Whenever it feels sticky, sprinkle flour.

6 Kneading must be done thoroughly—you need to push and pull and throw the flour until you have a dry, satisfying little ball. Roll it around to your heart's content. But after 10 minutes, the fun has to stop. It is nearly ready for baking.

7 Divide the dough into six equal portions. Grease the baking pans and shape your dough. Fill the pans just three-quarters full. Score patterns on top with a knife and leave covered for about a hour in a warm place.

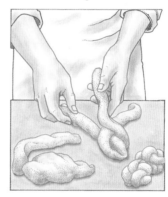

8 If you want to be more decorative, make a braided loaf. Divide the dough into three, make each sausage-shaped, and braid—just like that. If you want to, brush the top with milk to make it shiny and sprinkle with poppy seeds.

9 Shape little rolls with leftover dough. Put them on a baking tray and leave on top of the stove to rise. After 30 minutes, put them in a very hot oven 450°F (232°C). In 10 minutes you will have magnificent breakfast rolls.

Now take up your bread pans very carefully. If you jog them, they will collapse and you will have solid bread, so gently ease them into a hot oven 425°F (220°C). Half an hour later, take a look to see if they are cooking evenly. Turn them if necessary. Wait another 15 minutes, and they should be done.

10 To test them, tap the bottoms. If they sound hollow, they are done. Or push in a skewer—it should come out clean. If it doesn't, it is not a disaster; put them back for a few more minutes.

11 When you are sure your loaves are good and ready, take them out and stand on top of their pans to air.

TEMPERATURE AND TIME

Bread rises (and yeast ferments) best at 80°F (27°C). Yeast will die at any temperature much over 95°F (35°C), and it won't multiply under 48°F (9°C). So the place where you set the bread to rise must fall within these temperatures. Usually the top of the stove is ideal. The oven should be—well, hot. Apart from the time you spend waiting for things to happen, you probably don't spend more than half an hour working the dough, and the result is six beautiful wholemeal loaves.

Preserving

It is fall and you have a surfeit of all the crops you have been gathering through the summer. What could be more fulfilling than to can, pickle, and preserve it in all possible ways for the dark days of winter ahead? Now read on… The harvest season is short for most things, although in a mild climate it is possible to pick fresh green things every day of the year. Few things can equal the pleasure of coming fresh to new green peas at the beginning of their season after six months of pea-abstinence. The palate, jaded and corrupted by months of frozen peas, or quick-dried peas masquerading as fresh garden peas, longs for the delicious taste of freshly picked peas. True dried peas, cooked as pease pudding, or put in soups and stews, are quite another thing. They are a traditional, time-honored way of preserving plant protein for the winter months, and eating them all winter does not jade the palate for the fresh garden pea experience every June.

At the same time there is, potentially, a vitamin shortage in the dark winters, and those dark, cold days should be enlivened by nice tastes and odors besides that of salt bacon. So the self-supporter will wish to preserve certain things, preferably by a process that improves their natural flavor, such as canning, pickling, chutneying, or wine-making. There is nothing more encouraging in fall than the sight of shelves heavily laden with full jars and crocks. More than anything, they give you the feeling that you are likely to survive the winter. This may sound like a contradiction, but it isn't.

There is a legitimate role—and certain suitable foods, especially berries—for freezing (see pp.306–307). Although it is an effective storage system, you may not improve any food by deep-freezing, but you actually improve fruit and vegetables by making them into chutney, jam, and the like. Freezing meat is another matter: unless you are very hungry, you cannot eat a steer before it goes bad. In more sensible times, people killed meat and shared it. Now the whole principle of sharing with neighbors is forgotten and the cold of the freezer often replaces the warmth of neighborly relations.

Wine
Wine-making (see pp.326–329), much like beer-making (see pp.320–325), turns sugar into alcohol. Some fruits, such as grapes grown in a warm climate, have so much natural sugar in them that you don't have to add any. But many of the things you can make wine from are low in sugar. So you will have to add sugar if you want alcohol of a decent strength. And remember that weak wine won't keep, it just goes bad. Some "wine" described in books of wine recipes is simply sugar-water fermented and flavored with some substance. Most flower wines (see p.328) are made like this, and people even make "wine" of tea leaves—that sugarless substance!

Fruit wines have their own sugar, but usually not enough, so you must add some. The same goes for root wines. Parsnip, which is by far the best, has quite a lot of sugar.

What country wines do is to preserve and even enhance the flavor and bouquet of the things they are made of. They cheer us up in the dark days of winter and are very good for us, too.

Chutneys and pickles
You make both chutneys and pickles by flavoring fruit or vegetables, or a combination of both, with spices and preserving them in vinegar. The methods of preserving, however, do not resemble each other (see pp.310–311).

Chutneys are fruits or vegetables that have been cooked in vinegar, often heavily spiced and sweetened. They are cooked until all excess liquid has evaporated, leaving a thick pulp, the consistency of jam. The flavor is mellow. Pickles are put down whole or in large chunks in vinegar, but not heated in it. Anything that is to be pickled must not have too much moisture in it. So sometimes moisture must be drawn out first with salt. The resulting flavor is full and sharp.

Both chutneys and pickles are an excellent way of preserving things for the winter and of enhancing their taste as well. They are delicious with cold meats and meat pies, and also offset the taste of curries or cheeses.

Ketchups and similar sauces are strained juices of fruits or vegetables spiced and cooked in vinegar. These, too, if well made, can give a lift to plain food.

Canning
The principle of canning is very simple. Food is put in jars, and both jars and their contents are heated to a temperature that is maintained long enough to ensure that all bacteria, molds, and viruses are destroyed; at this point the jars are completely sealed to prevent any further pathogens from getting in, and then allowed to cool. Thus the contents of the jars are sterilized by heat, and safe from attack by putrefactive organisms.

The same principle applies to commercial canning, except that the product is preserved in an unattractive steel box. It is also a process that the self-supporter will find considerably less easy than using standard canning jars.

Fruit cans very well. Vegetables are far more difficult, because they are low on acid, and acid makes food preservation easier.

My own feeling about the canning of vegetables is: don't do it. What with salted runner (pole) beans, sauerkraut, clamped or cellared roots or cabbages, and, in all but arctic climates, quite a selection of the things that will grow and can be picked fresh outdoors all winter, there is no need for the rather tasteless, soggy matter that vegetables become when they have been canned.

On the other hand, tomatoes, which aren't, strictly speaking, a vegetable, are a very good thing to can. They give a lift to otherwise dull winter dishes like nothing else can. They are easy to can, you can grow a big surplus during their short growing season, they are rich in vitamins, and they taste delicious.

Freezing

Virtually all fruits, vegetables, and meat can be stored by freezing. Some freeze better than others, and you will discover just what you like and what you do not. Freezing preserves by making it too cold for bacteria and molds to function—but the downside is that ice takes up more space than water, so the cells within foodstuffs are broken, and the texture, and even the flavor, of foods can change.

You may think that by using freezing as a major method of storage, you are courting disaster if your electricity supplier cuts off your power, or if the weather or other natural elements disrupt it. There are two remedies for this: the paper remedy is to take out insurance; the practical remedy is to set yourself up with a standby generator. You can buy reliable standby generators at a reasonable price, and the power requirements of a freezer are fairly minimal. We are so dependent on electricity, which is a very convenient power source for many things, that a standby generator is well worth the effort.

As with all food storage, we should only process good-quality raw materials. Be fussy about this. Damaged fruit and vegetables will not freeze well, and you risk wasting time and space that could be better used for other things.

The chest freezer is like a bizarre frozen filing cabinet and, like all filing systems, it needs to be kept in order. Not only must you have your foods clearly labeled—with labels that do not come off when frozen—but you must also rotate your usage so the oldest items are used first. To give you some idea of how we manage, our smallholding has three fairly large chest freezers: one is kept for meat; the other two for fruit, vegetables, ice cream, and other delicacies we have a hankering for. At least once each year, we arrange to empty one of the freezers to give it a good defrosting—and almost every year we rush to use up or give away fruit we have been carefully hoarding through the winter because June has arrived and the next crop is due. Possibly we have links to prehistoric squirrel species.

TIPS FOR FREEZING

Do not skimp on the quality of raw foodstuffs.
Use foods in rotation.
Defrost freezers regularly.
The longer food is stored, the more moisture it loses, so pack in good-quality freezer bags. After much trial and error, we now use the expensive zip-lock bags because they are tough, lie flat, and can be used several times.

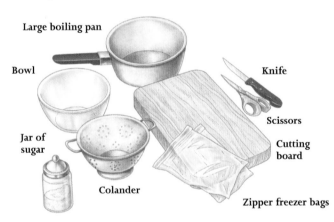

Large boiling pan

Bowl

Knife

Scissors

Jar of sugar

Cutting board

Colander

Zipper freezer bags

FLASH-FREEZING

1 For best results, many foods are best flash-frozen, especially mushrooms and soft fruits. Spread the fruit on a tray or on newspaper and put straight into the freezer, uncovered, for 24 hours.

2 Put the frozen foods into plastic bags. Since they are already frozen, they will not stick together, making them more attractive when cooked.

FREEZING BLACK CURRANTS

1 A freshly picked basket of currants is full of stalks, leaves, and bugs. Minimize these when you are picking and you will save time later.

2 Cut off stalks, take out leaves and debris, and throw bugs into the compost bin. This is a nice job to do socially after supper on a fine summer evening.

3 Fruit does not need any special treatment before being frozen, but it is a good idea to spread them out so they don't touch before flash-freezing.

4 Now the finished product is ready to put into good-quality plastic bags for storage in the freezer. Zip-lock bags are easier to open and close than tie bags.

PLUMS

Everyone looks forward to the plum harvesting season. After all, what can be better than a fragrantly fresh plum straight from the branch? I pick my plums by making sure the grass under the tree is well cut and cleared, then I simply give the tree or the branch a gentle shake. Ripe plums will rain down on your head—possibly with a few angry wasps to boot. Picking them up from the ground is a pleasant job—and if your turf is soft there will be little bruising. Watch out for dozy wasps, and get the plums inside for sorting and processing as soon as you can. Plums keep reasonably well for a few days, but the flavor definitely suffers over time.

BEANS, SNOW PEAS, AND SUGAR SNAPS

All these vegetable freeze very well, and the basic approach to preparation and freezing is the same. First of all, harvest your crop when it is perfectly ripe. Check the crop regularly, for you do not want food that is stringy. This may mean picking every day. Get into a good routine of picking and processing a little every day as the crop progresses. Young and tender food is the essential aim, and the more often you pick, the better the plant will respond by producing more. Different varieties of peas crop in different ways—there are dwarf varieties, which can crop for weeks on end, but others may produce almost the whole crop in just two or three pickings.

1 Split each plum with a sharp knife and take out the stones. It's a great excuse to sit down with friends and enjoy a chat while working.

2 Put the halved plums straight into your freezer bags, making sure that no leaves or stalks manage to creep in.

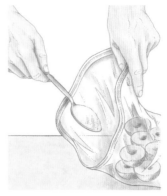

3 Add three or four tablespoons of sugar to each bag. Give it a shake to spread out the sugar, squeeze out the air, and seal for the freezer.

1 Sort and trim the pods, getting rid of unwanted leaves, damaged pods, and stalks. Cut off each end of the pods. You can slice three or four beans at a time, but watch out for your fingers!

2 Beans must be sliced diagonally into thin slices with a sharp knife or by using a bean slicer. Snow peas and sugar snaps are frozen whole.

3 Put a large pan of water on the stove to boil, and dump your pods into the boiling water. Leave for a minute or two until it comes back to the boil.

4 Drain off the pods after they have been blanched. Plunge them quickly in cold water to stop the cooking, shake them well to get rid of any water, and let them drain. You may need to plunge into cold water a few times to cool them enough.

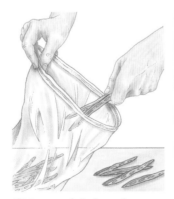

5 Once cooled, the pods are ready to bag up for freezing. Be careful to squeeze out all the air in the bag before you seal it. Specially made freezer bags with resealable tops and strong plastic that resists tearing are a great help for this.

SNOW PEAS

Simply cut off both ends of the snow peas or sugar snaps with a sharp knife before you blanch them in boiling water. Try to remove any strings from the peas at the same time.

PEAS

Ordinary peas freeze very well. Pod the peas, take out any leaves or pod, and blanch them before freezing. Have your pig bucket handy to put the waste in right away.

Canning

Glass jars for canning must have airtight tops, capable of supporting a vacuum, and arranged so that no metal comes in contact with the contents of the jar. If you examine the common Mason jar, or any of its rivals, you will find quite a cunning arrangement ensuring that the above requirements are met. A rubber ring compressed by a metal screw-cap forms an airtight seal, and only the glass disk inside the screw cap comes in contact with the jar's contents. Mason and other proprietary jars need the metal parts to be smeared with vaseline to prevent them from rusting, both when in use and when stored away. Keep the rubber rings in the dark, for light rots rubber.

For canning, you also need a container in which jars can be boiled. If you buy one, it should have a false bottom, so that the jars are not too close to the source of heat. Alternatively, put a piece of board in the bottom, or else just a folded towel. When canning fruit, pack the jars as tightly as you can; tapping the base of the jar on the table helps to settle the fruit, and drives air bubbles out.

CANNING FRUIT
Cold water bath method
Put the fruit into jars of cold brine or syrup and put the jars in cold water. Take an hour to bring water to 130°F (54°C), then another half hour to raise it to the temperature given on the chart below.

Oven method
Fill the jars, not putting any syrup or brine in them yet, and covering them with loose saucers only. Put them in a low oven at 250°F (120°C). Leave them for the time given in the chart, take out, and pack with fruit from a spare jar that has undergone the same process, then fill up with boiling brine or syrup, screw on the tops, and leave to cool.

Hot water bath method
If you have no thermometer, and no oven, use the hot water method. Fill packed jars with hot syrup or brine, put the lids on loosely, lower into warm water, bring to the boil, then simmer for the length of time shown on the chart below.

For fruit other than tomatoes, use a syrup of sugar and water if you wish. Water alone will do, and if you pack the fruit tightly you won't need much. But if the fruit is sour, a weak syrup does help.

CANNING VEGETABLES
I strongly advise against the canning of vegetables, but if you insist upon doing it, you must heat in a pressure-cooker, as boiling at atmospheric pressure is not enough to make it safe. Sweet corn can be canned (although I prefer the oven-drying method I describe on p.298):

Husk your corn, remove the silk, wash well, and cut the corn off the cob with a knife. If you force the cob onto a nail sticking up from a board at an angle, you will have it steady for slicing. This will leave a little of each grain on the cob, but that's all the better for the pigs. Pack the corn in the jar to within an inch of the top, add half a teaspoonful of salt to each pint of corn, fill up to half an inch from the top with boiling water, put the lid on loosely, and heat in a pressure-cooker at 240°F (115°C), at 10 pounds pressure, for an hour. Remove the jars from the cooker and seal.

Salting string beans
Use a pound (0.5 kg) of salt to 3 pounds (1.4 kg) of beans. Try to get "dairy" salt or block salt, though ordinary salt will do. Put a layer of salt in the bottom of a crock, a layer of stringed and sliced beans (young French beans do not need much slicing, whereas string beans always do) on top, another layer of salt, and so on. Press down tightly. Add more layers daily. When you have enough, or there are no more, cover the crock with an airtight cover and leave in a cool place. The beans will be drowned in their own brine, so do not remove it. To use, wash some beans in water and then soak them for no more than two hours.

Basic method	Cold water bath		Hot water bath		Slow oven	
	Take 90 minutes to bring water from cold to required temperature, then follow instructions given below.		Starting at 100°F (39°C), take 25–30 minutes to reach required temperature of 190°F (88°C). Follow instructions.		Preheat to 250°F (120°C). Leave jars according to times given below.	
Liquid in jars	Put cold syrup or water in before processing.		Put hot liquid at 140°F (60°C) in before processing. For tomatoes, liquid is optional.		Add boiling liquid at end of processing.	
	Temperature	Time	Temperature	Time	Temperature	Time
Soft fruit Blackberries, raspberries, currants, etc. and apple slices	165°F (74°C)	10 min	190°F (88°C)	2 min	250°F (120°C)	45-55 min
Stone fruit Cherries, plums, etc. **Citrus fruit**	180°F (83°C)	15 min	190°F (88°C)	15 min	Heat oven to 300°F (150°C)and put hot syrup in before processing them.	40-50 min
Tomatoes	190°F (88°C)	30 min	190°F (88°C)	40 min	250°F (120°C)	80-100 min
Purées and tight packs	Allow 5–10 min longer than times shown above and raise temperature a little.					

CANNING TOMATOES

Jars of canned tomatoes on your shelves in winter are a cheering sight. They are easy to can and it even improves their flavor.

1 Remove the green tomato stalks, and nick the skins with a knife.

2 Put the tomatoes in a bowl and pour over boiling water. Leave until the skins have loosened.

3 Drain and cover with cold water. Don't leave them very long or they will get soggy.

4 With a sharp knife, peel off the skins carefully so that the tomatoes retain their shape and do not lose any juice. Make up a brine by mixing half an ounce (14 g) of salt to a quart (1 liter) of water.

5 Pack tomatoes in jars very tightly. Push large fruit into place with the handle of a wooden spoon.

6 If sterilizing in water, fill the jars with brine, cover with sealing disks, and screw the lids on loosely; if in the oven, add brine afterward.

7 Put jars in a pan of water, or stand on newspaper in the oven. Now cook.

8 When cool, try lifting the bottle by the disk. The vacuum should hold.

MAKING SAUERKRAUT

Winter cabbages can be clamped, but if greens are scarce, make a sauerkraut standby.

1 Shred hard white cabbage hearts finely, and estimate ½ ounce (14 g) salt for each pound (0.5 kg) of cabbage.

2 Pack layers of shredded cabbage into a stone crock or wooden tub; sprinkle salt between the layers.

3 Spread one big cabbage leaf across the top, put a cloth over it, and cover that with a plate.

4 Weight down and leave in a warm place. In three weeks, put the cabbage in jars and sterilize as described opposite.

Making Pickles & Chutneys

Pickles and chutney are another way of preserving produce. They add flavor to cold meats, meat pies, cheeses, and curries. The principle of both involves flavoring fruit and vegetables with spices, and then storing them in vinegar. Ideally, you would make your own vinegar (*see pp. 330–331*), but if you cannot do this, and have to buy it, you should note that there are vinegars of different strength, cost, and flavor.

Distilled or fortified vinegar is by far the strongest (it is also the most expensive). Wine vinegar is the strongest natural vinegar, and more expensive than cider or malt vinegar. Remember that vinegar leaves its flavor in chutney, and even more so in pickles, so if you want to have the best-tasting accompaniments to your cold pies, you may find yourself paying for your vinegar. And the best-flavored vinegar is wine. However, when you make chutney, much of the liquid is evaporated during the cooking, so malt vinegar could be a more economic proposition.

PICKLES

The vinegar is first steeped with spices and sometimes cooked with sugar, to improve and mellow its sharpness. To make a spiced vinegar suitable for a variety of pickles, you can add any spices you like. Ground spices make vinegar turn cloudy, so if you want the pickle to be attractively presented, and clearly recognizable, use whole spices.

The ideal way of making spiced vinegar is to steep all the spices in cold vinegar for a couple of months, after which time the liquid is ready to be strained and used. Since this is not always practicable, here is a speeded-up version. For 2 pints of vinegar take 2–3 ounces (56–84 g) of spices and tie them in a little muslin bag. Include:

a piece of cinnamon bark
slivers of mace
some allspice
6–7 cloves
6–7 peppercorns
½ teaspoon mustard seed
Add garlic, or any herb, if you like the flavor, and for a hot taste add chili, ginger, or more mustard.

Now put the vinegar and spices into a pitcher or heatproof jar that can be covered with a lid or a plate. Stand it in a pan of water. Bring the water to the boil, then take it off the heat. Leave the whole thing to cool down for two hours, by which time the spices should have thoroughly flavored the vinegar. Remove the little bag and the vinegar is ready to use.

You can pickle fish, eggs, fruit, and vegetables, and pickle them whole or in pieces. Moist vegetables and fish are usually salted first to draw out some of their water. Crisp pickles like cucumbers, beets, cabbage, and onion are put straight into cold vinegar. Others, like plums, tomatoes, and pears, are cooked until soft in spiced vinegar; this is then reduced to a syrupy consistency before finishing.

When adding sugar to sweet pickles, use white sugar: it keeps the pickle clear and light. Pickle jars need close sealing to prevent evaporation, and the vinegar must not come in direct contact with metal lids. Eat all pickles within six months; after this, they are likely to soften.

Pickled eggs

Hard-boil as many new-laid eggs as you like; you need about a quart (liter) of vinegar for every dozen. Shell them. Pack them in jars and cover them with spiced vinegar. Add a few pieces of chili pepper, if you like. Close tightly, and begin to eat after one month.

Pickled onions

Choose small button onions. Don't skin them at once, but soak them in a brine of salt and water using 4 ounces (115 g) of salt to each quart (liter) of water. After 12 hours, skin them. Put them in fresh brine for two or three days, with a plate on top so that they stay submerged. Then drain and pack in jars or bottles with spiced vinegar. A little sugar added to the vinegar helps the flavor. They are good to eat after two or three months.

Pickled apples

This is a sweet pickle. Use small apples (crab apples are good). For 2 pounds (1 kg) of apples, use 2 pounds (1 kg) of sugar and 1 pint (0.5 liters) of spiced vinegar.

Cook the sugar and vinegar until the sugar is just dissolved. Prick the apples all over, using the prongs of a carving fork. If they are too big for the jar, cut them in half. Simmer in the vinegar/sugar mixture until they are soft but not falling apart.

Put them gently in jars. Reduce the syrup to half a pint (0.3 liters) by boiling. Pour it hot over the apples, but not so hot that it cracks the glass.

CHUTNEYS

Chutney is a concoction of almost any fruit or vegetable you like, flavored with spices and cooked with vinegar to a thick, jamlike consistency. Soft, overripe fruit and vegetables are suitable, as they turn into pulp quickly.

Possible ingredients for chutney are squashes, pumpkins, rutabagas, turnips, peppers, onions, beets, carrots, celery, eggplant, mangoes, tomatoes, apples, rhubarb, blackberries, pears, bananas, lemons, damsons, gooseberries, plums, dried fruit, peaches, elderberries, cranberries, oranges, and grapefruit.

The herbs and spices can be any of these: bay leaves, chili, cumin, coriander seeds, cardamom, cinnamon, cloves, ginger, allspice, peppercorns, mustard seed, horseradish, paprika, cayenne pepper, juniper, and garlic.

It is best to finely chop vegetables or fruit for chutney and then cook them slowly for a long time to evaporate the liquid. Sugar plays a large part in chutney. Most chutneys darken as they are cooked, so if you want an even darker one use brown sugar. Molasses is a possible alternative.

MAKING TOMATO CHUTNEY

The secret of good chutney is to use contrasting ingredients. In this example, the spice and garlic offset the tomatoes and apple.

You need: 2 lb (1 kg) tomatoes, 2 onions, 1 cooking apple, raisins, 2 cloves garlic, ½ oz (14 g) fresh ginger, 2 oz (56 g) brown sugar, ½ pt (0.3 liters) vinegar, salt, and some spices.

1 Skin the onions and peel and core the apple. Then chop them up finely.

2 Simmer the onion in a small pan with a little water. Add the apple and the raisins, and cook gently until they soften.

3 Skin the tomatoes, then chop them up roughly into chunks.

4 Crush the garlic and fresh ginger in a mortar and pestle with salt. If you are using dried ginger instead, add ½ oz (7 g) to the bag of spices.

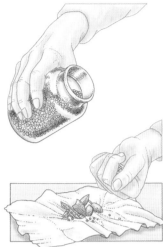

5 Tie up in a little muslin bag: 1 crushed bay leaf, 2–3 crushed dried chili peppers, ½ teaspoon mustard seed, 4–5 cloves; add cardamom, cinnamon, coriander seeds, or peppercorns as you wish.

6 Tie the muslin bag to the handle of a large saucepan, so as not to lose it in the chutney.

7 Pour the softened ingredients into the pan, then everything else.

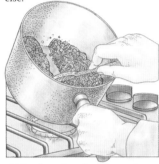

8 Cook on low heat for an hour or so, until mixture thickens, so when you draw a spoon through it you can see the pan.

9 Can at once in hot clean jars. Seal, and label when cooled.

Cooking chutney

Use stainless steel or enameled pans. Vinegar eats into copper, brass, or iron pans, so don't use them.

Simmer hard ingredients such as apple and onion in a little water before mixing with softer ingredients such as squash or tomato, and before adding salt, sugar, and vinegar, which tend to harden fruit or vegetables.

Put whole herbs and spices in a muslin bag, which you can tie to the handle of the pan so that you don't lose it in the chutney. If you prefer to use powdered spices, they can be added loose to the other ingredients. Crush garlic and fresh ginger in a mortar and pestle before adding to chutney. Soak dried fruit in water before cooking it. Use sufficient vinegar just to cover the ingredients. Cook until the consistency is of thick jam, and there is no free liquid. Be careful it doesn't burn toward the end. Stir well while it cooks. Can while still hot in clean hot jars, cover, and label.

Storing chutney

Chutney improves with keeping, so store it in a cool, dark place in glass jars. Make sure they are tightly sealed or the vinegar will evaporate, leaving an unappetizing, dry, shrunken mess. Cellophane papers such as those that are sold for jam covers are not suitable. I use twist-on metal caps from old jam or pickle jars. Check that the metal from the lid is well lacquered or protected with a waxed cardboard disk; otherwise the vinegar will corrode the metal. You can also use synthetic skins, or wax paper circles underneath a wax paper tie-on cover. Cover the jars with a cloth that has been dipped in melted paraffin.

Making Jams & Syrups

Jams and conserves of all kinds are a very useful way of preserving fruit. Usually the fruit is cooked first without any sugar, to soften it and to release the pectin, which is what makes it set. Sugar is added next, and the whole thing is boiled rapidly until setting point is reached. As long as jams are properly made, well covered, and kept in a cool, dry place, they keep for ages.

Fruit should be under- rather than overripe, and clean. Bruises on damaged fruit don't matter as long as they are cut out. It is important to weigh the fruit before you begin cooking; otherwise, you don't know how much sugar to add. Don't add more water than necessary to cook the fruit. The sugar should be fine sugar, since this dissolves fastest. Brown sugars are okay, but bear in mind that they add a flavor of their own and in some cases are damp; therefore, adjust the weight.

Some fruit has more acid and pectin in it than others. Fruit that is low in acid or pectin usually needs extra acid or pectin added to it (see below).

Basic jam-making

In general, jam-making goes like this: clean, sort, and prepare fruit. Weigh it. Cook it with sufficient water to make it tender. Put it in a large, wide pan, and when it is boiling, add the required amount of sugar. Stir until all the sugar is dissolved. Bring to a rapid boil. Don't stir. Test from time to time to see if setting point (see below) is reached. Stop cooking when it is, and allow to cool a little so that pieces of fruit will not float to the top of the jam in the jars. Fill hot clean jars to the brim with jam: cover, seal, label.

Testing for pectin

Put into a little glass a teaspoonful of strained, cooled fruit juice from the cooked fruit, before you add the sugar. Add three teaspoons denatured alcohol, and shake together. Wait a minute. Pour the mixture out into another glass. If the fruit juice has formed one solid blob, the pectin is good. If it is several blobs, it is not so good, so add less sugar. If it is all fluid, it is useless, in which case boil the fruit again. Even add commercial pectin if necessary.

Testing for set

Put a little jam from the pan on a saucer to cool. If the surface wrinkles when you push it with your finger, it is done. Examine the drips from the spoon: if a constant stream flows, it is no good; if large, thick blobs form, it is okay. The temperature of the boiling jam should reach 222°F (105°C). It is best to use all or at least two of these methods to be absolutely sure your jam is ready.

Canned fruits or conserves do not keep as long as jam, but because they are only cooked briefly, the flavors are very fresh. It is not so necessary to worry about pectin with conserves, so you can make them with low-pectin fruit like raspberries, strawberries, blackberries, and rhubarb. Also, note that there is more sugar per pound in conserves.

Damson or plum jam

Much of the pectin in plums is found in the stones, so if you can, extract the stones first, crack some of them, and tie the kernels in a little bag. If this is difficult, never mind; they will float to the top when the jam cooks, and you can skim them off with a slotted spoon at the end. You will need.

6 lb (2.7 kg) damsons or plums
6½ lb (3 kg) sugar
½ pint (0.3 liter) water

Wash the plums and cut them in half. Add them to a pan containing the water and simmer until tender. Add the sugar, stirring until dissolved, then boil hard until setting point. Remove floating stones, or if you put kernels in a bag, remove the bag. Leave the jam to cool a little so that the fruit will not rise to the top of the jars. Put in jars, seal, and label.

Raspberry conserve

4 lb (1.8 kg) raspberries
5 lb (2.5 kg) sugar

You can use damaged but not moldy fruit. Warm the sugar in a bowl in a low oven. Butter a large pan, put in the fruit, and cook over a very low heat. As the fruit begins to give up its juice and bubble, slowly add the warm sugar. Beat hard until the sugar is dissolved. It should remain a lovely, bright color and taste like fresh raspberries. It should be quite thick. Cool, put in jars, and seal in the usual way, but examine for mold after a few months. Another way is to put sugar and raspberries in layers in a large bowl. Leave overnight, and bring just to the boil the next day, before putting in jars.

Lemon curd

4 oz (114 g) butter
1 lb (0.9 kg) sugar
4 eggs
3 or 4 lemons, depending on size and juiciness

This is not a jam, but a good way of using up eggs. Grate the rind from the lemons and squeeze out their juice. Put rind, juice, butter, and sugar into a small pan and heat until the butter melts and the sugar just dissolves. Let it cool. Beat the eggs. Put them in a bowl that will just fit over a saucepan of simmering water, and stir in the juice. Beat over the saucepan of water, or use a double boiler, until the mixture thickens to curd consistency. Pour into a jar and cover. Lemon curd doesn't keep long, so use it up quickly. Don't make too much at a time. Richer curds can be made using eight egg yolks instead of four eggs. Variations include using oranges or tangerines instead of lemons. With sweeter fruit, use less sugar.

Lemon and carrot marmalade

8 oz (228 g) thinly sliced lemon
8 oz (228 g) shredded carrot
2 pints (1 liter) water
1 lb (0.9) kg sugar

Mix the lemon, the carrot, and the water. Cover and allow to stand overnight. Cook in a covered saucepan, bring to the boil, then simmer for about half an hour or until tender. Then add sugar, and simmer until it completely dissolves; boil rapidly until setting point. Try a little on a cold plate see if it jells; it may take 15 to 30 minutes. Pour into clean, warm jars, cover with wax paper and seal.

The flavor of carrot and lemon is very fresh and fairly sweet. Eat within three months.

Making fruit cheeses

Fruit cheeses are jams made from puréed or sieved fruit. (Softer versions are known as fruit butters.) Fruit cheeses, if they are firm enough, can be turned out of their molds as little "shapes."

THREE FRUIT MARMALADE

Make this from oranges, lemons, and grapefruit as a tasty change from orange marmalade.

1 Squeeze out the juice from eight oranges, two lemons, and two grapefruit. Strain it and save the seeds.

2 Shred the peel coarsely or finely, depending on how thick you like your marmalade.

3 Tie the seeds in a bag, and soak with peel and juice for a day in 12 pints (5.7 liters) of water. Boil for 2 hours.

4 Test for pectin: add 3 tsp denatured alcohol to 1 tsp juice. The juice should set.

5 Remove the bag of seeds from the pan. Boil the mixture, add 7 pounds (3 kg) sugar and stir until dissolved. Cook until it sets.

6 Let some marmalade drip from a spoon. If it falls in thick flakes, it is properly set.

7 Or cool a little on a saucer. It is done if the surface creases when touched.

8 Put into hot, clean jars, cover with wax paper and cellophane, seal, and label. Start eating it as soon as you like.

Fruit cheese is delicious eaten for dessert with cream or even spread on a slice of bread.

Blackberry and apple cheese

You will need equal amounts of blackberries and apples. Wash the apples but don't bother to peel or core them. Cut them up roughly. Pick over the blackberries and wash them if they are dusty. Put both fruits into a pan, just cover with water, and stew, stirring occasionally, until the apples turn mushy. Sieve the cooked fruit. You should have a fairly thick pulp. Weigh it. Add 1 pound (0.5 kg) sugar to each pound of pulp. Boil together. Stir all the time, since this burns easily. When it thickens enough for you to see the bottom of the pan as you draw the spoon across it, it is done. Can and cover like jam. It sets quite firmly, like cheese, and will last for ages.

Making jellies

Jellies are simply jams that have had all the solids strained out of the cooked fruit. When the juice is boiled up with sugar it forms jelly, which can be used in the same way as jam.

Blackberry and apple jelly

This recipe will suit any high-pectin fruit, such as crab apples, red currants, citrus fruits, quinces, gooseberries, sloes, damsons, and rowanberries. You can also experiment with mixtures of fruits. Cook them separately if one needs more cooking than the other.

Proceed as for blackberry and apple cheese to the point where the fruit is cooked and soft. Then strain the juice through a cloth. Don't succumb to the temptation to squeeze it to speed it up, or the finished jelly will be cloudy. Measure the juice and add 1 pound (0.5 kg) sugar to each pint (0.5 liter) of juice. Cook until setting point is reached, and can and label in the usual way. If you are very economically minded, you can stew up the residue of fruit in the jelly bag with more water, then either extract more juice or make a fruit cheese by sieving it. Follow the instructions given above if you want to do this.

Fruit syrups

Fruit syrups are made in the same way as fruit jellies, though you don't need to add so much sugar to syrups. To prevent spoiling by fermentation (when you would be on the way to making wine), you have to sterilize syrups and keep them well sealed. They make very refreshing drinks and milkshakes in summer, or you can use them as toppings for desserts and cereals.

Extract the juice from any unsweetened cooked fruit you fancy, as for jelly, or, if you wish, extract it by pressing, then straining. Measure the amount and then add about 1 pound (0.5 kg) sugar per pint (0.5 liter) of juice. Heat it until the sugar is just dissolved—no more or it will start to set like jelly. Let it cool. Sterilize the bottles and their lids, preferably the screw-cap type, by immersing in boiling water for 15 minutes. Drain, then fill with syrup. Screw shut tightly, then unscrew by half a turn, so that the heating syrup will be able to expand. Leave a 1-inch (2.5-cm) gap at the top of each bottle.

Stand the bottles in a pan deep enough for the water to come up to their tops. If possible, use a pan like a pressure cooker that has a false bottom. Bring slowly to the boil and keep boiling for 20 to 30 minutes. Take out the bottles and screw the lids on tightly as soon as they are cool enough. If you are doubtful about the tightness of the seal, coat with melted paraffin.

Bakery & Desserts

Cakes, cookies, and desserts—now this is where the real magic of cooking lies for me. Somehow, over thousands of years, dedicated humans have experimented with all sorts of mixtures and ovens, and today we can enjoy the results. I've no doubt the chemistry of flour, eggs, yeast, and baking powder is complex indeed—and I certainly never studied it in school—but the end products are straightforward enough. With modern mixing machines, there is no excuse for missing out on the excitement of a weekly session of making your own desserts and treats. So what is the key to all this magic? All equipment must be clean and cool. Try to keep one specific board, preferably made of marble or slate, for rolling pastry. The rolling pin should not be too heavy—in fact, a round glass bottle filled with cold water can be ideal. You have to make pastry in as cool a place as possible so that the cooking process creates lightness by expanding cool air trapped in the dough. People with warm hands simply cannot make good pastry! Keep plenty of flour on hand to dust over the pastry to prevent it from sticking. Roll it lightly and try to press evenly with both hands; always roll away from you, taking short quick strokes and lifting the rolling pin between the strokes. There are endless different recipes for baked goods and desserts, and I've suggested a few recipes, which follow. The key thing is to experiment. With a little practice, you will soon find recipes that your family and friends enjoy.

Lemon Drizzle Cake

If you like, you can use oranges instead of lemons in this zesty treat for the whole family. You will need:

shredded rind of 2 lemons (preferably organic), reserving some for decoration later
6 oz (170 g) granulated sugar
8 oz (225 g) softened, unsalted butter
4 fresh eggs
8 oz (225 g) self-rising flour
¼ teaspoon salt
1 teaspoon baking powder

Preheat your oven to 320°F (160°C). Grease a 2-pound (1 kg) bread pan or a round 7–8-inch (18–20-cm) cake pan and line with wax paper. Mix the lemon and the sugar together, reserving some for later. Cream the butter with the rest of the lemon and sugar mixture, and add the eggs. Mix the ingredients until the mixture is a smooth, pale yellow color. Sift the flour with the baking powder and salt into a bowl, and fold into the mixture one-third at a time.

Turn the mixture into the baking pan, smooth it out so that the top is level, and bake for 90 minutes, or until golden brown and springy to the touch. Turn it out onto a rack. When it has cooled, put a plate under the rack, pierce the cake all over with a fine skewer, and carefully drizzle the rest of the lemon and sugar mixture into the holes. The cake will absorb a surprising amount of liquid.

Farmhouse Carrot Cake

This is another great way to use eggs and carrots from your garden, as it makes a marvelously moist and flavorsome recipe. You will need:

1 lb (450 g) sugar
4 eggs
1 cup olive oil
8 oz (225 g) finely grated carrots
8 oz (225 g) all-purpose flour
1 heaped teaspoon baking powder
1 teaspoon ground allspice
1 teaspoon ground cinnamon

For the frosting you need:
8 oz (225 g) confectioners' sugar
1 cup of softened cream cheese
2 oz (56 g) butter
1 teaspoon vanilla extract
6 oz (170 g) chopped nuts (try walnuts)
A little milk if required

Mix together the sugar, eggs, oil, and grated carrots in a large mixing bowl. Sift all the dry ingredients together into a separate bowl. Add a small amount of the dry ingredients to the mixture a bit at a time and mix together up until you have blended all the ingredients.

Grease and flour two 9-inch (22-cm) cake pans. Divide the mixture bwteen the two pans. Bake for about 40 minutes in a preheated oven at about 375°F (190°C). Check for doneness by putting in a skewer or fork and seeing if it comes out clean. If it comes out, it is ready; if the mixture is attached to the skewer you need to let the cake cook for a little longer.

Once cooked, let the cakes cool in their pans for a few minutes and then tip them out on to wire racks to let them cool completely.

To make the icing, combine all the ingedients, except the walnuts, together until you have a smooth, spreadable consistency. You may need to add milk if the mix is too dry. Add the walnuts and blend together. Spread over the top of one cake layer, top with the other cake, and then spread the remaining icing over the icing.

Doughnuts

You won't eat another store-bought doughnut after you have made your own. The problem is you need a lot of very clean, fresh oil. They are made from a normal bread dough (see p.203) but also include the following ingredients, added during mixing:

2 oz (56 g) melted butter
1 egg

2 oz (56 g) sugar
milk (substitute this for the water used in making a normal bread dough)
pinch of salt
1 lb (0.5 kg) flour
1 oz (28 g) yeast or ½ oz (14 g) dried yeast

Mix the dough until smooth and soft. Cover with a cloth and leave it to rise in a warm place for about one hour. Knead it vigorously for about 4–5 minutes. Roll out the dough on a floured board. Use a large glass or cutter to press out a circular shape. To make the rings, use a bottle top and press down in the center of the circle. Don't worry if the holes look small as they will more than double in size during cooking. Cover them with a cloth and leave in a warm place to prove for 20 minutes. Once proved, fry them on both sides, a few at a time, in deep, boiling fat. The spherical ones will turn themselves over at half time, leaving a pale ring around the equator. Drain the doughnuts on paper towels and then roll in sugar. Eat at once.

Cheese Scones

Quick to cook and delicious to eat warm and crumbly from the oven, these savory scones make an appetizing addition to any teatime feast. You will need:

1 oz (28 g) butter
6 oz (170 g) self rising flour
3 oz (85 g) strong cheddar cheese, grated finely (reserve a little for sprinkling over the top)
¼ teaspoon of mustard
½ teaspoon of salt
1 egg
2 heaping tablespoons of water

Rub the butter into the flour and then add the grated cheese and seasonings. Add the egg and the water and mix together. Once you have a firm dough, roll it out so it is about half an inch thick. Sprinkle a little more grated cheese over the top and cut out circular shapes with a cutter or a glass. Place onto a greased tray and bake in the oven at 425°F (220°C) for 15 minutes.

Blackberry Charlotte

This is a classic pudding for fall when blackberries, walnuts, and apples are in good supply. You need:

2½ oz (65 g) unsalted butter (plus some for greasing the dish)
65 g (175 g) fresh white breadcrumbs
2 oz (56 g) of soft brown sugar
2 fl oz (60 ml) of corn syrup
finely-grated rind and juice of 2 lemons
2 oz (56 g) of walnut halves
15 oz (450 g) of blackberries
15 oz (450 g) of sliced cooking apples

Preheat the oven to 355°F (180°C). Grease a 15-oz (450-ml) dish with butter. Melt the butter and add the breadcrumbs. Sauté gently until the crumbs turn golden brown and slightly crisp. Leave to cool. Put the sugar, syrup, lemon rind, and lemon juice into a small saucepan an gently warm through. Add the crumbs. Chop the walnuts very finely and add to the mixture. Put a layer of blackberries in the dish, followed by a layer of the crumbs and another layer of sliced apples. Continue layering, finishing with a layer of the crumb mixture on the top. Cook in the oven for 30 minutes.

Flap Jacks

These make a wonderfully healthy and quick snack.

4 oz (112 g) butter
2½ oz (70 g) sugar
1 tablespoon syrup
6 oz (170 g) of oats

Melt the butter, sugar, and syrup into a pan. Stir in the oats and mix well. Spread onto a greased baking pan, press down firmly, and, with a sharp knife, divide into squares. Bake in a moderate oven at 375°F (190°C) for 15–20 minutes. Allow to cool and remove.

Meats

To the self-supporter, meat is not merely "flesh." Each animal has its own life saga with escapes, injuries, and always a shared sympathy between living beings. Seeing an animal happily content with its accommodation, its food, and its caretaker is a pleasure. But there will have been frustrations and furies, too—the day the beast escaped into the strawberry bed, or the time it broke its water trough and water flooded the food store. Finally comes the day when animal becomes meat to be eaten or preserved.

Smoking One very useful way of helping to preserve the meat is to smoke it. This also helps it dry out, and probably helps it mature quicker. It is also much easier than people seem to think. If you have a big open chimney, simply hang the meat high up in it, well out of reach of the fire, and leave it there for about a week, keeping a wood fire going at all times. There is a lot of mysticism about which wood to use for smoking: Americans swear by hickory, the British will hear of nothing but oak. In my experience it matters very little, provided you use hard woods and not pine.

Whatever you use, don't let the temperature go above 120°F (50°C): 100°F to 110°F (39°C to 43°C) is fine. Building a smokehouse is a matter of common sense and a little ingenuity. For years we used a brick outhouse. (We didn't use it for its original purpose, of course.) We had a slow-combustion wood-burning stove outside, with the chimney pipe poking through the wall, and we hung up the meat from lengths of angle-iron under the roof. It does seem a pity, though, not to make use of the heat generated by the smoking fuel, so surely it is better to have your burning unit inside a building, even if the smoke chamber itself is outside. Often a slow-combustion wood burning stove can heat a house and, with no increase in fuel consumption, it will automatically smoke whatever you like. There are two kinds of smoking: cold-smoking and cooked-smoking. The latter is common in the US and Germany but almost unknown in Great Britain. It consists of smoking at a higher temperature, from 150°F to 200°F (65°C to 93°C), so that the meat is cooked as well as smoked. Meat thus smoked must be eaten within a few days, because it will not keep as cold-smoked meat will.

Thawing meat Always take your meat out of the freezer in time to let it thaw before you cook it. Meat is much better thawed slowly at room temperature. Once thawed, the meat should be cooked immediately, since it will not keep.

Bones Many modern butchers like to "bone" joints of meat. This is not something I recommend. I know housewives hate the idea of paying for the bone, but if they would just pause for a moment, they would realize that boned meat actually costs more per pound and they are really paying for the butcher's time in doing the boning. The plain fact is that meat on the bone cooks better, and the marrow and presence of the bone add an extra flavor.

Larding and barding I don't hear these terms used much nowadays, because real bacon has become such a rarity. But if you make your own bacon from your own pigs, then you are likely to have a fair bit of "fatty" bacon that can be used in roasting other meats. Larding is simply threading pieces of bacon through a joint using a "larding needle." "Barding" means covering any lean or exposed parts of a roast with a few slices of fatty bacon. This provides fat to prevent burning, and also imparts an extra boost to the flavor.

Roasting I try to have an open-air roast over a fire once or twice a year, and very delicious and exciting it is, too. If you want to roast a pig or lamb like this, you need at least 12 hours' burning time: the longer, the better. So start your fire early in the morning. You will need two strong metal supports to hold your rotating spit rod, and you must fasten the carcass to this using wire. Keep the meat high up to start with, and progressively lower it during the day. Always have a good supply of well-dried timber for the fire, and appoint a responsible person to be in charge at all times.

If roasting in an oven, start with a relatively high temperature to "seal" the roast. Make sure the oven is at an even temperature all over and is well ventilated. Keep an eye on the meat to ensure it does not dry out, and baste with fat as often as necessary. If you want to make fat or skin crisp, then rub in some salt before cooking. If you suspect your oven temperature may be uneven, then use foil to cover parts of the roast exposed to "hot spots." Do not think that there are fixed times for making a perfect roast: each piece of meat will have its own characteristics and a long, thin, roast will cook much quicker than a fat, round one. Something like 20 minutes to the pound, plus 20 minutes extra, will not be far wrong. Pork, lamb, and veal should cook longer than beef.

Braising This is an excellent way of cooking the tougher, less attractive cuts of meat by effectively combining roasting and boiling. If possible, use a heavy cast-iron cooking pot with a close-fitting lid. Tie your meat up with string if necessary. Partially fill the pot with water suitably spiced up with whatever takes your fancy: I like dried tomatoes and black peppercorns. Then cook for however long it takes for the meat to become tender. Your oven temperature will not be as high as for a roast—perhaps 150°C (300°F). Make sure the liquid does not boil away. If the meat is fatty, you can allow the whole thing to cool overnight before reheating the next day. All the fat will solidify on the surface and can be removed.

Stewing Now we are talking about long, slow, cool cooking for tenderizing the less attractive and tougher parts of the animal. The first job is to cut up the meat into lumps less than 1 inch (2 cm) square, removing all unnecessary fat and gristle. These must now be "sealed" with a quick burst of strong heat, using good fat or olive oil and perhaps a few chopped onions.

Now make up your chosen mixture of vegetables and seasoning before allowing everything to simmer gently in a slow oven for three or four hours. You can keep a good stew going for several days simply by adding fresh vegetables and stock—but remember, it must be boiled up strongly once each day or it will go bad.

Fish

I vividly remember catching mackerel from a yacht as I entered a small anchorage on the Scottish island of Gomera, near Mull. Within a couple of minutes, I had the fish filleted; the sails came down and I dropped anchor. So quick was the journey from ocean to the grill that the fillets practically jumped off the grill. Freshly grilled with lemon juice, mackerel is delicious. What did this tell me? That well-cooked fresh fish is one of the great delicacies of the world. But how often have we been disappointed in restaurants to find the meal either pappy and overcooked, or almost raw?

So, aside from finding a good fish counter or local fisherman and timing to perfection, bear in mind these tips:

Gutting fish It is essential to clean and gut fish properly. For most fish, gutting is done by slitting the fish on the underside from the head halfway to the tail and carefully removing the insides. Always handle fish gently to avoid bruising. If there is a roe in the fish, you can either replace it if it is small or cook it separately.

Make sure you take out all of the guts, including any black skin lining the body cavity. Rub this out with salt if you have to, because if you leave it, there will be a bitter taste. Wash the fish out well with cold water; use a running faucet rather than soaking the fish, or you will find they become watery.

Scaling If there are scales on the fish, then these must be removed by scraping from tail to head with a sharp knife. Angle the knife slanting against the fish and scrape slowly so the scales do not fly everywhere. Sometimes the scales are tough to remove: if so, dip the fish quickly into boiling water. If you are going to serve the fish whole, then you should cut off the fins with a sharp pair of scissors. Either cut off the head or take out the eyes.

Skinning Round fish are skinned from head to tail. You make a cut along the sides of the fish close to the fins and then make a cut in the skin just below the head. Now start pulling the skin away downward, using a knife to hold down the flesh. Put your hands in salt if the fish is too slippery—or use a cloth to hold it. Flat fish are skinned in similar fashion but starting at the tail. The skin of flat fish can be pulled off quickly once the sides have been cut and loosened—just hold down the tail to keep it steady.

Filleting You will need a very sharp knife and a fair bit of practice to do a good job of separating the flesh from the bones. The basic technique is to make a cut down the whole of the back of the fish, down to the backbone. Then carefully scrape away the fillets of flesh from either side; you make two fillets from each side. It is usually easiest to work the first fillet from the left-hand side of the fish working from head to tail. Then turn the fish around and work the second fillet from tail to head. Now turn the fish over and repeat for the other side.

Fish stock Making a good fish stock is the essence of cooking a fine fish sauce. The best stock is made from fresh fish trimmings after filleting. Discard any black-looking skin and break the bones up into small pieces.

Put the trimmings into a saucepan with water and/or milk, a small piece of onion, white peppercorns, and some parsley. Simmer the mixture on a low heat for about half an hour and then strain off your stock. Add white wine instead of milk if you prefer.

Boiling fish This is a good way to cook large fish. They should be left unskinned with the heads on and eyes removed. Fish should be put into the water when it is piping hot but not boiling, and the water should be salted, with a little vinegar or lemon juice added. If you do not make the water slightly acid, the fish will not be white and firm when cooked.

A fish kettle is the best way to boil fish. This will have a drainer to take off the water and avoid breaking the fish. If you do not have a fish kettle, then you can use an ordinary large saucepan. Put a plate in the bottom and rest the fish on this, tied up in muslin. By hanging the ends of the muslin over the sides of the cooking vessel, you can remove the fish whole without breaking it.

Weigh the fish before you boil it: 8 to 10 minutes per pound, plus 10 minutes, is a good guide. Do not put too much liquid over the fish or the boiling will shake it around and damage the skin. About 2 inches (5 cm) above the fish should be sufficient.

Broiling fish This is a good way to cook smaller fish like herring, mackerel, and trout. Prepare the fish carefully and score the skin on both sides to prevent it from cracking when cooking. Season the fish with pepper and salt and brush it all over with oil or melted butter. Alternatively, you may want to split the fish open, removing the bone, and coat it lightly in flour or fine oatmeal. Make sure the broiler is hot before you start cooking. Allow 7 to 10 minutes for cooking, and turn the fish at least once. It should look nicely browned when ready and should be served immediately.

Frying This is probably the most popular way to cook fish, as well as one of the trickiest to do well. There are two important things to remember: first, make sure your fish is as dry as possible before you cook it, and second, coat the fish in some mixture that will prevent it from absorbing the cooking fat. There are several different ways of coating fish for frying. The easiest way is simply to dip the fish into sifted flour. Alternatively, you can use the familiar batter coating: this is a weak batter of flour, milk, and egg. I prefer to use egg and breadcrumbs, and this certainly looks the best when the fish is cooked. Make sure the fat is always kept very hot: do not put too many pieces of fish in the pan at any one time, and let the fat heat up again before putting in a fresh piece of fish. Drain the fish on paper towels before serving so as to remove excess grease.

Baking fish Fish can be baked very simply in an open dish at 350°F (180°C). Add the seasoning of your choice. Baking is a dry way to cook fish, so you may need to add some butter, fat, or milk to provide moisture.

Poaching or steaming With the correct equipment, these are two other excellent ways to cook fish.

Vegetables

We talk easily about "vegetables," but we are really talking about a huge range of completely different foodstuffs. At one extreme we have simple salads, fresh and uncooked. At the other end there are things like globe artichokes that need a lot of cooking and a lot of eating (*see below*). What we do know is that vegetables are essential for our supply of vitamins, trace elements, and roughage.

It is, alas, a sad fact that all vegetables begin to deteriorate the second they are picked, some much more than others: the vibrant sugars produced by the growing plant are quickly converted into starches as soon as the vegetable is taken from the soil. So vegetables must be stored properly in humid, cool, fly-free spaces, and they must have all damaged material carefully removed before cooking. Exactly the same priority attaches to the preparation of vegetables prior to storage in the freezer. So if you are a home producer, you should be able to take your veggies straight from the freezer all ready for a quick burst of boiling water (usually) to become deliciously ready for the table.

Generally, vegetables should not be washed until just before they are to be prepared for cooking. Close-leaved plants like Brussels sprouts and cauliflower can benefit from a short soaking in vinegared water, which will draw out slugs and bugs (if you use salt, it tends to toughen the leaves). Always carefully remove all damaged parts before cooking, and wash thoroughly in cold water to remove all traces of the garden.

If you do not have a good set of stainless steel pans for steaming vegetables, then this is something you should consider, for in my opinion most vegetables are best cooked by steaming rather than immersion in boiling water. Vegetables can, of course, be roasted, baked, fried, or grilled. Almost certainly the major sin when cooking vegetables is to overcook and boil into oblivion. Better a little crunchy than soggy, bland mush!

Artichokes

Brilliantly simple to cook and prepare, these make a most tasty and sociable starter. Choose the larger flower heads, but make sure they are still tender and there is no sign of the actual flower appearing. Soak these in water (probably one or two maximum per person) with a little vinegar added to bring out bugs. After half an hour, take out, wash, and drop into a large pan of rapidly boiling water for 5–6 minutes. Then lower the heat and simmer for another 40 minutes to an hour, depending on the size of the artichokes. You will know they are cooked when the leaves peel off easily. Remove from the water, drain, and serve with a choice of dressings. Butter is good or, alternatively, you can try our favorite, which is a mixture of good-quality soy sauce, lemon juice, and olive oil in equal parts.

Broad beans

Do not pod these until just before you are going to cook them. In all cases other than when beans are very fresh and young, you will have to remove the skins of each bean. Do this by dropping the podded beans into boiling water for a few minutes, then remove, and the skins will come off easily. Now you can boil in salted water. Remove any scum as it appears, and test regularly to see when they become tender. Drain and serve with melted butter and a good dressing of salt and pepper.

Green beans

Pick these before they are fully grown so you avoid the risk of the dreaded "string" bean. Small and tender is better than big and stringy!

If the beans are very small and young, you can simply cut off the heads and tails and serve them whole. Older beans must be thinly sliced diagonally into lozenge-shaped pieces. Drop the sliced beans into a pan of salted, boiling water. When the beans are ready, they will sink to the bottom of the pan. Serve with hot butter and plenty of salt and pepper.

Beets

Small, well-shaped beets make an excellent hot meal. Chose your beets carefully, scrub clean, and then boil in salted water for at least an hour, possibly more. Test if they are cooked and tender by using a finger—if you spear them with a fork, all the color will tend to leak out into your cooking water. Once cooked, remove from water and take off the skins. You can then quarter them and serve with a dressing made by frying a few well-chopped onions in butter and adding a little tarragon vinegar.

Carrot croquettes

Cook some carrots, but don't let them get too soft. Grate about 1 cup per person. Now melt together butter and flour in a saucepan (about equal parts, 1 ounce/30 g per person) together with about one cup of milk per person. Cook steadily until the mixture begins to draw away from the sides of the pan, stirring constantly. Now add your grated carrot plus the yolk of one egg for each person to be served. Add seasoning to taste (salt and pepper plus some sugar) and turn out onto a plate to cool. When cool you can form into shapes—use a little flour if you need to stop them from sticking together.

Baked eggplant

This is a very quick and delicious way to cook eggplant, especially if you have a large stove that is always hot. Wipe or wash the eggplant and cut off the stalk ends. Cut the eggplants down the centers to split into two halves. Put the halves into a baking tray, cut side up, and add a little olive oil to stop them from sticking. Now grate some cheese onto the upturned flat sides of eggplant. Bake at 350°F (180°C) for about 40 minutes.

Creamed leeks

Wash five or six leeks and clean them carefully. Cut off the roots and most of the green leaves. Split them open lengthwise and cut into pieces about 2 inches (5 cm) long. Throw these pieces into boiling water, slightly salted, and cook for 10 minutes, then drain. Now put them into a pan with half a pint of milk seasoned with pepper and salt. Simmer them slowly until they are tender. Now strain off the milk and arrange the leeks carefully in a warmed vegetable dish.

Melt 1 ounce (30 g) of butter in a pan and mix with a tablespoon of flour. Then pour in the milk you have strained off the leeks. Stir the mixture until it boils, and cook for a couple of minutes to make sure the flour has cooked through. Now add the cream at the end and pour the entire sauce over the leeks. Sprinkle with parsley and serve hot.

Baked mushrooms

Wash and peel your mushrooms, then remove the stems. Now put them hollow side up in a baking tray greased with a little olive oil. Sprinkle them with salt and pepper and a few drops of lemon juice, then add a small piece of butter to each one. Bake them for about 15 minutes at 350°F (180°C). Of course, you can add crushed garlic to the butter and produce the dish that is so popular in restaurants.

Potatoes *au Gratin*

Make mashed potatoes in the normal way, but add plenty of milk and butter together with grated cheese—add as much cheese as you like, depending on the strength of the cheese. Season with salt and pepper and add a little mustard. Now pour the mixture into an ovenproof dish. Grate cheese to cover the top, and add a few handfuls of breadcrumbs. Spread a little melted butter over the surface and then brown at 425°F (220°C). This is delicious.

Baked tomatoes

Choose moderately sized tomatoes and cut out the stalk and the hard part at the root of the stalk. Place the tomatoes on a buttered baking tray, and put a small piece of butter into the hole left after removing the stalks. Sprinkle with pepper and salt, and bake at 350°F (180°C) for about 15 minutes. Serve in a hot dish.

Baked cauliflower/eggplant

This is a quick and tasty way to cook large vegetables. Preheat your oven to 375°F (190°C). Grease a baking tray (I like to use olive oil). Place your prepared vegetable in the center (large lumps for cauliflower, cut in half for eggplant) and sprinkle grated cheese (cheddar is fine) over the top with a little pepper and salt. Bake it for about 30 minutes.

"Since we have been here, we have made wine of cowslips, parsnips, elderberries, crab apples, wheat, marrow, broom flowers, grapes, and sloes. The cowslip was superb, but never since the first year have we had enough cowslips. The crab apple was unfortunate. Firstly, the apples probably have quite a lot of native sugar in them and so we should not have added so much. Secondly, I added what we decided to add without telling Sally [John's wife at the time], and she then came along and added the same amount again! The yeast cannot turn all that amount of sugar into alcohol—because when the alcohol gets to a certain strength it kills the yeast. So the stuff tasted like very sickly alcohol grenadine. It was revolting and we gave it to the pigs which made them as drunk as people. Knowing what we now know we would not have given the pigs a treat. We would have tried refermenting it, mixing it first with another load of vegetable matter—adding some lemons, perhaps—anything the flavor of which would not have clashed with the apples and which would have given more non-sugar matter for the yeast to work."

JOHN SEYMOUR FAT OF THE LAND 1976

CHAPTER EIGHT

BREWING
AND
WINE-MAKING

Brewing Basics

Brewing, wine-making, and distilling have been major influences on the development of entire civilizations. Today they remain the cornerstone of success for several of the largest companies on planet Earth, not to mention vital sources of revenue for the national governments. How fortunate, then, that alcohol is so conveniently produced in the natural world by yeasts that are ever-present on the food we eat and the air we breathe. We may think wine, beer, and liquor are important today, but their value was even greater for our forebears, who faced a real challenge in storing foodstuffs through the winter. By converting sugars to alcohol, the value of food could be preserved and its flavor even enhanced.

Some plants and fruits seem to lend themselves particularly effectively for winemaking and brewing. Malt and hops have formed a staple part of Western diets as "beer" for many years. Meanwhile, in warmer climes, the grape is preeminent with its strong flavors, natural yeasts, and excellent health-giving qualities. In some very special way, the smell, taste, and presence of beautiful wine or beer seems to symbolize a very essence of bounty from the earth.

Yeast works in mysterious ways

Different strains of yeast behave in different ways, and we need to choose one that suits our purposes best—or at least encourage that type above all others. Some yeasts will float on the top of the brew; others will sink to form a mud on the bottom. Still others will remain suspended as a colloidal mess—definitely not the brewer's favorite. Some yeasts work quickly but cannot stand high temperatures or too much alcohol. Other yeasts work slowly but go on to produce much more alcohol over many months.

The first types of yeast are excellent, aggressive plants ideal for beer, while the second are what we want for wine but very easily displaced and upset by interlopers. This is why we can ferment beer quickly in relatively unsealed containers, while we have to treat wine much more carefully. And the whole brewing process involves managing the complex microfauna of a sugary fruit solution in the best way we can to achieve the results we want. Sometimes the power of an aggressive, early fermentation gives way slowly to the gradual pace of tough wine yeasts. And all the time the millions of fungal and bacterial spores that float through the air are awaiting their chance to contaminate our drinks. The vinegar flies lose no chance to splash their little feet in our future dream of wine, spreading harmful bacteria. And the oxygen of the air itself rapidly oxidizes many of the volatile flavors in our fruit soup.

Racking off

When we make beer (or wine, for that matter) we must carefully separate the delicious-tasting part from the buildup of sludge and yeast. A fine, clear end result can only be achieved by managing a process called "racking off." To do this well, the first point I would make is not to rack off beer or cider until the major fermentation process has stopped. While fermentation continues, the minute bubbles of carbon dioxide gas carry sediment with them into the body of the brew. As fermentation calms down, there are fewer bubbles and less sediment. With wines, we may want to rack off several times during the much slower fermentation—and we do this once a solid body of sludge has built up.

The second point I would pass on is that a cool liquid holds less sediment than a warm one. Put your brew in a cool place at last 24 hours before you finally rack off the finished product. And if possible, put the demijohn or fermenting bin on a high table in this position so it's ready for racking off without having to move it again. The more height you have, the more quickly you can siphon off the brew! Finally (and perhaps an obvious point), make sure you have some device for preventing the end of your siphon from going too far down into the sludge (or near it), for suction will pull it up. There are all sorts of special devices sold for this purpose in brewing shops, but I prefer to use a good solid copper nail fastened onto the pipe with elastic band. A copper or galvanized nail will not taint the brew and its weight helps keep the siphon pipe down.

Another important tip I have learned (from bitter experience) is not to put newly corked bottles straight into storage. Remember, you will be storing them horizontally with labels uppermost so that the cork breathes properly and the sediment settles on the opposite side from the label. In this position you will lose everything—and make a big, smelly mess—if the corks blow out. So leave freshly corked bottles upright for at least 48 hours, and examine them carefully to make sure the corks are secure before laying them down.

When pouring out your beer to consume and enjoy, it is best to decant the whole bottle into a suitable container for the dining room—this way you have something pleasant to look at on the table and you avoid stirring up sediment and wasting a good half pint of each bottle. I have long used a lovely old German 2-liter flask with a porcelain and rubber clip top.

Distilling

If you get a big copper boiler with a fire under it, half fill it with beer, float a basin on the beer, and place a shallow dish wider than the boiler on the top of the boiler, you will get whiskey. Alcohol will evaporate from the beer, condense on the undersurface of the big dish, run down to the lowest point of it, and drip down into the basin. It is an advantage if you can run cold water into, and out of, the top dish to cool it. This speeds up condensation. And if distilling is illegal in your part of the world and some inquisitive fellow comes down the drive, it doesn't take a second to be washing clothes in the boiler, making porridge in the floating basin, and bathing the baby in the big, flat dish. And what could be more innocent than that?

Malting Barley

Something that has contributed over the millennia to keeping humans human, even if it sometimes gives them headaches, is the invention of malt. One imagines that very soon after humans discovered grain, they also discovered that if you left it lying around in water, the water would ferment, and if you drank enough of it, it would make you drunk. In fact, you can make beer out of any farinaceous grain. (When I fought in World War II, we had a company brewer in every company of the King's African Rifles. He brewed once a week, and would brew beer out of absolutely any kind of grain he could lay his hands on. Most of it was pretty horrible stuff, but it kept us sane.)

Later on in history, some genius discovered that if you sprouted the grain first, it made better beer and made you even more drunk. He didn't know the reason for this, of course, but we do. It is because alcohol is made from sugar.

Yeast, which is a microscopic mold or fungus, eats sugar and turns it into alcohol. It can also do the same, in a much more limited way, with starch. Now grain is mostly starch, or carbohydrate, and you can make an inferior beer out of it before it sprouts by fermenting it with yeast. But if you cause the grain to sprout—that is, start to grow—the starch gets turned, by certain enzymes, into sugar. It then makes much better, stronger beer much more quickly.

So to make beer, we civilized people sprout our barley before we ferment it. This process is known as malting, and the sprouted grain is called malt. You can malt any grain, but barley, being highest in starch, makes the best malt.

Malting barley

Put your barley, inside a porous sack if you like, into some slightly warm water and leave it for four days. Pull it out and heap it on a floor and take its temperature every day. If the latter goes below 63°F (17°C), pile it up in a much thicker heap. In the trade this is called "couching" it. If the temperature goes above 68°F (20°C), spread it out more thinly and turn it often. Turning cools it. Keep it moist but not sodden: sprinkle warmish water on it occasionally. Remember, you want to make it grow. After about 10 days of this, the acrospire, or shoot of the grain (not the root, which will also be growing), should have grown about two-thirds the length of the grain. The acrospire is to be seen growing below the skin of the grain. Couch it for 12 hours when you think it has grown enough.

Kilning the malt

After this you must kiln the grain. This means bringing it to a temperature of 120°F (50°C) over either a fire or a stove, or in an oven with the door open to keep the hot air moving through the grain. Keep it moving in the kiln, which is simply a perforated steel plate over a fire, until it is dry.

Kilning for different beers

The color and nature of beer can be altered one way or the other by the extent of the kilning of the malt after it has been sprouted. This kilning is necessary to kill the grain. If you didn't kill it, it would go on growing into long, gangly shoots. Kilning also makes it keep, and you almost always have to keep it before you use it. If you just put it, wet and growing, in a bag, it would rot. Not only would it be useless, it would also smell nasty.

A light kilning makes a light-colored malt and consequently a light-colored beer, while heavier kilning makes darker malt and darker beer. If you want to make lager, keep the temperature down to slightly under 120°F (50°C). If you want dark ale, take it up as high as 140°F (60°C), but not over. Why not over? Because over would kill the enzymes that are to go on turning even more starch into sugar when you mash the malt.

The maltster watches his malt in the kiln, constantly turning it and looking at it, and he stops the kilning at the right stage for the kind of beer he intends to make. You can stop kilning when you can bite a grain and it cracks between the teeth, but if you want a darker beer you simply go on kilning until the grains turn browner. If you want stout, you actually go on kilning until the grain turns nearly black—but do not allow the grain in the kiln to go over 140°F (60°C). Just give it longer, that's all.

When you have kilned enough, just crush the grain in a mill: don't grind it fine. Now you have malt, and you are ready to start brewing your beer.

MALTING BARLEY

Soak the grain for four days. Pile it in a heap on the floor, and by alternately spreading it out and piling it up again, or "couching" it, keep it at a temperature between 63°F (17°C) and 68°F (20°C). You will need to do this for about 10 days, until a shoot about two-thirds the length of the grain can be seen growing beneath the skin of the grain. Dry the grain completely in a kiln (*below right*), crush it in a mill, and you have malt.

Making Beer

Before Tudor times, there were no hops in Britain, and the stuff people drank—fermented malt—was called ale. At about that time, hops were introduced from continental Europe and used for flavoring and preserving ale, and the resultant drink was called beer. Beer is more bitter than ale was and, when you get used to it, much better. Nowadays the nomenclature has gotten confused and the words beer and ale are used indiscriminately. But make no mistake: in our day and age, beer and brewing are big business—the lifeblood of huge transnational corporations and the source of billions in government taxation.

There are few areas where the self-supporter can make such large cash savings by creating a more delicious product to his or her own taste—at just a fraction of the commercial cost. And what self-supporter would be without a constant and ample supply of this great lubricant for sociability and wise reflection? Making your own beer is the ultimate activity for many a self-supporter, especially city-dwellers, for whom it can be a first small act of "freedom" from mass production. Of course, you can go further and prepare all the ingredients from your own land.

Soil for hops

Hops like a deep, heavy, well-drained loam and liberal manuring, preferably with farmyard manure. But they will produce some sort of a crop on most land, provided they are well fertilized and the land is not waterlogged, and if you grow your own hops for your own beer, some sort of a crop is all you need: you need pounds, not tons.

Planting hops

Clean your piece of land thoroughly. Make sure you get out all perennial weed roots and grass. Beg, borrow, or steal a dozen pieces of hop root from a female (cone-producing) vine. Sections of root about a foot in length are fine. Hops produce an enormous mass of roots every year, and an established hop plant just won't miss a foot or two of root.

Plant these pieces of root at intervals of 2–3 feet (60–90 cm), with plenty of farmyard manure or compost. Arrange horizontal wires, some high and others down near the ground. Put vertical strings between the wires for the hops to climb up, three or four strings for each piece of root. When the hops begin to grow, they will race each other up the strings, and you can place bets with your family on the winner—they grow so fast you can almost see them move. Watch for aphids. If you get them, spray with insecticidal soap, pyrethrum, or some other nonpersistent insecticide.

Harvesting hops

Pick the flowers when they are in full bloom, and full of the bitterly fragrant yellow powder that is the virtue of the hop. Dry the flowers gently. If you put them on wire, burlap, or some other perforated surface over a stove, that will do. When they are thoroughly dry, store them, preferably in some woven sacks.

Malt and malt extract

You can brew beer from malt extract, which you can buy from the store, or in "brewing kits" from various enterprises. The beer you brew will be strong (or can be), will taste quite good (or can), but it will not be the same as real beer brewed from real malt. The best beer will be the stuff you brew from the malt you have made yourself (see p.321). But you can also buy malt in sacks, and this is preferable to malt extract. The difference between beer brewed from malt and beer brewed from malt extract is great and unmistakable, and if you once get used to beer brewed from malt you will not be content to go back to extract beer—nor to the liquid you sip from a six-pack.

Brewing beer

In the evening, before you go to bed, boil 10 gallons (38 liters) of water. While it is boiling, make a strainer for your mash-tub, kive, brewing vat, or whatever you call it. This is a tub holding 20 gallons, but with the top cut off. You can make the strainer by tying a bundle of straw, or hay, or gorse leaves with a piece of string, poking the string through the taphole of the vat, pulling it tight so as to haul the bundle hard up against the hole inside, and banging the tap in. The tap then holds the piece of string. Or, if you like, you can have a hole in the bottom of your kive with an ash stick pushed down into it to close it. When you pull the ash stick out, of course, it opens the hole. If you lay a layer of gorse in the bottom of your vat, some straw on top of this, then a flat stone with a hole in the middle of it, and then poke your ash stick through this hole, you have a magnificent strainer.

GROW YOUR OWN HOPS
Hops must be given strings to grow up; otherwise they get into a hopeless mess and the harvest is drastically reduced. Fix horizontal wires to sturdy posts and then arrange vertical strings between the wires, three or four to each root planted. The hops will do the rest. You just watch and keep them clear of aphids if necessary. Harvest when the flowers are in full bloom (above). Inside, they will be full of bitter yellow powder—sweet nectar to a serious home brewer.

BEER-MAKING

To make consistently good home-brew, you must start off with scrupulously clean vats and barrels. They should be scrubbed, scalded, and then disinfected by exposure to wind and sunlight. Choose a quiet evening and boil up 10 gallons (38 liters) of water in your copper.

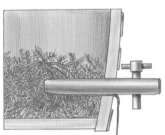

1 While you are waiting for the water to boil, make a strainer for the vat. Tie a small bundle of gorse, hay, or straw with a piece of string and drop it in the vat, poke the loose end through the bung-hole, and pull hard. Then bang in the tap (wooden cock).

2 When the water boils, let it cool to 150°F (66°C) and pour half into the vat.

3 Dump in 1 bushel (55 lb or 25 kg) malt, and the rest of the hot water, and stir thoroughly.

Then tuck the kive in for the night. Cover with a clean sheet and a blanket. The enzymes in the malt plus the water will then go to work extracting the malt sugar.

4 The next morning, open the cock and drain the "wort" (liquid) into a bucket, or even better, into an "underbuck," the traditional wooden vessel.

5 Now "sparge" (sprinkle) the spent malt with lots of kettles of boiling water to remove all the sugar, until 10 gallons (38 liters) of wort have drained out into the bucket. And thence into the boiler.

6 Pack 1 pound (0.5 kg) of hops into a pillowcase and plunge it into the wort. If you want to cheat by stirring in sugar, honey or malt extract (6 lb or 2.7 kg to 10 gallons or 38 liters of wort) now is the time to do it. Boil for at least one hour. Meanwhile, get on with cleaning out the vat. The mash makes splendid food for pigs or cows.

7 Draw a jugful of boiling wort and cool quickly by immersing in icy water. When it has cooled to 60°F (16°C), plop in your yeast—either packet beer yeast (about 1 ounce or 28 g will do) or a couple of tablespoons of "barm" that you have strained off the top of your last brew and kept covered in a cool place. Then transfer the rest of the boiling wort back into the vat.

8 Cool the bulk of the wort as fast as you can by lowering buckets of cold water into it, but don't spill a drop if you want your beer to be worth drinking.

9 As soon as the bulk of the wort has cooled to hand-hot, pour in the "starter," a jugful of foaming, yeasty wort, and stir. Cover with blankets to keep out vinegar flies.

10 Leave for three days. Then skin off the "barm." After fermentation (5–8 days), pour off without stirring up the sediment.

"Mashing" the malt

When the water has boiled, let it cool to 150°F (66°C). Then dump one bushel (about 55 lb or 25 kg) of cracked malt into it and stir until the malt is wet through. This is called "mashing," and the malt is now the "mash." It is most important that the water should not be hotter than 150°F (66°C) because if it is, it will kill the enzymes. Cover the vat up with a blanket and go to bed.

Early in the morning, get up and open the cock, or draw the ash stick, to allow the wort, as the liquid is now called, to run out into buckets. Pour it from the buckets into the boiler, together with a pound (0.5 kg) of dried hops tied in a pillowcase, and boil it. While the wort is dribbling out, "sparge" (brewer's word for sprinkle) the mash with boiling water. (You don't care about the enzymes now—they have done their work and converted the rest of the starch into sugar.) Go on sparging until 10 gallons (38 liters) of wort have drained out. Much of the original 10 gallons has been absorbed by the mash.

Boil the 10 gallons of wort, and the hops in the pillow case, for an hour. If you want the beer to be very strong, add, say, 6 pounds (2.7 kg) of sugar now, or honey if you can spare it. Or, another way of cheating is to add 6 pounds (2.7 kg) of malt extract. But you needn't add anything at all. You will still get very strong beer. Clean the mash out of the kive and set it aside for the pigs or cows.

Transfer the boiling wort back into the clean vat. Take a jugful of wort out and cool it by standing it in cold water. When it is hand-hot, dump some yeast into it. This can be yeast from a previous fermentation, or yeast you have bought especially for beer. Bread yeast will do but beer yeast is better. Bread yeast is a "bottom fermenting" yeast; it sinks to the bottom in beer. Beer yeast is "top-fermenting" and is marginally better.

The faster your bulk of wort cools now, the better. An "in-churn" milk cooler put into the wort with cold water running through it is very helpful. If you haven't got this, you can lower in buckets of cold water, but be sure no water spills out and that the outside of the bucket is clean. Quick cooling allows less time for disease organisms to get into the wort before it is cool enough to take the yeast.

When the main body of the wort has cooled to 60°F (16°C), dump your jugful of yeasty wort into it and stir. This is the time when you should pray. Cover up very carefully to keep out all vinegar flies and dust. Try to keep away from the stuff for at least three days. Then skim the floating yeast off. Otherwise it will sink, which is bad. When it has stopped fermenting, after five to eight days, "rack" it. That means pour it gently, without stirring up the sediment in the bottom, into the vessels in which you intend to keep it, and cover these securely. From now on no air must get in. You have made beer.

You can use plastic garbage cans instead of wooden or earthenware vessels; I don't like them, but they have their advantages for hygiene and accessibility. If you use wooden vessels, though, you must keep them scrupulously clean.

Beer from kits

Most good drugstores or health food shops sell beer kits, and usually all the equipment to go with them. The modern equipment is mostly plastic, but this is at least one beneficial by-product of the petrochemical industry. You will want to try quite a few different recipes—and do not think the most expensive is always the most delicious. For years I bought the cheapest cans of malt/beer extract made by Irish monks—they were delicious, but now, alas, the monks have died out. Always keep a note of what you have brewed and how you brewed it.

Your key items of equipment are a large fermenting vessel, normally 40 pints (19 liters), with a well-fitting airtight top, a decanting siphon tube with rigid pipes at each end and a tap at the end you will put into bottles, and a heating mat for keeping the fermentation at the right temperature. Your kit will come with its own yeast and its own instructions. All you need to provide is "love," plenty of hot water, and a couple of pounds of sugar—then plenty of thirst to drink the stuff.

I normally make one brew each week and somehow it all seems to disappear. First swish out your fermenting vessel (which should be kept nice and clean—replace it if it gets old and worn) with a kettle full of boiling water to kill any beasts and bugs. Pour in your malt extract (after prewarming it on the stove to make it pour easily), add 2 pounds (1 kg) of sugar, and then two kettles full of boiling water. Stir it all together and when well mixed, fill up the vessel with cold water before adding the yeast. Try to avoid leaving the top of the vessel open to keep out contamination and vinegar flies. Pop on the top and place on your heating mat in a calm place for about one week.

Modern beer kits have yeast that sinks to the bottom when fermentation is complete. Test your brew after seven days: it should be a clear brown, with all foam gone, and have a bitter taste (all the sugar gone to alcohol) and a lovely, beery smell.

If it is ready, turn off the heating mat and put in a cool place, preferably high up where you can decant into bottles, next morning. Get all your decanting equipment ready before you start. You will find clear plastic soda bottles ideal for storing your beer; make sure they are well washed and stored full of clean water. Smell each one as you pour out the water and toss out any doubtfuls. You will find many a friend glad to give you these items of "waste."

Siphon off your beer carefully to avoid disturbing the sediment. Put extra sugar into each bottle; the exact amount is a matter of taste and judgement. I like beer without too much fizz, so I put half a teaspoon in a 2-liter bottle before screwing down the lid. Keep the filled bottles in a warm place for 24 hours to get the secondary fermentation going before you put them out into storage. They will take another 10 days to fizz up. You can tell how much fizz there is by simply squeezing the bottle; a hard bottle means lots of fizz.

Making Wine

Strict cleanliness is essential in wine-making, for wine is made by a living organism (yeast), and if other living organisms (wild yeasts or other molds or bacteria) get into the act, either the tame yeasts that you want to use for your wine cannot do their job, or you get putrefaction, bad tastes, and odors. Aside from that important point, you can ignore the plethora of books about home wine-making, each one blinding us with science more effectively than the last. You really only need to remember the following few essentials:

1 *As already stressed, keep all wine-making equipment scrupulously clean. Use boiling water whenever possible.*
2 *You are unlikely to get more than 3 pounds (1.4 kg) of sugar to ferment in 1 gallon (4 liters) of water, so keep to approximately this ratio if you want strong wine.*
3 *You must ferment at the temperature most favorable to vital yeasts.*
4 *You must give your special cultivated yeast every help and an unfair advantage over the wild yeasts and other organisms that might ruin your brew.*
5 *You must keep all contaminants out of your wine, especially vinegar flies, those little midges that hang around rotting fruit, carrying the bugs that turn wine to vinegar.*
6 *You must "rack" or pour off the wine from the lees and sediments before the latter spoil its flavor.*
7 *You must allow the wine to settle and clear in the cool after the yeast has done its work.*
8 *Finally, having safely bottled your wine, you must try to keep your mitts off it for a year with red wine, if you can, and at least three months with white.*

Equipment

You need jars, barrels, or bottles for fermentation. You also need fermentation locks (if you can get them). The purpose of these is to allow the gases produced by fermentation to escape while keeping out air, which is always germ-laden, and vinegar flies. Many a vat of fine wine has been made without a fermentation lock and with just a plug of cotton balls stuffed in the neck of the vessel. Many a gallon of wine has been ruined this way, too. A fermentation lock is a very useful thing. A thermometer is not to be despised, either. You also need a flexible tube—rubber or plastic—for "racking" or siphoning, a funnel or two, and containers for the final bottling of the wine. A corking gun is very good for driving in corks, which have to be driven in dead tight or air gets in and the wine goes bad. Polythene sealers are quite a good substitute for corks if you do not want to invest in a corking gun.

Materials

You will need yeast. Old-fashioned country wine makers, including myself, have used all kinds of yeasts—bread yeasts and beer yeasts and so on—but undoubtedly it is best to buy wine yeasts from a store. For very good and strong results, some people use yeast nutrients, also bought from a store. Acid is another thing you may have to add. Lemons will provide this, as will citric acid, which you can buy. Tannin, too, can be bought, but tea or apples—particularly crab apples—will provide it. The reader may say that it is not being self-sufficient to buy all this stuff from a store. True, but I would say that a trivial expenditure on this sort of thing is necessary if you are going to make a great deal of fine, drinkable wine.

GRAPE WINE

There is no wine like grape wine. Red grape wine is made by fermenting the grape skins in with the wine. White wine is made by taking the skins out. White wine is often made with red or black grapes, for all grapes are white inside. It is easier to make red or rosé wine than white because the tannin in the skins helps the "must" (wine-to-be) to ferment better, and the quicker it ferments, the less chance there is of bad organisms getting to work.

Crushing

Crush your grapes any way you like. Personally, I could not drink wine if I had seen somebody stomping it with his bare feet, so l would use some sort of mortar and pestle for this job. If you want to make white wine, press the broken grapes in a press (a car jack will do), having first wrapped them in strong calico "cheeses" (*see* p.293). In the case of red or rosé, press in the same way, but then add a proportion of the skins to the wine. The more you add, the deeper the red color of the wine, but, in cold climates at any rate, the deeper red ones may contain too much tannin and will be a little bitter as a result. Now in real wine-growing climates (where you will not be reading instructions like this anyway, since your neighbors will initiate you), you don't need to add any sugar. In less sunny climates add 4–6 pounds (1.8-2.7 kg) of sugar to every 12 gallons (45 liters) of wine-to-be. If there has been a hot season and the grapes are sweet, you need less; if a bad season, more.

Fermenting

Let the juices and skins ferment in a vat. Grapes have their own yeasts in the "bloom" on their skins, but it is best to add a wine yeast culture bought from a store, if you can get one. Warm a bottle of the must (juice) to 75°F (24°C), dump the yeast culture into it, and stand it in a warm place with some cotton balls in the neck. Meanwhile, try to get your main body of must to 75°F (24°C). When the "starter" or culture in the bottle has started to fizz, pour it into the main body. If you keep the temperature at about 75°F (24°C.), fermentation will be so active that there is no danger of air getting to the must, for the carbon dioxide given off will prevent this. Don't let the temperature rise above 80°F (27°C) or some of your yeast will be killed. Don't let it fall below 70°F (21°C), or your yeast will get sleepy and foreign yeasts will gain advantage. Always keep the skins stirred into the must. They will float on top, so don't let them form a dry, floating crust.

WINE-MAKING EQUIPMENT

Don't attempt to make your own wine without arming yourself beforehand with plenty of containers, to hold the must at each of its many stages. Bottles and bottling are only the end stages of a long fermentation process, during which you will need at least several containers, such as jugs and jars—and quite possibly vats and barrels, too.

Key
1 Fermentation barrel
2 Corking gun
3 Jug
4 Bottle
5 Sieve
6 Bottle brush
7 Funnel
8 Hydrometer
9 Measuring cylinder
10 Screw-top bottle
11 Plastic or rubber siphon
12 Earthenware vessel
13 Barrel and tapped vat
14 Fermentation jar and lock
15 Cork and plastic sealer

Racking

When the first violent fermentation has ceased, rack off the must, squeeze the juice out of the skins so as not to waste it, and pour the juice into a barrel or carboy, so that the must fills it completely. Be careful not to leave an air space above it.

Let the temperature fall now to a temperature of about 60°F (16°C). Check, and when you think most of the sediment has sunk to the bottom, rack the wine into another container. At this stage, people in continental climates often put wine outdoors in winter so that it almost freezes, because this hastens the settling down of sediment. Now rack it again. After another month or two of it sitting quietly, you can then bottle it in the way I will now describe.

Bottling

Bottles must be completely cleaned and then sterilized. It is no good "sterilizing" anything with dirt in it; the dirt must first be removed. Sterilize by heating slowly so you do not crack the bottles. You can do this in an oven, if you like. Then pour in boiling water, or put in cold water and slowly bring to the boil and boil for five minutes. Hang the bottles upside down immediately to let them drain and stop dust from floating down into them. Either use as soon as they are cool or cork until you want them. Boil the corks before you use them and whack them in with a special corker. Store bottled wine on its side to keep the corks wet. If they dry out, they will shrink, and air and vinegar bacilli will get in. Store wine in the dark, at a cool even temperature. A cellar or basement is ideal.

COUNTRY WINES

I am going to give you some recipes for "country wines," that work, as I know from long experience. I would not discourage anybody from "scientific wine-making," which is reliable and produces good wines, but country people all over Europe and North America have used the sort of recipes I give for centuries, and very seldom have failures; indeed, their wines are very good. One point worth noting is that the larger the bulk of wine you make, the less likely you are to have a failure. My old friends in an English village, who all brew rhubarb wine in the summer and parsnip in the winter, in batches of 60 gallons (225 liters) stored in huge cider barrels, have never known what a failure is. Their spouses cry in vain for them to grow something else in their gardens, but their wine is superb.

Flower wines

Pour a gallon (4 liters) of boiling water over an equivalent quantity of whatever flowers you wish to use, cool, and press the water from the flowers. Add 4 pounds (1.8 kg) of sugar, ½ pound (228 g) of raisins (optional), and the juice of three lemons. The flowers don't give much nutriment for the yeast, and sugar alone is not enough for it, so add some yeast nutriment if you have some. A tablespoon of nutriment to a gallon of wine is about right. When the temperature has fallen to 75°F (24°C), add yeast. A bought wine yeast is best. Put the wine in a vessel with a fermentation lock, and leave to ferment. Rack off and bottle when ready. I have made wines from gorse and broom flowers, elderflower (superb), cowslip, and dandelion, and I have drunk good rose wine.

Here are some wine recipes to try for yourself:

Rhubarb wine

15 lb (6.8 kg) rhubarb stems
2 ½ lb (1.2 kg) sugar
1 gallon (4 liters) water
yeast

Chop up the rhubarb, pour boiling water over it, and mash. Don't boil it any further. Leave it to soak until the next day, strain off your liquor, and press the "fruit" to get as much out as you can. Stir in the sugar and bung in the yeast. Leave it to ferment, then rack it and bottle it.

Nettle wine

4 lb (1.8 kg) nettle tips
4 lemons
2 lb (0.9 kg) sugar (preferably brown)
1 oz (28 g) cream of tartar
2 gallons (8 liters) water
1 tablespoon dried yeast brewer's yeast

Put nettles and cut-up lemons in the water and boil for 20 minutes. Strain liquor out and add cream of tartar and sugar. When cool enough, add yeast and ferment for three days in a warm place. Then let it settle for a couple of days in a cooler place before bottling in screw-top bottles. You can drink it in a week, and it doesn't keep long. It is extremely pleasant and refreshing. If you add some ginger to it, it is even better.

Parsnip wine

4 lb (1.8 kg) parsnips
3 lb (1.4 kg) sugar
1 gallon (4 liters) water
some lemons or citric acid
yeast

Cut the parsnips up and boil them without letting them get too soft. They should just be easily prickable with a fork. Boil a couple of lemons up with them if you have them. Strain off the liquor, and while it is still hot, stir in the sugar, so that it dissolves. Put in some lemon juice or citric acid, and some raisins if you like. The purpose of the lemon juice or citric acid is to give the yeast enough acidity to feed on, since parsnips are low in acid. Put everything in a vessel, wait until the temperature drops to blood heat, then add your yeast and allow to ferment. Like all other wine, ferment under a fermentation lock, or put a wad of cotton in the neck of the vessel, to keep the vinegar flies out and let out the carbon dioxide. Rack it well a couple of times, and then keep it as long as you can keep your hands off it.

Elderberry wine

6 lb (2.7 kg) elderberries
3 lb (1.4 kg) sugar
1 gallon (4 liters) water
2 oz (56 g) citric acid or lemon juice
yeast

You are supposed to get all the berries off the stalks, but I have shoved in stalks and all and it has made no difference. After all, if you can save a lot of work by departing from slavish convention, why not do so? Pour the boiling water on, mash hard with a potato masher, cover and leave to soak for 24 hours. Put the sugar and yeast in and leave it alone. The longer you leave it, the better. When it has finished fermenting, rack it into bottles or other containers, so as to leave the sediment behind. You do this with all wines.

This recipe can be applied to any wine made from berries or currants.

Elderflower "champagne"

This is nothing like champagne, of course, but it is a very refreshing summer drink, and it does not have to be kept long before you can drink it.

12 heads of elderflowers (in full bloom and scent, picked on a hot day)
1½ lb (0.7 kg) sugar (white sugar is less obtrusive than brown in such a delicate drink)
1 lemon
2 tablespoons wine vinegar

Put blooms in a bowl with the juice of the lemon. Cut up the rind of lemon and put that in (minus the white pith). Add the sugar, vinegar, 1 gallon (4 liters) of water, and leave for 24 hours. Strain liquor in screw-top bottles, cork up, and leave for two weeks. Don't add yeast—weak yeasts on the flowers are enough. Drink before three weeks old.

MEAD

To supply what in your estimation is about 3 pounds (1.5 kg) of honey to 1 gallon (4 liters) of water, you want comb cappings, odd bits of "wild comb" that you can't put through the extractor, and perhaps some pure honey stolen from the main storage pot when your spouse isn't looking. Melt the honey in the water and ferment.

Honey is deficient in acid, so put the juice of two or three lemons in a gallon, or some citric acid. Mead also likes some tannin to feed the yeast, so some crushed crab apples are a good idea. I have heard of people putting tea in mead. I once dumped some rose hip syrup that the children decided they didn't like into my mead, which wasn't fermenting very well, and it started to ferment like crazy. Mead goes on fermenting for a long time, so do not try to hurry it, and if you can leave it in a bottle for a few years so much the better. But can you?

MAKING ROSE HIP WINE

The principle of wine-making does not vary much according to the main ingredient. The addition of a wine yeast to your brew starts off the fermentation process, which can take as long as three months.

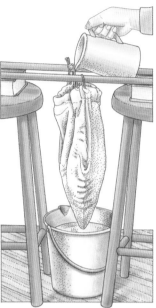

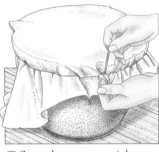

1 Take 3 quarts (3 liters) of rose hips, clean them, and chop them up finely. Crush with a wooden spoon or mallet.

2 Put the crushed hips into a deep bowl and pour 1½ gallons (6.5 liters) of boiling water over them. If you like, you can add the rind and juice of an orange.

3 Add 2 pounds (1 kg) of sugar and heat to 75°F (24°C).

4 Stir in a teaspoon of fresh yeast. You can put this first into a bottle of "starter," which you add to the brew when it starts fermenting. Add 1 teaspoon of citric acid and half a teaspoon of tannin.

5 Cover the must overnight to keep out vinegar flies and all other contaminants.

6 Strain the must from the hips through a sieve or muslin cloth. For even clearer must, use both these methods.

7 Or you can strain through a jelly bag, suspended from two stools. Don't press it, or it will go cloudy.

8 Strain the must into fermentation jars. Use a funnel. Keep at 75°F (24°C).

9 A fermentation lock keeps air out but allows gases to escape.

10 If you have no tube, use a hand jug and a funnel. Leave an inch (2.5 cm) at the top for corks when filling the bottles.

11 When fermentation stops, rack the wine off the lees into bottles. Use a rubber or a plastic tube for this.

12 A corking gun is excellent for driving corks in tight, but a wooden mallet will do. Date, label, and leave for a year.

Making Hard Cider & Vinegar

HARD CIDER

Hard cider should be made from a mixture of apples. The ideal mixture is a selection of apples rich in acid, tannin, and sugar, so a good combination mixes very sweet apples with very sour ones, perhaps with some crabapples thrown in to provide the tannin.

Hard cider can be made with unripe apples, but it is never very successful. Ideally, the apples should be picked ripe and then allowed to lie in heaps for two or three days, until they begin to soften a little. A few bad or bruised apples in the press don't seem to affect the quality of the cider. Apples vary greatly in juice content, so it is not possible to tell exactly how much cider you will get from a given number of apples. As an estimate, 10–14 pounds (45–6 kg) of apples make about one gallon (4 liters).

Over the centuries, cider-making was one of the best ways of preserving the "food" value of apples over the winter. Alcohol and the fermentation process are like a magic preserving process. By the miracle of nature, cloudy and dirty apple juice become a delicious (if slightly intoxicating) golden liquor. Apples are produced in great quantities during the autumn. Some varieties store fairly well—Coxes, for example—but most will only last a couple of months, and then only if they are picked in perfect condition (windfalls will be bruised and useless for storage). In the modern world, very few people know how to deal with their apple crops, and we find we have lots of friends who are only too happy for us to appear with a party of kids to gather up all their windfalls. Cider-making parties with kids are a pleasant way of enjoying an autumn day.

Crushing

When you have collected a pile of apples—a wheelbarrowful, at least—you're ready to start cider-making. A few strong helpers will be useful if you can find them. You will need chopping equipment, a crusher, a fruit press and a 5-gallon (20-liter) fermentation bin. You then crush the apples. Crushing is an arduous task. Traditionally, this was done by a horse or an ox pulling a huge, round stone around a circular stone trough. I did have one friend who used to put his apples through a horizontal mangle, which reduced them to pulp very effectively.

First, get all the equipment out of storage, cleaned, and set up. Make sure your fruit press is fastened to a solid, heavy object. I have made a small, heavy table for the purpose and screw the press down so strength can be exerted without knocking things around. The apples go from the wheelbarrow into a chopping box, where they can be chopped with a clean spade. Once chopped, the apples can be put through the crusher—watch out for fingers here. When your press is full, get squeezing. The first juice is exciting—and delicious to drink straight from the press.

THREE SIMPLE STEPS

1 **The chopping box** Use a strong wooden box for chopping your apples with a clean, sharp spade. Fill it full enough so the apples cannot move around, but not so full that the pieces spill out.

2 **The crusher** Put your chopped apples into the crusher when they are no more than 1 inch (2.5 cm) square. Crush the pulp straight into the fruit press—and be careful you don't catch your fingers.

3 **Pressing the juice** Fix your press to a sturdy table or work surface and squeeze the juice straight into the fermenting vessel. Remove the "cheeses" of squeezed pulp and feed a bit to the pigs, with the bulk going onto your compost heap.

Direct the juice from the press straight into your large fermenting bin, and do not worry too much at this stage about bits of apple or grass floating in the vat. When all the juice has been squeezed from the first batch of apples, you must undo the press to take out the "cheese" of crushed pulp. I keep a separate wheelbarrow on hand for this. You can feed the pulp, in moderation, to pigs and cattle, but most must go on the compost pile. Refill the press and repeat the process until your fermenting vessel is nearly full.

Your vat of apple juice is full of natural yeasts from the skins and the orchard. It will probably have a fair amount of other bits and pieces in it, too. The next step is to cover with a muslin cloth to keep out the vinegar flies, then leave the vat overnight in a sink. In the first day or so, there is likely to be a rapid fermentation, and you want this to bubble over the sides. This trick means that the bubbles carry with them large quantities of dirt and muck over the edge and down the drain. As soon as any violent fermentation has finished, you can decant the whole bin into another clean fermentation bin through a sieve. This removes any remaining bits and pieces of apple, and you can leave behind any heavy sediment that may have formed in the first vessel.

You should now have 5 gallons (20 liters) of reasonably clean apple juice ready to complete its fermentation. At this stage I normally add a couple of teaspoonfuls of commercial brewing yeast and 1–2 pounds (0.5–1 kg) of granulated sugar. The yeast makes sure that you get completion of a good fermentation, since you cannot altogether rely on natural yeasts. The sugar is added at your own discretion—more sugar makes a stronger cider that will keep much better than a watery version. Add the sugar by making up a syrup with a couple of pints of boiling water: pour this into your vat. Put a tight-fitting lid on your fermenting vessel and keep it warm; you can use a warming pad or an old waterbed heater.

The brew now needs to ferment completely so that all the sugars are transformed into alcohol. This may take anything from 10 days to three weeks. You can check on progress by looking at the brew to see if there are still bubbles coming up or by tasting it (if it is still sweet, then there is a long way to go). When fermentation is complete, the liquid will begin to clear and a brown scum of yeast will be left around the edges. You are now ready to rack off into bottles for storage.

Take the fermenting vessel into a cool place—preferably where you are going to rack it off. Leave it for at least 24 hours so it can settle, then rack it off into bottles just as you would beer. Add a little more sugar to each if you wish to ensure a secondary fermentation, but this often happens on its own. I have stored flattish cider throughout the winter months (in outside storage), then, when the warmer months come, a secondary fermentation starts and gives an excellent fizzy lift.

It is a great challenge to keep hard cider in storage much beyond Christmas but, in fact, it improves greatly with age. If it has good strength it will certainly keep for up to a year.

MAKING VINEGAR

Vinegar is wine, beer, or cider in which the alcohol has been turned into acetic acid by a species of bacteria. This bacillus can only operate in the presence of oxygen, so you can prevent your wines, beers, and ciders from turning to vinegar by keeping them protected from the air.

Yeast produces carbon dioxide in large quantities, and this expels the air from the vessel that the beverage has been stored in. But yeast cannot operate in more than a certain strength of alcohol, so fermentation ceases when so much sugar has been converted into alcohol that the yeast is killed or inhibited by its own action. This is the moment when the vinegar-forming bacillus, *Acetobacter*, gets active, and the moment when your beverages need protecting most rigorously from fresh air and bacterial infection.

However, if you want to make vinegar, you must take your wine, beer, or cider and expose it to the air as much as possible. If you just leave it in an open barrel, it will turn into vinegar in a few weeks. But it is better to speed up the process, to ensure that smells from the surrounding atmosphere do not taint the vinegar and hostile bacteria have little time to attack.

To hasten the process, take a barrelful of beech shavings. Beech is a traditional component for this stage of the proceedings but, really, any shavings will do as long as they do not come from a very resinous tree. First, soak the shavings well in a good vinegar of the type you are trying to make. Then, put a perforated wooden plate in the barrel over the shavings and pour your wine, beer or vinegar on to this plate.

The liquid will drip slowly through the holes, which must be very small—about the size of pinholes. Slowly, the liquid drips through the shavings. This ensures that the liquid is well exposed to both air and *Acetobacter*. At the bottom of the barrel, the liquid is drawn off through a cock. Just leave it in an open cask and it will turn into vinegar within a week.

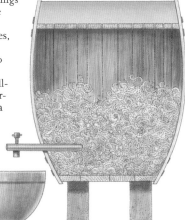

MAKING VINEGAR
Soak a barrelful of beech shavings in vinegar of the kind you are making. Put a wooden plate, perforated with pin-sized holes, on top of the shavings in the barrel. Pour your alcohol onto the plate. It will drip slowly through the barrel and be well-exposed to air and the vinegar-forming bacillus. After about a week in an open cask, it will turn into vinegar.

"Every householder should have several small bins: one for organic waste, one for aluminum, one for nonreturnable glass, one for tin cans, and one for plastic. Plastic, by the way, is hugely overused. It hadn't been invented 50 years ago, or most of it hadn't, and the world got on surprisingly well without it. We should refuse to buy goods which are overwrapped in plastic. As far as recycling goes, by far the best solution is one that has been developed in Germany: melting it down and turning it into building panels which are strong and good insulators. Our poor suffering old planet just cannot stand the wastage and pollution of rubbish dumping any more. We owe it to our children and our children's children to put an end to this scandal: we are rifling their inheritance."

JOHN SEYMOUR CHANGING LIFESTYLES 1991

CHAPTER NINE

ENERGY

AND

WASTE

Food for the Garden

MAKING COMPOST

If you pile vegetable matter up in a heap, it will rot and turn into compost. But to make good compost, and to make it quickly, you have to do more than this.

You can make the best compost in the world in 12 hours by putting vegetable matter through the guts of an animal. To make it any other way will take you months, whatever you do. But the principle of compost-making is this. The vegetation should be broken down by aerobic organisms. These are bacteria and fungi, which require oxygen to live. The bacteria that break down cellulose in plant matter need available nitrogen to do it. If they get plenty of available nitrogen, they break down the vegetable matter very quickly, and in doing so they generate a lot of heat. The heat kills the weed seeds and disease organisms in the compost. If there is a shortage of available nitrogen, it takes the organisms a very long time to break the vegetable matter down. So in order to speed the process up as much as you can, you try to provide the things that the compost-making organisms need: air, moisture, and nitrogen.

You can provide the air by having rows of bricks with gaps between them underneath the compost and, if you like, by leaving a few posts in the pile as you build it, so you can pull them out to leave "chimneys." You can provide the moisture either by letting rain fall on the heap, or by throwing enough water on it to moisten it

well. And you can provide the nitrogen by adding animal manure, urine, fish meal, inorganic nitrogen, blood, blood meal, or anything you can get that has a fairly high nitrogen content.

Dung and fertilizers

The natural, and traditional, way to make compost is to throw your vegetable matter (generally straw) at the feet of yarded cattle, pigs, or other animals. The available nitrogen in the form of the animal's dung and urine "activates" the compost. The urine also provides moisture and enough air gets between the straw. After a month or two, you dig the heap out and stack it carefully outdoors. More air gets into it and makes it rot down further. Then, after a few months, you cart it out and spread it on the land as fertilizer.

But if you don't have any animals, your best bet is to build compost piles by putting down a layer of bricks or concrete blocks with gaps in them, and laying coarse, woody material on these to let the air through. Then put down several layers of vegetable matter, sprinkling a dusting of some substance with a high nitrogen content between them.

Ten inches (25 cm) of vegetable matter and a couple of inches (5 cm) of chicken manure, or a thick sprinkling of a high-nitrogen inorganic fertilizer, would be ideal. Some people alternate lime with the nitrogen.

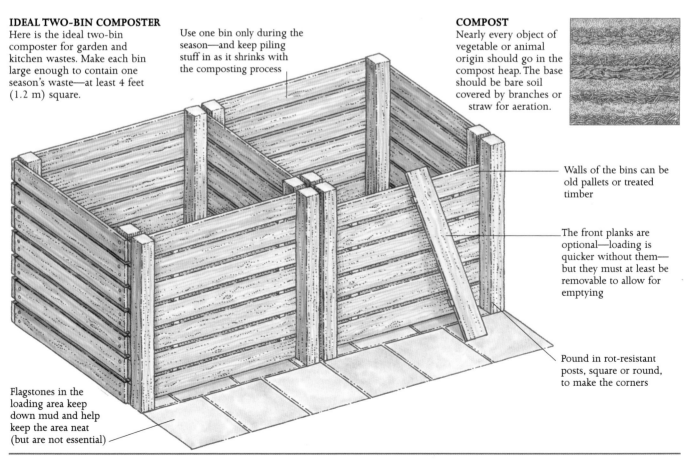

IDEAL TWO-BIN COMPOSTER
Here is the ideal two-bin composter for garden and kitchen wastes. Make each bin large enough to contain one season's waste—at least 4 feet (1.2 m) square.

Use one bin only during the season—and keep piling stuff in as it shrinks with the composting process

COMPOST
Nearly every object of vegetable or animal origin should go in the compost heap. The base should be bare soil covered by branches or straw for aeration.

Walls of the bins can be old pallets or treated timber

The front planks are optional—loading is quicker without them—but they must at least be removable to allow for emptying

Pound in rot-resistant posts, square or round, to make the corners

Flagstones in the loading area keep down mud and help keep the area neat (but are not essential)

Keep the sides vertical using walls of either wood, brick, or concrete, and keep it decently moist but not sopping.

Don't forget that anyone can pile up stuff to make a heap, but only a pro can make a good stack with vertical sides. You will be surprised how much material from the garden you can deal with in this way. Just make sure you spread out each addition into a thin layer rather than a heap. And mix plenty of rich green stuff (weeds, grass cuttings, and so on) with the more woody wastes so you keep a good mix.

Keep piling vegetable wastes in for a whole season. Make sure you allow enough space to do this—8 x 4 feet (2.5 x 1.2 m) does it for our half-acre of garden. The pile will grow with new material one week and shrink back down the next as the material decomposes; in fact, you will be surprised just how much shrinkage takes place.

At the end of the season (October/November), you will stop adding any further material to your season's compost. From now on you will use the second composting area, leaving the first to ferment undisturbed. When it comes to early spring (February or March, most likely) you will be able to take off the top and unrotted material from the outside of last season's pile and put this into the bottom of the second pile. You can then spread your rotted compost on the garden as you choose: some for your runner bean bed, some for the soft fruits, some for new deep beds, as you fancy.

Of course it is a great help if you can obtain farmyard manure from a local farmer if you cannot provide it yourself. You may see farm signs for compost or manure along the roads, but you'll need a trailer of some sort.

The closed urban composter

I like to keep a closed plastic composting bin for the richer kitchen wastes that attract flies and rats. You can have a closing top and a rat proof base and some municipalities are starting to supply suitable plastic bins for this. Of course, if you have a composting toilet then most of this stuff can go down that route.

Essentially the same principles apply as to the open garden compost pile: a good mixture and plenty of it. I put an aluminum sheet with holes punched through it as a base for my plastic composter and this keeps out rats but lets in worms. Once you have sufficient mixture to generate a good fermentation you will see the material rapidly shrinking. Add urine if you feel it needs extra nitrogen. The composting bin has a hatch in the bottom that can be opened to shovel out the rotted material after several months of fermentation. You may want to add this to your existing garden compost pile if it is not quite ready.

Worm composting

In warm climates worm composters are very popular and easy to use. These depend on small red manure worms that either appear naturally from nowhere or that can be bought from bait shops. Worms need moisture and warmth to thrive. And one neat way of providing this is to use a column of used motor tyres as a container for organic wastes—add manure worms at the bottom and they will steadily multiply and eat their way upward. You can then remove the lower tire (and its compost) as the column fills up. The worms will have moved upward by then, so you keep the process going.

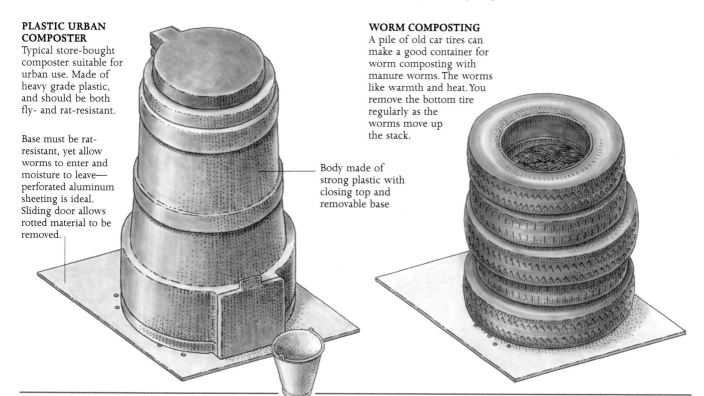

PLASTIC URBAN COMPOSTER
Typical store-bought composter suitable for urban use. Made of heavy grade plastic, and should be both fly- and rat-resistant.

Base must be rat-resistant, yet allow worms to enter and moisture to leave—perforated aluminum sheeting is ideal. Sliding door allows rotted material to be removed.

Body made of strong plastic with closing top and removable base

WORM COMPOSTING
A pile of old car tires can make a good container for worm composting with manure worms. The worms like warmth and heat. You remove the bottom tire regularly as the worms move up the stack.

The Dry Toilet

Our dry toilet has been the subject of many jokes, much interest, and a couple of TV documentaries. Amazing, really, considering the fact that the idea is not exactly new. What is new, of course, is that such things are no longer a common accessory, at least not for modern urban living. So great is the deep human emotion on this topic that we find media people simply unable to overcome their fear and open the door to the Killowen composting "throne." So if you find all this X-rated material, now is the time to stop reading!

This fear of basic functions seems to be part of the modern human condition, which finds the idea of dealing with waste and death extremely challenging. To illustrate the other extreme, I must tell you about a friend we have from the United States. He is, in fact, one of the founders of the growing bio-regional movement. David regards the flush toilet as one of the greatest sins of modern man, so much so that he takes a small shovel with him on all trips to "civilization" so that he can deposit his own waste carefully into the soil, rather than pollute the water table. Madness? I don't think so. The flush toilet is a remarkably expensive way to pollute fresh drinking water, while at the same time wasting the very nutrients that are essential to maintain fertility in the soil. One push of the lever and the waste becomes somebody else's problem. We just pay our taxes and allow our children to pick up the real inheritance of all this pollution. But for the self-supporter, there is great satisfaction in being able to deal directly with what he or she consumes and what he or she produces as waste. The composting toilet has a great role in this, and, as a way of explaining this role, I give you the text pinned up on the wall that introduces guests to the "Thunderbox."

Our Marvelous Thunderbox "Loo"

Now the human being is a very strange beast with capabilities good and bad
Not frightened of nature, no not in the least our follies are often quite mad
The toilet that flushes fills our souls with glee
A brainwave by Thomas Crapper
Mixes shit with clean water and pours out to sea
as if the dirt did not matter.

Out of sight, out of mind, muck shoots down the pipes
An incredible fabric of magic
Squandering food for the soil as the water we spoil
It's a tale that is terribly tragic.

But all is not lost for at a marginal cost
Another solution comes easy
The composting loo; yes that's our riposte
And your tummy need not feel too queasy.

The vent goes up high, sending gas to the skies
And the lid fits snug so no entry to flies
Two years it will take, our compost to make
and our river's not sorry the flush to forsake.
No water, no tricks—it's all built with bricks. The shit and kitchen waste too
All go together making food for the soil in our marvelous Thunderbox "loo."

Here are the short instructions that help them to help the Thunderbox do its job.

Using the Thunderbox

The Thunderbox is a dry composting toilet built to designs well-tested in tropical countries, but you must check your local regulations and building codes before building one for yourself.

To work effectively, its contents should always be a good mixture of organic materials, with a suitable blend of carbon and nitrogen within the mix *and* plenty of air to make sure the fermentation does not become anaerobic.

The toilet does not smell because it is vented above the roof height, and the composting process in any case is not particularly smelly.

When using the toilet, please:
—Try not to put in too much pee and use the bucket for pee (no paper, please).
—Do not use too much paper in the Thunderbox.
—Pour in a box of sawdust after use.
—Always close the lid when you are finished so that you keep out flies.

Kitchen and garden waste are regularly put into the toilet to give a richer composting mix—so you may see all sorts of vegetable material if you happen to peer down below. We also put in straw and well-rotted manure to help the process.

Design

The design of the Thunderbox derives from the dry toilets commonly used in many tropical parts of the world. So far, our toilet has eaten up wheelbarrowloads of waste—from humans, kitchen, and garden. For a family of six, with occasional guests, it has taken more than three years to fill the first chamber. There are thousands of different bugs, bacteria, and manure worms working away down there. Large quantities of water vapor and methane go up the chimney. It is such a pity the methane is wasted, but it would be difficult to process such relatively small quantities of waste in a methane digester.

The essential principle of the Thunderbox is that it is a two-chamber system. One chamber rests and composts while the other is in daily use. This means that the size of the chamber must be sufficient to take all use for at least one whole year to allow sufficient time for complete fermentation before the chamber is emptied after a minimum of two years since first use. The design must allow for the front of the chamber to be somewhat permeable so that any liquids can percolate slowly through if things are getting too wet in the mix. In practice, I have never found this to be a problem—possibly because I frequently add woody garden wastes. By using tongue and groove timber fronts we allow percolation and complete

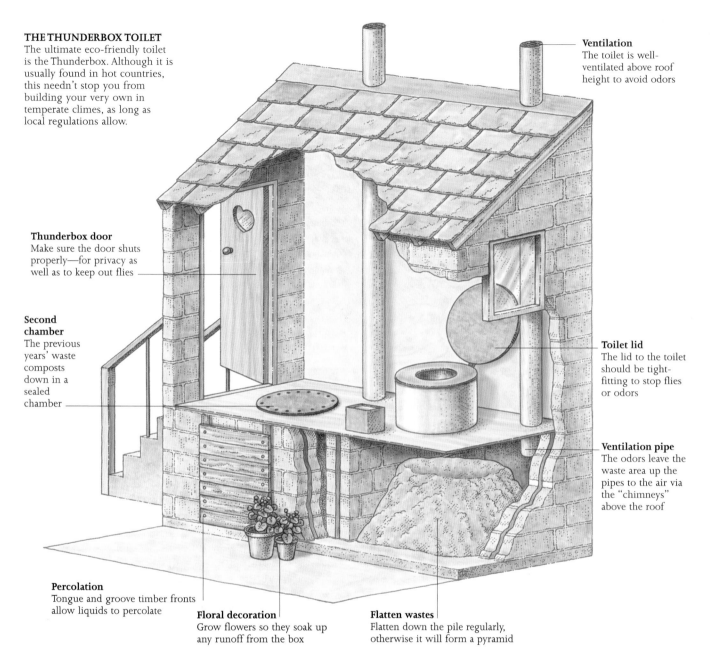

THE THUNDERBOX TOILET
The ultimate eco-friendly toilet is the Thunderbox. Although it is usually found in hot countries, this needn't stop you from building your very own in temperate climes, as long as local regulations allow.

Ventilation
The toilet is well-ventilated above roof height to avoid odors

Thunderbox door
Make sure the door shuts properly—for privacy as well as to keep out flies

Second chamber
The previous years' waste composts down in a sealed chamber

Toilet lid
The lid to the toilet should be tight-fitting to stop flies or odors

Ventilation pipe
The odors leave the waste area up the pipes to the air via the "chimneys" above the roof

Percolation
Tongue and groove timber fronts allow liquids to percolate

Floral decoration
Grow flowers so they soak up any runoff from the box

Flatten wastes
Flatten down the pile regularly, otherwise it will form a pyramid

replacement of the front (if necessary) after one cycle of use. With a stone or concrete runoff area in front of the chambers, it is a simple matter to grow a few geraniums or other container plants that can soak up any small runoff. If there is a great quantity of runoff, then action must be taken by adding more sawdust and stirring the mix (with a long pole inserted through the top opening). It is good practice in any case to stir the compost regularly—say, every month—to prevent a buildup of a pyramid under the opening.

Good ventilation is vital, with the chimneys positioned well above the roof. The warm gases create their own draft without the wind, taking away the water vapor and any odors. It is essential that the composting does not get waterlogged.

Varied feeding
Composting in a confined space benefits from a good mix of ingredients. Floor sweepings, dust, and succulent garden waste provide variety, while leaves and sawdust keep things from getting too wet. But, as always, composting is something of an art form—you get better with practice.

Close-fitting lid
Keeping flies out of the toilet is the hardest job, and some small fruit flies are almost inevitable. If the lid fits closely, keeping out all light, and the only source of daylight is down the chimney, then the flies should fly up to the mesh and drop back exhausted. It is vital to get this part of the design correct.

Managing Waste

Over the last 50 years, garbage collection and the processing of human waste have become a major challenge for urban civilization. We take from nature, we use (briefly), and we throw away—tons and tons of supposedly useless "waste." Most of this is put into landfills, which will, of course, become the mines of tomorrow, if not the methane power stations of the 22nd century. Much more than half of this "waste" is paper and kitchen waste, and lots more is glass, metal, or clothing that could be recycled. Every self-sufficient holding should take pride in producing as little waste as possible—indeed, zero waste should be the goal.

The first and most elementary step is to avoid buying in waste in the first place. Give up your daily newspapers, for a start; you probably have news blasted at you many minutes a day anyway from TV and radio. If you can't give up the newspapers, reuse them or recycle them. And avoid plastic packaging at every available opportunity.

The second step is to make sure you separate your waste into different containers. I have separate bins for:

1 Compost pile Your main compost pile takes bulk vegetable waste like potato peelings, weeds, leaves, fruit skins, apple pulp, and so on. Your closed composter takes stuff that would attract rats—for example, used tea bags, or rotten meat or fish unsuitable for pigs. (*See p.334 for more on the compost pile.*)

2 Pig or poultry bucket This takes waste food and scraps and must be emptied and washed out daily to keep it clean and hygienic. Stale bread and buns, meat fat, and fish skins are pure heaven for your pigs, who will convert the whole works into beautiful bacon. The more varied your pig's diet, the tastier the bacon and pork will be.

3 Paper Paper can be burned (if local regulations allow—check with your fire department), composted (if shredded first, which can be a nuisance), or recycled. Cut down on catalog and magazine subscriptions and stop buying the Sunday paper to help reduce the amount of waste paper coming into your household.

4 Plastic Plastic is almost impossible to avoid in the modern world, beholden as it is to the oil industry. Recycle plastic milk bottles, 2-liter soda bottles, and any other plastic that your community's recycling program will accept. You could also wash out the 2-liter bottles and keep them for bottling beer and hard cider.

5 Cans Most recycling facilities accept both aluminum cans and tin cans, but you should keep them separate. Aluminum cans are easily crushed to save space; tin cans can be flattened if you remove both top and bottom with a can opener.

6 Glass The smashing of bottles and jars is now a familiar sound at recycling centers around the world as people get rid of waste glass. Why we have to break perfectly good bottles when millions of kilowatts of energy could be saved by having a few standardized shapes beats me; for example, I remember a time when milk came in bottles that were used and reused without difficulty.

It's sensible to check with your local government first to find out what recycling they offer. But the best recycling is that of composting your garbage to use later as a fantastic fertilizer for your crops.

THE BLACK ART OF MOVING MUCK

We are told that the Zen master of housework spends a lifetime perfecting the job of doing the dishes so that the activity ultimately becomes an art form of sublime pleasure and satisfaction. What greater success could there be in life? What magic is it that can transform drudgery into high pleasure?

On the previous pages I've discussed how to make the best compost for your garden, but here I'd like to concentrate on an even better source of food for next year's vegetables. It may seem like a foul task: that of emptying out a winter's buildup of cow manure and straw. Let's face it, digging out and wheelbarrowing 10 tons of smelly manure does not sound immediately appealing. But in the art of self-sufficiency, the good student will enjoy great satisfaction from the sight of a beautiful heap of rotting manure. Just think of the hot, sweaty, smelly shoveling as being like riding a bike up a beautiful mountain; the pain of the climb is more than balanced by the prospect of whizzing downhill for many miles on the other side. In this case, the pain of the shoveling is more than compensated by for the prospect of a good pint of beer afterward and fabulous "food" for next year's vegetables.

The fork and wheelbarrow

The first requirement, as all students of Zen will know, is to get to know and love your tools—in this case, the manure fork and the wheelbarrow. The right equipment is vital. Your manure fork will have four prongs or tines made of spring steel and with curved shoulders, like a pitchfork. The tines should have a nice curve on them that not only allows you to carry more dung but also serves as a vital lever to prize up layers of heavy, downtrodden, wet straw. The curved shoulders mean that straw is less likely to stick to the fork when you toss it into the barrow. A heavy, square garden fork is absolutely the wrong tool for this job: it is straight, its tines are too thick, and its shoulders catch constantly on the straw.

Your wheelbarrow has to be strong enough to carry up to 250 pounds (100 kg) of muck at a time. The wheel should be of the inflatable type, since this runs more smoothly. And don't forget that you can purchase and use different grades of tires. The more expensive ones are less likely to go flat. A galvanized steel barrow is probably the best of all. You will also want your wheelbarrow to fit close to the cowshed gate so you do not have to take more than a couple of steps each time you put a forkful into the barrow. Minimize walking and save time and energy.

Now get yourself organized so that you have a clear run between the cowshed and the compost-manure pile.

You would not want this to be more than 25 yards (23 m). Make sure your manure heap has good strong sides that can take the pressure of a few tons of manure—drive in some extra preservative-treated posts with your post rammer, if necessary. We are talking here about a manure pile that might typically be 10 feet (3 m) across and 6 feet (1.8 m) deep. It will be open at one side and bounded on the other three by timber slats, held in place by more treated fenceposts.

If you have steps or similar to climb, then you will make sure any ramp is well-secured and supported before you start. The straw bedding will be heavily compacted by the weight and hooves of the animals. Each barrowload may weigh over 220 pounds (100 kg), so you will need a good run to get up any slopes.

The art of digging
You cannot dig out manure like sand. Instead, you must push in your fork tines at a low angle and use the curve of the tines to act as a fulcrum as you lever gently down on the handle of the fork. This will slowly lift up a layer of manure perhaps 3 inches (7.5 cm) thick with a sucking sound as the compaction is released. You can then lift this, with a bit of jiggling, and toss the forkful into your barrow. You can pile up the barrow pretty high, since the manure holds itself together well. One tip worth remembering is not to put your hand over the end of the fork handle. If you do and accidentally bump a wall, it'll hurt!

Making a straight-edged stack
Now you have the task of making a good stack of manure to compost. This is an art form in itself for, as every country person knows, anyone can make a pile, but only an expert can make a good stack. And a stack is going to be there for all to see as a work of art, or otherwise, for perhaps a year or more!

The key to making a good stack is to have the material (straw, in this case) sloping down into the stack from the edges. If it is sloping down from the center to the outside, then it's going to slip and you will not get a straight vertical side to your stack. In the old days of farming, the stacking of the crop was a vital skilled task, for a stack that slipped or let in the weather was a major disaster. Stacking your manure pile is not quite that important, but a neat stack will keep its shape and give you a better compost than a loose pile.

To make a straight-edged stack, you must start by putting material along the outside edge. You want a wide mat of material with plenty of long strands, ideally running at right angles to the edge of the stack. If you have a forkload of loose material that is in small pieces, then discard it for the moment: toss it to the back of the space. By building up a straight edge right across the front of the heap, about 9 inches (23 cm) high, and then working back from it, you will make sure your material is sloping down

away from the edge. Every time you have a good forkload with long strands, use this to strengthen the edge. The long strands will be trapped by the other material above them and hold the edge firm.

You have a major strategic choice to make when digging out your animal manure. Do you make a solid pile of manure that will compost itself? Or do you keep your good manure in reserve so you can take out a 6-inch (15-cm) layer every couple of weeks to add to your general compost pile? It depends on the amount of manure, the routine of your garden, and the need you have to clean out the cowshed quickly for more stock or whatever. By mixing manure with other material for composting, you will achieve an excellent result. The final choice is up to you.

There is a lot to be said for taking a little time over moving 10 tons of muck. Like many tasks in the world of self-sufficiency, a great deal can be achieved by regular application. When the eager beaver from the city tries to race into a long job, he or she will literally bust a gut if trying to hit some arbitrary target. Targets are a big feature of the business world, but they often become counterproductive in the world of self sufficiency.

The only way to tackle a huge job is to make a point of doing a little but doing it regularly. I often make moving muck a pleasant break from other daily chores by fitting in say, six barrowloads in one session. That might take about 30 minutes—and move about half a ton of muck.

Do this every day for about three weeks, it's better than going to the gym (certainly much cheaper) and the job will get done even though each day you can hardly see any change. It is the same logic for digging a large vegetable bed: little and often is much better than taking a huge bite at one time.

So that's the story. Good tools and the right attitude can transform drudgery into a sublime pleasure where you can bask every day in the beautiful light from the end of your metaphorical tunnel. And each day after the task is finished, you will pass your manure heap and enjoy the memory of your daily sweat and application.

MANURING
If your land has had proper additions of farmyard manure or the dung of animals added direct, or seaweed (which has in it every element), or compost, it is most unlikely to be deficient in anything. By getting your soil analyzed when you take it over, and adding once and for all whatever element the analysis shows the soil to be deficient in (nitrogen, phosphorus, potassium, or calcium), and thereafter farming in a sound organic way, the "heart" (fertility) of your land should increase continually until it is at a very high level.

There should be no need to spend any further money at all on "fertilizers." And, very often, if land is virgin, or if it has been properly farmed in the past, you may not even need to get it analyzed.

Saving Energy

THE ALTERNATIVES

Throughout this book I have advocated an integrated approach to the land: the encouragement of organic, beneficial interaction of soil, crops, and animals. When considering energy, we must adopt this same approach. We should look upon our holding of land as having a certain energy potential that we can use for our own good purposes, and we should aim to make our holding autonomous in this respect, as we have aimed to make it for food.

There is something wrong about burning coal to heat water on a hot, sunny day, or burning oil to warm a house when there is a fast-flowing stream next to it. Or, for that matter, using domestic electricity to drive a mill or a power loom, when there is potential wind or water power nearby.

Water power is most available in hilly, rainy countries and wind power in flat lands, but wind power should never be used where water power is available. The simple reason for this is that the wind is fickle, while water is relatively reliable and consistent. Where there is hot sun, it it is ridiculous not to use it. It is obviously unproductive to feed cold water into your water boiler when the corrugated iron roof over your shed is so hot you can't hold your hand on it.

A characteristic of natural sources of energy is that they lend themselves much more to small-scale use than to large-scale exploitation. For example, more energy can be gotten out of a given river more cheaply by tapping it with a hundred small dams and waterwheels right down its length than by building one enormous dam and driving one set of huge turbines. The wind's energy can be tapped better, and now increasingly is (thankfully for our environment) by a myriad of small windmills, rather than some gigantic wind-equivalent of a power station.

It doesn't need an "Earth Summit" to tell you that every house in a city could have a solar roof, and derive a great part of its energy requirements from it, whereas a solar collector big enough to supply a community is still in the realms of fantasy. Scattered farmsteads can easily make their own methane gas, but to cart muck from a hundred farms to some central station, make gas from it, and then redistribute it would be madly uneconomical. So these "alternative energy devices" commend themselves especially to the self-supporter.

HEAT LOSS

A house built in the traditional way loses vast amounts of heat through the roof, doors, windows, floor, and outside walls. Use a combination of the methods illustrated and you can save as much as two-thirds of your annual domestic energy requirement.

Shutters are insulated, to be closed at night in bad weather

Triple-glazed windows are now commonplace in Scandinavia, and gas-filled triple glazing is highly energy-efficient

Use at least 4 inches (10 cm) of high-quality insulation between cavity walls

Always put in as much underfloor insulation as you can in a new building

You can put 9 inches (23 cm) of insulation between ceiling joists

Solar water heaters are a simple and effective way to provide warm water for the hot water system

Board out the roof space with aluminum-backed drywall to save heat and protect against condensation.

Use 9 inches (23 cm) of insulation, glass or, mineral wool, or even treated sheep's wool for insulation between rafters

Filter and reuse "gray" water for the garden and toilet flushing.

A small porch creates an airlock effect to prevent heat loss when entering and leaving

Use the same central unit to cook food, heat water, and run central heating

Hot air and heat from the sun provide a great saving in winter with a south-facing conservatory

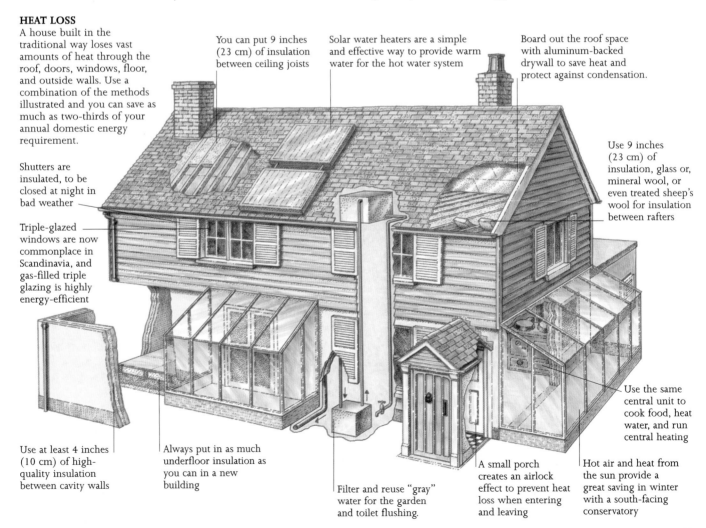

COMBINING NATURAL ENERGY SOURCES

Now it may well be that it is better for the self-supporter to combine several sources of energy, instead of concentrating on just one. For example, you could have a big wood-burning furnace (*see* p.387) that does the cooking for a large number of people, and heats water for dairy, kitchen, butchery, bathroom, and laundry. If you preheated the water that went into it with solar panels on the roof, you would need less wood to heat more water.

Then, if you had a methane plant to utilize animal and human waste and used the methane to bring the hot water from the furnace to steam-heat for sterilizing dairy equipment, better still. Then you could use a pumping windmill to pump up water from the clear, pure well below your holding, instead of having to use the very slightly polluted water from the hill above.

And what about lighting your buildings using the stream that runs nearby to drive a small turbine? All these things are possible, would be fairly cheap, and would pay for themselves by saving on energy brought in from outside.

SAVING ENERGY

There is little point in devising elaborate systems for getting heat from natural sources until you have plugged the leaks in the systems you already have.

For keeping heat in a house, there is nothing to beat very thick walls of stone, rammed earth, or brickwork with small windows and a thatched roof. The thin cavity walls of brick or concrete block housing only insulate well if plastic foam or some other insulating material is put between the walls and laid on the joists in the roof. The big "picture windows" beloved of modern architects are terrible heat-losers. Dual glazing may help, but it is very expensive. Country-dwellers, working outdoors for most of the day, as people were designed to do, want to feel, when they do go indoors, that they are indoors; they get plenty of "view" when they are out in it and are part of the view themselves. Therefore, for country housing, big windows are a mistake.

Huge chimneys, very romantic and fine when there are simply tons of good dry firewood, send most of their heat up to heat the sky. In a world short of fuel, they are inexcusable. Long, straggly houses are also great heat-wasters. A compact shape is more desirable. A round building will lose less heat than a square one, because it has a smaller surface area in comparison with its volume. A square building is obviously better than an oblong one. It is always best to have your primary heat source in the middle of the building, rather than against an outside wall.

Most insulation nowadays is achieved with high-technology products, and these are very expensive. What we can do is search for cheaper and more natural materials. Wherever the cork oak will grow, it should be grown, for it provides an excellent insulator and in large quantities.

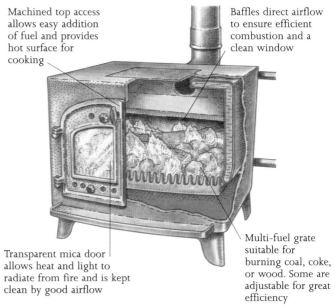

Machined top access allows easy addition of fuel and provides hot surface for cooking

Baffles direct airflow to ensure efficient combustion and a clean window

Transparent mica door allows heat and light to radiate from fire and is kept clean by good airflow

Multi-fuel grate suitable for burning coal, coke, or wood. Some are adjustable for great efficiency

CLOSED BOILER

Most wood stoves and ranges will burn almost anything combustible. Dead wood and all other inflammable garbage provide additional free fuel supplies that can be saved and stored during summer and fall for use in winter. A large, old-fashioned cast-iron stove can supply the major source of domestic heat as well as being used for cooking meals.

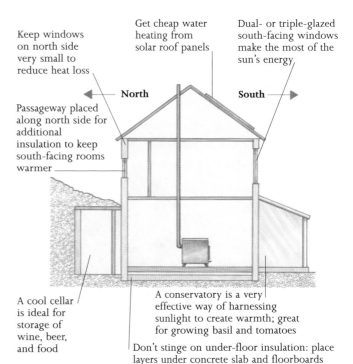

Keep windows on north side very small to reduce heat loss

Get cheap water heating from solar roof panels

Dual- or triple-glazed south-facing windows make the most of the sun's energy

North   **South**

Passageway placed along north side for additional insulation to keep south-facing rooms warmer

A cool cellar is ideal for storage of wine, beer, and food

A conservatory is a very effective way of harnessing sunlight to create warmth; great for growing basil and tomatoes

Don't stinge on under-floor insulation: place layers under concrete slab and floorboards

USING NATURAL FEATURES FOR ENERGY SAVING

By optimizing the orientation of your house, you can create a comfortable, energy-efficient living space. Building into a south-facing slope is the ideal: the effect can be magnified by careful tree planting to create shelter on the north and east sides. Before cheap fossil fuels, traditional builders took full advantage of all these possibilities. Both thatch and thick cob walls were excellent insulation. Today we can extend the principles by using modern materials.

Power from Water

Parakrama Bahu, King of Ceylon, as it was in the seventh century, decreed that not one drop of water that fell on his island should reach the sea: all should be used for agriculture. In wetter climes, where irrigation is not so necessary, the inhabitants would do well to take the same attitude, but change the objective a little: "let not one river or stream or rivulet reach the sea without yielding its energy potential."

Water power is completely free, completely non-polluting, and always self-renewing. Unlike wind, it is steady and reliable, although of course there may be seasonal variations, but even these tend to be consistent. Like wind, it is generally at its strongest in the colder months, and is therefore at its greatest strength when we most need it.

The primitive water wheels that have stood the test of centuries are not to be despised, and for many uses are better than more sophisticated devices. For slow-flowing streams with plenty of water, the "undershot wheel" is appropriate. With this you can take in the whole of quite a large stream, and thus exploit a river with a low head but large volume. Your wheel will be slow-turning, but if you use it for a direct drive to slow-turning machinery—a grain mill, for example—this is an advantage. It is a common mistake of "alternative energy freaks" to think that all power should first be converted to electricity and then converted back to power again. Energy loss is enormous in so doing.

If you want to generate electricity with your water power, you will need something more sophisticated than a waterwheel, for this requires high speeds to which more complex water engines are well suited. For small heads, from as low as a yard (1 m) to up to 20 feet (6 m), the propeller turbine is very good.

WATER WHEEL (OVERSHOT)
The oldest method of using water power, the overshot water wheel is up to 70% efficient. The water goes over the top, filling the buckets around its rim. Water wheels like this turn quite slowly but with considerable force, making them best suited for driving millstones or other heavy, slow-speed equipment. Depending on flow rate, power from this wheel might be from five to 20 hp (4–16 kW).

WATER WHEEL (UNDERSHOT)
Undershot wheels are less efficient than overshot, but are used when there is insufficient head of water for it to fall over the wheel. They can produce from two to five hp (1½–3 kW).

BREAST WHEEL (UNDERSHOT)
An undershot wheel with straight blades is up to 30% efficient; fitting curved blades increases this to 60%. A breast wheel makes twice the power from the same source.

WATER POWER

To calculate the available water power of a stream, measure the flow rate of the water, and multiply it successively by the density (62.4 lb/cu ft), the head of water, and the efficiency of the turbine or water wheel you will be using—e.g., in a hilly area the flow rate might be ½ cu ft water per sec. This flow falling 40 ft through an 80% efficient Pelton wheel would give:

$\frac{1}{2}$ x 62.4 x 40 x $\frac{80}{100}$ = 998 $\frac{ft}{lb/sec}$ $\frac{998}{550}$ (1 hp) = 1.8 horsepower.

If used for generating electricity, 60% of the turbine's power might be converted into electrical power: in this example 60% of 1.8 = 1.08 hp and as 1 hp = 746 watts, this is the equivalent of 805 watts.

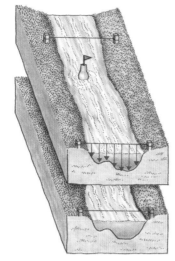

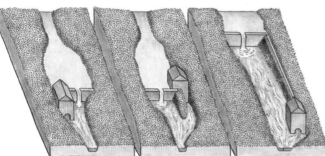

POSITIONING AND TYPES OF DAM

In order to build up a head of water and control its flow, it is often necessary to build a dam or a weir (*above*) across the main stream, usually at a narrow point or where there are rapids. A head race or leat, dug along a contour above the stream, will create enough head for a water wheel or turbine to function. A dam can be a pile of rocks in a stream, although wooden dams (*below right*) or combined wood and earth-fill ones (*right*) are effective.

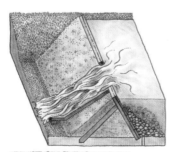

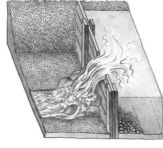

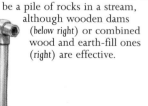

Flow rate

Water power depends primarily on the flow rate and available head of water. The flow rate of a stream therefore needs to be measured, along with its fall, to predict the available power. A simple method is to find a length of the stream that is straight and has as constant a cross-section as possible. The cross-section of flow is estimated by taking soundings at regular intervals across it and calculating the average depth: area equals average depth times width. This should be repeated at several points to arrive at an average cross-sectional area for the chosen length. A sealed bottle (*left*) is then timed as it drifts along the middle of the chosen section. Flow rate for the stream will be around 75% of the speed of the bottle times the average cross-sectional area of that length of stream. (*For an example of a water-power calculation using flow rate, see the caption, left.*)

HYDROELECTRIC POWER

If you are fortunate enough to have a stream available for use, then potentially you have the capability to produce a free and continuous supply of electricity. Don't use a water wheel to run a generator, because this turns so slowly that an enormous step-up ratio of gears or belts and pulleys is needed to arrive at the required generator speed. Small turbines turn much faster and need little more than a pair of pulleys and vee belts to connect them to a generator. They are less expensive to build because their smaller size means they need much less steel, and they are also slightly more efficient than water wheels. There are many different types of turbine. The Pelton wheel turbine (*top right*) is for high head applications where the fall is 40 feet (12 m) or more, and is up to 80% efficient. A special nozzle directs the water at high speed against a set of spoon-shaped deflector buckets set around the periphery of the turbine wheel. The Banki turbine (*center right*) is for medium head, up to 65% efficient and best suited to a fall of 15–40 feet (4.5–12 m). Again, a special nozzle directs water into the periphery of a spool-like wheel with curved blades. The propeller turbine (*bottom right*), up to 75% efficient, works best on heads of under 20 feet (6 m), right down to 6 feet (1.8 m). A propeller in a pipe, it is the best substitute for an old mill water wheel. For better efficiency, the water must be given a spin the opposite of that of the propeller. This is done by running it through a spiral volute before entering the draft-tube containing the propeller.

Pelton wheel turbine

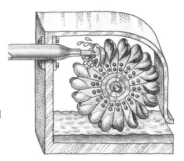

Banki turbine

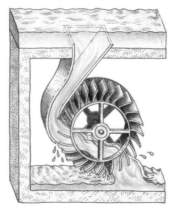

Propeller turbine

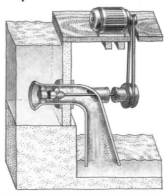

Heat from the Sun

The most practical solar collector is a wood, for woodland can collect the sun's rays from vast areas, and, properly managed, can continually convert them into energy, while to cover a few square yards with a man-made solar collector costs a lot of effort and money. But if collecting and storing the sun's heat can be done relatively easily and cheaply, as it usually can on the roof of an existing house or wall, then, if nothing more, solar energy can be used to reinforce other sources of energy. The drawback is that in cold climates we want heat in the winter and we get it in the summer, but if the winter gap is filled in with wind or water power (which may be at their best in the winter) a consistent system can be evolved.

The practical choices open in temperate climates are:
1 Heating water by letting it trickle over a black-painted corrugated roof under a transparent covering that turns the roof into a heat collector. You will have to buy your transparent covering and a pump to circulate the water. All the same, this will allow you to collect the sun over a large area.

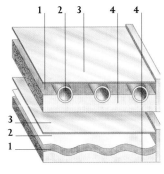

SOLAR ENERGY
Solar energy 1 is most abundant in midsummer, while our heating requirements 2 are greatest in midwinter. Most solar collectors provide more heat than we need in summer B and less than we need in winter A. The productive use of solar energy C reaches peaks in spring and fall. Received energy per day per square meter might be 4–5 kW-hrs in summer, and ½–1 kW-hr in winter in a temperate climate.

FLAT-PLATE SOLAR COLLECTORS
Most solar energy collectors use a black surface 1 to absorb the sun's radiation and produce heat. You transfer the heat into a hot water tank, or to heat space, by passing water, or air in some cases, through pipes or channels 2 behind the absorbing surface. A glass or plastic covering 3 prevents heat loss from the front of the collector; insulation 4 prevents it from rear and sides.

HEATING AIR: THE TROMBE WALL
Named after Professor Trombe, this is a clever method for making use of solar energy in winter. The Professor perfected the wall high up in the Pyrénées, where the sun shines quite often in winter, albeit weakly. You use a vertical dual-glazed plate glass window 1 that faces south, and allow a black-painted wall 2 behind it to catch and trap the sun's heat. When you require heat inside the house, you open ventilators 3, 4 and these allow warm air to circulate between the glass and the wall. An overhanging roof 5 prevents the high summer sun from striking the glass and also protects the building from getting overheated. An alternative to the Trombe wall is a glass-covered extension to your house—in other words, a sun room. This will warm the house if properly ventilated.

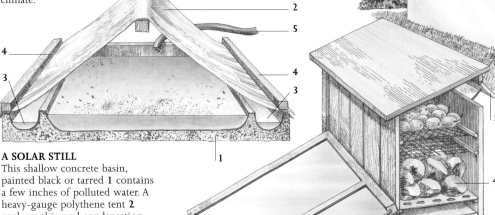

A SOLAR STILL
This shallow concrete basin, painted black or tarred 1 contains a few inches of polluted water. A heavy-gauge polythene tent 2 encloses this, and condensation runs down the inside surface of the tent into a pair of collecting gutters 3. The condensation is pure distilled water which you can siphon off. Hold down the plastic sheeting with heavy wooden battens 4 and close the cover ends rather like a ridge tent. You can replenish the polluted water through a hose 5.

SOLAR DRYER
An inclined, glazed, flat-plate solar air heater admits air through an adjustable flap 1. The air heats up as it crosses over a blackened absorber surface 2 because the heat is trapped by glass panels 3. The heated air rises through a bed of rocks 4 and then through a series of gratings that hold the produce to be dried. A flap 5 under the overhanging roof allows air supply to be adjusted or closed off. The rock bed heats up during the day and continues releasing a measure of warmth to the produce after sunset, thereby preventing condensation from occurring. There is a door in the unit's back to allow produce to be added or removed.

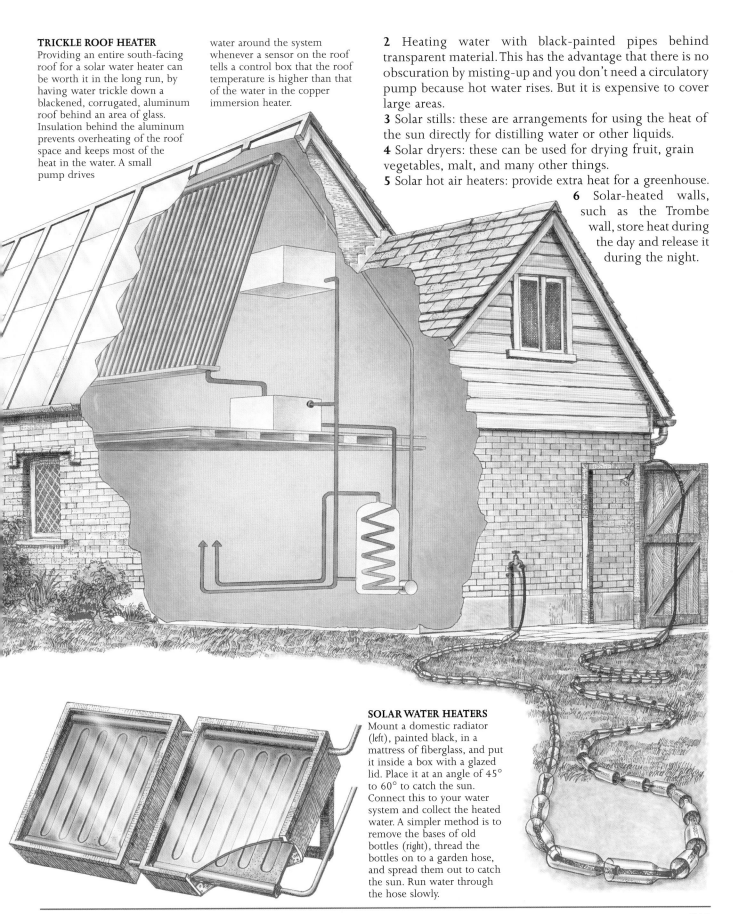

TRICKLE ROOF HEATER

Providing an entire south-facing roof for a solar water heater can be worth it in the long run, by having water trickle down a blackened, corrugated, aluminum roof behind an area of glass. Insulation behind the aluminum prevents overheating of the roof space and keeps most of the heat in the water. A small pump drives water around the system whenever a sensor on the roof tells a control box that the roof temperature is higher than that of the water in the copper immersion heater.

2 Heating water with black-painted pipes behind transparent material. This has the advantage that there is no obscuration by misting-up and you don't need a circulatory pump because hot water rises. But it is expensive to cover large areas.

3 Solar stills: these are arrangements for using the heat of the sun directly for distilling water or other liquids.

4 Solar dryers: these can be used for drying fruit, grain vegetables, malt, and many other things.

5 Solar hot air heaters: provide extra heat for a greenhouse.

6 Solar-heated walls, such as the Trombe wall, store heat during the day and release it during the night.

SOLAR WATER HEATERS

Mount a domestic radiator (*left*), painted black, in a mattress of fiberglass, and put it inside a box with a glazed lid. Place it at an angle of 45° to 60° to catch the sun. Connect this to your water system and collect the heated water. A simpler method is to remove the bases of old bottles (*right*), thread the bottles on to a garden hose, and spread them out to catch the sun. Run water through the hose slowly.

Power from the Wind

The common factory-built steel pumping windmill, seen by the thousand in all lands where water has to be pumped up from deep boreholes, is one of the most effective devices ever conceived. Many an old steel "wind pump" has been turning away, for 30 or 40 years, never failing in its job. Such machines will pump water comfortably from a thousand feet (300 m) and work in very little wind at all. The tail-vane is arranged on a pivot so that the windmill can turn sideways to the wind in a storm.

Wind power has followed the same trend as water power, in that low-powered but high-speed devices are now wanted for driving dynamos to produce electricity. But the wind, of course, is completely unpredictable, and so you must either accept that you cannot use a machine in calm weather, or in severe gales, or you must be able to store electricity, and that is very expensive. However, if you can use the power when it is available—say, for grinding corn—or store it—as heat, for example—the total wind energy available over a period of time tends to be fairly constant.

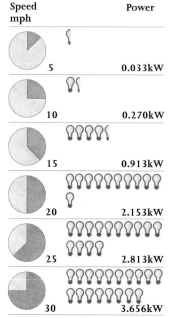

Speed mph	Power
5	0.033kW
10	0.270kW
15	0.913kW
20	2.153kW
25	2.813kW
30	3.656kW

HOW MUCH POWER?

The main problem in harnessing wind is that it carries very little power when it blows lightly, but offers an embarrassing surfeit in a gale. The power of wind is proportional to its velocity cubed: in other words, if the wind speed doubles, its power potential rises eight-fold. This means that a fairly large windmill is needed if useful amounts of power are to be extracted from a light breeze, and that the windmill must be protected from storm damage by having a hinged tail-vane that can swing the wind-rotor out of the wind. Or it can have removable sails or blades that can be made to twist into a "feathered" position where they act as air brakes to slow the rotor. The diagram shows how many 100-watt lightbulbs a 15-foot- (4.5-m-) diameter electricity-generating windmill can power.

Sail windmill

All-metal

Tubular steel

Triple-blade

This is a variation on a Mediterranean sail windmill. Used for irrigation water pumping by gardeners on Crete, it is readily improvised.

This typical all-metal windmill is used for pumping water. A swinging tail-vane turns it out of the wind in a storm. You might be able to renovate an old one.

A water-pumping windmill in which the rotor runs in the lee of the tubular steel tower; weights at the blade roots swing them into a feathered position in gales.

This windmill needs only three aerodynamically profiled blades. The machine trickle-charges a bank of batteries to supply low-powered appliances.

To be self-sufficient in electricity

Wind power is hard to harness and store, so you should always use wind-generated electricity sparingly. Never use it for heating appliances. To exploit wind power you must have an average wind speed of at least 9 mph (14 km/h), with no lengthy periods of low winds; even so, you will need battery storage to cover up to 20 consecutive days of calm. Apart from an electricity-generating windmill, you need a voltage regulator and a cut-out to prevent the battery from overcharging. Total battery storage capacity needs to be 20 x average current needed in amps (watts ÷ volts) x average usage time in hours per day, measured in amp-hours. Standard domestic electric appliances requiring 220 volts AC can be driven from a bank of 12-volt (DC) batteries by an electronic inverter. Alternatively, low-voltage appliances may be used directly. A typical 2-kW, commercially manufactured windmill will often generate at 110 volts DC to charge a bank of low-voltage batteries, wired in series. You might get 5,000 kWh annually from a 2-kW windmill. One kW is equal to one unit of electricity.

Generate your own electricity

The typical electricity-generating windmill is available in kit form or as a do-it-yourself design. The aluminum or fiberglass blades are pivoted from the hub: centrifugal force works on the balance weights and overcomes a set of springs attached to the hub shaft, so the blades feather automatically if the rotor overspeeds.

A toothed rubber belt drives a car alternator to produce up to 750 watts. Power is transmitted down the inside of the tower, either through a conducting slip ring and brush, or by a cable that can be released when it is twisted, thus providing a breakable connection. Similar arrangements might be improvised, though they might suffer in reliability.

ROTOR TYPES
Here are a selection of rotor blades running on electrical generators, pumps, and even a Dutch-style millstone—ideal for the self-supporter. Locally constructed and operated windmills have been highly successful in many rural communities in Denmark, as it happens. Sadly, incentives for small-scale windpower are few.

Rotor type		Typical load	rpm	Hp	Torque
Propeller (lift) double and triple		electrical generator	high	0.42	low
Darrieus (lift)		electrical generator	high	0.40	low
Cyclogiro (lift)		electrical generator or pump	moderate	0.45	moderate
Chalk multiblade (lift)		electrical generator or pump	moderate	0.35	moderate
Sailwing (lift)		electrical generator or pump	moderate	0.35	moderate
Fan-type (drag)		electrical generator or pump	low	0.30	high
Savonius (drag)		pump	low	0.15	high
Dutch-type (drag)		pump or millstone	low	0.17	high

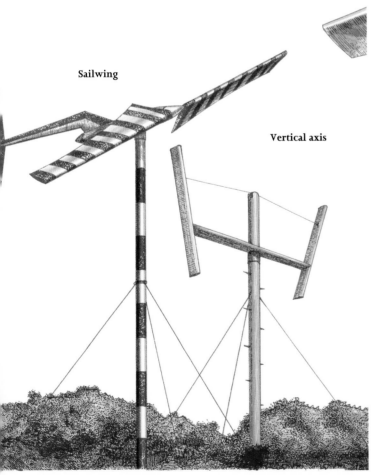

Sailwing

Vertical axis

This is the simple and cheap sailwing, developed at Princeton University. A fabric sleeve is stretched between the two edges of the "wings."

Reading University in England developed this vertical axis windmill. Airfoil blades are spring-loaded and fold outward to prevent over-speeding.

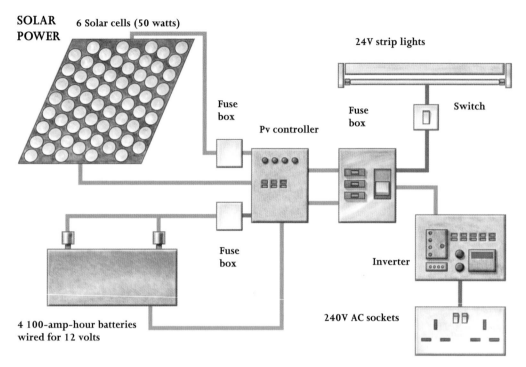

SOLAR POWER

6 Solar cells (50 watts)

Fuse box

Pv controller

Fuse box

24V strip lights

Switch

Fuse box

Inverter

4 100-amp-hour batteries wired for 12 volts

240V AC sockets

PHOTOVOLTAIC SYSTEM
These are the main elements of a typical photovoltaic system. A battery of cells is aligned to the sun. This is often tilted downward somewhat to optimize the performance in winter months when the sun is low. Power flows through to a bank of storage batteries through a control unit, which also links the batteries to domestic appliances. Lighting, audio, and computers can all work well from 24 volts. There is also an inverter for converting the power to 110 volts alternating current for occasional use in larger household appliances. As a guideline, a car battery produces just 12 volts across its terminals, whereas in your house there is 110 volts between the live and neutral wires. High voltage electricity (above 50 volts) is dangerous; low voltage is not. Solar cells normally produce low voltages.

SOLAR ELECTRICITY GENERATION
One of the greatest potential sources of electrical energy lies in the direct conversion of sunlight by photovoltaic cells. This is a remarkable piece of physics, and today's solar cells have become so effective that a gram of thin-film cell silicone will produce as much energy over its lifetime as a gram of uranium.

In modern photocells, purified silicon is used in its crystalline form. There are various grades of cell with different efficiencies and, not surprisingly, different prices. The best cells convert over 15 percent of the incident energy into electricity. They work by creating what amounts to a one-way valve for electrons: when light excites the electrons, they end up going more in one way than the other—hence electricity.

Photovoltaic cells are readily available today and will provide up to several hundred watts of electricity for a normal home. Obviously, they only work when the sun shines, so you must have some storage capability. Normally, batteries will serve for this. Lead acid batteries are the most common and well-understood form of storage. You must look after them carefully, keeping the electrolyte filled up and not leaving them uncharged.

The output of the photocells is usually limited to 24 volts, so an electronic device called an "inverter" must be used to convert the voltage up to normal domestic levels (110–120 volts). But the great challenge is in fact to limit your domestic use of electricity to such things as lighting, audio, and computing, which all work fine from 24 volts and use very little power. All space heating, water heating, cooking, and heavy machines, like washing machines and the hellish beast that is the tumble-dryer, have a heavy appetite for power.

In a northern climate, you are obviously not going to have constant recourse to sunlight in winter. So, as with all alternative energy sources, it is wise to plan your electrical system using several different sources of electricity. If you can combine wind power, water power, and standby diesel generation with your solar array, and put it all together through a modern control and storage setup, then you will be well on the way to success.

UNDERSTANDING ELECTRICITY
Volts Scientists think of electricity as electrons flowing down a wire, almost like water down a pipe. The higher you lift the top end of the pipe, the greater the pressure and the faster the water flows. It's the same with electricity. If you apply more "volts," you push the electrons harder and more "current" will flow down your wire.

Amps You measure the amount of electricity going down a wire in amps: like gallons of water per second in a water pipe. The more amps there are going down a wire, the hotter it gets and the more energy is being transmitted. All domestic appliances run on what is called alternating current—this changes backward and forward 50 times a second and produces power and heat whichever way it goes. Alternating current is easier to manage in the household supply and in motors, but solar cells and batteries produce direct current. This only goes one way, and it is the only kind of electricity that batteries can store.

Watts This is how you measure the power produced by electricity. It is an amount you calculate simply by multiplying the voltage by the amps. If you run a machine at 1,000 watts for an hour, then you have used one kilowatt-hour of energy. This would apply to something like an electric heater.

Fuel from Waste

The attitude that has grown up in the Western world that all so-called "waste" from the body, human or otherwise, is something to be gotten rid of at all costs and very quickly becomes harder to sustain as our planet's fossil fuel comes in shorter supply. If we can take the dung of animals or people, extract inflammable gas from it in quantities that make the effort worthwhile, and still have a valuable manure left over to return to the land, we are doing very well.

Methane is a gas that is produced by the anaerobic fermentation of organic matter: in other words, allowing organic matter to decay in the absence of oxygen. It is claimed that after the gas has been produced, the resulting sludge is a better manure than it was before, for some of the nitrogen that might have been lost as ammonia is now in a fixed form that will be used by plants. As the methane gas itself is as good a fuel as natural gas (in fact, it is the same thing) and is nontoxic and safe, methane production from farm and human wastes seems very worthwhile.

Methane is made with a methane digester, which is fine for animal wastes, but there's a limit to the amount of bulky vegetable matter that you can put into it. This precludes filling it either with tons and tons of straw or with the large quantities of valuable manure that result from the traditional practice (well-proven) of bedding animals with straw. The spent sludge from the digester is itself an excellent manure, but my own feeling is that, rather than dump it straight from the digester onto the land, it should flow onto straw or other waste vegetable matter. There it will undergo further fermentation, this time aerobic, and at the same time activate the bacteria that will break down the tough cellulose content of the litter.

Chicken
½ft³
300BTU

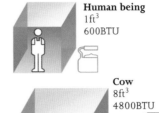

Human being
1ft³
600BTU

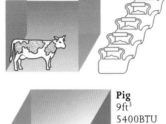

Cow
8ft³
4800BTU

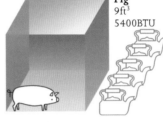

Pig
9ft³
5400BTU

HOW MUCH GAS?
The diagram above shows the amount of gas produced by the waste of different animals in a day. The gas is sufficient to boil the number of kettles shown.

THE METHANE DIGESTER
The process shown below involves the digestion of organic wastes by bacterial action in a sealed container from which all air is excluded. Animal manure mixed to a slurry with water is added to a holding tank **1** daily. The input is fed into the digester by gravity when a valve **2** is opened. The stirrer **3** has an airtight joint where it enters the digester and prevents scum from building up. The tank is well-insulated with straw or similar material **4** since the process only works effectively at temperatures close to blood heat. Each fresh addition causes an equivalent amount of digester sludge to overflow into the slurry collector **6**. The digestion process takes from 14 to 35 days, depending on the temperature of the digester, so the daily input should vary from $\frac{1}{14}$ to $\frac{1}{35}$ of a digester volume to achieve the desired "retention time." The gas bubbles up through the slurry into space **5**, and is siphoned along a delivery line **7** to the gas holder **8**. An important safety precaution is a brass or copper fine mesh flame trap at the entry to the delivery pipe to protect the gas holder if air gets into the line and causes a burnback. The gas produced, called bio-gas, is a mixture of about 60% methane (the inflammable fuel component) and 40% carbon dioxide, which is inert but harmless. The digested sludge makes a valuable fertilizer, being rich in nitrogen and trace elements.

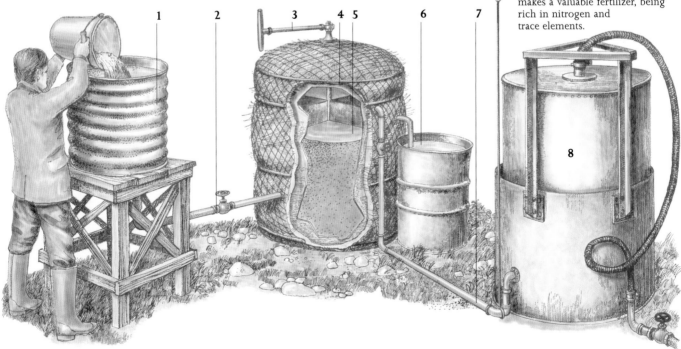

"No machine-made artifact can be beautiful. Beauty in artifacts can only be put there by the hands of the craftsman, and no machine will ever be built that can replace these. Machines might one day be made which will appreciate the beauty of articles made by other machines. People can only be truly pleased by articles made by other people. As far as possible we buy only things that have been made by people, not machines. I do not mean necessarily by the bare hands of people—hands can be magnified by tools and machines—but the hands must be there. Cloth woven on a loom by a person is fine. Cloth woven on a loom by an automatic device is dull. It is grudging…it only serves the one purpose."

JOHN SEYMOUR FAT OF THE LAND 1976

CHAPTER TEN
CRAFTS
AND
SKILLS

The Workshop

Some people meditate in their potting sheds; myself, I meditate in the workshop. You may think it is a form of overkill to consider making your own dedicated workshop, but believe me, you will find plenty of time to use it. In real life, things are always breaking and wearing out—usually just when you don't want them to. If you have all your tools on hand, in good shape, and a suitable place to use them, your blood pressure will benefit greatly. Make mending tools and equipment a source of satisfaction and you transform an irritating chore into a pleasure.

First things first: a workshop needs to have a good solid worktop. A half-inch (1 cm) of good quality plywood would just about do, but two-inch (5-cm) planking would be better. Make a few large holes in the worktop with an auger so you can put in wooden pins to keep work still. You will also need a good vise. You must have good light to work effectively—but you do not want hot sun coming through your window, so a big northern skylight would be ideal (you will see these in many old factories). The workshop does not need to be huge—even 8 square feet (2.5 m) would do. It should have electric power outlets in convenient places—at working height. The workshop should have a floor that is easy to brush clean, but it must not be slippery: plain concrete or unvarnished boarding is ideal.

It is true that one of the new portable workbenches can be a great help for the self-supporter. I have two and both have now reached a battered old age; believe me, these things suffer serious punishment. And that's the bottom line. Do not buy one unless it's robust: the deck should be marine-quality ply and not any form of chipboard. The fittings should be rust-resistant in some shape or form. Anything else will disintegrate pretty rapidly.

Sharpening stone and guides
Tools are worse than useless unless they are sharp. And being sharp in my book means blades with straight edges and no chips. The blades on chisels and planes have been heat-tempered on the edges and are very easily chipped if

they are dropped, put down carelessly, or used as scrapers or levers. All too often they are borrowed by would-be helpers who use them to scrape off paint or lever up nails—this spells disaster, and many hours of hard work to get back a decent edge. My tip to avoid this is to keep good chisels tucked away safely out of sight and leave an old chisel out in a rack or the workbench, where it will be an effective decoy for visitors/helpers who are searching for a tool!

If you want to have planes and chisels with straight edges, then you need to buy a first-rate carborundum or diamond stone: this will not come cheap, but your tools are no good without it. And the way you use the stone will affect the flatness of the surface and hence the straightness of the blade. To keep the surface flat, you must use the full width of the stone and turn it around from time to time so both ends get worn equally. You simply cannot do decent work without properly sharpened tools. I have to let you in on a secret here: I always have two sharpening stones. When a stone is worn and old, I leave it out on the bench as a decoy (much like my chisel duplication, as well as for sharpening kitchen knives) in the hope that any strangers visiting the workshop will not therefore be tempted into looking for my carefully manicured newer stone, which I have hidden. That is how seriously you need to take this crusade for properly sharpened tools.

When you sharpen chisels or planes, always use a rolling guide to keep the blade at exactly the correct angle. You can see whether you are on the right track by looking at the bright, shining area produced by the stone. If your angle is correct, this should cover the entire area of the blade. There is no way you can sharpen tools effectively without the guide.

Fixing a broken handle
Follow the steps illustrated below to make the repair. If the old handle will will not budge, even in the vise, after step 2, then I always try cutting off the end straight across at the end of the metal.

FIXING OLD TOOLS
We are talking here about spades, forks, axes, and sledgehammers. You can buy new handles for all of these at the home improvement store and save yourself a lot of money, as well as keeping your favorite tools going for another few years. It is a strange thing how familiar tools become so comfortable to use; it's a great help to develop and keep a good relationship like this. When you choose a handle, take care to find a good, straight piece of ash—the tighter the grain, the better. Do not be seduced into buying a clean, white piece of some tropical wood—it may look good, but believe me, they always break.

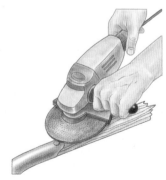

1 To get the steel spade, shovel, or fork off the broken end of the old handle, you will need a grinder to grind off the ends of the old rivets securing the broken wooden end.

2 You should then be able to hammer out the rivets using your punch. With a bit of luck, you may then be able to dislodge the broken wooden end and free it from the metal tube and blade.

3 If the broken handle still won't budge, put the whole item into a fire—wood burns but metal doesn't, and thus you will have a clean space to insert the new handle.

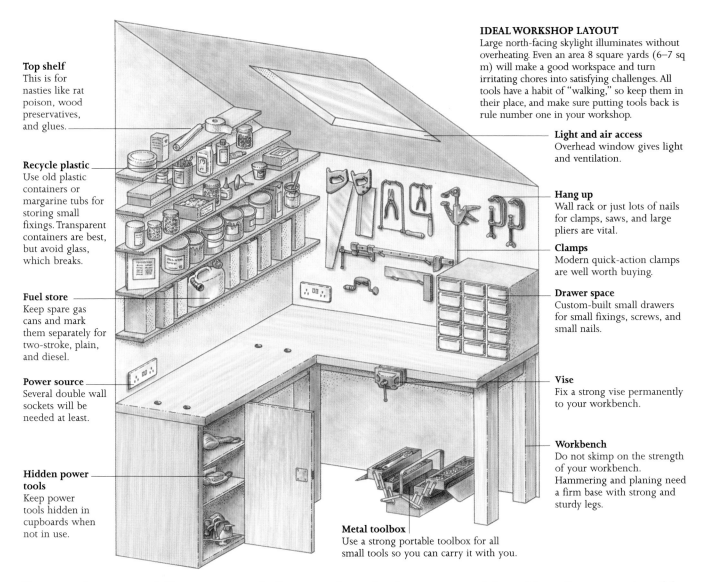

Top shelf
This is for nasties like rat poison, wood preservatives, and glues.

Recycle plastic
Use old plastic containers or margarine tubs for storing small fixings. Transparent containers are best, but avoid glass, which breaks.

Fuel store
Keep spare gas cans and mark them separately for two-stroke, plain, and diesel.

Power source
Several double wall sockets will be needed at least.

Hidden power tools
Keep power tools hidden in cupboards when not in use.

IDEAL WORKSHOP LAYOUT
Large north-facing skylight illuminates without overheating. Even an area 8 square yards (6–7 sq m) will make a good workspace and turn irritating chores into satisfying challenges. All tools have a habit of "walking," so keep them in their place, and make sure putting tools back is rule number one in your workshop.

Light and air access
Overhead window gives light and ventilation.

Hang up
Wall rack or just lots of nails for clamps, saws, and large pliers are vital.

Clamps
Modern quick-action clamps are well worth buying.

Drawer space
Custom-built small drawers for small fixings, screws, and small nails.

Vise
Fix a strong vise permanently to your workbench.

Workbench
Do not skimp on the strength of your workbench. Hammering and planing need a firm base with strong and sturdy legs.

Metal toolbox
Use a strong portable toolbox for all small tools so you can carry it with you.

You can then use a drill or auger to hollow out the wood—this often takes the pressure off and allows the shaft to come free. Now if all this fails, do not waste knuckle-scraping hours fighting with the broken implement—go straight to step 3. I use a power plane to pare down the new shaft to get a good fit. If you twist the shaft backward and forward slightly, you will see from the brown marks how well it fits. Plane away the brown marks. Bang the shaft hard down on a concrete floor to force the tool on before you put a couple of big screws through the empty fixing holes. Put the screws right through the tool by using a small pilot hole made with your drill; it is not as easy as you think to hit the hole in the steel at the other side of the handle. Finally, grind off the ends of the screws and file or hammer them down to make a firm fitting. Bingo: the tool is as good as new.

Machinery maintenance

Some people like flowers and vegetables, some love animals, and some even enjoy machinery. I must confess

that I am not one of them. My earliest memories of farm work are extremely uncomfortable ones of lying under broken pieces of machinery, trying to get rusted bolts loose. Machinery designers seem to have an uncanny knack for making their progeny almost impossible to get at to make repairs. As with so many things in life, prevention is much better than cure, and here are a few golden rules:
1 Check the oil regularly on all engines (and gearboxes, back axles, and the like) and change it according to the official maintenance instructions. There is research to suggest that for some strange reason, there are far fewer breakdowns of any kind on engines where the oil is checked regularly. Could this be some sort of emotional response to this form of love? I wonder.
2 If you hear any strange noises—stop! Check for loose nuts and check oil levels. Do not continue until you find the cause. Strange noises can be very expensive.
3 Be very wary of lending machinery to "friends": the level of care they have for your loved one may be less than you imagine.

Building

For some reason, the self-supporter often seems to spend considerable time building. Sometimes this amounts to repair work to keep existing buildings going against the ravages of damp and weather—or even the battering given by pigs or cattle. More often the self-supporter simply wants to extend his or her accommodation and storage space, whether for humans, animals, or equipment.

It's all in the planning

If you are building anything substantial, you ought to contact your local building inspector. You may also need a building permit—which means paperwork. Do not be deterred. In most cases, the building inspector can offer you very constructive advice about the pitfalls and peculiarities of local conditions. Far better to get advice early than have to knock down your prized blockwork and start again.

Building is labor-intensive, but much of the work is far less skilled than you might imagine. It is a great help if you have a good eye for straight lines and right angles, and you do need to be fairly systematic. The vital first step is to make sensible plans—sensible in terms of where you are siting your building, how big you are going to make it, what materials you are going to use, and how much of a financial budget you expect to have available. Last but not least, do not take on more than you can manage: start with a small, simple project and move on from there. A great deal of the work in building consists of lugging heavy, uncomfortable material from one place to another, often lifting up a considerable height. This will give you strong arms and a patient disposition; alternatively, you may make some new friends who have plenty of energy and good, strong backs!

There is a wide choice of materials available for building. Bricks, concrete blocks, breeze blocks, wood, and metal are the most common. Local stone may be an option if you are lucky and there is an abundance of suitable building stone. Of course, you can also use more outlandish materials, such as straw bales or rammed earth, but for most practical self-supporters, it is easier to make a trip to the home improvement store. For a cheap, strong, and long-lasting building my preferred material is concrete block: you can face this with cement, or plaster or wood, if you don't like the look of it.

Before you buy materials, ask around to find out which suppliers have the best quality and most reasonable prices. You will find enormous variations in both. Many suppliers will deliver much more cheaply if you buy direct from the factory. This means buying a truckload (and making sure

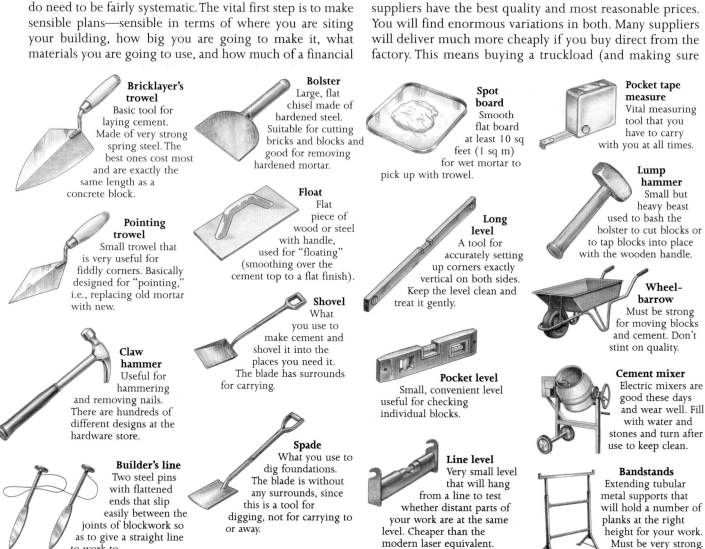

Bricklayer's trowel
Basic tool for laying cement. Made of very strong spring steel. The best ones cost most and are exactly the same length as a concrete block.

Pointing trowel
Small trowel that is very useful for fiddly corners. Basically designed for "pointing," i.e., replacing old mortar with new.

Claw hammer
Useful for hammering and removing nails. There are hundreds of different designs at the hardware store.

Builder's line
Two steel pins with flattened ends that slip easily between the joints of blockwork so as to give a straight line to work to.

Bolster
Large, flat chisel made of hardened steel. Suitable for cutting bricks and blocks and good for removing hardened mortar.

Float
Flat piece of wood or steel with handle, used for "floating" (smoothing over the cement top to a flat finish).

Shovel
What you use to make cement and shovel it into the places you need it. The blade has surrounds for carrying.

Spade
What you use to dig foundations. The blade is without any surrounds, since this is a tool for digging, not for carrying to or away.

Spot board
Smooth flat board at least 10 sq feet (1 sq m) for wet mortar to pick up with trowel.

Long level
A tool for accurately setting up corners exactly vertical on both sides. Keep the level clean and treat it gently.

Pocket level
Small, convenient level useful for checking individual blocks.

Line level
Very small level that will hang from a line to test whether distant parts of your work are at the same level. Cheaper than the modern laser equivalent.

Pocket tape measure
Vital measuring tool that you have to carry with you at all times.

Lump hammer
Small but heavy beast used to bash the bolster to cut blocks or to tap blocks into place with the wooden handle.

Wheelbarrow
Must be strong for moving blocks and cement. Don't stint on quality.

Cement mixer
Electric mixers are good these days and wear well. Fill with water and stones and turn after use to keep clean.

Bandstands
Extending tubular metal supports that will hold a number of planks at the right height for your work. Must be very strong.

your access is suitable for such) which probably amounts to over 1,000 blocks. One thing about blocks and building materials is that this kind of thing does not deteriorate, and believe me, you will always find uses for blocks. Make sure you think things through carefully before you tell the truck driver where to stack the blocks. The modern trucks have a very long reach with their hydraulic cranes. Get the blocks as close as you can to where they will be used.

Damp is the great enemy of the self-sufficient builder. If you have damp in your floors or walls, you can expect all sorts of trouble from rot. So a good roof, good damp-proof course, proper membrane under any concrete slab, and well-made cavities between walls are essential. Concrete and plaster act like blotting paper and seem to have an uncanny knack for absorbing any moisture.

Roofing

Materials for roofing also come in all shapes and sizes—from thatch at one extreme to fiberglass tiles or corrugated iron at the other. In between you have tiles and natural slates. Each type of roofing material requires a different approach. Your choice will obviously depend on the aesthetics of your design, your budget, and what is easily available locally.

If you are using heavy roofing materials, you will need to construct a strong wooden framework. Slates and tiles are extremely heavy—this is one reason they make a good roof that will resist the ravages of the wildest winter storms. Make sure the roof is well-ventilated to prevent damp from rotting the timber. Use stainless steel, aluminum, or copper nails for fastening roof coverings.

Basic block laying

First load out your blocks in piles close to where they will be needed. Make sure you have a couple of spot boards for dumping mortar ready for use. Mix your cement (usually a 4-to-1 mixture of sand and cement, respectively) and add some mortar plasticizer to make the cement flow better. With practice you will get the sloppiness just right: not too wet and not too dry (wetter is probably better than drier to start with). With your large trowel, lay a bed of wet mortar in the place where your first block is to go. Place the block carefully in position, exactly to the markers you have set up in advance (corner and line). Slide it backward and forward to ease it into the mortar. Check with your pocket level that it is level in all directions. Tap it with the lump hammer end if it refuses to settle correctly. Block after block, keep each one positioned accurately to your builder's line.

BUILDING FOUNDATIONS AND A WALL

1 Mark out the foundations with posts and lines. Corners and diagonals must be exact. Dig by hand or mark out with white lime for a small digger to work to. As a rule, dig to at least 2 feet (60 cm).

2 Tap your metal bars into the bottom of your trenches until their upper ends are in exactly the right place to give you the correct thickness of concrete.

3 Check your levels carefully across the tops of the metal bars. Use a long straight piece of wood in conjunction with your long level—and be fussy. Mistakes at this stage will cost you time and frayed nerves later.

5 When the foundations have set solid, you are ready to begin your "footings." Again, make sure you have your corners marked accurately and take great care to get the corners precise before you set up lines from them for the rest of the blocks.

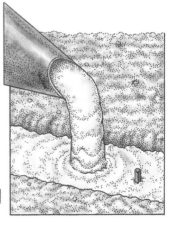

4 Pour your concrete to the tops of the metal bars and spread it out carefully. Tamp it down with a long, straight piece of wood, making sure the levels are correct.

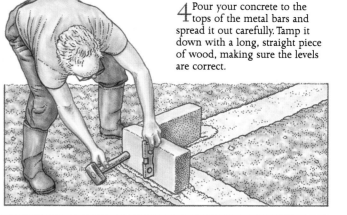

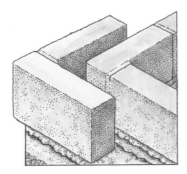

6 Place the inner course of blocks in exactly the right position inside the original blocks. Spacing must be exactly right for a substantial layer of insulation material (usually at least 4 inches/10 cm). Don't forget to put in wall ties to connect the two walls every few feet. And never let mortar drop down between the walls, since this can cause damp if it bridges the gap.

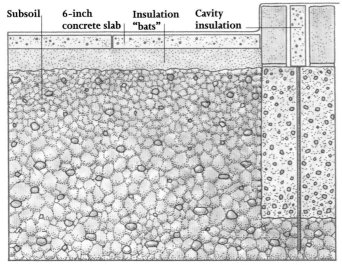

Subsoil | 6-inch concrete slab | Insulation "bats" | Cavity insulation

CROSS SECTION
This shows the foundations, footings, and layers of insulation. There is insulation under the concrete slab and between the two courses of blocks that form the walls. You also have a strong damp-proof membrane between the slab and the earth underneath.

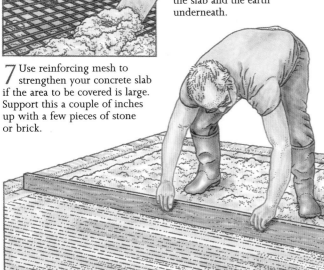

7 Use reinforcing mesh to strengthen your concrete slab if the area to be covered is large. Support this a couple of inches up with a few pieces of stone or brick.

8 Find or make a long, stiff wooden batten to extend right across the slab so you can "tamp" down the concrete to a perfect flat, level surface. Always pour a little more concrete than you need so you can pull off the excess with the batten.

9 Lay your damp course carefully over the top of the footings on a bed of wet mortar. The damp course must be well above ground level if it is to work effectively to keep out damp.

10 Split blocks to size using a lump hammer and bolster. Cut a shallow groove in each side of the block using a few blows at a time.

11 Use your long level with great care to make sure corners are exactly vertical on both sides. Don't fudge, or the project will go awry.

12 Once the corners are set, use a builder's line pulled tight between the pins at each corner. Check levels regularly using a hanging level at the middle of the line.

Springs & Plumbing

SINKING A WELL

The easiest way of finding water is to drill a hole with a drilling machine, and if you can get hold of one, it is well worth using it. But they are expensive, even to rent, and all they really save is time and energy. If you have got some of each to spare, you can dig your well yourself by hand.

Sinking a well in earth or soft rock is very easy, if laborious. You just dig in, keeping the diameter as small as you can, just leaving yourself room to use a shovel. As you get deeper, you send the spoil (dug earth) up to the surface in a bucket hauled up by a friend with a windlass, and you go up the same way. It is almost always necessary to line the well as you dig to stop the earth from falling in. The easiest way to do this is with concrete rings sent down from the top. As you dig down, you dig under the lowest concrete ring, which causes it to fall, and all the other concrete rings on top fall with it. From time to time you put another concrete ring on top. Where timber is cheap, you can use a timber lining on the same principle.

Sinking a well through rock is harder in that you have to blast it, but easier in that you probably don't have to line it. In days gone by, the rock was shattered by building a fire on it and then quenching this with water. The rapid contraction shattered the surface of the rock. Of course "powder" and modern detonants are the direct route to a well, and in the past I would do it myself, but nowadays you need to hire experts.

Whichever way you sink a well, when you come to water, go on sinking. Even if you have to spend half of each day winding up water in the bucket, go on sinking until the water beats you, because if you don't, when there is a drought and the water table sinks, your well will go dry. When you have got your water, the best thing you can do is install a steel pumping windmill (see p.346). It will pump water from 1,000 feet (300 m) and go on doing it for years, free, and with very little attention.

PLUMBING

I have no regrets about saying goodbye to the drama of hot solder and the mysteries of copper piping. Those cunning plastic gizmos that can join pipes, make T-junctions, and fix faucets have made plumbing a lot easier (and believe me, your labor is much cheaper than a plumber's).

A tip I will pass on: always put in-line service faucets into your new plumbing. These small faucets fit into the line of your piping and can be turned on or off with a screwdriver. By installing these, you can easily isolate new pipework from the rest of the house, so any leakage can be fixed without cutting off the entire water supply. If your garden is anything like mine, you will inevitably cut through or damage buried water pipes. So keep a range of plastic joining fittings in your workshop: this will save you a great deal of time, not to mention nerves, since water has to be turned off and kitchen, bathroom, and washing machine grind to a halt.

MANAGING A SPRING
Make good use of your spring as a source of clean fresh water. Explore the source of the spring carefully so you cover it effectively with the chamber, and make sure the outlet pipe is placed to avoid mud and soil contamination.

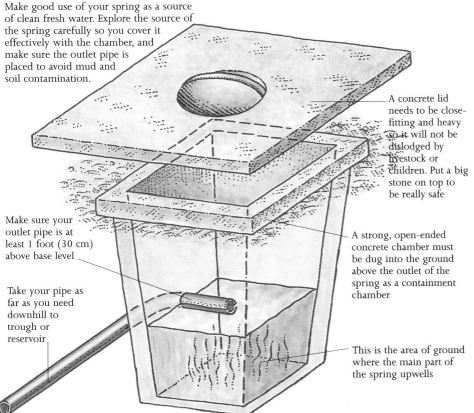

A concrete lid needs to be close-fitting and heavy so it will not be dislodged by livestock or children. Put a big stone on top to be really safe

Make sure your outlet pipe is at least 1 foot (30 cm) above base level

Take your pipe as far as you need downhill to trough or reservoir

A strong, open-ended concrete chamber must be dug into the ground above the outlet of the spring as a containment chamber

This is the area of ground where the main part of the spring upwells

PLUMBING FITTINGS
You will find a whole range of easily used plastic plumbing fittings at a good home improvement store. Make sure you know exactly the sizes of pipe you are using—take a piece in if you are unsure.

This is a typical all-purpose joint where the inserts can be of different sizes— very convenient as a spare.

This is a cheaper plastic joint that must be the correct size to fit piping.

There are many types of push-fit connectors for taps and pipes (left). A typical T-junction (below left) has brass "olives" compressed to make the joint watertight. Keep extra new olives for each different size of pipe so you can reuse the joints.

Knots & Ropework

The use of rope and string is probably older than the wheel. Their use is certainly one of the greatest of all human inventions. If string and rope came first, then knots, nets, and weaving came pretty soon afterward. Ropes and cordage are made in all sorts of clever ways by spinning and twisting strong fibers together. Hemp, linen, cotton, and wool are obvious examples of fibers used in making rope and cord. But today we are more likely to come across the modern plastic equivalents in terylene, nylon, and other synthetics.

Different kinds of rope and cord are suitable for different types of jobs. And there are a thousand different types of knots that humans have developed over the centuries for specific purposes. Learning about knots and cordage is one of the simplest skills, yet surprisingly few people know more than one or two knots and, even then, do not know their proper names. Those of you who have seen the movie *Jurassic Park* will know just how important it can be to tie a proper bowline that makes a loop that will not slip, or jam, or come undone. Our hero's truck was tied to a tree by some foul Hollywood hitch and was always destined to slip off into the clutches of the rampant waiting dinosaurs.

Knots—a life skill

They should teach knot-making to children in school: knots are cheap, they require dexterity, and they are extremely useful. Indeed, the right knot in the right place can be a lifesaver. Animals frequently pull and twist on any rope used to tie them. The wrong knot will either jam or come undone—in the first case needing a knife to free it, in the second leaving the animal free to cause havoc elsewhere. A stockman's hitch or falconer's knot is tied quickly with one hand, yet allows for quick release if the animal panics or has to be let free quickly. Using the right type of rope or cord can also be vital: some stretch and some do not, some are easy on the hands, some are as hard and sharp as sandpaper, some are stiff and some flexible.

The right knot is one that does the job it is intended for with minimum effort. An anchor bend, as its name suggests, is for securing an anchor, and it will never slip, even when it is allowed to tighten and slacken on every tide. It may jam and have to be cut free, but that is a fair price to pay for not losing your anchor. The knot is tied tight up against the anchor ring so that it will not chafe and rub. And so the list goes on.

One of the most satisfying moments a teacher can have on any self-sufficiency topic is the look of amazement on a student's face on seeing how years of struggling with rope can be swiftly brought to an end with the right knot. My father always used to tell the tale of how the "thief" knot was used instead of reef (square) knots to tie up important parcels. The reef knot is the simplest of knots: right over left and left over right and the sails are tied up tightly in place as the wind strengthens. It is so simple that the knot is invariably used to tie up parcels. On first glance the thief knot looks just like a reef knot: left over right and right over left—certainly sufficient to deceive a would-be snooper. But there is one crucial difference: the loose ends of string in a reef knot come out both on the same side of the tight string, while the ends on a thief knot come out on opposite sides. The simple logic of the story was that you could always tell if someone had meddled with your mail if it was tied with thief knot!

Just for the record, the reef knot is often used for tying together two pieces of rope, yet it is quite unsuitable for this because it will come undone if the tension of the rope is varied or jerked. The correct knot for tying together two pieces of rope is the sheet bend, or double sheet bend if the ropes are of different thicknesses.

Managing rope and cord

All ropes should be properly coiled when they are not in use. They should be kept free of knots and kinks, which will, in time, weaken them. And their ends should not be allowed to fray. Ends can be kept tidy in three ways:

1 *Using heat from a match or hot piece of steel if the rope is of synthetic material. Watch out if you are doing this and the rope catches fire: the molten material that drips off can cause very nasty burns, since it is sticky and extremely hot.*

2 *Applying strong twine in the form of a whipping that binds the loose ends together over at least an inch of the rope.*

3 *Undertaking a back splice on three- or four-stranded ropes, which makes the job much more permanent.*

Ropes have a nasty habit of getting twisted and knotted. There is one very simple reason for this. When a rope is made into a single coil, it has to be twisted to make it coil neatly. Consequently, if both ends are tied and the rope then unravels, it can only do so with all the twists intact. As soon as tension comes off the rope and it gets loose, then it seems to tie itself up in knots. You often have this problem with telephone cords. Even worse, the problem is often the final straw in the kite-flying exploits of young children.

There is a simple answer to this, which I learned when I was studying falconry. When training a young falcon, the falconer must tie a long, lightweight string to the falcon, so that on its first few flights it cannot simply disappear up the nearest tree. This line is called a creance. One of the essential skills the falconer learns is how to wind up the creance (one-handed, of course, as the falcon sits on a glove on the other hand). The only correct way to wind up the creance is in a figure eight on a special wide stick made for the purpose. Miracle of miracles, this figure eight system means that the falcon can pull out the string *without* making any twists. The twists at each end of the figure eight cancel each other out, and this makes running out the rope much, much easier. Remember this when you are flying a kite with kids and life will be much simpler!

ESSENTIAL KNOTS

BOWLINE

The bowline is the essential method of making a loop in rope that will not slip and will not jam—an important factor when stringing a bow (for which this knot was originally intended). If you can only learn one knot, this should be it.

FALCONER'S HITCH

Learn to tie this knot with one hand, since you have to hold the animal with the other. One pull on the loose end undoes the knot and lets a struggling animal free.

SHEETBEND

The sheetbend rivals the bowline in importance. It is the definitive knot for tying together two pieces of rope under tension. The thin rope can be passed around twice for extra security to make a double sheet bend. For extra security, whip the loose end of the thicker rope tight against the part under tension (the "standing" part).

ROLLING HITCH

A rolling hitch is used to fasten a rope to a pole or beam. The tension on the rope should be pulling against the double turn side of the knot, which jams the turns tight, preventing slippage.

CLOVE HITCH

This is a quick way to take tension on a pole or post. But it does slip, so it cannot be used for a permanent fastening without adding a couple of half hitches.

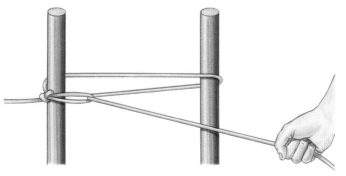

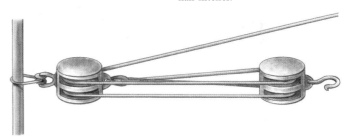

LORRYMAN'S HITCH

Use this knot to tighten up a rope already under tension. The loop acts like a block and tackle to double your force. You can then secure with a quick half hitch against the loop, or a slip half hitch if you want to undo it more easily.

This knot is now largely replaced by the use of woven straps with hooks at each end and a ratchet tightener. These are powerful tools; I always keep a couple in the workshop.

BLOCK AND TACKLE

Modern sailing equipment has produced some extremely light but powerful versions of the block and tackle. It is amazing what force you can exert, provided you have something to pull against. Remember, always

pull the free end in the same direction as the force you want to apply. Every self-supporter should have a block and tackle available for emergencies. The best ones even have self-jamming cleats to maintain tension when you let go.

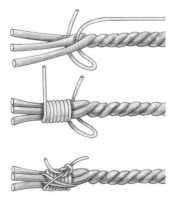

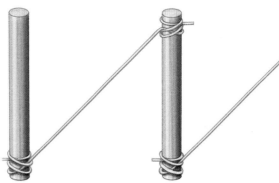

SPLICING

The art of splicing is worthy of a book in itself, but a simple splice is easy enough to understand. Simply weave the cords making up one rope through the cords making up the other. Even three or four tucks makes an extremely strong join. Pare the ends of the cords down gradually if you want a neat finish that will not jam in blocks or other guides or fasteners.

WHIPPING

A very useful technique for making a permanent neat end on ropes using strong twine so they cannot fray and come apart. Simply wind the twine over a loop of itself, then put the loose end through the loop and pull it under the turns you have already made.

HOLDFAST

By driving three posts into the softest mud or soil, you can achieve amazing staying power with this layout of holdfast. This is the way to pull a boat, machine, or animal out of the mud if you have a block and tackle but no convenient tree to pull on. It really works!

Each post should be at least 3 feet (about a meter) long and driven well into the ground. Use rolling hitches to fasten the ropes. You can use a similar configuration of posts and wire to anchor the ends of stock fencing before applying tension: drill holes through the center of the posts to fasten your wires.

Basketry

You can go for a walk in the country with no tools other than a sharp knife and come back with a basket. Traditionally, one-year shoots from willow (called osiers) are used for the strongest baskets, but you can use other materials, such as straw or rushes, too. Osiers are grown by pushing sturdy lengths of willow into the ground. These should be about a foot (30 cm) long and at least ½ inch (1.5 cm) thick, planted about 18 inches (45 cm) apart with rows a couple of feet (60 cm) apart. These will sprout roots at one end and rods at the other. The rods are cut in winter when the sap is down. Sort the rods into lengths after harvesting. You can let them dry naturally, or you can strip the bark, or you can boil to obtain different finishes. Rods are tied into "bolts" (bundles) for sale.

Basic basketry

Good willow should be smooth and straight, with nice, thin tips. It can only be worked when it has been soaked. Choosing rods the correct size for what you need is more critical than you might think. Even small variations in thickness can allow the stronger rods to dominate the work.

The base of your basket, the "slath," can be round, oval, or square. The base is the foundation for your work and must be firm and well-shaped. Choose strong, smooth rods and use "pairing" to form them into the shape required. The uprights are then pushed firmly into the base to begin weaving the sides.

To make uprights for a square basket, you must cut away the willow at the butt of the stake to make what is called a "slype." Otherwise, simply use the traditional bodkin (*see below*) to insert a stake into the weave on each side of each stick of the base. Push the stake right to the center of the base if you can. If the stakes are too stiff, then you will have to prick them—that is to say, make a small crease with your thumb or the back of a knife at the point about ¼ inch (0.5 cm) from the base edge where they are to turn up. Now tie the ends of the stakes together as you prepare to weave. The first few rows of your weave (the "upsett") are critical to the shape of the finished basket. The weave used for this is called the "waling." It is vital to get the stakes into the correct positions with this weave, and you will probably use a rapping iron to firm them down. You always finish a round with the tip ends.

Borders A good border is critical. We show one border here (another common border is the 3-rod-behind-1). Once you have three pairs of rods facing toward you from three consecutive spaces, you simply take the right-hand rod of the left-hand set in front of the next upright and behind the next. You can then bend the first upright down beside it and continue the sequence.

Handles A bow handle is made by forcing a rod down into the weave on each side of a basket. Use a bodkin and grease to ease the sharpened rod into position as far down the weave as you can. Now cover the handle bow with thin rods, taking four at a time, pushing them in beside the handle. Wind them around the bow three times as you go to the other side, where they can be woven in. Repeat with another four rods from the opposite side. Add more rods until the handle is evenly covered.

To make a twisted rope handle, take four rods long enough to reach across the handle twice with some to spare. Slype the first one and insert it beside one end of the handle. Wind the rod five times around the handle to the other side. Pass the rod through or under the border and bring it back, keeping the twist beside the first. Tuck the loose end through the weave to keep it in place. Repeat the process with the next rod. Twist the ends of the weavers together and weave them under the border to complete the handle.

BASKET-MAKING EQUIPMENT

The bodkin is a sturdy iron rod, tapered down to a pointed end to part the weave in order to insert a new rod. The grease horn stores the bodkin when not in use. Use cheesecloth soaked in tallow for the grease. A curved knife with a sharp point is really useful for cutting scalloms. Weights are heavy chunks of metal used to keep work in place. The rapping iron is a heavy flat strip of metal used to tap down each row of the weave. The screwblock is a clamp used to hold weaves flat, particularly for making bases. For a measure, use a rigid steel or retractable wooden rule. The pruning shears are for cutting rods.

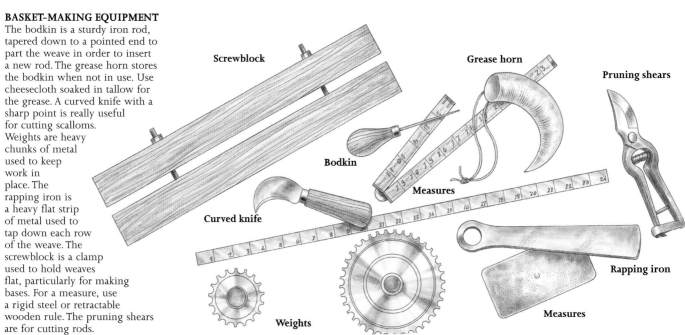

Screwblock

Grease horn

Pruning shears

Bodkin

Measures

Curved knife

Rapping iron

Weights

Measures

MAKING A HARD BASKET

You need three different types of rod: eight short, stout rods for the "slath," or base; a number of strong but flexible rods for your side stakes; and some weavers—the long, thin whippy rods that hold the basket together.

Side stakes are generally about 8 inches (20 cm) longer than the intended height of the basket. Weavers can be any length, but they should be at least long enough to go around the basket once. They come in varying thicknesses.

Soak all your rods for an hour before using them, in a container big enough to hold them all. They might need to be weighed down to keep them under water.

The base of the basket is the most critical part of your work, since it forms the foundation for all that follows. The size, shape, and number of sticks in your base will determine virtually the entire form of your basket.

The patterns and strength of your basketry comes from using different weaves—but the shape and quality comes from how well you perform each stroke of the weave and being vigilant about the shape and evenness of your work.

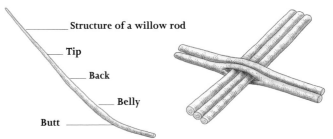

Structure of a willow rod — Tip, Back, Belly, Butt

1 Choose the best length of rod for your work: 3 feet (1 m) for small baskets, 4–6 feet (1.2–6 m) for shopping baskets, and 8 feet (2.4 m) for large items. Sort into four groups of matching thickness.

2 Soak all your rods for an hour before using them. Cut the rods for your slath, and cut slits in two of them. Poke the others through to form a cross.

ALTERNATIVE BASE
Instead of piercing or threading, you can start your base with sticks overlaid as shown.

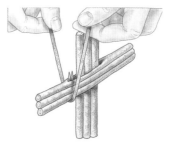

3 Begin the base weave (tie in the slath) by pushing the sharpened butt ends of two weavers into the split center of your base sticks.

4 Begin pairing (the most common weave for creating a base) and separating out the sticks so as to open them out into the correct configuration.

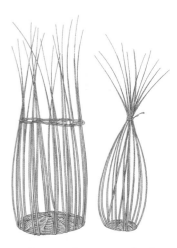

5 When your base is completed by tucking tip ends of the final weavers into the weaving, you are ready to stake up to form the basket sides. Try to make sure all your stakes are the same thickness. A tied stake (*above left*) and hooped stake (*above right*) are shown ready for the upsett (the first few rows of the basket side).

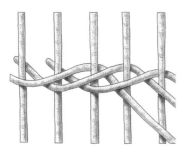

3-ROD WALE
Insert 3 weavers into 3 adjacent spaces. Here the 3rd rod is being woven. The twist in the weave locks the rods into position.

SCALLOMS
Each scallom goes over the "tail" of the one before and holds it in position. Start weaving easily from any base shape by using scalloms.

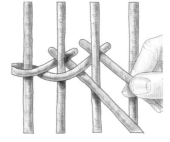

UNDERSIDES
Make all joints either tip to tip or butt to butt. Slip the ends of the new weavers under the ends that

are finishing—you can overlap with a few strokes if you are changing at the tips.

SLEWING
Quick and useful for using up odds and ends but not easy to control. This is a 4-rod slew: add a new new rod as the bottom is used up.

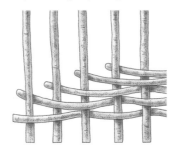

RANDING
A single weaver is used to go in and out of the stakes and it creates a spiral effect. Start each one off one space to the right.

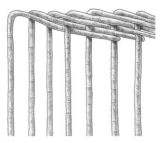

TRAC BORDERS
Trac borders are the simplest to understand: simply bend over the stakes and weave them through three or four stakes to the right.

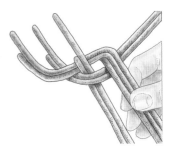

BRAIDED BORDER
For decorative effect on bowls or trays where there are no handles, work with pairs over each upright stake through to the inside.

Pottery

Clay is very often overlain with earth, and so you may be walking on it, or even living on it, without knowing it is there. Prospect where a cutting has been made, or a well, or anything that exposes the subsoil. If it looks like clay, and when wetted becomes plastic and sticky, it is clay.

Testing clay

Once you have found it, you have got to find out if it is any good. It probably isn't. Wet some down to a plastic state and then allow it to dry out. If it has a noticeable scum, usually a whitish stain, on its surface after it has dried, it contains undesirable alkali and probably isn't worth using. Drop a sample of the clay into a beaker containing a 50 percent solution of hydrochloric acid. If it fizzes, forget it—too much lime. If the clay looks dark brown or black and is very sticky, then there is too much humus. Clay very near the surface may be like this, but there is often better clay underneath.

To test for plasticity, which is important, make some clay into a stick the size of a pencil and see if you can bend it into a ring an inch in diameter without breaking it. If you can, it is good clay.

If there is too much sand in your clay it may be hard to mold or throw on the wheel. If this is so, mix a fatter, less gritty clay with your sandy clay and try that. You can screen sand out of clay, but it is a laborious job and probably not worth it.

Mixing and screening

If you want to mix it with other clay, or screen it, you must mix it with water to a pretty sloppy liquid. Throw the clay into a tank full of water (don't pour the water on the clay) and mix. You can do this by hand, or with a paddle, or in a "blunger," which is a special machine for the job, or in an ordinary washing machine. The semiliquid clay is then called "slip." The slip can be poured through a screen, to screen it. Use a 60 mesh per inch screen for ordinary earthenware and a 100 mesh for porcelain or china. If you want to mix two or more clays, make slip of them all and then mix them up in that condition.

The next job is getting the water out of the clay again. An easy method is to let your slip sit in a barrel or tank for a few days until the clay all sinks to the bottom. Then you siphon the water off, much as a wine maker racks his wine. There is a machine called a filterpress that will then extract the rest of the water, but if you haven't got one, you can place the slip in bowls of unglazed earthenware and leave these in a drafty place. The absorbent earthenware draws the water out of the clay. The water is then dried off by the air, and after a few days the clay is fit to work.

Preparing clay

If you are very lucky, you may find a clay that you don't have to combine with anything else, or screen, and all you have to do is dig it up and let it weather, or age.

All clay is better aged, even if only for two weeks, because bacteria do good things to it. Then you must mix it with water and "pug" it, which means you must tread it well with your feet. Finally, you must "wedge" it. This is the process of pushing the clay away from you on a board, pulling it toward you, rolling it, cutting it up, and recombining it: in fact, giving it a thorough kneading just as you knead bread.

Shaping pots

There are many ways of shaping a pot. Almost certainly pottery was discovered because baskets used to be plastered with clay to make them hold water. One day a basket got burned and the clay became hard and durable. This was the first pot made with a mold. Simple ways of making pots include "pinching," "coiling," and using "slabs."

The potter's wheel

The invention of the potter's wheel was the great breakthrough, and there is really no substitute for it. You "throw" a lump of clay on the wheel, "centering" it smack in the middle of the wheel by pressure from both hands as the wheel revolves. Then you shape it with pressure from your hands, fingers, tools, and so on. Remove the pot from the wheel: usually, you cut it off with a piece of wire. Set it aside to dry. Then replace it on the wheel by sticking it with a little water, and "turn" it, that is, spin it around and smooth off the rough edges with a steel cutting tool. Turn it twice: once with the pot the right way up, and again with it upside down.

Making a wheel

In primitive countries they still use wooden cart or wagon wheels as potter's wheels, and if you can get hold of one you can do this, too. You mount the wheel horizontally near the ground, ideally on a short section of its original axle. Make a hole in the side of the wheel toward one edge, or in a spoke if it has them. To use it you squat by the side of the wheel, put a stick in the hole and set the wheel turning. Because the wheel is very heavy it goes on turning by its own momentum and your hands are then free to throw a pot or two.

A more sophisticated potter's wheel can be made by casting a reinforced concrete wheel, say, 28 inches (70 cm) in diameter and 3½ inches (9 cm) high with a 1-inch- (2.5-cm-) diameter steel shaft about 30 inches (75 cm) long through it. The bottom of the shaft should protrude a couple of inches, and steel reinforcing bars should be welded radiating from the shaft so they can be embedded in the concrete. This wheel you kick to make the throwing wheel revolve. Then, build a table-high wooden frame that has a bearing let into it to house the top bearing of the shaft, and a thrust bearing at the bottom to take the bottom of the shaft. The frame should also include a seat for you to sit on, and a table to place clay.

Fix the concrete wheel and shaft into the frame. And now you must fix on your throwing wheel. Weld (*see* p.374) or braze a wheel-head, say a foot (30 cm) in diameter and ¼ to ½ inch (0.7 cm to 1.2 cm) thick to the top of a steel hub (a short piece of water pipe will do). Put this on top of the shaft and weld, or braze, it on. To use your wheel, just sit on the seat and kick the concrete wheel around with your foot. Being heavy, it has plenty of momentum.

Firing

Firing is necessary to harden the clay. With most glazed ware there are two firings: the "biscuit firing," which is just the clay and not the glaze, and the "glost firing," which is the biscuit ware dipped in the liquid glaze and fired again. You can fire pots to flower-pot hardness in a large bonfire, although you cannot of course glaze them like this. Lay a thick circle of seasoned firewood on the ground, lay your ware in the middle, build a big cone of wood over it, and light. Pull the pots out of the ashes when they are cooled.

Traditional kilns are "updraft" kilns, and you can build one yourself if you can lay bricks. "Downdraft" kilns are a more recent development and a little more difficult to build. The kiln is arranged so that the heat from the fire is sucked down through the pots before it is allowed to rise up the chimney. Much higher temperatures can be achieved using this method. Temperature can be a matter of experience, or can be measured with "pyrometers" or "cones." Cones are little pyramids of different kinds of clay mixture that are placed in the kiln and that tell us the temperature by keeling over when they get to a certain heat. You can buy them very cheaply, but if you plan to use them, remember to build some sort of a peephole in your kiln so you can see them.

Glazing

Most glaze is a mixture of silica, a "flux" (which is generally an oxide of some metal), and alumina (which is clay). China clay is the most usual form of alumina in glazes. The silica melts and solidifies on cooling to form a coating of glass on the ware. The flux helps the fusion, lowers the melting point of the silica, and provides color. The alumina gives the glaze viscosity so that it does not all run down the side of the pot when you put it in the kiln.

Anybody can make their own glazes. You must grind the components down fine, either with a mortar and pestle or in a ball mill. The latter is a slowly revolving cylinder that you fill with flint pebbles and whatever material you want to grind. You can make a raw glaze from 31 parts washing soda (the flux—sodium is a metal); 10.5 parts whiting; 12 parts flint (the silica); 55.5 parts feldspar. Grind this, mix it, and pass it through a 100 mesh per inch (2.5 cm) lawn, which is a piece of fine linen. There are hundreds of glazes, and the best thing you can do is get a book on the subject and experiment with a few.

BEFORE SHAPING YOUR POT
Let newly dug clay age for at least two weeks. Then pug it to get the air out. The easiest way is to mix it with water and trample on it.

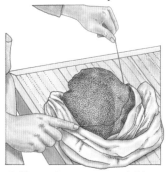

1 Use a wire to cut a workable lump from your store of pug.

2 Wedge the lump to make it a soft, homogeneous mass, free of air bubbles and foreign bodies like bits of stone and grit. You can wedge in the same way as you would knead dough for bread. Roll the clay toward you with both hands, twist it sideways, and push it down into itself. Press out air bubbles and pick out bits of dirt. If you are mixing two clays, wedge until your clay is one uniform color.

AFTER SHAPING YOUR POT
Most glazes are applied after the first firing in the kiln, the biscuit firing. The most common method is to dip your pot in a soup of powdered glaze and water, but it takes practice to avoid finger marks. You can pour glaze so that it flows over the pot. You can spray it, or paint it on with a brush.

A SOLID FUEL UPDRAFT KILN
You can get kilns that use electricity, gas, or oil, but a solid fuel kiln can be equally efficient, and you can build it yourself out of ordinary bricks. Updraft kilns are the simplest. You have your fire box at the bottom. If you burn wood, you can do it on the ground, but coal and coke should be burned on steel firebars so that the ash can drop through. Build your pot chamber directly above the fire, by supporting a system of shelves made of firebrick on steel firebars. Include a peephole so you can watch your pots' progress. And as long as you build the whole structure firmly, the chimney can be directly over the pot chamber.

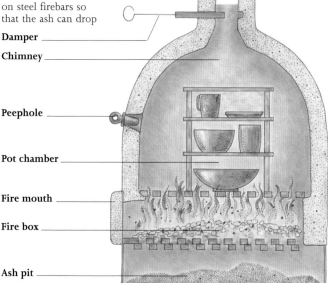

Damper

Chimney

Peephole

Pot chamber

Fire mouth

Fire box

Ash pit

Spinning Wool & Cotton

WOOL

Wool should be selected (or sheep should be selected) for the job to be done. Different breeds of sheep give wool of varying lengths of "staple" or fiber. Long staple wool is better than short for the hand spinner. Rough, hairy wool is fine for tweeds and rugs: soft, silky wool for soft fabrics like dress material. There are no hard and fast rules, though.

To turn raw wool straight from the sheep into yarn ready for weaving, you usually begin by "teasing" to straighten the wool out and get rid of dust, burrs, and other garbage. Then you "card" to create "rollags" (*see opposite*), which are rolls of well-combed wool ready for spinning. Spinning (*see opposite*) is done with a spindle, a hedgehog, or a spinning wheel, and whichever it is, the principle is the same: to stretch and twist the straight fibers of wool from your rollags to make lengths of yarn ready for weaving or knitting. The subtle feature of a spinning wheel is that the endless twine that acts as a driving band goes over two pulleys of different sizes. This means that the bobbin and the flyer, which the pulleys drive, revolve at different speeds. The flyer is therefore able to lay the yarn, as it is spun, on the bobbin at the right tension.

Roving

A self-supporting friend of mine wears the most flamboyant garments, very warm and good-looking, and he makes them entirely from wool, with no other tools but five sticks and a needle. He spins them on one stick and weaves them on the other four. Now it is possible to spin wool without carding first. Instead you have to "rove" it, which can be done with the hands alone. Take some teased wool in your left hand, release a little of it between your finger and thumb, and pull out in a continuous rope with your right hand, but not pulling so hard that you break or disengage the rope. This is not as easy as it sounds, and it takes practice. When you have pulled out all the wool, bend it double and do the whole operation again. Bend it double again (sometimes you might like to triple it) and go on doing this until you are satisfied that it is fairly parallel and well teased-out. This is now a "roving" and you can spin it directly.

Types of yarn

For weaving, you generally use single-ply wool. The warp yarn should be fairly tightly spun: the weft yarn less so. If you intend to knit with the yarn, double it.

PREPARING RAW WOOL

You can turn a fleece into spun wool with just a spindle, but it is easier to use cards, and a hedgehog, or spinning wheel.

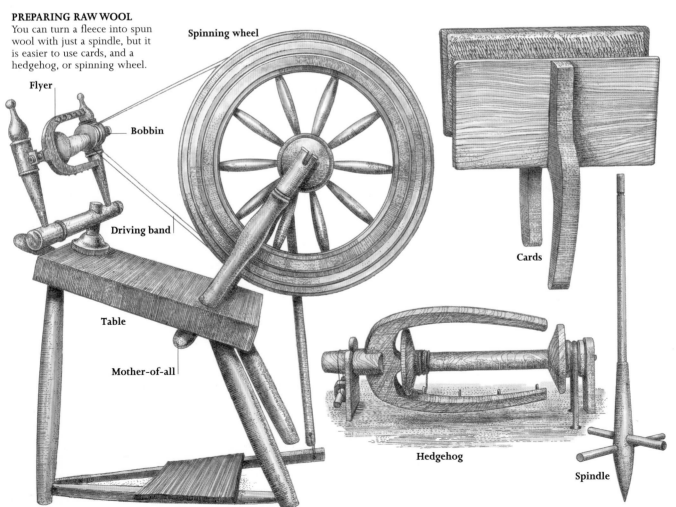

Flyer

Spinning wheel

Bobbin

Driving band

Table

Mother-of-all

Cards

Hedgehog

Spindle

To do this put two full bobbins on a "lazy kate," which is simply a skewer held horizontally at each end (two upright pegs will do just as well), put the ends of the two yarns together, feed them into the spindle on your spinning wheel just as if you were going to spin, put them around the flyer (*see illustration*), tie them to the spindle, and then turn the wheel backward, or from right to left. This will make two-ply wool. If you want three-ply do the same thing with three bobbins.

COTTON

Cotton is often "willowed" before being carded. In the West this generally means being put in a string hammock and beaten with whippy willow rods. The vibrations fluff out and clean the cotton very effectively. It is then carded just like wool, but it cards much more easily, the cotton staples being much shorter.

Spin it as if it were wool, but keep your hands much closer together, treadle more quickly, and don't hold the cotton back too much with the left thumb and finger or it will kink. Angora hair, if you can get it, is delightful stuff and can be treated just like cotton. It makes amazingly soft yarn, much softer than most wool.

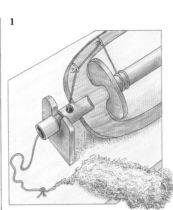

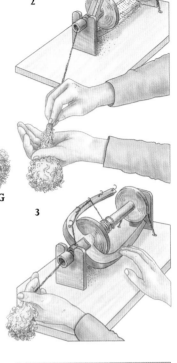

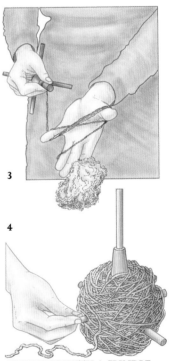

SPINNING WITH A HEDGEHOG

A hedgehog fits on to a treadle. **1** Tie a string around the bobbin, loop over first two hooks, poke through, and tie to your rollag. **2** Treadle, and pull unspun wool from your left hand with your right. **3** When you have a good length of spun wool, stop treadling, move the string on to the next hook, hold the outer bracket still, and treadle. The spun yarn will be drawn on to the bobbin.

TEASING AND CARDING

1 To tease take raw wool and pull out small pieces. **2** Lay teased locks evenly over your left card. **3** Stroke the left card with the right until the fibers are well combed. **4** Transfer fibers from left card to right. Comb and transfer about five times. **5** Get all the wool on one card and roll it off. Make a rollag, by rolling between the card backs or on a table.

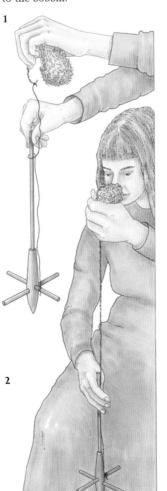

SPINNING WITH A SPINDLE

1 Tie spun yarn to spindle, take a turn around the hand, and tie to your rollag. **2** Spin spindle. Pull unspun wool out between index finger and thumb of left hand. **3** When spindle reaches the ground, haul it up wrapping newly spun wool around fingers. Transfer spun wool back to spindle. Spin new length of wool. **4** Pull out dowels to release wool.

Dyeing & Weaving

DYEING

Stock dyeing—that is, dyeing the fiber in the skein before it is woven—is best for the self-supporter. It is easier thus to get an even distribution of color.

Natural dyes will generally only dye natural materials: they will not dye nylon and the other synthetics. But the right natural vegetable dyes, used with the correct "mordants," will dye any natural fabric with good and fast colors. (Mordants are chemicals that bite into the fabric and give the dye something to fix on.) Although aniline dyes, which are derived from coal tars and other strange chemical substances, can get close to natural colors, they can never quite match them. But if you want very brilliant colors, then you will probably need artificial dyes.

Some plant-derived dyes don't need a mordant, but most do. The mordants that you should be able to make for yourself or come by very readily are vinegar, caustic soda, and ammonia. To get a greater range of colors you need substances like cream of tartar, alum, chrome (potassium dichromate), tin (stannous chloride), and iron (ferrous sulfate). Alum is the most useful one, and if that is the only one you have, you can still do a lot of dyeing.

To mordant with alum, heat 4½ gallons (18 liters) of water, dissolve 4 ounces (115 g) of alum and 1 ounce (28 g) of cream of tartar in a little water, and then add it to the 4½ gallons (18 liters). Immerse 1 pound (0.5 kg) of clean, scoured (washed), dried wool in the form of a skein and simmer for an hour, stirring occasionally. Lift the wool out and press gently.

To prepare your vegetable dye, cut up your vegetable matter into small pieces, let it stand in cold water overnight, and boil it for an hour. Then add more water if necessary. You will need 4½ gallons (18 liters) of dye for a pound (0.5 kg) of wool. Drop wetted, mordanted wool into the dye all at once. The dye should be warm. If it isn't, heat it. Leave the wool in for an hour, occasionally stirring very gently. Then take it out and drain.

A few materials that make strong color are listed below, but the field is open to endless experiments.

Yellow Bark of ash, elder, brickthorn, apple, pear, and cherry; leaves and shoots of broom and gorse; privet leaves; onion skins (not very fast in sunlight, though); marigold flowers; goldenrod; Lombardy poplar leaves; lily-of-the-valley leaves; bog myrtle leaves; dyers' chamomile; spindle tree seeds; pine cones (reddish-yellow); barberry roots and stems (no mordant required).

Green Purging buckthorn berries; heather leaf tips; privet berries (a bluish-green); bracken leaves; spindle tree seeds boiled in alum; elder leaves.

Brown Walnut roots, leaves or husks of shells (no mordant required); slow or blackthorn bark (reddish-brown); boiled juniper berries.

Red Spindle tree seed vessels; blood root.

Black Oak bark, which will dye purple if mixed with tin (stannous chloride). Oak galls make ink.

Purple Bilberries are much used for tweeds in the Highlands of Scotland and are a fine dye (no mordant required); willow roots.

Violet Wild marjoram.

Orange Lungwort lichen, *Sticta pulmonacea* (no mordant required).

Magenta Lichen makes a magenta on the first dye and other colors as you enter successive dye-lots into the same dye. When the dye seems exhausted, freshen it with vinegar and you will get a rosy tan.

BLEACHING

Fabrics can be bleached by soaking them in sour milk and laying them in the sun. A mixture of chlorine and slaked lime also bleaches and is good for flax and cotton. Wool and silk can be bleached with fumes of sulfur. Simply hang the skeins over burning sulfur in an enclosed space.

WEAVING

Weaving on a good hand loom is a magnificent accomplishment, and if you can do it, you have made a big step toward true self-sufficiency. Once you have the loom, and are proficient, you can achieve a considerable output of very good cloth. Machine-woven cloth does not compare with hand-woven, nor have machines yet been devised that can even imitate the hands of the weaver.

Fasten four sticks in a square frame shape, tie lots of threads over them all parallel with each other (the "warp"), and haul another thread (the "weft") through the threads of the warp with a needle or sharpened stick, going over one and under the next thread of the warp and so on. Then bring the needle back with another thread on it, going over the ones you went under before. Keep on doing this and in no time you will see your cloth appear.

If you need to make cloth seriously you will soon find yourself inventing ingenious devices to make your task easier and your cloth better. First, you will devise a comb (*see illustration*) to poke between each pair of threads in the warp and beat the threads of the weft together so that the weave is not too loose. You will have invented the ancestor of the "reed."

Then you will find that it is tedious to keep threading the weft through with a needle, and so you will invent an arrangement of two sets of strings, with loops in their middles, hanging from sticks, and you will thread each thread of the warp through the loop in one of these strings, each alternate thread going to a different set of strings from its neighbors. You will have invented the "heddle." You will lift each set of heddles alternately, on a frame called the "harness" and it will leave a space called the "shed" between the two sets of threads. You will be able to throw your needle through the shed so that you can crisscross, or weave, the threads without having to pick through each individual warp thread with your needle. Next you will find it a nuisance having to attach a new weft thread to your needle each time.

THE SQUARE WEAVER

The simplest loom is the 5-inch (13-cm) "square weaver." It makes 4-inch (10-cm) squares of cloth that can be sewn together as patchwork. String the warp as shown below and weave the weft with a 5-inch (13-cm) needle. Design your own patterns on graph paper (right): on black squares, the weft goes under; on white squares, it goes over.

Pattern with plain weave · **Simple checks** · **Diagonal weave**

Weaving comb

Stick shuttle

Boat shuttle

Warping frame

THE FOUR-HARNESS TABLE LOOM

A table loom takes up less space than a floor loom and does all the same things. It is a little slower because the harnesses are operated with handles instead of pedals.

1 Harness	**4** Cloth beam
2 Heddles	**5** Shed
3 Reed	**6** Warp beam

So you will carve notches at either end of a stick and wind the thread around it in such a way that the stick can turn and release, or pay out, the yarn.

You will have invented the "stick shuttle" (*see illustration*). As you get more inventive, you may invent the "boat shuttle" (*see illustration*), into which you can drop a reel of thread, ready wound. You will soon find that, with all your new gadgets, you quickly come to the end of your weaving frame and only have a small piece of cloth, so you will invent a roller at each end of your loom, one for rolling the threads of the warp on, the other for rolling the newly woven cloth on. This time you will have invented the "warp beam" or "warp roller" (*see illustration*), and the "cloth beam" or "cloth roller" (*see illustration*).

You will also find lifting the alternate harnesses to form your shed a nuisance. So you connect the harnesses up to some foot pedals with an elaborate arrangement of strings. You will have invented "treadles" with "marches" or "lamms" above them to transmit the motion to the harnesses.

Then, if your life depends on weaving an awful lot of cloth, you will devise a sling device worked by a handle, which will fling the shuttle backward and forward through the warp without your having to touch it. By this time, you will have invented the "flying shuttle" and, believe it or not, you will be getting dangerously near the Industrial Revolution.

Now, when you come to thread your new patent loom up with the warp threads, you will find that it is so difficult that you nearly go mad, so you invent a revolving spool, a "warping mill" to wind the threads of the warp around, or else a rack, a warping frame (*see illustration*), with pegs that serve the same purpose.

Finally, you will realize that by having four harnesses instead of two, you can greatly vary the pattern formed by the warp, for you can lift different combinations of warp threads. And by having two or more shuttles, with different colored weft thread in them, you can alter the pattern in other ways.

But to learn to weave you simply must get somebody who knows how to do it to teach you: you cannot learn it out of a book, although a good book on weaving will help.

FINISHING CLOTH

"Fulling" partially felts cloth and makes it denser and stronger. You do it by beating the cloth in water. Try putting it in the bathtub and stamping on it hard. If you add "fuller's earth" you will fill up the pores of the cloth.

"Raising" is done by picking the surface of the cloth, traditionally with "teasels," which are the heads of large thistles. You can often find them growing wild, or you can cultivate them yourself. The effect of raising is to give the cloth a fluffy surface.

Spinning Flax

Flax is the most durable of all the fibers available to us. Synthetic fibers haven't been invented long enough yet to know whether they will outlast flax: my guess is they won't, for quite good-looking pieces of flax linen have been dug up in Egyptian pyramids, and my corlene rope won't last two years.

The crop is harvested before the seed ripens, which is a pity because it means losing the oil the seeds would ultimately produce. It is pulled, not cut, then tied in sheaves and stacked.

Preparing raw flax

Flax must first be "rippled," which means pulling the heads through a row of nails with their heads filed to points. This removes the unripe seeds, which make a marvelous stock food. Then flax is "retted," which really means rotted. Lay it in stagnant water for two or three weeks, until the fibrous sheaf separates easily from the central woody portion. You can ret in running water, but it takes much longer, or you can spread your flax on grass for about six weeks and let the dew do the job. After retting, dry the flax carefully.

Then you must "scutch," which is the process of breaking the stems of the flax. Do this by beating the flax on a table with a broad wooden blade, or with a special "scutcher."

"Hackling" is the next step, and consists of dragging the flax across a bed of nails to remove the "tow," which is all the short fibers, and leave the "line," which is the long ones. The tow can be used for caulking deck seams on boats, or stuffing mattresses, or it can be carded and spun to make a rather coarse and heavy yarn. The line can be spun to make linen thread.

To spin (you don't card line) you have to dress the line on a "distaff," which is simply a vertical stick, or small pole, which can be stuck into a hole in a spinning wheel.

Dressing a distaff

Dressing a flax distaff needs considerable skill. Put an apron on (if you don't happen to be wearing your long bombazine skirt), tie a string around your wais, leaving the two ends a few inches long, and sit down. Take a handful of line, such as falls naturally away from the larger bundle, and tie around one end of it carefully with the two ends of the string around your waist and secure with a reef knot. Cut the two loose ends of the string. Lay the flax out full-length on your lap with the knotted end toward you. Hold the bundle with your left hand at the end farthest from you, pull a few fibers away from the main bundle with your right hand, and lay them on your right knee. Pull some more fibers away and lay them next to the first few. Go on doing this until you have made a thin, fine fan of flax on your lap. Remember that the end closest to you is tied fast.

Now grab the main bundle in your right hand and reverse the process, laying a second fan from left to right

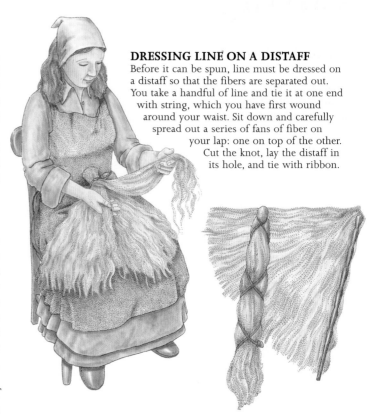

DRESSING LINE ON A DISTAFF
Before it can be spun, line must be dressed on a distaff so that the fibers are separated out. You take a handful of line and tie it at one end with string, which you have first wound around your waist. Sit down and carefully spread out a series of fans of fiber on your lap: one on top of the other. Cut the knot, lay the distaff in its hole, and tie with ribbon.

on top of the first fan, but be sure to pull from the same part of the main bundle. Go on doing this, alternating hands and directions, until all the flax of the bundle has been laid out, in crisscrossing fan shapes, one on top of the other. As you work, try to crisscross the fibers, otherwise they will not pull out properly when you come to spin.

Now cut the string, take it away, and slightly loosen the top end of the bundle where it was tied. Then lay the distaff on one edge of the fan, with its top where the knotted string was. Wind the fan up on the distaff, winding very tightly at the end near you but keeping the flax very loose at the bottom of the distaff. Then put the distaff, with the flax fan around it, upright into its hole and tie the middle of a ribbon tightly around the top. Then crisscross the two ends of the ribbon downward around the cone of flax until you reach the bottom. Tie the two ends in a bow.

Spinning flax

Take the yarn that you have already tied into the bobbin of the wheel and catch it in the flax at the bottom end of the distaff. Spin. Have a bowl of water by you and keep wetting your fingers so as to wet the flax. Use your left hand to stop the spin from going up into the distaff, and your right to clear knots and pull out thick threads. If you have done your dressing operation right, the line should steadily feed itself through the thumb and finger of your left hand into the spinning thread. Turn your distaff as required, and, when you have cleared the distaff as far as the bow in the ribbon, untie the latter and tie it farther up to expose more fibers. Keep doing this until you come to the very top of the distaff and the last few fibers.

Curing & Tanning

Animal skins become hard, like boards, when they have been pulled off the carcass and dried for some time, and then they are good for practically nothing. Early on, mankind found two ways to overcome this disadvantage: mechanical methods that produce rawhide, and chemical methods that produce leather.

To make rawhide, you must take hide straight off the animal and begin working it before it gets hard. In this way you will break down the fibers that set to make it hard, and it will remain permanently soft. A great deal of working is needed. Inuit women, we are told, do it by chewing the hide. Undoubtedly chewing, and working between the hands, for long enough (probably pretty constantly for about a week) will do the trick.

Curing

I use a method that is part mechanical and part chemical to cure sheepskins, fox skins, and especially rabbit skins, which come up beautifully. The end product is a cross between rawhide and leather.

Wash your animal skin well in warm water and then rinse it in a weak borax solution. Then soak it in a solution of sulfuric acid made by mixing 1 pound (0.5 kg) of salt with 1 gallon (4 liters) of water and pouring in ½ ounce (14 g) of concentrated sulfuric acid. Don't throw the water onto the acid, or you may lose your eyes and spoil your beauty.

After three days and nights, take the skin out and rinse it in water and then in a weak borax solution. If you put it in the washing machine and let it churn around for an hour or two, so much the better (after you have washed the acid out of it, of course). Next hang it up and let it half dry.

Take it down and rub oil or fat into the flesh side and work it. Scrape it and pull it around.

Pulling it with both hands backward and forward over the back of a chair is a good method. Leave it hanging over a chair and pull it around every time you go past. Rub more fat in from time to time. It will become quite soft and as good as tanned leather.

Tanning

Tanning with tannin is a purely chemical method, and the end product is leather. It takes half a ton of good oak bark to yield a hundredweight (50 kg) of tannin, and this will cure two hundredweight (100 kg) of fresh hides. Wattle, elder, birch, willow, spruce, larch, and hemlock also contain tannin. The bark must be milled: that is, pounded up small and soaked in water. The hides must be steeped in the resulting solution for four months in the case of small hides, a year in the case of big ones. For really perfect results, it is best to soak hides in a weak solution at first, putting them in increasing strengths as the months go by. A foolproof method is to soak the hides in a weakish solution for, say, a month, and then to lay them in a pit or tank with a thick layer of bark between each skin. Then just cover the pile with water. Leave like this for at least six months.

A quick way of tanning a skin is the "bag method." You make a bag out of a skin (or take the skin off whole). Hang the bag up, and fill it with tannin solution. After a week or two the hide should be tanned. To get the hair off skins, lay them in a paste made of lime and water for three weeks, or in a lime-sulfide paste for a day. De-lime by washing in a weak vinegar solution.

Sewing leather is as easy as sewing cloth: all you need are a few large needles (sailmaker's needles are fine), an awl for making holes in the leather, and some strong waxed thread. Any thread dragged through a lump of beeswax is waxed thread. *For stitches, see illustrations.*

STITCHING LEATHER
You need an awl to make holes, strong needles, and tough waxed thread. The strongest stitch is the opposing stitch. Put a needle on each end of a long thread. Push one needle through the first hole and pull half the thread through. From then on push both needles through each hole, but from opposite directions. The blanket stitch and the crossover stitch are both good for light leather.

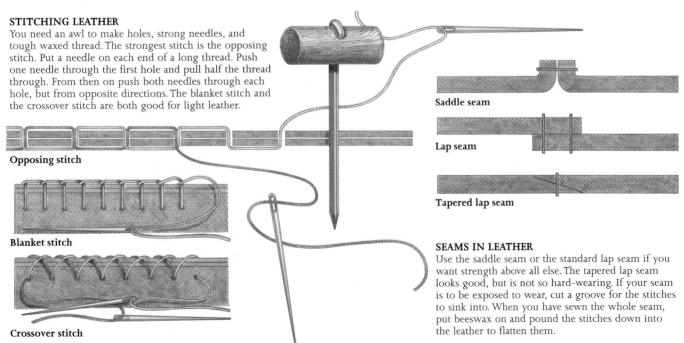

Opposing stitch

Blanket stitch

Crossover stitch

Saddle seam

Lap seam

Tapered lap seam

SEAMS IN LEATHER
Use the saddle seam or the standard lap seam if you want strength above all else. The tapered lap seam looks good, but is not so hard-wearing. If your seam is to be exposed to wear, cut a groove for the stitches to sink into. When you have sewn the whole seam, put beeswax on and pound the stitches down into the leather to flatten them.

Making Bricks & Tiles

If you can avoid it, don't buy clay to make homemade bricks. Instead, try the different clays on your land and in your locality. You are quite likely to find one that makes a good brick, and save yourself a lot of money.

When you have found it, dig the clay and puddle it. You can do this by laying the clay in a pit, wetting it, and trampling it for an hour or two with your feet. This method works very well, but any way of working the clay well with water will do. Then, when the clay is of the right consistency—that is, solid but malleable—you can make bricks using the method described.

Drying and firing bricks

In countries with a rainless, dry season the easiest way to dry bricks is to lay them out in rows on level sand and just leave them. In rainier climes, they must be under cover, and they are usually piled up about six courses high, crisscrossed to leave spaces for the air to circulate.

Bricks have to be left to dry for anything from a week to a month, according to the climate, and then they must be fired. To fire bricks, you must build a clamp, which is basically a rectangular pile, at least the size of a small room, made of bricks crisscrossed so as to leave cavities between them. There are two ways of using the clamp. The first is to leave fireplaces sufficiently large to contain fair-sized wood fires at roughly 3-foot (1-m) intervals on the two long sides of the clamp. Then you plaster the whole clamp with clay, except for some small chimneys at the top of the leeward side, and light fires in the fireplaces on the windward side. If the wind changes, block up the fireplaces on the new leeward side, open up the fireplaces on the new windward side, and use them.

The fireplaces can be rough arches of already burned, or half-burned, bricks, or false arches made by stepping bricks. After firing for a week, let the fires go out and allow the clamp to cool. Open it up, pull out the well-fired bricks, and keep the half-fired ones to be fired again.

The other method, which I think is easier and better, does not require fireplaces. Instead, you fill the gaps between the bricks with charcoal (coal, anthracite, or coke will do). The clamp can be smaller, 7 feet (2.2 m) high by any width or length you like. Plaster the whole clamp with mud, except for a hole at the bottom on the windward side and a hole at the top on the leeward side. Light a small wood fire in the hole on the windward side and go away and forget it. The charcoal will quickly catch. After five or six days, when it has cooled, open the clamp and take your bricks out. You get more completely fired bricks than with the other method.

Tiles

Tiles can be made of the same clay as bricks, but it must be carefully puddled and mixed. They can be flat, or they can be pantiles, which have a convex and concave side, or they can be, as most Mediterranean tiles are, half-cylinders. In Spain and Italy the latter are commonly tapered because, it is said, in Roman times they were molded on a man's thigh. These can be, and often are, made by throwing a cylinder on a potter's wheel and splitting it in half before drying and firing. Any other tile must be made in a mold.

Fire the tiles in the same clamp as the bricks and build it so the bricks take the weight. Tiles are not strong, so they must have holes for nailing or pegging.

BRICKMAKING: THE ESSENTIAL TOOLS

Most important is the mold, which you should make precisely the right size to allow for the shrinkage of your particular clay. Make it from jointed wood and, if you want it to last, put a steel pin secured with a bolt through each end. Make your bow by bending a length of hazel and stringing a wire across it. The cuckle is an excellent tool for moving large amounts of clay. Your sand tray should be deep enough to immerse the mold in. You need a knife for cleaning the mold and boards for drying bricks.

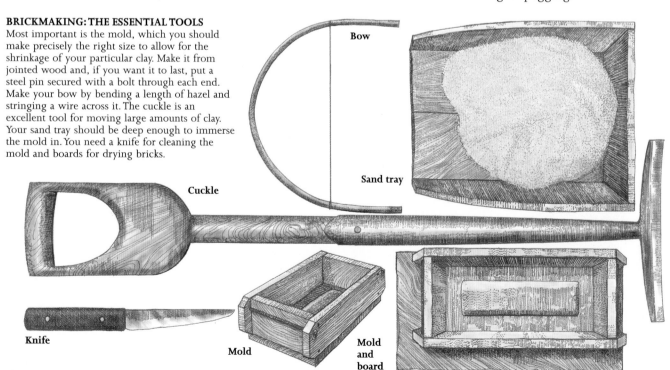

Bow

Sand tray

Cuckle

Knife

Mold

Mold and board

MAKING BRICKS IN A MOLD
Time and practice has determined that bricks should measure 9 inches (23 cm) by 4½ inches (11 cm) by 2¼ inches (5 cm). Depending on your clay and how much it shrinks, your mold must be marginally bigger. Experiment, and make a mold to suit your clay.

1 Clean the inside of your mold by scraping around with a knife.

2 Dampen the mold and coat the inside with sand as you would a cake pan with flour, by dipping in sand and shaking.

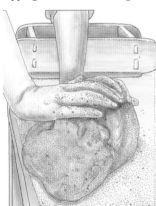

3 Take what you think is the right amount of clay and begin to form a "warp" (a brick-sized lump).

4 Work the warp into the right shape by rolling on a board. Sand the board and your hands to stop the clay from sticking.

5 Once you have the right shape, gather the clay toward you, rolling the ends in.

6 Drop the clay with a spinning action so that it thuds onto the bench. This will knock out all the excess air.

7 Throw the warp hard into the mold so the clay spreads out toward the corners.

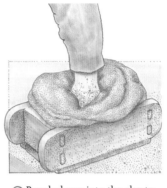

8 Punch down into the clay to push it into the corners and leave a hole in the middle.

9 Ram more clay in the hole and press down very hard into the mold.

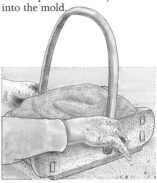

10 Cut off any excess clay by running your bow across the top of the mold.

11 Peel off the severed clay and return it to your pile.

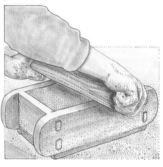

12 Dip a length of wood in water and use it to smooth over, or "strike," the top surface. Then sprinkle the top with sand.

13 Pick up the mould and tap its corners against the bench until you can see gaps on all sides of the clay.

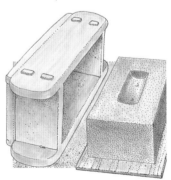

14 Dry the clay brick on a board for about a month.

Working in Stone

Some stone, particularly granite, is awkward for building because it does not split easily in straight lines. Other stone—most sedimentary stone, in fact—has been laid down in layers under water and therefore splits easily along horizontal lines, but they are not necessarily horizontal in the ground. The beds may have been tilted. Still other stone, which builders and quarrymen call freestone, splits easily both horizontally and vertically. This is what the builder is looking for and if he can find it he is a very lucky man. Much of the oolitic limestone from Britain's Jurassic sea is like this: the huge quarries of Barnack in the English county of Northamptonshire supplied much of the material for the great gothic churches and cathedrals of eastern England. In the United States, oolitic limestone quarried in Indiana has been used in many important buildings, including the Pentagon and the Empire State Building.

Freestone can often be split out with wedges instead of explosives. Holes are drilled in a line along the rock, the wedges are driven in, in sequence, farther and farther, until suddenly the rock splits along the line. If you are splitting off a big piece, you can use "the plug and feathers." The feathers are two pieces of steel that you put down either side of a hole drilled in the rock. The plug is a wedge that you drive in between them. The advantage is that the feathers exert a more even pressure than the plug alone, and so the rock splits evenly when it comes away from the parent rock.

Holes are driven in rock by a rock drill, which is a steel bit with an edge like a chisel sharpened at a very obtuse angle. You either hit the bit in with a hammer, turning it between each blow, or you drive it in with a percussion drill. You can drill the hardest rock in the world like this, and in soft rock go quite quickly even with a hand hammer. Put water in the hole for lubrication, and get rid of the ground rock dust by splashing. Wrap a rag around the bit so you don't get splashed in the eye with rock paste.

You can break out, subdivide, and dress to rectangle any rock, even the roughest and most intractable basalt or granite: the harder the rock, the harder the work. You can build with uneven, undressed boulders, and fill the inevitable spaces with—well, just earth, or earth and lime, or in these decadent days, concrete made with cement so the rats can't get in. But there will always be places where you need a solid, rectangular stone: doorsteps, lintels, hearth stones, and other similar things.

Slate is a metamorphic rock, which means it is a sedimentary rock that has undergone great heat and pressure. The original layerings or laminations have been obliterated and others have developed more or less at right angles to the first. It cleaves easily along these. Generally, there are faults or weaknesses in large masses of slate more or less at right angles to the laminations of the slate. These make it possible to break out large blocks without too much blasting. Slate is the very best roofing material, and thicker slabs are ideal for shelves in pantries.

HANDLING THE MASON'S TOOLS

To prepare stone you need two types of chisel and hammer. The points and the edging-in chisel are given sharp, direct blows with a steel hammer. Claws and other chisels must be given softer blows, so for these you use a wooden mallet.

POINTING
Hold the point at an angle and hit sharply with a steel hammer.

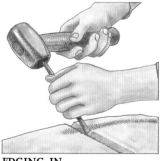

EDGING-IN
To help you control the edging-in chisel, place your thumb across it. Use small, hard, strokes keeping the chisel in position on the stone.

CLEAVING A LARGE BLOCK
Mark around the stone with a pencil. Drill and chisel deep V-shaped slots in the top and sides.

Crowbar the block up and place a steel section below

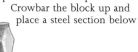

FINISHING A SURFACE
Skim rhythmically with the claw or chisel: **1** place tool on surface; **2** hit firmly with mallet; **3** draw back tool and mallet together and repeat.

1

2

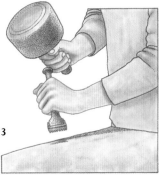

3

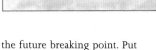

the future breaking point. Put steel wedges in the slots and hit in sequence with a steel hammer, listening to the ring of the stone. It dulls as the stone cleaves.

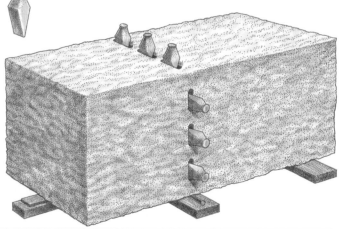

THE MASON'S TOOLS

The heads of the claw and chisel are specially flattened for use with the wooden mallet. The heads of the points and edging-in chisel round over as they are hit repeatedly with the steel hammer.

Brush for dusting away chippings

Large point

Edging-in chisel

Set square

Wooden mallet

Chisel

Steel hammer

Carborundum stone

Small point

Wet and dry paper

Claw bit

Spirit level

Steel rule

1 Dressing stone
To prepare a flat, smooth surface from an unprepared stone, you must follow five distinct processes.

2 Pointing
Use points to knock off large lumps until only small lumps remain.

3 Clawing
Claw in neat lines diagonally across the stone, always working away from any edge.

4 Chiseling
Chisel as though clawing. Very little stone need be removed to give a smooth surface.

5 Using a carborundum stone
To smooth out chisel marks, wet stone and rub surface with a coarse stone using a circular motion. Use water to stop clogging.

WET AND DRY PAPERING
On hard limestone, marble, and granite, you can get a polish by using wet and dry in the following grades: 150, 220, 320, 600 in this order. Use clean water between stages to avoid scratching.

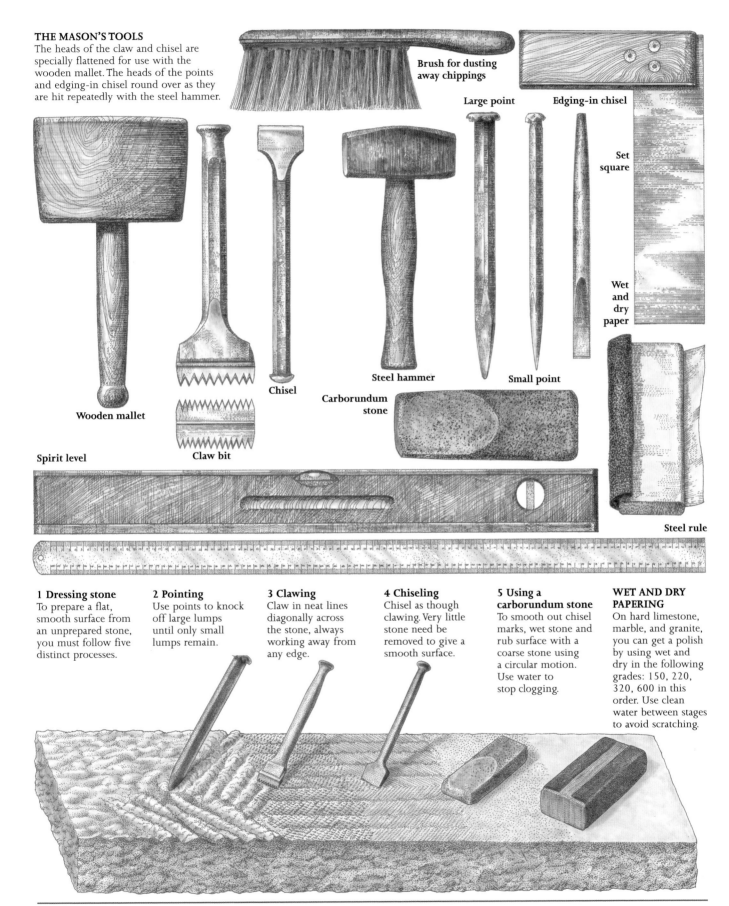

Working in Metal

BLACKSMITHING

To learn to be a proper blacksmith should take seven years, but you can learn to bend, shape, and weld wrought iron in a few hours. To do it well takes practice, though, and you will ruin plenty of iron first. If you are planning to work with iron a lot, you need equipment: a forge, an anvil, a bench with at least one good vise on it, and suitable hammers and tongs. But I have done simple forge work by crawling around on my hands and knees in front of an old cast-iron stove, poking bits of iron into the firebox, and hammering them on the head of a sledgehammer laid on the ground. A little knowledge may be a dangerous thing, but it helps sometimes.

Blacksmiths work with ferrous metal, and there are many kinds. Wrought iron is the blacksmith's classic material. It is made from pig-iron (the stuff that runs out of the bottom of blast furnaces) by persistent heating and hammering. It has enormous advantages for blacksmithing: you can shape it, split it, weld it—in fact, treat it as if it were clay or plasticine—provided you get it to the right temperature. When cold, it is hard (but nothing like as hard as steel), tough, and strong, ideal for much agricultural machinery, chains, shackles, split-links, and the iron components of carts and boats. It doesn't corrode easily.

Cast iron is what it says it is: cast in molds. It is extremely hard, but brittle. It will not stand hammering and it is no good for edge tools, since the edge would just crumble off, but it does not corrode easily. Malleable iron is only used for a few things, like the fingers of mowing machines, which have to be shaped when cold. Steel comes in many forms and qualities. "Mild steel" is much used by blacksmiths nowadays because they cannot get wrought iron. It is nothing like as good, because it is harder to work and it rusts easily.

For forging wrought iron, you need an ordinary blacksmith's forge. This is a fire tray, or hearth, with a pipe, called a tuyere, or tue iron, which blows air into the fire. The tuyere commonly passes through a water bath before it reaches the fire so that it keeps cool enough not to burn away, but sometimes it simply passes through a massive piece of cast iron. Cast iron can stand great heat without melting or burning. The fire can be of coal, coke breeze, or charcoal. If you use coal or coke, clinker will form and hamper your work. Let the clinker solidify and remove it.

Keep the fire as small as possible by wetting the fuel around its center, and place the work to be heated in the heart of the fire. Draw wet coal in sideways as needed: don't dump "green" coal on top of the fire. The blast can be provided by a bellows worked by hand, by an electric air pump, or by a vacuum cleaner turned the wrong way around so it blows instead of sucking, but don't use more blast than you need.

Different jobs require different degrees of heat.

Blood red is for making fairly easy bends in mild steel.

Bright red is for making sharper bends in mild steel, or for punching holes and using the hot chisel in mild steel.

Bright yellow is the heat for most forging jobs in wrought iron, and for drawing down and upsetting (making thinner or making thicker) both wrought iron and mild steel. It is also right for driving holes in or hot chiseling heavy work (iron or steel more than an inch or 2 cm thick).

Slippery heat is just below full welding heat and is used for forging wrought iron and for welding mild steel if it proves difficult to weld it at a higher temperature. It takes speed and skill to weld steel at this heat.

Full welding heat is for welding wrought iron and most kinds of steel. When you reach it, white sparks will be flung off the white hot metal, making it look like a sparkler.

Snowball heat is the temperature for welding very good quality wrought iron, but it is too high for steel. If you go beyond snowball heat, you will burn your metal.

Tempering

Tempering is the process of heating and then cooling metal to give it different degrees of hardness and brittleness. The general rule is that the higher you heat it and the quicker you cool it, the harder it will be, but the more brittle. When tempering a steel cutting tool, you harden it first, by heating it to somewhere between black and blood red and then plunging it into water. When you have done this you temper it by heating it again, dipping the cutting edge into water so as to cool it, then letting the colors creep down from the rest of it until exactly the right color reaches the edge, and then quenching it again.

Welding

To weld wrought iron or mild steel, first get the metal to the right temperature. Then take the first piece out of the fire, knock the dirt off it, and lay it face up on the anvil. Whip the other bit out, knock the dirt off it, lay it face down on the first bit, and hit it in the middle of the weld with a hammer, hard. Keep on walloping it: on the flat if it is flat work, around the beak of the anvil if it is, say, a chain link. But all this has to be done very fast. If the weld hasn't taken, put it in the fire again. If the center has taken but not the outsides, fire again, or "take another heat," as blacksmiths say.

To weld anything harder than wrought iron, more modern forms of welding must be used. From the point of view of the self-supporter, these are oxyacetylene and electric arc. Neither of these are as formidable as they sound: every scrap metal dealer uses oxyacetylene, and many a farmer has his own small electric welding set and uses it, too. But for either gas or electric welding, always wear goggles or a mask. You can blind yourself permanently if you gaze at an arc or a gas flame for just a second or two—it is very easy to do severe damage to your eyes.

Oxyacetylene

Oxyacetylene tackle consists of two pressure bottles, one of oxygen and the other of acetylene. The latter gas, in the presence of oxygen, gives off an intensely hot flame, and a

flame, furthermore, that acts as a protection against oxidation for the hot metal before it cools. The two gases are brought together by pipes and then burned at a nozzle. It is the inner flame that you must use—not the outer. The aim of the welder is to melt rod metal and use it to fuse two metal faces together, and also to fill in any spaces between them. Ideally the edges of the steel plates should be beveled where they meet, and the space left filled with the rod metal.

There are two methods, then, of oxyacetylene welding. One is "leftward," or "forward," welding. In this method the rod, which is made of metal of more or less the same type as the work to be welded, is held in the left hand and moved to the left, while the torch is held in the right hand and follows the rod. The edges of the pieces of steel are preheated. Be careful not to keep the flame in one place too long, or the metal will be distorted. In "rightward," or "backward," welding, the torch is moved to the right, and the rod follows it. Less rod metal is used with this method, and it is considered better than leftward welding, particularly for joining larger pieces of steel, anything over ¼ inch (0.6 cm).

Electric arc
Electric arc welding is a simple matter of using a very high voltage to create a spark at the top of a rod. Held between the two surfaces to be welded, the spark melts them and also the tip of the rod. The material to be welded must be earthed. You can buy quite cheap and simple AC welding sets that work off the domestic supply, and also portable sets that have a small motor to generate current for them.

Sharpening tools
The principle of sharpening is that, if it is just a freshening up of the edge you want, you use a "whetstone," but if the tool has begun to lose shape, then you put it on the "grindstone" first, grind it down to shape, and then hone it on the whetstone afterward. Whetstones come either as slipstones, which are shaped to be held in the hand, or as oilstones, which are mounted in a wooden box and used on a bench. Both should be oiled with thin oil when used. Grindstones are coarser and are frequently circular and mounted with a handle over a trough of water so that they can be kept wet.

Most sharpening stones that you can buy nowadays are artificial with carborundum embedded in them. They are undoubtedly better than anything except the best Arkansas stone, which is an almost pure quartz, grainless and hard.

You must grind your cutting tools at the right angle. This will be a compromise between the acute angle needed for easy cutting and the more obtuse angle needed for strength. A chisel to be whanged with a mallet must have a more obtuse edge than one to be used for delicate carving in the hand. You can buy a guide, or jig, to help set the angle.

USING YOUR ANVIL
If you want to work with metal, get an anvil. Most of your work is done on the anvil's "face," the flat section at the top. You should use the "table," the short step down, for pulling out nails or

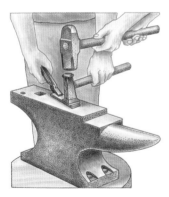

for cutting or chopping, because its surface won't damage. The "beak," the long pointed part, is for working anything that needs a curved edge. To flatten metal, or remove marks made by a hammer or other tool, you should hold hot metal on the face of your anvil with tongs, hold a flatter over it, and whack it with a sledgehammer until you achieve the desired effect.

THE HAMMER AND PRITCHELL
To make holes in any metal, and particularly in horseshoes, you should use a pritchell, which is a square-handled punch. Again, use this on your anvil's face and hit it with a heavy blacksmith's Warrington pattern hammer (*above*), or with a ball peen hammer. If you need to make a large hole, do it over the round hole in the "tail wedge" of your anvil to avoid damaging the table underneath. One of your most important tools will be your pincers. You need them for bending metal, and just holding

things. The longer the handles, and the smaller the head, the greater the leverage.

THE TOP AND BOTTOM SWAGE
The swages are for shaping circular rods from hot iron, or for bending rods or pipes. The bottom swage slots into the square "hardie hole" in the anvil's tail wedge.

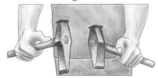

HOT SETT AND COLD SETT
The hot sett (left), with an edge sharpened to about 35 degrees, cuts hot metal. Place it on the metal and wallop with a sledgehammer. The cold sett (right), whose edge is about 60 degrees, will cut light iron or mild steel cold.

LEG VISE AND SCROLL WRENCH
The best vise for a smithy is a leg vise. It will stand up to heavy hammering because it is made of wrought iron, instead of the more normal cast iron, and some of the load is transferred through the leg to the floor. The front arm is held on a hinge and is opened by a spring. The leg vise is excellent for bending metal, because the leg will stand up to heavy levering. A scroll wrench has rounded jaws for pulling strip metal, especially wrought iron, into curves. Quite intricate designs can be made with it.

Building & Thatching

COB & MUD BUILDING

The cheapest way to construct a solid building is to use mud and thatch, and don't be put off by the way it sounds. Mud is rot-proof and fireproof, and it keeps sound out and heat in pretty efficiently. Mud for building should be fairly free of organic matter, so dig it from well below the surface: from 2 to 3 feet (60–90 cm) is best. Save your humus-laden topsoil for growing things.

Your building should be simple, with large areas of unbroken wall, few and small windows, all loads well spread on timber plates, and no outward-thrusting roofs.

An easy but effective method of building with mud is cob building. Cob is simply clayey or chalky mud, mixed with straw and laid in 1-foot (30-cm) layers with a shovel and trowel. Each layer is laid at a different angle from the one below it, so that there is a certain amount of binding. The wall should be at least 18 inches (45 cm) thick, 24 inches (60 cm) if your building is to be more than one story tall. You cannot build very fast with this method, for each course has to dry out to some extent before the next one is laid on it. The resulting wall is only weatherproof if you keep its "head" and its "feet" dry. In other words, give your building a good overhanging roof and solid foundations, using concrete if possible. And if you can, build a base wall of stone or brick, preferably with a damp-proof course (slate is impervious to water and makes a good one), on top of your foundations up to ground level. The outside, too, should be protected by cement rendering if possible: otherwise with a lime and sand mortar rendering, or at least a thick whitewash. Broken glass is sometimes embedded in the base of a cob wall to deter rats. Window sills must be protected by slate or other stone or concrete.

Rammed earth (otherwise known as adobe) blocks are an improvement on cob because shrinkage takes place in the brick before the wall is built, you can make smoother surfaces, and you can easily build cavity walls. The blocks are made by ramming a mud and straw mixture into wooden molds. Dry them in the shade, so that they don't dry too quickly and crack. The earth should be, like brick earth, of the right consistency for the job: that is, a benign mixture of clay and sand. The higher the clay content, the more straw you add—up to 20 percent straw by volume.

African hut

To make an African hut, dig a circular trench, stand straight, wall-height poles in it so that they touch one another, and stamp them in, leaving a space for the door. You can have one section shorter than the others if you want a window. Then, on the ground, make a conical roof of what is basically giant thatched basketwork. Get some friends to help you lift the roof and lash it on to the circular wall. Plaster the pole wall with mud, preferably mixed with cow manure. If you rub the earth floor with cow dung and sweep it every day, it will become as hard and clean as concrete.

BUILDING WITH MUD AND THATCH

You can build yourself a warm and solid house or barn mainly out of mud and straw. To make your building last you should build foundations. "Cyclopean concrete," which is large stones embedded in concrete, is effective and fairly cheap. On top of this, build a stone or brick wall to just above ground level and top it with a damp course, ideally of slate. Walls can be built of cob, which is mud mixed with straw. Make your wall at least 18 inches (45 cm) thick and lay in courses 12 inches (30 cm) deep. Allow two or three weeks' drying between courses. To keep rats out of your house, you can set broken glass in the wall at ground level. Use slate sills and timber lintels for windows. Render the outside with cement or lime "rough cast," a lime and sand mixture. Apply two coats of pitch at the base to keep it dry. Top the wall with a timber wall plate and to this attach your tie beams, which run right across from wall to wall. Each beam carries a king post, which supports the ridge and the struts, which in turn support the principals. The purlins run the length of the building, principal to principal, and carry the rafters to which you nail the battens that will key your thatch. Fix joints with strong bolts.

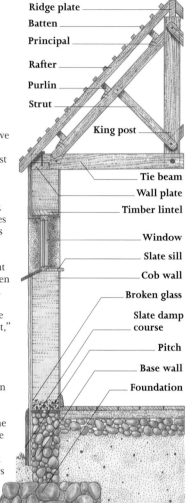

Ridge plate
Batten
Principal
Rafter
Purlin
Strut
King post
Tie beam
Wall plate
Timber lintel
Window
Slate sill
Cob wall
Broken glass
Slate damp course
Pitch
Base wall
Foundation

THATCHING

Phragmites communis, commonly called "Norfolk reed," is the best thatching material there is. A good roof of reed will last 70 years. A roof of "wheat reed"—simply wheat straw that has not been broken in the threshing—may well survive 20 or 30 years. Wheat straw that has been threshed and stored in a stack can be used for thatching ricks. To get it ready for thatching, you "pull" it by hauling some down to the foot of the stack and throwing several buckets of water on it. Then you pull the wet straw in handfuls from the bottom of the heap. Because the straw is wet the handfuls come out straight, with the straws all parallel to each other. Lay the straws in neat piles about 6 inches (15 cm) in diameter. Tie these with twine or straw rope to make your "yealms." The secret of thatching is that each layer should cover the fastenings that tie down the layer below it, so that no fastenings are visible or exposed to the weather. In practice this means that each layer must cover just over three quarters of the layer below it.

Ricks

Rick thatching is fairly easy and uses comparatively little material. You only need a coat of thatch 2 or 3 inches (5-8 cm) thick to shed the rain.

TOOLS FOR THATCHING

A shearing hook **1** and thatching shears **8** trim thatch, a rake **2** combs it, and a leggat **3** shapes it. A whimbel **4** is for making bonds, the long twists of straw for tying yealms. Brortches **6** cut from hazel with a spar hook **5** hold the thatch down, and iron hooks **7** secure it to the rafters. Protective knee and hand pads **9** are essential.

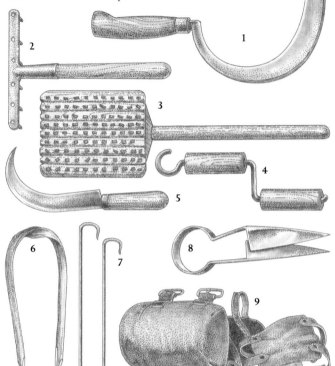

THATCHING A ROOF

Always begin thatching at the eaves on the right hand side. Secure a short row of yealms (straw bundles) to the roof with sways, lengths of flexible hazel held to the rafters with iron hooks. Gather the straw up at the upper end of each yealm by pushing in a brortch. Keep laying rows of yealms, each overlapping the one below, until you reach the ridge. Then move the ladder to the left and thatch another stretch of roof. Carry on like this until you reach the ridge on both sides of the roof.

To thatch the ridge, lay a row of yealms horizontally along it, and cover them with more yealms folded over the ridge and secured on both sides with sways, brortches, and hooks. You can use hazel sways to decorate the roof.

Lay the straw or reed, ears upward, in a row along the eaves of the rick. Hold this first row down with one or two lengths of string, and hold the string itself down with "brortches." These are 2-foot (60-cm) lengths of hazel or willow (I prefer hazel), twisted in the middle, bent into a hairpin shape, and sharpened at both ends. Ram your brortches down over the string and bang them into the rick with a mallet, so that they hold the string down tight. Space the brortches at the intervals that common sense suggests (every thatcher has his own ideas). Now lay your next layer of straw so that it overlaps a little more than three quarters of the first layer and covers the strings. Peg this down, too, with string and brortches. Go on, layer after layer, until you get to the top.

You then have the problem of ridging. Make bundles of straw about big enough to clasp in both hands, tie them tightly with string, and lay them along the ridge of the rick. Then lay long straw over these bundles so that it overlaps the top layer of thatch on both sides of the ridge. String and brortch this down on both sides. Or, better still, use hazel or willow rods instead of string here, and brortch them down. Make a pretty crisscross pattern if you like. Of course, with a round rick you don't have a ridge, but a point, and this makes the job much easier.

It is a very simple matter to fashion a conical cap of straw and fasten it down with brortches.

Buildings

You can thatch a building with a comparatively thin layer of straw laid on, much as in rick thatching, pretty well parallel with the slope of the roof. This makes a watertight thatch, provided the pitch is steep enough, but in a wet climate it is unlikely to last more than two years.

Thick thatching is quite different (*see illustration*). The bundles of reed are laid on much closer to horizontal, so that the coat of thatch is nearly, but not quite, as thick as the reed is long. Building such a roof takes an enormous quantity of material, a lot of time, the right equipment, and a great deal of skill. But if made of true reed, it will last a lifetime. It is completely noiseproof, very warm in winter, and cool in summer: in fact, it is quite simply the best insulation in the world.

If you are building a mudhouse or barn, use rough, unsawn, and unriven poles for the framework of the roof, and they don't have to be seasoned. Thatch is flexible and if the timber moves, it doesn't matter. The timber will season naturally in the well-ventilated conditions of a thatched roof, and generally last at least as long as the thatch.

Scything

The traditional scythe consists of a long blade of sharpened spring steel fixed by a simple ring and wedge to an ash frame (*see also p.248*)—and a well-swung, sharp scythe is a thing of great beauty. There is little that can beat the wonderfully satisfying scrunch of a really sharp scythe as it cuts the grass and magically peels it away to form a windrow. There are three quite distinct skills involved in scything: the first is how to set and sharpen your scythe; the second is how to perfect a smooth stroke to cut the grass; and the third is how to plan your attack to make best use of the lie of the vegetation.

Setting the Scythe

The set of the scythe must be adjusted to suit the size and style of the user. Traditionally, this was done by the local blacksmith, who could heat up the fixing pin and bend it to just the correct alignment. Today you might have to persuade your local garage to make any adjustments.

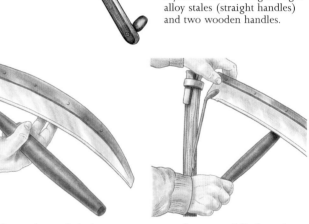

Pin prevents blade from flexing

English scythe

Northumberland A-frame scythe

SCYTHES
English sneads (scythe handles) were traditionally steamed and bent, and the trusty tempered blades were made by the village blacksmith. Modern scythes come with lightweight alloy stales (straight handles) and two wooden handles.

SHARPENING A SCYTHE

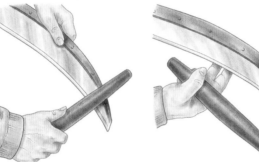

1 Turn the scythe upside down; grasp the back of the blade firmly in your left hand so the sharp side is facing toward your right hand. Press the sharpening stone firmly against the blade.

2 Sharpen at the shallowest possible angle so the stone is just touching the band on the outside of the blade. Move the stone along the blade in small circles, from tip to handle.

3 The result is a slight burr or sliver of metal pushed down off the blade's edge. Feel for this carefully by pulling your fingers at right angles to the line of the blade across the underside.

4 Feel very carefully from the outer edge. Now, strop (swipe back and forth) the blade quickly to remove the burr, and do this along both sides of the edge in turn.

USING A SCYTHE

1 Test the sharpness of the edge by resting the blade on the ground as if to cut. Gently press down and move backward and forward. It should cut even the shortest grass easily.

2 The scythe is pulled around in a short arc with the back of the blade in firm contact with the ground. Do not use it as a chopper, and remember, it does not need to move fast to cut.

3 Throughout the stroke you must keep the tip of the scythe up and the heel of the scythe pushed firmly down using the right hand. You are looking for a gentle rolling action.

4 The outside of the blade may be blunt, so slip the point between vegetation and a chosen tree and then slide the blade forward. Continue around the plant until you clear a full circle.

LIE OF THE LAND
Plan your cutting to take advantage of the lie of the grass produced by wind and rain. Always cut away from standing vegetation toward the cut area.

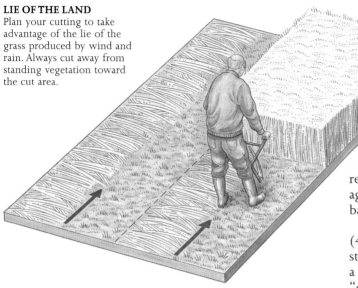

The objective is to have the blade of the scythe running parallel to the ground and lying comfortably on it when held in the scything position. Make sure the blade is very firmly fixed to the handles by getting a good fit between the wedge and the steel ring. You hammer down the wedge by turning the scythe over and resting the handle on the ground. The short stay should be a tight fit, being fastened to the frame by a single screw.

Sharpening your scythe

A good scythe blade is quite literally as sharp as a razor and will cut paper with ease. It is vital to keep the blade this way *at all times*—your scythe will not cut if it is blunt, and your efforts will almost certainly damage the instrument, as well as your self-esteem.

Be very careful to avoid touching the blade. The only time you will have to touch it is when you're feeling for burrs, followed by stropping with the stone, which simply takes off the burr and gives a nice, clean edge (*see illustration, left*).

If in doubt, I always recommend you try to watch someone with more experience first if you can. You will see the area you are sharpening become bright as the tarnished metal is worn away. But your scythe is nowhere near sharp until the bright area stretches all the way to the edge of the blade.

In tough grass you may have to sharpen the blade every 20 or 30 strokes—but you will waste much less time if you do this frequently, rather than waiting until the blade is really blunt, when you will have a tough time getting it sharp again. It may take 20 minutes or more to bring up a good edge the first time you get to work on a new blade. Sharpening is the hardest skill of all, but it is the essence of good scything. If you cut yourself, run your hand under cold water immediately and you will find it heals very quickly and neatly, since the blade must have been good and sharp!

Cutting grass

Set your scythe so that the blade runs comfortably parallel to the ground when you hold the handles. Take advantage of the lie of the grass produced by wind and rain. Always cut away from standing vegetation (*see illustration, left*). It is best to experiment with short, firm, little strokes backward and forward to give you that first feeling of how a sharp blade will sweetly cut the grass. You should gradually extend the length of your stroke, always remembering to keep the back of the blade pressed against the earth. You will only tire yourself and develop bad habits if you try to take too big a swing at first.

You can cut along by scything across about 18 inches (45 cm) of grass in each stroke, and by taking the next stroke just one or two inches farther on. You need to keep a firm grip on both handles and avoid any temptation to "chop." As soon as the scythe loses its edge, get to work with your stone.

Always keep a careful watch for stones or posts well to the sides of the row you are cutting. The tip of your scythe will extend maybe 3 feet (90 cm) and it is vital not to damage this important part of the scythe.

Carry your sharpening stone with you, preferably in your back pocket. These stones get lost, "walk," or break very easily. I always wear decent-length rubber boots, even in hot weather; if you cut through a nest of red ants, these little beasts make very uncomfortable companions inside ordinary shoes. You have been warned! You will quite often come across frogs when you are scything, so try to keep an eye out for them.

Tips for the tip

Beginners frequently have problems because they have not realized how important it is to have the scythe very sharp at the tip. You will always have to give this part of the blade special attention. The tip is the first part of the blade to come in contact with the grass, and if it pushes it over rather than cutting it, your stroke will be much, much harder. When a tip breaks off, you must grind down the end of your scythe to make a new tip—a scythe with a broken end simply will not work.

Special jobs for the scythe

It is a pleasant and important task to scythe around young trees in May. Once is usually enough to keep the grass down, provided you cut right to soil level. Using a sharp scythe is a pain-free way of clearing brambles and small scrub. The scythe will slice through bramble stems easily with firm pressure and a good edge. Use your scythe to cut weeds before rototilling the vegetable garden. This way you can rake off the vegetation and dump it straight on to the compost heap in a matter of minutes. For trimming grass edges along turf around the vegetable patch, you cannot beat the scythe for speed and simplicity.

Woodworking

Woodworking is a vital skill for the self-supporter. It may be making a small box to store apples, repairing stalls for animals, building a hen house, or making a roof. But it seems that hardly a day will pass without some activity connected to woodwork. You will need to have a good set of basic tools and you will need to take care of them. Not only do good tools get damaged easily, they are also prone to "walk" when other people are around. A locked storage space is one answer to this.

In addition to tools, you will need to keep a decent supply of screws and fastenings, glues and mastics, and paints and thinners. Generally, it is much easier to buy screws by the box, and you will be surprised how fast they get used up. There is a vast range of screws and nails available: nails are usually sold by weight at the hardware store. It is extremely important to have the right fixings for the job in hand.

QUICKFIT CLAMPS
A quick and easy alternative to the traditional (and heavy) vise, quickfit clamps are a relatively new product, and you will find that having a couple always to hand means you have effectively another pair of hands. You can clamp pieces of wood firmly and quickly to your bench (or simply a large plank if you are working on a construction site), and you can clamp pieces together easily to assist with fixing. The one-hand quick-release mechanism is very handy when you have several tasks going at the same time. I also keep a much larger pair of what are called "sash cramps," which I tend to use to hold together large pieces of work during fixing and gluing. Like all tools, these do not deteriorate over time, so having several is usually a good investment.

WOOD SCREWS AND NAILS
Here are the essential screws and nails needed for any woodwork projects. Keep a selection of these handy in your toolbox.

Countersunk wood screw
The traditional fixing for woodwork. This screw needs a hole drilled first to avoid splitting the wood, plus countersink to recess head. Use with a screw-cup for added strength.

Roundhead screw
Another traditional fixing that requires a hole drilled first and leaves the head proud.

Posi-drive screw
Now almost universally used with modern electric or cordless screwdrivers, the beauty of these screws is that no pilot hole is required. The fixing will also grip tight even if screwed into endgrain wood.

Coach screw
The coach screw is a very strong fixing for outdoor work. It requires a pilot hole and must be tightened with a wrench. Use the galvanized versions for long life.

Lost head nail
The "lost" element refers to the small round head that is easily knocked into the work, especially useful for floorboards. Use a nail punch to push it below the surface and make it invisible.

Clout-galvanized nail
A nail for external work such as for for fixing roofing battens. These nails also provide a cheap way to fasten slates. Clouts come in all shapes and sizes—both length and thickness. Make sure you know exactly which size you need, especially if fixing roofing where you do not want sharp ends going through your felting.

Flathead wire nail
The standard nail for fixing. It also comes in galvanized form for outdoor use. You can't have too many of these handy fixers.

Cut clasp nail
Often used for fastening floorboards, this square section nail is excellent for avoiding splits in the wood.

Roofing nail
A heavy, twisted and galvanized nail that will not pull out of roofing in wind or gales.

Masonry nail
Toughened steel nail for fastening directly into masonry. Can be difficult to use: watch out for sparks and splinters.

Ribbed flooring nail
A nail used to fix hardboard and chipboard flooring down so it will not loosen and squeak.

Staple
Comes in different sizes and is usually galvanized for fixing wire to fencing—such as chicken wire to posts for a run.

Anchor fixing
A fixing that is simply hammered into the correct-sized hole made by a masonry drill.

Expanding masonry bolt
The ultimate fixing for fastening into stone or masonry. Tremendous load-bearing capabilities. Requires the right size of masonry bit to make a good joint.

DOWEL JOINTS

For a neat, strong, and relatively easy joint between two pieces of wood, you can now buy dowel kits from most good hardware stores. The kit has short lengths of different-diameter hardwood doweling, a set of wood drills exactly the right size to take each size of doweling, plus a small plug cutter so you can seal and disguise doweling holes if you need to. To achieve workable dowels, holes of exactly the right size must be drilled in each piece to be joined.

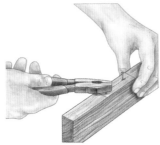

3 Drill holes in the piece to be joined and insert dowels with glue to half their length.

DOWEL JOINT

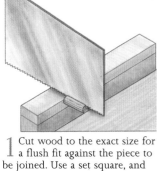

Dowel

Positioning must be exact, so the dowels (round pins) match up in correct alignment within the glued joint.

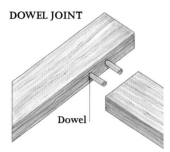

1 Cut wood to the exact size for a flush fit against the piece to be joined. Use a set square, and make sure you cut the correct side of the drawn line.

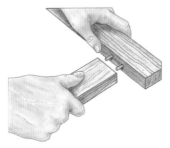

2 Mark the center of the end grain with a sharp scribe.

4 Now marry up the fixed dowels to the end grain of the marked piece. Mark centers exactly and use a square to drop down to center line.

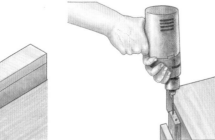

5 Now drill out the two final dowel holes, taking care to keep the drill perfectly perpendicular to the end grain.

6 Hand-join the two pieces of wood and tap the dowels home with a little glue, and your joint is complete. Clamp, if necessary, until the glue is set.

MORTISE AND TENON JOINTS

The basic joint for the "joiner" who graduates from using dowels is the mortise and tenon joint. This joint, or variants of it, would be useful for tables or gates. With a little practice and care, you will soon get the hang of it and produce strong and neat results. Accurate marking-out is vitally important, and you must learn to decide whether to cut lines off or cut inside them. Think about this carefully or your tolerances will be too great. Always use a good glue to finish the job.

MORTISE AND TENON JOINT

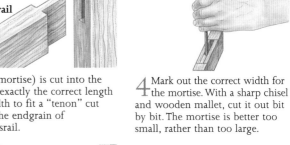

Siderail

Crossrail

A slot (mortise) is cut into the siderail exactly the correct length and width to fit a "tenon" cut out of the endgrain of the crossrail.

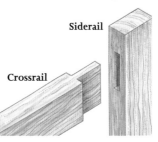

1 Mark out the length of the mortise carefully using the crossrail. Use a square throughout to extend lines across the rail.

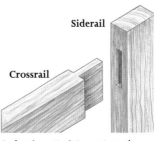

2 Mark off the length of the tenon (again, with a square). Don't make it too long or you may go through the back of the mortise on the siderail.

3 Carefully scribe the marks for the edges of the tenons at each end of the cross rails. Cut these out accurately with a sharp saw and a firm vise. Pare down with a sharp chisel if the saw goes awry.

4 Mark out the correct width for the mortise. With a sharp chisel and wooden mallet, cut it out bit by bit. The mortise is better too small, rather than too large.

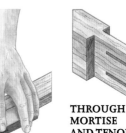

5 Offer up the tenon into the mortise to check for a tight fit. Use your chisel again if you need to perfect the fit. You will see why a smaller mortise is better.

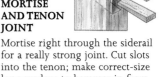

THROUGH MORTISE AND TENON JOINT

Mortise right through the siderail for a really strong joint. Cut slots into the tenon; make correct-size long wedges to hammer in from outside when joint is positioned.

A good quality power screwdriver will last for many years if you treat it well and use the battery sensibly. These batteries must not be recharged when they are only partially discharged. If you do this you will destroy the ability of the battery to store charge. So always run the battery down until it is absolutely flat and you will get many years of use from it.

Choosing your wood

For most of your tasks you will be selecting your wood from a lumber yard. And I mean selecting: do not trust the place to choose wood for you or you will certainly end up with all the lengths left by others. Remember, too, that each lumber yards will have its own standards. Some

managers will be very fussy about the lumber they will accept; others simply do not give quality of lumber any priority and get whatever is cheapest. Try to use an outlet that sets reasonably high standards if you can find one: it will save you a lot of trouble, even if it costs a bit more.

As a quick checklist, here is what to look for in your timber.

1. Timber that is straight. Use your good, old mark one eyeball, that is, inspect the wood thoroughly for any warpsor bends. You may be horrified by what you might have been fobbed off with.

2. Timber that has no splits.

3. Timber without many knots in the wrong places.

4. Timber that has, if possible, the grain running in a way

CHOOSING WOOD

Learning to understand the grain of wood and how it will affect its future importance is critical. All wood shrinks as it dries out and "seasons." If the grain runs straight through the wood (*below,*

left) then the wood shrinks evenly and will neither warp nor split. If the grain runs across or diagonally then the wood will warp (*below, right*). Choose wood which looks like the former rather than the latter.

MAKING A BOX

This is a simple but effective method of constructing a strong wooden box which will come handy in for all sorts of useful jobs on your farm. Use good-quality plywood and well-chosen 6-by-1 pine planking. For best results, add round beading around the inside after completion, and up the insides of the corners.

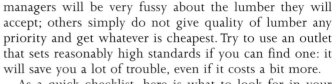

1 Cut your 6 inch (15 cm) planking to accurate lengths, using a set square to make sure the ends are exactly at 90 degrees to the sides. Next, cut the plywood base to the correct size.

2 When you cut the plywood base, make sure again that you have corners which are accurate right angles. Cut the base too big rather than too small so you can plane down later.

3 Take off any rough edges with sandpaper or a sharp plane. This applies to saw edges as well as the sides of the planking. You'll need to apply some pressure as you sandpaper.

4 Now screw the ends of the box onto the plywood base. Use countersunk screws either galvanized or brass for outdoor use. These are custom-made for weathering.

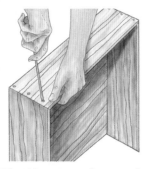

5 The sides can now be screwed into the end grain of the ends which have already been fixed. Posi-drive screws work well for this and will pull themselves into the wood.

6 Make sure corners fit exactly and sand off any rough or overlapping edges. You have to work quite hard at this, since the corners are quite tricky to make contact with.

7 Finish screwing on the base, and be sure to use plenty of screws to do the job effectively. A cordless screwdriver is the best tool for this job.

8 Cut hand holes as needed. First, use a drill to make a hole large enough to take the blade of the jigsaw. Then carefully cut out the hand holes. Finally, smooth them with sandpaper.

that will prevent future warping. This is particularly important for critical items like door posts.

5. Wood that comes in quarter-sawn planks for any kind of quality carpentry. When you look at the grain end-on, it should run at right angles to the side of the board all the way across. Remember that the businessmen are trying to get as many planks as they can from each tree, and this is a much more important consideration for them than cutting for stability.

Making a lathe

A simple wooden foot-powered lathe can be made very easily, and although it works slowly it works as well as any other lathe for wood-turning. Plant two wooden uprights in the ground, or if you live indoors attach them to the floor, about 3 feet (90 cm) apart; 6-inch by 4-inch (15-cm by 10-cm) posts are ideal. Nail a block of wood to each post, just at hand height, and on a level with each other. Drill a hole in each block big enough to take the ends of

the "stock," which is the piece of wood to be turned. (You will have to whittle down the ends of this with a knife to make it small enough to fit the holes.) Arrange a simple foot pedal below. This can just be a piece of wood, held at one end by a pin which is supported on two short stakes. Then arrange a bendy, horizontal pole of ash, or other springy wood, above the contraption, so that one end sticks out and can be bent up and down. You can use trees, stakes, or, if indoors, the rafters to support this pole.

Tie a piece of rope to the foot pedal, take one turn with it around the stock, tie the other end to the end of the whippy pole. Nail another piece of wood across the posts next to your stock to rest your chisel on, and you have a lathe. Depress the pedal and the stock turns one way, release it and the pole above your head straightens and turns it the other way. You only make your cut when it's turning the right way, of course. Wood turning is skilled work (*see illustrations below*). If you can, go and watch a skilled craftsman at work.

TURNING A BOWL ON A LATHE

These pictures show a bowl being turned on a simple lathe powered by electricity, but you can turn a bowl in the same way on a treadle lathe, or, rather laboriously, on a chair bodger's

pole lathe. If you use the latter you must replace the stock with a rod fixed to a chuck to which the bowl can be attached. For the heavy work of removing unwanted wood you need three gouges of differing thicknesses (*above right*), and for the more delicate shaping and smoothing you need scrapers (*above left*), Never press hard with any tool, particularly a gouge. If they stick, you are in trouble. Keep your tools sharp.

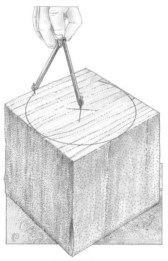

1 Take a block of wood, mark the center with a cross, and draw a circle with a compass slightly larger—say, ¼ inch (6 mm)—than the intended diameter of your bowl.

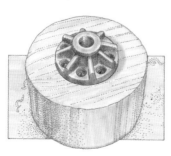

2 Cut roughly around your circle with a saw. Then establish the midpoint for your chuck and screw it on evenly.

Use short, strong screws because the base of your bowl must be thicker than your screws are long. Your work will be ruined if you come down to a screw when shaping the inside.

3 Round off edges with a large gouge.

4 Shape the outside with a smaller gouge. Use the handrest and keep the gouge moving slowly along it.

5 Smooth off the outside with your scrapers. Then, keeping the bowl on the lathe, rub with sandpaper, which will give the wood a gloriously smooth finish.

6 Move the handrest to work on the inside. The unbreakable rule for hollowing wood on a lathe is: begin at the outside and work toward the center. Start with a gouge, then scrape with rounded scrapers only, and finally sandpaper it smooth. Remove the chuck from the lathe, unscrew it, and fill the holes with plastic wood. Polish it all with beeswax and glue felt on the bottom.

Household Items

SOAP

The first lion I ever shot had been eating a friend of mine's donkeys in Africa. It had a thick layer of fat on it, and my friend's mother turned this into soap. She did it by the simple method of boiling the fat with caustic soda. It worked, but was pretty rough stuff.

The chemistry of soap-making is to boil an alkaline with fat, which is an acid. The alkaline, or lye, as soap-boilers call it, can be practically any alkali, and caustic soda will do. But there is a simple way of making your own lye. Knock some holes in the bottom of a barrel, lay some straw in the bottom, fill the barrel with wood-ash, and pour a bucketful of cold water on top of the ash. Pour on a bucketful every three or four hours on the first, third, and fifth day. The water that drips out of the bottom of the barrel will be lye.

Now, to make soap, take your fat and clarify it by melting it in a slow oven, straining it into cold water, and then skimming it off the water. If you haven't shot a lion, practically any fat will do: dripping, lard, chicken fat, goose fat, and so on. Melt the fat again and let it cool to lukewarm. At the same time, warm your lye to lukewarm, too. Then, very slowly pour the lye into the fat (if you pour it too fast, it will not mix) and stir it very gently with a wooden spoon. When the mixture begins to drip from your spoon like honey, stop pouring. If you want to make your soap stronger, pour in a solution of borax and water (8 tablespoons of borax to 1 pint (0.5 liter) of water) and a dash of ammonia. To half a gallon (2 liters) of soap mixture add 1 pint (0.5 liter) of the borax solution and half a cup of ammonia. Put a board over the mixture, cover it with a carpet, leave until the next day, and cut it.

If you want a soap that will make you and your friends smell good, use:

- 1 lb (0.5 kg) good fat or tallow
- 1 cup of olive oil
- 1 cup of peanut oil
- ½ cup of water with 2 tablespoons lye in it
- 1 cup of water with perfume in it

To perfume the soap, use the aroma of your choice from a range of essential oils bought from the drugstore. Use about 3 tablespoons of it. You can also make your own perfume out of lavender, rosemary, lemon balm, or a score of other flowers or herbs you can grow yourself, in which case you would probably add more. Melt the fat, add the oils and the scent to it, and warm to 90°F (32°C), stirring all the while, of course. Meanwhile, mix the lye and the water and pour it into the fat and oil mixture—and don't stop stirring. When the mixture thickens, pour it into molds of any fancy shape you like.

Saddle soap

To make saddle soap, use:

- 6 cups of tallow
- 1 cup of lye
- 2½ cups of water

Heat the tallow to 130°F (54°C). Dissolve the lye in the water and then let it cool down to 95°F (35°C). Once it reaches this temperature, pour it slowly into the tallow, stirring all the time. Just before it is ready for molding, pour in 1 cup of glycerine and stir.

SUGAR

From sugar beets

Cut the tops off your sugar beets and press the juice out of them any way you can: with a cider press, a car jack, or an old-fashioned mangle. Boil the juice until all the liquid has evaporated and you are left with unrefined sugar. Refining it is a complicated process involving lime and carbon dioxide. Anyway, it would be madness to refine this further, for unrefined sugar is nourishing and good for all the purposes of sugar, while refined sugar contains 99.9 percent sucrose, absolutely no vitamins, and nothing else that is of any use at all to body or soul.

From sugar cane

Sugar cane must be thoroughly crushed to produce syrup. Cane is tough stuff and full of long fibers, so you need either a lot of strength and a mortar and pestle, or a steel crushing mill. Put the syrup you've managed to extract into a copper boiler, over a fire that you can fuel with the spent cane. Boiling turns the syrup into what in India is called "gor," which is unrefined sugar. As I have said above, it is a waste of time to refine sugar any further, and it is much better for you like this.

Maple sugar

To make this you must tap the sugar maple tree in the chilly month of March, by drilling the trunk and driving in a "spile," which is a short tube you can buy or make yourself out of bamboo, willow, sumac, elder, or anything you can hollow out. Hang a container under the spile (an old can will do, or a bucket, or a plastic bag) and cover it to keep insects out.

As soon as the sap runs, carry it to the "arch" (leaving it too long will spoil it). The "arch" is a boiler placed over a wood fire that needs to be kept blazing by a strong draft. The arch must be outdoors, since a great deal of moisture is given off. Don't let the sap get more than a couple of inches deep. Keep the level by pouring in more sap. It is an advantage to have two boilers. Use one for the fresh sap and keep ladling the partially boiled sap into the other, from which you "syrup off," meaning take the syrup.

Skim the scum off from time to time, and watch constantly to see that the sap doesn't boil over. If it starts climbing up the pan, add some fresh sap, or drop some creamy milk on the climbing froth, or draw a piece of fat across the bubbles. Test the sap's temperature with a thermometer. When it is boiling at 219°F (104°C), it has turned into syrup. Strain it off into jars, cover while hot, and put away to cool. This is maple syrup—delicious with pancakes, ice cream, or, in fact, anything.

If you want sugar, go on boiling until the temperature is 242°F (117°C). If you pull a spoon out and the drip forms a thin, spidery thread, that is enough boiling. Remove from the fire, leave to cool for a few minutes, then stir with a wooden spoon. When the syrup begins to crystalize, pour it into molds and you have sugar.

SALT

If you live near the sea, you can make salt by simply boiling and evaporating seawater. You can use driftwood for fuel—and nowadays the oil spillage that coats most driftwood means it gives even more heat. A mobile iron boiler, such as those you boil pig-swill in, is ideal. Never use a copper boiler. The copper and salty seawater will react with one another.

PAINT

Very good paints can be made from a mixture of sour milk, hydrated (slaked) lime, and any colored earth pigment that you can find. The lime and the sour milk must have neutralized each other, and this can be tested with litmus paper: if the paper turns red, add more lime; if it turns blue, add more sour milk. The pigment you add to this can be any strongly colored earth, sediment or clay. Dig it out of the ground and boil it in water several times, each time in new water. Strain off the water and dry the sediment in a warm place. Pulverize it as finely as you can and store. Mix this powder with the milk–lime mixture until you get the color you want.

PAPER

It is possible to make paper from any fibrous plant, or wood, cotton, or linen rags. Nettles, flax, hemp, rushes, coarse grass, and tall fibrous plants like *Tagetes minuta* all make very good paper. Ret (moisten) the plants first by soaking them in stagnant water. Then chop them up as small as you can—into, say, ½-inch (1-cm) lengths. Put the chopped material into a vat and cover with a caustic soda solution made up of 2 teaspoons of caustic soda per quart (liter) of water. Boil until the material is soft and flabby. Put it in a coarse sieve and drain. Hold the sieve under the faucet, or plunge it up and down in a bath of water. This will clear the pulp away. If you want white paper, soak the fiber you now have left in a bleach solution overnight. If left unbleached, the paper will be the color of the material you are using. Drain the bleach off through a fine-meshed sieve (you don't want to lose fibers).

Next, you must beat the material. You can do this best with a mallet or any kind of pounding engine. When you have beaten it thoroughly dry, add some water and continue beating the pulp. A large food mixer or a large mortar and pestle will do very well for this stage. Put some pulp in a glass of water occasionally and hold it up to the light: if there are still lumps in it, go on beating. If you want to make interesting papers, don't beat too long and your paper will have fragments of vegetation showing in it.

You make the paper on molds, which can be simple wooden frames covered with cloth. Cover the molds with a thin layer of pulp by dipping them into it and scooping. As you lift the mold out of the pulp, give it a couple of shakes at right angles to each other. This helps the fibers to "felt" or mat together. If you find that the "waterleaf," which is what your sheet is called, is too thin, turn the mold upside down, place it in the vat, and shake the pulp off back in the water. Then add more fiber to your vat. Turn the mold upside down on a piece of wet felt and press the back of the cloth to make the waterleaf adhere to the felt. Take the mold away and lay another piece of wet felt on top of the waterleaf. Repeat the operation with another waterleaf. Finally, you need a press. Any kind of press will do. Make a "post," which is a pile of alternate felts and waterleaves, and put the post in your press. Press for a day or so, then remove the paper from the felt and press just the paper sheets. Handle the paper very carefully at this point, and then lay it out on racks to dry.

RESIN, ROSIN, AND WOOD TAR

Long-leaf pine, maritime pine, Corsican pine, American balm of Gilead, cedars, cypresses, and larches can all be tapped for their resin. To do this: clear a strip of bark, about 4 inches (10 cm) wide and 4 feet (1.2 m) high, off a large tree. This is called a "blaze." With a sharp ax, take a very thin shaving of true wood off at the base of the blaze. Drive a small metal gutter into the tree at the base of this cut and lead the sap, or resin, into a tin can. Every five days or so, freshen the cut by taking off another shaving. When you can get no more out of the first cut, make another just above it. Repeat until you have incised the whole blaze (this may take several years). Don't tap between November and February. If you grow conifers for tapping, clean the side branches off the young trees so that the trunks are clean for tapping.

If you distill resin—that is, if you heat it and condense the first vapor that comes off it—you will get turpentine. "Rosin" is the sticky stuff that remains behind, and it is good for violin strings, paints, and varnishes. If you heat coniferous wood in a retort, or even just burn it in a hole in a bank, a black liquid will run out of the bottom. This is wood tar, and it is the best thing in the world for painting boats and buildings.

CHARCOAL

Charcoal is made by burning wood in the presence of too little oxygen: you set some wood alight, get it blazing well throughout its mass, and then cut off the air. I have tried many ways of doing it and the simplest and best is to dig a large trench, fill it up with wood, and set it alight. When it is blazing fiercely, throw sheets of corrugated iron on to start smothering the fire, and then very quickly (you will need perhaps half a dozen helpers) shovel earth on top of the iron to bury it completely. Leave for several days to cool, then open up and shovel the charcoal into bags. You can use the charcoal for cooking fuel or making bricks.

Making a Pond & Fish Farming

MAKING A POND

If you are going to keep ducks, or if you want to try the highly rewarding process of fish farming, you will need a pond. You can just dig a hole, but if the bottom or sides are porous, it will probably be necessary to puddle clay and tamp it in so as to form an impervious sheet, or else bury a large sheet of thick plastic.

Simply piling earth up in a bank to form a dam to impound water seldom works. The fill material may be too porous, and "piping" will occur, meaning water will seep through and erode a hole. Or the material may contain too much clay and there will be drying, shrinkage, and cracking. If the soil is just right, and well compacted, and an adequate spillway to take off the surplus caused by rainwater is constructed, a simple earth dam may work, but where there is doubt, the dam should be made of porous soil with puddled and tamped clay embedded in it. Nowadays, plastic sheeting is sometimes used instead. If your pond is for fish farming, then good topsoil should be placed in the bottom for plants to grow on.

FISH FARMING

Fish are marvelously efficient producers of high-protein human food: far better, in fact, than other livestock. This is because they don't have to build a massive bone structure to support their weight (the water supports it), and they don't have to use energy to maintain their body heat (they are cold-blooded). In the tropics, particularly in rice paddies, they are a major crop. Modern commercial fish farming, in which only one species of fish is fed on expensive high-protein food in water that is kept weed-free with herbicides, is ecologically unsound and requires absurd inputs of expensive feed or fertilizer. We should all start experimenting with water ecosystems that achieve a proper balance of nature, and in which a variety of fish species can coexist with a cross-section of other marine life, both animal and vegetable.

Strangely enough, in the 16th century the matter was far better understood. In England at that time, a writer named John Taverner wrote that you should make large shallow ponds, 4 feet (1.2 m) deep and more, and keep them dry one year and full of water the next. When dry, graze them with cattle, and when wet, fill them with carp. The ponds grow lush grass because of the sediments left by the water, and the carp benefit from the fertility left by the cattle. This is the true organic approach to husbandry. You should have at least two ponds so that there is always one full of fish and one dry. Drain the wet pond dry in late fall, and take the best fish out then to put in your stewpond near the house, where they are ready for eating. Put a lot of young fish in your newly flooded big pond.

Carp

Carnivorous fish, such as trout, are poor converters of food into flesh. Vegetarian fish are far better. This is why the aforementioned Taverner and the monks of old in Europe had carp in their stewponds. Carp will give you a ton of fish per acre per year without any feeding if they are in a suitable pond. The way the monks farmed them was to let them breed in larger ponds, but then to catch them and confine them to small stew ponds near the living quarters in the fall.

The stewponds were just deep enough to stay ice-free, and the carp were therefore easy to net. As well as being vegetarian, carp are healthy, quick-growing, and they can live in non-flowing water. They need half their food from natural provenance, and can be encouraged by a certain amount of muck or rotting vegetation dumped in the water. This is transformed into the sort of food carp eat by bacterial action, but they will also eat oatmeal, barley, spent malt, and other similar food.

The Hungarian strain of the Chinese grass carp has been tried in England, with success. In China these fish grow up to 100 pounds (45 kg) in weight: in England 30 pounds (13.6 kg) is considered a good fish. Unfortunately, they need temperatures of 122°F (51°C) to breed, and so are propagated in heated tanks and released outdoors, where they flourish.

Tilapia

The best fish of all for fish farming are the African tilapia, but because they are tropical fish they need warm water. Nevertheless, putting yourself out for them may well be worthwhile. Research has shown that the average family could provide all its animal protein requirements in a 3,600-gallon (13,640-liter) covered and heated pool full of tilapia. The water should be about 80°F (27°C): less than 55°F (13°C) will kill them.

Tilapia mossambica, which is one of the best of the many species, can be bought from pet shops. The hen fish produce about 25 to 30 young, which live in their mothers' mouths for the first period of their lives, and the hens bring off several broods a year. Much of their food can be supplied free with a little labor by incubating pond water, slightly fertilized with organic manure, in tanks. After three weeks or a month, carefully pump this water into the tilapia pond with the organisms that it contains. The incubation tanks should be partially roofed with glass, but access for mosquitoes and other flying insects should be provided.

In temperate climates *Tilapia mossambica* can be kept in heated pools, and they don't require constantly running water. Using a combination of solar heating and wind/electric heating has proved successful for growing them in North America.

They will produce two tons of good meat per acre per year. As adults they will feed on algae or any vegetation you put into the water (within reason), or they will eat oatmeal. When young they need protein, which can be supplied in such forms as mosquito larvae, maggots, worms, fish meat, or blood meal. They are probably the most delicious of all fish to eat.

The All-Purpose Furnace

Firewood is a renewable resource, and the best solar energy collector in the world is a stretch of woodland. Woodland cut for firewood should be coppiced (*see* p.236). In other words, the trees should be cut right down every 10 to 15 years, depending on how fast they grow, and the stumps left to coppice, or shoot again. Cut over systematically in this way, two or three acres of woodland will yield a constant supply of good firewood and other timber.

To burn wood effectively and economically requires several things. The wood must be burned on the floor of the furnace, not on a grid. The fire must be enclosed, and there must be a means of carefully regulating the draft. A huge, open fire is a romantic thing, but all it does is cheer the heart, freeze the back, and heat the sky. Where wood is in limitless supply it may be justified, but not otherwise.

It is an advantage to burn wood in a dead end, admitting air from the front only. A tunnel with the back walled off is ideal. Logs can be fed into the dead-end tunnel and lit at the end closest to the door, and the fire then slowly smoulders backward into the tunnel. The draft control should be such that you can load the tunnel right up with dry logs, get a roaring fire going, and then actually put it out by cutting off the air. If you can feed your furnace from outside your house, you will avoid a lot of mess inside. And if you can organize things so that your furnace can take long logs, you save an awful lot of work sawing.

Now any decent, economical furnace should be capable of doing at least four things: space heating, oven baking, hot-plate cooking, and water heating, and if it can smoke meat and fish as well, so much the better. We built a furnace that will do all these things on my old farm, and since that farm was called Fachongle, I call it the Fachongle

Furnace. But don't try to build one like this unless you know you can get, for not too much money: firebricks, a cast-iron plate big enough to cover the whole furnace, and a massive cast-iron fire door.

BUILDING A FURNACE

We built a firebrick tunnel 4 feet (1.2 m) long inside the house. It is bricked off at the back, but the front falls 4 inches (10 cm) short of the exterior house wall. The house wall there is lined with firebricks. On either side of the tunnel we built a brick wall slightly higher than the top of the tunnel. The bases of these need not be of firebrick, but the tops must be able to withstand the heat. On top of the two outer walls we laid a steel plate. (This has since warped slightly, which is why I advise you to get a cast-iron plate.) This goes from the back of the furnace right to the wall of the building. On top of the steel plate away from the wall of the building, we built an oven, and at the very farthest end from the wall we built a chimney. We knocked a hole in the outer wall and in that set a furnace door with firebricks. The furnace is fed through this door, and the heat and smoke has to come back to the front end, curl up through the 4-inch (10-cm) gap, hit the iron plate, curve back, and go under the oven and on up the chimney. We built a back boiler into the back wall of the tunnel, and the pipes from it come back between the tunnel wall and the outer wall, and then come out through two holes in the latter. We partially filled the cavity between tunnel and outer walls with sand to insulate and store heat.

Managing your store of firewood is an essential part of operating any woodburning stove. The wood must be dry, that is to say, it must have been cut at least 12 months before burning. We constantly add to the woodshed, keeping two piles of wood: one new and one (for use) 12 months old.

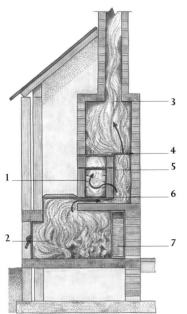

A VERSATILE FURNACE THAT YOU CAN BUILD YOURSELF
We designed and built the Fachongle Furnace with the idea of getting as much benefit as we could from burning wood. The furnace gives us space heating for a large area, a lot of very hot water, a hot plate and oven for cooking, and a smoke chamber. We burn the wood in a tunnel made from firebricks. The back is closed off and contains the back boiler for water. The front comes almost up to a hole in the house wall where we have built a fire door, so that the furnace is fed from outside. We built brick walls on either side of the tunnel right up to the house wall, and rested a steel plate across them. The front of the plate serves as a hot plate, and over the back we have built an oven. There is a slit in the steel plate so that heat circulates all the way around the oven. At the very back is the chimney, which widens out above the oven to form the smoke chamber. Heat from the fire comes forward along the tunnel, curls up under the hot plate and oven, and continues on up the chimney. It is likely that your requirements will be different and will necessitate a modified design.

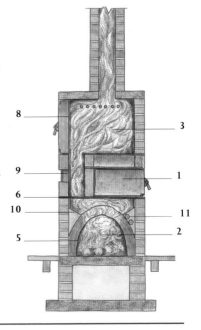

1 Oven	7 Back boiler
2 Fire box	8 Smoking box door
3 Smoking box	9 Access door
4 Damper	10 Sand filling
5 Firebrick	11 Water pipes
6 Flue passage	

Becoming a Self-Supporter

Making the break

One thing I have noticed is that the settlers who fail and have to go back to the city are generally the ones who tried to adopt, unchanged, the patterns of traditional husbandry in the areas they settled in. In this they are not aiming for self-sufficiency; indeed, they will buy much of their food from normal stores, like other farmers, and try to make money to do it by selling just one or two products. This simply cannot work. Traditional farming is up against the ropes; the farmers who inherited their land and their occupation from their families are finished. True, it will take a long time before they finally break up and disappear—and it will be an uncomfortable and sad process—but the industrial world that makes the rules has no time for traditional farmers.

I cannot tell you what patterns of activity will work for you in combining a self-sufficient lifestyle with money-earning activities, but I can give you some examples:

A retired couple (the man from engineering) has bought a house and a roughly a dozen acres. The wife milks the six cows and sells the milk to be made into cheese. The man keeps a herd of pigs in his woodland and buys some of the whey back to feed them. Besides growing most of their own food and brewing their own beer, they have a small pension. They work hard, have an enjoyable life, and live well.

A divorced lady lives on five acres of rough land with her 13-year-old son. She is a successful potter and earns the money she needs from her work. She can just afford to run an old van. She milks one cow and rears calves on another, kills one young steer a year for the freezer, keeps two sows, kills two fat pigs a year for bacon and ham, makes all her own butter, cheese, and so on, sells some, sells a few of her fat roosters and ducks, and buys wheat from a local farmer and grinds it by hand to make her own bread. The son is a great help, being utterly at home on the farm, a budding carpenter, and a good shot.

A salesman, who retired early, and his wife bought a very remote 25-acre (10-ha) holding. They have fixed up the house, and fenced and improved the land. They keep a herd of goats and some poultry from which they get all their milk and meat. They run a fine garden, and the man works part time as an engineer for a local firm. The wife does most of the manual work on the holding and loves it.

A music teacher in schools bought a 20-acre (8-ha) farm. He and his wife rear calves, milk a cow, run the farm very efficiently (taking good advice from their neighbors), and grow most of their own food. The man teaches the piano to local kids to earn extra cash. He turns down requests for more work because he has already as much as he wants to do and does not need much money anyway.

A group of people each put $10,000 into a kitty a few years ago and bought a good-sized farm, around 50 acres (20 ha), with a large house on it. Most of the originals have left now, but others have come, and they all live in the big house and work the farm cooperatively. They had enough capital at the start, so they have good machinery and farm well. They grow strawberries to sell, run a big market garden, make some pretty awful cheese, which they eat themselves, run a shop that sells their produce, and have a stall at the local market. They seem to live very well, although the house is not neat and tidy. There are lots of happy kids living there.

Now, I could go on like this for pages. The lesson to draw is that all the successful recruits to self-sufficiency have some skill or business that will provide cash for part of their living. And none of them have debts.

Checklist

It is useful to make yourself some kind of checklist that might include such items as:

Why—Get clear in your mind your major motivations for making a change.

When—There is a marvelous passage in Thoreau's *Walden* in which the writer relates that a certain young man, wishing to become a poet, went off for several years first to make money to support himself. Thoreau remarks, "He would better have gone up the garret at once." In other words, his years as a money-grubber would have made him completely unfit to write any poetry. His Muse would have been killed, and no amount of money could bring it back. If you have to buy land, then perhaps the sooner you get your foot in the door, the better.

Where—You may have to travel around extensively before you get a real feel for what you are looking for. Finding your ideal small farm is a matter of good research, cool judgment, and a great deal of luck. Many of the best homesteaders find their ideal spots by some process of serendipity. Maybe they get lost on a trip to friends, or their car breaks down, or they see a lucky ad. You just have to leave yourself open to this kind of adventure. And do not forget that you will have to live within the local culture as well as on the local land—try to take a dip into this by going to local restaurants, markets, and stores. Talk to people and see what it feels like. A local health food shop or library will have many notices of local events and services—that's a useful guide to what life there may have to offer.

Who with—Well, you could be alone, with a spouse and family, with one trusted partner, or in a community, or one of many other permutations. Many people have dreams of living in communes, but I can tell you this is much more difficult than it sounds. Decision-making, money, and sex are a trilogy of troubles that humans find it extremely difficult to deal with effectively in groups.

How much—Nearly all new settlers are too ambitious and go for too much land, spending too much money and taking on more than they can manage. We are all familiar with the television sitcoms showing city folk struggling with stubborn animals and uncooperative neighbors as the weather devastates their romantic rural

home. What you must remember is that you do not have to do all this at once. It is perfectly possible to start slowly. Many of our students have done just this—some begin by baking their own bread or making their own beer. Others may start with a few chickens or just a small vegetable garden. All of these are activities which give the would-be self-supporter a new feeling of achievement and a chance to experience the satisfaction of making your own requirements first hand.

What buildings—Do not be put off by poor-quality buildings or lack of buildings. In many ways it is better not to spend hard-earned cash on buildings that you could (in time) renovate or build yourself. What you absolutely do not want to do is to buy yourself a pile of work and trouble, especially in the form of old, damp buildings that will break your heart (and your wallet) to repair. And whatever the realtors may tell you, make sure you conduct some of your own research before committing yourself.

What money-earning activity—This is a matter of the most crucial importance and, as we have seen, there are many ways of approaching it. But do not despair if you cannot see how this will happen—life has a strange way of filling spaces. And you may, of course, be of that determined breed who say to themselves, "Well, my city profession as a poodle faker is not going to be in great demand, so I will learn a new trade." Remember, there are nothing like enough good craftsmen in the world—plumbing, electrics, mechanics, carpentry, basket-making, and so on are all things you can learn. But many city folk do have skills that find a use in the countryside—computer use, accounting, marketing, nursing, and teaching, for example.

What crops—To a large extent, this will depend on the type of land you have bought, the area you are in, and your own predilections. Once again, my advice is not to be too ambitious—make haste slowly and take care to keep a good diary, and learn from your own mistakes.

Getting it together with others

If you really want to make a change in your lifestyle, then you are going to need help from others. And, what's more, the bigger the spread of talents you can find, the better your self-sufficient lifestyle will become. It makes no sense, for example, to imagine you can milk a cow just for a single family. You will have far too much milk and far too much of a tie that means you can never take a day off. You are unlikely to have all the skills—to make clothes, shoes, furniture, buildings, pottery, and the like. But find others who can do these things and your life will become more interesting and much more comfortable.

This logic does not simply apply to those who are seeking the rural idyll; it applies probably even more strongly to those of you who live in towns and want to make some important changes in how you live. Of course some of you will be able to take on community garden plots or make vegetable gardens; others will keep bees, chickens, or rabbits; some will be experts at bicycle repair; others will know of local farmers who produce organic food; then there will be those who enjoy making bread, or beer, or wine. And so it goes on. Your challenge is to find such people and, having found them, to energize them and yourself to do things differently. By developing and using these different skills, you can make a richer, happier, and healthier lifestyle for you and your family. Yes, and even create more of your own entertainment, too—meeting socially for parties, music, walks, poetry readings, meals, and visits.

All this human interaction and mutual support is what we mean by "getting it together." Strangely, these skills in human relations have been all but destroyed by our modern urban lifestyle. This puts all the emphasis on tight little nuclear families and a separate social life at the workplace. Each family has to paddle its own canoe, so to speak, earning its own money, paying its own bills, and surviving its own crises. Work, school, and survival take up so much time it seems there is no spare time left to develop alternative human contacts. Now is the time you can begin to change all of that.

The first thing you will want to do is to find out whether a self-sufficiency group is already meeting anywhere on a regular basis. Try local papers, noticeboards, web searches, and the local library for starters. If nothing has been done to bring people together, then it is up to you to make the first moves. To some this will be second nature, but for others it may take quite a bit of courage. There are really a couple of sensible alternatives here: Try an "at home" evening or organize a local meeting place session. The important thing is to try. It is a great chance to exchange ideas, to laugh about your mistakes, and to find out what else is going on in your area. As you get to know each other better, you can plan more joint activities and develop a barter system of goods and skills. Once you have gotten the ball rolling, make sure you meet regularly; once each month is a good start. Now, here are a few tips and hints about how to have successful meetings:

1 The first thing you may want to do is to search out a local restaurant that seems suitable for meetings. A public place is good because it is neutral ground and does not involve anyone in having to "show off" or clean the house or prepare food at home. And you can go there without involving all the other members of your family in the meeting. A health food restaurant may be another option, or even a hotel. One way or another, my preference would be a place with real beer, real wood, and a bartender who is happy to have you.

2 Very often libraries have meeting rooms that you can book free of charge—but don't use these unless they have a good atmosphere. Somewhere that is cold and dusty, with no "buzz," is not going to make a pleasant meeting.

3 If you find a positive response from your first contact list, then try to find a convenient date for a first meeting.

Your first meeting will be quite exciting if you haven't met face to face before: like a scene from some spy movie where the plotters meet up using a secret sign. In your case this may be the color of your hat, the newspaper you are reading or, a copy of *The Self-Sufficient Life and How to Live It*.

4 To those who are confident and outgoing, it is a relatively simple matter to meet up with and get to know new faces. But to many it will be a daunting prospect, and you may have some tense silences while people try to figure out what they are supposed to be doing and what you all have in common. With small groups (six or fewer), it is pretty simple to have a joint conversation where everyone has a chance to take part.

5 If groups get bigger, then the conversations will split up or, alternatively, you will need more rules about how each person can make their contribution. Some groups will be very able to "police" themselves so as to make sure everyone feels included. Others will have to work harder and may need a bit of leadership, or what is called "facilitation," if they are to work successfully. It is really helpful if you have someone in the group who is used to working with people and has a sensitivity to the mood and the needs of the meeting.

6 If you have "called the meeting" and set things moving, then people will expect you to take a lead in getting things started. Usually people like to introduce themselves and say a little bit about what they and their family members do, and how they are coping with being self-sufficient.

If things are a bit sticky, you can invite people to speak either by starting with yourself and then taking each person in turn around the table, going alphabetically, or writing down names on slips of paper and pulling them out of a hat. This is not as far-fetched as it sounds and is actually more fun, because people will speak more spontaneously when they do not know when their turn will come. Remember, though, that the only important objectives of the first meeting are to get to know each other and to fix a date for the next meeting. Do not be put off if you find some of the people irritating or bizarre in some way. You have to remember that several of these people are likely to become very good friends as time goes by.

Building a community of support

Many modern people have simply never had the experience of working with others to create a community. You would be wise to work hard at making these friendships work. "Community" is an important aspect of self-sufficiency. It may take a real effort and much probing to find out the skills and talents of those who have come together around the table. People who may be hopeless at small talk may be wonderful carpenters, musicians, cooks, or gardeners—with skills to share. You need to take the view that all your new contacts have amazing hidden talents and it is up to you to find them. In the meantime you have to make allowances all around for the poor development of social skills that is so prevalent in the modern industrial world.

Your meeting may well be a rip-roaring success. If so, that's great. But do not be surprised if the first meeting seems to be rather hard work. And do not despair. Remember, the modern human has gotten used to having all the group work, team-building, and community activity provided in a package by the workplace. It is no accident that the most popular TV shows are the soaps, which provide what amount to virtual communities. The viewer can enjoy the ups and downs of these virtual communities at the turn of a switch and without any personal cost or effort. But now you have the challenge of getting the best from your group. Each of you will need to find ways of encouraging and using the varied talents and finding ways of enjoying yourselves together that strengthen and reinforce your friendship. If you can work as a group, then your chances of really achieving big steps towards self-sufficiency will be very much greater. But be under no illusions—creating a community is a fundamental human skill that has been largely destroyed by modern urban living. It is no accident that follow-up studies that have looked at the progress of over 1,000 ecovillages and organic communities have found that almost all of these initiatives failed. And the prime reasons for failure were not lack of skill in producing food, or lack of people with many diverse skills, or lack of a good local school, or failure to build ecohomes, process waste, or manage livestock. No, the prime reasons for failure were the lack of effective community decision-making procedures, and the inability to manage money. There are two routes you might take to build a community and avoid these pitfalls. One is following a self-selected leader—such communities can work very well in human terms, and they can continue for many years, provided there are effective arrangements to replace the leader on death or sickness. Alternatively, the "democratic" choice of leaders is much favored. But this "model" must work by consensus—general agreement—and the voices of concern listened to very carefully.

Making your contribution

By meeting regularly—as I have said, preferably once a month—you can build up confidence between the members. This is a great help in getting people to share their feelings and show their talents. You will want to meet in different circumstances and start to do things together. You can do things even as simple as arranging to visit some place of interest together or going for a walk. Or, even better, you can meet up to do a project at someone's home. Here are some examples:

—*Making cider from loads of apples to be chopped, crushed, and juiced*
—*Clearing waste; brambles and thorns to cut, trees to chop up*
—*Butchering a pig into joints and bacon*
—*Helping move livestock*
—*Hay-making or wine-making*
—*Building projects*
—*Digging and weeding*
—*Fruit harvesting and processing*

As your group develops its strength, you may want to experiment with new ways of being together and talk about matters rather more personal and of deeper meaning. You will have to find ways of short-circuiting emotional stresses that creep into all human relationships. You will have to find ways of building up your energies for particularly difficult tasks or local campaigns. For example, I would explore those excellent techniques, many developed over the centuries in the East, such as yoga, meditation, and the like. In the West, groups such as the Quakers or Alcoholics Anonymous have developed highly effective ways of using groups effectively in supporting the actions of each individual forming part of the group. It is well worth looking into the subject more fully if your group begins to grow bigger.

On a practical and economic level, by creating a group you also give yourselves the opportunity to bulk-purchase foodstuffs and equipment. There are excellent sources for bulk-buying organic products such as flour, fruit, and cheese. You can research the farmers in your area to see who would sell you organically reared meat such as pork, lamb, or beef. As a group you can afford to buy a whole animal and cut it up for your freezers. You can also explore and create recycling options—and urge others to do so—by composting more, experimenting with using less energy, or even sharing a car or buying some land together.

Rules for group meetings
1 Appoint one person to look after the way the group works for that meeting
2 Decide how the group is going to work during the meeting: you could use talking sticks, timed contributions, talking at random, talking around the table, or talking freestyle.
3 Try to set a maximum length for the meeting, and have a timescale if you need to limit each person's contribution.
4 Draw up an agenda of points people would like to see discussed at the meeting.
5 Decide how the group is going to make decisions—by consensus, by vote, by summing up, or by some other method.
6 Appoint someone to conclude the meeting (can be the same person as for Item 1): sum up, thanks, next meeting, short silence, hold hands around table, or other ceremony of your choice.

If your group settles down well, then you may begin to think about bringing in new members or contacting other, similar groups. However, never allow your group to grow too big: 12 people should be a maximum for a basic group. If the number of people coming to meetings increases beyond this, then you need to create separate groups. This does not mean you do not meet in larger groups, but it does mean that you do work differently in such groups. The small group will always be the powerhouse supporting your day-to-day self-sufficiency activities.

To make contact with other groups, you can simply ask one of your group to go along to neighboring meetings. There will be contact people in each group, and their details will be listed under self-sufficiency, self-supporter, or homesteading Websites. And as things develop, we expect to build up a skills directory and a bulletin board for each group, which can include "for sale" and "wanted" items as well as events and services. I would also make sure to have a directory of the groups in every region and town that are holding monthly self-sufficiency meetings.

In all of what we do in our groups and in our lives, we must constantly remember that the cardinal rule is that nature is bountiful and full of goodness, provided we stick to the rules. To coin a phrase: "it is fun to have fun but you have to know how." As far as I am concerned, the rules are very simple: love life, respect the earth, build human community, and work with nature, not against it.

We must also do what we can to celebrate our successes every year, and what better way than to have annual fairs in every region? If we say that each group of 12 groups makes up a region, then they can choose a couple of neighboring groups each year to organize their regional fair. Ideally this should take place in June, when the days are long and the hay is being made. It will last three days and have entertainment, produce, events, displays, book sales, speeches, and plenty of good food and drink.

MEASURING PROGRESS
The households of most modern consumers take in virtually 99.9 percent of their daily requirements from outside suppliers and, equally, they pass on 99.9 percent of their waste products back to outside agencies via the garbage can, the dumpster, the sewer pipe, the chimney, and the car's exhaust pipe. For the self-supporter, this is a profoundly unsatisfactory and even dangerous situation. Trying to measure the extent to which we depend on outside agencies (mostly the huge transnational corporations, government agencies, and supermarkets) is something we need to come to terms with. Below are some of the key "measuring units" by which we can judge our contribution to a self-sufficiency model.

Energy
Typically we will buy in oil, gasoline, natural gas, firewood, and electricity. We use these and export the waste, mostly carbon dioxide and pollution, to the world's atmosphere. For the ideal self-supporter, the household energy requirements would be provided by the solar economy, either directly through the sun or indirectly through wind, water, or self-grown firewood. The self-supporter can tackle energy dependency in a multitude of ways. Saving energy is the first step—more insulation, better design of houses, less travel, lower temperatures, and more clothes. Making sure your household heating and cooking arrangements are sensible is important—and never use electricity to heat anything because this is supremely wasteful.

Food

Huge quantities of food are transported thousands of miles and surrounded by acres of packaging material to make them attractive and available to modern households. This is the pride and joy of supermarket shopping. It is almost certain that there is a direct and unpleasant relationship between the look of the food, the quantity of poisons used to achieve this, and the resulting lack of taste for the consumer.

We can eat foods from all over the world anytime we want—but when we do so, someone has to pay a price sooner or later. The transportation costs in terms of pollution and energy are enormous. Worse still, we no longer have the excitement created by having to wait for foods to be in season. Absence really does make the heart grow fonder, and this applies just as much to strawberries as it does to sweethearts.

For the most part, modern consumers have no idea where their food comes from, who grew it, what was put on it to keep off the bugs, and what was done to the soil to make it grow. Nor do they know what has been done to color and preserve it. Enough said. The smallholder and even the community gardener can grow a large proportion of their own food. The results will be very satisfying, very healthy, and very tasty. We can measure progress toward self-produced food by costing our trips to supermarkets.

Household goods

The great snag with many household goods is that they are not designed to last. Sometimes this is because of style (which may rapidly go "out of date"), but often there is simple, old-fashioned, built-in obsolescence. The self-supporter will avoid these pitfalls at all costs.

Make sure you buy goods that are made to last—even if it costs quite a bit more in the short term. The classic choice for household items is, of course, the light bulb. Many other things are similar—there is a choice between a high initial cost that is offset by long life and cheap running costs, or a low-cost, high-operating cost.

Transportation

Most of you will know the old argument about using a car. It goes something like this.

Take your average car and look at the annual costs (always a sobering prospect!) You will find that depreciation, maintenance, and fuel costs for an average year's travel of, say, 8,000 miles breaks down like this: depreciation is about $50 per week, insurance around $25 per week, and fuel costs $20 per week. Add on a few extra bits and pieces and you have running costs around $100 per week. If your wages are around $8 per hour then you are effectively devoting 12 hours each week to pay for your journeys (the time taken traveling in modern traffic is probably 8 hours).

So 20 hours devoted to travel makes your average speed just 8 miles per hour, which shows you that you would be much better to take a bike at 10 mph! I look forward to the day when we can have family-sized, weatherproof, bike-cars powered by pedal power so we do not need to visit the gym. Quite why no one has produced such a vehicle is one of the great mysteries of the modern age. Downhill performance would, of course, be exceptional, with aerodynamic shaping of the bodywork, lightweight disk brakes, on-board CD, and rechargeable lightweight batteries taking charge from downhill braking and helping with the uphill sections. It doesn't hurt to dream!

SUSTAINABLE LIVING ON LAND

By understanding the nitrogen cycle and nature's law of return, we can steadily build up the fertility and production from our land. A healthy soil is the prime agent that we depend upon to convert natural wastes into fertility and food. But a healthy soil needs careful management and a constant supply of nutrients from animal wastes. A healthy soil must not be poisoned by strong chemicals or fed artificially with factory-made nutrients. If the soil is to increase in depth and fertility, then it must contain good quantities of vegetable material (humus). Without humus from decaying plant material, the soil will either blow away or wash away in winter rains or snow melt.

Recycling organic waste

Composting and animal manures are prime agents for recycling organic wastes. By learning the art of compost-making, we convert weeds, kitchen waste, and garden by-products into new fertility for the soil.

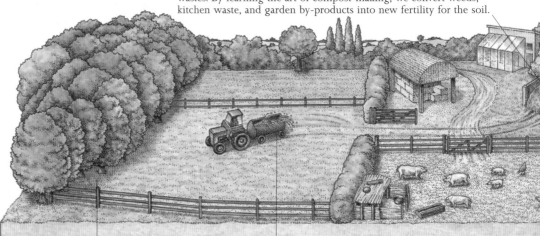

Crop rotation

Different crops need different nutrients and suffer from different diseases. To choose in which order to grow crops in rotation maximizes the available nutrients and minimizes the build up of disease.

Organic farming

For healthy soil and food we must minimize contamination from powerful chemical poisons. An organic farmer will avoid growing large areas of single crops and highly bred varieties.

Water and "gray" water

For many parts of the world water is the key scarce commodity, yet the modern western lifestyle uses thousands of gallons of purified fresh water every week in washing machines, dishwashers, toilets, garden sprinklers, and (increasingly rarely) drinking. Indeed, so careless are we that for the most part we do not even meter the quantity of water we use.

There are many ways to reduce dependency on piped and treated water. In the urban situation, great savings can be made by collecting rainwater in an old-fashioned rain barrel. This is, by the way, a really good way to get the water for your greenhouse, because if you put the barrel in the greenhouse the water will always be at the correct temperature for the greenhouse plants. We can also be even more creative and get to work with a plumber to use the so-called "gray" water. (Always be sure to check local regulations and building codes before you start.)

Gray water is what comes out of things like washing machines, sinks, and bathtubs. It may be a bit soapy, but the worst of the stuff can easily be removed with suitable filters. Your water company can possibly advise on this. The objective is to pump the used gray water back up into a special attic storage tank so that it can be reused for such purposes as flushing toilets, watering the garden, or cleaning the car. Huge savings can be made this way, and everyone benefits. Gray water systems will undoubtedly become the norm within the next 20 years. In the smallholder situation use of water is also likely to be a critical issue. Many self-supporters will use their own well water, water from a spring, or mountain stream water. Obviously, having your own independent water supply is good practice for the smallholder.

Using a gray water process will be very beneficial, as will use and collection of rainwater. But, and this is critical, the self-supporter will also be able to make enormous savings by avoiding the use of a flush toilet. Mr. Crapper's famous invention is a great way to pour away vital nutrients for the soil while, at the same time, creating massive pollution of the rivers and water-table. The liquid waste goes off down the sewer pipe to an industrial unit that tries to separate out the organic wastes and chemicals so it can be put back into the natural water cycle without too much danger to the environment (including humans who will have to drink it again before it reaches the sea). If you can use a composting toilet (*as described on pp.336–337*) then these problems are avoided.

Waste

When archeologists of the future try to make sense of this age we live in, they might well name it the "Garbage Age," as we named ages of the past—"Stone Age," and so on. For wherever they are likely to sink their spades into what were once high-tech countries, they will turn up garbage. We generate more of that than the people of any former age. Soon there will be no more possible landfill sites to dump our garbage in. We will be forced to stop looking upon it as garbage, and to look upon it as material that has been used once (or more) and will be used again.

In the conventional urban household, all solid waste goes off in cans of one kind or another, usually once each week. For the most part, it is still buried (although recycling and composting are slowly changing this). Simple separation of household waste is obviously the first step: glass, paper, metal, organic material, and plastic can all be reprocessed.

Sustainable timber
We must treat timber with a much longer timescale for planting and management.

Collecting and conserving energy
Energy resources must be conserved and sensible design and lifestyles adopted. Natural sources (wind and sun) must be harnessed.

Growing food
Grow as much food as land type and quality will support in your locality, and do away with expensive processing and huge transport costs.

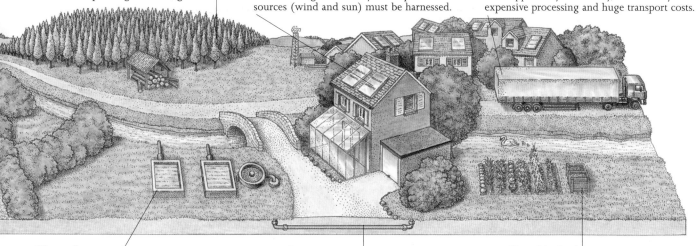

Nitrate-free water
By careful use of organic methods we prevent serious contamination of drinking water caused by farming's massive dependence on highly soluble cheap chemical nitrates.

Dual water systems
Current use of expensively treated drinking water for flushing wastes, washing cars, or watering must be stopped by creating dual water systems to collect "gray" water for reuse.

Fertility of the land
The challenge of constantly increasing fertility must be one of organic farming's highest objectives. Using chemicals for short-term profit can only damage long-term fertility.

Organic material can be composted in the garden by either bacteria or worms. I can remember an energetic charity worker who I met in Texas getting very excited about some fine-looking red worms she had seen in a local bait shop. Just the thing for a worm-composting program she was setting up in downtown New York City. The right sort of manure worms will work wonders on converting your kitchen waste to soil (and more worms for the fishermen). And you can easily have such a unit in your kitchen with no smell and no fuss.

Clothes

God forbid that you are a victim of "fashion." This is a strange disease that has been popular with humans for thousands of years. Essentially, it involves constantly wanting to wear the same kind of clothes as well-publicized role models. These models probably started out as emperors or kings, but today they are more likely to be rock stars or movie stars, celebrities, or models. The "disease" bears ample witness to the basic fact that your clothes say a great deal about the person you are.

Strangely, this was the main message I brought home after the 1992 Rio Earth Summit. Here we saw citizens' groups from all over Planet Earth wearing ethnic clothing (very beautiful and often handed down from generation to generation), or cheap T-shirts and shorts, while the government delegations and the well-heeled NGO representatives wore sharp suits and ties. Of course, they could only do this in their own artificial world of air-conditioned hotels, cars, and conference centers. Out in

Brazil, the suit and tie are about as sensible as a wool sweater in a sauna. The suit and tie have, of course, become the uniform of the merchants of greed. Wear one and you are immediately at ease in the company of other merchants of greed or their many and various acolytes and parasites. The tie in particular is some kind of symbol of servitude— slave to the status quo and runner on the wheel of greed. Now there can be few objections to the person who makes their own suit and tie, except for the obvious fact that they would have to be pretty crazy to try to do so.

In practice, there are few indeed in the modern Western world who make their own clothes in any shape or form. Yet for centuries this skill was always a feature of village life, and indeed, for some civilizations of the past, the residue of fabrics and clothes are major indicators of their sophistication. Today, most of our clothes are made effectively by machines and cheap labor in disadvantaged, nonindustrialized countries. Once they have a fashionable logo and a big advertising budget, they become desirable designer items selling at 10 times what they cost to make.

The true self-supporter will want clothes that are practical, sensible, and made as locally as possible. They will be made mainly from naturally occurring fabrics— wool, cotton, linen, silk, and leather being obvious choices. Fabrics created from by-products of the oil industry will be particularly avoided, especially plastics and nylon. But the self-supporter's clothes will be stylish as well as practical, for we take pride in our appearance and are proud to hold our heads high as we take more control over our own lives and our impact on the Earth.

Measuring your lifestyle changes

Family Units
—*Miles in the car*
—*Hours on the bus*
—*Time watching TV/DVDs*
—*Time spent working for someone else*
—*Per capita units (base amount divided by number of persons)*
—*Weight of garbage collected*
—*Money spent on energy (electricity, gas, fuel, wood)*
—*Number of toilet flushes/gallons of water used*
—*Money spent on food and drink (includes eating out)*
—*Money spent on new clothes/shoes*
—*Money spent on entertainment, e.g., movies, CDs, games*

These units are certainly not ends in themselves, just ideas of ways to show how your lifestyle may change over time if you are able to master any or all of the techniques of self-sufficiency. Making a weekly or monthly tally will help focus minds on questions of lifestyle, as well as giving a point of reference to compare notes with other fellow travelers on the road to self-sufficiency. Of course, the bottom line in measuring progress is the simple question of whether you end up feeling happier about your life and the thousands of activities that make up your particular jigsaw puzzle of living.

THINGS TO BARTER WITH
The urban dweller moving away from the cash world of the city may be surprised at how many people in the countryside offer favors and help. This is very much in keeping with the principle of "you scratch my back and I'll scratch yours." And it is not just fruit or vegetable produce or a joint of beef or half a dozen eggs. You can barter with your labor, tools, and skills as well and these are just as useful.

A word on barter and social credit

In our more idealistic moments, we may dream of a future where money is a rarely used commodity. Indeed, this may appear to be an extremely remote prospect. But we should remember that even 150 years ago, money was by no means a common medium of exchange in rural areas. In times when villages were more or less self-sufficient in all day-to-day necessities, there was relatively little call for cash. Everyone living in the community made their own contribution in some way with a particular skill or vocation. Living in close proximity, everyone was more or less able to "keep score" and avoid running up obligations to other members of the community.

In many rural areas these traditions live on. It is a natural feeling in the countryside to want to be in what might be called "social credit" with your neighbors. When my neighbor's tractor gets stuck outside my front door and I can pull him out of trouble. This is a great bonus for me; he is indebted to me and will certainly repay the favor when the time comes.

Whenever we visit friends (and we do so often, for what could be nicer than an unexpected visit?) it is always a good feeling to bring some of our own produce as a gift. Whether it be fresh eggs, elderflower wine, or a cut of beef, the pleasure of giving what we have worked with gives us a good feeling. And these exchanges of things—which are almost part of ourselves—cement friendships and bring their own bounty a hundred times over in returned favors. One of the greatest wisdoms I have learned since moving to Ireland is the importance of giving generously. If you are going to give, then do so with generosity and style—no penny pinching, handing out second-rate produce, or giving half measures. Make the same true of your time, too. If friends visit, then "roll out the barrel" and carve up the side of beef. All the very best parties come through serendipity, as one or two good friends or families show up unexpectedly. A good store of home brew and ample supplies of bread and cheese are the ever-ready foundations for such an occasion. And if there is music and singing to be had, then so much the better.

Don't limit your barter by restricting yourself to goods and produce: your labor, tools, and skills can be exchanged, too. Every fall our cider press, for example, "does the rounds" as our ever-increasing circle of cider-making friends take their turn in converting unwanted apples into the sparkling golden pleasure that comes in a bottle. When it comes to more sophisticated tools, always remember that you cannot depend on friends (much as you would like to) to understand their maintenance requirements, so if you want to "lend" these out, then it's better, in my opinion, to lend yourself out as well. Much better to be safe than to be sorry for a broken piece of machinery (that might easily ruin a friendship). Every self-supporter should want to be in social credit with his or her neighbors. Give your products and labor generously and sooner or later you will be generously repaid.

Nuts and bolts of self-employment

Bureaucrats strangled the Roman empire, and they are making a pretty fair job of strangling our present civilization. Somehow, paperwork has an extraordinary ability to grow and grow, like some invasive plant that has to be constantly cut away and dealt with. Those who are employed—and that means the majority of today's workers—are spared much of this because the State ensures that the employer fills in the forms. This is one of the stranger boons of being employed. Worse still, the embrace of conventional employment provides a whole range of easy comforts for the dependent employee. I can easily give you a host of examples: subsidized meals, health care, cheap gym membership, a company car, and so on.

For those who are contemplating major lifestyle changes, such as moving away from employment and into self-sufficiency and self-employment, all these comfortable aspects of employment will disappear. Not only will they disappear, but we will have to face up to the unpleasant realities of dealing with bureaucracy ourselves. And a very unpleasant and useless task it is, too. Some of my independent-minded friends make a feature out of letting their paperwork become a wild jungle of impossibility. Others (very few, I have to say) are models of quiet organization and efficiency. Probably most of us are somewhere in between. Whatever your own predelictions, I do recommend at least keeping your papers properly filed.

Taxes

The greatest difference between being employed and being self-employed is in the way we have to pay our taxes. Long, long ago, governments realized that it is much less painful to extract taxes from ordinary workers *before* they get their hands on the cash, and then refund any excess at the end of the year. The system works fairly automatically, with the employer acting as an agent for the government, filling out forms and paying in the necessary taxes after adjusting wages or salary accordingly. With self-employment, it is all quite different.

A self-employed person is required to pay estimated taxes quarterly in advance. Basically, you keep records of all the money you spend trying to run your business, as well as any money people have paid you for what you do or sell. There are plenty of tricky little rules about what kinds of costs you can count as part of your business. Obviously, you have to keep the little bits of paper you get as receipts. And, if you have a big enough business, you have even more complications in keeping records for the sales tax people (but this need not concern us here). The essential ground rule for those who are self-employed is to keep all the receipts you collect when you pay out money in the course of your business. You will find it a big help if you keep receipts for cash separate from receipts for checks. This makes it much easier to check your bank statements—and banks make mistakes, that's for sure.

To keep effective records for paying your own tax, every month you will need to tally up the receipts, entering the amounts either in a book or, if you can manage it, in a suitably user-friendly computer (these machines can do arithmetic, as well as driving you mad!). If you are debating whether to use an accountant (a sort of high priest who professes to understand the tax system), I would say it is generally wise to find one, at least when you are starting off on the self-employment road. He or she will tell you how to keep your records and, most important, how to fill in your annual tax return. With the help of your accountant, make a list of the headings that you are going to use for expenditure, such as heating and lighting, telephone, insurance, maintenance, fuel, and so on. Make another list for the different headings of income you may receive: goods sold, services offered, rental payments, and the like. When you write out your checks, make sure you enter all the correct details and then carefully file the relevant invoices.

Every month, enter the details for expenditure and income under the appropriate headings and add them up. You can then put the resulting monthly totals into summary form for the appropriate month. Use these totals to compare your figures with the figures sent to you in your bank statement. You must be able to reconcile them every month, and on some occasions it can be a surprisingly tedious piece of detective work to do so.

Keep separate records for cash expenditure, and keep these receipts in a separate folder month by month. If you use a personal credit card, then treat this the same as cash expenditure, because it does not come out of the business account. Keeping track of cash payments can become a nightmare in my experience, so watch out.

You may object to having to pay the accountant's fees after the first few years, when all this bookkeeping becomes so routine. Quite right, too. It pays a thousandfold to keep track of your own income and expenditures. Accountants can easily cost more than the taxes they save. I had one eccentric British friend who simply kept all his receipts and deposit slips in a big box, which he then sent to the Inspector of Taxes every couple of years. The inspector did the necessary paperwork, and my friend was charged the appropriate amount of tax. But he reckoned this was cheaper in the long run than employing an accountant. In the US, the Internal Revenue Service would not take kindly to such an approach and would undoubtedly make your life a waking nightmare, so you have to do the work whether you like it or not.

Tax and accounts really are most important if you are seriously making the big break. If you get it pretty well right at the start, then you will save yourself a great deal of trouble (and possibly money) later on. The main thing is not to be shy about putting down every item of expenditure that could possibly be thought of as being necessary for you to earn income from whatever trade (or trades) you are doing.

Claim, claim, claim

Don't hesitate to claim expenses: I can remember my first accountant telling me how important it was to put down plenty for taxi fares in the your first year, the logic being that taxis are not always going to give you a receipt, so the more you could justify under this head, the better off you would be (since all expenditure counts against income before tax). Of course, I am talking about tax avoidance here (quite legitimate) as opposed to tax evasion (which is prosecutable). You should seek professional advice, or ask the IRS itself, if you are in any doubt. Once the taxman's computer has registered a certain pattern for your expenses, then this pattern can (indeed, probably should) be continued for all time. Over the years, a regular few hundred dollars on taxi travel adds up to a small fortune of taxes you do not have to pay.

Pensions and life insurance

Other things to watch out for are pensions, life insurance, and bank accounts. I am specifically excluding any mention of borrowing money here, because it is one of the few things I would advise any self-supporter *never* to do. Borrowing can have great attractions in this world of having your cake tomorrow as well as eating it today. But it is a brave man who can predict the future, and being harnessed to work for a lending institution is no fun. If you look around in the big towns, you will soon see who has the swankiest offices and the biggest profits. Are they really the people you want to make even richer?

Pensions are important, and there are various tax-efficient strategies for putting money aside for this purpose. You will need to check out these rules carefully because your benefits and options may very well vary with what age you are. And if the government is going to help you save for your own future, then so much the better. But be warned, any pension plan will almost certainly involve handing your hard-won money over to someone else to look after it. Different outfits charge at very different rates for this service, as well as offering all sorts of different possible ways of saving. Do your homework and think very carefully before you agree to any saving plans that involve stock market investments (these are the ones that can go down as well as up).

Life insurance is another of the big scams that tends to be managed by people in suits in tall buildings. There are two main kinds of option—one is essentially a regular savings plan (linked to a final lump sum or a pension); the other is the completely different insurance deal where you pay a small monthly amount so that if you die before the plan ends (say, 25 years later) the company will pay your relatives a big lump sum. The former is a compulsory saving, which may or may not be more effective than something you could arrange for yourself (tax breaks aside). The latter is effectively a gamble on your own life expectancy. The "suits" do a few calculations based on your age and ask a few questions about family medical history.

You might also possibly have to have a medical examination. For your own peace of mind, it is a very good thing to have a decent-sized life insurance of this kind, normally called term assurance.

Bank accounts

Bank accounts are a necessary evil, but there is a lot you can do to give yourself peace of mind. Certainly some of the modern telephone and Internet banks are very much more cost-effective than old-fashioned banks. But all banks spend your money to make a profit for themselves, and the way they do this is something you want to find out about. At one end of the spectrum we have agencies like the credit unions that only lend your money to other local people. Then there are so-called ethical banks, which take a certain amount of care with what they spend your money on. Finally, there are the big, money-grubbing banks that will put your money where it will earn most, regardless of the activities it is promoting. As a self-supporter, I am very much in favor of local banking through credit unions, even if they do not operate credit cards or checkbook facilities. They make my money work for the good of others in my area, and they have the simplest of all criteria for lending money if you hit a seriously bad spot in your business life.

Insurance

Another subject that is "boring but important" is insurance. If you are going to keep animals, then you have to realize that the law is pretty fierce in the sense that you are likely to find yourself liable for any damage they do. And believe me, in the real world animals do escape, fences break, friends leave gates open, and animals decide they want to explore. It is also possible that animals or equipment may injure someone on your land. In all these cases, you certainly should be covered by insurance. The key point here is that many ordinary domestic insurers will not cover these types of damage. If you find this is the case, then try working through farming organizations. There are always a number of specialized firms that are used to these kinds of risks; they are the people you need to talk to.

Craft associations

Many of those who adopt a self-sufficient lifestyle will take up a craft as a sane and satisfying means of earning money. Whether you are a potter or a furniture-maker, this can often be a lonely occupation, where marketing your produce becomes very time-consuming and frustrating. One of the best ways of avoiding some of these problems is to join your local craft association. And if you cannot find one, then think very seriously about setting one up yourself. An active craft association will be a great support for you, not only emotionally, but also in the vital task of gaining access to markets. Many craft associations run their own markets, and this is an excellent way to sell your work.

IN SEARCH OF THE SELF-SUPPORTING LIFESTYLE

So what, then, does a sensible man or woman really need to be happy? How does the would-be self-supporter achieve this while walking lightly on this much-muddled world of ours? Health, of course, and real positive health, not just absence of disease. This can be achieved only by hard manual work or exercise, fresh air, sunshine, secure shelter, and unadulterated food. All but the last two items here are free (and we have forgotten how much in this world the best things, such as love, too, can be free). The inflated price of housing in Western countries (and unsustainable population growth) makes a warm, dry, and comfortable home, surrounded by a vibrant and productive natural world, elusive for many; but it is essential for the self-supporting lifestyle. Other prerequisites are good friends and neighbors and working to keep it that way. Working hard should be balanced by plenty of play with ample opportunity to enjoy good food, good beer, late nights with music, songs, and dancing. (Never let go of fun and conviviality.) It's about having control of your own time. It's about working with the great power of the natural world—just like a surfer works with the waves, or the skier with the snow—always aware that nature is bountiful but must treated with great respect. It's also about leaving the world a better place with healthier and happier animals, plants, people, and soil.

Making your own entertainment

Certainly when I talk of self-sufficiency, my ideas do not stop at the simple production of food and drink. We should also want to develop other talents and contribute whatever we can to the whole social fabric around us. The more we give to it, the more it will give back to us. And if we can have great entertainment, that is self-generated, and not subject to some huge international corporation, so much the better. I have been to wilder nights in the pub when the Gaelic music and audience have been fantastic. Musicians, singers, and dancers have enjoyed themselves mightily; and as for quality, well the audience is not paying directly for it, and it has been a great thrill to have been involved in the whole performance. Entertainment is only limited by the imagination, and you could encounter drama groups, singing groups, birdwatching groups, music groups, poetry reading, arts and crafts, cardplaying, and so on. Some of these groups will be more or less formal, others will exist only for their members (check your local newspapers and noticeboards). As for participating, do not be shy nor too modest. We all have talent and a capacity to respond to practice. It's taking the first step that can be difficult and, as the old adage goes, it's the taking part that counts. And do not forget that much of what we see in the media is recorded, mixed, and re-recorded until it is perfect. But in real life and in real human interaction it is not plastic perfection that we seek. On the contrary, it is honesty and commitment. When people are doing their best and putting their full soul into it, then that is all we can possibly ask.

Contacts & References

On the following pages you will find organizations, societies, associations, cooperatives, and the like who, in my opinion, have something to say to the self-supporter, however small. Bear in mind that web addresses, like telephone numbers, change with alarming rapidity, but they were accurate at press time. Certainly, the home computer can really help the self-supporter, especially for getting in contact with like-minded souls. Good luck and good searching!

Every effort has been made to check the accuracy of telephone numbers, and email and website addresses, at the time of going to press. However, the content, as well as the addresses, are subject to frequent changes, and the publisher can accept no responsibility for any inconvenience or distress arising from such changes

SCHOOL FOR SELF-SUFFICIENCY
The John Seymour School for Self-Sufficiency
The Self-Sufficient Smallholding, Killowen,
New Ross, County Wexford, Ireland

Tel/Fax: +353 51388945
www.self-sufficiency.net

Each year the "School" takes up to eight students at a time on week-long courses that provide hands-on experience of life on a small farm. There is accommodation on site and courses include occasional visits to neighbors, local pubs, and the nearby town. The Killowen homestead is 3.5 acres, with 1 acre taken up by the house and garden. Courses cover practical skills that vary depending on the seasons and include: Organic Vegetable Growing; Planning a Smallholding; Top Fruit and Soft Fruit Growing; Pig and Cow Husbandry; Poultry Management; Dairy Work; Beekeeping; Basket-making; Wine, Beer, and Juice-making; Jam and Bread-making; Scything and Grass Management; Composting; Blockwork and Basic Building Skills; Ropework and Knots. The school is run by William and Angela Sutherland.

COMMUNITIES & ASSOCIATIONS
Homestead.org
www.homestead.org

ENERGY
American Solar Energy Society
www.ases.org
Leading association of solar professionals & grassroots advocates; magazine.

American Wind Energy Association
Web: www.awea.org
Association promoting wind power growth through advocacy and education.

MAGAZINES
Backwoods Home Magazine
www.backwoodshome.com

Countryside & Small Stock Journal
www.countrysidemag.com

Mother Earth News
www.motherearthnews.com

FURTHER HELP
Adams County Nursery
P.O. Box 108
Aspers, PA 17304
www.acnursery.com
Fruit trees and orchard supplies

Bountiful Gardens
18001 Shafer Ranch Rd.
Willits, CA 95490
www.bountifulgardens.org
Gardening equipment and supplies; organic vegetable and herb seeds

The Cook's Garden
P.O. Box 535
Londonderry, VT 05148
www.cooksgarden.com
Specializes in gourmet and heirloom vegetables and flowers

Cumberland General Store, Inc.
#1 Hwy. 68
Crossville, TN 38555
www.cumberlandgeneral.com
A wide variety of supplies for the home, garden, and farm

Ed Hume Seeds, Inc.
P.O. Box 1450
Kent, WA 98035
www.humeseeds.com
Specializes in seeds for short seasons and cool climates

Edible Landscaping
P.O. Box 77
Afton, VA 22920
www.eat-it.com
Specializes in a wide range of fruits

Energy Outfitters, Ltd.
543 NE "E" St.
Grants Pass, OR 97526
www.energyoutfitters.com
Solar, wind, hydroelectric, and other "off-the-grid" power systems

Fungi Perfecti
P.O. Box 7634
Olympia, WA 98507
www.fungi.com
Mushroom-growing supplies

Gardener's Supply Company
128 Intervale Rd.
Burlington, VT 05401
www.vg.com
Gardening supplies

Gardens Alive!
5100 Schenley Pl.
Lawrenceburg, IN 47025
www.gardensalive.com
A wide range of organic pest control supplies and fertilizers

Gempler's, Inc.
100 Countryside Dr., P.O. Box 270
Belleville, WI 53508
www.gemplers.com
Tools and pest management supplies

Harmony Farm Supply & Nursery
3244 Hwy. 116 North
Sebastopol, CA 95472
www.harmonyfarm.com
A wide range of organic gardening and farming supplies

Henry Leuthardt Nurseries, Inc.
P.O. Box 666
East Moriches, NY 11940
www.henryleuthardtnurseries.com
Specializes in small fruits

Irish Eyes—Garden City Seeds
P.O. Box 307
Thorp, WA 98946
www.irish-eyes.com
Specializes in potatoes, garlic, onions, and shallots

Johnny's Selected Seeds
184 Foss Hill Rd.
Albion, ME 04910
www.johnnyseeds.com
Vegetable and herb seeds, plus gardening supplies

Lehman's
P.O. Box 41
Kidron, OH 44636
www.lehman's.com
Non-electric appliances, tools, grain mills, and much more

Native Seeds/SEARCH
526 N. 4th Ave.
Tucson, AZ 85705
www.nativeseeds.org
Southwestern native and heirloom vegetable and herb seeds

Natural Gardening Company
P.O. Box 750776
Petaluma, CA 94975
www.naturalgardening.com
A wide range of organic gardening supplies

New England Cheesemaking Supply Company
P.O. Box 85
Ashfield, MA 01330
www.cheesemaking.com
Home cheese-making supplies

Nichols Garden Nursery
1190 Old Salem Rd NE
Albany, OR 97321
www.nicholsgardennursery.com
Untreated herb and vegetable seeds

Nourse Farms, Inc.
41 River Rd.
South Deerfield, MA 01373
www.noursefarms.com
Specializes in small fruits, as well as asparagus and rhubarb

Peaceful Valley Farm Supply Co.
P.O. Box 2209
Grass Valley, CA 95945
www.groworganic.com
A wide range of gardening supplies

Pinetree Garden Seeds
P.O. Box 300
New Gloucester, ME 04260
www.superseeds.com
Inexpensive, small seed packets and many other gardening-related items

St. Lawrence Nurseries
325 State Hwy #345
Potsdam, NY 13676
www.sln.potsdam.ny.us
Specializes in hardy fruits and nuts

Seed Savers Exchange
3076 North Winn Rd.
Decorah, IA 52101
www.seedsavers.org
Heirloom fruits and vegetables; home of the Flower and Herb Exchange

Seeds Trust High Altitude Gardens
P.O. Box 1048
Hailey, ID 83333
www.seedsave.org
Specializes in seeds for high altitudes and cold climates

Southern Exposure Seed Exchange
P.O. Box 460
Mineral, VA 23117
www.southernexposure.com
Open-pollinated and heirloom vegetable, flower, and herb seeds

Territorial Seed Co.
P.O. Box 158
Cottage Grove, OR 97424
www.territorial-seed.com
Vegetable and flower seeds for the Pacific Northwest; gardening supplies

Whitman Farms
3995 Gibson Rd. NW
Salem, OR 97304
whitmanfarms.com
Currants and gooseberries

FURTHER READING
The Fat of the Land
John Seymour; Carningli Books (2007)
www.carninglipress.co.uk
This is the original personal story of how John and Sally Seymour developed their desire for self-sufficiency in rural Suffolk. Packed with anecdotes and real-life dramas, the book makes entertaining reading as well as giving a warning about some of the less expected consequences of searching for self sufficiency

Glossary

acrospire first stages of the shoot coming from germinating grain

aftermath short grass stubble left after hay-making

anaerobic fungal and bacterial action taking place in absence of oxygen

annual plant that germinates, grows, seeds, and dies in one year

ark small portable house or shed providing shelter for animals

awl sharp spike used to make holes in wood or leather

babbing technique for catching eels by tangling their teeth in threads passed through a bundle of worms

biennial a plant that grows in the first year and seeds in the second

blanch to dip fruit or vegetables in boiling water briefly before freezing

bloom surface coloring or sheen on plants or animals

blunger robust mixing device for merging different clays

bolt large bundle of reeds or willow twigs

brash to cut off lower branches of young, growing trees to make better timber

brassica plant in the family of vigorous vegetables including cabbage, sprouts, turnips

break growing a different crop for a season to reduce the likelihood of disease in the crop that is grown more regularly—e.g., a root break between cereal crops

breeching the part of the harness that goes around the backside of the horse to prevent a cart from over-running downhill

broadcast to sow seed by scattering
broiler chicken bred to be fattened up quickly into meat for the table

brood the eggs and young grubs of bees

brortch a length of flexible hazel rods used to pin down thatching

budding a useful way of propagating fruit varieties by grafting a single bud onto a compatible host tree

bulling the behavior of a cow when "in heat" and ready for the bull

cake the solid, crushed residue of fruit that is left after the juice has been pressed out

cappings the beeswax removed from the top of honey cells each time honey is taken from the hive

carding the process used to straighten out and align fibers in wool or flax before spinning

catch crop a quick-growing crop sown late in the season, after another crop has been harvested

caul the white, fatty membrane that supports the intestines

cheese a mass of chopped or pulped fruit that is placed into a muslin bag prior to being put in the juicing press

chitlings the stomach and intestines of a pig

churn a robust chamber or vessel used to create butter

clamp a pile of earth and straw that is built over a heap of vegetables— usually potatoes—to preserve them through winter

clean the term used to refer to land or soil that is free of weeds

cleave to split wood down the grain

come what happens when cream turns to butter

coping the act of splitting a small stone with a cold chisel

coppicing the technique of cutting back growth on mature trees to stimulate fast growth of smaller logs suitable for firewood

cordon a particular way of training fruit trees so the crop is convenient to pick

coulter the sharp, vertical knife positioned to cut turf in front of the plowshare

creep feed a feeder fenced in by a small opening that only allows access to small, young animals

crush device to contain and hold still large animals for veterinary work

curd the solid lumps that form in milk as it is attacked by bacteria or enzymes (like rennet in cheese-making)

curing preserving and softening leather by use of manipulation and chemicals, or the preservation of meat using salt and/or smoke

cutting a small piece of wood/plant removed from a mature plant with the objective of rooting it to create a new plant

decant to carefully pour off a clear liquid from a sediment

draw to remove the guts of an animal after slaughter

drill to sow seed in straight lines with a machine designed for this purpose

espalier a way of training a fruit tree along horizontal wires, making it easier to manage and pick fruit

fan a way of training a fruit tree into a fan shape for ease of management

fell the thin layer of translucent white skin that covers the outside of butchered meat after an animal has been carefully skinned

fisting the forceful removal of skin from a newly killed carcass by using the fist

fleece the wool of a sheep

flitch a term for a side of bacon

flocculation what happens when fine particles of material (usually soil) come together to form larger particles which are easier to manage

fold the process of turning grazing animals onto a piece of land where specific fodder crops have been

grown, usually with temporary fencing of some kind

fold pritch a heavy, sharp steel rod used to make holes in the ground that can be used to put up hurdles being used to "fold" animals

friable the description of soil that is pleasant to handle and breaks up easily into crumbly pieces

frost pocket a low-lying place where frost collects because of either the lie of the land or the existence of hedges or trees

fulling the process of creating felt from cloth by bashing it around in water

gambrel a strong twin hook used to hoist up freshly killed carcass

grafting the process of fastening one type of growing plant to a host rootstock so as to combine the virtues of both plants

hackling dragging retted flax over spikes to pull out the short fibers and leave the long ones

harden off to gradually expose a plant to outdoor conditions after it has been kept in a greenhouse

hardy frost-resistant

harrow to cultivate an area of land using a lightweight metal grid with downward-extending spikes

heavy the description of land which contains a high proportion of clay, making it prone to stay wet and create difficult conditions for cultivation

heddle a row of loops on a wooden batten that lift threads to allow the shuttle to pass through when weaving

heeling in putting plants in a trench to cover their roots while they are temporarily in storage

holding bed a part of the garden used to grow seedling plants before they are transplanted to their final positions

hulk *see* paunch

humus the largely decomposed masses of vegetative matter that make up a vital part of good soil structure

kive the large vessel used to contain and heat up beer during the brewing process

legume the family of plants that create their own fertility through nitrogen-fixing bacteria in root nodules (clover, beans, peas)

ley a special grass mixture sown as a temporary break for good grazing between cereal crops

light the description of soil that contains a high proportion of sand and is therefore quick to dry out and easy to work

linseed the seeds of the flax plant, which produce an excellent oil when crushed

lye alkaline chemical used to make dyestuff

mash the mixture of malt, hops, and water that is heated up and processed to make beer

mordant chemicals that bite into fabric as a key for dye

moldboard the large curved part of a plow that turns and shapes the furrow

mulch a layer of reasonably inert material that is spread onto soil to keep down weeds and prevent loss of moisture

must the remains of fruit that has been squeezed out in the process of making wine

pasteurize to eliminate harmful bacteria by heating

paunching the immediate removal of stomach and guts from freshly caught game such as deer or rabbit

perennial a plant that grows on from year to year without reseeding

poaching trampling of soil into mud by livestock in wet weather

pH a term used to measure acidity

pitching the act of putting yeast into a liquid that is being fermented for wine or beer

polled having no horns (usually said of cattle)

propagation the various techniques that are used to create new plants from existing mature plants

proving the process by which active yeast infuses carbon dioxide gas into dough to make it rise in bread-making

puddle to pour copious quantities of water onto newly transplanted seedlings

quack grass the persistent rhizome grass weed that is commonly found in light soil

rack to siphon off clear liquid that lies above sediment during the process of making beer or wine

rand a type of neat, strong weave in basket-making

render a thin covering of cement (usually 4 parts sand to 1 cement) used to finish off walls and floors

retting the process of rotting down fibrous plants (especially flax) to be used for making cloth

ripple to pull heads of flax through spikes to remove all the seeds

rive to split (rather than saw) a length of wood

roots crops that yield an edible root

rotation technique of changing crops grown on a piece of land every year to create a pattern that minimizes disease and boosts fertility

row crop crops that are grown in rows for ease of hoeing, weeding, and harvesting (as opposed to broadcast or deep-bed plantings)

runner a vegetative shoot produced by a "walking" plant to propagate itself

scion the piece of living wood that is grafted on to a rootstock to create a productive tree

screen to sieve soil (or any other material) to remove large pieces

scutching the action used to break up flax before the fibers are removed

served when a female stock animal has been inseminated by a male, she is said to have been "served"

sets the term for small onions that are planted as "seeds"

share the pointed, sharp end of the plow

shed the open space between threads created during the weaving process to allow easy passage of the shuttle

shuttle the heavy, two-ended needle that carries thread each way through the shed during the weaving process

singling the act of thinning massed seedlings with a hoe in the early stages of establishing a row crop

skep a small, round straw container used to contain a swarm of bees

slath term used to describe the base of a willow basket

slewing fast weave used in basket-making

slip watery mixture of clay and water

snood piece of stiff wire used to keep hooks away from line when sea fishing

sparge to pour hot water over spent malt and hops to remove the last of the flavor

spile to drive in stakes to hold out the sides of a well or hole being dug in sandy soil

spit depth of digging equal to the length of the blade of the spade

squab fledgling pigeon

stack a neat pile of material, quite different from a "heap"

standard the shape of a young tree where a single trunk extends at least 6 feet (1.8 m) from the roots to the first branches

starter a small brew of bacteria that is put into milk to make yoghurt or cheese

stook a bundle of newly cut cereal before the grain has been thrashed out

store adjective used to describe beef cattle reared on a low diet and needing fattening

stratify to expose seeds to frost in order to make them germinate

strike what happens to sheep when fly maggots attack their flesh

swaithe the row of cut grass/hay/cereal left after the scythe or mower

tailings small grain that is too small to grind into flour

tease to pull out wool into straight lengths using a board full of small spikes

ted to fluff up cut grass to allow it to dry into hay

tempering changing the spring and hardness of steel by alternate heating and cooling

tender sensitive to frost damage (said of plants)

throwing the action of a potter making a shape with clay on a wheel

tine a spike fastened to implements that are used to till the earth

tow the pieces of fiber that are too short to spin into yarn, often used for caulking the gaps in the hull of a wooden boat

truss to tie up a freshly dressed bird to prepare it for roasting

tug the part of the harness that takes the strain when a horse pulls a plow or cart

tuyere tube that blows air into a blacksmith's forge

volunteer a plant that grows on in the following year from a tuber or seed left behind from the previous harvest (typically potatoes)

waling a very strong and stable weave used in basket-making

walk-up what happens when game is disturbed from cover by a hunter walking on foot

wedge the shape created in threads during the process of passing the shuttle in weaving

whey what is left of the milk after the curd has been taken to make cheese

windrow the row of cut grass left fluffed up to dry after the mower or scythe in hay-making

winnow to separate grain from chaff using wind or blown air

wort the mixture of water, malt, and hops when it is ready for fermenting

Index

Acknowledgments

For this edition

The publisher would like to thank Pip Morgan for all his editorial help, Louise Waller for her design assistance, and Patricia Hymans for creating the index.

Thanks to the following for all editions of
The New Self-Sufficient Gardener:

Roger Bristow, Michael Carlo, Georgino D'Angelo, Christopher Davis, Jackie Douglas, Ariane Durkin, East Malling Research Station, Annelise Evans, Katherine Fenlaugh, Fred Ford, Ramona Ann Gale, Lesley Gilbert, Andrew Halstead, Dawn Henderson, K. Holmes of Cramers Ltd., Edward Kinsey, David Lamb, Mick Leahy, Peter Leech, Alan Lynch, Heather McCarry, Chris Meehan, Pip Morgan, Sue Rawkins, David Reynolds, John Rudzitis and the staff of Vantage, Sally Seymour, Dr. W. E. Shewell-Cooper, Geoff Smith and the staff of Cowells, Martin Solomons, Sybil del Strother, Kathryn Wilding, and Jenny Woodcock.

Thanks to the following for all editions of
The Self-Sufficient Life and How to Live It:

Susan Campbell, Cleals of Fishguard, Fred'k Ford, Peter Fraenkel, Barbara Fraser, Ramona Ann Gale, James Harrison, Christine Heilman, Clare Hill, Mel Hobbs, Patricia Hymans, Amanda Inness, Richard Kindersley, Edward Kinsey, Martyn's

Garden Services, Carla Masson, Peter Minter of Bulmer Brick & Tile Co., Mr. Fred Patton of Cummins Farm, Aldham, Peter Rayment and the staff at Diagraphic, John Rule, Rachel Scott, David and Anne Sears, Barry Steggle, Michael Thompson and the staff of Photoprint Plates, Louise Waller, Murray Wallis, Gary Werner, John Norris Wood, and Mr. Woodsford of W. Fenn Ltd.

Artists for both books

David Ashby, Norman Barber, David Bryant, Peter Bull Associates, Helen Cowcher, Michael Craig, Brian Craker, Roy Grubb, Julian Holland, Richard Jacobs, Peter Kesteven, Edward Kinsey and Alastair Campbell at QED, Ivan Lapper, Sally Launder, Richard Lewis, Kathleen McDougall, Robert Micklewright, Peter Morter, Dave Nash, Richard Orr, Nigel Osborne, Christine Roberts, Jim Robins, Simon Roulstone, Jeremy Sancha, Rodney Shackell, Kathleen Smith, Malcolm Smythe, Eric Thomas, Harry Titcombe, Justin Todd, Roger Twinn, Ann Winterbottom, John Woodcock, and Elsie Wrigley.

Acknowledgments to 1st edition
of *The Self-Sufficient Life and How to Live It*

I would like to thank the many people who have helped me with information and advice, particularly Sally Seymour, without whom this book would never have been written. The students on my farm, Fachongle Isaf, also assisted in many ways, especially Oliver Harding and David Lee, who helped with the drawings and diagrams.

John Seymour

Measurements & Oven temperatures

Weights and measures in this book, (including temperatures) have approximate metric and Imperial conversions (rounded up or down); this applies to the recipes, too. When referring to these measurements, including recipe temperatures (*see below*), do not mix metric with Imperial.

Gas Mark			
	1	275°F	140°C
	2	300°F	150°C
	3	325°F	170°C
	4	350°F	180°C
	5	375°F	190°C
	6	400°F	200°C
	7	425°F	220°C
	8	450°F	230°C
	9	475°F	240°C

The Authors

JOHN SEYMOUR

John Seymour was born in Essex, England, in 1914. He was schooled in Switzerland, and later went to Wye Agricultural College in Kent. At the age of 20 he left England for Africa to look for adventure. John traveled all over Africa; he managed farms, worked in a copper mine, and became skipper of a fishing boat off the Skeleton Coast. When World War II broke out, he joined the King's African Rifles and fought in Ethiopia and Burma—of the 40 officers who started the campaign he was one of only three who survived.

After the war he came back to England where he lived on a trolley bus followed by a Dutch sailing barge. By this time he had begun to write; mostly travel books about Africa and India and books and articles on sailing. He also started making radio programmes for the BBC.

John married Sally in 1953 and when they had their first child, they rented a remote cottage, without water or electricity, in Suffolk. With John's inspiration and knowledge and Sally's practicality they began to provide all they needed for the family from their five acres.

John wrote about their experiences in his first self-sufficiency book *The Fat of the Land*. It is still in print today.

After ten years in which they honed their methods for a self-sufficient life, they decided they needed more land and moved to West Wales to a 7-acre farm. There John wrote *Self-Sufficiency* and Sally drew the illustrations. From this book came the bestseller *The Complete Book of Self-Sufficiency*. In 1981, John, now in his late 60's, felt the urge for more

adventure and went further west to Ireland with his companion Angela Ashe. There he continued living a self-sufficient life, but became more active in environmental issues. In 1992 John and Angela started a school for self-sufficiency.

During 1998 he became one of the famous Arthurstown 7 who were arrested for destroying part of Monsanto's experimental GM, or as John preferred, "genetically mutilated", sugar beet trials.

John returned to Wales in 2002 to be with his family. He spent his last summer with Sally and they relived many of their adventures together. John died peacefully, surrounded by his family, on 14th September 2004. His burial was as self-sufficient as he could have wished; the gravestone came out of the grave that was dug by his friends and family, his byre was made of wood and his shroud was made from wool from his own sheep.

Throughout his life John wrote over 40 books and made many films and radio programmes for the BBC and RTE.

ANNE SEARS

John's daughter, Anne, lives with her family and her mother Sally Seymour on the farm in Wales where they still run a smallholding. Anne is a potter and has a craft and publishing business with her husband David.

WILL SUTHERLAND

Born in 1945, Will grew up on his father's traditional mixed farm in Northumberland. After taking a degree in Theoretical Physics and Law at Cambridge University, he went on to receive a Diploma in Farm Management and an MSc in Agricultural Economics before undertaking a year's apprenticeship on the family farm. Pursuing his fascination for insights into the reasons why countless human civilizations have failed to stand the test of time, Will then joined the Whitehall civil service becoming a Private Secretary and eventually a Treasury "Mandarin". In 1979 Will's public sector career was interrupted by twin desires to design and build his own organic golf course (The Millbrook Course in Bedfordshire) and to establish a worldwide organization for windsurfing in which he had been UK National Champion on a number of occasions. Having established both, Will returned to the public sector in 1983 becoming Head of the Policy Unit at Westminster City Council and later a Senior Management Consultant with Arthur Young (now Ernst and Young) in the City (of London's financial sector).

In 1989 Will left full-time management consultancy to edit and publish an alternative political magazine called *Ideas for Tomorrow Today*. Whilst organizing a conference prior to the Rio Earth Summit, Will met John Seymour in London. After taking part in the Citizens' Forum at Rio de Janeiro, Brazil, in 1992, Will devoted the next 18 months to editing and publishing the NGO (Non-Governmental Organization) *Alternative Treaties* which are now published in many different languages. Will moved to Ireland in 1993 to work with John Seymour and Angela Ashe, who were jointly running a school for self-sufficiency. Later Will married Angela and they continue to run the School for Self-Sufficiency.